DATE DUE

Investigative Psychology

Investigative Psychology

Offender Profiling and the Analysis of Criminal Action

David Canter and Donna Youngs

International Research Centre for Investigative Psychology, UK

A John Wiley and Sons, Ltd., Publication

8/2/10
Lan
#179.40

This edition first published 2009
Copyright © 2009 John Wiley & Sons Ltd

Registered office
John Wiley & Sons Ltd, The Atrium, Southern Gate, Chichester, West Sussex, PO19 8SQ,
United Kingdom

For details of our global editorial offices, for customer services and for information about how to apply
for permission to reuse the copyright material in this book please see our website at www.wiley.com.

Library of Congress Cataloging-in-Publication Data

Canter, David V.
    Investigative psychology : offender profiling and the analysis of criminal action /
David Canter and Donna Youngs.
        p. cm.
    Includes bibliographical references and index.
    ISBN 978-0-470-02396-9 (cloth) – ISBN 978-0-470-02397-6 (pbk.)
1. Criminal psychology.   2. Criminal behavior, Prediction of.   3. Criminal
investigation–Psychological aspects.   I. Youngs, Donna. II Title.
    HV6080.C3756 2009
    364.3–dc22   2009017246

ISBN 978-0-470-02396-9 (H/B)
ISBN 978-0-470-02397-6 (P/B)

A catalogue record for this book is available from the British Library.

Typeset in 9/13pt Kuenstler by Aptara Inc., New Delhi, India
Printed in Great Britain by CPI Antony Rowe, Chippenham, Wiltshire

Contents

Preface

This book is the first thorough account of the theoretical basis and professional applications of the newly emerging field of investigative psychology (IP). The field is characterised by an exploration of what offenders actually do – criminal actions – in order to develop an understanding of crime and criminality that will help to solve and manage crimes and contribute to prosecution and defence processes all over the world.

As the first academic text for this new strand of psychological science the book draws on over 20 years of research publications and professional reports and extensive unpublished material. These studies are set within the formal IP framework carved out by the authors and their students and colleagues since David Canter's first involvement in helping to solve a major serial murder case in 1986. His subsequent involvement in many aspects of police investigations laid the practical foundations for this new discipline.

The theoretical basis of IP derives from offence actions, the details of how the offender interacts with his/her surroundings and explicit or implicit victims, not inferred 'motives' or other assumptions about what the offender is trying to achieve. Within an action system framework, these interactions can be assigned to different modes that relate to the locus of what initiates the action and of where its consequence results. This builds on the initial framework for considering the roles offenders assign to their victims, first outlined by David Canter in 1994. Further, it gives rise to a broader based narrative framework of relevance to the full gamut of crimes. The implicit personal stories of offenders as applied to their modes of interaction with implicit and explicit victims are explored within the narrative framework in order to identify dominant themes from which inferences about offenders can be derived.

The book thus provides an integrated, wide-ranging, model for the differentiation of all forms of crime and criminals which is at the heart of the theoretical and practical applications and evolution of IP. This model has its roots in empirical research and particular analytic tools but it draws heavily on constructivist approaches within the social sciences and those perspectives that put active human agency at the core. Thus whilst acknowledging the value of some reductionist arguments about criminality the IP models that distinguish between crimes and criminals identify themes in criminal actions which start from the premise that offenders are fundamentally people not organisms.

These themes provide the basis for the profiling equations, linking offence actions and offender characteristics, which open up both the theoretical and practical implications of IP.

The book reviews the empirical research which is gradually providing insight into the inference processes at the heart of these equations. They are shown to be relevant to the full range of crimes; from arson or burglary to stalking and serial killing, drug networks and terrorism.

Throughout, the research is structured according to the operational challenges that it informs. The research questions are consequently not derived from purely academic concerns and then 'applied' to practical problems; they are developed within a spirit of solving real-world problems that do not owe their existence to arcane, ivory-tower debates. These extend beyond the central question about what can be inferred about a perpetrator's likely characteristics, to the identification of the salient aspects of a crime, the elicitation and prioritisation of suspects, the linking of offences to a common offender, the geographical locating of an offender's likely home/base and the prediction of where and when an offender will commit the next offence.

Investigative psychology is relevant to all aspects of the effective investigation and successful prosecution and defence of crime. It thus provides contributions to:

- The retrieval, evaluation and utilisation of investigative information.
- Strategic and tactical decision-making in investigations.
- The preparation and presentation of the legal case in court.
- Its relevance to the management of crime and treatment of offenders is also beginning to become apparent, although this is not addressed in the present volume.

This is a lively new area of activity in which very little has been determined with any certainty. The book captures the debates inherent in such a developing domain, emphasising the need to understand the psychological and social processes inherent in criminality if crimes are to be prevented or detected and criminals effectively comprehended and dealt with.

This is such a potentially vast area that the book does not pretend to be a general text on all aspects of psychology, crime and law. Rather, it is a comprehensive account of the highly distinctive IP approach to crime and criminality. This distinguishes it from other books that deal in detail with the clinical perspective on offenders and their treatment, or focus on such specialist topics as eyewitness testimony. However, this bias does put topics such as the causes of crime, the differences between offenders, the role of punishment and the treatment of offenders in an intriguing new light. In a concluding section the relevance of an investigative approach to psychology beyond crime and police enquiries is also explored.

Outline of the Book

The opening chapter provides an overview of IP and the issues it addresses. Its historical context is given, showing how current explorations in IP have grown out of many different strands of social and behavioural science contributions to the understanding of crime and criminality. Some of these strands have their roots in attempts to classify people in general and criminals in particular, as explored in Chapter 2. Other strands have grown more directly out of the work of informed detectives, as considered in Chapter 3. These two distinct roots came together in the early work of 'profilers', most notably a distinguished group of FBI agents at their training academy in Virginia in the 1980s as described in Chapter 4.

Having outlined the scope and origins of IP in *Part 1,* the fundamentals that form the basis of present-day IP are given in *Part 2.* This starts at Chapter 5 with an introduction to the central challenges to psychology posed by contributing to investigations. These revolve around the importance of determining the salience of any criminal actions. The conceptual structure of the *radex* is presented and the ways in which it is open to empirical test and development are illustrated. In Chapter 6 the *narrative perspective* on criminal actions is reviewed and its connections to radex models are explored. This provides the basis for considering the processes of making inferences about offences and offenders from their actions in the crime. As shown in Chapter 7, these inference processes are given further depth and clarity by recognising that criminal activity is an interesting example of an *action system.* The combination of the narrative perspective as developed with the framework of the radex as an aspect of an action system gives rise to the *narrative action system* which informs all areas of IP.

Chapter 8 focuses on where crimes occur and illustrates the underlying processes of propinquity and morphology that help in the understanding of crime location choice and its relationship to the offender's home/base. This provides a rich theoretical basis to decision-support systems such as those that make up geographical offender profiling, which are considered in the final chapter. It is shown that the relationship between base and crime location is elucidated by aspects of the narrative action system. This is revealed when offenders discuss the maps they have drawn of where they have offended.

Given their fundamental significance, the central demands of data and appropriate information in studying and investigating actual crimes are explored in Chapters 9 and 10 as the conclusion to Part 2. First the psychological procedures for improving the effectiveness of the information collected in an investigation are reviewed in Chapter 9; the subsequent chapter then considers the issues of deception and approaches to reducing its occurrence and detecting it.

Part 3 draws on the topics dealt with in the earlier parts of the book to consider particular aspects of criminality. The chapters start from the 'volume' crimes that are typical of many criminals and make up the majority of reported crimes, which are essentially centred on acquiring money or objects, in Chapter 11. The next chapter moves on to more violent crimes, especially those that have a sexual component. The more extreme forms of violence in homicide and serial murder are dealt with in Chapter 13. The final two chapters that focus on areas of criminality deal with larger scale offending that has strong social and cultural aspects; organised crime in Chapter 14 and terrorism in Chapter 15.

The final chapter summarises the material covered in the book by outlining the many areas of application, emerging topics being explored and the wider reaches of IP beyond crimes and criminality. The central message the book closes on is the one that runs throughout the whole book. Investigative psychology is a way of doing a particular kind of problem-solving research. It grew out of studies of ordinary, non-criminal activity with which it still connects. It is thus founded on the ambitious belief that psychology has a relevance to the way people deal with each other. An investigative psychology is consequently a natural product of making psychology worthwhile.

David Canter and Donna Youngs

Acknowledgements

Many of the people with whom we have had productive working relationships over the years are apparent in the following pages through the ways in which we have cited their work. The influence of many colleagues and nearly 200 graduate students has also permeated the following pages. We cannot hope to remember all those whose questions and contributions, pilot studies and projects have shaped our thinking and writing but we would like to mention four people in particular whose development of our work has informed and encouraged the growth of this pioneering new field: Craig Bennell in Canada, Gabrielle Salfati in the United States, Helinä Häkkänen-Nyholm in Finland and Katarina Fritzon in Australia. We hope the many others who will recognise their voices in the following pages will forgive us for not mentioning them.

Two very different people have to be mentioned because of their warm support for our early work and their personal encouragement. One is the much-missed late Professor Lionel Haward, the true father of forensic psychology in the United Kingdom. The other is special FBI agent Roy Hazelwood. Their magnanimous support for our early, faltering efforts has been a continuing inspiration.

We are extremely grateful to Laura Hammond for her sterling support in preparing this book and also to Maria Ioannou for her outstanding help in putting it together. We are also grateful to Dr Samuel Shye for his helpful comments on facet theory and related methodological issues.

We are further grateful to Tony Kelly for this expert guidance on legal issues, particularly those pertaining to the Scottish legal system.

The Road to Investigative Psychology

The Emergence of Investigative Psychology from Offender Profiling

John Bellingham assassinating the Right Honourable Spencer Perceval

Introducing Investigative Psychology

'You two characters been seeing any psychiatrists lately?'

'Hell,' Ohls said, 'hadn't you heard? We got them in our hair all the time these days. We've got two of them on the staff. This ain't police business any more. It's getting to be a branch of the medical racket. They're in and out of jail, the courts, the interrogation rooms. They write reports fifteen pages long on why some punk of a juvenile held up a liquor store or raped a school girl or peddled tea to the senior class. Ten years from now guys like Marty and me will be doing Rorschach tests and word associations instead of chin-ups and target practice. When we go out on a case we'll carry little black bags with portable lie detectors and bottles of truth serum. Too bad we didn't grab the four hard monkeys that poured it on Big Willie Magoon. We might have been able to unmaladjust them and make them love their mothers.'

(Raymond Chandler, *The Long Good-Bye*)

In This Chapter

- Learning Objectives
- Synopsis
- Psychology and Investigations
- The Emergence of IP
- Origins in 'Offender Profiling'
- The Investigative Cycle
- Disciplines Drawn On by IP
- Mind the Gap – Bridging Policing and Psychology

- System Integration versus Expert Opinion
- Questions that Investigative Psychologists Ask
- Beyond Crime and Criminals
- Linking Theory and Practice – The Book Ahead
- Summary
- Further Reading
- Questions for Discussion and Research

Learning Objectives

When you have completed this chapter you should be able to:

1. Understand what investigative psychology (IP) is and identify the main principles upon which it is based.
2. Detail some of the key contributions that IP can make to the management, investigation and prosecution of crime.
3. Identify the differences between IP and 'offender profiling'.
4. Appreciate the issues involved in investigative decision making.
5. Recognise the key stages of the investigative cycle and how IP can contribute to each.
6. Outline the key differences between police and academic cultures.

Synopsis

Investigative psychology is the study of offenders and the processes of apprehending them and bringing them to justice. It deals with what all those involved in crime and its investigation do, feel and think. The dominant objective is the understanding of crime in ways that are relevant to the conduct of criminal or civil investigations and subsequent legal proceedings. As such, IP is concerned with psychological input to the full range of issues that relate to the management, investigation and prosecution of crime. But it is also an approach to problem-solving psychology that has relevance far beyond crime and criminality.

It is based on the following principles:

- *All investigation is a form of decision making in which information is retrieved. Inferences are made on the basis of that information and actions result that, in turn, may generate further inferences to keep the cycle repeating until a resolution to the investigation is achieved.*
- *The contributions to investigations grow out of an understanding of criminal actions and the effective modelling of those actions.*
- *A key issue in contributing to all aspects of an investigative process is the identification of the salient aspects of any given set of criminal actions – of everything that happens in a crime and of the components of psychological and investigative significance.*
- *This modelling contributes to central problem-solving processes, which consist of making inferences about subsets of information, such as the characteristics of an offender, from other subsets of information, such as the details of what happens in a crime.*

- *In order to make effective inferences it is necessary to be able to make valid and fruitful distinctions between offenders and between crimes.*
- *The contribution of IP comes from the development of scientific principles and decision-support systems based on those principles not from the special intuitions or deductions of apparently gifted individuals. It thus feeds into many aspects of police training and the procedures that police use and is drawn on by many other people whose jobs require some form of detection or investigation.*

Investigative psychology is much more than the production of 'offender profiles' on serial killers, as is commonly believed. It provides a framework for the integration of many aspects of psychology into all areas of police and other investigations, covering all forms of crime that may be examined by the police as well as areas of activity that require investigation that may not always be considered by police investigators, such as insurance fraud, malicious fire setting, tax evasion, or customs and excise violations and even terrorism. The full range of offending activity is considered and analysed with the objective of informing the investigation, management, prediction and analysis of crime as well as the legal case. Through these explorations, IP seeks to advance the psychological understanding of offending activity, offenders and the investigative process itself.

Psychology and Investigations

Crime is everywhere. It dominates newspapers and news broadcasts. It constitutes a great deal of the fiction on television, in the cinema and in the bookshops. Governments stand and fall by how they cope with crimes and criminals. But what fascinates people most is how criminals are detected and brought to justice. No serious crime these days is solved without one or more journalists or the senior investigating officer subsequently writing a book to describe in great detail how the bad guy was caught, as illustrated by the examples given in Box 1.1.

Box 1.1 Recent Publications on Investigations into Crimes that Caught the Public Imagination

On the murders of five women in Ipswich:

Hunting Evil: Inside the Ipswich Serial Murders (2008)
by Paul Harrison and David Wilson

Cold-Blooded Evil: The True Story of the Ipswich Stranglings (2008)
by Neil Root

On the murders of two young girls in Soham:

Beyond Evil: Inside the Twisted Mind of Ian Huntley (2005)
by Nathan Yates

Soham: A Story of Our Times (2004)
by Nicci Gerrard

(continued)

On Josef Fritzl, the Austrian who kept his daughter captive in the cellar:

Monster (2008)
by Allan Hall

House of Horror: The Horrific True Story of Josef Fritzl, the Father From Hell
by Nigel Cawthorne

On the serial murderer Dr Harold Shipman:

Evil Beyond Belief: The Inside Story of How and Why Dr Harold Shipman Murdered More than 200 People (2005)
by Wensley Clarkson

On the Washington Snipers:

Sniper: Inside the Hunt for the Killers who Terrorized the Nation (2004)
by Sari Horwitz and Michael E. Ruane

Yet at the heart of detecting culprits and bringing them to court are complex patterns of human activity that can be elucidated and facilitated by drawing on concepts, theories, methods and results from psychology. It is the realisation that all aspects of the investigation of crimes can be made more effective by drawing on behavioural science that has drawn psychologists and other social scientists into the area of investigations. They are discovering the many fascinating challenges that investigations raise about human behaviour. Developments in our understanding of people in general are therefore emerging from the attempts to help solve crimes.

Many sciences are now contributing to the detection of crime and the management of criminals. Breakthroughs in DNA identification and a wide array of forensic procedures are as much part of real criminal investigations as they are of the fictional television portrayals such as *CSI* and *Silent Witness*. Contributions from psychology are slowly emerging to match these developments from the natural sciences. The many different ways in which psychology can contribute to police work are brought together in the field of IP. This is a rapidly developing discipline within applied psychology, which integrates a diverse range of aspects of psychology in ways that contribute to all areas of criminal and civil investigation.

IP is concerned with all the forms of criminality that may be examined by the police, from arson and burglary to murder, rape or even terrorism. The discipline also extends to cover those areas of activity that require investigation but may not always be conventionally within the domain of police services. These may include matters such as insurance fraud, corruption, malicious fire setting, tax evasion or smuggling. Increasingly, issues of crowd control and public order are also being studied by Investigative Psychologists. The military values of IP are also being recognised for dealing with insurgents in war zones as well as home grown terrorists.

The main concerns of IP are the ways in which criminal activities may be examined and understood in order for the detection of crime to be effective and for legal proceedings to be appropriate. As such, IP deals with psychological input to the full gamut of issues that relate to the management, investigation, prosecution of crime and defence of suspects.

The contributions that psychologists can make to police investigations have until recently been most widely known and understood in terms of 'offender profiles'. Offender profiling, as typically practised, is the process by which individuals, drawing on their clinical or other professional experience, or background as detectives, make judgements about the personality traits or psychodynamics of the perpetrators of crimes. They may also make other more operationally useful guesses about the demeanour, family background, or criminal history of an unknown offender. From the perspective of scientific psychology, however, such a process is flawed in its reliance on personal judgement rather than clearly defined aspects of criminal actions that have been empirically explored.

This comparison between the deductive, 'fictional-hero' approach and that of the scientific psychologist is not new to psychology. It has many parallels with the distinction between clinical and actuarial judgements that were explored by Meehl (1996). The clinician uses her or his judgements and experience to form an opinion about the patient. In contrast actuarial judgements are those based on careful measurements and the resultant statistical relationships. In a series of studies first published in 1954 and followed up over subsequent decades, it has been found that the actuarial decision processes were far more accurate and valid than those based on clinical judgement. In general the scientific approach proves to be far more effective than that based upon personal opinion.

The clinically derived theories upon which much 'offender profiling' has relied have been equally questioned by a number of researchers (such as Beauregard and Proulx, 2002; Egger, 1999; Smith, 1993). Of course it is possible to develop principles from research that can then inform the professional judgements of experts. Bennell, Taylor and Snook (2007) have illustrated this neatly by taking findings from Canter's (2005) geographical offender profiling studies as the basis for training people in thinking about offenders' home bases (Bennell, Taylor and Snook, 2007). They show that when such training is applied to (admittedly rather limited) sets of crimes, informed respondents could operate as well as some aspects of computer software.

The study of geographical offender profiling shows how 'clinical judgements' can be enhanced from research and how IP allows us to move beyond those offender profiles that were originally the drawing of a pen-picture to describe the likely characteristics of an unknown offender. As we shall see there are reasons why this may not be possible under some circumstances. There are also reasons why some aspects of the 'pen-picture' are more feasible to produce than others. A careful, systematic exploration of what is involved in contributing to police investigations needs to go far beyond personal opinion derived from the experience of any given individual.

The lack of scientific rigour evident in the profiling process has for two decades driven proponents of IP research to map out the scientific discipline that could underpin and systematise contributions to investigations. This more academically grounded approach is opening up the potential applications of psychology beyond those areas in which 'profiling' first saw the light of day. Early profilers insisted that their skills were only relevant to bizarre crimes in which some form of psychopathology was evident, notably serial killing and serial rape but investigative psychologists now study and contribute to investigations across the full spectrum of illegal activities.

Thus, although IP today is a very different discipline from the early attempts at 'offender profiling' it is nonetheless helpful to understand the origins of informed contributions to the work of detectives. These contributions can be traced back long before trainers at the FBI academy in Quantico came to public notice because they were fictionalised in Hollywood movies. The early work went through the same stages as all scientific activity. Thus, to understand the origins of IP we need to go back many centuries and examine the ways in which criminal investigators formed views of the crimes and criminals they were investigating.

The Emergence of IP

Most people learn about crime and about the potential contribution of psychologists to investigations from fictional accounts. However, fictional accounts of psychological contributions to police investigations are very misleading.

One problem with such fiction is that it almost invariably deals with the investigation of serial killers. These murderers provide such a simple icon of evil and depravity that they easily generate an apparently worthy foil for the hero of the story, the 'detective' who solves the case. But in order to create an appealing fictional hero who will detect and uncover the villain, the hero's wit and virtue have to be emphasised by contrast with the person who kills over and over again. To emphasise the power of the hero (or more recently heroine) the killer has to be shown not only to be callous and cold-blooded but also to be clever and devious. There is little dramatic mileage to be obtained from showing that the difficulty in detecting the serial killer is a product of ineffective record keeping, poor police training and the general anonymity that a free society affords.

Further, any account of serial killers, in fact or fiction, always runs the risk of sensationalising its subject and pandering to fiction writers', and readers', search for a plot that has an exciting momentum, with individuals who are clear antagonists pitted against each other. Processes and systems play little part in such accounts. In fiction research findings are assigned to the insights of the hero, not to painstaking study. So inevitably, fiction does not capture the scientific process at all and leads to the implication that all that is needed is an insightful person who gleans an understanding of criminals from experience or intelligence, not from an arena of established procedures and knowledge on which any professional can build.

The results of research can be used by anyone with the skills to understand them. They become part of the public domain of science. When the science deals with the actual people who carry out crimes, how their crimes differ, and the ways in which that understanding can be utilised by police investigators, then it can feed into many aspects of police training and the procedures that police use.

Origins in 'Offender Profiling'

The practice of producing 'offender profiles' became widely known when the special agents at the FBI Academy in Quantico started publishing reports of the procedures they were using (for example Ressler, Burgess and Douglas, 1988). They emphasised an objective approach based in experience of criminal investigations. As Hazelwood *et al.* (1987) put it very clearly, the view of these FBI agents was that: 'Successful profilers are experienced in criminal investigations and research and possess common sense, intuition, and the ability to isolate their feelings about the crime, the criminal, and the victim. They have the ability to evaluate analytically the behavior exhibited in a crime and to think very much like the criminal responsible' (Hazelwood *et al.*, 1987: 148).

This makes it clear that Hazelwood and his colleagues did not see a strong research basis to their activities. They saw the skills as residing in the 'profiler' rather than being the product of systematic social science. It is not surprising therefore that many researchers found deficiencies in the accounts that these FBI agents produced of their work. For example, Alison and Canter (1999), Coleman and Norris (2000), and Muller (2000) all draw attention to the misrepresentation of established psychological theory within the ideas of these FBI agents, the weaknesses of their methodologies and the lack of any convincing empirical evidence for their claims. However, the uptake of the idea of profiling by brilliant crime fiction writers, most notably Thomas Harris in his 1988 book *The Silence of the Lambs*, with the subsequent blockbuster movies, changed the common meanings of 'profile'.

The 1999 *Collins Concise Dictionary* gives two meanings for a 'profile' as either a 'short biographical sketch' or 'a graph, table, etc. representing the extent to which a person, field or object exhibits various tested characteristics'. However Thomas Harris promulgated the much more exotic idea of a profile, which Blau (1994: 261, attributing to Reiser, 1982) describes as '... an arcane art in which psycho-diagnostic assessment and psychobiography are combined with case evidence and probabilities from similar cases to draw a picture of a likely offender ...' Far from this being an objective biographical sketch or even a measure of the extent to which the offender exhibits various tested characteristics, Blau (1994: 261) makes it clear that, when he was writing in the early 1990s, 'contrary to hopes and expectations for a scientifically derived investigative tool, psychological profiling is merely an inferential process analogous to a psychological evaluation done with an ordinary client.'

In the decades since Blau was writing it has become clear that developing a scientifically derived investigative tool may be more difficult than the early writings by FBI special agents had implied (Mokros and Alison, 2002). Nonetheless, their promotion of the potential links between the actions associated with a crime and the characteristics of the person who committed that offence have drawn an increasing number of serious scientists to elaborate and find answers to the central psychological questions that are implicit within the concept of 'profiling' and associated activities.

The development of a scientific psychological approach to police work had its roots in the experience of David Canter when he found that his advice to a major police enquiry was seen to be of great value (Canter, 1994). His background was in applied social and environmental psychology so he did not approach the task of helping the police with their enquiries from the perspective of a clinician who could draw on memories of criminals he had dealt with, or experience of earlier investigations. He derived his views from what previous studies he could find and his own approach within applied psychology. So that when he realised how helpful such a contribution could be he did not think of himself as some sort of genius who could now offer his services to the police on the basis of his one big success. Instead he saw the opportunity for helping to develop a whole new area of applied psychology that he called *investigative psychology* in 1992 (Canter, 1995).

The Investigative Cycle

An important development in the emergence of IP as a distinct applied discipline was the overt recognition that the work of investigators is essentially a decision-making process. David Canter was very influenced in making this step by his early work as a psychologist in a school of architecture (cf. Canter, 1977). Architects had invited psychologists into their research and training activities in the 1960s with the emergence of a much more systematic approach to design. Part of this approach was to blow away the myth of architecture being a wholly intuitive, creative art and introduce the idea of architecture as a 'design process', which although it drew on creative insights nonetheless saw architecture as consisting of a series of decisions based on careful amassing of information, analysing that information and then making choices on the basis of the results of the analysis.

Canter and Youngs (2003) took this perspective into the consideration of what it is that the police do to which psychology can contribute. They posited that the challenges police face during the course of an investigation may be readily conceptualised as a series of decision-making tasks. This allows the investigation process to be informed by psychological studies of effective and ineffective decision making. The evaluation of the evidence and leads available in an investigation will similarly benefit from thinking of this information as the basis of some form of scientific 'data'.

Investigations as Decision-Making

The decision-making tasks that constitute the investigation process can be derived from consideration of the sequence of activities that detectives follow, starting from the point at which a crime is committed through to the bringing of a case to court. As they progress through this sequence of activities, detectives reach choice points, at which they must identify the possibilities for action on the basis of the information they can obtain. For example, when a burglary is committed they may seek to match fingerprints found at the crime scene with known suspects. This is a relatively straightforward process of making inferences about the likely culprit from the information drawn from the fingerprints. The action of arresting and questioning the suspect follows from this inference.

However, in many cases the investigative process is not so straightforward. Detectives may not have such clear-cut information but, for example, suspect that the style of the burglary is typical of one of a number of people they have arrested in the past. Or, in an even more complex example, they may infer from the disorder at a murder crime scene that the offender was a burglar disturbed in the act. These inferences will either lead them to seek other information or to select from a possible range of actions, including arresting and charging a likely suspect.

Investigative decision-making thus involves the identification and selection of options, such as possible suspects or lines of enquiry that will lead to the eventual narrowing down of the search process. Throughout this process detectives must gather the appropriate evidence to identify the perpetrator and prove their case in court. A clear understanding of the investigation process as a series of decision-making tasks allows the challenges implicit in this process to be readily and appropriately identified. The main challenge to investigators is to make important

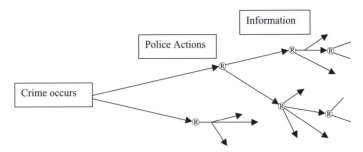

Figure 1.1   Schematic indication of the rapidly developing information in a major police investigation.

decisions under considerable pressure and in circumstances that are often ambiguous. The events surrounding the decisions are likely to carry a great emotional charge and there may be other political and organisational stresses that also make objective judgements very difficult. A lot of information, much of which may be of unknown reliability, needs to be amassed and digested. In decision-making terms the investigative process can be represented as in Figure 1.1.

In this diagram the lines represent investigative actions by the police while the nodes are the results of those actions – new pieces of information or facts. Immediately after a crime occurs, detectives often have few leads to follow up. However, as they begin to investigate information comes to light, opening up lines of enquiry. These produce more information, suggesting further directions for investigative action. The rapid buildup of information in these first few days will often give rise to exponential increases in the cognitive load on detectives, reaching a maximum weight after some short period of time. At this point investigators will be under considerable stress. Studies of human decision-making carried out by Flin, Slaven and Stewart (1996) in similarly stressful contexts, show that there are likely to be many heuristic biases and inefficiencies in decisions made under these sorts of conditions. The relevance of these issues to complex police investigations has been reviewed in a number of recent studies (for example, Alison, Barrett and Crego, 2007; Alison and Crego, 2008).

As the investigation progresses, detectives will eventually be able to start to narrow down their lines of enquiry by establishing facts that close off all but one of them, substantially reducing the general level of demand. The general diamond shape in Figure 1.2 represents

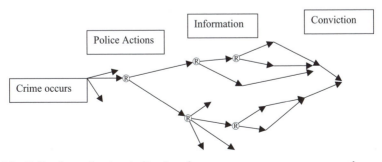

Figure 1.2   Police investigation indicating the convergence on a suspect and conviction.

the typical progression of an investigation. The diagram depicts the initial build up and then the subsequent narrowing down of the information (the nodes) under consideration and investigative steps related to these (the lines) as the investigation becomes increasingly focused to the point where an arrest occurs.

Areas of Contribution

Throughout all the activities of any investigation there are three distinct processes in play, each of which carries different implications of how psychology may be relevant to those processes. These can be represented by a simple framework for these three sets of tasks (as shown in Box 1.2). In essence they can be regarded as giving rise to IP.

Box 1.2 The Investigative Cycle

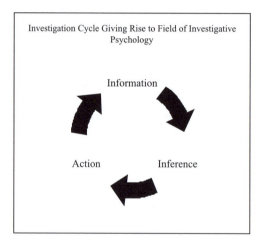

Investigation Cycle Giving Rise to Field of Investigative Psychology

Information

Action

Inference

Investigative psychology is the systematic, scientific study of

- investigative information, its retrieval, evaluation and utilisation
- police actions and decisions, their improvement and support, and
- the inferences that can be made about criminal activity

with the objective of improving criminal and civil investigations, and legal processes.

Effective Information

The decision cycle points to three main areas that investigative psychologists explore. One is the consideration of the information with which the police and other investigators work. All areas of applied psychology deal with the recording of information so there is considerable expertise to be drawn upon to make investigative processes more effective.

One approach is to consider the collection of any police information as similar to any other research instrument that may be developed, whether it is a questionnaire, an open-ended interview or even a psychophysiological test such as the 'polygraph' used in 'lie detection'. Any measuring instrument needs to have an established level of reliability. In other words two people using it under similar conditions should get similar results. The information-gathering procedures used by the police are not systematically put to this test.

Beyond reliability is the even more challenging issue of validity. Virtually all the studies that psychologists carry out assume that any informants will perform to the best of their ability and will try to be as honest as possible. This may be a naïve assumption for many psychologists but it is foolhardy for anyone involved with criminals to make this assumption. Even witnesses and victims may have understandable reasons for not telling the whole truth or even for lying. A growing amount of investigative psychological research is therefore aimed at developing ways of making sure the information is as valid as possible.

Reliability and validity are only the starting point for all the issues that are raised when considering the information the police retrieve. There is also the matter of obtaining more detailed and accurate information, which can be aided for instance by special interview procedures such as the 'cognitive interview' (Fisher and Geiselman, 1992; Geiselman *et al.*, 1985, 1986) as discussed in later chapters. The robustness of the information collection procedures, in other words how tolerant they are of being used by people under difficult circumstances who may not be very well trained, is a further aspect that psychologists explore (Hammond, Wagstaff and Cole, 2006; Memon *et al.*, 1997).

Appropriate Inference

Once there is some information to work with there is the significant challenge of determining what conclusions can be drawn from this information. These conclusions are inferences that claim that certain features are linked. The most obvious example is making inferences about the characteristics of the offender from some knowledge of how the crime was committed, as David Canter (1994) did in the investigation that led to the arrest and conviction of John Duffy. But there are many other inferences that are of interest and relevance to police investigations.

One inference that is often ignored, for example, is what an offender may have done with a weapon after a violent crime, or where that weapon may have come from. Such inferences can be based on probabilities from previous investigations without any knowledge of the characteristics of the offender. There are also very important inferences about which crimes may have been committed by the same person, sometimes known as comparative case analysis or 'crime linking'. Questions about what an offender may do next, or where he may be based, or how dangerous he is likely to be are also important and complex questions to which we will return in more detail in later chapters.

The exploration of inference implies an integrated set of psychological questions. Canter (1995) summarises these questions as the **A**→**C** equations, where **A** are all those actions that occur in and are related to a crime. In other words, they are known to the police before there is any recognised culprit. The **C** refers to the characteristics of the offender. The things the police want to know about him (or her) that will lead to identification and conviction. The scientific modelling that would allow inferences to be made about the characteristics from the actions is indicated by the → symbol. This simple symbol enshrines a complex and challenging set of issues.

The inferences that detectives make in an investigation about the perpetrator's likely characteristics, or possible next actions, or place of residence, will be valid to the extent that they are based on an effective understanding of the processes that can give rise to the key relationships that underpin these inferences. A number of potential processes are postulated within social and psychological theories. Any or all of these theories could provide a valid basis for investigative inferences if the differences in individuals that they posit correspond to real variations in criminal behaviour.

Valid inferences also depend upon an understanding of the way in which a process operates. Conceptually there are a number of different models that can be drawn on to link an offender's actions with his/her characteristics. One is to explain how it is that the offender's characteristics are the cause of the particular criminal actions. For example, if a man is known to be violent when frustrated, this knowledge provides a basis for inferring his characteristics from his actions.

A different theoretical perspective would be to look for variables that were characteristic of the offender and that would influence the particular offending actions. A highly intelligent person, for instance, may be expected to commit a fraud rather differently from someone with educational difficulties. The intelligence may be reflected in the style of action even if not in the actual cause of the action. A third possibility is that actions give rise to some consequences from which characteristics may be inferred. An example of this would be when particular types of goods are stolen that imply that the thief must have contact with other offenders who would buy or distribute those goods.

It is worth noting that the search for models of inference avoids unnecessary assumptions about what are often referred to as the 'motives' for an offence. Speculations about the reasons why an offence took place can be productive. However, they should not be confused with empirical exploration of the correlations that underlie the relationships between actions and characteristics. It is on these correlations that firm inferences can be based.

From an applied perspective, it is also important that the variables on which the inference models draw are limited to those of utility to police investigations. This implies that the A variables are restricted to those known prior to any suspect being identified, typically drawn from crime scene information and/or victim and witness statements. The C variables are limited to those on which the police can act, such as information about where the person might be living, his/her criminal history, age or domestic circumstances.

Focused Decisions

The third phase of the investigative cycle is to select from the various options that are revealed through the earlier stages and act on those options, either to seek further information or to prepare some action that will lead to an arrest or proceedings in court. These choices and decisions can be aided by 'decision support systems' that organise the information and possible inferences in ways that help investigators to visualise what is often complex material and to summarise patterns within that material.

Figure 1.3 Disciplines on which investigative psychology draws.

Disciplines Drawn On by IP

The variety of issues that IP deals with inevitably draws on many different areas of psychology, some of which are illustrated in Figure 1.3. Further, each of these areas do themselves draw on disciplines outside of psychology. For example, environmental psychology has a lot of interaction with geography, especially urban geography. The criminal psychology issues indicated here interact with more general areas of criminology, forensic psychology with forensic psychiatry, child psychology with issues in education and so on.

Mind the Gap – Bridging Policing and Psychology

One of the developments in policing that has contributed to the emergence of investigative psychology is the increasing openness of police forces to academic work and their embracing of scientific approaches to crime management. Drummond (1976) pointed out these emerging changes when he wrote 'the police are far more open with others than was the case a decade ago' (Drummond, 1976). These developments were encouraged when the need for a scientific perspective on large enquiries was identified by Byford (1981) in his review of the Yorkshire Ripper enquiry in which many weaknesses in police investigations were noted.

However, these contacts between police and scientists of all ilks are making it clearer that there are contrasts between the culture of the police and of academics. The difficulty of interaction between, on the one hand, the academic/scientific culture and, on the other, the culture of the police is not merely a matter of vocabulary or ingrained habits. As discussed in detail by Canter (2003), it is a set of fundamental differences in thought processes, typical modes of action and the central objectives that shape the institutions in which these cultures thrive.

The major areas of difference between the two cultures are summarised in Table 1.1. Five main areas of difference can be briefly considered.

Table 1.1   A summary of the differences between police and of psychology cultures.

	The Police	Psychology
Approach to information	Evidence	Data
Preferred methodologies	Due Process	Scientific method
Explanations of human actions	Individual Case	Mostly group trends
Attitude to knowledge	Secrecy	Publication
Temporal perspective	Short-term	Long-term

Data versus Evidence

Perhaps the most fundamental distinction between the police and academic communities is in what they regard as information. It was the Senior Investigating Officer of Operation Trinity, Superintendent Vince McFadden (reported in Canter, 1995) who first pointed out that what the police search for is evidence, something that can be used to prove a case in court, whereas what scientists want is data, material that they can work with, on which they can test their hypotheses. From the police point of view evidence is valid or not. For a scientist if data are suspect then they provide only lukewarm support for a particular hypothesis. Such data may not be dismissed but added to future data to help develop the argument further. Evidence makes or breaks the case. Data cumulate to help develop theories and models.

The significance of knowledge for the police is in what its consequences are. This contrasts with the interest that academics have in the process by which results were obtained. This means that information that is not actually used in a case may be put to one side by detectives. In contrast a scientist may look at it to establish whether it could be of value in understanding criminality and developing more effective processes in the future.

Canter (1995) gives an example of this from the work of Kind (1987) who demonstrated the potential of geographical profiling in relation to the Yorkshire Ripper enquiry. But his report arrived after the arrest of the 'Ripper' and so was not used in the investigation. However, rather than recognising its potential for the future, the UK police had to wait a number of years before Canter (1995) rediscovered the possibilities of geographical profiling, having never been told about Kind's earlier work.

When it comes to transactions between scientists and police officers over the information available from an investigation these differences in perspective take their toll. Law-enforcement agents are reluctant to make information available to scientists unless what can be done with it will help to turn it into evidence. There are even still police officers who cannot see the point in studying information from solved cases, believing that the central problem of each case is to find the evidence that will lead to a conviction.

As we shall see in subsequent chapters, the police do collect vast amounts of information in many forms that feeds their records. Canter and Alison (2003) have argued that improving the collection of this information and making effective use of it is a central challenge for developing a science that is relevant to police investigations.

Scientific Method versus Due Process

The training police officers get is, inevitably, focused on the law and its workings. This ties them into an appropriate concern that everything they do must be monitored and seek success. They evaluate their activities in relation to the process of law. They need to think of what is known as 'due process' to ensure that all that they do will eventually stand the test of what happens in court.

Academics, by contrast, have a fundamental commitment to intellectual freedom that is a luxury in which the police cannot indulge. Scientists are trained to test alternative hypotheses and to evaluate their success against the canons of scientific method. Science often moves forward by learning from failures. The approach to the nature of knowledge that distinguishes the two cultures is a consequence of the different relationships to the legal process.

Trend versus Case

The focus on legal outcome also gives emphasis to individual cases and the success or failure of procedures applied to them. This makes police forces exceptionally vulnerable to making decisions on the basis of unusual, one-off cases. There is considerable evidence that most people have difficulty in understanding probabilities without formal training and therefore the police are likely to dismiss the relevance of general patterns of criminality in favour of particular examples they remember, especially if these examples challenge the general statistical trends.

Even when social scientists use case studies they do so within frameworks that are built up from general patterns of activity and the broad trends that have been drawn from previous studies. They are comfortable with statistical probability and the ways in which the trends they find cohere with the logic of their unfolding theories.

Publication versus Secrecy

The importance of sustaining the development of scientific understanding through contributing to the scientific literature seems alien to many detectives. A number of people have commented on the 'defensiveness' of police culture. Hiding information from those who may destroy evidence, or use it to evade detection or capture, is a wholly appropriate habit for detectives.

The public expects an enormous amount of discretion from the most junior police officer. Police officers quickly learn that they have to wield this discretion with confidence if they are to be taken seriously. Police officers often do not understand that the processes of publication and peer commentary ameliorate academic anarchy that can be a side-effect of academic freedom.

For the ambitious police officer, solving the current case him/herself, or making an arrest, can have very direct career prospects. There are therefore pressures to hold on to information relevant to that case as it will be of direct benefit to the individual officer. If, on the other hand, police officers are at a stage in their career when academic recognition may be of some utility they can be very forthcoming and open to academic collaboration.

Academics often ignore these dynamics at their peril, thinking that the benefits of sharing information on which science is supposed to be based will be immediately recognised by their police contacts. For the police officer such openness to those outside the police is fraught with dangers and does not necessarily offer any direct career benefits.

Long-term versus Short-term

Overall the objectives of the police tend to be couched in the here and now. Academic life has a more leisurely pace. Members of the public want action from the police. Whereas academic life has unfolded with only minor changes over the half a millennium that universities and scientific laboratories have been in general existence there have been very considerable changes in the fundamental processes that characterise police work over the century-and-a-half that police forces have played a role in public life. Law enforcement agencies by their very nature must respond to the public concerns and integrate with evolving public bodies and other institutions. Academics really can survive in their ivory towers, still debating issues that exercised Greek philosophers 2000 years ago.

One further consequence of the very different contexts of police and academic work is the pressures to which they are prone. Crime and policing are so much on the political agenda and police forces, appropriately, need to respond so directly to pressures from elected politicians that an awareness of the current political concerns is essential for effectiveness at least in the higher echelons of the police. Traditionally academics, especially scientists, have been spared these concerns. Police officers are less likely to be aware of the fashions within the arcane debates of science than scientists are to know about the issues reported regularly in newspapers.

What this analysis shows is that the academic/scientific community and the police service need each other. The differences between them are generated by the overall missions of the different institutions and are usually consonant with them. Academics can benefit from taking on board some of the perspectives of the police. The police increasingly need academic and scientific input. Thus whilst both cultures have something to offer to society at large there is great benefit in them getting to understand each other so that they can work together more productively. It is out of the interaction between these cultures, a sort of miscegenation, that more effective policing will emerge and a fuller understanding of criminality will be developed.

System Integration versus Expert Opinion

The development of decision-support systems illustrates how the idea of the 'expert' who aids the police is giving way to a more integrated involvement between psychologists and the whole investigative process. The usual model that is assumed for the utilisation of psychological knowledge in a police investigation is that an expert is brought into the enquiry, rather in the way that Sherlock Holmes was, to interact directly with the investigation. The one to one contact between the 'expert' and the 'detective', so beloved of crime fiction, has found its way into police practice in the use of 'profilers' all over the world. Whilst there are probably some values to these contributions, as Copson (1995) pointed out in his review of their contributions, they are very limited.

A rather more productive model (discussed in more detail in Canter, 1995) is the one in which scientific psychology generates principles and procedures out of which processes can be developed which then become part of investigative practice. This does not have the drama to it that the 'heroic profiler' can portray. It also means that the 'expert' is not likely to be needed once the system is in place. There are therefore personal and commercial pressures that undermine the development of this model, but it is one that is gaining ground as IP takes root.

This raises fundamental questions for psychological offender profiling. Is it possible to assess those aspects of criminal activity available to police investigators and those characteristics of the offenders that are useful to help identify and prosecute those offenders? Can valid relationships between these be demonstrated? These are the questions at the heart of IP.

Questions that Investigative Psychologists Ask

Investigative psychology covers all aspects of psychology that are relevant to the conduct of criminal or civil investigations. Its focus is on the ways in which criminal activities may be examined and understood in order for the detection of crime to be effective and legal proceedings to be appropriate. Therefore, at the very heart of social and behavioural science studies are a set of fundamental psychological questions that researchers are exploring and which the remainder of this book unpacks and answers. It is therefore useful to summarise the major psychological questions that we will be dealing with in more detail throughout the book.

Salience

In order to generate hypotheses and investigative possibilities and to select from them, detectives and other investigators must draw on some understanding of the actions of the offender(s) involved in the offence they are investigating. They must have some idea or template of typical ways in which offenders behave that will enable them to make sense of the information obtained. A central research question, then, is to identify the behaviourally important facets of offences – those facets that are of most use in revealing the salient psychological processes inherent in any given crime.

Canter and Youngs (2003) have discussed this central psychological question in some detail. They draw attention to the need to establish the salient features of the crimes being examined. So many different aspects of a crime can be considered when attempting to formulate views about that crime, that there is the challenge, before any scientific arguments can be developed, of determining which of the crime features are behaviourally important. These features are important in the sense of carrying information on which reliable empirical findings can be built.

Determining salience turns out to be a much more complex issue than is often realised, with parallels in many areas of information retrieval. It requires the determination of base rates and co-occurrences of behaviours as well as an understanding of the pattern of actions that are typical for any given type of crime.

Consistency

One aspect of these salient features that also needs to be determined as part of scientific development is whether they are consistent enough from one context, or crime, to another such that they can form the basis for considering and interpreting those crimes and comparing them with other offences. The establishment of consistency is not straightforward. There are weaknesses in the sources of data, particularly its 'patchiness', whereby in some instances, certain features – or their absence – will be recorded and in others not. To deal with these problems with the data, as Canter and Alison (2003) have discussed, there is an emerging range of methodologies that focus on working with the sort of information that is available from police and other crime related sources (Canter and Alison, 2003).

It is worth emphasising here, though, that there are two rather different aspects of criminal consistency with which we will be dealing in later chapters. One is the consistency from the actions in a crime to the other aspects of the offender's life. This may thus allow some aspects of a one-off crime, such as the expertise involved, to be used to form views about an offender's previous training. So, the question here is which features of an offence are consistent with which, if any, aspects of an individual's background and personal characteristics.

A quite distinctly different form of consistency is that between one crime and another committed by the same person. This is often, rather loosely, referred to as an offender's *modus operandi*, or *M.O.* The question here then will be which features of an individual's offending behaviour are consistent across situations, separate offences and even across different types of offences. There are many aspects of this latter form of consistency that need to be clarified, but for the moment we just need to be aware of its relevance at the core of IP. Green, Booth and Biderman (1976) did demonstrate that M.O. could be given a precise definition and behavioural science statistics could be applied to help identify distinguishing offence patterns.

Development and Change

Any consideration of consistency will be against a backdrop of likely changes in a serial offender's activities. Some variation is a natural aspect of human processes. There therefore will be criminals who are consistently variable or whose behavioural trajectories demonstrate some form of career development, as well as those whose criminal behaviour will remain relatively stable over time. These issues are very similar indeed to those discussed in the more general personality literature about what is constant about people and what variable, as Youngs (2004) explores. Research around all these possibilities of consistency is therefore central to any development of a scientific basis for offender profiling.

The question of what is characteristic of an offender is one aspect of the operational problem of linking crimes to a common offender in circumstances where there is no forensic evidence, such as blood, fibres or fingerprints to link the cases. To date there has been remarkably little research on linking crimes (although interesting studies are beginning to emerge such as Woodhams, Hollin and Bull (2007) and Woodhams and Toye (2007)), even though this is a topic covered in the general personality literature (Shoda, Mischel and Wright, 1994).

The challenge to police investigations can be seen as the reverse of the personality question. Psychologists usually have a person and want to know what will be consistent about that person from one situation to another. Police investigators have a variety of situations, criminal events and need to know what consistencies can be drawn out of those events to point to a common offender.

Often consistency can also be found not so much in the individual as in the role he plays or is assigned in a criminal group. The social processes that underlie groups, teams and networks of criminals can reveal much about the consistencies in criminal behaviour and the themes that provide their foundation. A clear example of this was revealed in a study by Wilson and Donald (1999), which examined the different roles taken by teams of 'hit-and-run' burglars. They demonstrated, for example, that the offender who was given the task of driving the getaway vehicle was most likely to have a previous conviction for a vehicle-related crime. In contrast, the criminal assigned the task of keeping members of the public at bay, or controlling others who might interfere with their crime, often known as the 'heavy', was most likely to have a previous conviction for some form of violent offence. Other studies of group processes are beginning to show similar consistencies (Porter and Alison, 2006).

These findings of consistency between social role and forms of criminal endeavour are in keeping with the general thematic framework that is emerging through the studies of actual actions in a crime. They lend support to a general model of criminal activity that recognises the specific role that criminality plays in the life of the offender. It further supports the perspective that the style of criminality is an integral, natural part of the criminal's general lifestyle, not some special, atypical aspect of it.

Inference

Inferences about the likely perpetrator of a crime play a central role in driving the investigative cycle (as discussed above), so the drawing of inferences presents a key challenge in IP. Here we need to understand that exploration of inference implies an integrated set of psychological questions.

Differentiating Offenders

Although an offender's consistency is one of the starting points for empirically based models of investigative inference, in order to use these models operationally it is also necessary to have some indication of how offenders can be distinguished from each other. In part this reflects a debate within criminology about whether offenders are typically specialist or versatile in their patterns of offending (for example, Britt, 1994; Youngs, 2001). Research suggests that offenders may share many aspects of their criminal styles with most other criminals but there will be other aspects that are more characteristic of each individual. It is these rarer, discriminating features that are drawn on to provide a productive basis for distinguishing between offences and offenders.

The rarer features combine to create what may be regarded as a 'style' or 'theme' of offending. Therefore the production of a framework for classifying these different styles is a cornerstone of IP. The classification frameworks are ways of organising the themes that distinguish crimes which can then be drawn on in inference models so that, rather than being concerned with particular, individual clues as would be typical of detective fiction, the IP approach recognises that any one criminal action may be unreliably recorded or may not happen because of situational factors. But a group of actions that together indicate some dominant aspect of the offender's style may be strongly related to some important characteristic.

The most thoroughly developed empirical framework for differentiating criminals around themes is Canter and Fritzon's (1998) study of arsonists. They drew on Shye's (1985a) action systems general model of behaviour to identify four styles of arson and were able to show that the strongest statistically significant correlations were, as predicted, between actions and characteristics that exhibited similar action system themes (Shye, 1985a). We will therefore be exploring in some detail in later chapters how offending themes can be identified and what they imply.

Methodologies for IP

A range of research methods, approaches to theory and data collection and analysis devices have a special value in answering the central questions of IP: how research problems are defined, consideration of the implications for application of the methodologies chosen and the use of actual case material to elaborate on quantitative findings. By way of introduction some general points will help prepare for the remainder of this book.

The conventional data of much of psychology, in which students or general members of the public complete questionnaires or carry out tasks in laboratories, are not really appropriate for many of the issues that are relevant to investigations. Instead data have to be collected that are much closer to the sort of information that detectives and police forces work with. There are many demands in using this type of data that are not usually found within other areas of psychology. In many ways they are more similar to the data that historians, sociologists, archaeologists or anthropologists may use. They will tend to consist of archival information or reports of actual events. There will be legal and ethical constraints on what is available and what can be done with it. But as we shall see in later chapters there is a remarkable range of material available for research if you know where to look and the appropriate pathways to obtain it.

Research Strategies

The design of the research activities also tends to eschew the laboratory experiment which is so typical of many areas of psychology. Often studies that give a clear and coherent account of patterns of activities, which may be thought of as 'descriptive', are very valuable in new areas of research. Samples drawn from a wide range of different settings are also important because there is no guarantee that criminal patterns will be the same everywhere.

There can be no assumption that one study carried out with one set of data will give results that can be confidently generalised to all similar situations in different times and places, whether it be for instance a sample of serial killers, people who have defrauded their companies or terrorists involved in a series of attacks. Therefore every study counts. If it obtains similar results to previous research in the same area confidence is strengthened in the reliability of emerging patterns. If the results are different that is also very interesting because it adds to the richness of our understanding.

Furthermore, the sort of data that is collected carries direct and profound implications for the sorts of psychological theory that can be reasonably constructed. If theory is going to be about the active interpretations and purpose-oriented actions that a person brings to their environmental transactions then studies have to explore processes within the person. These will essentially grow out of correlations between aspects of what each participant being studied says or does. This leads to an important emphasis in research methodologies, including how the research is organised and the data collected, on fundamental assumptions about the nature of human beings. This is a most challenging paradox for any psychological research. What we are able to find out about people depends on the way we approach how we will find that out. The methodologies investigative psychologists use therefore impose the minimum set of assumptions on the data. They represent the underlying material as honestly as is possible.

Beyond Crime and Criminals

The tasks that investigative psychologists face are not uniquely tied into crime and police investigations. Many of the theories and methodologies inevitably relate to those evolving in other areas of psychology and related social sciences. The most obvious example is the study of criminals' geography. The models in use here can trace their descent to the emergence of epidemiology in the 1850s (cf. Canter, 2003). The classification of offenders and their offences draws on methodologies developed in social psychology and connects with debates in personality theory on personal consistency (for example, Shoda *et al.*, 1994). The work on interviewing draws directly on theories of memory and clinical psychology discussions of cognitive vulnerabilities (cf. Gudjonsson and MacKeith, 1988). It is therefore inevitable that the study of these issues in the context of investigations will feed back into the areas they connect with. The traffic of theories, methodologies and applications will certainly not be one way.

What distinguishes IP is its focus on problem solving. This makes the approach that is emerging in relation to criminal detection relevant to many other areas of psychology. It maps out a way of doing psychology that can be extended with value far beyond the criminal domain.

Linking Theory and Practice – The Book Ahead

The central challenge for IP is to keep its feet firmly within the realms of systematic, scientific psychology whilst still reaching out to applications and integration with the processes of investigation. This means that much of the research may have the form of action research or attempting to create the scientist-practitioner (Shapiro, 2002), as has been the goal of clinical psychology for many years. Some have even attempted to give this challenge the distinct label of pragmatic psychology (Fisher, 1999) although that sounds almost as if it were just opportunistic or with little base in psychological theories and methods.

This search for labels to characterise the nature of the discipline is partly because of the weaknesses in what psychologists do that emerge from the ways that many of them cow-tow to a simple-minded notion of science and scientific methodology. It is going beyond the conventions of much of psychology that the real contributions to police work and the opportunities for contributing beyond criminal investigations emerge. There is also the challenging fact that the quest to develop an IP grew out of the strengths and weaknesses of the ultimately applied activity of 'offender profiling'. The background to the development of 'profiles' provides many insights into the nature and demands there are on any behavioural science that would contribute to investigations, as we see in the following chapters.

Summary

The central questions that underlie the contribution of psychology to all aspects of many varied processes of investigation have been introduced.

* These are rooted in identifying what are the crucial aspects of any pattern of behaviour to consider; its *salience*.
* These features are the basis for developing ways of distinguishing between offenders.
* This allows systematic inferences to be made about crimes and criminals where relationships have been empirically established.

Investigative psychology takes the psychological contributions to investigations far beyond the idea of the lone, insightful individual who solves crimes on the basis of his or her special gifts of deduction. These were some of the origins of psychological contributions to police work but more often reflected in fiction than in fact.

By developing a scientific psychological study of criminal actions and detection processes, a much more challenging set of questions emerge than is apparent in fictional accounts of 'profilers'. These require consideration of what is actually consistent for an offender from one situation to another. There is also the challenge of dealing with how a criminal's actions may change over time due to many different processes of maturation and learning, as well as the variations introduced by any particular situation.

The challenges are so great that any methodologies and theories that are of value in relation to crime are probably also of utility in many other areas. The IP approach is therefore of relevance far beyond the consideration of crime and criminals, relating to issues as diverse as safety in industry or new product development.

Although IP is a new, rapidly developing discipline, it is already recognised within police forces such as Israel and South Africa which have dedicated IP units. It can trace one important strand of its origins to the process that has become popularly known as 'offender profiling'. An understanding of the origins and development of this activity is of value in gaining a full mastery of IP. The following chapters therefore review the emergence of this activity.

Further Reading

Books

Brewer, N. and Williams, K.D. (eds) *Psychology and Law: An Empirical Perspective*, Guilford, London.

Canter, D. (1995) *Criminal Shadows*, HarperCollins, London.

Canter, D. and Zukauskiene, R. (eds) (2008) *Psychology and Law: Bridging the Gap*, Ashgate, Aldershot.

Feldman, P. (1993) *The Psychology of Crime*, Cambridge University Press, Cambridge.

The *Journal of Investigative Psychology and Offender Profiling* published by Wiley InterScience is a major resource for current research and scholarship.

Articles

Canter, D. (2004) Offender profiling and investigative psychology. *Journal of Investigative Psychology and Offender Profiling*, **1**, 1–15.

Canter, D. (2008) Psychology and the criminal process, in *Criminal Psychology* (ed. D. Canter), Hodder Education, London.

Dowden, C., Bennell, C. and Bloomfield, S. (2007) Advances in offender profiling: a systematic review of the profiling literature published over the past three decades. *Journal of Police and Criminal Psychology*, **22** (1), 44–56.

Muller, D.A. (2000) Criminal profiling: real science or just wishful thinking? *Homicide Studies*, **4** (3), 234–64.

Youngs, D. (2008) Psychology and investigations, in *Criminal Psychology* (ed. D. Canter), Hodder Education, London, 177–92.

Questions for Discussion and Research

1. Watch any crime fiction episode that involves the use of an 'offender profiler' and consider the following:

   (a) What evidence is offered for the claims the 'profiler' makes? How does the 'profiler' support the opinion he (rarely she) offers?

   (b) If you did not know that the 'profiler' was supposed to be a psychologist what is there in his actions or opinions that would lead you to believe he was?

   (c) What contribution does the 'profiler' make to solving the case? If he had not been involved how might the investigation have unfolded?

   (d) Are you aware of any legal constraints that would have limited what the 'profiler' did if it had been 'real life'?

2. What aspects of your daily life do you think are reasonably consistent? If you were to commit a crime how do you think knowledge of those consistencies would be of assistance in determining you were the culprit?

3. Note how, in the quotation that starts this chapter, Ohls refers to how psychiatry will be used by the police. Why does he not say 'We'll all be reading Freud and Jung instead of the police procedures manual'?

4. Compare notes with others on how you go about having breakfast. What aspects of your breakfast routines do you think are particularly important in distinguishing what you do (the 'salient' aspects) from what others do?

5. If you really had to obtain money and the only way to do it was by illegal means, how would you go about doing it? What do you think the method you choose indicates about you and the sort of person you are? Compare your choice of crime with that of other people who you think are very different from you. Comparisons of male and female choices can be especially interesting.

CHAPTER 2

Foundations: Description and Classification

In This Chapter

- Learning Objectives
- Synopsis
- Psychology and Investigations
- Historical Background
- 'Profiling' Emerges
- The Significance of Inference
- Investigative Psychology and Offender Profiling
- Summary
- Further Reading
- Questions for Discussion and Research

Learning Objectives

When you have completed this chapter you should be able to:

1. Understand what are the key processes involved in detection.
2. Identify the misleading aspects of the 'profiling' mythology.
3. Detail the historical background of the relationship between psychology and investigations.
4. Discuss some of the origins of 'offender profiling'.

5. Evaluate some early examples of 'profiles'.
6. Appreciate the significance of inference.

Synopsis

Detection involves a number of different processes with description as its most fundamental and classification as a step further on in the utilisation of what has been observed. These processes can also be seen as the first stages in the development of inferences about offenders. They are illustrated by the early description of the characteristics of witches and subsequent proposals of the classification of people on the basis of their physical characteristics and the inferring of criminality from certain subsets of those characteristics. Even though these early attempts at identifying the indicators of deviance were fundamentally flawed they did point in the direction from which an investigative psychology could eventually emerge.

An important interim stage in the emergence of IP was the drawing of outline, pen pictures of offenders, which became known as 'offender profiles'. These descriptions of unknown offenders are based on inferences about what crimes can reveal about the criminals who commit them. The basis for such inferences and the broader implications of studying them open the way to the innovative science of IP.

Psychology and Investigations

Processes of Detection

The historical developments in the understanding of criminals and their consequent contribution to investigations reflect various stages in the investigative process. For example, investigation always requires careful *description* but that was also the first stage historically in the study of criminals. As investigations are becoming more sophisticated more advanced processes are becoming more involved. But these more advanced processes have only come to the fore in recent years. However, for an effective investigation each of the following is always necessary. The psychological issues they imply are thus also present, if implicit.

The processes that detectives need to carry out when they investigate a crime can be summarised as follows:

1. Description – they need to be aware of what is significant in a crime and to record effectively what they observe.
2. Classification – they need to be able to recognise what sort of crime they are dealing with and how it relates to other crimes.
3. Effective inference – they need to be able to derive valid inferences from what they have observed based as much as possible on scientific evidence.
4. Knowledge of criminals and their actions – their observations need to be informed by an understanding of how and why offenders act.
5. Effective decisions – they need to know how to make use of the inferences they have derived to seek further information and choose between the options for action available.

These five processes can also be regarded as stages in the evolution of what investigators have done throughout history. Early detectives, as we shall see, dealt directly with descriptions and deduced what they could from them without any systematic processes of classification or any scientific study of criminal behaviour. By contrast, present-day detectives have an array of computer tools to support their decisions and help them derive effective inferences. These inferences are increasingly being informed by the study of many crimes and criminals. In reviewing the origins of investigative psychology over this and subsequent chapters, we will therefore be considering the historical development through these five stages.

Beyond Mass-Media Mythology

Because fictional, mass-media accounts of 'profiling' are so widely available and because these often form the introduction that many people have to IP, it is essential to identify these myths directly and lay them to rest. Unfortunately many of these myths are not only accepted as factual but have led eager students to a distorted view of the realities of pursuing a career as a 'profiler'. Some of the most misleading aspects of the 'profiling' mythology are: (a) that it is an invention of the late twentieth century; (b) that its emergence was isolated from any other scientific developments and (c) that it is essentially an art dependent on the intellectual gifts of the person producing the 'profile'.

As the following historical review will demonstrate, all of these aspects have their roots in the consideration of 'profiling' as an activity that is distinct from the broader process of criminal investigation. We will therefore be showing that, on the contrary, the evolution of 'profiling' has actually been a process leading to the systematisation of detective work, marking out the ground for the behavioural science of IP that is now emerging as a new applied, evidence-based professional discipline.

Historical Background

Phase One: Description

Probably the earliest record of attempts to make inferences about people from their actions relied entirely on the description of salient behaviours that were assumed to be directly related to their characteristics. These assumptions were never put to the test but were deemed as self-evident. For example; it is reported in the Old Testament that the Jewish leader Gideon chose his army from those men who did not kneel to drink at the stream, cupping the water in their hands, preferring those who laid down to reach the stream and quench their thirst.

Gideon based his belief on the fact that orthodox Jews regard kneeling as an unacceptable, pagan act and therefore reasoned that the kneelers were secret idolaters who would be less likely to fight the infidel with total commitment. We are not given any hard evidence for Gideon's hypothesis. We do not know if at some points the banks of the stream were less deep so that kneeling was more or less feasible. Gideon selected one aspect of the observed behaviour of the men he was selecting and allowed that to guide his decision The description is recorded and the conclusion derived from it accepted without question.

Likewise, Shakespeare's Julius Caesar drew a direct conclusion from observing Cassius' thin build, saying :

Let me have men about me that are fat;
Sleek-headed men and such as sleep o' nights.
Yond Cassius has a lean and hungry look;
He thinks too much: such men are dangerous.

(William Shakespeare, *Julius Caesar*, Act 1 Scene 2)

As it turned out it was of course appropriate for Caesar to mistrust Cassius, but the generality of the claim is certainly open to question!

This approach of assuming that descriptions have natural and inevitable implications continues today in what are often referred to in detective novels as 'deductions'. Some poorly informed students, who have read more fiction than science, even think that it makes sense to refer to 'deductive profiling'. But of course this is nonsense. A deduction in this context is merely a guess about what an observation may imply. It may be possible to develop some argument as Gideon did, or state the implications categorically with great confidence as Shakespeare has Caesar doing but without further proof it is still a speculation. Do you think all thin people are untrustworthy as Caesar suggests? Or that it is even true that fat people tend to sleep well? The central pivot of IP, which takes it beyond such 'profiling', is the development of some validated principles that allow the criminal's 'shadows' to be interpreted, as Canter (1994) explained. Establishing validated principles turns out to be much more difficult to do than fiction implies or than some profilers' autobiographies would have you believe.

Nonetheless, these examples serve to draw attention to the first and fundamental component of IP and of all police investigation. This is the need to make careful observations. Even more importantly it is the need to determine what it is from all the possible things that can be observed in any situation that are the salient features to be taken account of. Sadly, throughout history people have been ready to jump to conclusions about what their observations imply and what the salient characteristics are that need to be focused upon. They have not unpacked the often complex processes by which valid inferences can be derived from what they observe.

The danger of jumping to conclusions on the basis of unchallenged but popularly accepted beliefs was particularly apparent in the witch hunts that swept across Europe for 300 years from the middle of the fifteenth century. These are salutary illustrations of just how dangerous untested and unproven 'profiles' can be.

European Witch Hunts

Cyriax (1993) estimates that between about 1450 and 1750 perhaps as many as 9 million women were killed because they were identified as witches. The main authorities in this campaign were 'witch finders' who developed what would now be recognised as a 'profile' that helped to identify who was a witch (see Box 2.1). This was a set of characteristics of a person that could be observed and which were then taken to imply that person was a witch, much as Caesar or Gideon identified untrustworthy people from their characteristics. To some extent the descriptions were drawn from incidents that were not directly aspects of the person, most notably the existence of 'impotence in the surrounding areas'. This is analogous to crime-scene information, regarding the description as the suggestion that there is someone in that area who is 'stealing men's potency'.

Box 2.1 Profile of a Witch

- Elderly female
- In meagre circumstances
- Lives on the edge of town
- Displays knowledge of herbal medicines
- 'Mark of the Devil' (insensitive spot)
- Steals men's potency, causing impotence in the surrounding areas
- Collects a great number of male members (penises) and keeps them in a birds nest or box

(Cyriax, 1993; Kramer and Sprenger, 1971; Ruiz, 2004)

The main emphasis of the witch profile is, however, on the characteristics of the person that are taken to 'prove' that she is a witch. They were drawn from stereotypes of what sorts of women were likely to be witches. These stereotypes were built up from the superstitions of the day and a complex belief system that accepted the presence of magic and that a collection of characteristics showed the person must be possessed by the devil. The characteristics of the woman were seen to be the salient features that separated her out from other people and pointed to her guilt. The stereotype of a witch is slightly different to the use of the concept of 'profiling' in present-day usage. The Witch-finders are using the profile as evidence to prove someone is a witch. Attempts have been made in court from time to time over the past decade to introduce profiles as evidence of guilt in much the same way but our modern judicial systems, fortunately, are very reluctant to accept such circumstantial evidence.

Although it was, of course, inappropriate to define a form of evil and list the features that would enable the evil person to be recognised, the systematisation of the process can be seen as a first step towards generating more objective features that could be used by investigators to identify a miscreant. The confident, yet erroneous listing of characteristics for witches has been copied in 'profiles' of offenders when witch hunts are no longer acceptable, yet a totally, empirically sound listing for all criminals is still as unlikely as the possibility that an elderly female can steal the potency of men around her.

Phase 2: Classification

The next stage in any scientific endeavour beyond the observation and listing of characteristics is to start to classify those features of interest and begin to build classification schemes, often known as taxonomies. The application of classification systems to the consideration of differences between people and thus to the consideration of criminality grew out of the powerful influence that classification was exerting in all area of science, gaining momentum in the nineteenth century. In 1859 Darwin showed that one central process, evolution, could explain the emergence of various classes of animals, in his world changing book *On the Origin of Species*. Not long after, in 1869, Mendeleyev showed that the variety of chemical elements could all be organised into a systematic form that could be explained by the weight of their atoms. This was therefore an age in which scientists believed that if only they could classify phenomena appropriately that would give them a profound understanding of the things they were classifying.

Anthropologists were carried along on this wave and many of them believed that they could understand the varieties of peoples and cultures by effectively assigning them to various groups and sub-groups. The most obvious basis for doing this was the physical appearance of each person. So leading anthropologists put a lot of effort into determining how different populations of *Homo sapiens* could be distinguished from each other by measurements of their body, especially aspects of the head and skull.

Influenced by a simple-minded view of Darwinism, which is still present in some current 'evolutionary psychology' (see the excellent discussion of this in Rose and Rose, 2000), those with an interest in criminality argued, in the nineteenth and early twentieth century, that some human beings could be assigned to subgroups of *Homo sapiens* that were closer to animals in their anatomy. They then drew the inference from this similarity that such people must therefore be more animal-like in their actions and morals. In other words that those who are criminal are genetic throwbacks in their physiology, thinking and actions to an earlier stage of human evolution.

This was a very confused argument on many levels. Perhaps the strongest challenge to it is that animals do not commit crimes, so suggesting that criminals are more like animals is to suggest there is some analogy, say between stealing property when the person knows who the owner is and foraging for food. Also the idea that there is some physical characteristic of a person that is close to that seen in, say, a great ape or chimpanzee, is very misleading because there are so many fundamental differences in the whole anatomy of non-human primates when compared with humans, as Marks (2002) makes clear in his thorough deconstruction of any claims of similarities between humans and other primates. There is also considerable evidence that early hominid societies were extremely peaceful for millennia.

But these confusions did not stop anthropologists who thought they could explain criminality and help identify criminals from declaring that physical characteristics of offenders are linked to their criminal actions. Moriz Benedikt was an early explorer of these issues, publishing *Anatomical Studies upon Brains of Criminals* in 1881. He claimed that criminals had very different brains from other people and that 'man acts, thinks, feels, desires, and acts according to the anatomical construction and physiological development of his brain' (Benedikt, 1881, vii; Henry and Einstadter, 1998). Of course, present-day neuroscience follows the same essential arguments, although usually more cautiously and often with rather more objective evidence.

There had been a series of discoveries in medicine that had led to the recognition that the brain was the most significant organ of the body in influencing thought and feeling and therefore character or personality. This idea was not prevalent until well into the eighteenth century, even though first proposed by Aristotle two-and-a-half thousand years earlier. With the growth in the study of anatomy during the nineteenth century it was increasingly possible to determine differences in the skulls of different individuals and the view therefore emerged that differences in the shape of the skull reflected differences in the shape of the brain and thus it was believed that personality characteristics could be inferred from the shape of the skull. This gave rise to a widely followed area of study called *phrenology*, which still has a popular following today, even though it has long since been discredited.

The idea was extended to cover other aspects of a person's anatomy, most especially their face and *physiognomy*. This gave rise to claims that criminals had distinct shapes to their faces. This was presented in detail in a book published in 1871 *New Physiognomy or Signs of Character*. These notions persist in some quarters today and are clearly in direct descent from Shakespeare's Caesar thinking that thin men are dangerous.

It was not a big step from believing the shape of the skull, or the face, reflected aspects of criminality to thinking that the argument could be reversed and criminals could be identified from their examination of their physical features. A number of people claimed that it was not just possible to identify whether individuals were criminal or not, but those who commit different *types* of crimes would be physically distinct from each other (Dugdale, 1877; Hooten, 1939; Lombroso, 1876; Lombroso-Ferrero, 1911; Talbot, 1898).

A Hungarian Psychiatrist, Dr Lipot Szondi (1952) took this idea even a stage further and claimed that he could determine a person's form of deviance by their selection from a set of photographs that Szondi put together of people with known psychological and criminal histories. Respondents are asked to say which picture they prefer and it is then inferred that they chose a person who has the same pattern of deviance as themselves. This test is still in use in some countries although evidence for its efficacy is difficult to find.

Box 2.2 Lombroso's (1876) Profile of Murderers (Lombroso-Ferrero, 1972)

1. An aquiline beak of a nose.
2. Fleshy swollen, and protruding lips.
3. Small receding chin.
4. Dark hair and bushy eyebrows that meet across the nose.
5. Little or no beard.
6. Displays an abundance of wrinkles, even in those younger than 30.
7. Four to five times greater taste sensibility than the average person.
8. A cynical attitude, completely lacking remorse.
9. More likely to bear a tattoo.
10. Attaches no importance to dress and are frequently dirty and shabby.

Source: As cited by Welch and Keppel (2006).

Cesare Lombroso

Although mainly of historical interest, it is worth considering the contributions of Cesare Lombroso and Ernst Kretschmer who pioneered approaches to creating typologies and profiles of criminals because they are often credited with inspiring the first generation of FBI 'profilers' (Blau, 1994; Brussel, 1968; Ressler and Shachtman, 1992; Teton, 1989).

As mentioned, Lombroso, who was trained as a doctor in Italy, was part of a movement who saw Darwinian evolution as applicable not just to the development of species but also to the creation of different types of people, some of whom he considered as essentially more primitive than others, in the sense that they were more like human's earlier animal forebears. His complex thinking also allowed him to propose distinctions between varieties of criminal, distinguishing for example rapists, thieves and murderers. This included differences in everything from their ears to the nature of their skin, but also proposed differences in their slang and the sorts of tattoos they had (Lombroso-Ferrero, 1911, 1972). Some of these are illustrated in Box 2.2.

Lombroso's ideas were based on the belief that criminals came from a particular class which was divided into subgroups of different forms of offending, an idea that still pervades many discussions of criminality. However, he did move the scientific process on by discussing types of offender and offending rather than focusing entirely on unique traits or attempting to develop an understanding of one particular criminal.

Not long after Lombroso's proposals were first published, a leading British physician, Charles Goring (1923) cooperated with one of the founder's of modern statistics, Karl Pearson, to examine more than 3000 entrants to English prisons over an eight-year period. He made very careful measurements of all the physical features of these prisoners to which Lombroso had drawn attention. He then compared these with measurements made on the law-abiding graduates of Oxford and Cambridge universities of a similar age. His conclusions were absolutely direct and unambiguous: 'Both with regard to measurements and the presence of physical anomalies in criminals, our statistics present a startling conformity with similar statistics of the law-abiding class. Our inevitable conclusion must be that there is no such thing as a physical criminal type' (Goring, 1923: 173).

A variety of other studies have had similar negative results. Furthermore, our understanding of genetics, as Marks (2002) has discussed in detail, now makes it clear that whatever it is that determines a person's physical features does not necessarily relate at all closely to what may determine other aspects of a person's characteristics. Furthermore, physical characteristics such as height and weight, lack of anomalies, and general health, which are reflected in what a person looks like – and many forms of mild deformity – are all very greatly influenced by social circumstances and environment.

Much of modern criminology (as outlined, for example, by Sutherland, 1978) has shown that criminals are often drawn from particular socioeconomic backgrounds. So the evolutionary, genetic basis for Lombroso's theories will always be confounded with the circumstances in which the person lives. But those circumstances are not unique to criminals. Not all people from poor backgrounds, who may be shabbily dressed and have wrinkled skins because of their circumstances, will become murderers.

The most fundamental flaw in Lombroso's work is his basic assumption that criminals are a distinct subset of people, especially what he called 'born-criminals'. This idea still pervades much of popular thinking about criminals but ignores the possibility of everyone being even the most violent of criminals given the appropriate situation. It presupposes that criminals are a distinct subspecies of humanity. In this regard it can be likened to the racist views that people from a particular cultural or ethnic subgroup are not human beings in the same way as people from other subgroups.

These weaknesses in Lombroso's theories are important to consider because, as has been pointed out, a number of early profilers (for example, Brussel, 1968; Ressler and Shachtman, 1992; Teton, 1989) think of their profiling activities as having been influenced by Lombroso's attempts to classify people and show how criminals may be distinctly different from other people. So whilst it is probably the case that these early profilers did not embrace the implicit evolutionary ideas behind Lombroso's thoughts, it is very possible that they were making similar assumptions about the possibility of there being distinct characteristics of various subsets of offenders.

The big difference, though, between Lombroso and the early FBI 'profilers' is that he operated in a mode that fitted his approach to science. He did measure criminals and make comparisons between them. It was just that he did this without the sort of clarity and statistical precision that Goring and Pearson (Goring, 1913) used to test his ideas. As we shall see, the early profilers were actually less scientific than this. They assumed that the characteristics of offenders could be inferred directly from crime-scene information rather than from general studies of criminals and their actions. It could therefore be argued their work might have been even more fruitful if they had followed through and developed Lombroso's methodology more carefully instead of building on his general theory.

Despite the obvious flaws and fallacies in Lombroso's theories and research, his determination to find types of people led many to believe that even if the particular characteristics he proposed did not reveal reliable types that nonetheless the search for such characteristics could be productive if carried out in other ways. He therefore helped to open the way to different attempts to classify people on the basis of their physical characteristics and to search for links between those characteristics and their personalities. By making the further assumption that personality is directly related to criminality (a leap, as we shall see in later chapters, that is neither logical nor valid) these attempts were used to try and go beyond Lombroso to identify types of person on the basis of their overall physical form.

Ernst Kretschmer

Although Lombroso did most in the last century to open up discussion on the physical features of criminals, the idea that bodily form relates to character or personality goes back to ancient antiquity. The person who is often credited with the basis of much of modern medicine, Galen, had proposed as early as 2000 AD that there were four main types of person. The labels he used are still recognisable in their English translations: choleric – which implies a person who is quick to express their emotions; phlegmatic, who is in modern parlance 'laid back'; melancholic, who we would call 'moody', and sanguine, who is sociable and outgoing.

Galen thought each of these typically had a particular build but was not very clear on exactly what those builds were.

Many others tried to develop Galen's ideas but it was not until Ernst Kretschmer the German psychiatrist published a carefully researched system of body types in his book *Körperbau und Character* in 1921, published in English as *Physique and Character* in 1925, that some of the ideas of Lombroso could be taken a stage further. As a psychiatrist, Kretschmer was interested in the various forms of mental illness. So he set out to show a relationship between types of build and types of mental patient. He then extended these ideas to claim that they could also be used to characterise criminals, on the assumption that criminality was also a form of mental illness (do not forget these were the days when people went to their doctors to get treatment for being homosexuals, in the belief that this, too, was a disease).

Kretschmer's typology of criminals had many similarities to Lombroso's ideas that a high correlation existed between physical features, personality type, and criminality. The big difference was that Kretschmer, harking back to Galen, focused on body type rather than features of the face or skull. A summary of his ideas about types of crime and types of body serves to show both how initially attractive his ideas are but how, on closer reading, they appear ambiguous and quite confusing, containing a number of internal contradictions (see Box 2.3).

Box 2.3 Kretschmer's Somatotypology (1925)

Cycloid personality	Schizoid personality	Displastic personality
heavyset, soft body type vacillate between normality and abnormality lack spontaneity and sophistication most likely to commit nonviolent property crimes	most likely have athletic, muscular bodies some can be thin and lean schizophrenic commit violent type of offenses	mixed group highly emotional often unable to control themselves mostly commit sexual offenses or crimes of passion

Source: Kretschmer (1925), Schmalleger (2004), as cited by Welch and Keppel (2006).

The great problem with his studies was that his definitions of both body type and mental illness were open to a lot of distortion. This meant that there was the possibility of unwittingly biasing his observations to get the results he was hoping for. He also took no account of the environment or circumstances of his particular patients and how that might have influenced his results. So although his ideas were taken up by others, most notably by the American psychologist Sheldon in his 1954 *Atlas of Men*, most experts these days do not regard the relationship between body type and personality as well established.

Whatever the fundamental flaws in the belief in the association between body type and types of criminality, many of the early profilers thought it appropriate to draw on these ideas when preparing their profiles. For example; Ressler claims that he used Kretschmer's body types in his profiles (Ressler and Shachtman, 1992). Brussel (1968) also claimed that he founded his profile of the Mad Bomber in 1957 on Kretschmer's work (Brussel, 1968: 33). Based on crime-scene details, Brussel believed that the Mad Bomber was suffering from paranoia. Kretschmer's study of 10 000 patients in mental hospitals indicated that 85% of patients suffering with paranoia had athletic body types, which led Brussel to conclude that the Mad Bomber most likely had a symmetrical build (Brussel, 1968: 32–3). The important development in Brussel's approach was that he was using information drawn from general clinical classifications to apply to a particular case. He may just have been lucky that the conclusions he drew happened to be correct in that case even though the information he was drawing on did not stand up to detailed scrutiny. Much more important was his methodology of looking for classification systems that he considered relevant then drawing conclusions from the research he could find. In doing this he was laying the foundations for IP.

'Profiling' Emerges

Investigators have always been willing to consider the guidance offered by others, although not necessarily to take any notice if it. These advisors have often been other more experienced detectives, or people with special expertise, most notably physicians, and such experts have often been willing to comment on characteristics of the offender or how the offender may be detected or caught, encouraged to confess or be shown to be guilty. With the development of psychology and psychiatry, the police increasingly turned to these professions for assistance.

In the middle of the twentieth century the summary of the characteristics of a person became popularly known as a 'profile', most frequently in newspaper descriptions of celebrities. Before that there was a mixture of terms in use. So that when, during the Second World War, in 1942 Colonel William J. Donovan of the United States Office of Strategic Services approached the psychoanalyst Walter C. Langer for a report on Adolf Hitler, Donovan said that what he needed was:

> a realistic appraisal of the German situation. If Hitler is running the show, what kind of a person is he? What are his ambitions? How does he appear to the German people? What is he like with his associates? What is his background? And most of all, we want to know as much as possible about his psychological make-up, the things that make him tick. In addition, we ought to know what he might do if things begin to go against him . . .
>
> (Langer, 1972: 3–10)

What Donovan was requesting was similar to the compilations that Roman Generals prepared of descriptions of the leaders of enemy forces in order to help plan their military campaigns.

If you find the description that Langer produced quoted today, you will see that it is called a 'profile of Adolf Hitler', although the word 'profile' does not appear to exist in any of the discussions in the 1940s. The creation of such a description of Hitler today would be called 'profiling', defined as the analysis of a person's psychological and behavioural characteristics. This definition clearly indicates that the term 'profiling' can be used to mean a 'pen-picture' of a person in any context, not just in relation to criminals.

It is worth noting that 'profile' also has a mathematical meaning. It is a set of values that typify a particular entity. This is usually the average measurements achieved on a number of different indices for a category of people or things. In this sense the environmental profile of a make of car would be its fuel consumption, carbon emissions, pollutant emissions and so forth.

The use of the term 'profiling' in relation to offenders probably began to be used in various law-enforcement agencies across the United States in the early 1970s but it gained a real impetus in the mid 1970s from the FBI's Behavioral Science Unit running training courses at the FBI college in Quantico, Virginia, specifically under the heading of 'criminal' or 'personality profiling'. But when Thomas Harris' 1988 novel *The Silence of the Lambs*, influenced by a visit he had made to Quantico, became a worldwide best seller, the term 'offender profiling' jumped into the popular imagination.

Since that time a growing body of accounts of profiling from autobiographies, newspaper articles and true-crime magazines of actual cases, academic reviews and an increasing number of scientific studies, have given rise to many different overlapping labels for 'offender profiling' and related activities (Box 2.4).

Box 2.4 Terms that are Sometime Taken to Mean 'Offender Profiling'

Applied criminology
Crime assessment
Crime scene analysis
Crime scene assessment
Criminal behavioural analysis
Criminal investigative analysis
Criminal personality profiling
Criminal profiling
Criminal profiling from crime-scene analysis
Geo-behavioural profiling
Geographic profiling
Geographical profiling
Geographical offender profiling
Investigative criminology
Investigative profiling
Investigative psychology
Personality profiling

> Psychiatric profiling
> Psychological profiling
> And various combinations of these.

The confusion this plethora of terms causes is made worse by the fact that for some people it is a rather casual activity based on experience as 'a method of identifying the perpetrator of a crime based on an analysis of the nature of the offense and the manner in which it was committed' (Teton, 1995). Here the perpetrator is 'identified' and all that is needed is an examination of 'the manner in which' the offence is committed. There is no hint here of developing a description of the offender. The task is simply to identify him. Nor is there any explanation of how the offence is to be 'examined' or on what basis that examination can be fruitful.

The emphasis here is on trying to identify the perpetrator when all that is available is the information from the crime scene. This is rather different from giving a description of what 'makes a person tick' as did Langer on Hitler. It also contrasts with John Faye's description in *The Police Dictionary and Encyclopaedia;*

> *Psychological profile:* a description of the personality and characteristics of an individual based on an analysis of acts committed by the individual. The description may include age, race, sex, socio-economic and marital status, educational level, arrest history, location of residence relative to the scene of the act, and certain personality traits. A profile is based on characteristic patterns of uniqueness that distinguish certain individuals from the general population. Regarding criminal acts, patterns are deduced from thoughtful analysis of wounds, weapon used, cause of death, position of the body.
>
> (Fay, 1988: 271–2)

Perhaps a little more poetically the process of making inferences about an unknown offender can be looked on as interpreting the psychological traces left at a crime. As Canter (1994: 4) puts it:

> A criminal may reveal what shoes he was wearing from his footprints. His blood-type can be determined by any body-fluids left at the scene. But as well as *material* traces, he also leaves *psychological* traces, tell-tale patterns of behaviour that indicate the sort of person he is . . . They cannot be taken into a laboratory and dissected under a microscope. They are more like shadows which undoubtedly are connected to the criminal who cast them, but they flicker and change, and it may not always be obvious where they come from. Yet, if they can be fixed and interpreted, a criminal's shadows can indicate where investigators should look and what sort of person they should be looking for.
>
> (Canter and Gregory, 1994). Reproduced with permission from Elsevier

The flickering shadow imagery serves to emphasise the problems of drawing profiles in contrast to Teton's confident claim that they identify the offender. Canter's caution is actually more in keeping with the original use of the term 'profile'. One of the earliest uses is Blount's 1656 description of illustrations in which places or objects are shown from a side view (Oxford English Dictionary, 2004). This use is derived from the obsolete Italian word *profilo*, 'a drawing or border', that in its turn has origins in the Latin *filum* for 'thread'. Thus the earliest use of the term emphasises that a 'profile' is not the full description of an object but is an outline sketch that captures its most salient features. It was in this sense that it began to be used to characterise a pen-portrait or summary verbal description of the distinguishing aspects of a person. In other words, an account of what they are like rather than a lengthy biography. From this meaning, of a filament or outline the terms 'profile' and 'profiling' have found their way into popular use, particularly in the context of police work, as a summary of the salient characteristics of an offender.

The Significance of Inference

The sketchy qualities of the profiles that are produced are one aspect that needs to be emphasised. They are outlines, indicators of the salient features of a person, not full-blown three-dimensional images. But they also imply a second crucial aspect. They are inferences derived from what is known about a crime. There is thus a crucial and fundamental difference between drawing a profile, whether of Adolf Hitler or the latest Hollywood star, and the process of 'offender profiling'.

In the case of a journalist or psychoanalyst considering a significant person in the public eye the person described in the profile is known. Walter Langer could interview people who had had close contact with Hitler. He could read Hitler's own autobiography and gather over 11 000 pages of information about the person he was describing. Similarly a journalist writing about a celebrity can gain access to the celebrity's friends and family, possibly personal documents, and may even be allowed to interview the person directly. None of this is possible in 'offender profiling'.

The central purpose of such profiles is as in the earlier quote from Canter (1994) to indicate for an *unknown offender* 'where investigators should look and what sort of person they should be looking for'. This means that profiles drawn for detectives are always speculative. They are hypotheses derived from inferences about the offender. These inferences are drawn from information available to the investigators, derived from details of the crime, where, when and how it happened and to whom. Shakespeare's Julius Caesar is making an inference when he claims that 'lean and hungry' looking men are dangerous, but at least Cassius is there for all to see. In a police investigation the inference is much more difficult because all that is available is the information – Canter's (1994) 'criminals' shadows'. This means that producing an offender profile is not a journalistic task, simply summarising what is known about a given person. It is the scientific endeavour of establishing what implications can be validly drawn from what happened during a crime.

This drawing of inferences has all the challenges, strengths and weaknesses of any new area of behavioural science because there are no well-established, universal principles that apply to all criminals in all situations. This is not like an area of the natural sciences like physics in which the properties of materials can be derived with great confidence from 400 years of study.

Investigative Psychology and Offender Profiling

Despite the vast media interest in offender profiling it is only in the twenty-first century that the first steps have been taken towards establishing how inferences about offenders can be made reliably. The scientific quest to develop reliable inference processes, going beyond the experiences of individual advisors and 'profilers' has given rise to the new discipline of IP. As we will see throughout the following chapters, by recognising that the process of 'profiling' is part of true scientific discipline it can be seen to take its place amongst a much wider range of contributions that psychology can make to police investigations.

Thus, although the impetus for developing IP was the potential that has been opened up by the possibility of drawing offender profiles, it would be misleading to equate IP with 'offender profiling'. The latter is the relatively informal activity of experienced police officers speculating about the characteristics of criminals. It was an activity that had its heyday in the training sessions at the FBI Academy in Quantico in the 1980s. Investigative psychology is a broad discipline that draws on many different aspects of psychology to assist in the understanding of crime and criminals and thereby contribute to all aspects of law enforcement.

Summary

Although the term 'offender profiling' has reached public attention most notably through blockbuster films and then through enormously popular television shows, such as *CSI, NYPD Blue, Millennium, Profiler, Law and Order, Missing without a Trace* and *Cracker,* and more recently *Fitz* and *Numb3rs* and *Wire in the Blood,* the activity of experts giving informed advice to criminal investigations can be traced back as far as Biblical times. This advice has inevitably drawn on knowledge and assumptions about offenders and their actions. Thus the emergence in the late twentieth century of 'offender profiling' as a distinct area of activity that is open to systematic study and improvement is most usefully understood as one stage in the evolution over many years of detectives' working practices. It is an interim stage on the way to the full-blown science of IP.

The activity of making inferences about offenders from the crimes they have committed shares its origins with the sciences on which detectives have always drawn. However, like the mainstream developments from physics, chemistry and biology, the psychological inferences about criminals have always been greatly influenced by psychological theories of the time. Initially there was no basis for these inferences other than untested assumptions and superstitions. The process of identifying a person who had done something wrong from overt characteristics that were believed to be associated with people who did such wrongs has been prevalent throughout history, reaching its apotheosis in the search for 'witches' but still being present today in racist beliefs and other stereotyped thinking. The move from the simple-minded belief that some salient feature of a person was an indicator of his or her guilt came when studies grew in medicine and the related biological and social sciences, that attempted to classify people into different types. These typologies were then drawn upon to build inferences about the links between various human characteristics, most notably between the form of their head or body and their personality. The proposals that each person could be assigned to a particular type paved the way for considering what type of person may have committed a particular type of crime. This gave rise to the drawing of pen-pictures of unknown offenders in a way similar to what had already been produced in the descriptions of well-known people, whose 'profiles' were a common journalistic practice from the middle of the twentieth century.

Investigators have always drawn on the sciences of their day to help them solve crimes and get convictions in court. With the widespread of psychology and related behavioural sciences throughout the twentieth century, it was inevitable that detectives would begin to draw upon the opinions and approaches of experts in these disciplines as they had drawn on experts in chemistry and medicine in the nineteenth century and of course still do today. It would therefore be wrong to assume, as portrayed in so many fictional accounts of 'profilers', that they were always some separate breed of specialists. The processes of profiling did not suddenly emerge without a long history of precursors in the interactions between investigators and those who claimed some insights into criminal activities and experiences. Nor did they emerge independently of developments in many other aspects of police work. Indeed, as will be detailed in the following chapters, one productive way of thinking about the 'offender profiling' process is as a systematisation of many aspects of investigations.

There were many weaknesses in the early attempts at assigning people to different types, whether it was witches in the 1500s or 'schizoid' personalities in the 1900s. Some of these weaknesses have without doubt become rooted in some present-day assumptions about criminals. But the most fundamental weakness is the extreme difficulty of confidently putting any person into one 'type' for all his or her activities. A parallel process has therefore always been present in science of building up an understanding of the mechanisms that give rise to particular phenomena. These are often thought of as 'theories' or 'models' and they are the bedrock of modern psychology. Yet they too have origins in the hesitant and not always particularly fruitful activities of scientists in earlier ages, to which we turn in the next chapter.

Further Reading

Books

The *Malleus Maleficarum* is available online from www.malleusmaleficarum.org.

Cesare Lombroso's *Criminal Man* Translated by Mary Gibson and Nicole Hahn Rafter, published by Duke University Press in 2006 is available from http://books.google.com/books.

Ellis, Havelock (1901) *The Criminal* is available as an Elibron Classic

Canter, D. and Alison, L. (eds) (1997) *Criminal Detection and the Psychology of Crime*, Ashgate, Dartmouth.

Harcourt, B.E (2007) *Against Prediction: Profiling, Policing and Punishing in an Actuarial Age*, University of Chicago Press, Chicago. (This may seem a curious choice but it explores the consequences of what may be regarded as modern day 'witch-hunts' driven by simple-minded 'offender profiling'.)

Questions for Discussion and Research

1. What are the origins of the term *profiling*? Do these origins have any implications for offender profiling?
2. Why are there so many different terms to describe the process of offender profiling?
3. Why is 'description' such a crucial stage in offender profiling?
4. What is wrong with offering a 'profile' of a witch? Are there any similar sorts of profiles offered today?
5. Can you tell people's characters from what they look like?
6. What are the main weaknesses in Lombroso's argument that criminals can be identified from their appearance?
7. Do you recognise Galen's types of people in those you know?
8. Are there any problems in assigning people to one type or another?
9. Can you come up with your own classification of criminal types?
10. Why is classification so important for a science of profiling?

The Coming of the Informed Detective

In This Chapter

Learning Objectives

When you have completed this chapter you should be able to:

1. Understand developments in science that led to individuals increasingly contributing to active police investigations.

2. Give some examples of cases where individuals made inferences about likely suspects and evaluate those inferences.
3. Discuss the value of some of the contributions made by key literary figures.
4. Distinguish between deduction and induction.
5. Evaluate the theoretical bases for the profiles of 'Jack the Ripper' offered by Conan Doyle and Thomas Bond.
6. Understand what is meant by the term 'reverse diagnosis'.

Synopsis

During the course of the nineteenth century the advancing developments in science encouraged a number of individuals outside of law enforcement to attempt to contribute to police investigations. They were usually physicians but also included imaginative writers, notably Edgar Allan Poe and then Arthur Conan Doyle. These advisors drew on careful consideration of the details of crimes and their knowledge of people to deduce aspects of the offence and offender that could be of assistance to the detectives trying to solve the crime. Although the recorded accounts of the reports they produced for the police did not lead to the major crimes of their day being solved, they did lay the basis for twentieth-century profiling and consequently cleared the path for present-day IP.

Medical Contributions

In the previous chapter we saw some examples of systematic description and classification emerging from studies of individual variation which were then applied to the consideration of criminality and the possible identification of criminals but that was only one route into the development of 'offender profiling' and from that the evolution of IP. Another equally important route was through imaginative contributions to police investigations.

These contributions came from people who had thought a lot about human actions, rather than the broader issues of categorisation that we dealt with in the last chapter. The main impetus for this activity was from the rapid development of medicine in the nineteenth century. Physicians saw their discipline as based in science but, unlike Lombroso and Kretschmer, they had very direct day-to-day contact with patients so were more willing to consider actual actions of individuals as the starting point for their inferences. Curiously, there was also considerable interplay between imaginative leaps in fiction and activities in practice; an interplay that is still with us.

This pathway to current psychological contributions thus reflects the third component of investigations and a further step towards the development of criminal behavioural science. This is the attempt to make effective inferences from observations and some knowledge of the categorisations that are appropriate to help understand those observations. These inferences are to be based as much as possible on scientific evidence.

From Fact to Fiction to Fact

The development of a more informed approach to inferences about criminals came with major developments in the investigation of crimes during the middle of the nineteenth century. In these early years of the reign of Queen Victoria, both in the United States and in Europe, detectives were moving out of an era of superstition and prejudice into the modern age where logic and the facts were held in much higher regard. But, as is so often the case in the area of scientific development, especially in the applications of science to criminal investigations, fiction writers were often ahead of the real-world practitioners they were claiming to write about.

In the summer of 1841 Mary Rogers' body was pulled out of the Hudson River near New York City. This was obviously a murder and the victim was an attractive young woman, whom it quickly emerged had some notoriety. Such a mixture of intriguing victim and horrific murder created a great deal of public interest so that many details of the case were reported widely.

Edgar Allan Poe

The young author Edgar Allan Poe was fascinated with this crime and studied the newspaper accounts closely. He was convinced that his writer's imagination could solve this crime where the plodding police could not. So he wrote a story set in Paris that he called the Mystery of Marie Roget. A few years later he added a prologue to this story that made his intentions in writing it clear:

> A young girl, Mary Cecilia Rogers, was murdered in the vicinity of New York; and although her death occasioned an intense and long-enduring excitement, the mystery attending it had remained unsolved at the period when the present paper was written and published (November, 1842). Herein, under pretence of relating the fate of a Parisian grisette, the author has followed, in minute detail, the essential, while merely paralleling the inessential, facts of the real murder of Mary Rogers. Thus all argument founded upon the fiction is applicable to the truth: and the investigation of the truth was the object.
>
> (Edgar Allan Poe *The Mystery of Marie Roget* 1850 – available from
> http://eserver.org/books/poe/mystery_of_marie_roget.html, accessed 10 May 2009)

It is interesting that his story is considered possibly the first modern detective story even though in many ways it is a desktop consideration of an actual case. Poe pored over the minutiae of how the victim was killed and how various clues were found, offering hypotheses and then seeking evidence to refute or support them. For example, there was an extended discussion by the police of how various articles belonging to the victim came to be in a particular location. The police had assumed they had been left there during a struggle but Poe argues that a careful examination of these articles shows that could not have been the case.

> And, now, let me beg your notice to the highly artificial arrangement of the articles. On the upper stone lay a white petticoat; on the second, a silk scarf; scattered around, were a parasol, gloves, and a pocket-handkerchief bearing the name 'Marie Roget.' Here is just such an arrangement as would

naturally be made by a not over-acute person wishing to dispose the articles naturally. But it is by no means a really natural arrangement. I should rather have looked to see the things all lying on the ground and trampled underfoot.

He came to the conclusion, from studying all the published material, that the murder was committed by a gang of villains, pouring scorn on the suggestions the police had of a suicide or even that the victim had eloped and it was not her body at all. Poe was trying to demonstrate that a highly systematic imagination could be brought to the consideration of the crime leading to an inevitable conclusion. The police were not too pleased with his attempts to better them from his armchair and he never had full access to all the actual details held by the police, so it is perhaps not surprising that the general consensus is that his conclusions of who had committed the crime were quite wrong. Unfortunately, though, as in so many crimes that grip the public imagination, the murder of Mary Rogers was never solved, so Poe's speculations still remain a possibility.

What is important about this recreation of an intense examination of a crime scene and the attempt to derive conclusions from it is that it provided a graphic impetus to the emergence of a much more scientific and methodical approach to investigating crimes. Rather than trying to establish whom witnesses had seen and obtain confessions from suspects through torture, or build up some general idea of what a criminal (or witch as discussed in the last chapter) would look like, Edgar Allan Poe laid out a process that started directly from the facts of the case and attempted to stick to them as closely as possible. He used his artistic imagination to try to make sense of those facts. He drew on some knowledge of the patterns of behaviour of criminals, but this was often more speculation than well-established facts. For example, there is an amusing discussion in the 'Mystery of Marie Roget' of whether petty criminals of the day carried handkerchiefs or not. So, despite the many weaknesses in his approach, he cleared the ground for an ever more scientific and systematic approach to crime investigation.

Dr Joseph Bell

Poe's detective work was an important harbinger of other fictional portrayals. Not least the detective who will be mentioned first if anyone is asked to name a famous investigator – Sherlock Holmes, the creation of the master storyteller Sir Arthur Conan Doyle. But Conan Doyle's skilful detective was not a totally fictional invention. As Conan Doyle was keen to point out, Holmes was based on the real-life professor under whom he had studied medicine in Edinburgh, Dr Joseph Bell (see Figure 3.1), in the middle of the nineteenth century (Orel, 1991). In a letter to Dr Bell in 1882, Conan Doyle wrote the following:

It is most certainly to you that I owe Sherlock Holmes and though in the stories I have the advantage of being able to place [the detective] in all sorts of dramatic positions, I do not think his analytical work is in the least exaggeration of some effects which I have seen you produce in the outpatient ward.

(Hall, 1983)

Figure 3.1   Portrait of Dr Joseph Bell.

As teacher and medical examiner for the courts as well as being a gifted surgeon Dr Joseph Bell also set up one of the first training courses for nurses (Liebow, 1982). In all this professional activity he highlighted the crucial importance of careful inspection of what could be observed in patients and detailed consideration of the implications of these observations. These considerations were informed by his encyclopaedic knowledge of illness and the ways of the world. It was not just the observation but the information he held in memory, informed by his many years as a medical practitioner, which enabled him to derive such powerful conclusions from what he saw and heard. He was thus able to show the young Conan Doyle how observation combined with detailed knowledge could be the bedrock for a much more powerful way of thinking about the detection of crimes.

The important point for us to remember is that Dr Bell was able to use his observations of the patients he encountered because of his knowledge of the regions, dialect, argot, patterns of speech and behaviour and other information such as tattoos and other visible marks to draw reasoned conclusions and diagnosis of the patient's illness. This is delightfully illustrated in the example that Conan Doyle gives in his memoirs (Orel 1991):

'Well, my man, you've served in the army.'
'Aye, Sir.'
'Not long discharged?'
'No, Sir.'
'A Highland regiment?'
'Aye, Sir.'
'A noncommissioned officer.'
'Aye, Sir.'
'Stationed at Barbados.'
'Aye, Sir.'

'You see gentleman,' he would explain, 'the man was a respectful man, but did not remove his hat. They do not in the army, but he would have learned civilian ways had he been long discharged. He has an air of authority and he is obviously Scottish. As to Barbados, his complaint is of elephantiasis, which is West Indian and not British.' To his audience of Watsons it all seemed very miraculous, until it was explained, and then it became simple enough. It is no wonder that after the study of such a character I used and amplified his methods when in later life I tried to build up a scientific detective who solved cases in his own merits.

(Hall, 1983: 79; Liebow, 1982: 132–3; Orel, 1991:5–6)

Note that Dr Bell had knowledge of patterns of behaviour in the army and of the prevalence of elephantiasis in the British colonies. He also was willing to make the intellectual leap and assume that the respect exhibited by the patient combined with an 'air of authority' indicated a military man who had reached the rank of non-commissioned officer. The sequence of questions is perhaps worth considering too. If Bell had been given a negative answer to his first question he would not have followed up with the other questions that built on the assumption of the patient being recently discharged from the army.

Another example is given by Emory Jones in an article in the *Lancet* in 1956. Jones had also been a student of Bell's and had recorded an example of the intriguing inferences he was able to make:

A woman with a small child was shown in. Joe Bell said good morning and she said good morning in reply.
'What sort of crossing di'ye have from Burntisland?'
'It was guid.'
'And had ye a guid walk up Inverleith Row?'
'Yes.'
'And what did you do with the other wain [child]?'
'I left him with my sister in Leith.'
'And would you still be working at the linoleum factory?'
'Yes, I am.'

'You see, gentleman, when she said good morning to me I noticed her Fife accent, and as you know, the nearest town in Fife is Burntisland. You notice the red clay on the edges of the soles of her shoes, and the only such clay within twenty miles of Edinburgh is in the Botanical Gardens. Inverleith Row borders the garden and is her nearest way here from Leith. You observed that the coat she carried over her arm is too big for the child who is with her, and therefore she set out from home with two children. Finally, she has dermatitis on the fingers on her right hand which is peculiar to workers in the linoleum factory at Burntisland.'

(Hall, 1983)

Here again, the knowledge Dr Bell had of local geography and soil conditions is combined with his knowledge of illnesses associated with working conditions in factories in the area, as well as simple conclusions from the observations he was able to make on the spot.

Sherlock Holmes

The similarities of these anecdotes about Dr Bell to examples in the fictional activities of Sherlock Holmes are easy to see. For instance, Sherlock Holmes has the following discussion with his associate Dr Watson:

> Upon observing two men, 'An old soldier, I perceive,' said Sherlock. 'And very recently discharged,' said the older brother. 'Served in India I see.' 'And a noncommissioned officer.' 'Royal Artillery, I fancy.' 'And a widower.' The amazed Watson, thinking he was being had, asked them to explain. 'Surely,' said Sherlock, 'it is not hard to see that a man with that bearing, expression of authority, and sun-baked skin is a soldier, is more than a private, and is not long from India.'
>
> (Liebow, 1982: 133)

Holmes' inferences always go a little further than is actually feasible in daily life, beyond the rather mundane, but engaging deductions that anecdotes about Bell illustrate. Nonetheless, these and other examples show the values that could be obtained from careful observations of patients that were interpreted with knowledge of anatomy and medicine, as well as knowledge of the various patterns of daily behaviour, to make appropriate inferences about the patient and what they were suffering from. This emphasis on obtaining the facts then deriving appropriate conclusions from them is rather neatly captured in one of Sherlock Holmes' famous retorts:

> 'This is indeed a mystery,' I remarked. 'What do you imagine that it means?'
>   'I have no data yet. It is a capital mistake to theorise before one has data. Insensibly one begins to twist facts to suit theories, instead of theories to suit facts . . .'
>
> (from 'A Scandal in Bohemia', 1891)

The facts are most often obtained from direct observation, so Sherlock Holmes and Dr Bell are often described as 'masters of observation'. Attention is drawn to what they observed but this is to underestimate the sense they made of what they observed. The often-quoted saying of Holmes 'You see, but you do not observe' (also from 'A Scandal in Bohemia') really emphasises the sense that can be made of what can be seen, turning the simple fact, of a coat over an arm or the way a person carries himself into an interpreted observation about the size of a child or military background. It is knowledge and understanding that turns seeing into observation.

It was this knowledge, coming from the sciences of anatomy, physiology and chemistry into the training of doctors and with it the emergence of a scientifically based medicine that had so greatly impressed Conan Doyle, so that when he started writing the Sherlock Holmes stories he made his central character more of a scientist making sense of the data available than a plucky hero or person with supernatural powers. Whenever Sherlock Holmes works out the meaning of some clue or other he explains to his friend and assistant, Dr Watson, the basis of his reasoning. There is always logic (at least apparently) in the conclusions Holmes draws that he makes clear to his audience. Revealing the logic makes the conclusions all the more impressive and also helps to provide support for them.

Distinguishing Deduction and Induction

Holmes' process of reasoning lays the foundation for scientific approaches to the investigation of crime. To understand how this approach works it is essential to be clear on the distinction between two different processes that we touched on in the previous chapter: deduction and induction. Science uses deduction to come up with inductive inferences. It works like this.

Consider the claim that 'all black birds are swans'. Well if I now see a bird that is black it is a logical *deduction* that it is a swan. However, if my initial premise is wrong and there are many black birds that are not swans then my 'deduction' will be wrong too. When the initial premise is in error, the deduction that the black bird I see is a swan is little more than a speculation. Knowing the proportion of black birds that are swans and indeed other characteristics that are distinguishing features of swans is the basis for an *inductive* process. Induction, in this context is usually defined as reasoning from detailed facts to general principles. In other words, by reviewing many known instances of swans, or in the criminal context criminals who commit certain types of crime (a process of empirical research), some general principles can be established, which can then be drawn upon to make inferences about some new instance, some new crime, that emerges.

Dr Joseph Bell was illustrating this use of inductive logic when he alerted his students to the key symptoms they should note when carrying out a diagnosis. Observation and careful description is the critical starting point, but without the knowledge of what processes may have given rise to the things observed, and the empirical evidence that shows these processes in operation, simple deduction on its own can lead to the errors of the witch finders, or the bad science of Lombroso and Kretschmer.

Reverse Diagnosis

Conan Doyle also made an imaginative leap that is crucial for the emergence of offender profiling. Dr Bell, like Dr Langer with his profile of Hitler, knew who the person was about whom he was drawing conclusions. The patient was standing before him, able to answer questions and revealing information by the mud on his shoes or his style of expressing himself. Langer interviewed many people who had met Hitler. The person these people were 'diagnosing' was present and the inferences were from the person to their actions.

Sherlock Holmes was really putting diagnosis in reverse. He did not have the luxury of the criminal in front of him. All that is available within Conan Doyle's fiction, as in real life detection, are the clues left by the criminal. He has to work backwards from the actions and traces at the crime to formulate a view of the person who carried out those actions. It is necessary for the detective to do something even more impressive than Dr Bell. The detective has to use his knowledge and understanding of crime and criminals to work from the traces left at the crime scene to propose important characteristics of the offender. This is like doing a reverse diagnosis, knowing the disease, who is likely to be the sufferer?

Therefore, one important step in all scientific investigation of crimes, and a crucial stage in the development of IP, is the consideration of what is actually known about offenders and the use of that knowledge to make empirically based deductions of relevance to police investigations. Perhaps not surprisingly, given the development of medicine and related natural sciences in the nineteenth century around the time that Conan Doyle was penning his Sherlock Holmes stories, some medical practitioners, including Dr Bell and Conan Doyle, were starting to provide guidance to police investigations in a form that we can now recognise as the first glimmerings of 'offender profiling'.

In his review of Conan Doyle's contribution to actual investigations Costello (1991) identifies at least 28 cases on which the author advised. One interesting example was when Conan Doyle contacted the police to suggest that he thought that a man had killed two women, one after the other, having married the first after the second one's death. Conan Doyle was particularly interested in the disappearance of the husband after the second woman's death. He wrote to his contacts at Scotland Yard 'you might put more men on his track. If these deaths are not sheer coincidence, then this business isn't finished ... You will have a creature to deal with who will be as rapacious a human as a pike that escapes being devoured by its parents – ruthless beyond all conjecture' (1991: 141). There is no record of whether the police took any notice of such elegantly written advice.

Serial Killers

When a series of killings have been linked to one offender, especially if that offender does not appear to have had any prior contact with the victims and thus these are regarded as 'stranger killings', there is great public concern and interest in these crimes and consequently great pressure on the police to do everything they can, and be seen to do everything they can, to find the perpetrator quickly. It is in such cases that investigators seek, and are offered, guidance from those who may have some special knowledge about criminal behaviour. Therefore there is no surprise that 'offender profilers' have typically been brought into such investigations.

This concern and fascination with serial killers is widely illustrated by the many popular films in which the plot is to find a serial killer. *Silence of the Lambs, Copycat, Taking Lives, Murder by Numbers, Along Came A Spider, Kiss the Girls, The Bone Collector, Kalifornia, Seven* and many other films all illustrate this. They almost inevitably utilise 'offender profiling' as a cornerstone of the plot. As Canter (2004a) has pointed out, the fascination with serial killers is probably partially to do with the disquiet caused by the idea of a predatory human being who can pick on anyone at random (which is not actually true of real-life serial killers as we shall see in later chapters). People deal with this disquiet through the exploration of fictional accounts. But also the dramatic power of murder and its significance in keeping the plot moving should not be underestimated. How many bodies are left on the stage at the end of Shakespeare's *Hamlet*? How many people are murdered in his play *Macbeth*?

In real life, too, serial killers have made the headlines, as long as there have been newspapers widely available. A great deal of effort is put into tracking them down – far beyond the effort put into a similar number of one-off murders where there is likely to be some known connection between the victim and culprit. This interest and concern is well documented for very many serial murder cases, but none more so than what many regard as the first serial killer of modern times, known as 'Jack the Ripper'. There are records of a number of people advising the police on the likely characteristics of this, still unknown, killer of five or more women in the Whitechapel area of London in 1888. These included Conan Doyle but because the dominant applied human science of its day was medicine these advisors were typically medical examiners who were also involved from time to time in carrying out autopsies for the court. They did not have an integrated role in the investigations, like Sherlock Holmes or fictional profilers. The investigations themselves were also far less thorough, lacking scientific support of the kind taken for granted today. The intelligent approach they took to their task should therefore be admired, despite the lack of success in the actual investigations.

Jack the Ripper

Between 31 August and 9 November 1888 at least five women were killed in an apparently unusual but very similar way. A killer in a major city murdering a number of vulnerable female victims over a short space of time was big news, as it would be today – especially because the body of each of the victims was mutilated, leading to the unknown offender being given the sobriquet 'Jack the Ripper'. The rapid growth in literacy had meant that many more people were buying newspapers and those publications that aimed at a mass market vied with each other for stories that would help them sell. Thus when it became clear that what we would now recognise as a 'serial killer' was wandering the streets of central London killing women at will there was a plethora of publication and speculation that stoked public interest even further. The fact that the killer was never caught keeps these crimes alive to this day, with literally hundreds of books published on them and countless movies. It has also grabbed the attention of investigators, motivating a number of investigations into the unsolved murders (most recently Keppel *et al.*, 2005). There is a certain poetic justice in this link between the search for Jack the Ripper and early profiling because possibly the first recorded offender profiles were produced to help that investigation.

Conan Doyle's Profile of Jack the Ripper

The author of the Sherlock Holmes stories did not want to be left out of the hunt for the 'Ripper' and according to Costello (1991) and Orel (1991) he speculated on the following characteristics of the perpetrator:

- He has been in America.
- He is educated, not a toiler.
- He is accustomed to the use of a pen.
- Likely has a rough knowledge of surgery.
- Probably clothes himself as a woman to approach victims without arousing suspicion and to escape the crime without detection.

- There will be letters where he has written over his own name or documents that could be traced to him.
- Facsimiles of his handwriting from letters sent to the police should be published in the newspapers so that someone may recognise the handwriting.

We have no indication of the basis for these speculations but of particular interest is that the famous author was ready to invent a clever deceit for the criminal, well worthy of detective fiction, by claiming he would dress as a woman. He also was keen to advise the police on the actions to take in order to try to identify the criminal using the mass media to seek the help of the general public, an idea that is standard police practice today in many countries. The letters to which he refers were those apparently sent by the killer to taunt the police. Interestingly, they were posted from the north of England; about 200 miles away from London, and one of the key suspects discussed by Canter (2004) lived in Liverpool near the place where the letters were sent. So Conan Doyle's recommendation certainly had some possibility of success.

Dr Thomas Bond's Profile of Jack the Ripper

However, another established medical practitioner, Dr Thomas Bond, gave an even more thorough profile of Jack the Ripper, which can probably be regarded as the earliest known profile of a killer. These speculations only came to public knowledge with the release in the late 1990s of the British Home Office files on the investigation by the 'London police into the Jack the Ripper Murders in the Whitechapel area of London'. In those files a letter was found from a doctor who had carried out various legal roles with the police, most notably as a coroner. This letter was dated 14 November 1888, following the murder of Mary Jane Kelly, who was probably the fifth victim of the Whitechapel killer.

Dr Bond visited the scene of Kelly's murder and subsequently carried out an autopsy on her. He also had available earlier reports of the descriptions of the murders of four other victims who were widely believed to have been killed by the same man. From this information he speculated on the crimes and the most likely features of the killer:

> The murderer must have been a man of physical strength and great coolness and daring. There is no evidence he had an accomplice. He must in my opinion be a man subject to periodic attacks of homicidal and erotic mania. The character of the mutilations indicate that the man may be in a condition sexually, that may be called Satyriasis. It is of course possible that the Homicidal impulse may have developed from a revengeful or brooding condition of mind, or that religious mania may have been the original disease but I do not think either hypothesis is likely. The murderer in external appearance is quite likely to be a quiet inoffensive looking man probably middle-aged and neatly and respectably dressed. I think he might be in the habit of wearing a cloak or overcoat or he could hardly have escaped notice in the streets if the blood on his hands or clothes were visible.
>
> Assuming the murderer be such a person as I have just described, he would be solitary and eccentric in his habits, also he is likely to be a man without regular occupation, but with some small income or pension. He is possibly living among respectable persons who have some knowledge of his character and habits and who may have grounds for suspicion that he is not quite right in his mind

at times. Such persons would probably be unwilling to communicate suspicions to the police for fear of trouble or notoriety, whereas if there were prospect of reward it might overcome their scruples.

(cited in Rumbelow, 1987:140–1)

This is probably the first recorded account of the features of an offender that are derived from the nature of his crimes. Yet although it was penned over a century ago it still recognisably contains all the constituents of a 'profile' that might be produced today. Indeed with the exception of the diagnostic categories, such as satyriasis and erotic mania, which today may be absorbed within a diagnosis of some form of 'personality disorder' (cf. for example Blackburn 1993), the description provided by Dr Bond is remarkably similar to that which may be found in many profiles of sexual murderers over the last few years (see, for example, Ressler, Burgess and Douglas, 1988).

Further, as many have pointed out (for example, Blau, 1994) Conan Doyle's fictional detective gave a lot of support to the possibility of an 'expert', external to the police, being of some assistance to an investigation. Blau (1994) mentions that some of the features to be found in modern profiles were first noted by Sherlock Holmes, such as 'the criminal returns to the scene of the crime'. Certainly, by the early 1970s the provision of psychological advice about offenders to investigators was common in both the United States (Reiser, 1982) and the United Kingdom (Canter, 1994) as we will see in later chapters.

Dr Bond's analysis of the crime scene and related material is an important milestone in the evolution of offender profiling because it moved beyond the uninformed jump from observation to accusation of earlier investigators. The report was specific to the crime, unlike the unsupported generalities of the early attempts to classify people into broad types. However, he is willing to draw upon the typology of medical classifications of his day referring to *satyriasis,* which can be defined as 'excessive, abnormal, or uncontrollable sexual behaviour, desire, and excitement in the male', although this is a little at variance with Bond's claim that the purpose of the attacks was to mutilate the victims, unless Bond thought that the Ripper found the mutilation to be sexually arousing.

Dr Bond's proposals make other contributions as well. Part of what Dr Bond is doing is to prepare a clear and precise account of the circumstances of the crime that can be derived from direct observations. This may be of use in many ways later in the investigation and even today is helpful to us in considering the crime. But he is also thinking through how the offender approaches his victim without causing alarm and manages to get away without being noticed. By looking at the injuries and considering the nature of the attacks he formulates a view on the character of the killer too. However, he is careful to make clear when he is describing what is known and observable and when he is speculating beyond the facts. (This is an attention to good scientific practice from which many who advise the police today could learn.)

Beyond Speculation

Edgar Allan Poe had shown as early as 1841 that careful attention to the detail of a crime could possibly help detectives to make sense of otherwise puzzling events. By the time of Jack the Ripper, 47 years later, a medical officer like Thomas Bond was willing, within a few days of a vicious murder, to offer an informed opinion about the characteristics of the perpetrator. They were both reflecting the vision that was so well encapsulated in Conan Doyle's master sleuth, Sherlock Holmes. It is no accident that the magnifying glass, to this day, represents detective work, showing the importance of attention to detail.

What began to emerge during the nineteenth and early twentieth centuries was a realisation that, despite the clever inferences of remarkable people such as Dr Bell, there are many facts that just do not give up their meanings directly. Professionals wishing to advise the police became aware that clever speculation was not enough. Some sort of induction process is necessary whereby the results of many examples are distilled to offer up general principles that can be applied to any new case that emerges. The identification of these principles has to be based on knowledge of actual criminals and their actions, not imagined ones. This search to understand criminals more fully is another component in the evolution of detection.

Summary

The detailed report that Dr Thomas Bond produced as assistance to the search for Jack the Ripper is an excellent illustration of how a medical officer can work with the material available from the crime scene and an autopsy to produce a systematic account of what he thought had occurred in the crime and what he thought would be the characteristics of the offender that would help the police to find him. This report, as a consequence, illustrates the interplay between detailed information about a crime and inferences that can be based mainly on knowledge about human behaviour. At that stage in the development of behavioural science the inferences were little more than speculations, but they were part of a growing belief in the power of such contributions. It was crime fiction, most notably that featuring Sherlock Holmes, which gave most impetus to the belief in the powers of informed deduction. However, further more detailed understanding of criminals and their actions was necessary for the contributions of behavioural science to law enforcement to develop more productively.

Further Reading

Books

The Adventures of Sherlock Holmes by Arthur Conan Doyle are widely available in many formats.
The most informed books on Jack the Ripper are by Donald Rumbelow.
Summercale, K. (2008) *The Suspicions of Mr Whicher*, Bloomsbury, London, is a very readable account of the emergence of modern detective work.

Article

Gross, H. (1997/1962) Certain qualities essential to an investigator, in *Criminal Detection and the Psychology of Crime* (eds D. Canter and L. Alison), Ashgate, Dartmouth, 5–10.

Questions for Discussion and Research

1. Why do you think Edgar Allan Poe wrote about the murder of Mary Rogers as if he were writing a fictional story?

2. Read any Sherlock Holmes story (*A Scandal in Bohemia* is a good one to use).

   (a) Identify the main deductions Holmes makes.

   (b) What is the basis on which Holmes makes these deductions?

   (c) How much of the basis is special knowledge that Holmes has?

   (d) How much of it is pure logic?

   (e) Under what conditions could Holmes' deductions be wrong?

3. What developments in modern science would have helped Holmes?

4. Read the quotations from Dr Bell and Sherlock Holmes and consider what other interpretations may have been made of the things they observed.

5. What are the processes of violent criminal activity that Dr Thomas Bond was drawing on to develop his profile of Jack the Ripper?

6. What are the main differences and similarities between Dr Bond's profile of Jack the Ripper and Conan Doyle's? Why do you think these similarities and differences occur?

CHAPTER 4

The Age of Profiling and the Road to Investigative Psychology*

A famous scientist exclaimed to a student in his laboratory: 'what do you want here? You know nothing, you understand nothing, you do nothing – you had better become a lawyer.'

(S. Goldschmidt: *Rechtestudium und Prüfungsordnung*, 1887)

In This Chapter

- Learning Objectives
- Synopsis
- Understanding Criminal Actions
- The Emergence of Investigative Advice
- The FBI Behavioral Science Unit
- The Emergence of Investigative Psychology
- Summary
- Further Reading
- Questions for Discussion and Research

---

* The lists of characteristics provided in the various 'profiles' in this and earlier chapters rely heavily on the excellent summaries provided by Welch and Keppel (2006).

Learning Objectives

When you have completed this chapter you should be able to:

1. Discuss some of the key areas of research that led to the development of IP.
2. Appreciate the contributions made to the development of informed detections by those such as Vidocq and Gross.
3. Describe some of the key works by criminologists and criminal psychologists in the early part of the twentieth century.
4. Evaluate the profiles that were offered of Peter Kurten, the 'Mad Bomber' and the 'Boston Strangler'.
5. Outline some of the key stages in the emergence of IP as a discipline in its own right.
6. Understand what is meant by the idea of the 'Hollywood Effect'.

Synopsis

In parallel with the developments in behavioural science and the increasing sophistication of detectives that have been reviewed in earlier chapters was a growing awareness that it was of great value to study criminals and their activities directly. This came out of the direct experience that detectives had of criminals, in some cases (most notably that of Vidocq) because they had originally been criminals themselves. This practice continues today, as we will see in Chapter 11, where the FBI employment of an experienced fraudster to help detect frauds is described. This opened the way for investigators to seek advice directly, especially on very bizarre cases such as the 'Dusseldorf Vampire' and the 'Boston Strangler'.

Initially the input to these very unusual cases came from psychiatry, being strongly flavoured with psychoanalytic interpretations of criminal actions. These early 'profiles' achieved great public interest but close examination of their role in catching the killers reveals that their impact was extremely limited. Perhaps of more long-term significance was their establishing of the basis for more systematic consideration of criminal behaviour and the encouragement they gave to the development of training courses at the FBI college in Quantico out of which came the FBI Behavioral Science Unit.

The worldwide interest in this unit was greatly stimulated by fictional accounts of its work. This in turn led to the British police at Scotland Yard seeking out a professor of psychology, David Canter, to help with a major enquiry into a series of rapes and murders across London. When the police heralded Canter's success in contributing to that investigation the ground was prepared for the development of the new discipline of IP.

Understanding Criminal Actions

Looking at the minutiae of a crime and making deductions about those details from general common sense can contribute to an investigation, especially if it is informed by some effective understanding of the variety of offenders in existence. However, there is a further process that is crucial to successful detection – developing in-depth knowledge of criminals and their actions. This process of detailed study of actual criminals was evolving in parallel with the other rather more distant considerations that were explored in previous chapters.

The use of the knowledge of criminals and their wiles as a route to catching miscreants can be traced at least to the Apocrypha of the Bible. An account is given there of how the Prophet Daniel showed that the priests of Bel were cheating King Cyrus into believing that their god was actually eating the offerings left in the sealed temple. As probably the first recorded detective story it interestingly reveals that Daniel was aware of the tricks that the false priests were perpetrating. For although the temple was closed at night, Daniel knew there had to be some hidden way for the priests to gain access to the food that so mysteriously had disappeared by morning. He therefore had ashes secretly scattered over the temple floor before it was closed for the night. In the morning the footprints left on the ashes revealed the route to the concealed access to the temple.

Daniel knew he would only convince King Cyrus if he had clear evidence of the cheating actions of the priests. He had to develop some hypothesis derived from his understanding of how criminals go about committing their crimes and then set up a test of that hypothesis by scattering ashes. The crucial point for us here is that Daniel had some knowledge or understanding of the nefarious activities of the priests. This knowledge enabled him to rise above mere suspicion and a general desire to challenge superstitions and idolatry. The knowledge enabled him to go beyond the observed facts of the disappearing offerings and to develop some ideas about what the priests must be doing.

Putting it another way, the experience of criminal processes allowed Daniel to make inferences about what he had observed. He drew on the notion that the people he was dealing with were probably drawn from the category of 'cheating priests', but the observations and categorisation alone did not allow him to make strong inferences that enabled him to propose a plan of action. It was his understanding of criminal processes that was crucial. This understanding of criminals and their actions has always been a significant part of detective work, being at the heart of the experience they build up over their time investigating crimes. It therefore plays a crucial role in any assistance they may get from behavioural science. But it is only recently that it has gone beyond the anecdotes that one detective passes on to another about how crimes may be perpetrated. Before such systematisation was possible it was the detective with the most experience of crimes who had most to offer the investigative process. Perhaps not surprisingly, therefore, some of the earliest informed detectives had once been criminals themselves!

Francois Eugene Vidocq (1775–1857)

One of the most significant people to influence the development of informed detections was Francois Vidocq. He had been a petty criminal himself and drew on that criminal past to contribute to many police investigations in his native France, first as an undercover informant but then as a recognised police officer. Eventually he was very influential in giving shape to the whole process of detective work, which still has many parallels today. It is to him that we owe the whole idea of a branch of policing that does not wear uniforms, 'detectives', and uses

Figure 4.1 Francois Eugene Vidocq.

Source: http://www.mtholyoke.edu/courses/rschwart/hist255/popcorn/vidocq.html

'undercover' police officers to become part of criminal networks (Edwards, 1977; Rich, 1935; Stead, 1953). He also showed the value of keeping a record of people who were suspected of crimes or were known to have committed them.

He thus prepared the groundwork for detailed accounts of who were criminals and what their patterns of behaviour were. This extended to building meticulous inventories of their beliefs and superstitions. Edwards (1977) gives an amusing example, drawn from Vidocq's memoirs (see Figure 4.1) of the sort of information espoused:

> The Sureté and the uniformed police had less to do on Fridays than on any other day of the week, Vidocq said, because no criminal ever initiated a major enterprise on Fridays. If the first person passed on the street when a criminal went off to do a job was a priest, the project was postponed for at least twenty-four hours. This rule was observed by Protestants, Jews, and atheists, as well as Catholics. If the first person passed at the beginning of a work day was a nun, the job had to be put off for a week . . . If he saw and retrieved a piece of iron, his enterprise would not fail. When a murder was planned, the killer had to sleep the previous night with some woman other than his wife or regular mistress, but he could go to bed only with his accustomed mate the night before perpetrating a major robbery . . . A swindler drank no wine for three hours before fleecing a victim, and a wise burglar always drank a glass of caraway-flavoured water before going to work.
>
> (Edwards, 1977: 93–4)

Vidocq also illustrates the fifth component of effective investigations. The need to know how to make use of the inferences that have been have derived and to seek out further information that will enable detectives to choose between the options for action available. He did not stop his investigation when he knew who the culprit was but put them under surveillance to ensure that as much as possible was known about them before they were charged and brought to trial. As he puts it in his memoirs, 'I was interested in knowing as much as possible about all the professional thieves, both men and women' (Rich, 1935: 405). This interest was not only to assist future investigations but to ensure there would be a clear conviction in court.

In this regard Vidocq was taking a further step along the road to influencing police procedures by recognising the importance of thinking through to the final stages when a case has to be presented to court. Daniel saw the need to present the evidence to the King, but even today many people who seek to advise the police do not take into account that it is essential to have evidence to ensure a conviction. Assigning an offender to a particular type is of little value in front of a jury. Noting salient features of a crime may move the detective closer to the offender but will not convince a judge that a particular person is guilty of the crime. Any advice to an investigation therefore needs to be alert to the available possibilities for obtaining information that will be relevant for direct use in court.

Unusually for a man who started as an undercover police officer, Vidocq became a prolific writer. He wrote books to inform other detectives and memoirs for a more general readership. His experience and writings informed the creation of plainclothes detective units in a number of countries outside his native France, notably the New York detective bureau in 1854, Britain's Bow Street Runners and Scotland Yard detectives (Edwards, 1977: 170–1; Rich, 1935; Stead, 1953).

However, this close involvement of detectives with criminals in order to understand their ways and to gain direct information has always been fraught with risks, when it is carried out independently of professional training and with no sound scientific basis. The main risk is one of bias and corruption. Poachers turned gamekeepers may be prone to be too confident in their own judgements and too willing to bend the facts to fit their own view of the circumstances, rather than giving objective, unbiased opinions. Also by using informants there is a real danger of police officers stepping over the line and being corrupted by the people they think are helping them. These matters have caused problems throughout the history of the various detective squads since they were first established. In their history of the first Scotland Yard detectives, Begg and Skinner (1992: 76) put it thus: 'The distinction between the allowable turning of a blind eye and the unallowable giving active assistance to a criminal sometimes becomes blurred. The opportunity for being compromised is often great.'

Begg and Skinner (1992) report numerous scandals in the early days of the Scotland Yard Criminal Investigation Department. Indeed, few of these early detective units set up around the world escaped such problems in their early stages. Often they were shut down within a few years of being established and reopened later when much better controls had been put in place. But it is not until their procedures rely as much, or even more, on carefully formulated operational rules that are informed by testable scientific methods that their activities can be confidently within the law.

Hans Gross 1847–1915

The incorporation of more detailed understanding of psychology into detective work, rather than relying entirely on native wit and personal experience as Vidocq did, was given particular momentum when the Austrian jurist and examining magistrate, Hans Gross, published his book *Criminal Psychology* (Gross, 1911), which was soon translated into many languages. He shared many of Vidocq's views about developing information on criminals, their activities and habits. He also stressed the importance of knowing everything about the criminal subculture and how they operated, using crime-scene details to develop an understanding of the possible offender, but he took all this a stage further by laying out a way of thinking about crimes and how they should be investigated.

In developing his 'criminal psychology' he drew on many of the rapidly developing scientific disciplines, the most important of which was psychology. This framed a broad perspective on how we know about crimes and make decisions both about investigating them and prosecuting the culprits. Of great significance was Gross's emphasis on assessing witnesses and related information:

> Let this be our fundamental principle: That we criminalists receive from our main source, the witnesses, many more inferences than observations, and that this fact is the basis of so many mistakes in our work. Again and again we are taught, in the deposition of evidence, that only facts as plain sense-perceptions should be presented; that inference is the judge's affair. But we only appear to obey this principle; actually, most of what we note as fact and sense-perception, is nothing but a more or less justified judgment, which though presented in the honestest belief, still offers no positive truth.
>
> (Gross, 1911: 16)

This clarity of vision that all the information that is the basis of an investigation needs to be carefully assessed follows through the whole of Gross' consideration of crimes and criminals. He sees the whole investigative and judicial process as an endeavour that should be rooted in the empirical sciences. This meant that investigators had to learn from scientists how to record crime scenes and any related information as carefully as possible, but always to be assessing the meaning and implications of what they were recording. This extended to careful consideration of the words a person uses, for example; pointing out that a criminal denying a crime may still refer to 'we' when discussing his activities, thereby implying he is part of some criminal group. He also explored what we would now call 'non-verbal' communication, discussing at great length the possible interpretation of facial and hand gestures.

These considerations led Gross to consider all the aspects of the person who might be involved in crime and to develop accounts of how they may live their lives, which has direct relevance to investigation and prosecution.

> The real criminal is different from the majority of other people. That this difference is great and essential is inferred from the circumstance that a habit, a single characteristic, an unhappy inclination, etc., does not constitute a criminal. If a man is a thief it will not be asserted that he is otherwise like decent people, varying only in the accidental inclination to theft. We know that, besides the inclination to theft, we may assign him a dislike for honest work, lack of moral power, indifference to the laws of honor when caught, the lack of real religion, – in short, the inclination to theft must be combined with a large number of very characteristic qualities in order to make a thief of a man.
>
> (Gross, 1911: 245)

This approach to examining all aspects of criminality did eventually enable him in a later book, published in English after his death (Gross, 1934), to consider the ways in which offenders may differ. He emphasised the patterns of behaviour that would be typical of any given criminal and how useful it was to identify them as an aid to detective work.

> ... for in nearly every case, the thief has left the most important trace of his passage, namely, the manner in which he committed the theft. Every thief has a characteristic style or modus operandi which he rarely departs from; and which he is incapable of completely getting rid of; at times this distinctive feature that even the novice can spot it without difficulty, but ... Only a practiced, intelligent, and fervent observer is capable of distinguishing those traits, often delicate but identical, which characterise the theft, and drawing important conclusions from them.
>
> (Gross, 1934: 472)

An important step beyond this was to recognise that these distinct ways of acting could be drawn on to provide inferences about other features of the offender:

> Note the differences between the various methods, according to the trade to which he belongs. The locksmith will attack the lock itself, the joiner the wood of which the almirah or table is constructed; the locksmith will open the lock with a master key or if that does not do it, he will smash it; the joiner will try to raise the top of the table or lid of the cash box without touching the lock, or perhaps he will turn his attention to the joinings of the planks, or try to pull out the nails which hold the hinges to the doors; in short each workman works in his own way and when a workman of one class has done a job, the specialist can immediately say what that class is.
>
> (Adam and Adam, 1934: 481)

Gross showed that it was possible to think of the crime scene as a source of information from which inferences could be made, provided the observer noted the appropriate details and had the understanding to enable the inferences to be drawn reliably. He was, in effect, setting up hypotheses of the relationships between particular aspects of a crime and particular characteristics of the perpetrator. He drew on his extensive experience to propose these relationships. Although he did see the need, as a social scientist would today, to carry out systematic tests with carefully drawn samples to show that the proposed relationships between criminal actions and offender characteristics really did occur with enough consistency to be drawn upon in investigations. However, that research did not really begin to happen until much later in the twentieth century.

Criminal Psychology

It would be wrong to think that all the developments in the understanding of criminals were emerging from those actively involved with the police. A whole field of criminology and forensic psychology was evolving in the early part of the twentieth century. Much of this was concerned with preventing crime, especially through trying to treat or rehabilitate offenders. For example, Bowlby (1949) compared the characteristics of 44 serious juvenile offenders with a group referred to a Child Guidance Clinic who did not steal. He established that children given less affection at an early age were significantly more delinquent than the control group, were more likely to have mentally disordered parents or were separated from their parents, or they had parents that openly displayed their hostility. Burt, in the same year, provided similar explanations of delinquency:

> Judged by the coefficients, the following proves to be the order of importance of the various conditions we have reviewed.
>
> (1) Defective discipline (2) specific instinct (3) general emotional instability (4) morbid emotional conditions, mild rather than grave, generating or generated by so called complexes (5) a family history of vice or crime (6) intellectual disabilities such as backwardness or dullness (7) detrimental interests such as passion for adventure . . .

These conclusions by Burt and Bowlby could be used as 'profiles' of the typical delinquents of their day and could certainly have been used to focus a police enquiry.

Gehnert and the Düsseldorf Vampire

The ideas put forward by Gross were influential in alerting German police forces to the possibilities of seeking help by obtaining suggestions about the characteristics of offenders from the details of their crimes. So when a number of violent attacks and murders occurred around Düsseldorf in 1929, the police sought help to find the culprit, for although they had quite a few clues and tips, they had no viable suspects.

The Düsseldorf police found themselves at a standstill as the crimes and victims increased so they brought in Professor Ernst Gehnert, asking him to help them identify the man known only as the 'Vampire of Düsseldorf' and the 'Düsseldorf Monster'. As it later emerged, the man responsible, Peter Kurten, had been killing since his childhood, in the 1890s, but it was in Düsseldorf that he earned his greatest notoriety as a multiple rapist, vampire, killer, and arsonist (Berg and Godwin, 1993). Many of Kurten's crimes went largely undiscovered until his confession following his apprehension.

Professor Gehnert produced an informed summary of the characteristics of the killer:

- The killer is familiar with Dusseldorf.
- The level of closeness achieved upon approaching his victims prior to attack suggests that he is perceived as friendly and good natured by those around him, they would never suspect him.
- He shows exceptional cruelty in attacks
- He is sexually abnormal, with a history of mental illness.
- He must be mad.

(from Welch and Keppel, 2006)

This did no more to help catch the culprit than Dr Bond's profile of Jack the Ripper 40 years earlier. It was Kurten's wife who finally came forward in 1930 to implicate him in the murders that had terrorised the community. Her assertions were corroborated by a living victim who described Kurten to the Düsseldorf police following his attack on her. His trial in 1931 created an international sensation (Jenkins, 1994). Forty-eight-year-old Kurten was charged with nine murders, seven assaults and implicated in over 60 additional crimes. He was revealed as a sadist who killed, slashed, tortured and mutilated countless young victims.

Gehnert's inferences about the way the killer went about his crimes were appropriate. In particular the understanding of the bizarre and deviant nature of the crimes that led to the assumption that the killer was psychologically abnormal drew on Gehnert's knowledge of the processes that give rise to different forms of criminal behaviour. But it was a mistake to confuse the obvious sadism in the crimes with the concept of insanity. The particular aberrations that are reflected in getting pleasure from hurting others are not necessarily or usually associated with the obvious lack of contact with daily reality that is the essence of 'madness'. Indeed the assumption that the offender would be familiar with the area and not threatening in his appearance, both reasonable assumptions from how and where the crimes were committed, also suggested that the killer was able to present himself to others as a normal, plausible person. It is not easy for insane people to simulate these characteristics. Central to Kurten's crimes was his desire for blood. His known crime scenes were soaked in blood and he is reported to have asked the prison doctor if he'd be able to hear the blood gushing from his torso when he was decapitated for that would give him a final moment of pleasure (Berg and Godwin, 1993).

The Emergence of Investigative Advice

Vidocq, Gross, and to a lesser extent Gehnert, provide a pathway to the later psychological contributions to police investigations. But their routes into investigative advice have some important distinctions from the other routes we have outlined in earlier chapters. None of them drew upon any clearly established framework of categorisations, such as Kretschmer's or Lombroso's. However, they did all emphasise the significance of careful observation and the need to make informed sense of those observations. Their contribution, though, was to emphasise the need to get to understand criminals from direct study and observation, and not rely solely on speculation and second-hand anecdotes. In addition, they also followed up the earlier attempts to derive assistance to the investigation, like Dr Bond and Conan Doyle, by providing suggestions as to how the investigation could be moved forward, going beyond mere descriptions of the likely characteristics of the offender.

The process of bringing in experts to advise the police in difficult cases built up momentum after the Second World War, especially in those cases in which the actions of the offender were apparently bizarre and difficult to make sense of. Consequently the police tended to turn to psychiatrists who had some experience of offenders with some form of mental illness. Probably the most significant of these post-war advisors was the New York psychiatrist Dr James Brussel.

Brussel and the 'Mad Bomber'

Over a 16 year period in the 1940s and 1950s, homemade bombs were left in many different places around New York including Grand Central Terminal, Pennsylvania Station, Radio City

Music Hall, the New York Public Library, the Port Authority Bus Terminal and the RCA Building. These devices were even secreted into the cut upholstery in cinemas. The bomber sent letters to newspapers such as one on October 22nd 1951 to the *New York Herald Tribune* pencilled in block letters, stating

> BOMBS WILL CONTINUE UNTIL THE CONSOLIDATED EDISON COMPANY IS BROUGHT TO JUSTICE FOR THEIR DASTARDLY ACTS AGAINST ME. I HAVE EXHAUSTED ALL OTHER MEANS. I INTEND WITH BOMBS TO CAUSE OTHERS TO CRY OUT FOR JUSTICE FOR ME.

The police had kept information about these bombings relatively quiet but when Brussel was called in he recommended that they use the news media to see if anyone could identify the bomber. It was generally recognised that the perpetrator was annoyed with and extremely resentful towards the Consolidated Edison Company, but Brussel put some flesh on this simple idea.

In his *Casebook of a Crime Psychiatrist*, he explained the ideas behind his description of the bomber, claiming that: 'by studying a man's deeds, I have deduced what kind of man he might be' (Brussel, 1968: 4). From a close examination of the letters the bomber had sent and other information about his actions Brussel proposed the following characteristics:

- Male (because most bombers are male).
- Has knowledge of metalworking, pipefitting, and electricity.
- Suffered an injustice by Consolidated Edison, which had rendered him chronically ill.
- Suffers from an insidious disorder, paranoia, and has a persistent and chronic disorder.
- Is pathologically self-centred.
- Has no friends, male or female, is a loner.
- Symmetric athletic body type, neither fat or skinny.
- Is middle-aged (due to onset of illness and duration of bombings).
- Good education, likely high school education but not college.
- Unmarried, possibly a virgin.
- Distrusts and despises male authority, hates father.
- Never progressed past the Oedipal stage of love for his mother due to her early death or separation from him.
- Lives alone or with female mother-like relative.
- Lives in Connecticut, is of Slavic descent, Roman Catholic and attends church.
- Neat, tidy, and clean-shaven.
- Quiet, polite, methodical, and prompt.
- Has chronic illness, either heart disease, cancer, or tuberculosis, most probably heart disease.
- Would be wearing a buttoned double-breasted suit when caught.

(Brussel, 1968: 30–46)

In fact, as is so often the case, it was not the rich description that Brussel provided which led to the bomber being caught but an assiduous clerk at Con Edison, Alice Kelly. She had read the newspaper reports and decided to look carefully through the company's worker compensation files, especially looking for those who had serious difficulties with their health. The company actually kept special files on those employees who had earlier made threats as part of their requests for compensation. This drew attention to George Metesky who had been injured at the factory in 1931. There was correspondence in these files that showed similarities of wording to the anonymous letters the bomber had been sending to the police, leading the police to him and his eventual conviction.

Newspapers later reported that the investigators claimed they had been stopped from examining the Con Edison employee files, although the company said this was a misunderstanding. So although much of what Brussel proposed turned out to be quite accurate the crucial point was one that investigators had assumed from the beginning that the bomber was a disgruntled employee. This was derived from what the bomber had actually written in his letters and where he had put bombs. Indeed the often-quoted reference by Brussel to the fact that the bomber would be wearing a buttoned up suit was little more than a description of what most men of his age and generation wore. Metesky's claimed Oedipal love for his mother was also of far less use to finding the bomber than Alice Kelly's diligent search through the records that contained details of a disgruntled employee.

The Boston Strangler – Experts Disagree

The dangers of expert opinion as the basis for identifying an offender and the growing variety of approaches to inferring characteristics of an unknown criminal became very apparent in the 1960s when Brussel was once again brought into a major investigation in Boston. Thirteen women had been violently raped then murdered between mid-1962 and early 1964. The killer became known as the 'Boston Strangler' (Brussel, 1968; Petherick, 2004).

The attacks varied in a number of ways, both in terms of the different ages of the victims and the different forms of sexual activity and violence. This caused investigators to consider the possibility that there was more than one offender, but also to seek out assistance. They did this by putting together a panel of experts in April 1964, which Brussel joined (Brussel, 1968).

The panel supported the police view that there were probably two independent killers. They came up with the following set of characteristics for the offenders:

- two separate killers as indicated by changes in M.O., both male;
- one male strangles and kills only elderly females;
- one killer is homosexual and focuses on younger women;
- both men are teachers;
- the killers live alone;
- they kill on scheduled holidays;
- sexually inhibited;
- products of traumatic childhoods with weak, distant fathers and cruel seductive mothers.

(Brussel, 1968; Cyriax, 1993; Newton, 2000)

Brussel did not agree with this believing that only one killer was involved, who changed his actions as he gained experience in committing murders (Brussel, 1968). He consequently claimed that the offender had the following characteristics:

* One man whose pattern of criminal actions has changed as he has matured and grown through the crimes.
* He transferred his schizophrenic feelings for his mother to his younger victims.
* His approach to the victims in their apartment did not frighten them; he had possibly befriended his victims and was invited there or he knocked on their door offering a plausible story such as he was taking a poll or checking the plumbing.
* He attacks when the victim turns her back on him, because he views this as a symbol of rejection.
* He is a paranoid schizophrenic.
* Based on Kretschmer's studies and the strength exhibited by the strangling, he is a well-proportioned, muscular and powerful man.
* Late twenties or early thirties.
* He'd be described as the average man and goes largely unnoticed, fading into the background.
* He is a cautious, neat, clean shaven, and tidy individual, he never leaves fingerprints or other clues, he has clean fingernails and dresses neatly.
* His hair is always combed and he tends it lovingly; girls would envy his hair.
* Obsessed with his relationship with the opposite sex; he wants women to be attracted to him rather than reject him.
* Italian or Spanish descent.
* Average or better intelligence.
* Unmarried and a loner.

A rapist who was known to have previously been convicted of many assaults was arrested in November 1964 for further sexual offences. His name was Albert DeSalvo. He was committed to a psychiatric hospital where he told a psychiatrist he was the Boston Strangler (Brussel, 1968; Cyriax, 1993; Frank, 1966). This confession and the similarities between his earlier crimes and the murders led investigators to accept that DeSalvo was the Boston Strangler and no further investigations were carried out. It was also widely accepted that the close similarity between DeSalvo and the description proposed by Brussel was also crucial in the police believing DeSalvo was the killer.

Albert DeSalvo was indeed athletic and muscular and in his early thirties at the time of his arrest, also being Italian and average looking (Brussel, 1968). Albert DeSalvo was very neat and clean. Brussel (1968) reports that he had 'meticulously combed and shaped' hair (Brussel, 1968:161) with scrubbed and clipped fingernails. He bragged about his sexual conquests, being firmly heterosexual (Brussel, 1968; Cyriax, 1993; Newton, 2000). However, contrary to Brussel's prediction, he had a wife and children with whom he lived. As a consequence, the basis of Brussel's conclusions and the extent to which they should have been relied upon are still open to question.

As Welch and Keppel (2006) point out, DeSalvo was never officially charged with the Boston Strangler murders so there was no direct test of the proposals that Brussel had put forward. DeSalvo's subsequent death in 1973, being killed by another prisoner, also meant that no further examination of his culpability was possible (Cyriax, 1993; Frank, 1966). There thus continued to be many questions raised about the investigation into the Boston murders and whether the 'profile' provided by Brussel was given too much credence (Sherman, 2003). Indeed in 2001 new DNA tests indicated that the semen retrieved from the last known victim was not DeSalvo's (Sherman, 2003).

The British Dimension – Dr Patrick Tooley

The contribution of Brussel to the history of 'offender profiling' is well documented, not least through his own detailed autobiography (Brussel, 1968) but, as Canter (1995) reports, by the late 1960s psychiatrists' involvement with criminals in treatment programmes and giving evidence of the fitness of defendants to plead in court was so widespread that from time to time they were asked their views on the possible characteristics of unknown criminals. One instructive example of this was the role that Dr Patrick Tooley played in helping the police find the murderer of Susan Stevenson who was attacked on Great Line Common in Kent. Dr Tooley proposed:

> The man is aged between twenty and thirty-five years, possibly a psychopath with previous convictions. Generally one would expect from his record that he had made a number of court appearances, was convicted at an early age and had possibly been in a special home; likely to be a manual worker and either unemployed or frequently changing jobs. Previous convictions could include unlawful sexual intercourse, drunkenness, robbery and assaults generally.
>
> Father absent – mother restrictive, sexually prudish and devoted to her son and spoils him. He, in turn, resents this and has a hate complex towards women. Despite that, he wants an affair with a woman but cannot make a normal approach. He does not mix socially and walks alone, in open spaces. He could be a 'peeper' but seldom resorts to indecent exposure.
>
> (Tullett, 1987: 155)

When the murderer, Peter Stout, was arrested these comments turned out to be generally accurate. Stout was 19, single, went for long walks on his own and did not mix well with others. Both his parents were dead, but his father had been a drunkard and a bully who was disliked by Peter, whereas his mother had been loved by her children. At the age of 14 Peter Stout was convicted for indecently assaulting a woman and he had been a victim of attempted buggery when he was 10 years old (Tullett, 1987).

However, this contribution to the investigation from Dr Tooley went largely unremarked. The British police did not see the potential benefits of such insights until they approached Professor David Canter over 10 years later. As so often with European inventions, it was necessary to wait for the developments of ideas that had their origins on one side of the Atlantic to take root and develop on the other side, with the attendant public relations and media presentation of these developments, before their potential was subsequently taken up and developed further, back in Europe.

The FBI Behavioral Science Unit

Howard Teton, who is credited with being the prime mover pushing forward 'offender profiling' as a contribution to major investigations (Egger, 1999; Petherick, 2004), makes clear that he was greatly influenced by what he saw as Brussel's successes (Teton, 1995). He referred to Brussel as the 'first practitioner' of profiling in modern times and 'a true pioneer of the field' (Teton, 1995: 476). Teton therefore spearheaded the drive to incorporate behavioural science into criminal investigations by setting up training courses at the FBI Academy in Quantico, Virginia in 1972.

It was thus initially as a course for FBI agents and other law enforcement investigators that 'offender profiling' became established as part of major investigations in the United States. The early work of this Behavioral Science Unit focused mainly on serial killers because it was thought the number of different crime scenes and the very unusual behaviour would provide a stronger basis for making inferences about offenders (Holmes and Holmes, 1996). It is interesting to note the strong influence, in this focus on serial killers, of the psychiatric and somewhat psychoanalytic orientation of Brussel. They tended to undervalue the possible contributions to more mundane investigations that Vidocq and Gross had pointed out many years earlier.

However, a crucial aspect of the FBI Behavioral Science Unit was that they realised in a way that had never been appreciated so clearly before that it was necessary to study serial killers if they were to improve and develop contributions to investigations. They did therefore carry out interviews with some convicted serial killers and serial rapists (Ressler *et al.*, 1986). These were rather informal discussions that have still never been fully analysed or given rise to detailed publications. Instead they tend to have been drawn on when giving advice to law enforcement agencies and as fascinating anecdotes in autobiographies of the early members of the Behavioral Science Unit (for example, Douglas and Olshaker, 1997; Ressler, Burgess and Douglas, 1988). Nonetheless, even though these interviews have been criticised by a number of scholars, they did lead others to recognise the importance of going beyond personal experience and the real potential of empirical research. This work was thus a very important stage in the emergence of IP.

The FBI team also broadened the base of contributions to police investigations by making clear that their analysis of criminal activities could be used to link cases to a common offender and by their readiness to suggest lines of enquiry that law enforcement agencies should follow. This advisory role has become so significant that in recent years the people at the FBI Academy prefer to call themselves 'behavioral investigative advisors' rather than 'profilers'.

Because of their general orientation to seeking evidence for their claims, the FBI did encourage a number of projects to evaluate their contribution to investigations. Teton conducted one of the first of these in 1981, examining 193 cases to which the Behavioral Science Unit had given guidance. He reported that 45% of the cases had been solved and that investigators claimed that in 77% of the cases the 'profile' had been of value in helping investigators to understand the person they were looking for. This review also came up with the finding that in 17% of the cases the contribution from the FBI has helped to identify the actual suspect

(Teton, 1995: 476). However, in subsequent studies it was found that there is little difference between 'professional' profilers, detectives, psychologists and college students (Pinizotto and Finkel, 1990) in the accuracy or effectiveness of their contributions. The possibility remains, therefore, that any reasonably well informed and intelligent advisor brought in by investigators can make a useful contribution to an investigation, but that a much stronger research base is needed for this advice to go beyond educated opinion.

The investigators at the FBI Academy at Quantico were aware of this need to move beyond the perceived successes of the early 'profilers'. They started to follow up the possibilities for systematic data collection that were becoming apparent. As Welch and Keppel (2006) report:

> Following a 1981 conference at Sam Houston State University, and spurred by the efforts of Pierce Brooks and Robert Keppel, the FBI established the Violent Crime Apprehension Program (VICAP). VICAP is a computerised database of characteristics of specific violent crimes that assists agencies in sharing information and linking cases (Howlett, Hanfland and Ressler 1986). Technological advances have led to the development of computerised programs, such as VICAP and the Homicide Investigation Tracking System (HITS), that assist in crime-scene analysis and investigation
>
> (Keppel and Weis, 1993).

The creation of a database and the practice of drawing on it for linking crimes and providing guidance to investigations has over the past 20 years become common practice for many law enforcement agencies around the world. However, it is still relatively rare for these agencies to recognise the research potential of these databases and to therefore open them up to empirical study. Such interaction between researchers and police agencies is, though, beginning to build in momentum. A large part of the impetus for this has grown out of the emergence of IP.

The Emergence of Investigative Psychology

By the mid 1980s there was widespread interest in police circles around the world in what they had heard about FBI 'profilers' at the Academy in Virginia. When between 1982 and 1986 a series of rapes and murders took place around London, which had been linked together to a common offender by police because of descriptions by surviving victims and details of what went on in the crimes, as well as blood typing, the police looked for someone who may be able to assist by commenting on the implications of the behaviour of the offender. As Professor David Canter (1995) reports, they found their way to him because of his earlier work studying human behaviour in fires and other emergencies. He was asked in a rather forceful way if he could help the investigation: 'Can you help us catch this man before he kills again?' (Canter 1995).

It is worth noting here that Professor Canter had had at that time no direct involvement with studies of criminals or their treatment. He was a social psychologist with experience in the applications of social psychology to many areas of real world activity, especially people's experience and use of the physical environment (cf. Canter 1977). This meant that as Canter (1995) describes it he had to 'pull himself up by his bootstraps'. He had to help as best he could by working from first principles without being able to test the veracity of those principles in the particular context of violent crime. It was only when his contribution to the investigation was declared by the police to be helpful that they then began to open access to police records that allowed him to start doing proper research, testing out his hypotheses and developing the theories and models that are central to the present book.

Without any detailed knowledge at that stage of the work of all the people before him who had been in similar situations, from Thomas Bond through to James Brussel, and with only a sketchy idea of the work at the FBI academy, Canter set about examining the details of what had happened in the offences. He reasoned as a social psychologist that the forms of personal interaction that the offender exhibited in his crimes would be characteristic of him in other situations. But he also hypothesised that the act of committing a series of crimes over such a long time period would itself have generated some sort of development in the criminal's actions that could be of use to the investigation. This was supported by the fact that the murders had occurred after the offender had been raping for many years.

As he describes it;

> As an environmental psychologist, interested in how people make sense of their surroundings, it seemed to me that there was likely to be some sort of process involved . . . in 1982 a series of rapes had happened in one limited area, in 1984 there had been a few more in a broader area, in 1985/86 there had been some more spreading out even wider . . . There were three murders that happened really further away. It seemed just painfully obvious that there was some development in this process, with the murders occurring round the edge, and . . . the movement out from the area of the earliest crimes. When we looked at the details of the behaviour there also seemed to be a psychological development.
>
> The early crimes were committed by two individuals. They tended to be at the weekend. One of the individuals even seemed to be a bit remorseful and on occasion apologised to the victims that they had raped. The later crimes tended to be during the week, appeared to be by an individual alone, were much more determined, much more planned. This indicated the possibility of a developing commitment to a criminal life, and related criminal activity. That psychological development seemed to be reflected in the growing geography of the crimes. Therefore it was very likely that what we should be thinking of is the early stages of the crimes being in a sense more amateur, almost 'recreational', if you can describe rape in that way, and less committed, less determined, less part of a convinced career than in the later part. If that were the case then if we ran the crimes backwards we would actually be able to end up with the idea of the area circumscribed by the initial three 1982 crimes being where the individuals started from. Within that area, I thought, perhaps they were less likely to be thinking through what they were doing, acting as part of their day-to-day activities. I thus suggested to the police that they were looking for individuals who might be based in the Kilburn area of North West London in 1982.
>
> (Canter, 2003). Reproduced with permission

In addition to these comments about location, Canter also proposed that 'an individual who had raped and murdered young women probably had a history of being violent against women and was quite a nasty character and would be known to be so'. He also drew on

Profile:

- Lived in area of early offences in 1983
- Arrested after October 1983, for violence not necessarily sexual.
- Lived with wife/girlfriend – childless
- Mid to Late 20s
- Light Hair
- 5'9"
- Right Handed
- 'A' secretor
- Semi-skilled
- No public contact
- Keeps to himself, with one or two close friends.

Figure 4.2   Picture of John Duffy taken at the time of his arrest for assaulting his wife.

general information about rapists and descriptions from the victims of the offender's actions to indicate the offender would be in his mid to late 20s, was in a semi-skilled job that did not bring him into contact with the public, would be known as keeping to himself with only one or two close friends. The offender had considerable sexual experience, Canter suggested, and had probably been arrested by the police around 1983 when no known offences occurred (Canter, 1995).

All of these hypotheses turned out to be important because one of their suspects, John Duffy (see Figure 4.2), was in the police records and being looked at only, as far as they were concerned, because he had violently attacked his estranged wife at knifepoint and raped her. It was this that had brought him on to the list of suspects but at that stage some police officers considered this to be 'just' *a domestic*; they thought it was a tussle between a married couple and they could not see this individual going off to commit a series of rapes and murders. Consequently, the comment that the individual they would be looking for would actually have some history of that type of violent interaction with women was something that led the police to reconsider that particular suspect (Canter, 1995).

It turned out that Duffy had indeed lived in area that Canter had derived from the analysis of the location of the crime scenes. The police therefore put their surveillance resources on to John Duffy, and that gave them the information of where he was moving around and how he was watching and following women. He was also seen in the areas where crimes had been committed. When they arrested him they found some very strong forensic evidence that led to a conviction. Duffy had indeed lived at the centre of the area marked out by the three rapes committed in 1982 at the time of those rapes.

Because of the success of this contribution to a major investigation Canter was requested to contribute to many other investigations. But as a social psychologist he was reluctant merely to repeat the mistakes of the past and survive on intelligent, informed opinion. He saw the need to set in motion a wide range of research activities on which could be built an effective scientific discipline. His worthwhile contributions to many police investigations opened doors to information and data on crimes and criminals from which many studies emerged (Canter, 1995, 2004; see also Youngs 2009 for a selection of Canter's students' and colleagues' work).

The Broadening Range of 'Profiling' Activities

Many writers about 'offender profiling' follow the claim put forward by the initial FBI agents that this type of advice is only relevant to offences with overt sexual activity, or reflecting the offender's severe emotional disturbance (Teton, 1989). Typically this is taken to mean sexual homicide and serial rape. This also led to the assumption that profiles would inevitably draw upon approaches typical of the clinical psychology consulting room and psychiatric diagnostic categories.

However, although profiles are still offered for cases of serial homicide and rape, there has been a rapid broadening of the types of crime for which psychological commentary is deemed as applicable, as will become clear in later chapters. The psychological contribution to investigations now runs the full gamut of crimes from arson to terrorism, by way of burglary and fraud, extortion and robbery, child abuse and shoplifting. This in turn has helped to loosen the grip of mental health professionals on the frameworks in use and has also encouraged a development of considerations beyond the individual criminal to the offenders' social networks and related social psychological processes (Canter and Alison, 1999).

Investigative psychology explores a wide range of crimes but also contributes in many more ways than the creation of a hypothetical description of an unknown offender. These contributions grow out of the identification of what it is that is really significant in any crime, which will often have operational implications in its own right. The salient features can guide interviewing strategies as well as scene of crime examinations. Furthermore, once the framework for considering the characteristics of offenders is properly structured it can be integrated with police systems to help elicit and prioritise suspects. There is also the task of predicting what an offender may do next that can be of great significance without any 'profile' of that offender.

Summary

As mentioned, public awareness of the contributions that psychologists can make to the investigation of crimes grew out of the general fascination with serial killers. These vile and determined murderers have become the stuff of urban myths. They are the mainstay of fictional crime drama and are guaranteed to steal the headlines if they break into fact. They seem to epitomise the essence of evil and to symbolise the darkest corners of the psyche. With such a load resting on the images of people who kill again and again it is perhaps not surprising that the images have been distorted and that fantasy and invention often hide the facts about their nature.

Many of the popular beliefs about serial killers that substitute for real knowledge have their origins in the much-quoted but under researched writings of the Behavioral Science Unit of the FBI, based in Quantico, Virginia (Ressler *et al.*, 1986; Douglas and Olshaker, 1997; Ressler, Burgess and Douglas, 1988; Ressler and Shachtman, 1992). The fascination that Hollywood has with the FBI gives the musings of FBI agents a currency that far outweighs their validity. Leading film actors are given lines to quote that repeat confused and misinformed opinions and as a consequence audiences from Alaska to Zanzibar gain the mistaken impression that what is said with such conviction and apparent authority must be the truth.

Out of this 'Hollywood Effect', of gracing personal opinion with dramatic illustration and thereby giving that opinion inappropriate validity, have emerged a great range of statements about serial killers. As discussed in Chapter 13, not one of these general statements survives close scientific scrutiny. So, for example, serial killers are thought to be considerably above average intelligence, they are not thought ever to be of African-American extraction. The phenomenon of serial killing is presented as an almost uniquely American one that had virtually no existence until the last quarter of the twentieth century. Serial killers are claimed only to attack victims of the same ethnicity as themselves and a strongly sexual component is assumed always to be present. Most curiously of all, the complex sets of processes that underlie serial killings are apparently reducible to the simple if rather ambiguous dichotomy of being 'organised' or 'disorganised' (Ressler et al., 1986).

In Chapter 13 studies are reported that make clear, all of these claims about serial killing are false. The claims fall at the first hurdle of systematic study. Even the most elementary reading of the world's newspapers shows that serial killing occurs all over the world in many different forms, committed by many different sorts of people. The claims that emanate from 'research' by FBI agents are false precisely because that research is so flawed. In any other context the results of such badly conducted studies would not have been published. It is only because of the hunger that the mass media and Hollywood have for anything that touches on the evil of serial killing that these claims are so widely broadcast.

The weaknesses of the early activities of FBI agents, when they produced 'offender profiles' are inevitable consequences of the context in which they operated. They were part of a culture in which the dominant mission was to solve crimes. They were not part of the more leisurely and thoughtful milieu of academic researchers. In such a 'go-get-'em' atmosphere it is natural to use whatever is available and offer that as the best guess at the time, even if the information on which conclusions are based is very limited. That is still true today in the applications of IP. Relatively limited findings from exploratory studies may be seized to provide guidance to police enquiries that go far beyond the validity of the original material. Therefore, the continuous development of research based, evidence-led studies is essential if the whole field is not to drift back into tradition and hearsay of little long-term value.

Further Reading

Books

DeNevi, D. and Campbell, J.H. (2004) *Into the Minds of Madmen: How the FBI's Behavioral Science Unit Revolutionised Crime Investigation*, Prometheus Books, New York.

Douglas, J.E., Burgess, A.W., Burgess, A.G. and Ressler, R.K. (2006) *Crime Classification Manual A Standard System for Investigating and Classifying Violent Crimes*, 2nd edn, John Wiley & Sons, Inc., San Francisco.

Keppell, R. (ed.) (2004) *Offender Profiling: Readings in Crime Assessment and Profiling*, London, Thompson/Custom Publishing.

Ressler, R.K., Burgess, A.W., Douglas, J.E. et al. (1986). Sexual killers and their victims: identifying patterns through crime scene analysis. *Journal of Interpersonal Violence*, **1**, 288–308.

Youngs, D. (ed.) (2009). The Behavioural Analysis of Crime: Studies in Investigative Psychology in Honour of David Canter. Ashgate: Aldershot, UK.

Articles

Canter, D. and Youngs, D. (2003) Beyond offender profiling: the need for an investigative psychology, in *Handbook of Psychology in Legal Contexts* (eds R. Bull and D. Carson), John Wiley & Sons, Ltd, Chichester, 171–205.
Douglas, J.E., Ressler, R.K., Burgess, A.W. and Hartman, C.R. (1986). Criminal profiling from crime scene analysis. *Behavioral Sciences and the Law*, **4** (4), 401–21.
Muller, D. (2000) Criminal profiling: real science or just wishful thinking? *Homicide Studies*, **4** (3), 234–64.
Rizinger, D.M. and Loop, J.L. (2002) Three card Monte, Monty Hall, modus operandi and 'offender profiling': some lessons of modern cognitive science for the law of evidence. *Cardozo Law Review*, **24**, 193–285.

Questions for Discussion and Research

1. Why are undercover police officers so prone to corruption?

2. What should you beware of in using 'a thief to catch a thief'?

3. What difficulties might Vidocq experience today in a major city if he tried to use the same procedures as he used in Paris in 1811?

4. Is there any difference between an M.O. and a habit?

5. For what of your actions would you say you have a characteristic M.O.?

6. Why do you think Professor Gehnert thought the Dusseldorf Vampire was mad?

7. Can you identify any ways in which the profile provided by Professor Gehnert could be directly used by the police to help find the killer?

8. Why in this book do we tend to put the words 'profile', 'profiling' and 'profiler' in inverted commas?

Fundamentals

A Framework for Studying Criminal Actions and Inferences about Offenders

William Sapwell stabbing Police Constable Long

Source: The New Newgate Calendar © The Folio Society Ltd 1960

5

The Radex of Criminality

In This Chapter

- Learning Objectives
- Synopsis
- The A→C Equations
- The Hierarchy of Criminal Variation
- A Model of Criminal Variation
- The Radex of Criminality
- Development and Change
- Summary
- Further Reading
- Questions for Discussion and Research

Learning Objectives

When you have completed this chapter you should be able to:

1. Explain the complexities in the process of drawing offender inferences from offence behaviour (also known as solving the A→C equations).
2. Identify the different levels within the hierarchy of criminal variation at which inferences may be drawn.
3. Describe the radex of criminality and explain what it tells us about how differences in offending behaviour are structured.

4. Understand the potential forms of development and change in an offender's behaviour that need to be integrated into models of inference.

Synopsis

*Investigative psychology moves beyond the informed speculation of earlier 'offender profiling' by identifying and elaborating central scientific questions about criminal actions. It focuses on those questions which have special relevance to investigations and understanding criminals. All these questions relate to the **A** → **C** equations. These are the relationships between offence actions and offenders' characteristics.*

Central to these equations (indicated by the →) is the task of making a variety of inferences about offences and offenders. Inferences can be developed in a number of different ways but in essence an inference is a conclusion that derives from a premise by using an argument. Other aspects of this process of argument can be added but the crucial starting point is that the premise must be valid. In the scientific context this is the empirical results on which the argument is built.

The operational applications of IP add further complications to this framework. The claims may not be about the character of the offender but about whether crimes are linked, what may be the most fruitful direction for investigative searches, either through physical space or the virtual space of records, or where to carry out house-to-house enquiries.

There are many reasons why deriving such inferences empirically is not as straightforward as might be expected. One relates to the hierarchy of criminality. It is necessary to determine at which scale of criminal actions, from general illegality to precise details of what happens in a crime, the inference is being drawn and how the inferences from different levels may interact.

Once the scale of crime is in focus it is necessary to determine what is salient about the actions being considered. This cannot be determined in isolation from the various processes that influence criminal activity. Salience can only be determined against the backdrop of what happens in similar events. The rarity of any event or action is one aspect that helps to determine its salience. The other is its particular distinguishing theme. These are the distinctions of quantity and quality that characterise all measurement processes.

The combination of qualitative and quantitative aspects of crimes can be conceptualised in a model that is known as a radex. The radex summarises the major ways in which crimes can differ and so serves to emphasise the great variety of criminal actions and the often unique quality of offences. The model encapsulates all possibilities, even though any example within it may be unique.

Further complexity is added by the recognition that most human action is subject to development and change. This does not rule out the possibility of making inferences but points to the very real difficulty of producing simple empirical relationships between A and C variables which will be universal. It is extremely unlikely that empirical evidence will be available that will be directly relevant to every special circumstance.

Investigative psychology goes beyond informed speculation then by developing theories and models of criminals' actions and experiences. Although these frameworks draw on data and individual cases, they allow inferences which will be relevant across time and place, and which are open to development and refinement as new empirical results become available.

The A→ C Equations

The growing use of offender profiling in the 1990s drew attention to a number of fundamental questions within psychology that had not been appreciated in earlier considerations of crimes and criminals. These were summarised in the central IP questions about how 'actions' in a crime relate to 'characteristics' of the offender, as noted in earlier chapters. The actions (or A variables) include *where, when* and *how* a crime is committed. The characteristics (or C variables) cover all aspects of an offender that may be of value to the investigative process or court proceedings. These relationships can be the A→C equations encapsulated within (Canter, 1993).

Although this relationship is not an 'equation' in a strict mathematical sense it is helpful to keep the looser meaning implied by this simple formulation. Thinking of the relationships as a family of equations simplifies the discussion of what the central questions of IP are. It also helps to clarify the many challenges and complexities that arise in trying to establish empirically any relationships implied by these equations. It is important to emphasise, though, that specifying the problem as a set of equations does not mean that there is necessarily a purely mathematical or statistical way of carrying out profiling. Quite the opposite is the case. By studying what would be involved in solving these equations it becomes clear that we have to use more conceptual, theory-driven approaches if we are to have any hope of producing a scientific basis for psychological contributions to investigations.

Canonical Relationships

A starting point for understanding the challenges inherent in the A→C relationships is to recognise that the A→C mapping will rarely take the form of simple one to one relationships (see Box 5.1), (Canter and Youngs, in press, d). For instance, it is not the case that the age of an offender is revealed entirely by, for example, how careful he is not to leave clues, but not at all by the use of a weapon; similarly use of a weapon can never be the single indicator of, for example, whether the criminal has been in prison. Rather, there are a range of complexities in the ways that As relate to Cs.

These complexities can be thought of as 'canonical equations', which are 'the relationships between two sets of variables' (Tabanick and Fidell, 1983: 146), as illustrated in Box 5.2. There is always a mixture of criminal actions that are being related to a mixture of characteristics or other criminal actions. The relationships are between combinations of action variables and combinations of characteristics variables.

The 'equation', though, is best thought of as an analogy, or even a metaphor, a form of representation more useful in illustrating the nature of the 'profiling' problem rather than

Box 5.1   Reasons Why One Clue Cannot Usually be Used to Predict One Characteristic (adapted from Canter and Youngs, in press, d)

The canonical equations emphasise some of the crucial problems in 'profiling' as a form of inference of characteristics from a single clue.

- The relationship between the two domains takes the form of a given *combination* of criterion variables that map on to given *combinations* of predictor variables.
- The same action can, on a consistent basis, indicate more than one characteristic.
- The same characteristic can be inferred from different actions – for example, extreme violence may be threatened in a robbery carried out by an inexperienced *or* a highly experienced offender. Conversely, both rapists and robbers will tend to have criminal histories that include burglary convictions.
- The same action can indicate different characteristics in different contexts or at different points in an offender's criminal progression – for example, carrying a gun by a lone offender may indicate a rather different individual than would the carrying of a gun as part of a group offending event. As another example, the use of an accelerant may indicate an above average intellect in the young arsonist but less so as he or she became more experienced.
- Changes in any one predictor variable (the actions) can destabilise the relationship of any other predictor variable with any criterion variable or set of criterion variables (the characteristics).
- The exclusion of pertinent variables or indeed, the inclusion of superfluous ones, can distort the relationships between A and C variables. For example, knowing how a burglary was initiated may be a crucial action variable that sets all the other actions in context. Or, the pattern of extensive damage and disruption to a property may suggest a desperate offender on drugs but if it was known that a 'con' initiation to the offence this may suggest a rather different, perhaps particularly vicious, offender.
- Minor variations in the variance or the inclusion of particular variables in the A set may radically change the weightings in the C set. So, for example, leaving out an action because a witness or victim was not sure about it could produce a markedly different description of the offender.

offering a direct way for dealing with that problem. The whole concept of a 'canonical equation' shows that small changes in any one variable can influence the overall outcome. A change in the range of crimes considered, or age of victims, or length of time over which the crimes are examined could produce very different predictions of, for instance, criminal history.

Box 5.2 A Technical Account that Illustrates the Criminal Canonical Equation

On one side of this equation are variables derived from information about the offence, which would be available to investigators. On the other side, there are the characteristics of the offender that are most useful in facilitating the police enquiry. So, if $A_{1......n}$ represents n actions of the offender (including, for example, time, place and victim selection) and $C_{1...m}$ represents m characteristics of the offender, then the empirical question is to establish the values of weightings ($F_{1...n}$ and $F_{1...m}$) in an equation of the following form:

$$F_1A_1 + \ldots + F_nA_n = F_1C_1 + \ldots + F_mC_m$$

If such canonical equations could be established for any subset of crimes then they would provide a powerful basis for police investigations as well as raising some fascinating psychological questions about criminal behaviour.

In mathematical terms there are many solutions to the equation. In other words, a variety of combinations of A weightings can just as validly give rise to a variety of combinations of C weightings. There are many possible relationships, not just one, within any data set linking the As to the Cs. In concrete terms this could mean for instance that one pattern of behaviour could indicate a young man with a long criminal history or just as readily an older man with little criminal experience. One relationship may be stronger than the other within any sample, but research is required to establish that and detailed enough data may not be available.

There are two related ways around these central problems. One is to conduct a large number of studies that cross-validate the links between the A and the C variables. The other is to put more reliance on theoretical perspectives that will guide the heuristic search for stable relationships. These two approaches, the empirical and the conceptual will feed on each other, as they do in all scientific activity, but in the short term the conceptual may prove more cost effective.

This means that we should give emphasis to empirical procedures that facilitate theory production. Massive, number-crunching data analyses will always be limited in their applicability to individual cases. But if those analyses allow us to go beyond any specific set of data by helping to generate broadly relevant principles, models and theories then they will contribute to the development of the whole field of IP, rather than just helping us to understand what is happening in a particular set of data.

Investigative Inferences

At the heart of the A-C questions and the models that we derive to answer them are inference processes. The → at the centre of the A → C equations implies an inference is being made about the likely relationships between A and C. The most obvious of these is the inference about the characteristics of an offender being derived from aspects of the crime. But the linking of crimes to a common offender is also an inference that may be thought of as an '$A_n \rightarrow A_m$ equation' (where n is one set of actions and m another). There are also crucial inferences central to all questions about offending that deal with the identification of the aspects of an offence or an offender that are to be the focus of attention, an issue we will explore under the heading of 'salience'.

There are many ways of making inferences. Indeed, there is a whole area of logic devoted to the study of how inferences may be made. But in general they can usefully be thought of as arguments that can be simplified as a form of 'if . . . then' statements. For example; *if* the crime happens during the working day the conclusion may be drawn that *then* the offender does not have a fixed job from which he would be missed. This argument always requires some sort of 'warrant' that supports the logic of the argument. In this example, that warrant may be that if a person were missing from a job then they would be noticed and this could cause questions to be asked that could lead to their identification for the crime. So only those who would not be missed would have committed the crime. But, as can be readily appreciated, such a warrant is embedded in assumptions about a culture or job situation and requires some empirical test before it can be accepted without question. For instance, the absence of a self-employed person and/or one who travels for his work activities may not be noticed.

By examining closely the nature of these arguments we can see even more directly how challenging it really is to put offender profiling and the understanding of criminal actions on a scientific footing. One detailed consideration of the structure of arguments and thus of what is involved in making inferences is given in Box 5.3. It can be seen that there are at least six different components to an argument. This shows that there are many more aspects of the 'If . . . Then' process than simply claiming that a case has a particular set of qualities therefore it was perpetrated by a particular sort of person.

Tight versus Loose Couplings

In considering the process of making inferences as part of an investigation it is important to keep in mind that inferences may vary in how precise they can be (Canter and Youngs, in press, d). So, for example, it may be possible to infer some sort of military background from the general level of control used in rape. But there could also be a more exact correspondence, such that the use of bindings in particular to control a victim was related to a particular type of military training.

At the same time, the strength of the correspondence between any two variables can vary. An example of a strong relationship would be one which shows that if a rapist enters a house in order to assault his victim and takes some of her property with him then there is a very high probability that he will have some previous experience, and a conviction for burglary. However, the preparedness of a burglar to enter an occupied house may be only very weakly related to his previous criminal activity.

The combination of these variations in precision and strength produce mappings that can be understood in broad terms as either tight or loose couplings. Where the mapping is both precise and the relationship strong the coupling is tight; where the mapping is less precise and the relationship weak, the coupling is loose.

Box 5.3 Inference and Argument

There are many ways of drawing inferences. Philosopher Stephen Toulmin (1958) developed a tidy graphic model for describing arguments which is helpful in understanding the components that an inference can contain.

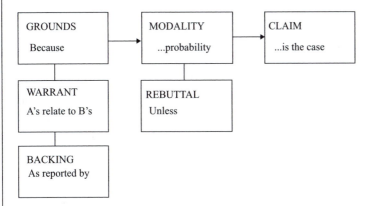

This has been useful in many areas, including the study of 'profiles' (Alison *et al.*, 2003). The model serves to illustrate that, for example:

* The *claim* that an offender will be a recognisably 'organised' person is derived from . . .
* The *grounds* the crime scene of killing is an 'organised' one because it is . . .
* *Warranted* by the relationship between 'organised' crime scenes and 'organised' criminals . . .
* The *modality* of this relationship is assumed to be a very high probability.
* Unless it is *rebutted* by the lack of any clarity in whether the crime scene can be designated as 'organised'.
* All this being *backed* by earlier studies.

Each of these six components is open to challenge, as will become apparent in later chapters. But breaking down the inference process in this way also draws attention to the need to have a robust and very clear way of defining the central issues, in this case the meaning of 'organised' and 'disorganised'. If this cannot be done then the rebuttal undermines the whole argument.

Looser coupling may be anticipated when talking for example of the criminal history of an offender being revealed through the particular precautions he makes to avoid detection when committing a crime. There may be broad relationships between carefulness in offending and criminal experience. An obvious example of this would be when casual young opportunist offenders take no care to avoid leaving fingerprints, whereas an offender who knows his fingerprints are already in the police system will be much more cautious about leaving such evidence. But there may be also be rather tight couplings between specific aspects of an individual's criminal history and specific forensically aware behaviours. So, for example, physically aggressive rapists may be expected to have much more violence in their criminal background than those rapists who coerce their victims through verbal threats. In later chapters we will explore the ways in which inference can be developed, but always keeping in mind that not all inferences are of the single clue = particular characteristic variety (see Box 5.1).

Of course the tighter the coupling, that is the more precise the relationship and the stronger the relationship, the more immediate application it can have to police investigations and the more readily can it be built into detailed models of criminals' actions. But loose couplings can still be of great value in clarifying the major conceptual parameters of a theory and in giving some form of guideline to police investigations (Canter and Youngs, in press, d). For example the indications that most violent, overtly aggressive and impulsive offences are committed within close proximity of an area with which an offender is familiar may be only a 'loose coupling' relationship. However, if there are limited resources to carry out an investigation, as there usually are, this general finding does suggest that the emphasis should be put on local investigations, house to house enquiries and following up suggestions offered by local people, rather than more widespread possibilities that may be brought to police attention.

The Hierarchy of Criminal Variation

Probably the most crucial part of an argument is that which is usually buried deep in fictional formulations and often ignored in factual accounts. This is being clear what the actual constituents of the issues being considered really are. A good illustration of this is what really is meant by a crime being 'organised' and how clearly it can actually be distinguished from one that is 'disorganised'? We shall return to this sort of question over and over again in subsequent chapters because if we are not even clear about the basic definitions and descriptions of the constituents of criminal action around which our inferences are based then there is little hope of building defensible or valid arguments.

The first step in specifying which aspect of criminality is going to be considered in any attempt to make inferences is to determine at what level of generality the explorations will be carried out. For example, it may be simply the type of offence – that the offender is a burglar rather than a robber or an arsonist. Or it may be the very particular details of how a window was forced open that should be the focus of concern. This leads to the need to consider what might be regarded as different levels of magnification of the criminal action, from the lowest magnification in which we just consider whether the action was a crime or not, to a very high magnification that focuses on the details of very specific behaviours. We will therefore now move on to what may be best thought of as a *hierarchy of criminal differentiation*.

There is a ladder of possible distinctions between crimes. At the most general, highest level we can consider the difference between the fact that a crime has been committed as opposed to some action that is legal. Once we step down from the general level of whether an activity is criminal or not, there is a continuum of variations (or further steps on our ladder) from this general matter of illegal versus legal actions at one extreme to the consideration of

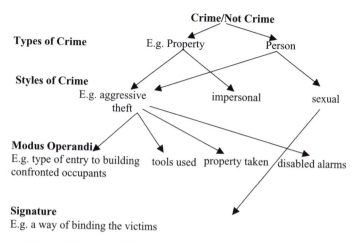

Figure 5.1 Typical frequencies of criminal differentiation.

distinguishing between events on the basis of very detailed examination of the precise actions involved. It is useful to identify a number of points along this continuum, as shown in Figure 5.1.

Determining whether or not something is criminal may not be as easy as it may seem at first sight. There are differences of opinion even over serious crimes as to whether they should be regarded as illegal. One example brought this home to us when as teachers we saw the horror on the faces of most students in our graduate class when one of the overseas students said with calm equanimity, believing what he was saying was self-evident, that 'of course it was not possible for a husband to rape his wife'. Even today in Britain prostitutes report police officers telling them that no assault on them can be regarded as a rape. Indeed, it is only in recent years that UK and US courts have accepted the possibility of rape within marriage and against any victim no matter his or her occupation.

This does mean, though, that in considering any set of actions that are regarded as a crime it is necessary to be clear how and why that is regarded as a crime and by whom. As discussed in Box 5.4, crime is not defined psychologically, but legally. This can have big implications for the meanings of that crime for the offender and thus the offender's likely characteristics and whether s/he may have committed other similar crimes. Another clear illustration of this is insurance fraud. Many people just do not regard it as a crime to exaggerate an insurance claim. Consequently, the sorts of psychological analysis such as the characteristics of who may commit such frauds and how to prevent them is going to be rather different from the consideration of events such as robbery, which most agree is criminal.

Any inferences about an offender may therefore start from considering what sort of people commit crimes (see Table 5.1). The criminological literature is replete with accounts of the makeup of offenders. In essence, the great majority of offenders are male and in their mid-to-late teens (see Figure 5.2). Most crimes are committed by people who come from a criminal environment, typically a criminal family. They are more often than not poorly educated and

Box 5.4 What is a Criminal?

The starting point for any psychology of crime is to recognise that crime is a socio-legal, rather than a psychological concept. What makes a behaviour a crime is the fact that it is defined in law, or by society, as such, rather than any intrinsic quality of the behaviour itself. Therefore, if we are to understand criminal actions and the underlying processes that give rise to them we cannot look to legal definitions to illuminate those processes.

Although, one common psychological basis that criminal behaviours do have is that they are all characterised by individuals choosing to infringe the rules of society, crime does cover a diverse and varied range of human behaviour.

To move on from the purely legal definitions, criminal activity needs to be construed as modes of interaction with people and objects to achieve a great mixture of objectives. This leads to the need to develop psychologically meaningful ways of distinguishing between criminal activities.

somewhat below average intelligence. This is the backdrop against which any understanding of offenders and inferences about them has to be made. Often therefore we need to look at how any subset of offenders differs from what may be thought of as the 'typical offender'.

Classes of Crime

At the first step down in our levels of differentiation there is the issue of general classes of crime, for example; whether they are against a specific person, or against an institution. This

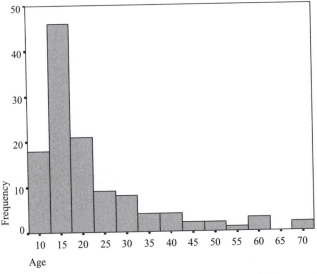

Figure 5.2   Frequencies of ages of offenders at the time of first conviction.

Table 5.1   General characteristics of offenders.

Characteristic	Findings

Age	From UK National Statistics figures:
	Peak age of offending = 17 (males), 15 (females)
	Slightly higher proportions of male than female offenders (59% compared with 56%) were aged 21 and over.
	People aged 35 and over, particularly women, are much less likely to be found guilty of, or cautioned for, indictable offences.
	For male offenders in 2005, 15-year-olds received more cautions than any other age group while 19-year-olds received the most convictions. Among female offenders, 14- and 15-year-olds received the most cautions and the most common age to be convicted was 16.
	
	From FBI Uniform Crime Reports 2007 (United States):
	Arrests by age (n = 10 698 310):
	    Aged under 15: 4.3%
	    Aged under 18: 15.4%
	    Aged under 21: 29.5%
	    Aged under 25: 44.4%

Gender	From UK National Statistics figures:
	Men commit more crimes than women.
	In 2002 male offenders in England and Wales outnumbered female offenders by more than four to one.
	In 2006, 1.42 million offenders were sentenced for criminal offences in England and Wales. The majority of these offenders, 80%, were male and of these 7% were aged under 18.
	
	From US FBI Uniform Crime Reports 2007:
	Arrests by gender (n = 10 698 310):
	    Males: 75.8%
	    Females: 24.2%

Ethnicity	From US FBI Uniform Crime Reports 2007:
	Arrests by ethnicity (n = 10 656 710):
	    – White: 69.7%
	    – Black: 28.2%
	    – American Indian or Alaskan Native: 1.3%
	    – Asian or Pacific Islander: 0.8%

would also include questions about subsets of crimes, such as the comparison between violent and property offenders. Many studies show that one of the clearest distinctions between people who commit a number of crimes is whether they commit crimes against property, such as theft, or against a person, such as violence or sexual assault (cf. Farrington and Lambert, 1994). Although the distinction between person and property crimes is important, it is not always that straightforward.

Consider the example of robbery. In essence the legal terminology indicates that any theft that involves violence or the threat of violence is known as 'robbery'. It is distinct from burglary, although it does overlap with a situation in which a burglar confronts a resident, which may be known as 'aggravated burglary'. Thus robbery may be regarded as having a primary objective that is to take property, making it clearly a 'crime against property', but it also includes a strong, direct interpersonal component in the attack on the individual whose property is being stolen, making it a 'crime against the person'. Arson is another example where the boundary may not be as clear as it may first appear. If the arson is carried out to hide a burglary it is clearly a 'property' crime, but if it is an act of vengeance against an individual perhaps it should be thought of as a crime 'against the person'. The details of the crime may assist in making these distinctions.

The distinction between person and property crimes has crucial implications for investigative inferences not least because of the well established findings in psychology about the important differences between people in terms of how they relate to others. The most well known personality distinction is between those who are high on one end or the other of the dimension of introversion – extraversion. Extraverts are seen as sociable and ready to relate to others. Introverts apparently prefer reading a good book to going to a party. A more directly relevant distinction is found in the less well known work of Little (1983) and his idea of personal projects. He shows that some people's lives are more clearly devoted to projects that involve objects and others to projects that involve people (Little, 1983).

This is not to suggest that property criminals are all introverts and that people convicted of violent assaults will be found to have person-oriented life goals. However, it does indicate that the distinction between property and person crimes does have parallels in other areas of human experience. It is therefore likely to be a reflection of more profound aspects of ways of dealing with the world.

One productive way of thinking about this is that property crimes relate to outcomes that are clearly external to the individual. Wealth and the possession of objects may be a manifestation of personal desires but they are outside of the person. By contrast, violence and aggression have the purpose of resolving something that the offender feels; something inside him. This is the same as Fesbach's (1964) distinction within violence between 'instrumental' and 'expressive' crimes. We can generalise this to all crimes considered in a broad sense.

In some crimes it is claimed that there is no external victim. These 'victimless' crimes may include, for example, possessing and taking illegal drugs, or driving offences such as driving without a licence. They may have the potential for leading on to crimes that affect others, but of themselves the only person who experiences the crime is the person who commits it. This therefore is a rather different crime from those that target a person or property.

Types of Crime

The assignment of crimes to broad classes is rather different from thinking of them in ways that are closer to the legal definitions. We will reserve the term 'crime type' for classifications that come close to distinctions that underlie the law such as residential burglary, armed robbery and homicide. But as we have noted, legal definitions of crimes and the way they may be coded in police records may not accord closely with the details of the criminal's actions or with crucial psychological features of the offence. There will be dozens of different police codes for many different types of burglary, for example, distinguishing between domestic and

Box 5.5 Discussion Topic – Motives

Do We Need Motives?

In all crime fiction, in proceedings in court and when police are discussing cases and the actions they should take, invariably the discussion turns to a consideration of the 'motive' for the crime. Indeed the FBI Crime Classification Manual claims that it is classifying crimes on the basis of their motive. But what is meant by motive? However, it will have been noted that there has been no need here to raise the spectre of 'motives' in considering the differences between crimes.

There are many problems with using the idea of motives:

- The term 'motive' can take on many different meanings, e.g.
    - Explanation, such as 'I had to kill him before he killed me'.
    - Purpose, 'I needed the money to pay for health care'.
    - Reason the offender may offer, 'it was an accident'.
    - Unconscious urge or psychological process of which the offender may not even be aware, 'he hated women because his mother had committed suicide'.
    - Set of actions of which the crime is a part, e.g. 'we were all drunk and having a laugh'.
    - The narrative that gives shape and meaning to a crime. 'I don't let people push me around, so I decided to teach him a lesson'.
- How do we know what is the reason for a person's actions. The person may not know himself!
- Most human action is not caused by just one 'motive'. Can you explain why you are reading this book? Is there only one reason?
- It has been argued very convincingly by Mills (1940) that we tend to use the idea of 'motive' when we cannot really understand why something has happened.
- Often 'motive' is used to mean the implicit narrative that gives shape to a series of actions. It is probably therefore better to try and make that narrative explicit.

So does it ever make sense to consider some crimes as 'motiveless'? Or do we just mean that we cannot explain why they happened?

commercial burglary, aggravated burglary, burglary 'artifice' (in which an offender pretends to be an official to gain entry to a house), damage to property as part of a burglary and many others. But if we are to understand the implications of the crime it will often be necessary to combine the police categories together in order to create a list that provides enough distinctions to be of value for psychological analysis but does not hide the behavioural picture by focusing on irrelevant details.

So even though there is some value in organising studies of crime and criminality under the broad headings of crime types there will never be a simple or single sub-set of crimes that have just one constituent in the legal code. Crime types will always be a creation by the researcher or investigator to meet their particular goals. This is so central to developing an understanding of criminality that providing an organised framework for thinking about crime types opens a door into a radically new way of thinking about crime and criminality. We will return to this when we have completed our review of the hierarchy of criminality.

Patterns of Action – Styles of Offending

At a more specific level than the type of crime are questions about patterns of criminal behaviour, such as the comparison of offenders who prepare carefully in advance of a crime with those whose actions are impulsive and opportunistic. Here the quest is to identify behaviours that co-occur to form interpretable groupings. This may be regarded as the *style* of offending. This is a major focus of IP research and much of the subsequent chapters explores the patterns of co-occurrence of criminal actions.

Modus Operandi

A somewhat more contentious subset of activities are those that are relatively unusual and may be regarded as typical of a certain offender. Although the term *modus operandi* (M.O.) is somewhat ambiguous it may be suitable for this level of specificity, distinguishing it from patterns of behaviour.

The term M.O. is very widely used and that is part of the reason for its ambiguity. Some authors try to get round this by giving a rather more involved definition. They claim that M.O. refers to the behaviours of the offender that are required to successfully complete a crime. Turvey (1999) elaborates on this by proposing that M.O. serves the purposes of protecting the offender's identity, ensuring successful completion of the crime and facilitating escape (Turvey, 1999: 152).

Unfortunately, the most elementary consideration of even the simplest crime reveals that that there are many aspects of a crime that do not have any of these obvious functional purposes even though they are typical of what an offender does. For example, if a burglar does not ensure that a house is empty, being willing to tackle any occupant who is present, then that is a crucial aspect of his pattern of behaviour even though it does not achieve any of the obvious purposes suggested as being part of an M.O. Indeed, in many cases it is not at all clear what the purposes of the criminal's actions are. So as with any categorisation scheme that relies on interpreting *why* something happens rather than focusing on *what* happens there will be uncertainty in determining exactly what is covered. This is similar to the use of the concept of 'motive' as presented in the discussion Box 5.5.

The M.O. may therefore be best thought of as a pattern of behaviour that is rather more specific than the general 'style' of an offence, such as, for example, whether a particular type of weapon was used (Lobato, 2000). The overlap with our idea of 'style' does mean that in many studies of patterns of behaviour the authors may use the term M.O. We will therefore have to learn to live with this confusion in the recognition that M.O. is popular terminology for particular patterns of behaviour.

Signature

The most distinct set of actions in a crime that are unique to that crime or criminal may be graced with the term *signature*. Various studies (Keppel *et al.*, 2005) have used this term although it implies very distinct features and a precision, like a written signature, that may not be directly paralleled in criminal actions. It is most unusual for a criminal to leave some very obvious trace in a crime that is unique to him or her. There is the further problem that it is rare indeed for an offender to carry out any uniquely distinct actions in every crime he commits. It is thus extremely unusual to find something like a behavioural fingerprint for an offender. Leaving a calling card, or the death's head moth as in the *Silence of the Lambs*, makes for exciting fiction but hardly ever happens in real life. On those very unusual occasions when it does, as in the puzzles that the 'Zodiac Killer' sent to newspapers, there is the risk that this 'signature' will become public knowledge and other offenders may be able to copy it to add further confusion.

The only context in which a signature action may be observed with some regularity is when a crime is perpetrated through the use of language, notably through threat letters or fraudulent documents. Then there may be some idiosyncrasy in the writing, a curious set of misspellings or grammatical errors that are unique to the person. But as we shall see over and over again there is always the important requirement of determining that the aspects of the writing being considered are not shared by many others. For example, in one case on which we consulted it was claimed by a linguistic expert that the author of a contested text was unusual in writing 'all though' instead of 'although'. However, a quick web search showed that this was not unique to this person at all.

A Multi-Dimensional Framework

Although Figure 5.1 provides notional levels in a hierarchy, the linear ordering implied by this is an oversimplification. It is not meant to indicate that there is some set of modus operandi features particular to each pattern of criminal behaviour and that, in turn, some sets of patterns of criminal behaviour are particular to each type of crime. Many empirical studies show that these various degrees of specificity can interact with each other in complex ways. For instance, the criminological literature indicates that offenders are not necessarily specialists in one particular type of crime (Piquero, Farrington and Blumstein, 2003). As a consequence the difference between an offender who came prepared to carry out his/her crime and one who just grabbed what was available may be more pertinent than differences in say whether it was a robbery or a burglary. In effect, this makes the description of any given crime multidimensional. The different levels of precision may be regarded as an inter-related set of dimensions for describing crimes, rather than a simple hierarchy.

The focus on highly specific patterns of behaviour in popular, anecdotal crime publications as well as in the limited research literature is in part due to the many complications and unanswered questions within these multivariate issues. Some relate to the versatility of offenders; the likelihood of them committing a mixture of crimes in different ways. Some relate to the limited knowledge that exists about what really is typical of offences in general, or of any particular subset of offences. These raise questions of just what may be regarded as typical or characteristic of any given crime or criminal.

Such a complex structure is extremely difficult to examine in total. Researchers have therefore usually focused on one or other of the 'levels' of this hierarchy. For example, there are many studies examining the differences between offenders and non-offenders or between classes of violent and non-violent offenders (for example, Canter and Ioannou, 2004; Farrington, 1995; Farrington *et al.*, 2001; Stephenson, 1992). There are fewer comparing the differences between those convicted of crime of different types. Eysenck's (1987) work on personality differences across crime types is an interesting exception although he points out that the behavioural variation within crime types is such that his findings can provide only crude indications of any differences. Within specific crimes such as arson or homicide, as we shall see in later chapters, there are now a number of studies of the offender characteristic correlates of offending style differences. However, a starting point for developing any inferences is the understanding of how crimes differ from each other in terms of who is likely to commit them.

A Model of Criminal Variation

When dealing with complex multidimensional problems it is useful to try and think how the conceptual issues may be represented visually. The human ability to make sense of visual information is usually much more highly developed than the ability to handle complex arguments or mathematics (see Roam, 2008 for a witty account of how to use this ability). In the present case when thinking of differences between crimes we could put on one side of our visual representation crimes that are against the person, for simplicity we can call those murder and violence, although it is also appropriate to put sexual violence such as rape within the violence category. To the other side we can place those crimes that are strongly linked to property and do not include any direct attack on a person, which we can illustrate with arson and theft.

If we further consider in very broad terms whether the offence may be for personal, emotional benefit or having some instrumental objective then we may agree that the violence and arson could be put together because of their personal, emotive quality and the theft and murder may have a more objective focus. This would give a four-way partitioning as shown in Table 5.2.

This table enshrines a number of different hypotheses about criminality that are open to direct empirical test. These hypotheses may be premised on the assumption that a criminal

Table 5.2 A general form of relationship between 'types' of crime.

	Person	Property
Emotional	VIOLENCE	ARSON
Instrumental	MURDER	THEFT

who carries out crimes in one cell of our table would also be more likely to carry out crimes in an immediately adjacent cell. So, for example, we would hypothesise that people convicted of murder would be more likely to have convictions for violence than for arson, but that arsonists would be likely to have convictions for theft or violence.

This idea is so crucial to forms of analysis that will be presented over and over again throughout the rest of this book that it is worth elaborating on what is being proposed here. The core of the argument is that the conceptual similarities between the entities, in this case the crimes, are a reflection of their actual co-occurrence. Our hypotheses are about which crimes will be associated with each other across a range of offenders.

These associations are one version of the → in our A → C equations. So in the very simple example we have started with above, the table actually proposes a whole set of inferences about which crimes will be related to each other. A number of hypothesised inferences are present, for example; if a murder has occurred we hypothesise that the offender will have a previous conviction for violence. If our empirical research does not support this then we have to change the model that Table 5.2 summarises and test it further against other data.

The list in Table 5.2 is just the briefest simple example of only four crimes. To illustrate the important issues here it is fruitful to take a longer list. Table 5.3 provides an indication of the major types of crime that are often distinguished for use in behavioural research. But each researcher is likely to use a framework that is distinct. Driving offences may be left out entirely, for example, or the varieties of sexual offence given much more differentiation. The list does serve to show, however, that the distinction between person and property crimes can only be sustained with clarity for the crimes at either extreme of this list. Burglary and theft clearly relate directly to property and may involve no contact with a person at all. Violence, sex crimes and murder are assaults on a person and need not involve any aspects of property. But, as already noted robbery is theft or burglary with violence, so it can be thought of as sitting between the two forms of crime.

Arson, as we have seen, also covers a range of different types of offence that may be an attack on property in some abstract sense, as when a child sets fire to his school, or may be a more direct assault against an individual, being an emotional act of revenge. Thus, although property is damaged most significantly in arson the crime may find a place closer to acts of violence in terms of its psychological significance.

Table 5.3   Major types of crime.

Burglary
Theft
Robbery
Fraud
Motoring offences
Drug related
Arson
Violence
Sex crimes
Murder

Motoring offences run the gamut from illegal parking to killing someone in an accident. Depending on the classification process they could also include the theft of a vehicle. They are usually distinguished from other crimes by researchers because they seem to be offences that are a product of very personal aspects of the offender that do not really imply either the desire for property or an attack on a person. They may be a direct product of an offender's emotional state. There may often be some very particular characteristic of the person such as alcoholism that is influencing their actions.

These personal possibilities lead to a recognition that some types of crime are really perpetrated against the offender by the offender. They are sometimes called 'victimless crimes' but that is a rather narrow view of their consequences. The most obvious example of these is illegal drug abuse. All the associated drug related crimes such as possession and selling of drugs could be part of this framework too but that would depend on the details of the crimes.

A Model of Variations between Crimes

These considerations show that there is no simple ordering of crimes from the most property-related through to the most person-oriented. Rather there are different modes of offending. At least three modes may be identified, to do with gaining property, to do with actions against other people and thirdly in relation to some personal aspects of the offender. Any particular crime may draw on more than one mode depending on exactly what it consists of. Arson, for example, may be carried out for the excitement an individual gets from setting things alight, or as an act of revenge against others. Similarly a motoring offence may be an indication of the excitement an offender gets from stealing a car, or may be directly related to the money that can be obtained from selling the stolen vehicle.

It is therefore more appropriate to represent the relationship between the offences in Table 5.3 as locations in a notional circle that distributes the offences across three broad modes of action relating to the target of the offence, as in Figure 5.3. The circular sequence implies that there is no simple ordering of the crimes from least to most, but that the sequence can start at any point and move round. This is analogous to the circle of colours that is often used to explain complementary and contrasting colours. It has no simple order to it but moves round logically from any start point back to the same place. For example, starting at red you can go through orange to yellow. From yellow you can go through brown and green on to turquoise and blue and then through the purples back to red. We may think of these colours as warm or cold, natural or not and can organise them in other sequences, but there is a logic to the circular ordering that any artist will understand. For those of a musical turn of mind, what is known as the 'circle of fifths' has a similar quality to it. We may therefore recognise that this circular way of representing experience has value in many contexts.

Co-occurrence of Offences

It therefore emerges that the organisation of offences into some framework as illustrated in Table 5.2 may not be as simple as might have initially appeared. Further, the simple order of Table 5.3 from property to personal crimes may not be as empirically valid as may have

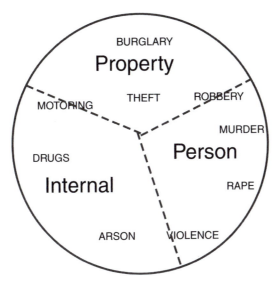

Figure 5.3 A model of variation between crimes.

been hoped. There are therefore important questions about what the actual associations are between these different crimes. The models in Table 5.2 and Figure 5.3 are therefore best regarded as a set of interrelated hypotheses that are open to direct test by looking at which criminal activities share aspects in practice.

These models are based on two assumptions. One is that offenders typically commit more than one crime. This is usually a valid assumption although of course it does mean that many of the inferences and other applications of studies based on these assumptions have to be treated with caution when a criminal commits only one crime. The second is that crimes that are conceptually similar to each other will typically be committed by offenders who share characteristics. Thus, it is this *co-occurrence* of crimes that is the empirical test of whether they should be thought of as similar to each other. To be clear, co-occurrence means that across a range of crimes and offenders there will be subsets of crimes that are carried out by the same people. In the great majority of cases where there are a series of crimes with the same culprit then their co-occurrence can be used as a basis for subsequent analysis and the development of models of criminality.

In later chapters the strengths and weaknesses of police databases will be discussed as well as the utility of working with offenders' self-reports of their criminal activity. The latter allows rather more complete account of offending because it tends to include a lot of crimes for which the person was not charged. It is therefore a useful basis for considering the co-occurrence of crimes and the determination of their underlying structure. There have therefore been a number of studies that examine the self reports of offenders by asking them to complete confidential questionnaires about their criminal activities (Junger-Tas and Marshall, 1999). There is reasonable evidence that their answers do relate to the crimes for which they have actually been convicted (Youngs, 2001), although as Youngs, Canter and Cooper (2004) show they are more likely to report less serious crimes for which they have been convicted and to underreport serious crimes for which they have not been convicted. These studies allow us to illustrate further the development of models of criminality.

A Study of Criminal Differentiation

Studies of offences that offenders themselves admit to provide results of great practical as well as theoretical value. The reasonable validity and reliability of self-report offending measures has been established (for example, Farrington (1973); Farrington *et al.* (2001); Hindelang, Hirschi and Weis (1981); Huizinga and Elliot (1986)). One such major study is that reported by Youngs (2004). It is helpful to understand the details of how such studies are carried out so that their strengths and weaknesses can be more fully appreciated.

She approached 207 young males (14–28 years) in probation centres, prisons, young offenders institutions and in the general population. Ninety per cent of the sample had at least one criminal conviction, having been involved from an early age (median age at first conviction = 15 years). Their mean age was 19 years old at the time of the study. Nearly half the sample reported more than 10 convictions; 12.2% reported more than 40 convictions. Many had a family history of crime; around a quarter revealing that at least one parent had a criminal conviction. Nearly two-thirds of the sample reported no academic qualifications. The sample thus revealed many of the characteristics typical of criminals in the United Kingdom (Youngs, 2004).

Youngs prepared a self-completion questionnaire that had 45 items relating to various forms of criminality and delinquency. The items were based on those used by Furnham and Thompson (1991), Elliot and Ageton (1980), Nye and Short (1957) and Hindelang, Hirschi and Weis (1981), Shapland (1974).

The questionnaire thus consisted of statements describing criminal and deviant acts and incidents. Respondents were required to indicate the frequency with which they had carried out those actions from never, through once to twice, a few times, many times, to very often (more than 50 times). For the purposes of developing a general understanding of criminality responses were initially dichotomised in terms of whether they had ever committed each of the 45 acts, or never committed each of those acts.

The questionnaire was completed anonymously in groups as large as prison or probation security procedures would allow. Typically this meant groups of three, although in some institutions it was necessary to give the questionnaires to the offenders to fill in on an individual basis. Care was taken to ensure that their responses could not be read by others. They completed the questionnaire in their own time. Youngs assisted some respondents who had reading or comprehension difficulties.

There are many ways of revealing styles of offending within the 45 self-reported criminal and deviant behaviours. These processes consist of seeking a meaningful structure underlying the co-occurrence of the responses across the sample. The most common is some form of factor analysis (the origin of factor analysis is generally ascribed to Spearman, 1904; see Harman, 1976, for a detailed discussion of its use). Other researchers favour a form of cluster analysis (first detailed by Tryon, 1939). These procedures have a number of weaknesses which are discussed elsewhere (cf. Grimm and Yarnold, 1995). However, their major weakness for the criminal context is that they do not facilitate the development of our understanding of the underlying structure as research evolves. They tend to be restrictive in the form of structure that they reveal.

Multi-Dimensional Scaling

A number of IP studies have found another approach to be productive. It is a type of multi-dimensional scaling (MDS) (see, for example, Canter and Fritzon, 1998; Canter and Heritage, 1990; Salfati, 2000). While the value of MDS for the study of crime and criminality was first identified by David Canter and his colleagues at the University of Surrey, research teams around the world have now taken it on board at the analysis of choice (for example, Gerard, Moemont and Kocsis, 2007). MDS shares a basic common mathematics with both factor analysis and cluster analysis and so will usually give broadly similar results, however it has the advantage of representing the relationships between variables in a strongly visual way. In essence, it represents the variables as points in a notional space such that the stronger the association between the variables, the closer the points that represent them in the derived MDS space. Many studies have made particular use of the non-metric MDS procedure known as Smallest Space Analysis (SSA-I) (Lingoes, 1973). The particular power of SSA-I comes from its representation of the rank order of the co-occurrences as ranks of the distances in a geometric space (hence it being called 'non-metric' MDS). This emphasis on the relative differences rather than the absolute values tends to makes the visual spatial representation easier to interpret. It also makes the analysis less sensitive to biases in any particular sample that might have generated particularly high or low absolute frequencies. A technical account of what SSA does is given in Box 5.6.

Box 5.6 An Account of What Smallest Space Analysis (SSA) Does

Smallest space analysis (Lingoes, 1973) is a nonmetric multidimensional scaling procedure, based upon the assumption that the underlying structure or system of behaviour will most readily be appreciated if the relationship between every variable and every other variable is examined. However, an examination of the raw mathematical relationships between all the variables would be difficult to interpret so a geometric (visual) representation of the relationships is produced.

In essence, when using an SSA the null hypothesis is that the variables being examined have no comprehensible relationship to each other. In other words, for example when considering the actions of rapists it is possible that those offenders who change their actions in response to the reactions of the victim are not the same as those who talk to the victim and encourage her to indicate her reactions to the attack. It may be a common-sense assumption that these two variables will relate to each other because they both indicate a desire to initiate some relationship with the victim, but the

(continued)

SSA allows a test of this assumption and all the other possibilities suggested by the relationship every one of the variables has to every other variable.

Although there will often be background theories that provide a set of hypotheses for the interpretation of the SSA, the use of SSA also allows the generation of hypotheses both about the components of the domain under study and about the relationships between those components, the *system* that exists within the domain. In other words, SSA may best be regarded as both hypothesis testing and also of heuristic value in helping to indicate if there are any directions from the results that can be used to focus future studies.

Smallest space analysis, then, is one of a large number of procedures that represent the correlations between variables as distances in a statistically derived geometric space. Although it was first used a number of years ago (Guttman, 1954) only recently have developments in computers made it readily available for general use. As described by Guttman (1968), SSA was so called because, when compared with other approaches to multidimensional scaling, it produces a solution of smallest dimensionality. This is primarily because it operates on the rank order of the original correlations rather than their absolute values.

The SSA program computes correlation or other association coefficients between all variables, then rank orders these correlations, in this case the columns of a data matrix are the variables that we are working with. Typically these are action categories derived from a content analysis process. The rows of this matrix are the individual cases or crimes. The first step is to correlate every variable (the columns) with every other. This produces another matrix that records all these correlations. Because the correlation of variable A with variable B is the same as that of variable B with variable A the matrix of every variable correlated with every other can be regarded as having a mirror image along its diagonal and therefore is often referred to as a triangular matrix.

It is these correlation coefficients that are used to form a spatial representation of items with points representing variables, the rank order of the distances between points being inversely related to the rank order of the correlations. Iterations are performed comparing the rank order assigned to the correlations with the rank order of the distance while adjustments are made to the geometric representation.

The closer the two rank orders, the better is the 'fit' between the geometric representation and the original correlation matrix, or as it is called technically the lower the 'stress'. The iterations continue until the minimal 'stress' possible is achieved, within the predesignated number of dimensions. A measure of stress called the coefficient of alienation (see Borg and Lingoes, 1987, for details) is used within the computing algorithm as the criterion to use in bringing the iterative procedure to an end. It can therefore be used as a general indication of the degree to which the variables' intercorrelations are represented by their corresponding spatial distances. The smaller the coefficient of alienation, the better is the fit – the fit of the plot to the original correlation matrix.

However, as Borg and Lingoes (1987) emphasise, there is no simple answer to the question of how 'good' or 'bad' the representation is. This will depend upon a complex combination of the number of variables, the amount of error in the data and the logical strength of the interpretation framework.

In the SSA configuration, then, in broad terms, the more highly correlated two variables are, the closer will be the points representing those variables in the SSA space. Since the configuration is developed in respect to the relationships among variables and not from their relationship to some given 'dimension', or axis, the orientation in space of the axes of the resulting geometric representation is arbitrary, even though the relationships between the points are replicably determined. Therefore, the pattern of points (regions) can be examined directly without the need to assume underlying orthogonal dimensions.

The testing of the evidence for ways of classifying variables by examination of the regional structure of an SSA is part of an approach to research known as facet theory (Canter, 1985). The 'facets' are the overall classification of the types of variables. The spatial contiguity of the points representing them provides a test of the major underlying differences amongst these variables as revealed through their co-occurrence in actual incidents, and is therefore a test as to whether the 'facets' are empirically supported. The SSA representation therefore offers a basis for testing and developing hypotheses about the structure of relationships between variables.

The postulation of facets goes beyond the rather arbitrary proposals of 'grouping', by using the principle of contiguity (Foa, 1958; Guttman, 1965; Shye, 1978), which states that because elements in a facet will be functionally related their existence will be reflected in a corresponding empirical structure. In other words, variables that share the same facet elements would be more highly correlated and thus should appear closer together in the multidimensional space than variables not sharing the same element.

This idea of contiguity can be extended as a general, regional hypothesis. Items that have facet elements in common will be found in the same region of space. Likewise, variables that have very low intercorrelations will appear in different regions of the plot, indicating dissimilarity, and no membership of the same facet element. Contiguous regionality in a multidimensional space is a quite specific identification of a facet element, provided a clear statement can be made of what the variables in that region have in common. Of course, once the exploratory phase of hypothesis generation has led to the establishment of facets, or when a literature suggests facets, then the existence of contiguous regions can be used as a strong, precise test of the hypothesised facets. The usual processes of scientific replication can also be carried out.

Areas of the SSA plot that contain few or no points are also of interest. Cases such as this may indicate weak areas in the data or in fact missing facet elements. Subsequent studies may then be carried out with new data sets to test for the existence of these missing elements. In this way the interplay between the formal theory, as specified in the facets, and the empirical structure, as revealed in the regional contiguity, can lead to the identification of issues not within the original set of data.

To reiterate for clarity, in MDS each point in a theoretical space represents a distinct variable; in this case whether or not the offender reported he had committed a particular offence. The closer any two points are to one another on the spatial configuration, the higher their associations with each other; in this case the higher their frequency of co-occurrence. Similarly the farther away from one another any two points are the lower their association with each other. In most studies of offending (e.g. Canter and Fritzon, 1998; Canter and Heritage, 1990; Salfati, 2000), the measure of co-occurrence that is used is Jaccard's coefficient (Jaccard, 1908). This calculates the proportion of co-occurrences between any two variables as a proportion of all occurrences of both variables.

The Facet Approach

To test or develop hypotheses the SSA configuration is visually examined to determine the patterns of relationships between variables. The configuration of points representing variables also allows of direct examination so that hypotheses can be generated as to possible distinctions between sets of variables that may be tested by other analyses in the future. The structure of the relationships among variables is reflected in the configuration of points, such that, in the Youngs' (2004) study, regions in the space represent patterns, or 'styles', of offending. The substantive interpretation of these regions draws on a facet theory approach (see, for example, Canter (1985); Shye *et al.*, 1994). Within this approach all variables are classified in terms of some number of underlying conceptual distinctions known as facets (Guttman, 1982). The term 'facet' comes from the Greek for 'face'. By referring to the *facets* of any entities that are being described we are considering different ways of looking at them. Thus, for instance, the unusualness of any action may be one *facet* of a crime and a second *facet* can be derived from the four dominant modes of interaction that we are considering. These two different facets of an action must relate in some systematic way and there is a very productive approach to research that allows us to create testable models of this complex set of approaches.

Evidence for these facets as the basis for the differentiation of the phenomenon in question is considered to exist where the mutually exclusive and exhaustive set of categories which describe the facets (the elements) are located within different contiguous regions of the space.

The structure of offending behaviour revealed by the SSA-I in Youngs' study is presented in Figure 5.4. The labels are brief summaries of the 45 behaviours. The full items these relate to can be found in Table 5.4. The lines are drawn on the resulting configuration by the researchers to help interpretation, within the principles of facet theory (see Box 5.7).

The central principle for interpretation is often referred to as the 'regionality hypothesis'. This is the idea that items that have similar meanings will be closer together in the configuration. It accepts that some items may share aspects of their meanings with a variety of items, or that a slight change in the way an item is phrased could mean it would be placed in a slightly different part of the plot. So the plot can only be interpreted in terms of regions, not clusters or dimensions, unless they are obviously revealed in the configuration.

The regions are indicated by boundary lines. It is therefore important to keep in mind that these lines indicate boundaries between regions. They are only meant to draw attention to changes in the meaning of the points around the plot. They are not intended as hard-and-fast

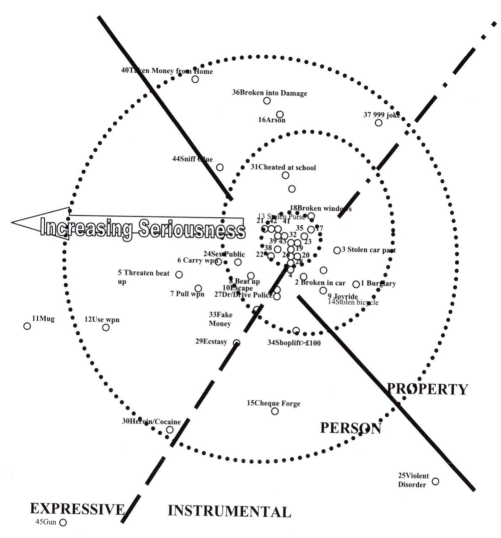

Figure 5.4   Smallest space analysis of offending behaviours. Full item description for the central variables can be seen in Table 5.4. Numbers on the figure refer to items in Table 5.4.

Source: Youngs (2004). Reproduced with permission.

indicators as would be generated by, say, regression lines. Indeed, it is in the nature of boundary lines that there will be some points close to any boundary that may draw on meanings from one side of the boundary or the other, whereas points far away from the boundary would be expected to be 'purer' in defining a region. Those familiar with factor analysis may think of the distance from the boundary as an increase in 'factor loading'. Those more comfortable with conventional inferential statistics may think of the clarity of the boundary and the intelligibility of the distinctions to which it draws attention as analogous to reductions in the probability ('p value') that the boundary is arbitrary.

Table 5.4 The forty-five offending behaviours used by Youngs (2004, 2006).

Full behaviour/item	Analysis label
1. Broken into house, shop, school and taken money or something else you wanted?	Burglary
2. Broken into a locked car to get something from it?	Broken in car
3. Taken hubcaps, wheels, the battery or some other part of a car without the owner's permission?	Stolen car part
4. Taken things worth between £10 and £100 from a shop without paying for them?	Shoplift (>£10<£100)
5. Threatened to beat someone up if they didn't give you money or something else you wanted?	Threaten 'beat up'
6. Carried a razor, flick-knife or some other weapon with the intention of using it in a fight?	Carry wpn
7. Pulled a knife, gun or some other weapon on someone just to let them know you meant business?	Pull wpn
8. Beat someone up so badly they probably needed a doctor?	Beat up
9. Taken a car belonging to someone you didn't know for a ride without the owner's permission?	Joyride
10. Tried to get away from a police officer by fighting or struggling?	Escape police
11. Used physical force (like twisting an arm or choking) to get money from another person?	Mug
12. Used a club, knife or other weapon to get something from someone?	Use wpn
13. Taken things from a wallet/purse (or the whole wallet/purse) while the owner wasn't around or looking?	Stolen purse
14. Taken a bicycle belonging to someone you didn't know with no intention of returning it?	Stolen bicycle
15. Tried to pass a cheque by signing someone else's name?	Cheque forge
16. Intentionally started a building on fire?	Arson
17. Taken little things (worth less than £5) from a shop without paying for them?	Shoplift (<£5)
18. Broken the windows of an empty house or other unoccupied building?	Broken windows
19. Bought something you knew had been stolen?	Bought stolen goods
20. Refused to tell the police or some other official what you knew about a crime?	Refused police information
21. Picked a fight with someone you didn't know just for the hell of it?	Picked fight with stranger
22. Been involved in gang fights?	Gang fight
23. Been loud, rowdy or unruly in a public place?	Acted rowdy
24. Had sex in public?	Sex public
25. Attended a demonstration or sporting event to cause a disturbance or be violent?	Violent disorder
26. Smoked marijuana (grass/pot)?	Marijuana
27. Driven a car when you were drunk or high on some drugs?	Dr/Drive
28. Taken barbiturates (downers) or speed (or other uppers) without a prescription?	Barbiturates/speed
29. Taken ecstasy ('E's)?	Ecstasy
30. Used heroin (smack) or cocaine?	Heroin/cocaine
31. Cheated at school in tests?	Cheated at school
32. Not returned extra change that a cashier gave you by mistake?	Excess change

Table 5.4   (*Continued*)

Full behaviour/item	Analysis label
33. Used fake money in a machine?	Fake money
34. Taken things of large value (worth more than £100) from a shop without paying for them?	Shoplift (>£100)
35. Been drunk regularly when you were under 16?	Drunk u/16
36. Broken into a house, shop, school or other building to break things up or cause other damage?	Broken in to damage
37. Dialled 999 just for a joke?	999 joke
38. Let off fireworks in the street?	Let off fireworks
39. Deliberately travelled without a ticket on a bus, train or the tube?	Travelled without paying
40. Taken money from someone at home without returning it?	Taken money from home
41. Deliberately littered the streets?	Litter
42. Annoyed or insulted a stranger?	Insulted a stranger
43. Not gone to school when you should have been there?	Played truant
44. Sniffed glue or other solvents (for example, tippex thinner)?	Sniff glue
45. Used or carried a gun to help you commit a crime?	Gun

Source: Youngs, Canter *et al.* (2004). Reproduced with permission.

Box 5.7 The Facet Approach

Louis Guttman (1916–87). We are grateful to Professor Manabe for this photograph.

Louis Guttman who invented the 'Guttman Scale' for measuring attitudes when he was 24 years old devoted much of his career to elaborating his theory of how science most

(*continued*)

effectively could progress and discover findings to be consistent enough to be regarded as 'laws'. He called his approach *facet theory* (Guttman, 1950).

The fundamentals of this theory are that any scientific laws consist of four components: (a) a definitional system that specifies the key concepts and their relationships to each other, (b) a set of relationships or 'structure' in observed data, (c) some regular correspondence between the definitional system and the observed structure and (d) rationale, or explanation for why there should be that correspondence.

Using this framework, a number of laws have been established, most notably in the arena of attitudes, intelligence and wellbeing.

These laws typically have two components; a 'first law' that specifies the conditions under which the entities being studied will tend to be non-negatively correlated. For example, all attitudes towards a common object, or responses to all questions that have a correct or incorrect answer. A 'second law' that specifies the conditions under which some sets of entities will be more highly related to each other than to other sets of entities. For example, emotional responses to objects would be expected to be more highly correlated with each other than to actual actions. Or answers to questions demanding numerical calculations will be more highly correlated with each other than to questions dealing with the meaning of words.

Within many domains of non-negatively relating items that can be distinguished into different subsets, such as intelligence and attitudes, it has been found that there is a meaningful structure that relates aspects of the degree of focus of the entities and differences in the sub-sets that Guttman called a *radex* in a crucial paper (Guttman, 1954). This was revealed using SSA, which Guttman (1968) developed. Thus researchers using facet theory tend to use SSA and related multidimensional scaling procedures even though they are not an inevitable component of facet theory.

Further references to texts on facet theory and related methodologies are given in Chapter 16 and at the end of this chapter.

To make sense of this plot, consider the two kinds of offence in the centre of the plot – shoplifting of objects of low value and truancy (Items 17 and 43; see Table 5.4). This is a clear indication that the people who report doing one of these things also tend to report doing the other. This accords well with common experience that school truants will often indulge in shoplifting. However, truants do not seem to get involved with guns very often, at least not in this sample, because the location of that activity is on the bottom left of this plot, away from the central core.

A further examination of the offences close in the lower left area reveals a grouping that clearly has the implications of violence; being involved in a fight, beating up someone, threatening to beat up, mugging, carrying or pulling a weapon as well as having a gun. These all suggest what might be thought of as 'crimes against the person'. What needs to be understood here, though, is that we are interpreting these crimes in that way because of their proximity in the space. For example; having a gun could have been part of a commercial transaction, such as selling firearms, not directly involved in violent crime. But because it does co-occur close to threatening to beat up and other activities that involve violence more obviously it seems reasonable to interpret it as implying aggression towards others.

The issue of interpretation is problematic because no questionnaire item or coding category is totally unambiguous. Therefore the items will incorporate a range of meanings. The interpretation process seeks to determine which of the possible meanings should be taken as dominant. Making sense of an MDS configuration, such as the SSA is thus always a mixture of two activities. One is to draw on the *a priori* meaning of items then see if the plot reflects these by items with similar meanings being close together. A second and complementary process is to inform the interpretation of the items by the other items that are close to them and far from them in the plot.

This process of interpreting regions of the SSA output is characteristic of all use of multidimensional scaling, but is somewhat different from other statistical approaches in which a table of numbers is derived that offers more limited information on the underlying relationships between the variables being studied. To make it clear again, at the risk of repetition, this form of regional interpretation is based on the idea that if the variables had been described slightly differently, for example; if we had specified the type of firearm differently or specified its use in a crime, the location of that variable might have been slightly different. Items are consequently treated as representatives of all possible similar items which could have been in that region of the configuration. We are using them to make sense of what that region is, as in our notional circle of colours we may be trying to decide if we should call a particular shade of turquoise blue or green.

So we are trying to make sense of the regions that the variables fall into, expecting, as with all 'maps', that there will be boundary conditions where items could be interpreted as falling into one region or another depending on the details of their interpretation. For example, in the SSA the act of arson is near 'fight' and 'drunk under the age of 16'. It could therefore be interpreted as either an aspect of aggression or some activity that related more to casual vandalism. It is only by building up an understanding of the patterns of co-occurrences that the regional structure in the SSA can be established. Then the key test is whether that structure is replicated with other data sets.

At a more general level of interpretation, the regions of the space in Figure 5.4 can be seen to reflect the joint action of three facets. The first facet divides the space into regions according to the focus or target of the behaviour. In the top right half of the plot are behaviours carried out against some form of property, so, for example, acts such as breaking in in order to cause damage and stealing a bicycle are in this region. Behaviours that have people rather than property as their focus (such as threatening to 'beat someone up' and using or carrying a gun) are found in the bottom left half of the plot. Drug-use behaviours, because they target the self, are considered to fall within this person region too. Interestingly, 'cheque forge' falls within the person rather than the property only region. This is consistent with the hypothesis that this is a more personal act than is stealing from anonymous institutions. Some exceptions to the property-person distinction can be found and these outlying items need further investigation but the general themes within the plot are clear.

Distinct regions of the space can also be identified according to the underlying mode of operation reflected in the behaviours, independent of the focus. Two modes of operation can be distinguished: expressive and instrumental. Behaviours reflecting the expressive mode are located in the top left section of the plot, for example; acts such as breaking into empty buildings to cause damage, arson and having sex in public are in this region. For these behaviours the execution of the particular act itself is the primary aim; the behaviours carry rewards of their own. These behaviours may be understood, then, as *direct* expressions of some goal or need.

The behaviours found in the bottom right section of the plot reflect a more instrumental mode of operation. In direct contrast to the expressive behaviours, instrumental behaviours are carried out, not for their own rewards, but in order to achieve some secondary goal. This region contains behaviours such as forging a cheque, shoplifting (more than £100) and burglary. 'Joyride', which it seems was probably interpreted by the respondents as the permanent stealing of a car, is also in this region. Interestingly, the behaviour 'attended a sports event or demonstration to cause a disturbance or be violent' is also in the instrumental region, suggesting that this violence has a rather different premeditated quality than other forms of violence.

The third facet divides the conceptual space into concentric rings. This facet orders the space from the centre to the periphery in terms of seriousness or psychological intensity. This is reflected to a large degree in the frequencies of involvement reported. In the inner ring are the high-frequency behaviours, acts committed, at least once, by 70% or more of the sample. Moving outwards the behaviours are more serious and the percentage of the sample reporting ever having committed each act decreases. The peripheral ring is a serious/intense crime region, consisting of behaviours that have been committed by less than 30% of the sample. As Figure 5.4 shows, the 'Seriousness' facet cuts across the other facets. It acts to modify these facets, creating a central core in which the behavioural styles are not differentiated but rather criminal involvement is generalised. Particular styles of offending emerge then, as seriousness or intensity increases, relating to the expressive-property, expressive-person, instrumental-property and instrumental-person themes.

Fundamental Incentives (Gains)

In a further extension of this work, Youngs (2006) has shown that these broad patterns of offending behaviours reflect the different fundamental incentives to human action described in Bandura's (1986) social cognitive theory. Different offending actions provide different combinations of gain in respect of these fundamental incentives. She identifies three of these general behavioural incentives as the basis for the differentiation of the set of offending behaviours she explores.

One of these, the power or status incentive, is about the desire for control over others. In a criminal context, Youngs argues that violence and threats of violence represent means of attempting to acquire this form of gain.

The sensory incentive is a desire for novel, pleasurable, stimulating experiences and the avoidance of aversive experiences including boredom. Youngs argues that criminal means of achieving this will include the destruction of property and other acts of vandalism. She notes further that sensory stimulation is also derived from 'rebellious' behaviours, so many status offences and minor rule infringements should also be considered part of a sensory offending pattern.

A third pattern of offending is tied into a material (or monetary) incentive. Bandura argues that this is about acquiring the ability to obtain whatever one desires and the possession of particular goods. As Youngs notes, in the criminal context this incentive will underpin the range of behaviours where the acquiring of this gain means taking it from others in some form.

As such, then, the argument is that the variations in patterns of offending are a reflection of differences in the gain the offender seeks. This is in turn tied into patterns of vicarious experience as well as cognitive factors, providing a theoretical basis for patterns of criminal specialisation and versatility.

The Radex of Criminality

Beyond 'Types' to 'Themes'

The general representation of the co-occurrence of offences indicates that any individual criminal may be thought of as committing a subset of all the possible deviant actions. Some of this subset will overlap with the subsets of many other criminals and some with relatively few. The SSA configuration demonstrates that there are no totally separate clusters of offences that form distinct 'types' of offending. It follows that assigning criminals or crimes to one of a limited number of 'types' will always be a gross oversimplification.

For over a century psychologists who studied the ways in which people differed have struggled with this problem of the inappropriateness of trying to classify people in terms of distinct types. Their research has led to the identification of underlying *dimensions* of personality in which people are described according to their levels on a number of distinct, relatively independent, aspects of personality. The most well known of these classifications are those that came out of Eysenck's studies (Eysenck, 1980). They covered the dimension of 'extraversion-introversion' and 'normality-neuroticism'. In recent years rather more complex models have emerged that do not require the simplifying assumption of independent linear dimensions (Plutchik and Contel, 1997).

As hinted at earlier, an analogy that helps in understanding this debate is the problem of classifying colours. Colours come in a virtually infinite variety, but in order to describe them some points of reference are necessary. These points of reference must cover the full spectrum of colours and they must be distinct enough for people to understand the reference. So, for instance, it would be unhelpful to try and discriminate colours merely on the basis of how much grey they contained and how much turquoise. Many differences between colours could not be accommodated in this scheme and many people may be unclear as to what colour turquoise actually is.

Another approach may be classifying colours along dimensions of blueness, redness and yellowness. Indeed, many computer colour manipulation systems use just such a dimensional approach. These three hues do account for all colours and they do have very clear meanings to people who are not colour blind. The psychological parallel of the personality dimensions of extraversion and neuroticism, or in intelligence of spatial, numerical and verbal ability, also seek to describe people in their combined position along all the identified dimensions. As with colour naming, a great deal of research has gone into determining what the major dimensions of personality or intelligence are, and into specifying how they may be measured as clearly as possible.

But whilst the dimensional approach has some values various difficulties arise in using it that can be clearly seen when applied to crimes. This will become clearer by first returning to our colour analogy. Colours are not perceived along distinct dimensions but rather as blending into each other. Various oranges sit between red and yellow, shades of olive and avocado between yellow and green, turquoises between green and blue, purples and pinks between blue and red, and so on. Indeed for some purposes, such as printing, it is more useful to think of the 'between' colours, or 'secondary colours' as they are known, as the defining dimensions: i.e. cyan, magenta, and yellow. This switch from one set of axes to another is only feasible because they all merge into each other in a continuous colour circle (as first pointed out by the artist Albert Munsell (1960).The existence of a circle of colours does not deny the value of defining the major points of this circle. But rather than treat them as independent dimensions, they are dealt with as emphases, or themes, from which other combinations can be readily derived.

All this can be illustrated by thinking about the concentric circles of offending indicated in Figure 5.4. The central circle encompasses the crimes that most offenders are involved in. That is why they are central, because they share co-occurrences with most other offences. They are the muddy grey of colours that contain a mix of all the primary colours. The crimes at the edges will be those that are most distinct from each other and from the more generally committed crimes. They are 'purer' like the distinct hues that give colours their vibrancy.

Therefore, if the general 'central' forms of criminality are used for assigning offenders to 'types' then most criminals will be very similar and there will be few types – as happens in black-and-white photographs, where differently coloured objects all look similar. But if more specific features are selected then the same criminals, regarded as similar by general criteria, will be regarded as different when considered in relation to more specific criteria.

If we return to our analogy of colours we can see that colours come in very many shades; aquamarine, cerise, violet, avocado and so forth. This means that it makes little sense to talk about distinct types of colour, except in the rare cases where there are 'pure' colours. However, it is still very useful to be able to talk about a range or reds or blues. These 'primary' colours give a focus to our discussions and help in making sense of mixed, or hybrid colours. The same holds true for conceptualising criminality. However, instead of discussing crimes in terms of the 'primary types' that make up any offence it makes more sense to think of the 'themes' that go to make up offending. These themes help us to describe, understand and make inferences about any particular offence.

So, for example, a burglary in which a house is broken into and the occupant attacked has much in common with both a street mugging in which the victim is hit in order to grab their handbag and with a break-in to a warehouse when no-one is present. A very violent sexual assault shares much with other violent assaults as well as sexual abuse in which no overt violence occurs. So, in order to move forward it is essential to identify and describe those actions that are most useful in specifying the dominant themes that help us to conceptualise variations between criminals and their actions but it would be unproductive to regard these themes as independent dimensions. It would be even more misleading to regard them as pure types, just as it would be misleading to think that colours can only be pure red, yellow, green or blue. In line with the colour circle analogy, differences in styles of criminal action would be expected to take the form of varying thematic emphases within an overall systemic model of criminal differentiation, rather than independent dimensions of crime.

The Radex Model of Criminal Differentiation

These considerations of themes that radiate out from a 'core' of criminality produce a conceptual model of criminal differentiation within which the variations in offenders' styles are the product of differences in two aspects of criminal behaviour. The first, described by the 'thematic facet', are differences in qualitative aspects of the behaviour. So, for example, in the present case, we have thought of these in terms of the targets of the offence being property or people and the degree of emotionality expressed. The second, described by the 'specificity facet' are quantitative differences in the specificity as opposed to generality of the offending across the areas of criminality being considered. A number of studies have shown how these two processes interact such that the qualitative variations in style emerge in relation to the more 'specific' behaviours, while the more 'general' behaviours remain undifferentiated, forming a subset of behaviours that tend to be common to all offences.

This model was recognised by Guttman (1982) as a powerful summary of many forms of differentiation between people and named a *radex* (cf. the radex of intelligence, Guttman, 1965; the radex of wellbeing, Levy and Guttman, 1975). A radex is made up of a quantitative and a qualitative facet, producing the 'dart board', target-like structure that is illustrated in Figure 5.4. Within IP, the radex of criminality consists of (a) the quantitative variation in the specificity of crimes, which relates to their rarity and the particularity of the psychological processes to which they relate, and (b) the differentiation into criminal themes relating to the target of the offending and whether it has strongly aggressive components.

The radex is a very useful clarification of the debate on criminal specialisation or versatility within the criminological literature, as Youngs and Canter (in press, a) have discussed. Some claim that offenders are specialist in their focus on particular types of crime, whilst others have argued that they are strictly generalist and versatile (Soothill *et al.*, 2000). The radex shows that virtually all criminals are both! There are certain forms of offending that they share with each other, whilst there are others that are relatively distinct for different subsets of offenders.

Development and Change

One fundamental weakness of any model of criminal differentiation, when used to make inferences, is that the way a person commits a crime will change over time, even if there is a background of consistencies. However, if the basis of these changes can be understood then they can be used to enhance the inference process. As we develop our understanding of criminality it is therefore essential to identify the major processes that underlie variations within criminals across their lifespan.

There are many forms of change. This adds an important complication to establishing the A→C links because the way a person commits a crime will change over time and the offender is also likely to change. However, this does not deny or reduce the possibility of making inferences, quite the contrary. If the basis of these changes can be understood then they can be used to enhance the inference process, as can be seen in the following forms of change which are an elaboration of those that were identified by (Canter and Youngs, 2003).

Responsiveness

A criminal's actions may not be the same on two different occasions because of the different circumstances he or she faces. An understanding of these circumstances and how the offender has responded to them may allow some inferences about his or her interpersonal style or situational responsiveness to be made that have implications for the conduct of the investigation.

Maturation

The physical and physiological growth and decay that occurs over the life span in all living beings is directly relevant to offenders. A young man who can happily climb a drainpipe in his teens may not be able to do it in his fifties. Maturation is an essentially biological process of change in a person's physiology with age. Knowledge of what is typical of people at certain ages, such as sexual activity, or physical agility, can thus be used to form a view as to the maturity of the person committing the crimes. For example compare the age distribution of sexual activity in the male population in general (Figure 5.5) with the graph of the age distribution of those convicted of sexual assaults (Figure 5.6). The similarity in shape of these graphs shows that to some extent sexual vitality is likely to be an aspect of a rapist's actions.

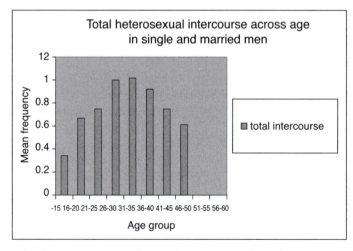

Figure 5.5   Graphs demonstrating total sexual intercourse of single men across different age groups.

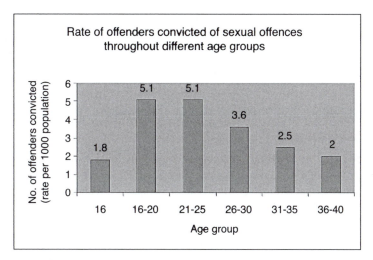

Figure 5.6   Graph demonstrating number of offenders convicted of sexual assault across different age groups.

Source: Soothill, Francis *et al.* (2000). Reproduced with permission.

Cognitive Development

This is the process whereby an individual's understanding evolves. One reflection of this is an increase in expertise in how to create the conditions for crime – notable, for example, in fraud. But serial rapists who grow in their understanding of how to locate and control vulnerable women are also an example of this. Evidence of such expertise in a crime can thus be used to help make inferences about the stages in a criminal's development that he/she has reached and indeed to indicate the way their crimes might change in the future.

Learning

Learning refers to those changes brought about by the consequences of previous actions. Most offenders will learn from their earlier offending in the same way that learning theorists have shown that behaviour generally is shaped by experience. So, for example; an offender who struggled to control his first victim may be expected to implement some very definite restraining measures during subsequent offences. Indeed, for offenders the particularly salient, potentially negative consequences of their actions (such as prison) may make this a powerful process for change in the criminal context. An inferential implication of this is that it may be possible to link crimes to a common offender by understanding the logic of how behaviour has changed from one offence to the next.

   Some of the learning process may be more a form of *familiarisation* – changes brought about by the actual circumstances of the offence such as knowing his way round after having got lost. This is particularly important in considering the geography of a criminal's activities, as we shall see in Chapter 8.

There may also be changes brought about by specific criminal educational or training processes. This is illustrated by the use of firearms that do require some instruction. It is of even more obvious significance in acts of terrorism where the explosives and other devices used may or may not indicate a particular stage in the criminal's development.

Careers

The most general form of change that may be expected from criminals is one that may be seen as having an analogy to a legitimate career i.e. those changes that come from the changing position within criminal subgroups and cultures. This would imply stages such as apprenticeship, middle management, leadership and retirement. Unfortunately, the criminology literature often uses the term 'criminal career' simply to mean the sequence of crimes a person has committed (for example, Farrington, 1986), ignoring its implicit metaphor.

The concept of criminal career is also sometimes confused with the idea of a 'career criminal', someone who makes a living entirely out of crime. As a consequence, much less is understood about the utility of the career analogy for criminals than might be expected. There are some indications that the more serious crimes are committed by people who have a history of less serious crimes and that, as a consequence, the more serious a crime the older an offender is likely to be. But a commonly held assumption that serious sexual offences are presaged by less serious ones does not have a lot of empirical evidence in its support.

Cultural Shifts

There are also important changes that come about from developments in society. Increased security precautions will lead offenders to change their behaviour. For example, most cars manufactured recently have built in security devices that make them extremely difficult to start without the key. They often require other conditions as well, such as placing the foot on the brake. This has led to some offenders who wish to steal cars to have to gain control of the owner of the car to be sure of being able to drive it away. Closed-circuit TV has given rise to more criminals wearing hoods to hide their faces, which they may not have done in earlier times.

Summary

In one rape enquiry in which we were involved, the victim was very clear that the man who attacked her had long fingernails on his right hand but very short nails on his left hand. Communing with the spirit of Sherlock Holmes and his origins in the observations of Dr Bell we were very pleased to remember that some serious guitar players deliberately keep their fingernails in this state. Should the investigation team therefore put all their efforts into finding a guitarist who was known to have violent tendencies, especially towards women? Fortunately we did not force that conclusion on the detectives. When the man who committed the rapes was eventually identified it was found he worked removing tires and his particular way of working generated the pattern of long and short nails.

The single clue being used as a direct indicator of a particular feature of the offender is a favourite of detective fiction. It has been taken to many extremes. A particularly amusing one occurs in the recent crime novel by Frank Tallis (2008), which is set in Vienna at the time when Sigmund Freud's work was becoming popular. One of the fictional characters, Liebermann, is presented as a student of Freud's and so interprets clues drawing on witty, rather simplified, Freudian ideas. One of these 'clues' is that an apparently minor character, Sommer, is not available for interview because he is indisposed by falling down the stairs and breaking his leg soon after the death that is at the centre of the plot. Liebermann interprets this accident as a product of Sommer unconsciously wishing to keep himself out of the investigation and therefore determines to interview him as soon as possible. This moves the plot forward but a moment's thought gives rise to many other possible interpretations of the report of Sommer's accident that do not fit the Freudian interpretation of this 'clue'.

These two examples, one factual the other fictional, illustrate the central problem of deriving inferences about a person from single details about them. Yet this is often regarded as the essence of 'offender profiling'. There are many and various reasons why such 'Sherlock Holmes' type of inferences are rarely likely to be valid. Therefore to develop a scientifically based IP it is essential to move beyond this 'clue = feature' approach to contributing to investigations. Wide-ranging models of inference need to be developed that help us both to understand crimes and that, although general, can still be drawn on to illuminate any particular crime.

This chapter has shown how the radex model provides a framework that has considerable empirical support for studying crime and criminals, providing a basis for understanding criminal activity and contributing to investigations. The model shows how combinations of criminal actions can be recognised as themes that distinguish crimes and draw attention to the salient variables. By this means, the distinctiveness of any illegal activity can be identified. This, in turn, allows differentiation in terms of the focus of the crime, whether it be against a person or is purely acquisitive. The variation in the emotional, especially aggressive qualities of offending also maps on to the general radex model.

This framework provides the initial basis for any inferences about an offender that may be drawn for his crimes. In the most direct form, this is inferences about what other sorts of crimes he may have committed. But it also opens the way to considering what the distinguishing features of the offender are likely to be. These considerations are inferences about the offender's characteristics drawn from his offences.

Such inferences can operate at a number of levels of generality, from the broad features typical of most offenders, through the classes of crime and then on into patterns of criminal action, styles of offending. In later chapters we will develop accounts of how this inference process may function at the different levels of specificity. However, the brief discussion in the present chapter on the ways in which offenders may change over time does point to the need for a more dynamic model of criminal variation, to which we will turn in the next chapter.

Further Reading

Books

Borg, I. and Shye, S. (1995) *Facet Theory: Form and Content*, Sage, London.
Canter, D. (ed.) (1985) *Facet Theory: Approaches to Social Research*, Springer-Verlang, New York.
Shye, S., Elizur, D. and Hoffman, M. (1994) *Introduction to Facet Theory: Content Design and Intrinsic Data Analysis in Behavioural Research*, Sage, Thousand Oaks, CA.

Articles

Canter, D. (1983) The potential of facet theory for applied social psychology. *Quality and Quantity*, **17**, 35–67.

Shye, S. (1998) Modern facet theory: content design and measurement in behavioral research. *European Journal of Psychological Assessment*, **14** (2), 160–71.

Youngs, D. (2004) Personality correlates of offence style. *Journal of Investigative Psychology and Offender Profiling*, **1**, 99–120.

Youngs, D. (2006) How does crime pay: the differentiation of criminal specialism by fundamental incentive. *Journal of Investigative Psychology and Offender Profiling*, **3** (1), 1–20.

Youngs, D., Canter, D. and Cooper, J. (2004) The facets of criminality: a cross-modal and cross-gender validation. *Behaviormetrika*, **31** (2), 1–13.

Questions for Discussion and Research

1. The wide use of the term M.O. introduces many confusions and ambiguities. What exactly does it mean and how can it be specified? To take this further, seek out academic journal articles that incorporate the use of the term M.O. and compare the different uses of the term by different academics.

2. Consider one criminal action, such as entering a house through a window as part of a burglary. Under what conditions might the significance of this be modified and how might that influence any inferences made about an offender from that action?

3. From a psychological point of view should aeroplane hijacking be considered a separate type of crime or fit one of the existing categories?

4. Review how you might have committed a crime when you were ten years younger than you are now compared with exactly how you might commit a similar sort of crime now.

5. How might a criminal's career unfold? Is there any evidence for this?

6

Personal Narratives of Crime

In This Chapter

Learning Objectives

When you have completed this chapter you should be able to:

1. Understand how the roles that are central to any criminal storyline give meaning to offenders' crimes.
2. Recognise the ways in which the role that offenders assign to themselves within their overall criminal plot enables them to legitimise the acts that they perform and to neutralise in their minds the destructive consequences of their actions.
3. Discuss the significance of offenders' personal narratives in providing a means of exploring offenders' own agency and of understanding their actions.

4. Appreciate that many aspects of police investigations can benefit from a fuller understanding of offenders' personal narratives – for example, interviewing, linking crimes and making inferences about a likely perpetrator.
5. Describe the four main criminal narrative themes that characterise how offenders see themselves.

Synopsis

Life stories, just like any fictional accounts or literary tales, may be analysed in terms of plots, settings, scenes and themes as well as characters and their dominant roles. These stories can be seen as falling into different themes, reflecting the role that the key individual takes within the overall context.

This process of embedding the view of the self in an unfolding personal story is referred to as an 'inner narrative'. Such narratives help to explain many aspects of criminal activity. The present chapter therefore explores the idea of 'criminal narratives', considering the life stories of offenders and the roles that they perceive themselves as playing within the particular episodes of their crimes. Examples are drawn from different offenders whose criminal narratives are dominated by one of the four major themes that recur throughout many different forms of criminality. They may be summarised as seeing their role as being:

- *victim (irony narrative)*
- *hero (quest)*
- *professional (adventure) or*
- *taking revenge (tragedy).*

These criminal narratives imply particular roles assigned to the victim, such that a person role is assigned within the victim (irony) narrative, an object role within the professional (adventure) narrative and different variants of the victim as vehicle role are implied by the hero (quest) and revenge (tragedy) narratives.

If narratives are thought of as dramas people live out then it is a short step to consider the scripts that these dramas may typically follow. A consideration of offending scripts consequently concludes the chapter.

Box 6.1 A 'Romeo and Juliet' Murder

In the early hours of November 2005 a 33-year-old hospital radiographer, Gavin Hall, killed his daughter Amelia, who was a few days away from her fourth birthday, as her mother and sister slept upstairs in their home in Northamptonshire. He was deeply distressed at having discovered that his wife was having an affair with a married judge and had determined to take his own life and that of his daughter. He sedated her with antidepressants then suffocated her with chloroform.

But before he did that he said in court:

> "We talked about heaven and we talked about no more crying, no more sadness."
>
> "It seemed very Romeo and Juliet, we were distraught, we were distressed,"

In letters written to his wife, Joanne, Hall claimed that he was taking their two children to a place where they would be loved.

More information at:

http://news.bbc.co.uk/1/hi/england/northamptonshire/6103118.stm

The Narratives of Criminality

The event reported in Box 6.1 is a stark example of how a father thought of his role in the murder of his daughter. It is a chilling example of the way in which he saw himself and his actions in relation to some well-known story that is an integral part of our culture. It illustrates that a powerful way of understanding an offender's agency is to draw on the narrative perspective. Out of this has grown the view that, like literary constructions, personal life stories can be analysed in terms of plots, settings, scenes and themes as well as characters and their dominant roles.

McAdams (1988) is one of the clearest writers on the narrative approach in psychology. He proposes that life stories are organised around themes of intimacy (or communion) and power (or agency). Individuals high on intimacy express a 'recurrent preference or readiness for experiences of warmth, close and communicative exchange' (McAdams, 1988: 77). The communal themes could be the helper, lover, counsellor, caregiver, and friend. In contrast, people high on power speak frequently of self-protection, self-assertion and self-expansion; they express needs for achievement, force and action. This indicates 'a recurrent preference or readiness for experiences of having impact and feeling strong (potent, agentic) vis-à-vis the environment' (McAdams, 1988: 84). The agentic characters could be the master, father, authority, or sage, who are forceful and have great determination as well as drive.

Criminal Narratives

Canter (1994) was the first to explore criminal behaviour using narrative theory. In his book *Criminal Shadows* he suggests that 'through his actions the criminal tells us about how he has chosen to live his life. The challenge is to reveal his destructive life story; to uncover the plot in which crime appears to play such a significant part ...' (Canter, 1994: 299). Criminal activity can only be understood through in-depth analysis and understanding of those personal stories that Canter calls (1994) 'inner narratives', and by connecting those narratives to characteristic roles and actions.

This process of embedding the view of the self in an unfolding personal story, an individual's 'inner narrative', helps to explain many aspects of criminal activity. Whilst it is especially helpful in explaining those crimes that are not of obvious financial benefit or are extremely high risk, the narrative perspective has also been shown to be of value in understanding many aspects of non-criminal behaviour. It has even given rise to a major form of psychotherapy (Crossley, 2000; McLeod, 1997).

Illustrations of criminal narratives help to show their power in providing insight into offenders' actions. The white-collar criminal may see himself as obtaining redress for earlier slights; an unwilling victim rather than a manipulative villain. The member of a criminal gang may view himself as a dashing leader or professional 'hard-man', rather than the dishonest bully that others may recognise. The roles which are central to any storyline give meaning to offenders' lives, but they are not just private and personal. They are embedded in a social matrix. They are supported and refined in the contacts the criminal has with others. They also connect with the notions of antagonist and protagonist that are present in the larger culture in which the criminal participates. This enables the criminal to legitimise, in his own eyes and those of his associates, the acts he performs and to neutralise in his mind their destructive consequences.

One further important aspect of the narrative perspective, as discussed in earlier chapters, is that the law and daily discourse about crime put great store on the active and conscious involvement of the offender as a person. It does not break the offender down into aspects of personality or hormonal processes but treats him as an active agent. It is therefore incumbent on investigative psychologists to connect with this perspective. To do this we need to understand more of what the radex of crimes described in the previous chapter implies because although it is a powerful summary of many different relationships between offences it lacks an obvious dynamic quality and is limited in its psychological richness. It underplays direct involvement with the ways in which the offender is likely to see the world. As with the great majority of accounts of criminality, just considering what a criminal has done fails to connect with offenders' own agency and understanding of their actions. Exploring the offender's personal narratives is one pathway into this.

In recent years a number of researchers have begun to explore these aspects of criminality. Maruna (2001), for example, argues that a true understanding of criminal behaviour can only come through in-depth analysis of such narratives, being especially helpful in making sense of how people desist from crime. He points out that criminals' personal narratives may lead them to consider their actions as acceptable and not 'criminal'. Or they may revel in being part of an 'outlaw' group that lives by rules that break conventions. Thus these narratives of offending embed self-identity in a social matrix. As Berger and Luckman (1991) put it, in what has come to be known as the social constructionist perspective:

> Identity is formed by social processes. Once crystallised, it is maintained, modified, or even reshaped by social relations. The social processes involved in both the formation and maintenance of identity are determined by the social structure. Conversely, the identities produced by the interplay of organism, individual consciousness and social structure react upon the given social structure, maintaining it, modifying it, or even reshaping it.
>
> (Berger and Luckmann, 1991: 194)

Vygotsky (1978) noted that mental functioning is shaped by and situated within social life. This socio-cultural approach emphasises how interpersonal contact shapes individual and mental processes. This can also be seen as a natural psychological consequence of Sutherland's seminal argument that criminality emerges out of differential association (see, for example, Sutherland and Cressey, 1974). To the psychologist, Sutherland's criminology implies that it is not just the actions of the criminal that are shaped by his social network but the whole way in which the criminal sees his world and makes sense of himself. Like all cognition, criminal cognition is socially situated. The social context of any criminal therefore has a profound relevance for the way in which that criminal's self identity is determined.

Maruna (1999) develops the implications of this social construction of criminality a stage further. He contends that proposals for the existence of criminal 'genes', neurophysiological damage, traits or any other pathogenic explanation of criminal behaviour must deal with the fact that the overwhelming majority of individuals stop offending. He emphasises that there is nothing stable about most criminals' careers. The fact that so many individuals desist from crime presents a serious problem for any stable trait theory as an explanation of criminality. Instead, Maruna asserts that a narrative perspective helps to explicate the changing dynamic features of the individual's life – the way in which identity is formed as a product of each individual's 'storyline'. This internalised autobiographic narrative is continually evolving to help promote coherence and meaning in individuals' lives. These processes of 'self-telling' (Bruner, 1987) have the capacity to shape events and therefore result in an interaction between the individual and his social environment. This joint construction of identity, as shaped by the social environment, clearly does not involve pathological diagnostic criteria though the routes through which individuals develop their identities may be deviant and destructive. Criminogenic socialisation processes therefore are not, as Maruna puts it, 'created in a vacuum' but are shaped by the opportunities of each individual's social world.

McAdams (1988) argued that life stories take on their shape in late adolescence. Such a view is consistent with the fact that most offenders commit themselves to a life of crime or avoid embarking on such a career in their late teens (Canter, 1994). Many acts of violence seem to erupt at a time when the perpetrator is searching for identity. This is possibly one of the reasons why so much crime is committed by teenagers. In terms of future crime, adolescence is a crucial period in determining which narrative will become dominant.

McAdams also draws attention to another important point. Life stories may be confused or clear, or as he calls them 'well-formed or ill-formed'. There is likely to be more tension and confusion in the ill-formed life story. Ill-formed stories may split into very separate, possibly conflicting narratives. They may also be changed dramatically by episodes in which the central character experiences relatively minor mishaps. 'Perhaps here is the clue to the hidden nature of the narratives that violent offenders live: their dominant narratives are confused and sensitive to episodes that most people would ignore' (Canter, 1994: 307–8).

It seems very likely that violent offenders' narratives are distorted from their earliest years. When a growing child is unsure about his or her identity, and as to which life story is appropriate, he or she will turn to the possibilities offered by the narratives around which often include violence and exploitation of others (Canter, 1994). Canter (1994) argues that criminals are limited people. He suggests that the limited narratives of a violent criminal share the common constituent of treating the victim as less than human. In other words, they are assigned a subservient, exploited role in the account the offender tells himself.

Implications for Police Investigations

All of this may sound rather abstract, being only of interest to social scientists, but there are many aspects of police investigations that can benefit from a fuller understanding of offenders' personal narratives. Knowing how offenders are likely to see themselves can have value when interviewing them. Interviews can be shaped to draw from suspects the roles they were playing, indicating the earlier episodes that they consider relevant, providing details as they make sense to the interviewee rather than having questions imposed on them by the interrogator. An unfolding narrative process across crimes may also be of value in linking crimes to a common offender because the emergence of a dominant narrative may be apparent as the offender sees himself, for example, as ever more heroic or indicates his feelings of being a victim. However, probably the most important role is in providing a basis for inferences about the characteristics of the offender from understanding the narratives that are implicit in his actions. As we shall see, this feeds into a framework of inferences that is open to empirical test and development.

Frye's Theory of Myths

The essence of the narrative approach within psychology is that implicitly, or explicitly as in the case of the father who murdered his daughter described in Box 6.1, we all draw on storylines that are available within our culture to give meaning to ourselves and our actions. The question that therefore arises is what sorts of stories do criminals live?

Some narrative psychologists such as Polkinghorne (1988) and McAdams (1988) argue that there is a limit to the variety of possible structures for all life stories. They see important connections with studies of literature, most notably the four archetypal story forms that Northrop Frye (1957) discussed in detail in his *Anatomy of Criticism*. He took a lead from Aristotle's *Poetics* to propose that all stories take one of four dominant forms which he called the 'mythic archetypes', labelling them *comedy, romance, tragedy* and *irony*. Kevin Murray (1985) equated Frye's 'comedy' (which many today would call a 'romantic comedy') with the films of the medical unit in Korea, *M.A.S.H.* What Frye calls 'romance' (which may be better understood as an 'adventure') Murray (1985) claims is typified by *Star Wars. The Elephant Man* is a classical tragedy. *Monty Python's Life of Brian* is typical of 'irony'.

More recently Booker (2004) has suggested there are seven basic plots. Underlying them is the fundamental distinction of whether the story has a happy ending or not. This puts tragedy in a distinct subset of narratives and develops separately the stories of adventure and derring-do into subdivisions such as 'overcoming the monster', 'rags to riches' and 'the quest'. This latter is illustrated most fully by *Lord of the Rings*. These quests seek power in various forms, consistent with McAdams' (1988) major theme of dominance. What Frye sees as comedic narratives, for which *Cinderella* is a clear example, are more concerned with what McAdams summarises as the search for intimacy (often reflected in notion of 'love'). Thus some of the mythoi place the individual in an active role, agentic in McAdams' sense; taking on the world to achieve personal objectives. Most notably in *Romance* and *Comedy* that are characterised by satisfying endings, the protagonist achieves some resolution through his own actions. By contrast, in *Tragedy* and *Irony* the central character is reacting to circumstances, either a general disquiet with society as in irony or fighting the Gods as in Tragedy. From this perspective the dominant axis of personal narratives runs from being professional, bringing existing skills, knowing what you are doing, across to feelings of being a victim who cannot operate in any other way, responding to the depredations of others.

It has to be emphasised that both Frye and Booker are concerned with invented, fictional stories, and Frye in particular is at pains to call attention to his view that fiction is always tidier and more clearly structured than real life. Polkinghorne and McAdams are therefore making something of an intellectual leap to propose that the way a person thinks of his or her life will have parallels to fictional accounts. We therefore have to proceed with caution if we are to claim that there is a subset of recognisable narratives within the actions of criminals. However, Frye's framework does offer an intriguing basis for thinking about offenders' narratives.

What is especially interesting about Frye's argument is that he claims that 'the fundamental form of narrative process is cyclical movement' (Frye, 1957: 158). From this he derives an elegant model of how his four dominant mythoi relate to each other as shown in Figure 6.1. He derives this sequence by analogy with the four seasons. Using Frye's original terminology then comedy being spring gives rise to the summer of romance, which can lead to tragedy, that is autumn. This in turn can decay into irony, which is like winter.

This structure has a strong dynamic quality. It is what propels each narrative archetype into the next. It is therefore a 'circular order' of the form we saw when we considered the radex in the previous chapter. It implies that there will be many hybrids as one type merges into another but there will be a dominant theme within any area of activity. That theme is hypothesised to reflect one of Frye's mythoi. It is exciting to realise that this framework derived from intense study of literature has a form to it that may be directly open to empirical test within the context of criminality.

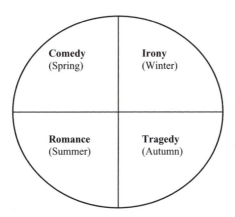

Figure 6.1 Theory of mythoi.

Empirical Study of Criminal Narratives

Given the origins of narrative perspectives within literary criticism it is perhaps not surprising that there has been little strongly systematic or quantitative research into the topic by psychologists. How can you characterise something as complex as a narrative in the form of a structured questionnaire? Of course you cannot but it is possible to capture something of the essence of a personal narrative by a carefully organised questionnaire that is supplemented by an open-ended account of an offender's life story. One way of doing this that is producing some interesting results is by exploring the idea of the 'roles' people think they have played during the commission of a crime (Canter, Kaouri and Ioannou, 2003).

Seeing yourself in the role of victim or hero, professional or revenger implies that you are part of a particular unfolding storyline. These roles are therefore productive shorthand summaries of much more complex processes. The complexities of those processes can be drawn from open-ended interviews in which people are asked to describe their own understanding of a crime in which they have been involved and to put it into the context of their life in general. Open-ended responses are extremely difficult to work with systematically and are challenging to develop into distilled themes. This is especially true when the material comes from offenders who it may be expected have rather 'ill-formed' narratives, but combined with questionnaire responses, fruitful patterns can be discerned.

In all these explorations of criminal narratives, though, some fundamental distinctions both from earlier narrative psychology and from much of literary criticism need to be borne in mind. The narrative perspective has most frequently been applied to the consideration of very effective law-abiding citizens (cf. McAdams, Josselson and Lieblich, 2006). However, in the criminal context we are typically dealing with people who are in many ways rather ineffective and of course not law abiding. Their actions may therefore often be of an inherently destructive form, but need to be understood from the perspective of the actor rather than from their consequences. This sometimes turns narratives on their head. The most obvious form this takes is when thinking of narratives that are dominated by intimacy, as in those that Frye calls 'romances'. For the violent offender 'intimacy' may look like aggression, revenge, or even rape, rather than the gentle forms that a love story typically takes.

Roles as the Encapsulation of Dominant Narratives

A recent major study of imprisoned criminals serves to illustrate the potential for studying offenders' personal narratives by exploring the roles they assign to themselves when committing a crime (Canter, Youngs and Ioannou, 2009). They developed a questionnaire that built on earlier studies by Canter, Kaouri and Ioannou (2003), which in its turn had been derived from interviews with offenders and explorations of the roles they saw themselves as acting out during crimes. Each of the questions was therefore shaped to imply a narrative of some form together with some indication of the offender's understanding of himself. This gave rise to the questionnaire in Table 6.1.

The roles questionnaire was completed by 71 male offenders who each used it to describe how they felt when committing a crime they could remember well. The crime was usually the

Table 6.1 Questionnaire used to indicate roles that criminals saw themselves as playing whilst committing a crime.

	Not at all	Just a little	Some	A lot	Very much
1. I was like a professional	1	2	3	4	5
2. I had to do it	1	2	3	4	5
3. It was fun	1	2	3	4	5
4. It was right	1	2	3	4	5
5. It was interesting	1	2	3	4	5
6. It was like an adventure	1	2	3	4	5
7. It was routine	1	2	3	4	5
8. I was in control	1	2	3	4	5
9. It was exciting	1	2	3	4	5
10. I was doing a job	1	2	3	4	5
11. I knew what I was doing	1	2	3	4	5
12. It was the only thing to do	1	2	3	4	5
13. It was a mission	1	2	3	4	5
14. Nothing else mattered	1	2	3	4	5
15. I had power	1	2	3	4	5
16. I was helpless	1	2	3	4	5
17. It was my only choice	1	2	3	4	5
18. I was a victim	1	2	3	4	5
19. I was confused about what was happening	1	2	3	4	5
20. I was looking for recognition	1	2	3	4	5
21. I just wanted to get it over with	1	2	3	4	5
22. I didn't care what would happen	1	2	3	4	5
23. What was happening was just fate	1	2	3	4	5
24. It all went to plan	1	2	3	4	5
25. I couldn't stop myself	1	2	3	4	5
26. It was like I wasn't part of it	1	2	3	4	5
27. It was a manly thing to do	1	2	3	4	5
28. For me, it was like a usual days work	1	2	3	4	5
29. I was trying to get revenge	1	2	3	4	5
30. There was nothing special about what happened	1	2	3	4	5
31. I was getting my own back	1	2	3	4	5
32. I knew I was taking a risk	1	2	3	4	5
33. I guess I always knew it was going to happen	1	2	3	4	5

one for which they were currently in prison. They were also asked to describe what happened in the crime in their own words, which were written down.

As indicated in the previous chapter, a fruitful way of exploring the structure of responses to the 'roles questionnaire' is to carry out a smallest space analysis (SSA). The hypothesis here is that the emerging structure should have some interesting relationships to Frye's mythoi. Given that his mythoi are derived from studies of literature and do not emphasise criminality, we would not expect a very close relationship. Further, the items in the questionnaire were derived from criminals' own accounts rather than from the study of fiction, so that would also be expected to reveal somewhat different emphases to those summarised in Frye's writings.

Criminal Narrative Themes

Figure 6.2 shows the interesting results of the SSA of the roles questionnaire completed by the prisoners. What is immediately clear here is that the dominant horizontal axis distinguishes between the role of 'victim' to the left and the 'professional' to the right. The vertical axis has a rather more subtle distinction. It is characterised by variables, at the bottom, of 'revenge' and having to commit the crime with nothing else mattering, in contrast to variables at the top in which the offender expresses a heroic bravado, reporting feeling he was not really part of the event and that it was nothing special. As we will explore, these represent four key roles that encapsulate the different criminal narratives: the victim, the professional, the revenger and the hero.

The structure of this configuration serves to illustrate further the power of this approach in both testing hypotheses and enabling the researcher to develop a further understanding of the material being explored. For instance, on the face of it the statement 'It was the only thing to do' would appear to mean something rather similar to 'I couldn't stop myself'. However, their separation on the plot and their closeness to other rather different statements helps to reveal the differences in how they are being interpreted by the respondents.

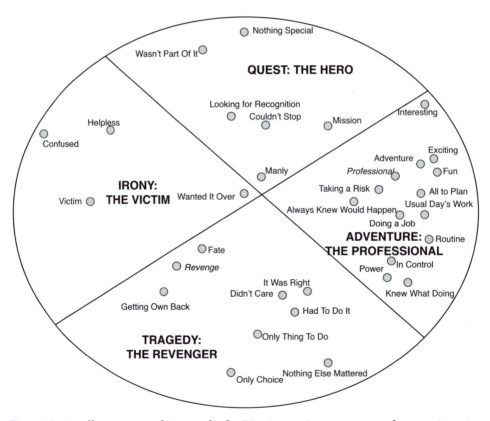

Figure 6.2 Smallest space analysis results for 71 prisoners' responses on roles questionnaire.

The statement 'I couldn't stop myself' is close to both the statements 'I was looking for recognition' and 'it was a mission'. This shows the active search that is inherent in not being able to stop. So that rather than a passive manipulation from the outside this is an active 'mission' to achieve some end. By contrast, agreeing that the crime was the 'only thing to do' is placed close to it being 'the only choice' and 'nothing else mattered', seeming to imply a more reactive role that interestingly accords with the notion of revenge and getting one's own back, which are in a similar region. The statements of revenge and also fate can be seen to be close to the boundary of the region with the statements that centre on feelings of being a 'victim'. This helps to illustrate that the statements relating to revenge do draw on some of the victim status as well as some of the feelings of having no choice as these offenders see it.

Many of the statements form a region to the right of the configuration, indicating how pertinent they are in the lives of offenders, because they produce so many different ways of talking about similar matters. They capture various aspects of adventurous risk-taking, with distinctions in the lower right that are more directly aspects of a routine job and those higher on the right relating to the excitement of this process. Here again statements at the boundary are particularly interesting. Note, for example, the role associated with being on a mission. As already mentioned this could be interpreted either as something that the respondent just could not stop doing, or it could take on the meaning of an interesting adventure.

All this exploration serves to show that the interpretation of the SSA is a heuristic framework for trying to understand the different themes available to offenders. These interpretations are, from one point of view, a set of hypotheses that can be elaborated in future studies. But in the present case they can also be compared with the framework that Frye proposed in order to determine if such a comparison gives us any richer insights into criminals' narratives.

Relating Roles to Mythoi

Irony: The Victim

In the left area of the plot are role descriptions that may be understood as manifestations of the irony narrative. This is the life story in which nothing makes any sense; there are no rules and nothing matters. The term refers equally to a genre or a style of film characterising 'a dark, corrupt and violent world'. The seemingly tough characters often found in *Film Noir* seem to represent Frye's idea of irony. His definition of irony is rooted in Socrates as an *eiron* or self-deprecator (Frye, 1957: 172). This general framework for life would produce offender accounts of the roles they were playing in terms of the confusion ('confused') and powerlessness ('helpless') seen in the region. An extension of this sense of powerlessness, given a world-view where normal social and moral codes do not apply, will be the inverted notion that it is in fact the offender that is the main victim in the event ('victim'). This is the generalised sense of impotence characteristic of irony rather than the angry conviction that one has been wronged seen in the adjacent region, although in some cases these will overlap. The role of being a victim is essentially associated with negative emotions. They point to endings that just dissipate into nothingness and are certainly not happy ones.

This is illustrated in Example A from an interview with one prisoner who saw himself totally at the mercy of his son's misdemeanour. This all came out of a confused, helpless lack of understanding of what he was involved in. The hallmarks of the victim narrative are strongly indicated also by the comment the offender makes that the person he thought was to blame, his son, got out of prison before he did.

Example A
A victim narrative in which the offender expresses helpless confusion (46 years old)

I was supposed to drive my stepson to the scrap yard but he wanted to stop at the bet shop. I drove to the bet shop and waited in the car. He comes running out with a bat and money bags, he'd done an armed robbery. He got in the car and I drove away. I was screaming, 'what have you done' and he was screaming, 'drive Dad drive'. As I'm driving I'm screaming and the money is going everywhere. The police were chasing us in their cars and the helicopter was following us as well. Chasing and sirens. It was a 25-minute chase, everywhere I went they were chasing me, I was going the wrong way on the roads. I crashed into a bollard and ran away. Police caught me. I got seven years and my son got five years. My son pleaded guilty and I didn't know it was happening so I pleaded innocent and got two years extra.

I would not have gone to the bet shop. He had a bat up his sleeve so I didn't know what he was planning to do. I should have drove off, but I couldn't as I would have got a hard time from the mother, but I got a hard time anyway. He apologises for what he'd done. He did it and got out before me. But he's done it to me again. I had my own flat and he had hidden drugs in there. He got five years and I got four years and he got out before me again! This isn't me, armed robbery and drug possession. I usually get charged for driving offences. I don't touch drugs and don't go to bet shops.

Adventure: The Professional

In contrast with the ironic, victim roles is the area to the right of the plot consisting of roles that reveal an underlying 'adventure' narrative, (which Frye calls 'romance'). This is the archetype of the sun's zenith, summer, and the triumph phase. Stories of the hero's great exploits, of apotheosis, and of entering into paradise are manifestations of this mythic archetype. In the romance, an aspect of life is configured as a successful hunt, or a pilgrimage to some desired end, consisting of three stages: a perilous journey with preliminary minor adventures, then usually some kind of battle in which either the hero or his foe, or both, must die, and finally exaltation of the hero. The protagonist is an ever-moving adventurer who tries to overcome adversity and take control of the new challenges in order to emerge victorious throughout life's journey. He or she embarks on a long and difficult journey in life in which circumstances constantly change and new challenges continually arise. In the criminal context this accords with offending being seen as an opportunity to gain satisfaction and pleasure by effective interactions with others and mastery of the environment.

The roles in this region capture the sense of competency and power that the control and mastery of the environment yields ('in control', 'power', 'knew what doing'). The offenders' accounts of the roles they were playing, and their activity as an 'adventure', 'exciting', 'fun' and 'taking a risk', point to the satisfaction derived from this mastery of the external circumstances that is central to the adventure narrative. At the same time, the calm, neutral approach to tackling life challenges is indicated by the offenders' descriptions of their activity in terms of 'doing a job', 'usual day's work', 'all to plan' and 'routine' roles. The emotional climate of the adventure narrative is calm but positive.

Example B is typical of adventure narratives, which are often provided by burglars and robbers. Here, the confident feeling of being a 'professional' is clearly expressed. He is pleased to point out his expertise, mentioning how he foils the expectations of the authorities and his awareness of the need to avoid CCTV cameras. The excitement of this adventure is mentioned directly, to the extent that he even feels 'excited when talking about it'.

Example B

An adventure narrative showing the contribution of being in control and how it relates to the excitement – the offender was convicted of theft and robbery and was 23 years old

Going into a shop and picking a rack of watches worth £5K–£10K. I ask the sales man to see the watch I put it on and just walk out. I would sell it for money but not for drugs, but to buy nice clothes. Sometimes I go out with the intention of doing it but sometimes I'll just do it then and there if it looks nice, or I'd go back the next time. If I go on my own I'll stay local but if I'm with someone else then I'll go out of town like to London or York.

The planning is done in the car, we'll discuss where they'll wait for me, have the car parked and which way I'll run. They'll never chase you.

I feel excited when talking about it, preparing to do it and thinking about when you get the money and where you'll go and what clothes you'll buy. It is an adrenaline rush. I always laugh when I run it's a nervous thing, the buzz. When there is no customers in the shop I'll run out but if there are customers then I'll walk and then run. In the car you think is it going to happen and then afterwards you have it. Park the car out of the way and plan a route. They don't expect you to be in a car but on foot. Feel safe when I get in the car.

I usually go for small things that are high value, something you can conceal and run with. I split the money with my mate and we party for the weekend. I've only been caught for the little things and not for the big things.

It takes 5 mins to plan the theft because we go there and have a look around, then do it and leave ... if you walk around town then you get yourself on CCTV.

Tragedy: The Revenger

The roles grouped together in the bottom centre of the plot are readily understood as close to Frye's tragedy narrative in which the hero is overpowered by the fates. In tragedy, there are wrathful gods or hypocritical villains who attempt to manipulate the tragic hero to evil ends. The protagonist is generally pessimistic and ambivalent as he has to avoid the dangers and absurdities of life, in which he finds that pain and pleasure, happiness and sadness are always mixed. The recurring emotions are sadness and fear. He is perceived as a victim of his nemesis. In the tragedy, the 'extraordinary victim' confronts inescapable dangers pursued by life's doom. Included in tragedy are stories of 'the fall', dying gods and heroes, violent death, sacrifice, and isolation. In the classic tragedy, the hero finds himself separated in some fundamental way from the natural order of things. The separation makes for an imbalance of nature, and the righting of the balance is the tragic hero's downfall. Like Oedipus, the tragic hero may be supremely proud, passionate, and of soaring mind; yet, these extraordinary attributes are exactly what separate him from common people and bring about his eventual demise. Frye (1957) remarks that tragedy evokes in the listener 'a paradoxical combination of a fearful sense of rightness (the hero must fall) and a pitying sense of wrongness (it is too bad that he falls)' (Frye, 1957: 214).

The tragedy narrative, then, is a story of the inevitable retaliation of the individual who has been unfairly treated, deprived or wronged. The protagonist has no choice but to avenge this wrong, as revealed in the 'only thing to do' and 'had to do it' roles seen here. It is the story of angry revenge, the offender is 'getting (his) own back'. The narrative is driven by the conviction that the protagonist is right and his actions are justified (captured by the 'only choice' and 'it was right' roles). The individual is not to blame for his response, believing it is 'fate'. This captures the individual's egotistical sense of his own significance as the 'extraordinary victim'. That this avenging story is ultimately doomed, as in all tragedy, is indicated by the lack of choice that the protagonist has and his need to proceed as if 'nothing else mattered'.

The account given in Example C shows the justification which is the hallmark of a tragedy. The offender saw his actions as being the right thing to do 'to let him know he just couldn't do that', although it ultimately leads to disaster. There is a total commitment to a life of violence that is so chillingly portrayed in this narrative, emphasised by the killer having an unknown person's tooth in his knee. Many people would actually describe this man as on a tragic life course from his early years or as 'a disaster waiting to happen'.

Example C

A tragic narrative in which the offender can see no other way of acting and the act was everything, nothing else mattered – he was convicted of murder, and was 26 years of age

I am in here for murder; there are other little crimes with it as well, like assault and sexual assault.

I walked into this house and was having a drink and my victim was slagging one of my mates' girlfriends off. I thought 'that's not right'. The lad whose girlfriend it was was there, I said 'you better say something to him'. He didn't and so I got up and just started laying into him while he was on the chair. There are parts of the incident I just don't remember. After beating him up for a bit, I took him to the bathroom, filled the bath and told him he would either die by drowning or I was going to fucking kill him. I was stabbing him for an hour or so. I didn't take any weapons with me, I was not out to cause trouble, that's not my lifestyle, I try and avoid trouble. I can't remember where I got these knives from.

The reason I did it was just because of what he said about my mates, to let him know he just couldn't do that.

Afterwards I went and got a wheelie bin from outside and brought it in the house. I told him to climb in it from the bath but he fell on the floor. He was there for about 20 minutes, I thought he was dead. I stabbed him in the back of the neck again when I realised he wasn't and he got in the bin. I threw white spirit all over it set it on fire and took him in this bin down to the canal. I kicked it over and he fell in the water, he was screaming so I picked up a brick and hit him over the head to shut him up.

I went back to the flat, borrowed clothes and went out on my own then, that was my night ruined. I seen a bouncer at this club that all bouncers go to when they are not working. This one I saw had broken my leg before, I got into a fight with him and hit him over the head with a piece of scaffolding and kicked him a few times. I can't remember where I slept that night. I handed myself in two days later and what I was in police custody I was all black and blue. They had the police doctor look at me and they found a tooth in my knee, it was not my victim's or the bouncer's, so it could be anyone's.

The Quest: The Hero

The roles in the top centre of the plot do not correspond so readily to the underlying narrative theme that Frye calls 'comedy', or what might be more clearly understood as a love story. In *comedic* fiction, the main characters are young heroes, usually in the pursuit of true love, happiness and stability in life with others, which is achieved by minimising interference from environmental and social obstacles and constraints. They seek simple and pure pleasures, are generally optimistic and the recurrent emotions that they experience are generally positive, such as joy and contentment. They are free from anxiety and guilt and are given the opportunity to provide a happy ending to their story on earth.

It is difficult to think that any but a very small minority of criminal activities could be fully incorporated into such a happy fairytale ending. Perhaps instead we need to look to Booker's (2004) development of the various forms of Romance that narratives may encapsulate. His idea of a heroic quest, a metaphorical 'voyage and return', as with *Alice in Wonderland*, may provide an appropriate narrative framework for understanding the criminal actions of some offenders.

The roles in the top centre of the plot are in line with this notion of the individual on an heroic quest. The offenders see their actions as part of a righteous 'mission', which is driving the offender to act ('couldn't stop'). In the criminal context, this mission may take the form of defending his manly honour ('manly'); the offender may feel he has been dishonoured so now his pride demands there will be consequences, which are framed by the offender in terms of obtaining respect ('looking for recognition'). The sense of bravado and casualness central to this narrative is revealed in the description of the actions as 'nothing special'. The fantastical, unreal quality of this type of story is hinted at within the 'wasn't part of it' role description.

This criminal narrative form is illustrated by the account given in Example D. The respondent had been given a life sentence for a very violent assault. He describes the assault he committed almost like a *Gunfight at the OK Corral*. To restore his manly pride, wounded in the insult to his mother, he waited for his victim and then attacked him. But, as in agreeing that he 'had to do it' on the questionnaire, in his narrative he said 'whatever happened, happened' as though it was part of a bigger mission and he was really not to blame. Although he claimed it 'was not really a vendetta' it is clear from his account that there was a history to his anger and that despite his claim that he 'didn't make any preparations' he did indeed create a vicious weapon and wait for his victim. He admitted that he had been drinking and 'taking coke' all day so that he was already in a heightened state, losing contact with reality. He seemed to think that he could assuage the insult and return from the violence, but now realises what a weak storyline that was to follow.

Example D
A 'Quest' narrative; this shows the significance of not being able to stop whilst on a manly mission – he was convicted of GBH with intent and was 24 years old

'My mum had a grievance with this fella next door, he was putting pressure on her and bullying her. I used to think he was a family friend but he kept knocking on her door with bottles of brandy and stuff hassling her to have a drink with him. I used to play football for him when I was a kid. My mum told me what he had been doing and I vowed to front him, something had to be done. I didn't make any preparations as it was not really a vendetta. On the night it happened I had been taking coke for six hours and had been drinking all day. He came into my local with his mate. It was all in good spirits until he came in. He said, 'your mum is just a slut anyway.' I told my friend that he was getting it, he snapped a cue in half and I put two snooker balls in my sock, we waited outside in my mate's car. I knew I wanted to hurt him, I was going to run at him when they came out. Whatever happened, happened. There was a scuffle on the floor and my victim tried to run away. I got up before him and hit him five or six times. I saw all the blood and stopped hitting. He got up and said I was getting killed, I started to chase him again but he ran in through his flat door. I was fuming. I realised what I had done and was caked in blood.

> I was given life with a three-and-a-half year tariff. The alternative to this would have been to just not do it. It did no good anyway, I am in here and my kids have got no dad there. I know how it feels to have no dad around and I promised myself that I would be there for my kids, that's the biggest thing that's done my head in. I had to eat my words, they have no dad, well only once a week when they come and visit me in here.

Victim Roles in Criminal Narratives

These different narratives imply not only roles for the offenders but also the assignment of roles to the victims in crimes. This is particularly important in our understanding of violent and sexual crime (see Chapters 12 and 13). Canter (1994) identifies a number of particular roles an offender may assign to his victim. These are the product of variations in the way the offender tries to maintain the control he requires to conduct the offence and also in the offender's style of interpersonal treatment of the victim. They produce a complex framework that Canter simplifies into three key roles: Victim as Object, Victim as Vehicle and Victim as Person.

Within an adventure narrative, the offender seeks, as part of his competent mastery of the event, simply to control the victim. The offender is focused entirely on achieving his objectives and the victim is irrelevant; just something to be forcibly managed to allow him to do what he wants. The victim is merely an *object* without feeling or significance.

Within an Irony narrative, the offender desperately seeks some kind of intimacy with the victim in a distorted attempt to address his sense of emptiness. In line with the sense of pointlessness and meaningless, this attempt to achieve intimacy relies on an abusive and coercive treatment of the victim, outside of any acceptable social conduct. The victim here then is recognised as fully human, a *person*, who has significance as such.

Different forms of the victim as *vehicle* role are assigned to victims within the Tragedy and Quest narratives. For the Tragic offender, the victim plays a symbolic role as a target against which he can exact his revenge. There is then sufficient empathy or recognition of her humanity that through the exploitation of her and her reactions, the offender can achieve his sense of retaliation. For the offender on a Quest, the attack on the victim is not about retaliation but is rather part of his bigger heroic mission; she is a vehicle for the expression of his desires. Although, unlike the victim as Object role, there is recognition of her humanity that is an important part of the purpose she serves for him, the focus is entirely on the offender's expression here.

Scripts and Narratives

The narrative model that has been presented has some important relationships to the influential perspective within psychology that explores the notion of 'scripts' (Abelson, 1981). The roles that a person plays, after all, imply that he is following some sort of script that determines the relationships between people and the succession of episodes. Storylines do follow particular sequences and there are well-established expectations of how they will unfold. In the criminal context these scripts would be expected to be drawn upon so that offenders may think that there is a particular way of carrying out a robbery, rape or murder, depending in part on what they think their role is. Even if they are not thinking consciously of what they should do their actions will be shaped by their expectations of 'what happens next'.

In a number of studies Canter and his colleagues have shown the value of considering the implicit scripts that underlie life-threatening circumstances (Canter *et al.*, 1990; Donald, 1993, 1995; Donald and Canter, 1990, 1992). The significance of these studies is that they show how people hold on to their pre-existing roles and patterns of behaviour even in extremely challenging situations. It is therefore to be expected that offenders will also shape their actions in relation to storylines that are popularly available.

Wilson and Smith (2000) propose one intriguing implication of the general availability of scripts in their discussion of hostage taking. They point out that breaking the expected rules of a script can give participants particular power. As they report:

> On the part of the terrorists, 'bluffing' is one type of rule breaking. Examples include hostage takers' claims to have specific hostages when they do not, or to have wired the building with explosives when they have not. A faked show of strength by hijackers in Tehran in 1984 may well have been the factor that led to the plane being stormed. After actually killing an American and dumping his body onto the tarmac they pretended to kill two Kuwaitis. After taking them back inside the plane and pouring 'catsup' on them, they invited journalists to photograph the evidence. In the following rescue mission by Iranian security forces the authorities bluffed back. One security officer posing as a doctor came on board in response to the request to attend to a passenger. Two others came on as cleaning men and disarmed the hijackers.
>
> (Wilson and Smith, 2000: 147)

In considering any crimes, then, the scripts that may be shaping them can be a valuable perspective to help not only to understand what are the processes that give rise to the criminal's actions but also may help to clarify the implicit narratives that the offender is living. This in turn will open the way to inferences about the sort of person he thinks he is and what are the psychological roots of his actions.

Summary

A somewhat innovative and challenging framework has been offered in the present chapter for considering offenders and their crimes. In order to recognise that offenders carry out conscious acts and are not just a product of their genetics and environment, ideas have been drawn on from the study of literature. It has been proposed that, like everyone else, criminals make sense of their lives through formulating some sort of narrative in which they play the main role. This storyline also assigns roles to their victims.

Following one of the major formulations of the archetypal forms that stories can take it has been proposed that criminals' personal narratives may be dominated by one of four mythic themes: irony, adventure, tragedy and the quest. Each is associated with various types of state-ments or assertions made by the offender. Key offender roles as victim, professional, revenger and hero inform understanding of the manifestation of these narratives in the criminal con-text. Empirical study of these roles has proven possible by asking offenders to describe how they felt when committing a crime that they can remember well.

The themes underlying these narratives also imply particular roles for the victim within the criminal narrative. In terms of Canter's role of the victim framework (1994), the Irony narrative assigns the victim a *person* role, the adventure narrative implies an *object* role, while different variants of the victim as *vehicle* role are implied within the tragedy and the quest.

The narrative model presented also has some important relationships to the notion of 'scripts', which may be drawn upon by offenders in determining the appropriate course of action in a given situation. Taken all together, the framework presented here offers a rich set of possibilities for developing inferences about offenders and generating hypotheses for future study that engage directly with criminals as active agents.

Further Reading

Books

Canter, D. (1995) *Criminal Shadows*, HarperCollins, London.
Crossley, M.L. (2000) *Introducing Narrative Psychology: Self, Trauma, and the Construction of Meaning*, Open University Press, London.
Laszlo, J. (2008) *The Science of Stories: An Introduction to Narrative Psychology*, Routledge, London.
McAdams, D.P. (1997) *The Stories We Live By: Personal Myths and the Making of the Self*, Guilford Press, London.

Articles

Bruner, J. (1987) Life as narrative. *Social Research*, **54**(1), 11–32.
Canter, D., Grieve, N., Nicol, C. and Benneworth, K. (2003) Narrative plausibility: the impact of sequence and anchoring. *Behavioral Sciences and the Law*, **21**, 251–67.
Canter, D.V. and Ioannou, M. (2004) Criminals' emotional experiences during crimes. *International Journal of Forensic Psychology*, **1**(2), 71–81.
Canter, D., Kaouri, C. and Ioannou, M. (2003) The facet structure of criminal narratives, in *Facet Theory: Towards Cumulative Social Science* (eds S. Levy and D. Elizur), University of Ljubljana, Faculty of Arts, Center for Educational Development, Ljubljana.

Questions for Discussion and Research

1. Review the event reported in Box 6.1 and discuss what forms of narrative it encap-sulates. What does this tell us about the killer?

2. Consider any crime film or novel. Which of the dominant narratives discussed does the storyline follow? What role does the main offender play within the overall storyline? Can you give examples of their speech or action to illustrate this role?

3. Consider the questionnaire to try and capture an offender's inner narratives, and to determine what role he sees himself as playing. If you were developing such a questionnaire to cover your own life what similarities and differences would it have? What issues would you need to consider and what problems might you encounter in developing such a questionnaire to cover your experience and that of your associates? What types of questions might you include?

4. Take any of the questions in the questionnaire in Table 6.1 and discuss the criminal story line that may be implied by that question. What sort of offences and offenders might be expected to see their lives in that narrative?

5. Review any or all of the examples A to D. What script is implied in each of these examples?

7

Finding Action Patterns and Drawing Profiles

In This Chapter

Learning Objectives

When you have finished this chapter you should be able to:

1. Understand how IP focuses on patterns of criminal actions.
2. Be aware of the implications of behavioural salience.
3. Know the consistency principles.

4. Discuss the theoretical foundations for investigative inferences.
5. Recognise the limits of 'profiling'.
6. Distinguish action system modes of inference mechanisms.
7. Comprehend narrative interpretations of inference processes.

Synopsis

Any class of crime, whether burglary, arson, robbery, fraud or murder, can take many different forms. The detailed actions can make one burglary or one murder very different from another. So if we are to generate a more detailed understanding of crimes and to develop more specific inferences about offenders then we need to look much more closely at the actions within an offence.

A generic basis for differences in offending style is proposed in terms of Shye's Action System model integrated with the different forms of criminal narratives. This produces four modes of offending action: the professional's adaptive adventure; the hero's expressive quest; the victim's integrative irony and the revenger's conservative tragedy. This narrative action system (NAS) model of criminal differentiation underpins variations in offending style across and within different forms of crime.

Inference processes will have their roots in the various pathways to crime: within (a) aspects of an individual's cognitive or dispositional characteristics, (b) their interpersonal interactions, (c) the subcultural and social learning processes of which they are a part, or (d) the emotional characteristics of the individual. These pathways reflect the four action modes of the narrative action system. Therefore each mode of the narrative action system model offers a framework for considering different inference processes; a different mechanism whereby actions can relate to characteristics. Different forms of inferences will be most productive depending on the particular NAS mode of the offending actions. The NAS inference model therefore provides a generic basis for developing deductions about offenders from information about their offending; an integrated model of crime differentiation and criminal inferences.

Criminal Actions

In previous chapters we have been mainly concerned with different classes and types of crime. Whether an individual commits a burglary or a rape carries implications about the nature of that person and about the other forms of offence in which he might have been involved. But to take our understanding of criminality further, it is necessary to look more closely at what actually happens in any crime.

The term 'action' is preferred in general for describing what goes on in a crime rather than describing what happens as 'behaviour'. An action implies intention whereas the term 'behaviour' can mean just a motor movement. Hurting a person is an action but banging them with a fist is behaviour. Often, for stylistic reasons, we use the terms interchangeably but it should always be kept in mind that we are rarely interested in mechanical behaviour but rather in the meaning of what is being done.

Table 7.1   Matters that an offender must determine.

1. When to commit the crime; time, day of the week, time of year
2. Where to commit the crime; general area, exact location
3. What to target; person, property, object
4. How much planning or preparation
5. How to initiate the crime
6. Style for carrying out the offence; for example, aggressive, devious
7. Tactics for achieving the main purpose of the offence; for example, use of weapon, tools
8. Form of relating to the victim e.g. avoiding, ignoring or attacking
9. Whether to control the possibility that criminal actions will be detected
10. How to conclude the offence

Matters that an Offender must Determine

A productive starting point for thinking about criminal actions in a psychologically richer way is to consider what is under the offender's control to any degree. For even the simplest offence to occur the offender must make a number of choices whether consciously or not as listed in Table 7.1. All of these aspects of an offence have to be reviewed and filtered if they are to be drawn on to help understand the crime and contribute to law-enforcement activities.

Taken together the issues listed in Table 7.1 show that many aspects of an offence carry significant information about the offender and his or her actions. They show that it makes a great deal of sense to consider the active agency of the criminal and draw from that some deeper understanding of what his criminality is about. This enables us to go beyond the broader issues of the class or type of crime that we considered in earlier chapters, to dig more deeply into the meanings of any given subset of crimes.

When we deal with actions in a crime many challenges emerge. Consider the burglary described in Box 7.1. The most immediate challenge is deciding what to look at. There are so many aspects to a crime. The challenge to the police officer, as for the researcher, is to identify those features that are of most relevance to deriving inferences about the offender. So, the question is which aspects of everything that has gone on in this burglary may reveal something about the offender.

Box 7.1 What Are the Salient Features of This Crime?

In the early hours of Saturday morning, the ground floor flat of a two storey house in Manchester was burgled. The burglar disabled the alarm, then entered through a downstairs window, stole cash and jewellery without making any mess but leaving fingerprints. The larger electronic goods in the house were not stolen. Just as he was about to leave the offender encountered the occupant and reacted violently punching her in the face several times before running off.

Not all of the aspects of the burglary will be equally revealing of the individual who carried out this offence. Should we, for example, consider the fact that he accosted the occupant rather than just running away when she discovered him? Should we pay more attention to what was taken or give equal importance to what was *not* taken? Is it of significance that it was on the morning of a day on which most people do not work? What about disabling the alarm? Is that of particular importance?

Deciding what is relevant is not straightforward. Does the damage done to property by the offender tell us something about him or her, but not the way in which the offence was initiated or what time of day it happened? Is the offender's readiness to be violent a key consideration for investigative psychologists but his choice of a ground-floor flat rather than a house unimportant? There are so many questions that in any research project or police enquiry many hours may be spent discussing what to take note of and what to ignore. Often detectives will jump on one or two aspects of the offence, say the violence, or the time of day, which strikes them as particularly significant and then proceed to build inferences on the basis of those features. Similarly a researcher may decide that she wants to focus on the violence that occurs in a crime because that seems most interesting or socially important. But selecting aspects of a crime in these somewhat arbitrary ways can be very misleading for many reasons.

In some places the police are alert to the potential for exploring the details of what happens in a crime. So much so that they put considerable effort into recording a lot of detail of what seems to have occurred even in crimes that are relatively common such as burglary. Increasingly around the world very large databases are created that are meant to record the minutiae of what offenders do. Table 7.2 gives a list of the actions typically recorded by a major UK police force of all the burglaries in a specific area over a three-year period, together with the frequencies of those actions across all the offences.

In Table 7.2 it can be seen that some actions are very commonly recorded such as a 'tidy search', 'untidy search' or entering through a window or door. In contrast, other actions are very unusual indeed, such as the offender changing clothes or turning on the TV. The table therefore throws into high relief the difficulty the police face of what on earth to do with all this information! Determining the pertinence of a criminal's actions requires an overall understanding of the incident within which the individual behaviours occurred. Some behaviour may only occur in direct response to situational stimuli so what it tells us about the offender may be limited. For example was the entry method important or was this method adopted just because a window was open? Are apparently incongruous acts that run contrary to the general style of the offence particularly significant? For instance, should the fact that an offender who was experienced enough to disable an alarm then also left fingerprints be regarded as crucial or incidental? Should we focus just on the behaviours that did happen or are there things that the offender did not do that are relevant? For example, is it significant that the offender did not carry any tools with him?

As discussed by Youngs (2008), a very important point here is that each aspect of a crime is open to different forms of examination and analysis. The way we determine whether the location is salient is rather different from how we make sense of the implications of the time of day. The behaviour in relation to any possible victims may have to be evaluated rather differently from considerations about the property taken. Indeed, the range of considerations

Table 7.2   Frequencies of actions recorded for burglaries in a police database.

Description	Frequency	Percentage
Tidy search was made	3636	28.6
Untidy search was made	3063	24.1
Entered through window	2709	21.3
Entered through door	2686	21.1
Sharp instrument	1368	10.8
Blunt instrument	1332	10.5
Climbed in to commit offence	1225	9.6
Entered through locks	939	7.4
Bag was used to carry away property	653	5.1
Security alarm activated	411	3.2
Tool used to enter	273	2.1
Exit prepared by suspect	233	1.8
Furniture forced open, e.g. drawers, desk	220	1.7
Building attacked other than entry	210	1.6
Door secured by suspect, e.g. locked or obstructed	185	1.4
Illumination provided by matches or lights, etc.	175	1.4
Suspect posed during offence	167	1.3
Keys used	135	1
Entered through bars	122	0.9
Alcohol was consumed	106	0.8
Entered through hinges	92	0.7
Till raided	87	0.7
Specific words used that could identify suspect	87	0.7
Security systems bypassed, e.g. wires cut	74	0.6
Curtains closed by suspect	74	0.6
Food consumed by suspect at scene	66	0.5
Suspect hid at scene	63	0.5
Suspect toileted either in WC or not	62	0.5
Suspect smoked at scene	54	0.4
Suspect used bed	47	0.4
Suspect was accompanied	45	0.3
Safe forced open	36	0.3
Putty removed	30	0.2
Victim threatened	28	0.2
Criminal damage, e.g. paint or graffiti at scene	28	0.2
Meter forced open	22	0.1
Security lights disabled/broken	21	0.2
Telephone tampered with by suspect	18	0.1
Suspect took drugs before offence	18	0.1
Victim physically attacked	15	0.1
Lookout used	13	0.1
Audio/TV turned on by suspect	11	0.08
Security cameras disabled/broken	11	0.08
Security lights activated	9	0.07
Suspect changed clothes	5	0.03

and their implications are potentially so complex that any *ad hoc* attempt to make sense of a criminal's actions is fraught with the risk of missing the point.

Without having some broader framework for the criminal activity, the selection of issues for consideration is arbitrary. The selection may be insightful on some occasions but misleading on others. Without knowing the behavioural context of which it is a part it is not possible to know the basis of any insights and whether any successes or failures on one occasion will be of relevance when a similar crime occurs in the future. Indeed being clear on what makes one crime similar to another requires some knowledge of the range of ways in which crimes vary. In other words, without some scientific principles to work with each investigation is a one-off exploration that does not cumulate to generate an investigative psychology.

Salience

A central research question, then, is to identify the behaviourally important facets of offences – those facets that are of most use in revealing the *salient* psychological processes inherent in any crime. There are many reasons why we may be interested in distinguishing salient aspects of crimes:

- As part of the exploration of psychological processes involved in committing crimes.
- To link a number of crimes to one offender.
- To develop crime prevention strategies.
- Another issue may be to determine if the offender is likely to move on to more violent and/or serious crimes.
- It may be as a basis for distinguishing who from a series of possible suspects is the most likely culprit.
- To develop a clear picture of the essence of a crime on which to base the presentation of the case to a jury.

Each of the many possible uses of the analysis of crimes and criminal actions makes different demands on that information.

Determining salience turns out to be much more complex than is often realised, with parallels in many areas of information retrieval. As we shall see, it requires the determination of base rates and study of co-occurrences of behaviours across crimes as well as an understanding of the pattern of actions that are typical for any given type of crime.

The behaviour that is typical of a pattern of criminal action is actually a way of defining a subset of classes of crime, or even of making clear what crime has occurred. Non-consensual sexual activity would be typical of a rape, helping to distinguish it from a robbery, but it does not help us to distinguish one rape from another. For that purpose we need to know more about the behavioural patterns. Such behavioural patterns may help us to distinguish classes of crime, for example whether they are against property or a person, but will be of even more help in distinguishing types of crime such as forms of sexual assault.

The more specific the legal focus, the more likely are the actions to be particularly distinct as well. Nonetheless it is helpful to keep these two aspects separate in our considerations because they imply different forms of examination of investigative material. Legal specificity takes us into examinations, for instance, of criminal histories and the versatility of offenders, determining styles of criminality. In contrast, as actions become more specific we are moving towards more characteristic aspects of criminal behaviour.

All of this points to the significance of understanding what aspects of a crime are being considered as pertinent when trying to discriminate one crime from another. It is just too simple-minded to utilise any aspect of a crime, pulled out of the plethora of possibilities, for example, whether there is a young woman involved, whether objects of personal significance to the victim have been stolen, whether there was forced entry to the house and so on, without understanding the role of that aspect within the possibilities for variation between crimes. Salience ties into the underlying conceptualisation of the criminal activity. The identification of the behaviours that are significant comes from understanding what the offence is about psychologically.

Salience also depends on how distinct the criminal's actions are. Are they typical of broad criminal lifestyles, for instance like smoking cannabis, or are they distinguishing aspects of their criminal activities, such as only burgling houses when no-one is present, or something even more specific like only stealing gold jewellery, or attacking young women wearing grey jeans?

In the burglary scenario in Box 7.1 although the stealing of cash may be thought of as potentially revealing of the offender, it may not be of much discriminatory value because it is typical of most burglars. As such, it is not a behaviour that is of use in building inferences that discriminate between types of burglary, or of linking burglaries to a common offender. The rape example in Box 7.2 shows a determination to continue with the assault despite being seen by two strangers. How typical is that of sexual assaults, or does it perhaps raise questions about the veracity of the victim's statement?

Box 7.2 What Are the Salient Features of This Crime?

The following is a police account of information they were given by a 16-year-old girl, K. What are the salient aspects of this offence?

> K states that she got off the bus at 16:30 in High Street and was in a hurry as she was already late home. She was crossing over to catch another bus when she was approached by the suspect who said 'excuse me' and tried to ask her a question. As she was late she continued on her way and ignored the suspect who then reached out and grabbed her by her right wrist. He then started to pull her towards the green door on the street and tried to pull her inside.
>
> An unknown female interrupted and asked the victim if she was OK. The victim said that she did not know the male and that he was touching her. The female member of public asked if she needed any assistance. The victim told this female that she didn't; she felt that she would be able to get the suspect off her. The member of public then left.

(continued)

The victim was forced into the front door which was open. This led through another door and on to a flight of stairs. She was forced up two flights of stairs into a corridor of doors. She was being held around the waist and across the mouth to prevent her from screaming. At the second flight of stairs they were approached by a second person. A male who appeared to work at the venue, he came from an office. He asked what was going on. The suspect stated that nothing was going on but that the victim was his daughter and that she was playing up. This second male then carried on about his business in the office.

The victim was taken to one of the doors along the corridor. All she can say is that it is a door on the left. She does not feel she will be able to pick out which one it is and cannot describe the doors in any detail. The suspect opened the door with key and went inside to what she describes as a bed sit.

Here she was locked in and the suspect stripped from the waist down whilst in the bathroom. The victim was then forced on to the bed, face down. Her knickers were pulled down to around her ankles and her school skirt was lifted and the suspect penetrated her anally. He penetrated her in this way for approximately an hour, until he told the victim that she was bleeding. He allowed her to pull her knickers up and threw her out of the room, telling her to never come back.

She ran from the venue and went to her bus stop. As she was getting her bus pass out of her pocket she noticed that she had £35 in her pocket that was not there before. She assumed it was from the suspect, and considered going back to give it back to him but was too afraid to return.

She went home and she was afraid to tell her mum why she was late and so said that she had been to make a dentist appointment.

Typicality

Those actions that can be found in the great majority of crimes of a given class can be regarded as *typical*. But they are also usually the aspects of the crime that lead to its definition both in any research context and in law. For example, a violent assault that involves sexual activity will be classified as a sexual assault or a rape. Therefore there is no surprise to find that all crimes classified as sexual assaults include non-consensual sexual acts. However, there are likely to be other associated actions, such as control of the victim, necessary to carry out the offence. Taking these all together will provide an account of what is typical of any subset of offences. As we shall see, determining what is typical of an offence is an empirical as well as a definitional question that is often a crucial starting point for any research project.

Base Rates

The frequency of actions across crimes is a practical starting point for understanding salience. These are often referred to as *base rates*. They are the basic rates at which anything of relevance may happen. For example, 90% of offences are committed by men. So it may not add much to our understanding of a crime if a man is cited as having been seen running away from the crime. By contrast, information that a woman was involved does open up other corridors of consideration. The police often ignore the importance of base rates. For example in the series of bedsit rapes of students in Manchester described in *Criminal Shadows* (Canter, 1995) the police had initially assumed that the offender was targeting students. But in that area of Manchester just about all young women living in bedsits were students. This base rate meant that the offender could more readily be assumed to have been targeting an area with many potential, vulnerable victims, not victims with a particular occupation.

Rarity is not of itself a guarantee of the significance of an action when it does occur. A simple count of exactly how frequent an action is has to be regarded with some caution. The significance of an action being rare or common depends on its meaning. In a general sense, for example smoking cannabis on 50 occasions does not equate psychologically to carrying out an armed robbery 50 times. So frequency may best be regarded as a symptom of the potential for discriminating between crimes, not as a cause of them.

All of this adds up to the fact that the determination of the salient characteristics of a crime is an empirical question, not simply a matter of definition or intuition. Some knowledge of the base rate of behaviours of particular classes of crime is essential before the characteristics that are particularly important in understanding a given offence can be explored.

Contingencies

Another crucial factor is the circumstance of the crime. Particular aspects of the situation may make certain sorts of activities far more likely, or even necessary. For example, a bank robbery is difficult to carry out without some sort of weapon, but burglaries usually rely on avoiding the victims so a weapon is not an important requirement. So the carrying of a weapon tells us something different about the offender in these different circumstances, Youngs (2008) refers to this as 'contingency destabilisation'. Similarly a rapist who attacks a person in her bed in a house occupied by others may be expected to insist on the victim keeping quiet, but not make such demands if he attacks a woman walking alone in deserted woodland.

The issue of circumstantial influences is a potential minefield for considering the significance of criminal actions, especially if the response of any victim is taken into account as well. One solution is to focus on those aspects of the crime over which the offender has most control or are likely to be least influenced by the circumstances.

There are also variations within the offender, who may on some occasions, for example, be under the influence of alcohol or drugs, but not other occasions. Indeed drug addicts have told us that that they typically commit a quick theft in which little money is stolen in order to get their first supply of drugs for the day. Then once they feel a bit more in control from having taken the drug they will commit more serious crimes to be able to buy a larger supply. So they will be in a different emotional and psychological state depending on how recently they have taken drugs.

These variations within the offender will interact with the particular circumstances of the crime and criminal opportunities but they all centre on the offender and his interactions with the situation into which he puts himself. These interactions themselves and the situations the offender chooses may therefore be typical of his actions. So, it is curious that some commentaries on offender profiling, for example in the recent very brief review by Alison and Kebbel (2006), suggest that the influence of situational factors greatly reduces the possibility of any sort of contribution to police investigations from analysis of criminal actions. If we were all totally thrown by the vagaries of circumstances, or big changes in our moods, we would never be able to achieve anything. Criminals, like everyone else, will often choose the circumstance over which they believe they will have control. Indeed as an intriguing study by Nee and Meenaghan (2006) demonstrates, some criminals may be regarded as experts in their own domain. Part of that expertise consists of managing the contingencies of the situation in which they choose to commit crimes or the skills of dealing with the situation as it arises, including dealing with their own psychological state.

The role of contingencies is beginning to emerge in studies that treat them as part of the criminal activity. Goodwill and Alison have shown (Goodwill and Alison, 2007) that the amount of planning that is indicated in the offender's actions interacts with the age of the victim as a basis for inferring the likely age of an offender. In other words, their study suggests that understanding the implications of any relationship between victim age and offender age needs to be informed by consideration of how other aspects of the offence may influence this relationship.

Interactions

The complication of the way in which different aspects of a crime will interact with each other is a recurring concern in making sense of offenders' actions. Dealing with each aspect of a crime as if it were independent of all others can be very misleading. In the burglary scenario in Box 7.1 we drew attention to the combination of an alarm being disabled but fingerprints being left. It is this mix of features that was being considered rather than each being examined on its own. The combination may tell us something more than each action on its own. Of course, to make sense of this, the circumstances would need to be taken into account, such as how sophisticated the alarm system was, as well as base rates – for example how common it is for burglars to exhibit both these actions. Ideally this would also take account of the context so that we would know if burglars in that area disabled alarm systems because local people actually took notice when they were set off.

The Basis for Inferences

Are Criminals Consistent in their Actions?

It is sometimes assumed that the investigative inference process relies on the consistency of criminals' behaviour. This is not entirely the case. Of course if the offender has a distinct style of offending, acting in a virtually identical way from one offence to the next, then this simplifies the process of categorising his actions in order to derive from them some possibilities that will contribute to investigations. However, if there are unique aspects of an offence that distinguish it from any other and therefore can be regarded as equivalent to a 'signature' then even if this is not found in all a given criminal's offences it can still be drawn on for deriving inferences. There may also be salient aspects of one or more offences

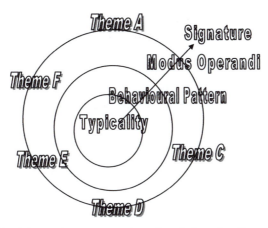

Figure 7.1 Schematic representation of variations in offence actions.

linked to a particular offender, which although they are not completely consistent, do indicate some characteristic of relevance. Taken together, then, these considerations show that behavioural consistency is not essential for deriving inferences from crime series although it can make matters easier. Conversely, if an offender is entirely consistent in certain actions but that consistency is something that he shares with many other offenders it will not help to provide inferences of particular utility in selecting an offender from a range of possible suspects. A proposed model for the commonalities and differences in offenders' action patterns is shown in Figure 7.1.

The extent to which behaviour generally is consistent has been the subject of considerable debate in psychology. This debate has been led by the assertions of Mischel and colleagues (for example, Mischel, 1968) that how people behave is determined not by the sorts of dispositional or personality tendencies proposed originally by trait theorists such as Allport (Allport and Allport, 1921) and Cattell (1946) but, rather, by the constraints of the situation. In fact it is worth nothing that one of the origins of environmental psychology was the work of Barker and his colleagues (for example, Barker and Gump, 1964) who studied what they called 'behavioral settings', where actions occurred, precisely because they thought this would help to understand and predict human behaviour much more effectively than studying individual differences.

In the investigative context, then, it may be hypothesised that opportunity and circumstances will determine the type of crime that is committed such that the particular act or the way in which it is carried out will be as much due to chance aspects of the context as to the propensities of the criminal. Such a perspective would argue that really any criminal could commit one of a great variety of different types of crime in any of a wide range of styles and no criminal could be distinguished from any other on the basis of his/her behaviour. For violent and obviously emotional crime, this inconsistency might be hypothesised not just because crime is seen as opportunistic but because these offences are committed in a state of impulsive, unplanned action. For these crimes, it would be postulated that people react in such an unstructured way that no aspect of their characteristics is likely to be revealed, other than possibly their characteristic impulsivity. So, for instance, the location chosen for a crime would be expected to be a haphazard one that bears no relationship to other aspects of the offender's life. Similarly, their victims would be expected to be of no particular significance.

However the complete inconsistency of offending behaviour implied by these processes of opportunism and impulsivity does not find support in the empirical work. As long ago as 1976, Green used cluster analysis and multidimensional scaling to demonstrate that burglars were consistent enough for what he called their M.O. to be used to distinguish between their crime series. In more recent studies, direct explorations of consistency in styles of offending do reveal regularity in some of the actions an individual carries out from offence to offence (see, for example, Bennell and Canter, 2002; Canter, Goodwin and Youngs, 2006; Salfati and Bateman 2005; Goodwill and Alison, 2005; Grubin, Kelly and Brunsdon, 2001). Furthermore, even momentary consideration of the history of detective work reveals that many crimes have been solved and linked to the same offender in the absence of forensic evidence because of consistencies in the offender's actions, often referred to as the offender's M.O. So although the potential for variation in a given criminal's actions is always present it should not be assumed to be so great that no inference can be derived from knowing their actions.

Studies showing the successful behavioural linking of offences to common offenders have tended to draw on some degree of consistency in those behaviours (for example, Canter, Haeritage and Kovacik, 1989; Santtila, Junkkila and Sandnabba, 2005). At the level of type of offence, as described in Chapter 5, Youngs, Canter and Cooper (2004) have shown that, where conceptualised and analysed appropriately, specialised tendencies can be identified within offending histories. These findings in the criminal context are backed up by the studies of Shoda and colleagues exploring the stability of general behaviour in relation to the personality-situationism debate (for example, Cervone and Shoda, 1999; Shoda, 1999). Their studies show that behaviour is consistent where the psychological properties of the situation are comparable. We would therefore expect that there may well be more consistency in a criminal's actions during a crime than in many other less comparable situations.

Often consistency can also be found, not so much in the individual as in the role he plays or is assigned in a criminal group. The social processes that underlie groups, teams and networks of criminals explored in later chapters can reveal much about the consistencies in criminal behaviour and the themes that provide their foundation. A clear example of this is a study by Wilson and Donald (1999), which examined the different roles taken by teams of 'hit-and-run' burglars. They demonstrated, for example, that the offender who was given the task of driving the getaway vehicle was most likely to have a previous conviction for a vehicle-related crime. In contrast, the criminal assigned the task of keeping members of the public at bay, or controlling others who might interfere with their crime, referred to as the 'heavy', was most likely to have a previous conviction for some form of violent offence.

One interesting possibility is the consistently inconsistent offender; an individual who always acts in different ways in committing his offences. In such cases it is this very inconsistency that tells us something about the personality of the individual, the kind of non-criminal life he leads and the likely role of offending as a challenge and diversion rather than, for example, a functional or job-like activity within his general narrative.

Are a Criminals' Actions Consistent with their Non-Criminal Actions?

We have been discussing the consistency, or similarity of actions, between one crime and another committed by the same person. Another form of related consistency is between the actions in a crime and the other aspects of the offender's life. The 'heavy' in a bank robbery who has convictions for violent crimes and is known to be aggressive in social interactions is revealing a consistent pattern to his life. This could well be a person who sees his life as some sort of tragic story in which he needs to be constantly seeking revenge for the wrongs done to him. This may thus allow some aspects of a one-off crime, such as the nature of the violence involved, to be used to form views about how others might recognise the culprit.

These findings of consistency between social role and forms of criminal endeavour are in keeping with the general narrative framework presented in Chapter 6. They lend support to a general model of criminal activity that recognises the specific role that criminality plays in the life of the offender. It further supports the perspective that, for the sorts of offenders considered in the studies cited, the style of criminality is an integral, natural part of the criminal's general lifestyle, not some special, atypical aspect of it.

Consistency or Displacement?

The search for some form of coherence between offenders' actions and the rest of their lives is at odds with a popular view of how criminality arises, which like so many other confused popular perspectives has its roots in the writings of Sigmund Freud. This is the view that criminal behaviour is a form of displacement activity, a cathartic reaction against psychological deficiencies. Such a perspective would predict that the offender's criminal activity will therefore differ markedly from his ordinary activities so the processes by which the two are linked will operate inversely. At its most basic this is the idea that a person without any money will steal to obtain the money. More psychologically, it is the notion of the mild and timid individual who commits horrifically violent offences as a way of expressing his suppressed, hidden anger. As Stephenson (1992) demonstrates in some detail, on close analysis there is little support for such a view.

Are Criminals Normal?

The assumption that criminals are dealing with some inner personal conflicts, which is inherent in any 'compensation' hypothesis, is often taken a step further to view criminals as psychologically distinct from other members of society. This was the common view in the nineteenth century, reflected in such books as Ellis' 1901 book called *The Criminal*. All the searching for body types for criminals and other overt distinguishing features discussed in Chapter 2 reflects the belief that offenders are not 'normal'. This idea still underlies many of the present day searches for biochemical or neurological differences between some offenders and others. However, the consistency perspective puts these assumptions in a rather different light. It sees criminal actions as reflecting more extreme aspects of normal behaviour. At a fundamental level criminals are only different from other members of society in so far as they break more rules. It is not assumed that there is something special about their basic psychology that separates them off from the rest of society. They may in general, for example, be more impulsive and typically less well educated than the average person but these differences are nearly always within the normal range for the population at large. So, just as there are many variations between people who are not regarded as being criminal, there will be variations between criminals. Some of them will be mentally disturbed, as would be the case within any sample of people; some will be introverted; some more extraverted and so on.

Rather, the indications are that criminal behaviour can be understood in terms of normal psychological processes and behavioural frameworks. This is clearly illustrated in Bennell *et al.*'s (2001) study of sexual offences against children, in which they examined the occurrence of 19 offence behaviours including behaviours such as how the child was approached, types and levels of violence, types of sexual activity and general treatment of the victim. These researchers found styles of behaviour in committing the sex offences that mapped on to conventional adult-child interactions of autonomy, hostility, control and love (cf. Schaefer, 1959, 1997). So, for example, one style of offending that emerged involved behaviours such as violence, threats and anal penetration that were a clear manifestation of a more standard controlling adult-child interaction. Similarly, an offending style was identified that could be understood, in the context of a sex offence, as reflecting Schaefer's love adult-child interaction. This was indicated by behaviours such as the giving of gifts and the offender performing oral sex on the child. The appropriateness of such normal rather than bizarre interpretations led Bennell *et al.* (2001: 155) to conclude that child abuse is comprised of 'abusive and manipulative variants of more conventional relationship processes that exist between adults and children.' In similar vein, Porter and Alison (2004) showed that the interpersonal behaviour that characterised the offending of gang rapists could be understood as an extreme form of normal patterns of interpersonal interaction.

This notion that normal rather than abnormal models of behaviour are appropriate to offending is one of the core principles of IP (Canter 1994, 1995). Criminals are not seen as qualitatively different from the general population in terms of the broad psychological influences on how they act on or react to the world. Of course, criminal actions may be extreme or distorted versions of normal conduct but the assertion is that almost invariably it will be possible to tie them back to standard psychological frameworks.

The possibility that in some cases the offender will be mentally ill should not be confused with the notion that criminal behaviour is a bizarre and unpredictable phenomenon. For these individuals it certainly may be the case that aspects of their criminal behaviour, as with their non-criminal behaviour, will be understandable within clinical or psychiatric models. To date, however, there is no consistent evidence of any strong impact of psychiatric diagnosis on crime style.

There is little support at present for the suggestion that mental illness overrides the more prosaic processes that govern fundamental decisions about, for example, where to offend, what the offender immediately seeks in offending or what general approach the offender adopts. Certainly, any idea that offending is a simple, direct expression of mental illness seems to be inappropriate. For mentally ill and non-mentally ill offenders alike, then, the view within IP is that most criminal actions can be understood within normal bounds. Because crimes are defined within a framework of legal rules and offending is therefore, by definition, the breaking of these rules, then it follows that one of the main implications of the consistency principle is that being criminal will tend to be an aspect of a person's life. In other words, people who offend with any frequency will be expected to break many social rules.

Psychopathy

It is necessary to mention one caution to this general perspective. There is much discussion in forensic psychology of what is called the 'personality disorder' of *psychopathy* (see Box 7.3). The behaviour of psychopathic offenders is clearly extreme and very often has obviously criminal components. These individuals are characterised by a lack of remorse and a readiness to lie. Sometimes they can be very violent but they will often be superficially charming as well. So people who are given the diagnostic label of 'psychopath' may seem to defy the general principle that criminals should be regarded as 'normal', although they may frequently be at the extremes of normality.

However, it is clear that people labelled psychopathic are not out of touch with reality and are not 'mentally ill' in the usual senses of that term. Their ways of dealing with others are extreme but they still act on the world in terms of what it means to them. Therefore, although they expand the boundaries of what we are considering in subsequent chapters, they are not outside the envelope.

Box 7.3 Focus on Psychopathy

Psychopathy is a psychological construct or a form of personality disorder characterised by serious deficits in a person's ability to interact effectively with others, pathological lying, lack of remorse or guilt, callousness and lack of empathy, poor behavioural controls, irresponsibility and impulsivity. Psychopaths are defined as individuals who have no concern for the feelings of others, a complete disregard for any sense of social obligation and an inability to form lasting emotional ties. They are predators who use charm, manipulation, intimidation and violence to control others and to satisfy their own selfish needs. Psychopaths are selfish, callous and remorseless in their use of others. They often have an impulsive, chronically unstable and antisocial lifestyle (Hare, 1991, 2003).

Psychopathy is most commonly assessed using Hare's Psychopathy Checklist-Revised (PCL-R). The checklist comprises 20 items, each of which is scored on a three-point ordinal scale (0 = no, 1 = maybe, 2 = yes). There is no official 'cutoff score', but in most research studies a score over 30 has been used to identify someone as a psychopath. Factor analysis of the PCL-R indicated that it consists of two factors. Factor one describes the interpersonal and affective deficits of the psychopath (for example, pathological lying and lack of remorse). Factor two assesses lifestyle and antisocial deficits (such as impulsivity and juvenile delinquency). Hare (2003) and Neumann, Vitacco, Hare and Wupperman (2005) have argued that a hierarchical model comprising two factors and four facets (interpersonal, affective, lifestyle, and antisocial) has strong empirical support.

(continued)

Psychopathy Checklist-Revised (PCL-R) (Hare, 1991, 2003)
PCL-R Items in the hierarchical two-factor, four-facet model

Factor 1: Interpersonal/Affective

Facet 1: Interpersonal

Glibness/superficial charm
Grandiose sense of self-worth
Pathological lying
Conning/manipulative

Facet 2: Affective

Lack of remorse or guilt
Shallow affect
Callous/lack of empathy
Failure to accept responsibility

Factor 2: Social Deviance

Facet 3: Lifestyle

Need for stimulation/proneness to boredom
Parasitic lifestyle
Lack of realistic, long-term goals
Impulsivity
Irresponsibility

Facet 4: Antisocial

Poor behavioural controls
Early behavioural problems
Juvenile delinquency
Revocation of conditional release
Criminal versatility

Items not loaded on to any factor or facet

Promiscuous sexual behaviour
Many short-term marital relationships

While Hare (2003) estimates that about 1% of the general population are psychopaths Cooke (1998) reports levels of psychopathy in British prisons of 8 to 22%. Coid (1992) found 77% of violent prisoners to be psychopathic. According to FBI reports, 44% of all police officer murders in 1992 were committed by psychopaths (Hare, 1993). Psychopathy appears to be particularly high within samples of rapists, with reports as high as 43% among serial rapists or rapists who killed their victims (Hare, 1996). Thus, as would be expected, psychopathy is disproportionately indicated among offenders.

Psychopaths also differ from other offenders. The indications are that they begin offending at an earlier age, commit a wider range of crimes and reoffend sooner once released (Hare, 2003). Research studies report that the recidivism rate of psychopaths is very high. In their study of 299 offenders, Serin and Amos (1995) found that 65% of the psychopaths were convicted of another crime within three years while only 25% of non-psychopaths had been reconvicted. In similar vein, Quincey, Rice and Harris (1995) report reconviction rates of 80% within six years of release from prison for psychopathic sexual offenders, compared to 20% for their non-psychopathic counterparts.

Beyond Simple Empiricism

It is worth repeating that every crime and every criminal is different. Therefore it is very unlikely that we can create empirically based, scientifically developed, detailed, but generic 'profiles' that will describe, for example, every burglar who breaks in through a window, or every murderer who uses a knife brought to the crime scene with him.

In principle, it would be possible to conduct numerous analyses of the relationships between all the different sorts of offender characteristics and all the different possible offending actions for every type of crime. There are studies that have approached the determination of the profiling equations in such an atheoretical way, simply attempting to establish A-C relations empirically, for example Farrington and Lambert (2007). But the accumulation of empirical relationships without any overall guiding framework is somewhat haphazard and extremely sensitive to the vagaries of any particular data set. This is in part a product of the canonical nature of the relationship (see Chapter 5) such that changes in one offending action can alter the whole pattern of characteristics implied by a criminal event. Therefore a fundamental challenge in developing solutions to the profiling equations is to identify the substantive nature of the processes that underlie any relationships. The narrative framework developed in Chapter 6 is a start in this direction.

What is being advocated here is the need for some general principles and processes that can be drawn on for any given crime, or series of crimes. In combination these can contribute both to the understanding of what is happening in a crime and have practical, operational utility. This is really using the idea that a 'theory' or 'model' is a way of going 'beyond the data' (Burch, 2006). It is a way of drawing out principles that are not simply a reflection of any given study or the results of a single analysis or a particular set of data.

The basis for making inferences, then, can be sought in the theories that explore the differences between individuals, theories of personality differences or of forms of individual variation, theories about how people come to be criminal. It is helpful to review these theories and consider the way they may be applied to the inference problem. But in keeping with our focus on criminal actions we will see how these explanations of criminality can be related to models of what it is that criminals actually do.

An Action System of Crime Differentiation

One framework, which allows us to go beyond any particular data set to make generalisations and to help the search for further relationships, that seems to be very fruitful for considering crime and criminality, is the action system approach.

The action system model is derived from Parsons' (cf. Parsons and Shills, 1951) exploration of sociopsychological systems. Their work is rooted in cybernetics and related attempts to model social and psychological processes as systems of interactions. Parsons and his colleagues were much criticised for the abstruseness of the model and difficulties in operationalising its central concepts but Shye (1985b) developed a robust and relatively straightforward conceptualisation of behavioural action systems that is directly open to empirical test.

Parsons' starting point was that all living systems are essentially:

- 'Open' in that they must interact with their surroundings in order to survive.
- Organised in that they contain distinct entities that can be distinguished from each other but that contain a recognisable relationship to each other – they are 'structured'.
- They have some stability in these components and their relationships over time.

Any system containing these properties is regarded as an 'action system'. Shye argues that the definition of an action system implies that any event in which the living system is engaged will have a source for its emergence and a location of the actualisation of that event. Furthermore the source may be within the system or external to it, as may be its manifestation. This gives rise to four possible forms of event:

INTERNAL SOURCE – EXTERNAL ACTUALISATION

Those events that emerge inside the system and are actualised outside – which Shye called the *expressive mode*, which often reflects individualistic aspects of the system.

EXTERNAL SOURCE – EXTERNAL ACTUALISATION

Events emerging outside and manifested outside – *adaptive mode*, which typically focus on shaping physical aspects of the environment,

INTERNAL SOURCE – INTERNAL ACTUALISATION

Events emerging within and actualised within the system – *integrative mode*, relating to intrapersonal processes, and

EXTERNAL SOURCE – INTERNAL ACTUALISATION

Events emerging outside and manifested inside the system – *conservative mode*, having cultural significance.

Criminal Action Systems

A very interesting implication here is that the different modes reflect different forms of criminal behaviour and explanations for crime. Canter and his colleagues (for example, Fritzon *et al.*, 2001) have demonstrated the utility of such an approach when applied to criminal behaviour. They further developed the action system model by linking it to dominant theories in the explanation and differentiation of arson, showing its power in combining a number of different theoretical perspectives.

The widely cited distinction between crime as having some instrumental purpose as opposed to being 'expressive' (of significance in its own right) is apparent in the division between the Integrative and Conservative modes, which are concerned with the impact on the individual, and the Adaptive and Expressive action modes that are externally directed actions on the environment, thus better understood as instrumental. It is important to note here that the meaning implied by Fesbach's (1964) original use of the term 'expressive' does not correspond to the action system meaning.

Theories of crime that distinguish between individual/personal and social/interpersonal mechanisms relate to the action system in a different way. The social/interpersonal theories

Table 7.3 Action system modes related to theories of crime and Fesbach's distinctions.

	'Expressive' (Fesbach, 1962)	Instrumental (Fesbach, 1962)
Individual theories	Integrative	Expressive
Interpersonal theories	Conservative	Adaptive

relate more readily to Adaptive and Conservative modes of actions that are a response to factors external to the individual whereas the more individually oriented theories of criminality are more in accord with the Expressive and Integrative modes that have their origins within the person.

The relationship to established frameworks and broad theories of crime therefore redefines the modes of action in a criminal context, drawing these together in a way that provides new insights into the different forms of criminal functioning or style.

- The *Integrative* mode is identified as a mode of functioning that has individually focused, expressive components. This implies interactions between the target of the crime and the criminal will have personal significance or a form of 'pseudo-intimacy' (cf. Canter, 1995).
- By contrast the *Adaptive* mode is a social/interpersonal but instrumental activity in which the individual is seeking direct gain from the world and others.
- The *Conservative* mode within a criminal context reflects interpersonal processes that are instrumental in nature, most commonly including the manipulation of others as a dominant objective.
- The *Expressive* mode is a targeting of others as a demonstration or expression of individualistic issues rather than as retaliation. Overt hostility against others would be a typical manifestation of this distinct mode of criminal functioning.

The Example of Arson

The differences in offending style that these generic action system modes produce are most readily understood with a specific illustration. One of the clearest is a study of 230 arson incidents by Fritzon, Canter and Wilton (2001), which was a development of the earlier study by Canter and Fritzon (1998). They identified 46 features that could be drawn from police and fire brigade records of arson on which they carried out an SSA, the results of which are given in Figure 7.2. The SSA readily lends itself to interpretation in terms of the action system. The style of offending produced by the adaptive mode, where both the source and the actualisation is external, is one in which the behaviour is an attempt to change aspects of the external environment for some instrumental purpose. Typically, these will be arsons that are attempts to hide evidence of some other criminal activity or arsons for insurance fraud purposes.

A rather different style of offending is produced by the expressive mode (internal source, external actualisation). Here, the behaviour is an attempt to impact on the environment for a more expressive purpose. This will be typically revealed as arsons that are attacks on buildings of significance to the person.

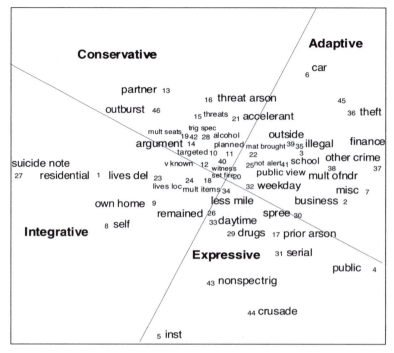

Figure 7.2 Smallest space analysis of 46 features of arson cases across 230 cases.

Source: Fritzon and Canter (2000). Reproduced with permission.

The style of offending produced by the conservative mode, where the source of the action is external but the actualisation internal, is one in which the behaviour is an attempt to redress an aversive internal state produced by some external factor or person. The desired impact is on the self, through revenge against someone. This underpins arsons that are targeted attacks against specific individuals, as a form of retaliation.

The integrative mode (internal source, internal actualisation) produces a style of offending that is an attempt to target and destroy the self as a response to a state of emotional distress, revealed in self-destructive, often suicidal forms of arson.

The action system model goes further than just being the identification of four modes of action. The basic definitions of the modes give rise to conceptual interrelationships that can be represented as regions of a notional space as illustrated in Figure 7.3.

This figure indicates that the integrative mode is hypothesised to contrast with the adaptive and the expressive with the conservative, so that in any study there would be higher correlations between any variables reflecting adjacent modes than modes that are opposite each other. Further, Expressive and Conservative can be thought of as products of the Adaptive and integrative modes so that the latter two would tend to be more highly correlated than the former two. This is captured in Figure 7.3 by having Expressive and Conservative further from each other than integrative and adaptive.

A simplified version of the SSA in Figure 7.2 is given in Figure 7.4, derived from a variety of different data sets, including acts of terrorism (Fritzon, Canter and Wilton, 2001). This is

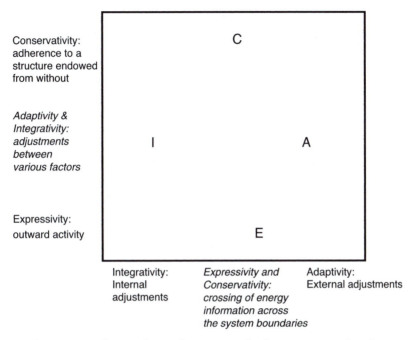

Conservativity:
adherence to a
structure endowed
from without

*Adaptivity &
Integrativity:
adjustments
between
various factors*

Expressivity:
outward activity

C

I   A

E

Integrativity: *Expressivity and*   Adaptivity:
Internal   *Conservativity:*   External adjustments
adjustments   *crossing of energy*
                          information across
                          the system boundaries

Figure 7.3 The conceptual interrelationships among the functioning modes of an action system, represented by means of geometric-spatial proximities.

represented as an ellipse rather than a circle. In other words, it is between the Expressive and Conservative modes that the conceptual distinction is most marked, Conservative actions being an inward absorption while expressive actions are an outward expulsion.

Linking to Offender Characteristics

The strength of this model is revealed in the opportunity it provides for hypothesising characteristics of the offender that may be inferred from the dominant mode the arson indicates. This provides a scientific basis for elaborating the 'profiling equation' central to an investigative psychology approach to evidence-based models for deriving offender characteristics from crime

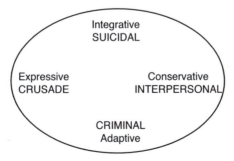

Integrative
SUICIDAL

Expressive   Conservative
CRUSADE   INTERPERSONAL

CRIMINAL
Adaptive

Figure 7.4 The schematic representation of the relationships between the modes of an action system and themes in arson and terrorism derived from empirical study.

scene information. So that, for example, in the case of arson it would be hypothesised that those who exhibit a strongly adaptive mode may well have a recognisable criminal background, but those whose mode is integrative are more likely to have a known history of mental illness.

Fritzon, Canter and Wilton (2001) explored these hypotheses by analysing the characteristics of arsonists and so that they could identify the main themes that distinguished them.

- Adaptive: delinquent. These were offenders who had been cautioned previously for criminal activities and had come to the attention of the social services, usually because of problems either in the home or at school.
- Expressive: repeat arsonist. These were people for whom arson was a significant aspect of their ways of dealing with others. As a consequence this would be reflected in their 'going missing' from routine daily activities such as work or school in order to set fires, as well as making fire alarm telephone calls.
- Integrative: psychiatric history. This theme is seen as fundamentally disintegrative, in which arson emerges out of the person's self-destructive emotions; suicide attempts and a history of mental illness are strongly inter-correlated in this theme.
- Conservative: failed relationship. Here the arson is seen as a direct means of affecting a person significant to the arsonist.

The central hypothesis, then, is that the action modes that relate to offender characteristics will relate most closely to those behavioural action modes that are most similar to them. By deriving scores for each of the four characteristics and each of the four action themes it was possible for Fritzon, Canter and Wilton (2001) to demonstrate the power of this hypothesis as shown in Figure 7.5. There the relationship between the Actions and Characteristics can be clearly seen to reflect the posited model. Figure 7.5 can thus be thought of as one illustration of what the A→C equation looks like with actual data.

Each of the action variables forms a region with the characteristic variable that has the same action system mode. Furthermore, the Expressive and Conservative modes are further from each other than the Adaptive and Integrative. This study therefore provides a benchmark for developing Investigative Psychology research. It has direct theoretical implications as well clear practical value. By knowing the target of arson, a reasonable set of inferences can be made of the characteristics of the offender.

Narratives as Action Systems

The action systems framework sees the key distinctions in behaviour as lying in the source of the action and where the effect or actualisation of that action is directed. Once we recognise that in narrative terms these are aspects of the offence that will relate to the offender and his interpretation of his role and other aspects that relate to the target and the impact that is desired, it becomes clear that the criminal narratives will inevitably imply particular action system modes. The adventure, tragedy, quest and irony narratives described in Chapter 6 can

Figure 7.5 Smallest space analysis of arson actions and characteristics.

each be understood then as elaborations of a core action system mode of functioning (Canter and Youngs, in press, d).

The adventure narrative is one in which life is seen as an opportunity for mastery of the environment and effective interactions that will provide the protagonist with satisfaction and tangible reward (key criminal role: 'professional'). The actions produced by the adventure narrative are direct exchanges of effort and skill for the acquisition of material gains (external effect), prompted by their availability in the environment (external source of the action). The mode of functioning fundamental to this narrative then is an Adaptive one.

The tragedy narrative is a story of the wronged or deprived hero whose fate it now is to seek vengeance to redress this hurt (as epitomised by the key 'revenger' role). Underlying the adoption of these roles is a conservative action system mode of functioning. The behaviour is a retaliation, the offender's response to having been wronged (external source) but the concern, whether the actual target of the action is the self or another, is only with the impact on the self and the individual's internal state (internal effect).

The quest narrative describes an individual on a mission, seeking heroically as a demonstration of his manliness, to salvage his honour by imposing his will on events and situations within the world (as epitomised by the key 'hero' role). Within the quest narrative then the underlying direction of the action is outwards, aimed at changing aspects of the external environment. This action, rather than being a reaction to an external wrong, as in the tragedy, has its origins in the offender's own sense of entitlement. The fundamental mode of functioning of an individual pursuing a quest narrative then is an Expressive one (Canter and Youngs, in press, d).

The Irony narrative is one of a generalised impotence and meaninglessness in which nothing makes any sense and there are no rules (encapsulated by the key 'victim' role). The offences characterised by the playing out of this narrative role will be Integrative events (Canter and Youngs, 2009). In a meaningless and senseless world, the only impact desired will be on the self (internal actualisation) and if nothing matters the only origin or prompt to any action will be the internal sense of emptiness and need (internal source).

This gives rise then to an integrated *Narrative Action System* model of criminal differentiation (Canter and Youngs, 2009) in which four styles of offending are identified in terms of key role, action system mode and criminal narrative:

- the Hero's Expressive Quest
- the Professional's Adaptive Adventure
- the Revenger's Conservative Tragedy
- the Victim's Integrative Irony.

Forms of Inference: Towards a Narrative Action System Model of Inference

The mythology of 'profiling' implies near psychic proposals about precise details of unknown offenders, such as whether they will wear a buttoned double-breasted suit or drive a pick-up truck. Often these are simple extrapolations from base rates, or inspired guesses. Wrong guesses are not reported, so the impression is given that all guesses are correct. A more scientific approach recognises the complexity of deriving any inferences from offence activity. But fundamentally the scientific perspective requires a theory or model that helps us to understand and explain how and why relationships exist on which inferences can be based.

Psychological explanations draw attention to a variety of processes or forms of consistency that could link criminal actions to characteristics (see Table 7.4).

Table 7.4 Main forms of investigative psychology consistencies.

Explanations	Inference process	Mode of action	Narrative	Key role
Individualistic – emotional	Characteristics cause the actions	Integrative	Irony	Victim
Social: interpersonal interactions	Interpersonal context links actions and characteristics.	Conservative	Tragedy	Revenger
Social: subcultural/ experiential	Subcultural context shares actions and characteristics.	Adaptive	Adventure	Professional
Individualistic – dispositional and cognitive	Actions are the characteristics	Expressive	Quest	Hero

Table 7.5   The narrative action system model of inference.

Consistency	Main inferences
Intellectual	Intellect
Emotional	Emotional state
Interpersonal	Role of victim
Instrumental	Skills
Experiential	Forensic contact
Offending	Antecedents
Spatial	Location

The specification of this range of types of inferences that may be drawn is not meant to imply that each type of inference will be possible from every crime scene. As Canter and Youngs (in press, d) note, the types of characteristics that can be inferred depend upon the type of psychological process that underpins the offending behaviour. In simple terms, a highly aggressive offence may tell us something about the interpersonal style of the offender but the assumption that intellect will also be indicated may be a mistake. This recognition allows us to move beyond these separate processes for relating actions to characteristics to develop an overall model of the different forms of inference process (Canter and Youngs, in press, a). This is integrated with the narrative action system model (NAS) of the differences in offending style to show what sorts of inferences are going to be possible in relation to which sorts of NAS offending styles (see Table 7.5).

The starting point for developing a formal model for inferences is this identification of the dominant emphases of any criminal actions. In order to develop inferences from these variations the agency that they are part of then needs to be elaborated. It is the active role of the criminal that links his actions to his characteristics. The criminal narratives and the key roles that are central to these provide a particularly interesting way of developing an understanding of this agency. This draws on the discovery that it is fruitful to consider four major narrative forms, which in the criminal context can be labelled professional (adventure), hero (quest), revenger (tragedy) and victim (irony). As outlined above, each of these implies a different dominant mode of acting, giving rise to a narrative action system (NAS) model.

Careful consideration of each narrative mode leads to specification of the particular form of consistency out of which A→C coherence can emerge for any crime, although one of these may dominate for any given crime. It should be emphasised that although all crimes contain some aspect of all these modes of transaction, the one that is dominant for a particular crime will typically be the focus for developing the most important inferences. Canter and Youngs (in press, d) propose that these most productive routes to investigative inferences will be:

- *Cognitive and dispositional consistencies* between actions and characteristics that are particularly relevant for offenders who see themselves as heroes on a quest, overcoming challenges. These demonstrative aspects of offending will relate most clearly to the approach the offender has to dealing with the world, including the social and other skills he has. This may also be revealed in aspects of his general lifestyle and interests – for example, an interest in survivalist recreation.

- *Instrumental and experiential consistencies* relate to the job-specific competencies and abilities of the offender who sees himself as a professional involved in an adventure. The instrumental issues revealed in the actions of the offender who offends in this way may indicate aspects of his criminal history and criminal contacts.
- *Interpersonal consistencies* of how the offender deals with others, particularly relevant to a person who feels he lives a tragedy narrative in which he tries to redress his sense of being demeaned by others. The interpersonal character of the crime would be expected to relate to the offender's social relationships and in some case may indicate gender.
- *Emotional consistencies* are especially relevant for offenders for whom life makes little sense and believe they are helpless and confused, as in the irony narrative. The emotionality of the crime relates to the offenders' psychological state and is also often related to his age.
- *Spatial consistencies* – all these consistencies above relate in various ways to the crime location and the implications that has for where the offender may be based, as discussed in Chapter 8.

Summary

- In deriving inferences from an offence, those actions which the offender determines directly will be most useful.
- Drawing inferences depends on identifying the salient aspects of the crime – those actions that are behaviourally important. Salience is influenced by issues relating to the typicality and base-rate occurrences of the actions. Determining salience also requires an understanding of the circumstances upon which any action may be contingent and the significance of interactions between actions.
- There is sufficient consistency in criminal action to allow inferences.
- The style of criminal action will be consistent with noncriminal aspects of the individual and his behaviour rather than representing a form of displacement activity.
- With the notable exception of psychopathic offenders, an individual's patterns of criminal action can be understood in terms of normal psychological and social processes rather than requiring special models of abnormal behaviour.
- The action systems framework provides a basis for understanding differences in offending style.
- The different criminal narratives imply and are consistent with particular action systems modes. As such, a narrative action system model of criminal differentiation can be elaborated. This identifies four offending styles, referred to as (a) the hero's expressive quest, (b) the professional's adaptive adventure, (c) the revenger's conservative tragedy and (d) the victim's integrative irony.

- Criminal narratives provide the active underlying processes by which aspects of the individual can be linked to their offending actions.
- A narrative action system model for inferences is therefore proposed. This highlights different inference pathways according to the specific offending style.
  - Inferences based on cognitive and dispositional consistencies are identified as significant for Expressive Quest forms of offending.
  - Instrumental and experiential consistencies will facilitate the inferences that are possible in Adaptive Adventure offending modes.
  - Interpersonal consistencies will underpin the inferences that are most productive in relation to Conservative Tragedy forms of offending.
  - Consistencies in individualistic emotional factors will be most productive in Integrative Irony forms of offending.

Further Reading

Books

Parsons, T. (1968) *The Structure of Social Action: Weber*, Free Press, New York. A digital version is available via Google books.

Articles

Almond, L., Duggan, L., Shine, J. and Canter, D. (2005) Test of the arson action system model in an incarcerated population. *Psychology, Crime and Law*, **11** (1), 1–15.

Canter, D. and Fritzon, K. (1998) Differentiating arsonists: a model of firesetting actions and characteristics. *Legal and Criminological Psychology*, **3**, 73–96.

Fritzon, K., Canter, D. and Wilton, Z. (2001) The application of an action systems model to destructive behaviour: the examples of arson and terrorism. *Behavioral Sciences and the Law*, **19** (5–6), 657–90.

Shye, S. (1985) Non-metric multivariate models for behavioural action systems, in D. Canter (ed.) *Facet Theory: Approaches to Social Research*, Springer-Verlag, New York.

Shye, S. (1989) The systemic life quality model: a basis for urban renewal evaluation. *Social Indicators Research*, **21**, 343–78.

Questions for Discussion and Research

1. Consider the crimes described in Boxes 7.1 and 7.2. Could they have been committed by the same person? Explore the similarities and differences using the 10 pointers in Table 7.2.

2. As discussed in Chapter 5 the term *modus operandi* or M.O. is widely used both in fictional accounts of offences and in real life discussions by detectives. Although this Latin phrase literally means 'method of operating', which could vary from one crime to another, it is usually taken to mean the characteristic patterns and style of

committing crimes that any given offender has – but exactly how can these 'patterns and styles' be clearly defined and identified? Consider the 10 aspects of a crime that an offender has influence over, listed in Table 7.1, and review how they may be reflected in an M.O. Does this imply that M.O. is probably too ambiguous a general term to be used in any psychological research?

3. Why might there not be total similarity in criminal actions from one offence to the next? What implications does this have?

4. Consider how the narrative action system modes might produce differences in offending patterns for a crime of your choice. What inferences are likely to be possible in relation to the different offending styles?

5. Why do you think that the study of arson has revealed some of the clearest results so far in the study of criminal action systems?

CHAPTER 8

Criminal Psychogeography

In This Chapter

Learning Objectives

When you have completed this chapter you should be able to:

1. Understand what is meant by the terms 'propinquity' and 'morphology' when used to describe criminal spatial behaviour.

2. Compare and contrast the behavioural and cognitive approaches to understanding criminal geography.
3. Evaluate 'route-following' and 'mental mapping' approaches.
4. Describe the routine activities and rational choice theories of geographical behaviour.
5. Appreciate the relevance of the issue of 'locatedness' to the study of criminal spatial activity.
6. Identify some of the key factors which may influence an offender's crime location choices.
7. Understand the notion of 'domocentricity'.
8. Appreciate how narrative theory relates to criminals' 'mental maps'.

Synopsis

The principles that shape where an offender acts can be elucidated by consideration of the narrative that is implicit to all aspects of the offending. Narratives, after all, have a physical context. Personal life stories are bounded by the locations in which events occur. How those events unfold in space is derived in part from the nature of the storyline. For example, it is rare for an adventure narrative to take place in one fixed area. The various episodes require different settings to keep this type of drama moving. On the other hand, an impulsive act of revenge, or seeking out of opportunistic targets, is likely to cover a limited domain and to be focused on particular areas. This framework allows the consideration of how offence locations relate to the lives of offenders.

A commonly cited framework that integrates the offender's non-criminal life with his criminal life gives emphasis to the routine activities and related paths that offenders follow. This focuses on the criminal opportunities come across as part of daily life. However, the IP viewpoint that offenders shape their lives around a personal perspective puts more emphasis on their internal models of the opportunities for crime, which they may actively seek, and less on passive learning shaped by their surroundings. Such a perspective is informed by exploring the offender's map-like representations of where he lives and carries out his crimes.

Two major aspects of offence location choice emerge from consideration of how they are shaped by the offender's personal narrative: propinquity and morphology. The first deals with the closeness of the crime locations to key places in the offender's life, notably his/her home or base. The second explores the pattern or overall geometry of the distribution of the offences, being a reflection of internal mental maps of possible offence locations.

Being able to model criminal spatial behaviour has special investigative value because of the way in which it helps the police to channel resources. It can thus provide direct help for a number of investigative strategies. Such models also lay the groundwork for developing sophisticated decision support systems for police investigations. But to be really effective it is essential to look beyond the dots on the map that indicate where a crime has occurred and understand the processes that take an offender to any given location.

Box 8.1 Where Does the Offender Live?

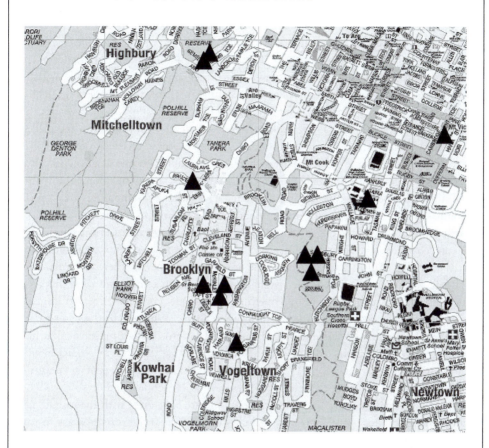

The triangles indicate the locations in which an aggressive prowler was seen. Can you estimate where he might have been living? Would it be within the area covered by the map? Why do you come to this conclusion? His actual residence is indicated at the end of the chapter.

We are grateful to Samantha Lundrigan for the analysis and case details.

Modelling Criminals' Use of Space

One of the most interesting and productive areas of IP to emerge in recent years has been the exploration of *where* crimes happen. It might have been expected that crime locations are either just a consequence of the opportunity for any particular criminal activity, or due to some idiosyncratic characteristics of the offender. At the very least, many would assume that criminals would take care to ensure that the place they choose to offend would have no obvious association with other aspects of their lives, especially with such crucial information as where they live. However, a set of remarkably consistent findings about the distances and distributions of offenders' crime site locations has emerged from many studies (as brought together by Canter and Youngs, 2008ba). The theoretical and practical importance of these consistencies does indicate that there is value in a closer consideration of how people make use of their environments and the implications that this may have for where they offend.

The starting point for considering offence locations is the assumption that, whether they are aware of it or not, offenders are making some sort of active choice about the places in which they will commit their crimes. Running through all these considerations is the idea that the offender has some influence over where he commits his crime. It also does assume that the crime location is not totally random. Even if it were a spur of the moment impulse, it would still have to be in a location where the offender was when that impulse is acted on. True randomness would only be possible if the offender was randomly in a variety of locations.

The patterns that emerge out of these implicit choices are not necessarily assumed to be under any conscious control of the offender. There may be conscious choices about avoiding an area where the criminal may be recognised, or seeking out an area where particular targets are possible, but how this shapes the spatial geometry of their crimes and what this reveals about them is not usually likely to be something the offender considers. Even an impulsive, unplanned offence gives rise to an inherent location choice. What might the bases for such choices be? How might an offender develop behavioural patterns that are reflected in the places in which offences are committed? It is worth emphasising that these are questions about the offender's psychological processes. They relate to, but are distinct from, general concerns in environmental criminology (as reviewed in books such as Hirschfield and Bowers, 2001).

Criminologists who explore the geography of crime are concerned with the overall distribution of where crimes occur. This may include examination of the sorts of areas in which offenders tend to live, but the information they deal with is about overall aggregates of criminality. This work has proven very valuable in identifying the sorts of areas most at risk of crime, often referred to as criminal 'hotspots' (cf. Sherman *et al.*, 1989), which in turn can guide policing and schemes such as 'Neighbourhood Watch'. However, that is rather different from exploring the actions of the individual criminal, which are the focus of the present chapter.

Contrasting Models of Environmental Learning: Route Following or Mental Mapping?

Two rather different fundamental models of how people build up patterns of spatial activity can be found in the mid-twentieth-century discussion of how learning takes place. Although this early work was rooted in studies of laboratory rats finding their way through mazes, the general principles that emerged still provide a useful framework for distinguishing between prevalent approaches to the modelling of criminal spatial activity.

The debate over how learning to deal with our surrounding takes place was often characterised as between Hull (1943) and Tolman (1948). Although the arguments are linked to the names of specific psychologists they were actually articulating two different traditions in psychology. These different traditions are still the basis for discussions about criminal geography, even though the people putting forward their models of offenders' location choices often do not make clear (and may not even realise) the sort of psychological assumptions they are making.

In essence, Hull (1943) proposed that learning was based on the buildup of a series of habits derived directly from experience. For Hull, there was little need to form any sort of internal mental representation of an environment. All that was needed was to incorporate a set of routine actions. This is fundamentally behaviourist in the sense that the learning process is seen as a set of linked behaviours that are acquired over a number of journeys. By contrast, Tolman (1948) argued for the development of internal representations ('mental maps') that allowed the individual to make choices that go beyond his/her immediate experience.

Detailed consideration of their arguments reveals that Tolman and Hull had much more subtle ways of considering human learning than this oversimplification of 'habit learning' versus 'map learning', but the broad differences between them offers a way of thinking about distinctions between models of criminals' spatial activity. Both approaches draw on the assumption that, rather than being entirely opportunistic, offenders' crime locations have a discernable logic and are anything but random.

The arguments of both Hull and Tolman have some validity. The route-following and mental-mapping perspectives can each be shown to apply under different conditions or in combination in certain circumstances. Each does however draw attention to different aspects of location choice. It is therefore helpful to think of the behavioural approach of Hull being most compatible with the processes of *propinquity* that lead to the tendency for criminals to have an optimal range over which they offend which is often not far from their home or other base. The mental mapping approach of Tolman, on the other hand, draws attention to the overall *morphology* of the crime locations; the general patterns, structures, or geometry of where the crimes occur.

The Behavioural Approach and Propinquity

Although little recognised, established theories of offender geography proceed from one or other core psychological standpoints. The model favoured, at least implicitly, in North America, notably by Brantingham and Brantingham (1981) is more Hullian, in that the assumption is made that the offender moves along familiar paths and learns of criminal possibilities along these paths. It is out of this perspective that the notion of a 'journey to crime' emerges. Offenders' spatial decision making is assumed to relate very strongly to established routes and actual journeys. Within this framework emphasis is put on the actual streets and pathways that offenders may follow.

Brantingham and Brantingham (1981) developed the consideration of the familiarity a criminal has with an area beyond the home. They included job and recreational experiences, drawing attention to an 'action space'. This consists of a network of paths and nodes which an offender would know well.

Routine Activity

In proposing an action space for criminals, Brantingham and Brantingham (1981) saw crime as a byproduct of other activities in which the criminal engages. Originally developed by Cohen and Felson (1979), this has become known as 'routine activity theory', seeing crimes as opportunities taken within the awareness space of day-to-day life. The central hypothesis is that criminals learn of possibilities for crime, or seek them out, as part of their daily, legitimate actions; visiting friends, going to work, recreation, shopping and the like. Recently, Wiles and Costello (2000) have reported results from interviews with burglars and those stealing cars that lend support to the earlier speculations of the Brantinghams. The interviewees indicated that even when they travelled some distance from their place of residence to carry out a crime, the places they went to were influenced by contacts they had in those areas. The routine activity explanation for offender spatial behaviour has usually been put forward to explain the target or victim selection stage of an offence. The approach focuses on the discovery of 'opportunities' in the form of victims and targets during non-criminal activities.

It has also been suggested that routine activity theory can equally be applied, for example, to the body disposal stage of a murder, especially in stranger and serial murders, where the offender has to identify an appropriate location to leave the body. The difference lies in the temporal stage of the offence. The likely offender has become an actual offender, the suitable target has been located and the crime has been committed. For the offender the search moves from that for a victim to that for a disposal location. These same arguments could thus be applied to many other spatial aspects of an offence, such as where stolen materials may be hidden, or where an abducted victim may be kept.

Rational Choice

A different emphasis to routine activity that gives more credence to the decisions an offender makes has been referred to by Cornish and Clarke (1986) as the 'rational choice' explanation of criminality. This has direct applications to spatial behaviour. The key premise here is that at any stage of a crime the criminal makes choices which exhibit a tradeoff between increased opportunity/greater reward on the one hand, and the costs of time, effort, and risk, on the other. At its most elementary this leads to the argument that the further an offender travels from home the greater the risks and costs, so an increase in benefits would be expected. The risks or costs of crime are those associated with formal punishment should the offender be apprehended. The benefits of a criminal action are the net rewards of crime and include not only material gains, but also intangible benefits such as emotional satisfaction. For example, a serial murderer may place a great distance between his home and the place where he disposes of a victim's body in order to distance himself from the offence, or to reach a particular location with which he associates some emotional satisfaction (the benefit). However, the risk of apprehension may increase the further he travels (the cost).

The 'rational choice' framework is actually a form of economic model in which decisions are the result of an analysis of the relationships between costs and benefits. Like all such simple-minded economic models, the fundamental assumptions are that the decision maker has complete knowledge of the costs and benefits and is indeed making a simple logical, 'rational' choice amongst the options. In recent years, economists have realised what psychologists have always known. People are not completely informed of the options and consequences for their actions, nor do they make unemotional decisions. Spearheaded by Daniel Kahneman, who won the Nobel Prize for economics in 2002 for 'having integrated insights from psychological research into economic science, especially concerning human judgment and decision-making under uncertainty', a new area known as 'behavioural economics' has emerged (recently overviewed in popular form by Thaler and Sunstein (2008)). This emphasises all the ways in which judgements are not simply rational.

Bennett and Wright (1984) pre-empted these ideas in relation to criminal activity when they suggested that the concept of limited rationality best explains the spatial behaviour of offenders. Here, it is not presumed that offenders weigh all the relevant factors every time an offence is contemplated, but other factors (moods, motives, perceptions of opportunity, alcohol, the influence of others, and their attitude toward risk), apparently unrelated to the logic of the decision, often take over. Bennett and Wright conclude that offenders are behaving rationally as they see it at the time but what might be perceived as rational on one occasion might not be so perceived on another. However, Kahneman's studies suggest that there will be common biases in offenders' decision processes so that the 'rationality' of the decision may not be an issue that the offender considers.

Integrating Routine Activity and Rational Choice

The proposal of limited rationality implies some random process in crime site selection. This would mean that offenders would not be expected to move systematically through an area committing crime. By drawing this together with a rational choice approach then a domain of operation would be hypothesised in which the central influences of familiarity were having an effect but with the subjective factors introducing some degree of randomness into the selection of sites. In so far as routine activity was the dominant influence, the home/base and routes frequently used would play a pivotal role. In so far as rational choice was dominant, the actual qualities of the crime location, such as the risks involved in gaining access, and the opportunities for benefit it provided, such as appropriate victims or property, would be primary.

However, all of these considerations of offenders' choices draw attention to their limited contact with and knowledge of opportunities for crime. This leads to an emphasis on the likelihood that offenders will commit crimes close to the places with which they are familiar, most notably where they have their base or home. This gives rise to one of the main principles that characterises offender geographical activity – *propinquity* – especially closeness to home. From the narrative perspective, this illustrates the very limited personal storyline of many offenders, for whom their everyday settings act as constraints on where they will travel and the possibilities they will explore.

Locatedness

These considerations of the behavioural and cognitive processes that underlie criminal activity assume that the crimes have a distinct location. This may seem an obvious assumption for a burglary or a robbery but it becomes more open to question if, for example, the crimes consist of telephone calls or fraud carried out over the Internet. However, there are examples of these crimes, which apparently lack a specific geographical location in physical terms but that, nonetheless, still reveal meaningful spatial patterns (Canter, 2005). These crimes exist in a 'virtual', or cognitive, space that the offender uses. For instance, he may only telephone local numbers, or even though the fraud is perpetrated over the Internet, the fraudster will still use local banks to establish fraudulent accounts.

The issue of 'locatedness' also becomes more complicated when there are a number of different locations associated with any given crime. For instance, in a murder case there may be a point of first contact with a victim – a location to which the victim was taken and assaulted, another location where the victim was murdered and yet another location where the murderer disposed of the body. There may even be other locations where clothing or stolen material is left. All of these locations are of interest to investigators, as is the relationship between them. All of them may also have some systematic relationship to the place where the offender is based.

The locatedness of the offender's base is a further complication. Generally it is assumed to be where the offender lives, or at least typically sleeps at night. But the term 'base' or even 'anchor point' is often used because the key point of relevance may not be where the offender lives. The offender may be a vagrant with 'no fixed abode', or be venturing out from a friend's or partner's house. Criminals may also use pubs or nightclubs as a base, or commit their crimes more directly near to where they can obtain a supply of illegal drugs than to where they are living. All of these possibilities, and many others, add challenges to attempts to explain and model criminal spatial behaviour.

Box 8.2 Crime Location Choice

A fundamental assumption in understanding offence behaviour is that the crime locations are not random. Of course the whole of geography and psychology are based on the premise that human behaviour has some pattern and structure to it but it is only in recent years that there has been a determined, systematic search for the geographical patterns within crime locations.

It must also be assumed that the patterns are not solely a function of the opportunities for crime or broad social processes. There has to be some aspect of any given individual offender's ways of dealing with the possibilities for crime that influences where his criminal acts take place.

Consider the locations of your own (presumably non-criminal) activities. What sorts of patterns do they reveal? How do they relate to fixed 'anchors' in your life, for example where you sleep, where you work/study, where you eat, places for recreation or shopping, friends? What opportunities for crime are present around these locations?

Without consulting any published map draw a sketch map of these key locations in your life. Having done that compare your sketch with an actual map. What do the differences between your sketch and the actual map reveal about you and your activities?

The Decay Function

One important constituent of models of crime location choice is the proposal that the further criminals are from home, the less likely they are to commit a crime. The relationship between distance and frequency of offending, explored over 30 years ago by Turner (1969), has become known as 'distance decay'. It gets this name because of the negative exponential relationship that tends to characterise aggregate summaries of the relationship between distance from home and frequency for any given sample, as shown in Figure 8.1. The existence of such geographical decay functions was mooted by Jarvis (1850), and as Hunter and Shannon (1985) make clear, from its earliest days researchers were aware that many resource and geographical issues would modify the form that any decay function took, affecting the steepness of and variations in the slope.

In the context of crime, Turner (1969) also pointed out there are potentially a large family of functions which could characterise distance decay. Eldridge and Jones (1991) considered this in detail pointing out the behavioural implications of different functions. For example, the home could have a very strong influence on the activity of the offender, in which case the function would be expected to be very steep, decaying quickly. Or there could be a much wider area in which the offender based himself leading to much shallower functions in which the distances decay very slowly. Figure 8.1 illustrates one set of 19 functions that Canter *et al.* (2000) explored as part of their consideration of these matters. The practical and technical implications of these functions will be dealt with in Chapter 16.

Resources, Opportunity and Criminal Range

Another important set of contextual parameters are those relating to the psychological and other resources the offender has available. These reflect both his experiences as a criminal and what he has available to him to support his activities. The more resources he has, the further he is likely to travel but there will be some balance of benefit against effort. This balance will also be adjusted by the focus of his activities. If he is targeting specific types of person or object this will also distort his geographical pattern. This can be seen as a further difference between

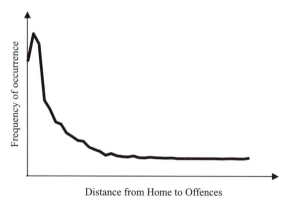

Distance from Home to Offences

Figure 8.1   Typical frequency decay function.

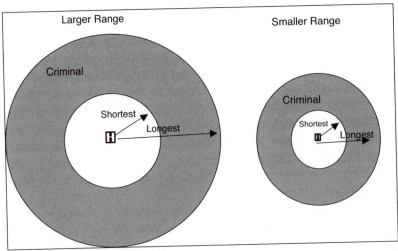

Figure 8.2   Illustration of how shortest and longest distances to crimes may be related depending upon the typical range of an offender.

the narratives of offenders who are seeking out success over a series of exciting episodes as opposed to those who feel the need to respond to pressures within themselves. The targeting of offences can take the offender far and wide on his adventures, whereas the emotionally involved offender is likely to be operating much closer to home. This emotionality can take many forms, recognisable within and between different types of crime.

All of these factors – personal resources, familiarity and opportunity, as well as the narrative drivers for a crime – lead to the expectation that most serial criminals will operate over a comfortable size of area and/or a large distance from home. This can be demonstrated by a direct consideration of the average distances offenders travel and the range for each offender as illustrated for example in Figure 8.2.

A further test of the existence of this range is to correlate the minimum distance an offender travels with the maximum distance. Do those offenders whose shortest distance from home is small tend also to have a small longest distance, and vice versa? Figure 8.3 shows one such correlation for a set of offenders. This shows a very strong correlation indicating that offenders do indeed act over an area the size of which is characteristic for them.

The Cognitive Approach and Morphology of Crime Locations

The emphasis on routine activity and a rational, if limited, set of decisions shaping crime location choice gives relatively little importance to the ways in which people actively construct their understanding of places. These frameworks tend to assume that people only act in relation to routes and journeys rather than having an overall idea of where places are in

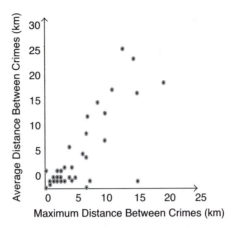

Figure 8.3 Correlations between the average and maximum distance between crimes indicating how the parameters of series tend to be high supporting the idea of a criminal range; 45 serial rapists (r = 0.8).

relation to each other. Routine activity theory puts the offender in a rather passive role in relation to the environment, only becoming aware of opportunities for crime by what the environment reveals whilst the offender is going about non-criminal activities. For although Brantingham and Brantingham (1981) had referenced the significance of criminals' mental maps, with direct citation of the original work of Lynch (1960) who explored how people made sense of cities, their models of criminal spatial patterns do not recognise the psychological implications of the process of cognitive representation of environments as was articulated by Canter (1977).

In contrast, the European perspective, most readily described by Canter (2005) explicitly takes the Tolmanian viewpoint that the offender makes choices on the basis of his/her mental map of the opportunities for crime. The theory here is that an offender builds up knowledge of an area by moving through it and carrying out crimes. The offender is not just learning a route with opportunities along it but is also creating a mental picture of the area that will fill in gaps between locations that s/he has visited. Like all of us, offenders will have an idea of where certain places are likely to be although they have never actually visited those locations, only the area around them.

In other words, rather than just knowing a linked set of routes, the assumption is that the offender has some notion of a domain, or region, of activity. Offenders may not even have a clear notion of a specific route of relevance to their crimes but they do have an idea of general locations and the broad directions in which they need to travel to get to them. Furthermore, because they are part of a general cognitive representation the offender has, they are open to influence from many different sources, including comments and suggestions from other offenders or even the consideration of transport or other maps.

Of course the offender's understanding of the risks involved will also help shape where crimes are committed. The exact journey will, from this perspective, be less significant than the overall knowledge of the possibilities for, and implications of, offending in the location/area. This perspective adds the idea of a structure or shape to where crimes will be committed – a *morphology* that goes beyond issues of closeness that are dominant from the routine activity perspective.

One particularly important consequence of this 'mental map' approach is that it is not necessary to consider the offender's actual journey to crime, with its putative routes, as the dominant way of modelling the spatial distribution of his offence locations. The overall conceptualisation of the area and opportunities is what needs to be modelled. So the relative position of locations is what is crucial and the straight-line (often called 'Euclidian' or 'crow flight') distance between them is an effective a way of representing them. This draws heavily on Canter's (1977) explorations of how people come to understand and make sense of places. He emphasised that there are two interacting psychological processes that contribute to a person's internal model of his/her surroundings. One is the process of encoding the information. This leads to various forms of distortion in the mental image. The second is how people actively make use of their surroundings. Together these give rise to an internal model that the individual draws on – a 'mental map'. This is a constantly updated setting that the person has available for acting out his personal narrative.

The mental image or 'map' is derived from the interaction between the active storing of information and the passive availability of environmental cues. The mental image that is formed influences what a person thinks is possible and where that possibility lies. This is a developing, cyclical process. The direct interaction with the surroundings in turn shapes the person's conceptualisations. Where a person does various things is consequently partly a product of what that person knows to be possible and where. Their experience shapes what they know to be possible. This will be a dynamic process that takes the offender beyond their 'routine activities' as they get to explore the possibilities for crime. It is out of these dynamic processes that the offender selects opportunities for crime.

The Map Within – Criminological Cognitive Cartography

There has been little examination of the mental representations that criminals have of the locations in which they commit their crimes, so the suppositions outlined above about individual crime location choices have yet to be thoroughly tested. This limitation is in part because the exploration of their essentially subjective, internal, mental representations is notoriously difficult. But this has not stopped psychologists and other social and behavioural scientists from at least gaining approximations for the way people cognitively structure their non-criminal transactions with the world. One procedure of interest that has been widely used actually owes its scientific origins to an urban planner, Kevin Lynch (1960). He used the device of asking people to draw sketch maps of their cities as a way of exploring their mental representations, or 'images' as he called them, of those cities. His early studies of Boston, Jersey City and Los Angeles have encouraged many other people to follow his lead, in the main because of the distorted and limited maps that people draw. These distortions and limitations are seen as indicators of the cognitive processes that shape people's transactions with their surroundings.

When considering the mental maps produced by offenders there are interesting questions about the sorts of details that offenders may recall or choose to symbolise in their representations of their geographical experiences. Do these indicate a studied examination of their surroundings or a haphazard, opportunistic approach to their selection of locations in which to offend? Of course the nature of the crime may be expected to relate to how the environment is conceptualised by the offender. Crimes that are closely tied to particular locations, such as burglaries, may be hypothesised to have stronger geographical structures than those that follow the possibilities for finding vulnerable victims, such as rape. Furthermore, some crimes may be location specific, such as targeting a specific warehouse. In all these cases the question arises as to whether the offender has some mental representation that reflects the selection of crime locations and, in turn, possibly helps to enhance the geographical focus of his crimes.

Of course, as was illustrated in some detail many years ago (Canter, 1977) and has subsequently been elaborated with great precision by Kitchen (1994), there are a number of methodological difficulties in basing psychological models solely on 'sketch maps' (Canter, 1977). The skills of the producer may distort what they draw, the ability to understand the nature of the exercise may relate to cartographic training and the precise details of the instructions may have a very strong influence. However, there can be little doubt that important aspects of the respondent's conceptual system are indicated by what they choose to draw and how they choose to draw it when asked 'to draw a map from memory' of any particular area.

The instructions, to 'draw a map', do assume some understanding of the mapping process. In the British education system children are given such exercises throughout their school career. It may start at the age of seven or eight with being required to draw a map (or more accurately a plan) of their classroom, or to draw a map of their route to school. It is therefore reasonable to assume that British offenders have some idea of what is required from an early age. Indeed in the few explorations carried out no individuals have ever not understood the instructions, even though they may have found it challenging to follow those instructions in relation to their own criminal activity.

There does therefore appear to be considerable potential for understanding criminals' ways of thinking about their crimes and the locations in which they commit them by asking them to 'please draw a map that indicates where you have committed crimes'. What follows are some illustrations of the results of such explorations. They indicate the potential for this line of research. At the present time these results are presented as indications of the possibilities for such a methodology in the hope that they will stimulate others to develop them further.

Canter and Shalev (2008) and Canter and Hodge (2000) explored the mental representations that criminals have of their surroundings, following up the studies of non-criminal populations mentioned above (Canter, 1977; Downs and Stea, 1977). They studied the strategies offenders use for choosing crime locations by asking them to draw 'mental maps' of their offence areas. This mental mapping approach did indeed reveal a variety of locational decision processes that offenders utilise. It also illustrates the way in which different personal narratives could be seen within these representations of spatial behaviour, ranging from those characterised by impulsive, opportunistic strategies to those that were carefully planned as we shall now consider in more detail.

Domocentricity

When crime is an integral part of the offender's day-to-day activities, the sketch maps that they draw can be taken as indicators of how they see their local world to be structured. This can be seen clearly in D's map in Figure 8.4, which is not atypical for young, prolific burglars. His home is in the middle of the map but the Grand Union Canal to the right very distinctly demarcates the area he chooses to draw; a very direct representation of the no-man's land into which a criminal will not venture to commit crimes.

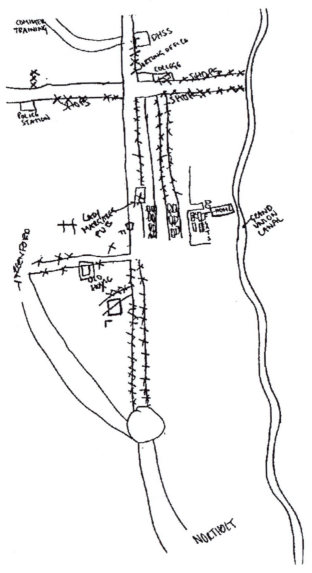

Figure 8.4 D's sketch map of where he committed his crimes, indicating the centrality of his home and the mental constraints on the area of his offending.

In contrast, the area around D's home is marked in some detail. The salient locations in it, his local pub, which interestingly forms the centre of the map, the DHSS office where he gets his welfare cheques, and the police station, are all marked as well as the sets of tower blocks that create the area in which he has an apartment. But what is particularly noteworthy is his memory of the locations in which he has carried out a burglary, each carefully marked with a cross. The prolific crosses are clearly on the main routes he takes between this home and the DHSS office and out towards the main road junction that defines for him the edge of his domain.

D's map reveals a dense world of criminal opportunity. The crosses that mark his crime sites are not casually placed there. The thinner pattern of crosses around the 'old house', and on the way to the police station, show that he has carefully marked actual sites. The street in which he has burgled virtually every house or shop are also so marked that they reveal the assiduousness with which he has broken into every place on both sides of the road. This map reveals a burglar for whom all the properties that he has easy access to are feasible targets for his criminal activities. But this is also a constrained world that he knows, bounded by the limits of his familiarity, the police station, the DHSS office, and the canal.

Sometimes young burglars like D produce maps with even more detail, proud to mark on every building the particular form of security devices and burglar alarms it has. For these people the sketch map reveals the plan of work that shapes their deeds. It can almost be regarded as an action plan that will be drawn on in the future as well as a record of what they have enjoyed doing in the past.

Settings for Personal Narratives

As already indicated, an approach that draws on both the direct experience of routes and opportunities for crime but includes an active development of an internal model of how places relate to each other in providing the possibilities for desired actions, is to consider crime locations as the settings for personal narratives. All stories, factual or fictional, derive some of their power and significance from a physical context. Personal life stories are bounded by the locations in which events occur. How those events unfold in space is derived in part from the nature of the storyline. For example, it is rare for an adventure to take place in one fixed area. The various episodes require different settings to keep the drama moving. On the other hand, an impulsive act of revenge, or seeking out of opportunistic targets, is by its focused nature, likely to cover a limited domain and to be centred on particular areas. This framework allows the consideration of how offence locations relate to the lives of offenders. The following mental maps show how three different forms of personal narrative underlying the offender's criminality can produce very different spatial patterns.

A Heroic Mission

An interesting illustration is Figure 8.5. J, who had a heroin habit from the age of 14, drew this. He had a long history of offences such as drug dealing, burglary and car theft all over England. He would often spend 24 hours away from home on a burglary spree, travelling

Figure 8.5 Map 1 – J's 'map' of his crimes, showing his excitement with being chased by the police.

along country roads over great distances to commit crimes. Drawing a map of these activities would be very demanding for any person. J therefore had to choose some aspect of his criminal activity to represent. He chose to draw a number of sketches of particular locations without any indication of the links between them, perhaps illustrating something of his haphazard approach to his criminal activities.

Figure 8.5 is especially instructive. As can be seen, he chose to draw a bird's eye view of a particularly dangerous moment in a car chase. He wrote on the 'map' 'many car chases all over most areas'. The drawing has strongly emphasised skid marks and even the numbering on the top of a police car. The drawing captures the excitement that J obviously feels in the chase and serves to illustrate the importance of the 'mission' underlying his criminal activities.

J's 'map' also indicates the metaphorical qualities of attempts to represent the locational qualities of thoughts and feelings. This is worth bearing in mind even when a map appears to be an attempt at some cartographic exactitude. It is really just one set of symbols that aims at reconstructing experience. The geographical cross-reference in the symbols will always refer to or mask many other psychological associations. Of course, care must be taken in treating the drawings offenders produce as a 'projective' technique, like a Rorschach inkblot. But, as Lynch (1960) stressed, sketch maps and related drawings may often function as a fruitful focus for a more extended interview, exploring the emotions and conceptualisations associated with the image produced (Lynch, 1960). J's drawing therefore serves to illustrate that even the most impoverished attempt at a sketch map may emphasise important aspects of the offender's relationship to his crimes and the targets he selects.

The Professional

Figure 8.6 shows a map which is just a set of routes as might be sketched out by a delivery employee seeking to make a note of the journeys that need to be made to various drop-off

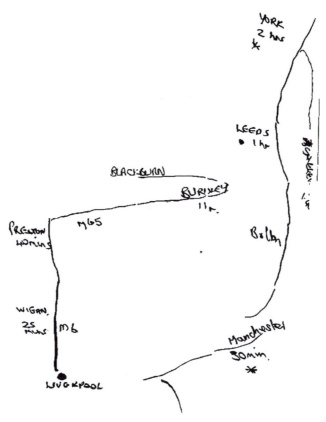

Figure 8.6   Map 2 – F's 'mental map' of the routes she takes to steal from chain stores in small towns around Liverpool, indicating her focus on the routes to crime.

points. The names on the map are names of small towns and cities in the north of England. The numbers are those that designate the main inter-city highways (or 'motorways' as they're called in the United Kingdom, hence M6, M65). The times are the journey times from the base in Liverpool. In some senses a job route timetable is what this sketch is, although for F it was the routes she took to go shoplifting; stealing from stores rather than delivering to them!

For her, stealing from well-known department stores was a job that she did to collect goods that people had ordered from her. So she visited the well-known chain stores aware that they would have what she wanted, preferring those in the smaller towns because their security was more lax. A mother with seven grandchildren, she rarely visited the places on her map except 'on business'. She just parked in the central car park near the stores where she did her thieving, leaving each load in the car while she moved on to the next shop, and then returned straight home.

For F, then, her mental image of crime scenes is a set of opportunities distributed throughout a network of available small towns. The reliability of goods on offer in chain stores across the country means that the only thing she needs to know is whether any small town had a Woolworth's or Marks & Spencer. If it does then the particular town name implies a standard pattern of activity. She would even steal from the shops in a standard sequence that she had developed over her years of theft.

It is also noteworthy that F gives no details of Liverpool, where she is based, or the link roads from her home in Liverpool to the motorways. She just sets off out of there on the road to crime. Indeed, she reported that she would never steal in her local shopping centre, in part because she only goes there on her 'days off' from 'work' and also because she does not want to risk losing membership of her local golf club if she should be caught . . .

Routes to crime

One very interesting implication of these different mental maps is the broad difference between those offenders for whom their home/base is a very distinct focus and those for whom some transit route is a dominant feature (see Figure 8.7). If there is a dominant axis to the crimes then the points would be expected to lie along some line as in a regression equation. This is also true of the offence pattern shown on maps (Figure 8.6), where the influence of the main road is clear. The offender is using the road to structure his actions. The contrasting Figure 8.8 indicates an offender whose distribution of offences is much more likely to be based on his mental representation of the possibilities for offending and, as we shall see in the next example, may imply that he will have a base within the area of his crimes.

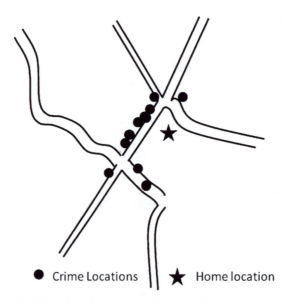

● Crime Locations   ★ Home location

Figure 8.7   Example of burglar whose crimes lie strongly on an axis created by a road.

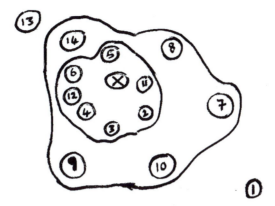

Figure 8.8 Map 3 – P's indication of the locations across a UK city where he had raped women he saw walking in the street.

The Egocentric 'Victim'

When the crimes become an all embracing drive which takes over the offender's life then the sketch maps offenders draw can be chilling in the sense they give of dominating the offender's way of relating to the world. Figure 8.8 was drawn by a man in his mid 20s to indicate the locations in which he had raped 14 different women, all strangers to him, over a period of a few months.

P has taken the trouble to mark on the locations of his assaults their chronological order as well as indicating with an X the location of his home during the period he was attacking these strangers. It is remarkable, not to say unnerving, to see how closely this schematic pattern reflects the model put forward by Canter and Larkin (1993) on the basis of the crime locations of serial rapists in the South of England. The home is clearly at the conceptual centre of P's map. He is also aware of a process in which his first attack is some distance from his home but then a wave of attacks happens in the closer area around his home, which he has bounded with a line. He then sees himself moving out from that location, after his sixth crime, to a further region before moving back again for the eleventh and twelfth and further on again for the thirteenth, before attacking closer to home for the fourteenth, where he was caught.

After his initial rape of a girlfriend, he took to following women as they left railway stations on their way home, attacking them as they walked through an area where there was no one to witness his assault. For P the whole of the city around where he lived became his stalking ground, moving from one locality to another in case he was recognised. The sequence shows clearly that he would never carry out more than a couple of assaults in adjacent localities before moving on to somewhere distinctly different. He was very aware of doing that and felt he had been caught because he moved back to an area where he had committed crimes earlier and where the police were therefore waiting for him.

The lack of any other detail in P's map than the rape sites and his home show how important these assaults became in defining his existence. He could move anywhere he liked and find possible victims. The only thing that brings significance to a location appears to be whether he carried out an attack there. Within this framework he seems to have a notion of boundaries that relate the offence to his home location. This gives the impression of his being aware that he had been moving into unknown territory, although interestingly he puts a lot of space between his first assault and any of the others.

The Value of Imaginary Maps

The examples presented here were selected to illustrate the ways in which criminal activity can be more fully understood if the mental representations that criminals have of where they commit their crimes are explored. It has been shown that asking offenders to draw maps of where they commit their crimes does reveal some interesting insights into their approach to offending. However, the sketch maps on their own, without any other background information, can be very misleading. They are best as a focus for an interview that explores the criminal's lifestyle and offending career.

Nonetheless, despite the difficulties inherent in exploring what is going on in the minds of criminals, this brief examination of their mental representations does show that there is another side to the maps that fill a generalised atlas of crimes. Such an atlas is the product of the amalgamated activities of many individuals. Without knowing how those individuals see the geography of their crime, the maps produced by cartographers can only be seen as a relatively superficial account of the effects of criminals' actions. Such maps give only indirect hints of what gives rise to them.

Indeed the distortions between a cartographer's map and a sketch of a 'mental map' do reveal further issues of how anyone's spatial cognitions, especially a criminal's, incorporate distortions that themselves may influence where he offends. Figure 8.9 shows the actual map for the area indicated in X's sketch in Figure 8.4. There it can be seen that the canal is not parallel to the dominant road that X indicated. The sketch map is an overall simplification of the actual map, but not a random simplification. It turns the area of crime into a much more distinct territory than would be obvious from the actual map. There are many ways across the canal to the right of the sketch map but that is such an alien area to the offender, with such a different mixture of property around it, that this prolific burglar indicates it is not a part of his personal world. By acting on the area around his home to carry out burglaries he has developed his understanding of the opportunities for criminality that area provides, but that in turn this helps to give more focus and precision to the area of his actions.

By understanding the limited horizons of some criminals, the way others shape their lives around their criminal activities and the dominant roles that some offenders assign to the routes and pathways to criminal opportunities, it is possible to begin to see the psychological processes that underpin an atlas of crime. Development of this work will help us to understand not just the way criminals' mental geography shapes their activities but how such processes shape the transactions that we all have with our surroundings.

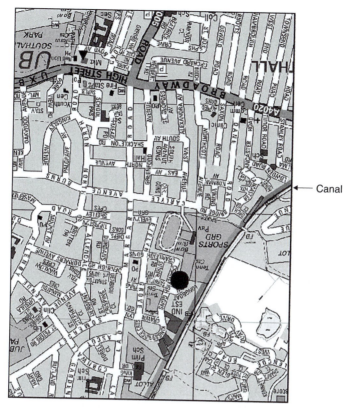

← Canal

Figure 8.9   Actual map of the area sketched by D as shown in Figure 8.4. What are the similarities and differences between the actual and the 'mental' map? (Note that the map is oriented in the same direction as the sketch with south at the top.)

Mental Buffers

The canal in burglar X's area is a clear example of a mental buffer. It illustrates how the mental representations a person has of a place are often greatly distorted by particular aspects of geographical experience. This helps to demonstrate how an environment takes on symbolic qualities and has emotional significance. Baker and Donnelly (1986) referred to the symbolic distances of relevance in understanding the distance travelled by offenders, pointing out that crossing boundaries may be conceived of as being a longer journey than one that does not cross boundaries. The environmental psychology literature (reviewed by Canter, 1977) provides many examples of how geographical features such as rivers, main roads, parks and other overt boundaries can have a distorting effect on internal representations of the environment. In criminal terms, this may lead to an offender having a base rather closer to his offences than might otherwise be expected, but on the other side of some boundary. In this case the boundary acts as a kind of 'mental barrier' in the criminal's cognition of the area in which he is operating. In his mind's eye, these hedges are barriers that protect him from recognition.

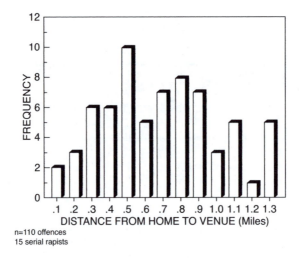

n=110 offences
15 serial rapists

Figure 8.10   The frequency of distances from home of a sample of rapists.

Figure 8.10 illustrates the practical implications of such a mental buffer. The offender carried out a series of assaults in tower blocks. He lived in a tower block, so he was familiar with how to move around them and the anonymity they provided. However, the sites of his attacks were on the other side of busy major roads from where he lived. As described in detail by Canter (1995) before the offender was caught, the possibility that he was operating in a nearby tower block but separated by some sort of buffer was the hypothesis that was the basis of guidance to the police of where to find the offender. It turned out to be remarkably accurate.

Safety Zone

Figure 8.1 and Figure 8.10, which gives a more detailed representation of the short distance over which a sample of rapists travel, both show that there is often a tendency for offenders to maintain a minimum distance from home. This is in accord with the study of Turner (1969), who found that juvenile delinquents in Philadelphia were less likely to commit crimes in the immediate area around their homes. Phillips (1980) explains this phenomenon by the apparent desire to travel far enough away so as not to be easily recognised. This is illustrated for example in Figure 8.10 where the distance from home to crime location for 110 offences occurring within a mile from home is represented. The tendency to not offend within the first half mile or so from home is quite clear in the frequency distribution. Indeed, over the first half mile there is what might be regarded as an inverse decay effect.

Temporal Buffers

Besides the mental buffers that are created by geographical barriers there are other constraints that find their way into some offenders' cognitions of where to offend. A significant set of these relate to where the offender has committed crimes previously. If the offence attracted attention or the crime raised the possibility that the offender might have been seen or could be recognised then he may well try to keep away from the location of his previous offence. This is illustrated by the Lundrigan and Canter (2001) study of the distance between crimes carried out by US serial killers. Their analysis used an approximation to explore what could be thought of as these temporal buffers but it supports and illustrates the general process.

Lundrigan and Canter (2001) compared the distance between crimes that occurred directly after each other (chronologically adjacent crimes, such as first to second, second to third and so on) with crimes that were chronologically alternate (such as first and third, second and fourth, and so on). As predicted, even for this simple exploration that takes no account of the actual time between offences or other factors that may influence intercrime distance; they found that the adjacent crimes were further apart than the alternate crimes. In other words, overall, offenders were keeping further away from the location of their most recent crime than from the crime they had committed before that.

Marauders

When three important processes, discussed so far, combine together in an offender's choice of crime locations an interesting and important geographical pattern emerges. The processes are:

- The dominant role of the home/base rather than of some route or pathway.
- The presence of a preferred characteristic range of distances over which to offend.
- Temporal barriers, whereby the offender will avoid going back to the location of a recent crime.

In effect, these offenders move out from their base to offend, returning to that base then out again in a different direction, avoiding the earlier crime locations, seeking out opportunities as they find them around that base. This gives rise to a particular distribution of great interest and practical value, whereby the crimes surround the serial offender's base (see Figure 8.11). It is the prevalence of offenders who exhibit this form of criminal geography that makes possible the major approach to geographical profiling and the development of systems to facilitate such processes, as will be discussed in Chapter 16.

Canter and Gregory (1994) proposed that the simplest way to define the area circumscribed by the crimes was to identify the two crimes furthest from each other and use the line joining them as the diameter of a circle. They then hypothesised that the offender's home would be within the circle so defined. They labelled such offenders 'marauders'. This notion has been so widely adopted that it is important to note that the assertion was not that the circle was necessarily the most precise geometry for describing an offender's domain – just that it was the simplest and most direct way of indicating the area covering offenders' 'mental maps' of criminal opportunities.

The frequent reference to the concept of 'marauding' offenders does mean that the term is sometimes discussed without consideration of Canter and Gregory's (1994) emphasis that it was merely a 'technical' term, not meant to imply any particular psychological search

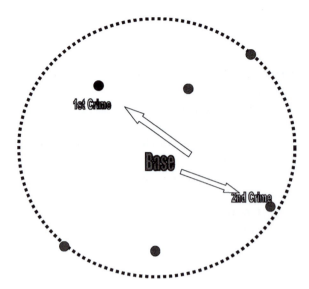

Figure 8.11   The marauder model of offending.

processes. They simply defined it as covering those offenders whose home was within the area circumscribed by a circle that covered all the crimes they committed.

Various studies have lent support to this 'circle' hypothesis. The proportion of offenders who are 'marauders' in this sense varies for different studies, as shown in Table 8.1. This can vary within one area of Australia from 35% for a sample of burglars to 93% for a sample of

Table 8.1   Summary of the percentage of 'Marauders' found in various studies.

Australia (Meaney, 2004)	
Arson	90
Rapists	93
Burglary	35
Australia (Kocsis and Irwin, 1997)	
Arson	82
Rape	70
Burglary	49
England (Canter and Larkin, 1993)	
Rape	87
England (Lundrigan and Canter, 2001)	
Serial murder	86
India (Sarangi and Youngs, 2006)	
Burglary	57
Tokyo (Tamura and Suzuki, 2000)	
Arson	70
United States (Warren et al., 1998)	
Rape	57
United States (Lundrigan and Canter, 2001)	
Serial murder	87

sex offenders (Meaney, 2004). The reasons for such variations have not been explored but as more studies emerge a clearer picture will become possible.

Even at lower proportions there are still enough offenders with bases within the areas of their crimes for this finding to provide a systematic basis for prioritising known offenders, or the places to look for them. This assumption of 'domocentricity' helps to demarcate the area to be searched in order to find an offender. As a consequence, the general principle of crimes being centred on the home of the offender has been at the heart of geographical profiling systems. Thus most geographical decision support systems work on the assumption that the offender is operating within the area of his/her crimes.

The 'Windshield Wiper' Pattern

Using a circle as the basic geometry for describing 'marauding' offenders was always recognised as an oversimplification that enabled early research to make a start. It has many weaknesses but a major challenge to it is that it ignores the actual geography of an area by assuming that offenders will travel equally in any direction. However, it is a commonly recognised process in all studies of transport, as well as everyday experience, that there are many more journeys into centres of population than away from them. This bias leads to the likelihood that offender's will also probably have a predisposition to travel in the direction typical of non-criminal journeys in general in their area when they travel to offend.

This possibility is opening up some interesting research and practical developments. One hypothesis that this generates is that the angle subtended from his home between his crime sites would tend to be acute rather than oblique. In other words, rather than radiating out from his base in all directions, the majority of his sites would be expected to be biased in a particular direction, probably in relation to centres of population density. This is illustrated in Figure 8.12.

This pattern was characterised as a 'windshield wiper' effect by Warren *et al.* (1998). It was studied in more detail by Lundrigan and Canter (2001) who looked at the average angle between crimes for 79 US serial killers. As shown in Figure 8.12, the typical angle is about 60°.

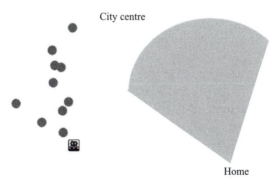

Figure 8.12 (a) Example of location of crimes. (b) Area covered by crimes in typical 'windshield wiper' pattern.

A more recent study by Goodwill and Alison (2005) has also indicated the practical potential of taking this 'windshield wiper' effect into consideration.

Probability Analyses

The idea that offenders follow routes typical of other journeys and indeed typical of other offenders, is opening up another approach to modeling offenders' crime location choice. This uses the calculation of the probability that an offender will be based in a particular area by considering the overall probability that known offenders who offend in any given location will be based in any other location. By deriving these empirical probabilities for existing known, solved crimes in any given locality, using Bayesian probability theory a number of researchers (notably Levine, in press) have been able to identify accurately where any given offender may be based.

This approach may well have considerable practical applications. It is also of theoretical interest because it shows how similar offenders may be to each other in their geographical behaviour. However, the theoretical benefits are limited if the studies only rely on the outcomes of probability analyses without the more detailed consideration of the underlying psychological and spatial processes that give rise to these probabilities.

Temporal Changes

The two theories that have been put forward to explain spatial behaviour predict the possibility of a change over time. The difference between them lies in the nature of this change and why it may occur. Routine activities would keep a criminal in an area unless the activities themselves took the person further afield. This could be due to changes in legal employment, going on holiday or a developing network of associates. A more strongly cognitive perspective would include, as mentioned when discussing the *marauder* process, change in order to avoid risk of detection because of greater vulnerability due to increased vigilance from the police or public. It could also be a consequence of the criminal developing his understanding of the possibilities for crime. An interesting example of this is the offender who stole from golf clubs around the country. When asked how he knew where to go he answered that he just obtained a map which had all the golf clubs listed on it.

A variety of studies have been carried out to explore whether there was change over time in the spatial behaviour of serial offenders. For example, the mean distances travelled by US serial murderers to each successive site in each series were examined (Lundrigan and Canter, 2001). A change in the size of criminal domain over time would be reflected in a gradual increase or decrease in the mean distances travelled. They found a general increase in the distances travelled up to and including the sixth site. It appears that the offender may then backtrack to within the previously established range.

In order to determine whether the overall changes were significant, a non-parametric version of the repeated measures ANOVA was used. This non-parametric test was used because results show the distances travelled do not have a normal distribution or even a symmetric distribution. Analysis using Friedman's ANOVA gave a significant result

Table 8.2   Disposal site numbers where a significant change over time was found.

Site numbers	Significance
1st and 5th	$z = -2.25, p = 0.05$
1st and 6th	$z = -3.03, p = 0.01$
1st and 10th	$z = -2.31, p = 0.02$
2nd and 6th	$z = -2.71, p = 0.01$
2nd and 8th	$z = -2.33, p = 0.02$
5th and 8th	$z = -2.39, p = 0.02$
5th and 9th	$z = -2.48, p = 0.02$

($X^2 = 14.95$, $p < 0.01$). In order to determine which of the changes in distance travelled were significant, Wilcoxon matched pairs signed ranks tests were carried out between each site and each other site. The sites between which significant differences in the distance travelled were found are shown in Table 8.2.

As Table 8.2 shows, there is no significant development until the fifth site is selected. This suggests that the offender will exploit the areas closest to him before moving to locations further afield. Interestingly, although the offender appears to 'retreat' into an already-established area after the sixth offence, there is still a significant difference between the first and last (included) disposal location. This gives support to a general increase in scale across a series despite the relative decrease in distance after the sixth site. However, caution must be exercised in generalising from this one study. There are many processes that might influence changes in distance travelled over time and there are hardly any published studies to show it is a common occurrence across all crimes.

Differences in distance travelled will vary with individual development and with the details of the geography. There are also likely to be changes that are a direct function of the time in the series at which an offence occurs. Some offenders may be expected to become more bold and adventurous as their series progresses but others may be expected to stay within an area with which they are familiar. Considerations of these variations will be related to other aspects of offenders' behaviour and characteristics, possibly even more than the geographical issues. A considerable amount of data will therefore be necessary to unravel the different aspects underlying temporal change in distance travelled to commit an offence. The opportunities that offenders seek out are also likely to influence these journeys but variations relating to different forms of crime may also be very important. The casual crime committed locally to provide funds or instant access to drugs may be very differently located from subsequent crime by the same offender that is planned more thoughtfully.

Emotionality, Crime Type and Distance

A further aspect of the distances offenders travel relates to the nature of the crime and their involvement in the crime. As we have seen, a deep involvement in an egocentric narrative in which the offender sees himself as driven by a desire for revenge or anger is far more likely to be acted out close to where the offender is based. In contrast, the excited adventurer may be expected to travel further afield in search for opportunities. Broadly, published studies support these hypotheses. Offenders travel further to commit property crimes than to commit crimes against the person, as Rhodes and Conly (1981) illustrate. In another study, Van Koppen and Jansen (1998) showed that within property crimes in Holland there is some indication that the greater the value of the property stolen, the greater the distance travelled. A quarter of a century earlier, in the United States, Capone and Nichols (1975) showed that the distance robbers travelled is directly related to the value of the property they steal. Again, it may be hypothesised that this is because more extended searches or specific targeting is involved in stealing higher value goods. But, such findings are certainly not uniform, which is unsurprising as the opportunities for property crime vary considerably from one area to another. Such variations do draw attention to the relevance of the contextual backdrop for the spatial patterns.

Longer distances may also reflect a more general commitment to the course of action. Such a process is suggested by Capone and Nichols' (1975) report that armed robbers travel further than those who are not armed. Similar processes have been demonstrated within other types of offence. For example, Fritzon (2001) has shown for arson that the more emotional arsons are committed at a shorter distance than those that have a very instrumental purpose. LeBeau's (1987) finding is also interesting here. He reports that rapists travelled furthest if they were using a vehicle, a mean of 11.7 miles. Given that Wiles and Costello (2000) showed that the general increased mobility of society did not lead directly to longer home to crime distances, LeBeau's finding here may again be understandable in terms of levels of commitment.

The details of exactly how and why the crime is committed need to be considered, not just its legal definition. For example, Warren et al. (1998) showed that different styles of stranger rape tended to be carried out by offenders who travelled different distances. Le Beau (1987) showed similar results considering the way the rapist approached the victim. He also showed that rapists' journeys to crime were shortest if the offence involved illegal entry, being less than a mile and thus similar to burglary distances.

All of these aspects of criminal behaviour draw attention to the limitations in focusing just on the locations of crimes without considering the nature of the crime and the details of how it was committed. The implicit narrative that energises the criminal's activity needs to be a more integral part of how we explore and understand the geography of criminality. This is one direction in which future research will undoubtedly develop.

Challenges to the Study of Criminal Geography

Challenges of Data Sources

Before we get too carried away with the exciting prospects that geographical profiling offers crime analysis and detection, a number of important cautions need to be emphasised. Many of these cautions derive from the fact that the whole domain of geographical profiling is based on the development of empirically tested principles. As discussed in detail in Chapter 9, this means that it draws from information about crime and criminals. But the challenge is that illegal activities, of course, are not normally in open public view. They can thus usually only be turned into data once the crime has been identified. Also, much information – notably where the offender lives – only becomes available once the offender is apprehended. This means that many of the studies may be biased because they must ignore those crimes that are not reported to the police or solved.

Broadly, the crime and criminal can give rise to data for research in one of two general forms. The most common is when the details become part of official records, held by the police, various legal agencies or government departments. Although, as Canter and Alison (2003) have argued, these records have a great deal of value for research and subsequent operational use, they are not normally produced with the idea of detailed analysis in mind. They are typically incomplete and often unreliably recorded. Their greatest weakness is that they only record information about crimes that have been drawn to official attention and the full details are only present for crimes for which an offender is known. It is certainly possible that the offenders who are not caught have different patterns of behaviour to those who are. This possibility however, assumes that offenders are caught through very focused and systematic police processes, rather than the random trawls that will catch offenders if they commit enough crimes.

A second source of information is the offenders themselves. This relies on the vagaries of offenders' memories as well any particular distortions they may introduce by way of justification or caution, or even to make themselves appear to be more significant criminals than they actually are. This source of information therefore probably has different biases from the official sources. Fortunately the few studies that compare these two sources of information indicate that they do not contradict each other, but rather the self-reported activities tend to be a clarification and elaboration of the much sparser official records (Canter *et al.*, 2004; Farrington, 1989; Youngs *et al.*, 2004).

Weaknesses in Study Methodologies

One further assumption that it would be disingenuous to ignore is that the researchers in this area are all working to the highest standards. As the discerning reader will quickly become aware, the various papers cited have a mixture of strengths and weaknesses. For example, often information that we now know to be of great interest is just not reported. Sometimes basic facts like the exact nature of the crime or the average distances travelled will not be reported in studies that otherwise have very useful ideas and findings. In some cases overly complex statistics are presented that hide more basic results, which are theoretically of considerable significance. No study or report is perfect. However, it is by drawing on the strengths of very different published reports that consistent and enlightening theories and findings are emerging.

There are many reasons why research in this area and accounts of it will be weak. Often studies are funded for direct practical reasons so the researcher has to balance an exploration of some relatively straightforward set of facts with the development of a richer understanding of what is giving rise to those facts. Another complication is that the data are never collected under the purified and controlled conditions of laboratory research. This can give rise to curious anomalies. For instance police records may only allow the ages of offenders to be extracted in subgroups rather than the actual ages, so the researcher is doomed to work with these subgroups, which may not allow some important differences in behaviour to be revealed. Or the police recording of addresses may be so vague that only general areas can be indicated rather than precise points. A particularly challenging problem for geographical analysis is that police records may only record where the offender was living when arrested, not when committing the crimes.

Such problems and difficulties are ever present, so it is noteworthy that so many consistent and clear findings have been produced. It is also the case that, as law-enforcement agencies around the world become aware of the potential practical values of studies of criminal geography, and researchers become more aware of the contributions to our understanding of human behaviour that can be made from studying criminals' geography, an ever more productive interaction between researchers and the police is developing. Out of these interactions much more reliable, precise and detailed information is emerging so that the quality of research is constantly improving.

Research Agenda

The links between the patterns of offence activity revealed by environmental criminologists and the individual patterns of offending discussed in the present chapter are crying out to be explored. It ought to be possible to produce combined models of the actions of a representative sample of known offenders and demonstrate how that relates to the overall patterns of crime found in a given area. Such models would allow bridges to be built between the general considerations for crime prevention and the management of individual offenders that have so far been difficult to construct.

The opportunity geographical analyses of crime offer for creating decision support systems is being explored in a variety of computer systems. However, most of these systems are limited to what are essentially geometric, or probability analyses of crime locations in an undifferentiated space. Future research therefore needs to explore more fully the opportunities for crime. Most current systems also take no account of the particular actions associated with any given crime. Future research therefore is required to build bridges between the behavioural issues of earlier chapters and the geographical patterns that have been explored in the present chapter. A step in this direction is illustrated in Chapter 16 where the iOPS system (Canter and Youngs, 2008b) is mentioned. This is a decision support system based on geobehavioural profiling, not just the spatial geometry of crimes.

Summary

Analysis of the spatial distribution of any given serial offender's crimes tends to show two broad processes. One is the propensity towards propinquity, as revealed by a decay function.

This characterises the bias across offenders towards committing crimes close to where they live. The second process has been described as a morphology or structure to offence locations. In an interestingly high proportion of cases a 'marauding' structure has been found to operate around the offender's home, but travelling offenders, including those who operate strongly along an axis, also occur in many cases. These aspects of the geospatial activity of offenders are consistent with their different narratives being the basis of their criminal activities. The power of these narratives is revealed when asking offenders to draw sketch maps of where they have offended. They show how for some offenders their daily lives do shape where they commit their crimes in accord with 'routine activity theory' and the 'marauder' framework, but for others who find excitement and adventure in their crimes the opportunities for crime and the pathways to offend give a rather different pattern to the geography of their offences.

Further Reading

Books

Brantingham, P.J. and Brantingham, P.L. (eds) *Environmental Criminology*. Sage, Beverly Hills, CA.

Canter, D. (2003) *Mapping Murder: The Secrets of Geographical Profiling*, Virgin Books, London.

Canter, D. and Youngs, D. (eds) (2008a) *Principles of Geographical Offender Profiling*, Ashgate, Aldershot.

Canter, D. and Youngs, D. (eds) (2008b) *Applications of Geographical Offender Profiling*, Ashgate, Aldershot.

Chainey, S. and Tompson, L. (eds) (2008) *Crime Mapping Case Studies: Practice and Research*, John Wiley & Sons, Ltd, Chichester.

Wiles, A. and Costello, P. (2000) The 'Road to Nowhere': The Evidence for Travelling Criminals (Home Office Research Study No. 207). Available at http://www.homeoffice.gov.uk/rds/prgpdfs/brf400.pdf, accessed 28 May 2009.

Wortley, R. and Mazerolle, L. (2008) *Environmental Criminology and Crime Analysis*, Willam, Cullompton.

Articles

Canter, D. and Hammond, L. (2007) Prioritising burglars: comparing the effectiveness of geographical profiling methods. *Journal of Police Practice and Research (US)*, **8** (4), 371–84.

Canter, D. and Hodge, S. (2000) Criminal's mental maps. In L.S. Turnbull, E.H. Hendrix and B.D. Dent (eds) *Atlas of Crime: Mapping the Criminal Landscape*, Oryx Press, Phoenix, AZ.

Canter, D. and Larkin, P. (1993) The environmental range of serial rapists. *Journal of Environmental Psychology*, **13**, 63–9.

Sarangi, S. and Youngs, D. (2006) Spatial patterns of Indian serial burglars with relevance to geographical profiling. *Journal of Investigative Psychology and Offender Profiling*, **3** (2), 105–15.

Questions for Discussion and Research

1. Compare your map as drawn following instructions in Action Box 2 with someone whose experience of where you live is much greater or much less than yours. What

does that reveal about the differences in where each of you might go if you were thinking of committing a property crime?

2. What are the main ways in which we learn our way around places? What implications do these have for how we may build models of offence location choice?

3. How do the resources of time, transport and knowledge influence where offenders carry out their crimes?

4. Consider different types of narrative and discuss the implications they have for where the action of the plot may occur. Does this have any relevance to understanding the relationship between offender behaviour and crime locations?

Answer to Problem in Box 8.1

The offender lived on Dorking Street which is in the centre of the bottom half of the circle defined by a diameter linking the two crime locations furthest from each other.

CHAPTER 9

Investigative Information

In This Chapter

Learning Objectives

When you have read this chapter you should:

1. Be able to discuss the quantity and quality of information that becomes available during police investigations.

2. Be able to identify the main potential sources of error in the information collected as part of an investigation.
3. Understand the basis for and organisation of the cognitive interview.
4. Be aware of the problems in relying on eyewitness testimony.
5. Understand the differences between 'data' and 'evidence'.
6. Be aware of the PEACE approach to interviewing.

Synopsis

The information that is the starting point for an investigation or for IP research must be carved out of real-world events and treated with great respect and considerable caution. A continuum of trustworthiness can be regarded as running from the most trustworthy evidence (the hard evidence at the crime scene) through to the least (the statement of a culprit who denies guilt). However, the trustworthiness of the information available in an investigation cannot ever be assumed, thus distinguishing investigative information from the sources of data with which psychologists are familiar. The statements and forensic records the police have cannot be treated at simple, face value as if they were derived from a questionnaire or from subjects in a laboratory.

The hurdles in the way of trustworthy evidence are present at every stage of an investigation from initial witness statements, through comments from suspects, to how evidence is presented in court. A psychologically significant proportion of these challenges relate to problems in human memory. It is possible to increase the accuracy and detail of the information as well as its reliability and validity, reducing biases, distortions and errors by drawing on psychologically informed procedures, notably in relation to interviewing witnesses, victims and suspects.

The variety of procedures that have been developed to improve the effectiveness of investigative interviews relate to the assumed level of trustworthiness and cooperativeness of the interviewee. The cognitive interview is mainly for cooperative witnesses, emphasising help in improving memory. For interviews that may have important evidential significance, the PEACE approach, used in England and Wales, draws attention to appropriate preparedness and interpersonal interactions.

Overall the central concerns of IP, when considering the information available through the work of the police and other agencies, are the ways in which material collected can be regarded not just as evidence that can be used in legal proceedings but also as data that are amenable to the explorations of scientific research, the results of which feed back to improve the investigative process. The great amount and variety of information in many enquiries can benefit from the sort of systematisation and distillation that are common in the social sciences. Beyond the challenge of information management, further challenges come from deliberate distortion or falsification of information. This is dealt with in the next chapter.

The Challenges of Investigative Information

Trustworthiness

The statement in Box 9.1 made by a potential witness, P, seems rather mundane and of little dramatic power. Yet it was crucial in a case of international significance. The police were interested in the items that had been bought because they had connected them to a major incident in which a great deal of money had been stolen and two people had been killed. By tracing the items back to the shop where P worked, the police believed that whoever sold them would be able to identify the customer who had bought them and would therefore be a crucial eyewitness to identify a significant suspect for the police investigation. P's memory of the items being sold, and to whom they were sold, was therefore extremely important in influencing the progress of the trial.

Box 9.1 Statement of P Taken 2 October 1998 by Detective A

I assist in the running of a general store, which is a family business.

On the 25 September 1997 I was interviewed by police officers regarding items stocked and sold in the shop. I was first asked about souvenir scissors, which the police said had been delivered as part of a batch to the shop on 18 November 1996 as part of an order from Y Equipment. I was shown a handle from the scissors, which has an unusual design on it. I checked my stock and found two pairs of scissors with the same colour and a similar design. They had Y Equipment labels attached. I was told by the police that the shop had 20 pairs of these scissors delivered. Therefore we must have sold the other 18 pairs. The label on the scissors showed the order number as 23/27/D. I sold these to the police and signed a label which the police said would be attached to them.

I do not remember the delivery date of this batch of scissors to the shop. A photograph shown to me by the police showed equipment I recognised as gardening forks stocked in the shop. I checked my stock and found that I had this type in stock and I sold one to the police. I signed labels which the police said would be attached to the fork and scissors. I cannot say exactly when the shop got delivery of the items I sold to the police but I know the shop had the items in stock in November and December 1996.

I do not remember personally selling any of the items referred to in my statement.

From the other photographs of material shown to me by the police I do not recognise anything else as being sold in the shop.

I was present when my brother T told the police that he remembered serving the man who bought these items. A took from stock shears and a spade which he said were similar to other items the man bought at the time. My brother also gave the police

(continued)

---

some string and brown paper which we use to wrap up parcels. I signed labels which the police said would be attached to these items.

I was again interviewed by the same police officers on 2 January 1999. I told the police that the gardening fork I have previously mentioned as being sold in the shop had a fox logo engraved in black on the back of the handle. The only people who normally work in the shop are myself, my brother T and sometimes my father E who owns the shop. Although my father owns the business he is now 70 years of age and suffers bad health after having a stroke about two years ago. As far as the business is concerned T normally does the selling in the shop and I do selling and administration.

SIGNATURE P

Such statements are the basis of most investigations. They provide the facts from which further information is sought. For example P was eventually asked to identify a key suspect from a lineup. But statements are also evidence in their own right, which can be used in court to support the claims of guilt.

Investigations are not really based on a crime *occurring* but on the *reports* that help to build up a picture of the relevant details of what happened. An horrific killing as part of a large robbery may be obviously a crime but the actual investigative process is not driven by the event of the offence itself but by the information that becomes available to the police about that event and associated matters.

This creates the central challenge of all investigations. The indirect nature of the material being dealt with means that it is always only partial and can never be assumed to be totally reliable or valid. There is great potential for discrepancies in the information through distortions, inappropriate additions and omissions. Some of these problems relate to the inadequacies of the recording and storage of the information, some to the weaknesses of human memory and recall that require the reconstruction of events after the crime, and some to deliberate distortions and falsifications on the part of those involved. Unlike data arising from scientific activity, which we can generally assume to be valid and reliable by definition, trustworthiness is not an integral part of investigative information. Indeed it is peculiar to the investigative context, compared with most other areas of research, that it can often be assumed that some of the information involved will *not* be trustworthy.

In many areas of research involving responses from people, the integrity of the initial information is taken for granted. Few opinion pollsters assume that the answers offered on the High Street are deliberately distorted. Historians examining early documents may well expect the authors of those documents to be biased but rarely will they consider how the trauma, for example, that the authors might have faced during the events they describe may have distorted their attention at the time.

It is helpful to keep in mind a notional continuum from the most trustworthy information to the least as illustrated in Box 9.2. Whether this sequence really is as simple as indicated is a matter for serious consideration. Crime scenes can be disturbed, suspects may wish to 'spill the beans', victims may have nefarious intentions and so on, but as a general framework this continuum is helpful to keep in mind as we progress through the consideration of how the information obtained can be improved.

Box 9.2 The Continuum of Trustworthiness

Crime scene material → victim statements → eyewitness statements → suspect statements

---

Hurdles to Evidence

There a number of hurdles that the police have to get over in order to be sure that what they end up with is sound evidence, or related information on which they can act (see Box 9.3). The first challenge comes from the actual report of the events that initially raises the possibility that a crime has occurred. This report will be based on what someone has seen or heard and what that person remembers about that experience. There may be many different reports from different people, all of whom have different perspectives on the events in question. Some may be lying, distorting or withholding information to hide their guilt, to protect others, or just because they are part of a subculture that does not support assisting the police, or they

Box 9.3 Hurdles to Evidence

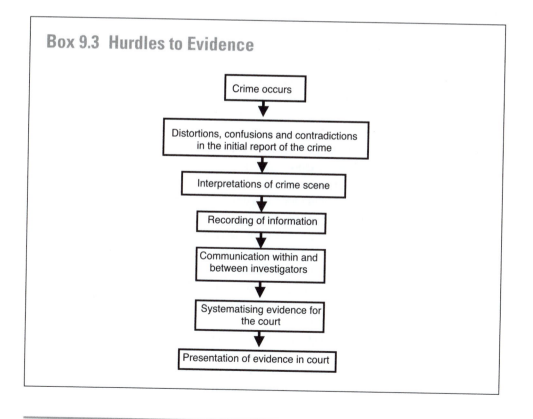

are afraid to do so. Or in an alleged rape there may be absolutely crucial matters, such as whether the victim consented, which can only be determined from the accounts given by those involved. The details of these accounts and how they may be supported or challenged by other information thus can become the central exploration of an investigation. In other words, the whole investigation is focused on determining if a crime had occurred or not.

In many – although not all – crimes, a place can be identified where the incident happened. This crime scene does not inevitably give up its story, even when there is a closed-circuit television recording of what happened. Interpretations have to be made of what went on where. This may require specialist expertise, such as making sense of blood splashes or analysing insect presence to determine how long a body had been in that location. The whole art of forensic science can play a part here. Even in burglaries there may be trace evidence or other information that can help to indicate what happened and point to the identity of the offender. But none of this information is necessarily totally reliable. Even fingerprints, the most seemingly unambiguous source of crime-scene evidence, can be smudged or confused. Police officers may leave traces of their own attendance at the crime scene, which then have to be removed from suspicion. In some crimes, officers may get to the scene so late that it has already been disturbed. If there is a great deal of media interest around the case then the vast amount of superfluous information this generates from the public can swamp the authorities trying to manage and make sense of it.

All the information available has to be organised and stored so that it can be drawn on and made sense of. This can be an enormous challenge with information being misrecorded, lost or omitted. The colour of a car may be put into the police records as blue by one person but as navy or purple by another, and their computer search processes may treat these as totally different vehicles. There may be different interpretations of what the crime was. So, for instance, while one person might decide it is criminal damage, another may decide that what has gone on constitutes a theft. Enquiries looking for particular types of crime may be confused by these differences. There may also be even simple inputting errors that have great significance. For example, Canter (1995) describes how a suspect was initially omitted from an enquiry in a crime that occurred in February because it was recorded that he had not been let out of prison until June. However closer examination of other records showed that he had actually come out of prison in January but that there had been a simple typing error in the abbreviation of the month, 'jun' having been typed in instead of 'jan' (Canter, 1995).

Often it will also be necessary to draw on information from diverse sources and multiple distinct law-enforcement agencies. In the well-known case of the murder of two girls, Holly Wells and Jessica Chapman, in Soham, two major police forces, Humberside and Cambridgeshire, had not shared information about allegations against an individual who had known the girls, which would have taken them to this culprit more quickly. Many researchers report that this is not always a matter of incompetence or inefficiency but that, because police promotion is based on solving crimes, some police officers may, on occasion, keep important information out of the official records so that they can nab the bad guy before anyone else.

Once a suspect has been charged with a crime and is being taken to court the information the police have needs to be organised and prepared for the legal process. This will often be carried out by lawyers who have had no contact with the original material and are working entirely on the basis of what the police have presented to them. This can lead to further omissions and distortions in the information available as well as information just simply being lost. One important example of how this can happen is indicated by Canter (2005) when he describes the process of seeking to obtain material about one of Britain's most notorious serial killers, Fred West, who had killed himself. The collection of documents and other artefacts was kept by the UK 'official solicitor' in an office in central London. The material, consisting of photographs, tape recordings, and West's memoir, as well as other evidence, was all piled into a metal cupboard that was also used to store parts of malfunctioning computers. There was no systematic listing available of what was in the cupboard relating to Fred West or any other process for archiving or protecting the material either for future research or any possible future court case.

When the case finally reaches court it then has to be presented to the judge and/or jury in accordance with the due process of the law. An expert, for example, is not allowed to give a lecture on what she did to come to her opinion, as she would be used to doing at a professional conference, but instead is treated like any other witness and has to answer questions put by the lawyers in court. Yet often in this process it will be difficult for the expert to convey the subtleties in the expertise given to the lawyers or the jurors. If lawyers do not understand the subtleties of the expertise and therefore do not know how to ask the most appropriate questions, experts may find it difficult to explain fully the basis of their opinion.

A full record of the whole court proceedings is rarely publicly available, although developments in electronic recording are changing this in important cases, rather summaries are produced in various forms. The outcome of the case and the details of the offender will then be incorporated into various databases and other police records. There may be newspaper reports that derive from the court proceedings and other information obtained by journalists. So any distortions or omissions that have been introduced along the way will find their way into the information that may be drawn on for future cases or research.

The Plethora of Information

Even the broad term 'information' does not do justice to what the police have to work with. It may be various forms of material, objects, data, statistics, records, speculations or processes. But for simplicity in this chapter we will tend to imply all of this by the word 'information'. The information that investigators use, though, will not only be about the actual case at the focus of their enquiries. Along the way a great deal of other information will have to be used that will throw light on what happened, or relate to possible suspects or other witnesses, possible experts and advisors, both in relation to material being considered and its legal implications. Consider, for example the background information the police in the enquiry relating to the witness statement featured in Box 9.1 had to explore about shops, stock and shopping patterns just to locate P's shop.

The volume and variety of information that accumulates during an inquiry (as summarised for some major enquiries in Boxes 9.4 and 9.5) poses its own challenges, so that one of the most crucial tasks of any police activity is the effective handling of information. These very large volumes of information are a double-edged sword in that, while such information is necessary to further the case, it leaves investigators with the unenviable task of having to evaluate every lead and scrap of evidence in order to find the proverbial needle-in-the-haystack that can lead to an arrest. Failing to pick up on one detail can mean an investigation goes off in an entirely wrong direction. Another example from the case in which P was such a crucial witness illustrates how important details can be. The gardening fork that was linked to the robbery and murder had a particular logo on it of a fox in a particular colour. The linking or not of the suspect to the crime depended in part on P remembering the details of the design on the forks he sold to be sure it was exactly the same.

Box 9.4   Volume of Information

Here are some basic figures from well-known cases to show the number of sources of material that had to be dealt with.

- The Yorkshire Ripper. Beginning in 1975, Peter Sutcliffe murdered 13 women and brutally assaulted another seven. During the course of the investigation police interviewed 175 000 people, took 12 500 statements, checked 10 000 cars and issued six photo-fits based on descriptions given by victims and witnesses.
- Jill Dando murder. On 26 April 1999 the well-known television presenter was shot once at close range on the doorstep of her London home. The information that investigators had to sift through included 1300 letters, 1100 messages, 2500 statements to police, the footage from almost 200 CCTV cameras, and the whereabouts of nearly 80 000 individuals who had used their mobile phones near the murder scene that morning. This left the police with a list of approximately 1900 suspects to interview and eliminate.
- 9/11 On September 11, 2001 three passenger jets were hijacked and flown into buildings in New York City and Washington, DC, while a fourth plane was crashed into a field in rural Pennsylvania. The result was the death of over 3000 people and the injury of thousands more. Within two-and-a-half weeks authorities received more than 100 000 telephone and Internet tips.
- D.C. snipers. For three weeks in October 2002, John Muhammad and John Lee Malvo carried out a series of random, sniper-style shootings in the suburbs surrounding Washington, D.C. Later linked to three additional incidents in other parts of the country, the spate of attacks left 13 people dead and three others critically injured. After requesting assistance from the public, police received over 100 000 phone calls, Internet tips and letters from the public. At the height of the investigation more than 1000 calls an hour were flooding into the hotline, at one point crashing the phone system.
- Suffolk murders. In December 2006 the bodies of five young women were found in woodlands and streams around Ipswich, in England. Police spoke to over 400 motorists in the area from which the women had disappeared, reviewed 10 000 hours of CCTV footage and received 10 000 calls – over 400 calls per hour for the duration of the investigation.

Box 9.5 Some Types of Information Available to Police

- biological evidence
  - blood, semen, excreta and other body fluids, hair and skin from which DNA and other biochemical and genetic information can be obtained
- trace evidence
  - cloth and other fibres, soil particles, plant materials, gunshot residue, explosives residue, and volatile hydrocarbons (especially relevant in arson, for example); insects are also a valuable indicator on dead bodies
- impression evidence
  - fingerprints, footwear impressions, and tyre tracks, or writing indentations
- ballistic evidence
- crime scene records
  - photographs (taken by police officers or members of the public), pathologists' reports and scenes-of-crime officers' reports
- geographical locations of offences
- running records
  - hospital records, records of births, deaths, marriages, etc.
- personal records
  - diaries, letters, suicide notes, computer searches, e-mails
- polygraph / truth verification systems
- witness statements
- victim statements
- informers' reports
- criminal records
- criminal intelligence
- transcripts of police interviews

For a less serious crime, say the theft of a bicycle, it may only be details of what was stolen, when and where, that need to be effectively recorded and organised by police. For major enquiries, such as those into serial murders, a vast amount of information accrues and will be necessary for police to solve and prove the case, using this information to draw on and filter out lines of enquiry. In some cases, such as terrorist bombings, whole warehouses are set up just to store all the information collected and a team of dedicated personnel is assigned just to the task of recording, archiving and managing this information.

The Variety of Material

On top of the demands of the amount of information that the police have to deal with is the great variety of material (summarised in Box 9.5). Each different type of material has to be managed and examined in different ways, requiring different skills and different assessment processes. It can include:

- Photographs or other recordings derived from the crime scene or near to the scene, such as CCTV tape.
- There may also be records of other transactions such as bills paid or telephone calls made.
- Increasingly there are also records available within computer systems used by witnesses, victims or suspects.
- Often there will be witnesses to the crime or there will be results of the crime available for examination.
- There will be transcripts of interviews or reports from various experts.
- Further, there will be information in police databases and other records that may be drawn upon to provide indications for investigative actions.
- There may also be clandestine information from informants.
- Once suspects are elicited there is further potential information about them either directly from interviews with them, or indirectly through reports from others and central or local records on offenders.
- In addition there may be information from various experts that has to be understood and may lead to further actions to develop the details of what happened in a crime.

By understanding the challenges of this task of managing and evaluating the information obtained, as well as improving what is actually collected, it is possible for investigative psychologists to generate processes that can greatly enhance investigations. These processes may run from help with the effective storage, systematisation and distillation of the information collected, through to techniques for improving the quality of what people remember on to, at the other end of the trustworthiness continuum, processes to detect lying and deception.

Prioritising Suspects

As many enquiries progress, especially in a major investigation, a large number of potential suspects emerge. Unlike in crime fiction, where there may be only a handful of possible culprits, in real life detectives may have to sift through dozens or even hundreds of possibilities (as illustrated in Box 9.6). Each of these suspects needs to be carefully evaluated, firstly in simple terms of whether he or she could have been unavailable at the time of the offences, for example by being in prison. Then alibis offered by suspects would need to be reviewed. Finally the possibility of guilt would need to be examined. At this latter stage, in particular, any IP advice could be of great assistance in helping to put suspects in some order of priority for being likely to have committed the crime. The resources of time and effort involved in looking at each suspect are considerable, as well as the risk that the culprit will escape or destroy important evidence before the police are in contact. Therefore help in getting to the culprit as efficiently as possible can be a significant contribution from psychology.

Box 9.6 The Number of Possible Suspects

Besides the number of contacts shown in Box 9.4, a large number of suspects usually need to be considered in a major enquiry. Here are some examples:

- The Railway Murderer. Between 1982 and 1987 at least seven women were raped and many more were sexually assaulted by the same men. Three women were also murdered in the same series. At one point in the investigation there were 1999 suspects although some estimates put the total number of individuals considered as suspects at one point or another during the investigation as high as 5000 men.
- Wimbledon common murder. On 15 July 1992, Rachel Nickell was sexually assaulted and stabbed 49 times while walking with her two-year-old son and the family dog. Police questioned 32 men as suspects and over 20 were arrested and questioned under caution. None of them was convicted of the crime.

Sources of Distortion

As illustrated in detail by Canter and Alison (1999a), the distortions that can occur at any stage of an enquiry in the emergence of information and evidence, can be thought of as being produced by cognitive, presentational, social or pragmatic processes. These broadly follow the sequence of evidence indicated in Box 9.7 (Canter and Alison, 1999a). Those aspects that relate to the earlier stages where the evidence from witnesses is being obtained have been most fully examined by psychologists. At the later stages, there is still a great deal to be done on how evidence is evaluated and organised for effective use by investigators.

For instance, the development of interview techniques has focused on reducing the distortions brought about by cognitive processes associated with memory that will influence the account a witness can give of an incident. Research on the detection of deception has also been very cognitive in its orientation, concerned with the intellectual pressures on people to maintain a deceptive account. However there is more recent work that examines social transactions between people in an interview context that can lead to biases and confusions. Some consideration of the use of expert testimony also highlights the ways in which material can be inappropriately used by investigators or the courts.

Box 9.7 Some Sources of Distortion in Police Information

Cognitive

Distortions brought about through processes of attention or remembering

Presentational

How the material is summarised

(continued)

Social
> Distortions that arise from interpersonal transactions

Pragmatic
> Misuses of information

The picture is not all negative though. Quite rich information may be obtained that is not normally available to psychologists except under very particular conditions, such as the details of the sexual behaviour of a rapist. It is highly unlikely that a researcher would think of trying to obtain this sort of information about exactly what happened in a rape for the purposes of his or her study. But the statement given to the police by a rape victim can be very detailed indeed.

Police records will also include such crucial factors as the time, place and details of the victim but they will not include the sorts of material that is the stock in trade of psychologists, such as the mental processes of offenders or their personality characteristics, as may be indicated in personality questionnaires. Equally, while the information available does have certain strengths (such as the fact that it may have been given under oath), it does not come from material that has been collected under the careful controls of laboratory research. It is therefore often incomplete, ambiguous and unreliable, as illustrated in Box 9.8.

Box 9.8 Examples of Distortion Difficulties in Actual Cases

Problems with using computerised databases

- The 'South Auckland Rapist' – the initial profile of a man aged between 25 and 35 excluded the killer, who was aged 36, from the list of suspects until the upper age limit was eliminated. The suspect also moved around a lot and this was probably not very well followed up on the database.
- The Soham case – the database was not updated to include the other surname Huntley started to use although police were aware of this change of surname. A report was also filed about Huntley on the database saying he was a 'serial sex attacker' but this report was later deleted.

Different interpretations by different people – how information is coded and/or information that is not first hand (hearsay) and/or errors in eyewitness recall or recognition

- Calling a car green when another will call it blue and the investigators are looking for a 'blue' car.

Problems in sharing information

- The Soham case – two police forces (Humberside and Cambridge) not sharing information (about allegations of rape, indecent assault, sex with underage girls) which causes a lack of information.

Problems of too much information – media-generated frenzy

- Jill Dando case – a lot of people came forward with irrelevant information, which hid other useful information for a long time.

Problems with the gathering of evidence – tampering with crime scenes and inadvertent contamination

- Jon-Benet Ramsey case – police officers' late arrival at the crime scene allowed it to be contaminated and altered.

Evidence that has become distorted due to time and physical conditions and/or lab-errors – mishandling of forensic evidence

- The O. J. Simpson case – the glove that may have fitted Simpson because of shrinkage due to the blood that had dried on it.

Focusing on a single suspect

- Elizabeth Smart investigation focused only on handyman Richard Ricci (despite the fact that the witness sister said that he was not the culprit) – this drew away attention from other suspects.

Weaknesses in Identification and Eyewitness Testimony

The distortions that can occur in the account that is given are not only likely to be due to deception, lapses of memory or simple confusions on the part of the witnesses or victims. Even when a person is not being required to generate an account of what has happened by recalling events, but is given the much less demanding task of recognising the perpetrator or other key actors, there is still the possibility of innocent errors being made. Psychological research has therefore examined the processes that can influence the validity of traditional 'identity parades' and related ways of identifying the culprit. Various procedures have been introduced by many police forces around the world to ensure that the recognition task set for the witness is appropriate and not open to bias. In particular, these take account of the need to protect the suspect against the possibility of the witness's memory being modified by experiences subsequent to the crime, such as meeting the suspect in other circumstances (see, for example, Haber and Haber, 2000).

On the whole eyewitness identifications are not very accurate. Cutler and Penrod (1995) conducted a 'meta-analysis' of eyewitness accuracy in 'natural settings' in 1995. In a typical study they reviewed, a person enters a convenience store and performs some memorable action (such as paying in pennies) to ensure the clerk's attention. Soon afterwards the clerk views a photo spread and identifies the 'customer'. The percentage of correct identifications ranged from 34%–48% and the percentage of false identifications from 34%–38%. The implication of this is that, even after a relatively short interval, eyewitnesses are as likely to be incorrect as correct when attempting to identify strangers (cf. Brigham *et al.*, 1982; Naka, Itsukushima and Iton, 1996).

Thus, although the courts have typically relied heavily on eyewitness identification of suspects, in which the witness is asked if they recognise individuals presented to them in vivo or as a photograph, there is growing evidence that such identifications can be unsafe. Indeed in 2001, MacLin *et al.* published a major review showing that, out of 62 people who had been exonerated by DNA evidence, 52 had been imprisoned on the basis of faulty eyewitness identification (Huff, Ratner and Sagarin, 1986; Wells *et al.*, 1998). There is a growing belief that a majority of false convictions are due to errant eyewitness testimony (Overbeck, 2005; Rattner, 1988).

The reasons for errors in identifications are complex and not fully understood but a large number of academic studies do point to factors, beyond the simple period of time between the alleged event and the identification, which may be relevant.

One such process that has been examined is the pressure to perform. When a witness is brought in by the police to attempt identification he is likely to assume that the police have a suspect in mind or even in custody. He is therefore under pressure to pick someone, even if the officer showing the photographs or running the lineup is careful not to force the issue (Buckhout, 1974). Further, in an identification situation the witness is subject to pressures generated by the desire to be correct, observant and helpful and to not appear foolish (Loftus, 1979).

Wells (1993), among others, has documented the influence of lineup administrators on eyewitness identification. They can inadvertently communicate their knowledge about which lineup member is the suspect and which members are fillers through various verbal and non-verbal cues. This is illustrated by the study of Phillips *et al.* (1999), in which they manipulated lineup administrators' assumptions about the identity of the culprit and found that this affected the identifications that the eyewitnesses made.

These studies point not only to weaknesses in the accuracy of the identification but also to the way the process of seeking an identification can inappropriately influence the confidence the witness has in his selection. For example, Bradfield, Wells and Olson (2002) found that postidentification suggestions made to eyewitnesses by lineup administrators led the witnesses to develop high levels of certainty that they had made an accurate identification. This is important because later in court such witnesses would be expected to give their evidence with more confidence. It is also worth repeating here that Wells and Olson (2003) also pointed out that it is common for lineup administrators (usually the detective in the case) to give confirming feedback. This appears to distort the eyewitness's recollections of the certainty they had in their identification, further confounding any relationship between confidence and accuracy. This effect may be exaggerated by the tendency for people to seek evidence that confirms their beliefs (Kebbell and Wagstaff, 1999).

Using Eyewitness Identification Research in Court

In a recent survey of 64 experts on eyewitness evidence for the *American Psychologist*, 30 eyewitness-research derived phenomena were evaluated in terms of their appropriateness for use in court. Eighty per cent of the experts agreed that a number of the phenomena were sufficiently robust to be presented in court. These 'reliable' phenomena included effects of the wording of questions, lineup instructions, mugshot-induced bias, attitudes and expectations, confidence malleability, suggestibility, cross-race bias, the forgetting curve (memory decay) and unconscious transference (Kassin *et al.*, 2001).

However, the difficulty of drawing on academic research evidence is complicated by the fact that this area of psychology lends itself to tidy 'classroom'-, or 'laboratory'-based experiments. These do not necessarily reflect the realities of the much more complex 'real' world. Thus an artificial event can be readily staged or a video shown and students can then easily be asked to identify the perpetrators or characterise the actions that occurred. Most of the published studies use this framework and the main findings to emerge about witness testimony have been drawn from the results of such studies. A recent extensive field trial in Illinois is therefore of particular significance because it raises questions about the applicability of laboratory studies to 'real-world' applications (Wells and Olson, 2003).

The Illinois study had the specific objective of comparing the conventional lineup, or its photographic equivalent, with the sequential presentation of possible suspects. The published literature predicts that the sequential process would generate more valid results, but this was not found in these field studies of actual cases. However, it was also found that the purity of the laboratory study was exceedingly difficult to replicate in an actual police investigation, so that debate is likely to continue on the robustness of the results found in the Illinois study.

Good Practice Recommendations

In response to the current level of understanding about the potential for errors in identification evidence and the processes that can generate these, a number of recommendations for good practice have been advanced. These provide a benchmark against which to consider any procedures and the possibility that those procedures may have introduced bias or inaccuracies.

In 1996 the American Psychologist/Law Society and Division 41 of the American Psychological Association made recommendations that:

- double-blind testing should be used – in other words the person managing any identification procedures should be ignorant of who was thought to be the culprit;
- eyewitnesses should be forewarned that the culprit might not be present;
- distracters should be selected based on the eyewitness's verbal description of the perpetrator – that people who look like the person described by the eyewitness should be present in any selection of possible suspects;

• confidence should be assessed and recorded at the time of identification.

(Detailed in Wells and Olson, 2003.)

Similarly, the Innocence Project specifies that identification lineups:

• should be presented sequentially;
• the individual conducting the lineup should not know the identity of the actual suspect;
• witnesses should be warned that the suspect may or may not be in the lineup;
• there should be a minimum of eight photographs in a photo identification lineup;
• no feedback should be given during or after a lineup;
• witnesses should provide confidence ratings at the time of making their identification.

It is important to note that all of these recommendations are broken when the witness is asked to indicate in court whether the defendant in the dock is the person he remembers. In this case the person believed to be the culprit cannot be hidden; there is no strong indication that the suspect may not actually be present for identification; there are no other people present whom the witness may confuse with the main suspect; the legal formalities can hide any lack of confidence the witness is willing to admit. Therefore a dock-based identification is the most unsafe means of seeking to obtain an opinion from a witness.

Unconscious Transference

Memory can be distorted by exposure to other similar individuals or situations in the period between an alleged event and its recall. Moreover, as recognition is facilitated by context, out-of-context witnesses can be aware that an individual is familiar but be confused about where they know that individual from. This is a process that gives rise to what has been termed 'unconscious transference' (Loftus, 1976), whereby the witness remembers seeing a person but wrongly assigns that person to the criminal context under consideration (Rossi et al., 1994).

Loftus (1979) gives as an example of this process: the case of a railroad ticket agent who had been robbed at gunpoint and ended up identifying a sailor as his assailant (Loftus, 1979). On the day of the robbery, however, the sailor had been away at sea. To the psychologists who reviewed this case, the sailor had been an obvious victim of the *unconscious transference* phenomenon. He was the one picked out from the lineup because his face was the most familiar one to the ticket agent. As it turns out the sailor was based near the railroad station, and had purchased tickets from that very agent three times before the robbery.

Loftus (1979) explains this phenomenon in the following terms:

> Unconscious Transference is a by-product of the integrative, malleable nature of human memory. It appears that brief exposure to a person can cause that person to look familiar when he is seen later. For example, an incidental character seen prior to a crime [incident] will be familiar to a witness who is attempting to identify the perpetrator of a crime from a set of photographs. The character looks familiar and his familiarity is interpreted as being due to the perception at the time of the crime

[incident], when in fact the familiarity is due to an observation made at a time prior to the crime [incident]. The familiar trace of the incidental character becomes integrated into the witness' memory for the crime [incident]. So, unconscious transference may take place when a witness identifies a suspect from a line-up. A person whose photograph has been seen before (for example; in a photo identification line-up) will look familiar. This familiarity may be mistakenly related back to the crime or incident rather than back to the photographs. The chances of a mistaken identification increase dramatically in these situations.

It is not clear how widely this process may occur or what degree of familiarity is necessary under what circumstances for it to surface. However, psychologists generally agree that it is a process that needs to be guarded against when considering witness testimony.

Earwitness Testimony

How people remember and recognise auditory material is a neglected area that has been developing. There is an increasing amount of research, reviewed for example by Huss and Weaver (1996), which indicates that many of the problems of eyewitness testimony are also present when the source of the memory is auditory rather than visual. This includes the rapid decay in memory over time and the weak relationship between confidence and accuracy.

Investigative Interviewing

Currently far and away the most common source of information about what happened in a crime is the open interview. Police interviews are 'open' in the sense that no standard questions are asked that allow only selection from a number of predetermined responses as the answer (except of course for the 'closed' question 'Did you commit this crime?' which only allows a yes/no answer). For example, a social scientist carrying out the study of a person's likely culpability may formulate closed question as follows.

On the night of the 18 October between the hours of 8 p.m. and 10.30 p.m. were you

(a) with somebody else who would provide an alibi
(b) on your own not involved in any criminal activity but unable to provide any corroboration
(c) involved in some other activity that would provide corroborative evidence, such as shopping or at the cinema or
(d) involved in the criminal activity in question.

It is intriguing to ask why it is that a question of this form which could be standardised across all interviews of culprits has not emerged. The most likely reason is that it is believed that it is much easier to be deceptive when answering such questions or that so much follow up detail would be necessary that it might as well be approached by asking the person the open ended question 'What where you doing a few nights ago? We're interested in 18 October.'

However, there are many cases in which the person being questioned is not assumed to be predisposed to lie. Would a structured questionnaire be appropriate in those circumstances? For example in a house-to-house enquiry, some key facts about what people have seen may be more readily obtained by asking everybody a very carefully structured set of questions. Although such questionnaires are used now in some enquiries it is still very rare, mainly because the statement that a person gives is seen as being evidence that could be used in the legal process. Therefore structuring the material too carefully may lead to the challenge that these were 'leading' questions that suggested the answers that they should give.

As a consequence of this sort of consideration the open interview loosely formulated around a set of topics relevant to the investigation is the characteristic way of gaining all the key information in an investigation. These days, in many places, such interviews are normally audio-recorded and then eventually transcribed, although video recordings are becoming more common. In the past, tape recording was not the norm and so there are a large number of interviews based on taking what are often called contemporaneous notes or other ways of trying to record what was said and then converting this into a statement that the witness, or suspect, can sign.

There is a large literature on the whole interview process and in recent years this has been developed to consider the police interview. For our present purposes we shall consider three aspects of this. The first relates to techniques for ensuring that the individual who is giving the account can remember as much as effectively as possible. The 'Cognitive Interview' has become a fashionable approach to this general issue (Fisher and Geiselman, 1992; Geiselman *et al.*, 1985, 1986).

The second aspect to be considered is the interpersonal relationship that is at the heart of any interview. This issue is of particular importance when interviewing suspects because this relationship influences whether the suspect may be prepared to give the facts carefully and clearly. Of course, suspects may have difficulty remembering so issues to do with memory may also be relevant.

There is a subgroup of witnesses, or victims, for whom this is particularly important. These are what we will refer to as vulnerable interviewees. They are people, for example, who have been traumatised by the horror of the offence; people who may be mentally ill or for some other reason unable to give a clear and coherent account of their experiences. For example, people suffering from drug withdrawal, or in a very different way, people of low intellectual ability. Children provide yet another area of vulnerability, both because of the difficulties they may have with memory processes and the relationship in the interview but also because of the legal implications of a child's evidence.

The third area is the assessment of the validity of the account that is given. It is important to know how much credence can be given, for example, to an allegation or an account given by a suspect. These issues of validity have two discernible constituents. One is the detection of deception. This may be attempted on the basis of all aspects of the information available, including, in particular, the nonverbal and paralinguistic aspects of what might be said. These aspects will tend not to be well recorded by investigating officers and so they can only be derived at the time of the interview. Tape recording may add a little to this, as may video-recording of an interview but the research suggests that people are so poor at detecting deception even when they have the person in front of them that these recording devices will hide much that may be relevant (cf. Eckman, 2001).

The second psychological constituent is concerned not with the detection of deception but rather with the identification of the plausibility of accounts (Canter *et al.*, 2004). So here the question of validity assessment is approached from the opposite endpoint, which may be more useful and appropriate in some cases. These approaches to evaluating accounts are considered in more detail in the next chapter.

Interview Procedures

In crime fiction, the witness or suspect often sits with a detective, answering direct questions as if the formulation of those questions and the whole interview process was some natural common-sense procedure requiring little preparation and even less training. That may have been the case in the past but police forces and other investigatory agencies all over the world are coming to realise that much can be learnt from the general psychological understanding of the interview process as well as the results of specific studies on investigatory interviewing. A variety of interview strategies have been developed out of these realisations.

The procedures that have been developed to provide a framework for police interviews range from those that focus mainly on facilitating memory processes, such as Geiselman *et al.*'s (1985, 1986) cognitive interview (CI) (detailed fully in Fisher and Geiselman, 1992), through socially oriented approaches that emphasise the detection of deception, most notably the IEE technique (Frank, Yarbrough and Ekman, 2005) through to procedures that emphasise getting some sort of confession or indication of guilt, often more closely associated with the idea of 'interrogation' rather than an interview as advocated by Inbau and Reid (1962) and their followers, which encourage procedures such as deception by the interviewer, some of which may be illegal in some jurisdictions. These different interview procedures will be more-or-less appropriate at different points along a continuum of inherent trustworthiness of the interviewee and their account of the events at issue. Those procedures that tend to assume more trustworthiness are considered in the present chapter while procedures targeted towards the other end of the continuum are considered in the next chapter.

All these procedures, though, can only be as effective as the witnesses' memory can be. If people do not notice anything untoward happening, for example, then it is unlikely that they will have any detailed memory. A variety of studies over the past 130 years since the seminal work of Ebbinghaus (1913) have shown just how limited human memory can be. A number of factors have been found to affect the reliability of eyewitness recognition, which can be broken down into situational variables and factors that are to do with the witnesses themselves.

Perhaps the most obvious situational factor is how well the witness saw the event, which will be greatly affected by lighting conditions, with witnesses recalling much less information if the event took place at night than in daylight (Yarmey, 1986). Witnesses also have difficulty estimating the duration of events and typically overestimate time (Buckhout, 1977). Other factors include the type of information being recalled – for example witnesses find it hard to make accurate judgements of speed and distance (Leibowitz, 1985) and colour (Weale, 1982), and the violence of an event, with witnesses recalling less information when an event is very violent (Loftus and Burns, 1982).

Witness factors include the effects of stress. Some studies have found that high stress leads to a decrease in the amount of information recalled (for example, Peters, 1988), whereas others have found no influence of stress on memory (for example, Deffenbacher *et al.*, 2005; Yuille and Cutshall, 1986). One consistent finding relating to the effects of stress is that the presence of a weapon during the commission of an offence generally leads to a focusing of witness attention on that weapon (Loftus, Loftus and Messo, 1987). The expectations or biases of witnesses can also influence the way they remember events (for example, Allport and Postman, 1947) so that events that conflict with preconceived expectations are remembered less accurately. Age is a very important witness factor, with young children generally being prone to suggestibility (Ceci, Ross and Toglia, 1987) and therefore less accurate than adults. Eyewitness performance has also been found to decline in the elderly (Yarmey, 1984). Studies examining the effects of gender on eyewitness abilities have found various results. For example, Clifford and Scott (1978) found that men were better at recalling the details of a violent event. Powers, Andriks and Loftus (1979) found that men and women pay more attention to items that catch their interest. Yarmey (1993) also reports gender differences in eyewitness accuracy. Finally, some research has shown that specific details may be remembered more easily by people who have been given training, such as police officers (Yuille, 1984).

Another practically important finding that has been of great interest to psychologists has been the very weak relationship between how confident witnesses are and the accuracy of their accounts. The importance of this is that the police may often take more notice of a confident witness. Yet confidence appears to be a characteristic of the witness rather than of his or her memory (Sporer *et al.*, 1995).

The Cognitive Interview

One of the most important aspects of the information obtained during an investigation is that it should have as much relevant detail as possible. Psychologists have therefore helped to develop processes, especially for police interviews, which maximise the information obtained. In doing this, the perspective is taken that there are two issues that need to be as effective as possible. One is based on the assumption that the respondent in an interview is essentially trying to remember what occurred. Therefore anything that can help the memory process should be of value. The second issue is the relationship between the interviewer and the interviewee. If this relationship can be as supportive and helpful as possible then more effective information is likely to be obtained. The cognitive interview (CI) has been developed to enhance both of these processes (Fisher and Geiselman, 1992; Geiselman *et al.*, 1985, 1986). The components of this are given in Box 9.9.

Box 9.9 Components of the Cognitive Interview

(Geiselman *et al.*, 1985)

- Establish rapport.
- Listen actively.
- Encourage spontaneous recall.
- Ask open-ended questions.
- Pause after responses.
- Avoid interrupting.
- Request detailed descriptions.
- Encourage intense concentration.
- Encourage the use of imagery.
- Recreate the original context.
- Adopt the rememberer's perspective.
- Ask compatible questions.
- Encourage multiple retrieval attempts.

The cognitive interview (CI) derives directly from the ideas first elaborated by Bartlett (1932) in his book aptly named *Remembering*. This developed the theory that human memory was an essentially constructive process. Information was not taken out from a file store (where it may have faded with time) but was actively constructed by a variety of psychological processes. Therefore to help people remember, procedures are recommended that help the respondent to reconstruct the events as effectively as possible.

A number of studies have shown that the cognitive interview generates significantly more detailed information than conventional police interviews (Fisher, Geiselman and Amador, 1989). Some studies show that the information obtained is more accurate and also more relevant information is obtained, but it is difficult to measure relevance or accuracy precisely, so the full value of the cognitive interview is likely to vary considerably between situations.

The CI was developed from experimental studies of memory. Consequently it offers a tidy framework for psychological research. These studies typically consist of a student audience being shown a video recording of an event then being questioned in one of a number of experimental conditions about what they remember of the event. The amount and accuracy of what they remember provide the dependent variables to test the impact of the different conditions. One of the conditions will be one or more components of the CI with other comparison conditions consisting of other interview approaches.

The possibility of clear results has meant that an industry has emerged in carrying out these studies, with many different variants of the experimental conditions. Explorations of the procedure in real use as part of police processes, or even in relation to real events, have been much fewer. When Clarke and Milne (2001) examined the actual practice of police interviews they found not only that ideas from the CI are very rarely drawn upon, but that there is a great reluctance to make use of them. A large part of this reluctance comes from the increased amount of time and effort the CI requires (despite attempts to develop shorter versions – cf. Kebell, Milne and Wagstaff, 2001) but possibly more importantly because the whole approach derives from a laboratory setting for the generation of data, not the demands of the police investigation and its search for evidence.

Nonetheless, it is important to note that the results of many studies using these procedures show that with no increases in error rates, the cognitive interview enhances information up to 35% more than for controls (Kohnken, Thurer and Zoberbier, 1994). Kebbell and Wagstaff (1999) consider in some detail the forensic effectiveness of this technique and illustrate how the process connects not only with the psychology of memory but also with social and communication issues. For example, they note that interruptions, inappropriate sequencing of questions and mode changing – whilst undoubtedly techniques that interfere with recall – are social processes that disrupt communicative flow between police officer and eyewitness.

In an attempt to single out the most constructive aspects of the CI, it is perhaps significant that, in light of comments in earlier chapters on the importance of context in understanding criminal events, that context reinstatement (cf. Hammond, Wagstaff and Cole, 2006) and the social components of the CI are the two areas that Kebbell and Wagstaff and others before them (Memon and Stevenage, 1996) identified as the issues on which to concentrate. Reinstating the context places witnesses back in the role that they played in the event and adopting professional social standards places the investigating officer in the role that facilitates him or her in maximising the amount of information elicited.

As Clarke and Milne (2001) pointed out in a careful consideration of what actually went on in police interviews, the main activity usually in an interview is the writing down of a statement by the interviewer for the witness to sign eventually. Even with the increasing uptake of recorded interviews the end result is still to obtain something that can be presented to the court as a written document. This has meant that many of the aspects of good general interview practice in any context are not followed. Police officers tend to ask closed questions that do not allow the witness to give an account in a way that makes sense to the witness. The interview is often shaped around what the interviewer believes to be the circumstances, further limiting the detail and accuracy of the information obtained.

A number of researchers have pointed out the purpose many police officers see for interviewing of suspects, rather than witnesses, is to obtain a confession. Yet research shows that an admission on the part of the culprit is related mainly to the quality of the evidence that indicates guilt. Williamson (1993) reports, for example, that in a study of 1067 cases there was an admission of guilt in 67% of the cases with strong evidence but a denial in 77% of cases with weak evidence. Yet it should be appreciated that the amassing of evidence and organising it to show its significance is part of the whole investigative process – not a special aspect of how questions are phrased or whether the interviewer carefully listens to the interviewee (Bull and Milne, 2004; Kebbell, Milne and Wagstaff, 2001). For these reasons other approaches have developed that are more directly related to the actualities of the investigation and of policing, most notably the PEACE procedure that is considered below.

Face Recollection

Attempts have also been made to use similar psychological processes to improve the recollection of faces and other details (Koehn, Fisher and Cutler, 1999). This has proved less successful, in part because human recall of faces is so poor. Psychologists have therefore been involved in a variety of studies of how faces are reconstructed from memory and the procedures that can facilitate this. This has led to developments beyond the traditional 'photo-fit' approach. But the training involved in the use of these new systems and their heavy reliance on effective interviewing has meant they have not had the uptake that would have been expected from the scientific findings.

Psychological research has also contributed considerably to the improvement in the validity of the traditional 'identity parade'. Various procedures have been introduced by many police forces around the world to ensure that the recognition task set for the witness is appropriate and not open to bias. In particular these take account of the need to protect the suspect against the possibility of the witness's memory being modified by experiences subsequent to the crime, such as meeting the suspect in other circumstances (see, for example, Haber and Haber, 2000).

PACE and PEACE

Concern with many aspects of police investigations in England and Wales led in 1984 to an overhaul of the law governing police investigations that became known as PACE, The Police and Criminal Evidence Act. This instituted a legislative framework for the powers of police officers in England and Wales to combat crime, as well as providing codes of practice for the exercise of those powers. The aim of the PACE Act was to ensure that police evidence was acceptable in court and to establish a balance between the powers of the British police and the rights and freedoms of members of the public. Maintaining that balance is a key element of PACE. As a consequence the Act does indicate the conditions under which interviews of victims or suspects should take place and provides rules relating to visual and audio recording of police interviews.

This drew attention to the need to provide a framework for police interviews and a training procedure that helped investigative interviewers to develop the skills for carrying out interviews effectively. The people formulating this framework were aware of the cognitive interview approach but wished to develop a system that related directly to police practice and the need to obtain information that could be used effectively as evidence in court.

The procedure that was developed deliberately went beyond a focus on improving the recall of the witness to deal with the social transaction or what Shepherd (2007) called 'conversation management'. In practice such matters as building rapport are considered as part of the CI, but the formalities of including consideration of the personal interactions, which are central in the training and definition of an interview process, were given much more strength in the PEACE procedure.

The interview procedure that was developed became known as PEACE, to summarise its main components as listed in Box 9.10. It gives weight to what the police do before and after the actual interview as well as highlighting the importance of engaging with the respondent, building rapport and listening carefully. As with the CI and Eckman's approach, discussed later, the main questioning procedure is to encourage the interviewee to give an uninterrupted account in response to open questions of the kind 'tell me what you remember'.

Various studies (for example, Bull, 2002; Milne and Bull, 2002) have shown that although training in this procedure does have beneficial effects on police interviews there is still a tendency for police officers to interrupt and ask focused, closed questions. This seems to be, in part, because the framework goes against the grain of police culture, which is to make strong assumptions about what happened and then use the interview to get confirmation of that.

Box 9.10 The PEACE Components

P	Preparation and planning
E	Engage and explain purpose of interview and process
A	Account – free recall
C	Clarify, challenge and conclude
E	Evaluate – new lines of inquiry?

Vulnerable Interviewees

An awareness of the vulnerability of some interviewees has also led to the legal requirement that now exists in many jurisdictions for an appropriate adult to be present at police interviews. A number of witnesses may be regarded as vulnerable because of their age, emotional state or intellectual ability. Such witnesses may be particularly open to suggestion or may be made especially anxious or confused by the interview process. Special interview procedures have therefore been developed for interviewing such people. They give emphasis to the relationship established between the interviewee and the interviewer and the need to phrase questions and facilitate answers in ways that make sense to the respondent.

Research Approach to Investigative Information

Treating Evidence as a Non-Reactive Measure

The information collected in a police investigation may productively be thought of as analogous to the 'unobtrusive' or 'non-reactive' measures that social scientists have utilised (cf. Webb *et al.*, 1966; Lee 2000). By thinking of the information as a form of 'data' that is being 'measured' it becomes clear that many of the psychometric issues that have been explored to improve the quality and utility of psychological tools are directly relevant to police investigations. In some circumstances, social science approaches may even expand the range of information that detectives may consider.

This data acquisition reflects all three modes reviewed by Lee (2000). This includes:

* The *retrieval* of victim, suspect and witness statements and criminal histories of offenders and a variety of other clandestine and official records.
* Information is *captured* from crime scenes through photographic and other records, including pathologists' reports and how the scene was disturbed by the offender and what was taken from there.
* Details of offenders' patterns of association with others are also *captured* from surveillance and covert telephone auditing.
* A considerable amount of material is also *found* by police officers and others involved in investigations, such as offensive and other relevant letters – for example suicide notes – files from suspects' computers, information on victims and their lifestyles and patterns of activity.

Organising the Material: Distillation

The amount and variety of material that the police have to deal with in an investigation, as well as its unreliability and potential biases and distortions, opens up many opportunities for contributions from IP. One very important contribution comes from the psychological exploration of deception and lying, particularly within the context of investigative interviews. This is such a large, interesting and significant topic that we devote most of the following chapter to it. But even when there is no deliberate deception there are many ways in which information from IP procedures can be valuable for the police.

One important contribution that may come as a surprise, given how much material is potentially available, is to help investigators to collect more information that is appropriate. The decision of what data to collect has grown up over years of police custom and practice, influenced by requests from government and other agencies who require particular details, say on 'street crimes', because of policy objectives. Frequently, a few experienced police officers sit down and draw up a list of the information they think it will be necessary to collect. There is no clear overarching plan for this and often many conflicting demands on what to collect. For example, some information is needed for official reports on crime levels and police performance whereas other information is needed to record what actions the police have taken. Yet other information may have direct implications for where to seek out further forensic clues, such as clothing, or exactly where a victim was grabbed. The mix of information collected can therefore be very idiosyncratic. We know of one police force whose record keeping at one stage kept a careful note of whether a bicycle had different colour pedals and what those colours were but kept no direct note of the ethnic appearance of a murder victim! Furthermore the collection of information does take time and resources. It has been calculated by some police forces that, on average, for every extra piece of information that is collected about a crime one further employee is required in the collection process. The sort of information collected by a police force on existing data management systems is given in Box 9.11.

Box 9.11 A Typical Police Database Record of a Rape Incident

(Names and other irrelevant details have been modified to maintain anonymity.)

CR No: 0328167/07

================================ =====================
==============================

General Info :

IU [WH] Allegation [Rape]

Summary :

Crime last updated [02/12/2007 9:39]

Totals - VIW [1] PROP [0] VEH [0] SUSP [1] ACC [0]

Details of investigation :

The following was entered by [POLICE OFFICER]

This incident was reported to police via the CSU OFFICER. I took the initial call and contacted the Sapphire team. I called the victim back and went to see her at the COLLEGE where she is a dance student in her second year.

VIW1 (VICTIM) explained that she is a second-year student who attended a party in the courtyard of the college on 10 November with a friend. They went into the courtyard from her room in the halls of residence which is just below her block.

Her friend know only at this time as FRIEND 1 went to the bar and VIW1 (VICTIM) was spoken to by the suspect who approached her. She said that the conversation was light and he said that he was an ex-student. She can recall nothing much more. FRIEND 1 returned and the man left them. During the evening she drank two snakebites and a gin and diet coke. At about 12 midnight she went to the ladies toilets in the corner of the courtyard under the arch way. She came out and the man she had spoken to earlier grabbed her from behind and forced her in to the gardens out the back of the archway to the rear of the residential block.

He then forced to a bench in the gardens and then over to the wooded area. Here he made her perform oral sex and then raped her vaginally. He ejaculated in her vagina.

She cannot recall where he went after or what happened. She knows that she next met up with FRIEND 1 outside her room in the residential block. She did not say to her what had happened.

The following Monday she told the STUDENT NURSE that she needed the morning-after pill, which she prescribed. She vomited afterward and is anxious that she could be pregnant.

CCTV covers the courtyard area where the gathering took place but does not cover the arch way where the suspect took her or the gardens ground where the assault took place. There is no lighting in the ground at night.

The suspect is described as male white aged between late twenties and early thirties, wearing a grey/blue T shirt and jeans. He had dark hair and spoke in a London/local

accent. He has an athletic physic and was taller than the victim. He had a drink with
him at the gathering but did not appear drunk.

The following was entered by [POLICE OFFICER]

Scene not preserved – unable at this time to pinpoint location other than general
area.

SUSPECT:

No leads at this stage.

An additional complication is that the records are often in a much-abbreviated form with many codes and acronyms. These are prone to error in use and not immediately meaningful to anyone who is not an expert in the system. This makes the research use of this information especially challenging but also opens up many possibilities for confusion and distortion.

One area in which IP is beginning to make some inroads is in providing a framework for considering what different sorts of criminal actions could potentially be carried out in a crime type so that there is a behavioural scaffolding on which to build police information systems. Later chapters show how such frameworks can be derived. They also show that the great range of information that can be collected in any given crime needs to be distilled in some way. It is just not possible to make sense of and remember all the details of a crime – and even if it were possible, then there could be confusion over which details were relevant. Sometimes experienced detectives will boast that they have investigated hundreds or even thousands of homicide cases. But they do not appreciate that it is not humanly possible to remember all the details of all the cases. The detective is likely to remember some salient aspects of memorable cases but the others will all blur into a confused mixture. Without a framework in place for considering the salient aspects of a case, memories are very unreliable and records can be more confusing than helpful.

As well as possessing a framework for considering the information that needs to be collected it is also necessary to have clear summaries of that information. These summaries are most useful if they draw attention to significant or salient features of any particular crime. As discussed in previous chapters, 'salience' is not obvious but requires theoretical development and empirical evidence.

Data or Evidence?

This use of information by investigative psychologists is distinct from the official statistics on crime and criminals that have been the mainstay of criminology from its earliest days. These criminological studies have tended to be at the aggregate level, facilitating the understanding of the societal processes that underlie criminality, the impact of different government policies on the management of crime, or the significance of judicial decisions for patterns of offending. By contrast, forensic psychology and psychiatry have tended to focus on offenders once they have been through the judicial process and find themselves as 'patients' or 'clients'. They are concerned with psychological explanations of criminality, often seeking to relate these to abnormal mental processes. The practical tasks that these forensic practitioners face are often concerned with decisions about individual 'patients', such as their fitness to plead in court, their ability to control their actions during the crime, or the risk that they may pose if released. The data for such research therefore relies heavily on interviews with offenders and their assessment using psychometric procedures (cf. Blackburn, 1993; Wrightman, 2001). This, of course, complements the official statistics, not least because there will be crimes that are revealed in the consulting room that never appear in official crime reports. Yet the clinical data tend to be collected to understand the cognitive and affective aspects of the lives of people dealt with as clients or patients, not as a way of obtaining details of the actions that actually occurred in a crime or relevance to investigations.

From their different perspectives, the aggregate data drawn from official statistics and the cognitive and emotional details of individual offenders are somewhat removed from the actions that occur in crimes and the experiences of the offenders and their victims. Yet agents of law enforcement often record these direct aspects of crime most immediately. Furthermore, the official statistics and the presence of a person within a clinical or penal setting are a product of the material collected during criminal investigations. Therefore studies that draw directly on the material available to law-enforcement agencies have the potential for contributing an important and distinct perspective that complements those of other areas.

By providing a different perspective on crime and criminals, the use of police material also has the potential to increase the practical applicability of any results that emerge. As Canter (2000b) has argued, findings that are directly derived from the sort of information with which a practitioner has daily commerce are far more likely to make sense to that practitioner and are far more likely to be relevant to her/his concerns than are findings based upon some special, arcane form of data collection. For instance, police officers are more likely to take note of psychological studies of what goes on in police interviews than results derived from trained observers' assessments of micro-movements revealed on video recordings of student subjects.

However, as we have discussed in some detail above the utilisation of the material drawn from police investigations is not without many difficulties. The challenge, then, is to work with police information and establish a framework that will aid the development of robust scientific measures derived from this so that it can be treated as scientific data.

There are many contributions psychologists can make to the improvement of the accuracy and validity of the information available in an investigation. A number of formal validity assessment techniques have been developed to assess the truthfulness of witness accounts when no objective means of doing this is available. Most of these techniques are based on the assumption that honest accounts have identifiable characteristics that are different from fabricated accounts.

By conceptualising and treating this information as 'data', and by treating the ways in which it is obtained as research processes, psychologists can make a further broad contribution to investigative activity. Understanding it in this way allows us to use psychological principles and knowledge to evaluate and improve the information that detectives need to progress an investigation or to support a case in court.

Summary

With the plethora of crime fiction and fact that fills our newspapers and television broadcasts it is easy to assume that information about a crime is inevitably and uncontroversially available.

This is rarely the case. A dead body may be found but there can be considerable discussion about whether the death was from natural causes or not. A woman may claim she was raped but there can be many challenges as to whether the courts would consider there had in fact been consent. A person may report property stolen but exaggerate what was stolen to enhance his insurance claims. Then there may be issues about what the police have recorded. Breaking into a garden shed and stealing tools of little value may be listed as malicious damage by one police officer, but a different policeman may record it as a form of theft. The details that are recorded will almost certainly vary depending on who is recording them. Even if the offender himself is interviewed about what he did he may present the account in a way that will justify or exonerate him rather than giving detailed, objective information. All of these examples show that the nature of the information recorded or obtained about a crime is potentially problematic.

There is a great deal of information potentially available to the police. It is very varied and has many problems in its reliability. The challenges this poses for investigations have a different emphasis from those that are posed for research. The biggest problems for research are the biases in the sampling and the gaps and lack of detail in the data. It is rare to be able to observe a crime as it happens (although CCTV recordings sometimes make this feasible). So the researcher always has to work from a record made of the events by some third (or fourth, or fifth) party. Such records are inevitably selective but the selections made may not be those that the psychologist would have made. The whole nature of IP research therefore needs to take account of these challenges to the integrity of the data that emerges when studying crimes. These are more fundamental issues than those of reliability and validity that are presented as at the core of psychometric studies. They are issues of robustness and how to clean 'muddy' data.

Investigators are not interested in *data*. They need *evidence*. Their concerns are therefore more directly focused on the detail and trustworthiness of the information they collect and how well it will serve their primary objective of getting a conviction in court. The detail is centred on what it reveals of the crime that has been committed. Is this rape or sexual assault, first degree murder or accidental homicide, theft or fraud, criminal damage or burglary? But overarching all of these questions is the one of 'who can be believed?'

There can be inaccurate recording, innocent confusions, self-serving distortions, malicious falsifications as well as various forms of police corruption, just to list the most obvious. There are also legal and ethical constraints on what can be sought or recorded.

Improving the Information

Most research in the social sciences assumes that any information that is made available whether it be through interviews, questionnaire or recordings of actions in laboratories, is provided and obtained in good faith. It is not usually assumed that students being asked anonymously about their attitudes towards religion, for example, will lie when they answer. Researchers do sometimes take account of biases due to the respondents wishing to present themselves in a good light but do not usually work on the assumption that people will deliberately falsify the information they provide. This may well be naïve on the part of social scientists but in the context of investigations it would be regarded as silly to assume that everyone tells the truth all the time. Rather the 'data' are vulnerable to influence through every stage of information gathering and analysis, from first contact with the victim or crime scene to how the material is summarised for the court.

Research Agenda

Most of the research to date that has looked at improving police information retrieval has relied very heavily on laboratory paradigms. In this way, rather restricted scenarios are explored in controlled conditions. There has been limited, although growing, consideration of the actual processes that go on in a police investigation to obtain information. Little has been done, for example, to explore all the stages from criminal action to the presentation of an account of that action in court. There are many stages to this process and each of them has the potential to produce distortions. The laws and guidelines concerning the nature of evidence are one way of managing this process but these take little account of what is known about memory or the interview process. Future research therefore is sorely needed to unpack these issues of what really does happen as investigators build up an account of a crime. This is the study of investigative actions, which parallels the study of criminal actions.

Further Reading

Books

Bull, R., Valentine, T. and Williamson, T. (eds) *Handbook of Psychology of Investigative Interviewing: Current Developments and Future Directions*, John Wiley & Sons, Ltd, Chichester.

Fisher, R.P. and Geiselman, R.E. (1992) *Memory Enhancing Techniques for Investigative Interviewing: the Cognitive Interview*, Charles C. Thomas, Springfield, IL.

Kebbell, M.R. and Wagstaff, G.F. (1999) Face Value? Evaluating the Accuracy of Eyewitness Information. *Home Office: Police Research Series Paper 102*.

Loftus, E.F. (1979) *Eyewitness Testimony*, Harvard University Press, Cambridge, MA.

Articles

Canter, D. and Alison, L. (2003) Converting evidence into data: the use of law enforcement archives as unobtrusive measurement. *The Qualitative Report*, **8**, 151–76. Available at http://www.nova.edu/ssss/QR/, accessed 28 May 2009.

Fielding, N. (2000) Social science perspectives on the analysis of investigative interviews, in *Profiling in Policy and Practice* (eds D. Canter and L. Alison), Ashgate, Dartmouth.

Geiselman, R.E., Fisher, R.P., McKinnon, D.P. and Holland, H.L. (1985) Eyewitness memory enhancement in the police interview: cognitive retrieval mnemonics versus hypnosis. *Journal of Applied Psychology*, **70** (2), 401–12.

Hammond, L., Wagstaff, G.F. and Cole, J. (2006) Facilitating eyewitness memory in adults and children with context reinstatement and focused meditation. *Journal of Investigative Psychology and Offender Profiling*, **3**, 117–30.

Kebbell, M., Milne, R. and Wagstaff, G.F. (2001) The cognitive interview in forensic investigations: a review, in *Psychology and Law in a Changing World: New Trends in Theory, Research and Practice* (eds G.B. Traverso and L. Bagnoli), Routledge, London.

Wells, G.L. and Olson, E.A. (2003) Eyewitness testimony. *Annual Review of Psychology*, **54**, 277–95.
Williamson, T.M. (1993) From interrogation to investigative interviewing: strategic trends in police interviewing. *Journal of Community and Applied Social Psychology*, **3**, 89–99.

Questions for Discussion and Research

1. In a police investigation into a murder the police have found a distinctive shoe print that has allowed them to identify the type and size of shoe. They are carrying out house-to-house enquiries to determine if anyone recognises the shoe. Discuss how an investigative psychologist would deal with information from the enquiries as data compared with how the police might use it as evidence.

2. What are the strengths and weaknesses of the statement from P in Box 9.1? What sources of challenge to this statement can you hypothesise? What procedures could be used to improve the quality of the statement?

3. What are the strengths and weaknesses of the information in Box 9.11? What are the likely sources of distortion in it?

4. What are the implications for the evaluation of evidence that comes from CCTV film of events as they actually unfold?

CHAPTER 10

Suspect Interviewing and Deception

In This Chapter

Learning Objectives

When you have completed this chapter you should be able to:

1. Understand the different relationships and involvements that people might have to the accounts that they are giving or examining.

2. Outline and evaluate Ekman's IEE approach.
3. Discuss the use of psycho-biological lie-detectors and their potential values and weaknesses.
4. Identify the steps taken using the Reid Technique to obtain a confession and their legal implications.
5. Outline some of the factors that may lead to false confessions.
6. Evaluate the use of statement validity analysis.

Synopsis

Unlike other areas of psychological research, it cannot be assumed that the information made available from respondents in investigations suffers only from incompleteness or innocent biases. There may be deliberate attempts to hide or distort the information. A number of procedures have therefore been proposed for more intensive investigative interviewing, which seek to minimise distortions and detect deception. This family of techniques for determining if a person is lying have various origins both in psychological research and police practice, with varying degrees of sound support for their efficacy or legal acceptability.

Ekman's IEE (Improving Interpersonal Evaluations) procedure draws heavily on research into emotions and their assumed prevalence when attempting to lie or deceive. The 'polygraph lie detector', emerging from EEG procedures, and voice stress analysis systems both have similar objectives but draw on psychophysiological phenomena that have a limited relationship to the complex emotions that may be involved in deception. Reid's approach to interrogation is even more controversial than the psychophysiological procedures. It actively seeks to obtain confessions, being proposed as especially relevant for use with suspects when the interviewer is confident they are guilty.

The pressure to obtain a confession that is present in many investigations raises questions about the conditions under which false confessions occur. The psychological focus on the susceptibility of an individual to provide his interrogators with a confession has generated widely used assessments of such susceptibility. But there has been little exploration of the social and institutional pressures and procedures for obtaining a false confession outside of the earlier interest in the military use of 'brain washing'.

So far the exploration of deception and false confessions has not been extended into the related, but rather neglected, consideration of false allegations. However, there is growing evidence that falsely claiming to have suffered from a crime is an important topic for examination in areas as far-ranging as insurance fraud and the manipulative insistence on the lack of consent in sex that gives rise to charges of rape. In this area, consideration of how accounts come to be considered plausible can be important especially in determining how a jury makes a decision about guilt. Written documents are open to other sorts of analysis to examine their validity, most notably through statement validity analysis. When they are anonymous they pose further challenges such as the determination of authorship or the characteristics of the authors.

The People of the Drama: Explanatory Roles in the Investigation of Crime

The people providing investigative information have different relationships to and involvement in the account they are giving or examining. This 'role' that they play in the 'drama' carries implications for the accounts they give. Understanding the role and context of an account therefore helps to alert us to the possibilities for distortion and to set up procedures for reducing those distortions.

At each stage of the enquiry individuals (whether members of the enquiry team, witnesses, suspects or barristers) 'play' different roles. Each 'player' will have varying degrees of involvement with, and skill in conveying or eliciting an account of the offence and each individual will 'play' his/her role as a function of the context in which the event occurred and in which the account is given. For example; a witness to a fire, which is later revealed to be an arson attack has only incidental involvement and no expert knowledge when giving his/her version of events. The fire-setter, in contrast, has a personal involvement and a degree of expertise peculiar to his/her own particular goals. These facets of 'involvement' and 'expertise' have been considered by Brown and Canter (1985: 232) as highly influential on what features are highlighted in any given account:

> . . . Just as the researcher will have special reasons for collecting his explanations, so will the person providing the explanations have a variety of purposes for giving them . . . This is not to say that the individual is going, necessarily, to bias or distort his account for the different recorders. It is rather to point out that it is precisely because they are an aspect of interaction between individuals, that they will be expected to take on different content and structure for different purposes.
>
> (Canter and Brown, 1985: 221–42)

Harré (1979), for example, discusses the importance of the elicitor of the account understanding the scenario or context of the account given. Therefore, if account giving is seen as only being fully comprehensible when considered in context, the nature of the account is likely to vary from one context to another. It is not difficult to recognise in this process, how an account given by a witness to a police officer may vary from the same account given by a police officer to the courts. The interdependent features of context and role and their unfolding impact on the enquiry are therefore the prime concerns at every stage of the assessment of an account.

Strengths and Constraints of Investigative Information

There are constraints on the information available to the police during an investigation and also on the type of information on which they can act. The constraints on the information available about the crime relate to the fact that only an account of what has happened, who the victim is, where it took place and when, is available to investigators. There is not often any direct observation by the investigator, or the possibility of direct contact with the offender during the commission of the crime, although increasingly CCTV may give some record of the crime even though it may be the back of the offender's head or a rather poor quality black-and-white image.

As mentioned in our opening chapter, this is very different from most of the areas of psychology, where the person of focal interest is available for close, direct observation and detailed questioning. If there is a victim who survives a crime then that victim may be able to give details of what occurred. But even in this case, it is unlikely that the victim can give any reliable information about the internal, cognitive processes of the perpetrator during the criminal acts. So the predictor variables (the important features of the offence) are limited to those that are external to the offender.

The criteria variables (the important features of the offender) are also restricted because the information on which the police can act is limited to what is available to them in the investigative process. Details of a person's characteristics and domestic circumstances are all potentially available to investigating officers for any particular suspect. However, personality characteristics, detailed measures of intelligence, attitudes and fantasies are all more difficult for investigating officers to uncover.

Similarly, in relation to giving guidance as to where detectives should look to find possible suspects, information about residential location, or recreational activities, for example, is more likely to be of immediate value than the issues with which psychologists are more conventionally concerned, such as locus of control or sexual predilections. In order for the inferences to be of value to investigators they must connect directly with things that police officers can actually act on. Where an offender could be living is a clear example of useful information to an investigator, but more subtle material such as how others may regard the offender or his/her likely skills and domestic circumstances may also be of value. However, intensive psychodynamic interpretations of the offender's motivations that might only become available during in-depth therapeutic interviews are less likely to be of direct assistance to police investigators. For example, detectives were able to arrest and secure a conviction against Barry George for the murder of Jill Dando in the absence of any clear ideas about why he had committed this crime (although a subsequent appeal found that conviction unsafe).

Unlike in many crime novels the motivations, or possibly more accurately the reasons why an offender carried out an offence can be of general interest to investigators but they are only of value if they allow inferences to be made that will facilitate the detectives' decision-making process. In practice, though, police typically draw on ideas about the possible motive in any direct way only when they have no obvious lines of enquiry.

However, in many cases the investigative process is not so simple – detectives often have information that is rather more opaque. For example; they may suspect that the style of the burglary is typical of a number of people arrested in the past. Or they may infer from the disorder at a murder case that the offender was a burglar disturbed in the act. These inferences will either result in a decision to seek further information or to select from a possible range of actions including the arrest and charging of a potential suspect.

Box 10.1 Getting a Confession

The police had been looking for the killer of two boys, whose bodies had been found near ponds in open parkland. To provide some idea of how the police eventually obtained a confession, here is an account based on an interview with the investigating officer.

The police officer started by saying:

> If he hadn't of come forward we would have found our way to him anyway. Through house-to-house enquiries we had a description of the man from two boys that had seen him earlier. They knew who he was and where he lived. We found out that about 15 minutes before we went to talk to one of these boys he had gone and knocked on their door and said 'you shouldn't go fishing up in those ponds anymore because there has been a murder up there.'
>
> The boy had told him that the police were coming to talk to him about that in 15 minutes anyway. He carried on cleaning his car, but when the police knocked on the door opposite he went over and said 'will you be wanting to talk to me'
>
> He told us that he had directed the boys to the pond. He choked when he said this but it was only at this point that he choked everything else was calm. He kept on cleaning his car after coming across to tell us that he had directed the boys.
>
> I thought it was significant that he had initially carried on with his normal activities. This meant that the man, if guilty, was really guilty and could not plead any form of diminished responsibility. It was this aspect of being able to carry out his normal activities that I found most surprising.

The man had offered to come and talk to the police about what he knew but they were being a little distant about dealing with him. This seemed to be a mixture of being not sure if he was just an interfering irrelevancy or thinking he might have something important to say. But the police officers were aware that if he did have something important to say they needed to interview him in their own time and place so that they could do it properly. So he was told that a car was not available to take him where he could give a statement. He nonetheless drove to the station himself and was there waiting to say what had happened.

Photographs of the man showed there was nothing unusual about him. He was moderately handsome man, looking younger than his mid-thirties with a dark short beard. One was a photograph of him standing in his shorts leaning against his door. This was a police photograph revealing scratches on his legs that it was assumed had occurred in the undergrowth near where the boys' bodies were found.

> I thought the way the man had behaved during the interview was very significant. He rambled on about the boys being sent to the pond, but he seemed choked and poured with sweat. At one point, when it was put to him that he was responsible for what happened, the man had fainted on to the desk he was sitting at. I was sure that he was still listening. His breathing

(continued)

was still quite normal but when he got up from the table there was a pool of moisture from the sweat that had poured out of him. I think a lot of this was just kidology. The fainting was a defence mechanism.

He said he had first gone to the pub after fishing and had gone home to wash up before going to get a lottery ticket. The follow up enquiries all suggested that this account was accurate and the timing reasonably correct, but what had been left out of this was the twenty minutes or so during which he had killed the boys and the time he had taken on the way to buy the lottery ticket and to throw away the murder weapon, at least the knife and the mallet, which were later recovered. The piece of wire that he had wrapped around the boys necks has not been recovered.

What he told us early on was that he had directed the boys to a further pond and then gone along to see them. He said that the boy was up a tree and came down with the wire tangled around his neck. In trying to get the wire off, he claims, he strangled the boy and then he stabbed him many times for reasons that he didn't know.

It is worth emphasising that any quest for motivation or motive, as mentioned in earlier chapters, is best seen as an informal attempt to develop some explanatory model that will help to link the crime behaviour to the offender. So, for example, if the motive were thought to be monetary gain then someone who would have a need for such money or who recently seems to have acquired a lot of money would be assumed to be a viable suspect. However, without clear empirical evidence on the particular types of behaviour that are associated with financially motivated crimes and that the people who carry out these crimes do indeed have a need for such financial gain, the interpretation of the motive and the inference drawn from it are little more than speculation. The weakness of such speculation can be demonstrated by the finding that those who have carried out insurance fraud have usually not been in particularly straitened financial circumstances. Dodd (2000), for example, demonstrated that only 13% of the 209 fraudulent insurance claimants he examined were in financial difficulties, whereas 57% were earning a regular income. In the same way, the commonly expressed view that rape is *not* motivated by the need for sexual gratification (for example, Godlewski, 1987) again draws attention to the point that one cannot equate the gain derived from a crime with its motivation, or by extension, with a particular type of individual.

Suspects

When the suspect is the source of investigative information it is quite likely that he or she will deliberately provide invalid information, so encouragement to tell the truth is an important investigative skill. As Moston, Stephenson and Williamson (1992) found some time ago, probably the best way to get the truth from offenders is to deal with them in a direct honest way, presenting clearly the evidence of their guilt. The stronger this evidence the more likely they are to confess.

However, in situations where the evidence is not so clear and there is suspicion of deception then attempts to detect falsehoods are important. There are many objective, conventional

police strategies for detecting deception, most obviously determining if the known facts contradict the suspect's claims, but behavioural and psycholinguistic cues to deception may also
be helpful. However, many researchers are sceptical as to the possibility of any generally available indexes of deception from the actions or words of the suspect during a police interview
(cf. Milne and Bull, 1999). Vrij and his colleagues (2008) have shown that developments in
the interview procedure itself may be an important way forward for detecting deception rather
than relying entirely on cues from the interviewee.

Other researchers have explored related approaches to setting up interview procedures that
will increase the likelihood of being able to detect deception or encourage the truth, but these
have their difficulties too, as we shall see in the following pages.

Ekman's IEE Approach

The cognitive interview emerged directly out of university-based studies of memory processes
and the PEACE system was derived from considerations by police officers with a background
in the psychology of the procedures for carrying out effective interviews. Ekman (2001) took
a different approach. For over a quarter of a century Ekman has been systematically studying
the expression of human emotions. As part of this research he became aware that some of
the issues he was studying had relevance for detecting deception because of the emotions
generated in many people when they are lying. In the late 1990s the relationship of this work
to the aspirations for improving the effectiveness of a range of interview situations became
apparent, especially in situations where the interviewee may be deceptive. The wide interest
in the cognitive interview was probably part of the stimulus for creating a process that would
go beyond memory enhancement and give the interviewer tools that would help him/her to
evaluate what was being said.

They therefore carried out studies of how good investigative interviewers worked, combining
their examination of what happened in the cut-and-thrust of real police work with background
material from experimental research on both the detection of deception and the enhancement
of human memory. Out of these considerations emerged the IEE (Improving Interpersonal
Evaluations for Law Enforcement and National Security) technique.

Like the CI and PEACE processes, the IEE approach emphasises a search for the truth
through open questioning. Attention is given to exploring whether the answers given, although
believed to be truthful by the interviewee, are not accurate accounts of the fact. Within this
framework there is also the possibility that the respondent does not believe the answers to be
truthful. This is where Ekman's approach to lie detection comes into its own.

Growing out of his studies of emotions he has argued, from a lifetime of research, that
lying tends to generate emotions in the liar. These emotions are typically very difficult for the
liar to conceal. Ekman proposes that this difficulty comes from the evolutionary basis for the
expression of emotions that are reflected in neuropsychological structures. So the experienced
interviewer can be trained to detect small indications of emotional responses that might at
least indicate the emotional significance of what a person is saying even if they do not indicate
lying.

A particularly interesting aspect of Ekman's proposal for observation of emotions that may be of investigative significance is that we express our emotions through many different 'communication channels'. What we say, the paralinguistic and non-verbal aspects of how we say it, the bodily gestures and facial expressions, are all potentially independent of each other. A person can describe a sad event with a big smile on their face or say 'yes' whilst gently shaking her head. The claim from the IEE procedure is that if there are discrepancies between these different channels then suspicions should be roused as to the real meaning and truthfulness of what is being said.

Part of the emotional response in deception relates to the cognitive load of creating deceptive information. Rather than recalling what has happened, the liar has to invent an account that he then needs to maintain, requiring a clear memory of what has been invented and the ability to create logical and consistent elaborations of that invention in the face of questioning. The cognitive and emotional demands of deception therefore may be revealed in self-manipulatory gestures, such as scratching, hesitancy of speech as well as repetition and other account dysfluencies. However, all researchers who have studied this emphasise that there are no generally available indexes of deception from the actions or words of the person during a police interview. The interviewer needs to take account of the normal reactions of the respondent, who may twitch or stroke her hair, or be rather hesitant in his speech even when not under the pressure of telling lies. By developing an understanding of the baseline, nonpressured reactions of the interviewee it may be more possible to determine when he or she is struggling to create a convincing account of the events and people being described. The interviewer who is aware of this can therefore listen very carefully for inconsistencies that may be a sign of fabrications, or vagueness that may be an indicator that the person is trying to avoid the need for further invention.

As noted earlier, one of the most significant findings from studies of investigative interviews is that a culprit is most likely to admit to a crime when there is clear incriminating evidence. This puts pressure on investigators to elicit that evidence and not rely solely on what may be said within an interview. But this also means that the interview itself can be a very useful source for determining where such evidence can be found. The IEE technique therefore explicitly proposes that the interview be integrated with other investigative activity.

Box 10.2 Basic Principles of IEE (Frank *et al.*, 2006)

- Awareness – knowledge of ways in which information can be inaccurate.
- Baselines – study of the normal mode of behaviour of the respondent.
- Changes – note reactions of the respondent that are different from the baseline.
- Discrepancies – observe variations in reactions in different channels of communication.
- Engagement – create a comfortable context for continuing rapport.
- Follow-up – explore corroborating evidence from other sources.

Psychophysiological Lie Detectors

In circumstances in which the truth of what is being claimed is absolutely crucial to an investigation and there is little opportunity for corroborating evidence, there is a desire in some jurisdictions to use procedures that it is believed will directly detect whether a lie is being told. There is some evidence to indicate that many people give psychophysiological responses that may be indicators of false statements. The procedure for examining these responses is often referred to as a polygraph or 'lie detector'. In essence this procedure records changes in the autonomic arousal system – emotional response. Such responses occur whenever a person perceives an emotionally significant stimulus. The most well-established indicator is when the respondent is asked to consider information that only the perpetrator would be aware of, known as the 'guilty knowledge' test.

A more controversial procedure is to ask 'control questions' that many people would find emotionally significant, in order to determine if they elicit responses that can be distinguished from those questions relating directly to the crime. However, in both these applications of psychophysiological measures, the most important element is the very careful interview procedure before measurements are made and during the process.

In general 'lie-detection' is more productive in supporting a claim of innocence than in providing proof of guilt (Elaad, 1999; Kleiner, 1999). For this reason, many jurisdictions do not allow 'lie detector' results to be presented as evidence in court. Its value is thus in eliminating possible suspects. This is how it is used in a variety of jurisdictions around the world.

Interestingly, the belief in the power of lie-detectors may be their greatest value. As Grubin (2004) for example describes, work with sex-offenders has shown that they are more likely to admit to breaking the rules of their probation if they are questioned in relation to lie detection procedures. It is their belief that they will be found out by 'the machine' that leads to them tell the truth!

Other procedures, such as hypnosis, the use of the 'truth drug' sodium pentathol, voice-stress analysis and developments in measurement of the electrical activity of the brain emerge from time to time as the basis for detecting deception. There is little doubt that each of them can contribute something of value to an investigation but the claims for them usually far outstrip any evidence in support. Often there are also very real practical as well as human rights concerns about applying them to ongoing investigations. However, this does not stop enthusiasts in some countries from trying to make use of these techniques quite inappropriately. There are even cases in South East Asia in which suspects are given sodium pentathol, hypnotised and then wired up to electroencephalogram equipment as part of an interview process. Not only would it be difficult to evaluate the products of such a cocktail of procedures but many people would regard it as a form of torture. The lack of effectiveness as well as the moral depravity of torture is a significant issue that is discussed in a very informed way by Pearse (2006).

The Reid Approach to Interrogation

When the FBI agent in the cult TV drama series *Twin Peaks* confronts a suspect with the challenging question of whether he is guilty or not, then decides confidently on the basis of the answer that the man is innocent, it is clear that the script writer knew something of the Reid technique. This process of obtaining a confession or determining guilt had its origins in the systematisation by US law enforcement officers during the 1940s of procedures that were widely believed to be of value when dealing with suspects (Buckley, 2006). Since those early days, the techniques have been developed further and converted into a formalised training package that has been delivered to 'hundreds of thousands of investigators' (Buckley, 2006: 190).

The Reid technique responds directly to the often-mentioned purpose that investigators have in carrying out an interview of a suspect; that is to gain an admission to the crime. This contrasts with the 'search for the truth', which is the stated objective of other processes described in the previous chapter, most especially the PEACE procedure. The reason for this difference in emphasis is partly due to the different rules regarding evidence in different countries, especially the much more cautious approach that the British courts take to confession evidence and the very distinct attempt to avoid any obvious coercion that is enshrined in the PACE law. Under US law, for example, deception of a suspect in order to obtain evidence is allowed under certain circumstances. This means, for instance, that the awareness that a confession is more likely if the suspect believes there is hard evidence against him can be used to deceive the interviewee into thinking there is evidence when actually there is not. Such practices used to be accepted in England and Wales but were outlawed under PACE. One important reason for denying interrogators the option of misleading their suspect was the large number of false confessions that the courts became aware of over many years, often produced by inappropriate interview techniques.

But although there are many criticisms, especially from United Kingdom-based experts (for example, Gudjonsson, 2006; Williamson, 2006) it should not be assumed that the advocates of the Reid technique are gung-ho, shoot-from-the-hip, cops totally oblivious to the human rights of the people they are interviewing. Advocates such as the President of John E. Reid & Associates, which provides the training in the technique, are at pains to insist that it 'scrupulously honours the rights of the individual and the guidelines established by the courts' (Buckley, 2006: 190).

The whole approach deriving from Inbau and Reid's initial (1962) proposals is to distinguish between a non-accusatory interview of a witness and a fundamentally accusatory interrogation of a suspect. Most legal systems recognise this distinction proposing specific guidelines especially for how an interview of a suspect should be carried out. For example; Section V of the PACE Act 1984 deals with the Questioning and Treatment of Persons by Police and the Codes of Practice C and H set out the requirements for the detention, treatment and questioning of suspects in police custody by police officers. Therefore the Reid proposals for an interrogation do reflect distinctions that are present in the minds of investigators and legal processes.

The Reid approach, then, is very much a set of procedures developed by police officers for the daily practice of police officers. In the training, attention is given to every detail, even how the chairs should be arranged in the interview room and the physical environment can be set up to establish a sense of privacy with minimal distractions. The process itself is then organised around nine 'steps'. The fundamental assumption of this technique is that the interrogator has very strong grounds for being convinced that the suspect is indeed guilty and that if pressed about the offence in a firm and informed way he will admit to the crime, or at least offer admission to enough aspects of the crime to provide the basis for further investigation and eventual prosecution. As is the case with so many procedures used regularly by law enforcement around the world, it is difficult to find any independent evidence of the efficacy of the Reid technique.

Box 10.3 The Main Steps in the Reid Technique for Obtaining a Confession

1. Step one: direct positive confrontation:

The suspect is told with absolute certainty, that he has committed the alleged crime.

2. Step two: theme development:

Reasons are given aimed at minimising the moral implications of the crime.

3. Step three: handling denials:

Denials are interrupted and the suspect told to listen to what the interrogator has got to say.

4. Step four: overcoming objections:

The interrogator overcomes the objections the suspect may give as an explanation or reason for his own innocence.

5. Step five: procurement and retention of suspect's attention:

When the suspect shows signs of withdrawal, the interrogator reduces the psychological (and if necessary physical) distance between himself and the suspect to regain the suspect's full attention.

6. Step six: handling the suspect's passive mode:

When it looks like the suspect's resistance is about to break down the interrogator focuses on a central theme concerning the suspect's reason for the crime, displaying signs of understanding and sympathy. The interrogator appeals to the suspect's sense of decency and honour and maybe religion.

7. Step seven: presenting an alternative question:

The suspect is presented with two possible alternatives for the commission of the crime, one being face saving and the other some repulsive or callous motivation.

(continued)

8. Step eight: having the suspect orally relate various details of the offence:
When the suspect has accepted one of the alternatives given to him he is asked tell about it in further detail.

9. Step nine: converting an oral confession into a written confession.

False Confessions

The greatest challenge to the Reid technique and to a lesser degree the IEE procedure is the possibility of people admitting to an offence they did not commit. Leo, Costanzo and Shaked (2009) have recently reviewed the challenge posed by the possibility of false confessions and how psychological input can be of value to the courts. Gudjonsson and MacKeith (1988) have drawn attention to the possibility that some individuals may confess to crimes they have not committed as a consequence of characteristics similar to those that make witnesses vulnerable, such as heightened emotional state and low intellectual ability, making the suspect more willing to accept suggestions from the interviewer (cf. Gudjonsson, 2001).

One approach to dealing with this has been Gudjonsson's development of a measure of a person's 'suggestibility', which has been drawn on by the courts around the world to support claims of a false confession (Gudjonsson, 1984). As Leo, Costanzo and Shaked (2009) emphasise, these may also be a product of cultural processes rather than aspects of personality, in which, for example, groups from certain ethnic minorities may deem it essential to agree with whatever a person in authority, such as a police officer, says to them (cf. also Gudjonsson, Clare and Rutter, 1995). Investigative psychologists have also considered the ways in which false confessions may be produced in response to various forms of psychological or physical coercion. However, all this work suffers from the practical difficulties of ever being certain that a confession really was false, so the impact of this approach often owes more to the predilections of particular jurisdictions than to the unchallengeable validity of the research on which it is based.

False confessions have been rather underemphasised in the past. The awareness that there are indeed a variety of circumstances in which people will confess to crimes that they have not committed is growing. Yet although there are various legal procedures in place in different countries to guard against false confessions there is still remarkably little psychological research on this topic, although the recent review by Leo, Constanzo and Shaked (2009) is opening the way to a more informed approach to this important topic.

False Allegations

Sometimes the concern will be not with the veracity of the suspect's account but with that of an alleged victim. In recent years there have therefore been explorations of the various conditions under which people will falsely allege that they have suffered at the hands of others. Often, but not always, this is an allegation of sexual abuse or harassment (see also

Chapter 12). The various procedures for detecting deception may be relevant in these cases but because the complainant is not a suspect the more intrusive processes of lie detection are rarely used. Instead there have been attempts to indicate the circumstances under which such false allegations are made and use those as guidelines for more intensive examination of the circumstances of alleged offence (Mikkelsen, Gutheil and Emens, 1992; Tate, Warren and Hess, 1992). However the validity of these procedures is still highly questionable.

Box 10.4 Some Reasons for False Allegations of Rape or Harassment

(from O'Donohue and Bowers, 2006)

- Financial gain
- Gain from 'victim status'
- Excusing inappropriate behaviour
- Gaining desired change in circumstances
- Hurting an individual or institution
- Gaining power in a relationship or institution
- Mentally disturbed understanding of experiences
- False (recovered) memory

These procedures sometimes deal with the nature of people who are most likely to make false allegations, which includes recognition that people with certain sorts of personality disorder may be prone to false allegations (O'Donohue and Bowers, 2006). Reasons such as extortion or blackmail cannot be discounted as well as the financial benefits that can sometimes come directly from compensation payments made to victims or indirectly from the support that victims can gain. This can include circumstances such as a desire to be rehoused by a local authority, which can lead to a person claiming they have been assaulted in their present accommodation. The much more complex issue of false memories being generated within the context of them being 'recovered' during therapy sessions has also been a source of false allegations that the 'victim' may genuinely have believed to have occurred. McNally's fascinating (2003) book on *Remembering Trauma* makes very clear the conditions under which false memories of trauma can occur, which in some instances can lead to false allegations and consequent disturbing miscarriages of justice.

Mention should also be made of those people who will appear as victims at televised news conferences, calling for help from the public, when in fact they are the culprit. A list of websites showing videos of their appeals is given in Box 10.5. These videos demonstrate the effectiveness with which many such people can lie convincingly. This has been demonstrated directly in a study by Vrij and Mann (2001) who showed how readily such appeals were believed, once more showing the difficulty of setting up procedures that will reliably detect lying even in high-stakes situations that have not been generated for laboratory purposes.

Box 10.5 Websites with Videos of False Appeals

Penny Boudreau's daughter went missing on February 2008 and her body was found a few days after this appeal:

1. http://southshorenow.ca/newsnowclips/play.php?vid=81

Penny Boudreau was arrested June 2008 and pleaded guilty Jan 2009. Her statement is at:

1. http://thechronicleherald.ca/News/9010584.html

Matthew Gretz's wife, Kira Simonian, was murdered June 2007. He made an appeal several weeks later:

1. http://wcco.com/topstories/Minneapolis.police.Kira.2.369066.html

He speaks at time 0.43–0.58 and again at 1.38–1.56.
Gretz was arrested Sep 2007 and confessed June 2008. It is reported here:

1. http://www.kare11.com/news/news_article.aspx?storyid=513048

Leah Walsh disappeared Oct 2008 and her husband Bill made this appeal:

1. http://abclocal.go.com/wabc/story?section=news/local&id=6474387

He speaks at time 0.45–0.49 and again at 1.48–1.55. Leah's body was found soon after and he confessed to her murder. His lawyer has now claimed that Walsh made a false confession:

1. http://abcnews.go.com/TheLaw/story?id=6147680&page=1

This is Nisha Patel-Nasri's husband who was later convicted of her murder:

1. http://news.bbc.co.uk/1/hi/uk/7388731.stm

(We are grateful to Clea Whelan for drawing up this list.)

Written Accounts

Although many of the nonverbal and paralinguistic aspects of the spoken word, as well as the other gestures and indicators to which Ekman particularly draws attention, are lost when words are written down, nonetheless most of the material with which an investigation deals is stored in the form of written words. Yet despite its limitations, material in written (or printed) form offers a variety of options for careful analysis that are not so readily applied to the spoken word. This can be a consideration of the veracity of the written material, its actual authorship, or even characteristics of the author.

In some cases the written material is the actual 'crime scene'. This would be true of extortion and blackmail documents, offensive or libellous material and many documents used in fraud. It is the record of what a person has done. If the document is written by a police officer then doubtless distortions will occur but even a photograph of a crime scene will be taken from a particular angle and objects might have been disturbed between the crime occurring and the photograph being taken. So there is every value in considering material written by an offender, or suspected victim, in great detail, very carefully.

Intrinsic Statement Validity Analysis

The problem of determining the truthfulness of statements is particularly important when there is the possibility of false allegations. There have been a number of attempts to develop procedures that will allow assessment of the validity of any claims from victims. These procedures draw on the central ideas of how deception may be detected, which are relevant to any account, most notably the difficulty of creating a coherent consistent account of something that has not happened.

The most frequently used approach to statement validation is that developed by Undeutsch in 1989 known as statement validity analysis, which draws upon detailed consideration of the content of a statement, a procedure referred to as criteria-based content analysis. Undeutsch hypothesised that accounts based on real events would contain certain features that would be absent in false allegations. These features were called 'Reality Criteria' and later came to be known as 'Content Criteria' (Steller and Kohnken, 1989).

The whole process of SVA consists of three phases: (a) a structured interview of the child witness, (b) criteria-based content analysis (CBCA) and (c) a validity checklist (Raskin and Esplin, 1991). It is important to note that the purpose of SVA is to provide an assessment of the validity of the recorded statement, not of the general credibility of the child witness. The basic purpose of CBCA is to determine if the specific content of the child's statement is indicative of a report produced by attempts to recall actual memories or if they appear to be the result of invention, fantasy or influence by another person. The verbal content of the statement is analysed by applying a set of criteria to the transcript of the interview.

As we have noted, there has tended to be a focus upon the role of the individual in the sequence of action associated with the event. However, as Tully (1999) points out, Undeutsch's breakthrough in the 1950s was to concentrate solely on an assessment of the account of a crime rather than on the background (or profile) of the witness/suspect giving it. The Undeutsch hypothesis therefore appears to make no judgement about the explanatory role of the account giver. A closer examination though reveals that this is not the case.

Undeutsch's fundamental criteria (for example, degree of detail, details of offender-victim relationships, contextual embedding) are all concerned with features that make for a convincing and coherent 'storyline'. Part of what convinces the listener is the role that the interviewee portrays themselves as playing within that account. For example, if the role player does not indicate the setting of the story (contextual embedding) this can be an indication that the individual is fabricating. Furthermore, as Tully (1999) points out, developments in criteria-based content analysis have centred around details outside of the statement itself with additional assessments being made on the psychological characteristics of the statement maker, characteristics of the interview, motivation and issues involved with investigative questions.

These additions beyond the sole consideration of the content material are employed to test the plausibility of various alternative hypotheses by examining different parts of the information. The process focuses on the role of the statement maker within the context in which the statement was produced. In doing so the individual carrying out the assessment is looking for a coherent set of relationships between the details of the account and the context within which the events purportedly occurred. For example, children often accurately report details of sexual acts from a framework not yet equipped to report such violations – so ejaculation may be reported as 'his snake spat at me'.

However, CBCA is not a sufficient basis to form a definite conclusion concerning the validity of the allegations. Additional factors must be analysed to consider all the other relevant information required to make a credibility assessment. This is done by means of the Validity Checklist.

Box 10.6 Content Criteria Used in Statement Analysis

These consist of five categories containing 19 criteria that have been found to differentiate between false and genuine statements.

General characteristics

1. Logical structure
2. Unstructured production
3. Quantity of details

Specific contents

4. Contextual embedding
5. Descriptions of interactions
6. Reproduction of conversations
7. Unexpected complications during the incident

Peculiarities of content

8. Unusual details
9. Superfluous details
10. Accurately reported details misunderstood
11. Related external associations
12. Accounts of subjective mental state
13. Attribution of perpetrator's mental state

Motivation related contents

14. Spontaneous corrections
15. Admitting lack of memory
16. Raising doubts about one's own testimony

---

17. Self-deprecation
18. Pardoning the perpetrator

Offence-specific elements

19. Details characteristics of the offence

Validity Checklist

Steller and Kohnken (1989) developed rules that were designed to enhance interrater reliability in applying SVA, including, for example, not increasing the rating of a criterion just
because of repetition in a passage. On the other hand some passages may fulfil more than
one criterion. This is known as the Validity Checklist. It is employed to test the plausibility
of various alternative hypotheses by examining particular aspects of the information. Steller
and Kohnken's (1989) checklist is shown in Box 10.7.

Box 10.7 Validity Checklist (from Steller and Kohnken, 1989)

Psychological characteristics

1. Appropriateness of language and knowledge
2. Appropriateness of affect
3. Susceptibility to suggestion

Interview characteristics

4. Suggestive, leading or coercive questioning
5. Overall adequacy of the interview

Motivation

6. Motives to report
7. Context of original disclosure or report
8. Pressures to report falsely

Investigative questions

9. Consistency with the laws of nature
10. Consistency with other statements
11. Consistency with other evidence

(From Steller and Kohnken, 1989)

These criteria have been validated by both simulation and field studies (Esplin, Boychuk and Raskin, 1988; Steller, Wellerhaus and Wolf, 1988). They have shown both very good interrater reliability on the presence or absence of criteria, and that the criteria are more often found in genuine cases than false ones. Other studies have also pointed to the effectiveness of this approach. For example, in their study of 43 interview statements from genuine and false rape cases, Parker and Brown (2000) showed that the CBCA factors did differentiate the two groups (as corroborated by forensic evidence, guilty pleas and withdrawal of allegation). However, in a Dutch study of 103 child sexual abuse allegations, Lamers-Winkelman (1999) reports only a weak relationship between the CBCA measure and case outcome, leading her to conclude that Statement Validity Analysis should not be used to assess sexual abuse accounts from children.

Summary

Investigative interviewers are required to do more than help the person being interviewed remember events as clearly as possible in a comfortable atmosphere in which they can give a clear account. Typically there will also be the need to encourage the respondent to tell the truth and to be able to determine if this is indeed the case. This does not only apply to interviewing suspects, who may have a variety of reasons for lying, but also to witnesses and victims – even when a person confesses to a crime this may not be the whole truth.

As a consequence various procedures have been and continue to be developed that encourage and test the veracity of interview statements. Some of these rely very heavily on the actual interview procedure itself. Such procedures, often thought of as 'interrogation', may get close to forms of coercion or seriously misleading the interviewee that are not allowed in many legal systems. Other processes rely on human psychophysiological responses generated by forms of emotional arousal that are assumed to be associated with not telling the truth. However, these procedures also have limited validity especially with skilled liars, although they can be useful in encouraging people to tell the truth.

Detailed analysis of exactly what has been said, using stylistic indicators of veracity, is also widely employed, but evidence for their effectiveness is not as widespread as might be hoped. What emerges is that most people are very good at lying and very poor at detecting deceit. It therefore remains the case that the best checks on truthfulness are those that draw directly on known facts in a case and corroborative evidence and that all inferences derived from police interviews need to be treated with caution.

Further Reading
Books

Canter, D. and Alison, L. (2000) *Interviewing and Deception*, Ashgate, Dartmouth.
Ekman, P. (2001) *Telling Lies: Clues to Deceit in the Marketplace, Politics and Marriage*, W.W. Norton, New York.
Granhag, P.A. and Stromwall, L.A. (2004) (eds) *Deception Detection in Forensic Contexts*, Cambridge University Press, Cambridge.

Gudjonsson, G. (1992) *The Psychology of Interrogations, Confessions and Testimony*, John Wiley & Sons, Ltd, Chichester.

Shepherd, E. (2007). *Investigative Interviewing: The Conversation Management Approach*, Oxford University Press, Oxford.

Vrij, A. (2008) *Detecting Lies and Deceit: Pitfalls and Opportunitites*, 2nd edn, John Wiley & Sons, Ltd, Chichester.

Articles

Baldwin, J. (1993) Police Interview techniques: establishing truth or proof? *British Journal of Criminology*, **33** (3), 325–52.

DePaulo, B.M., Lindsay, J.J., Malone, B.E. *et al.* (2003) Cues to deception. *Psychological Bulletin*, **129**, 74–118.

Parker, A., and Brown, J. (2000) Detection of deception; statement validity analysis as a means of determining truthfulness or falsity of rape allegations. *Legal and Criminological Psychology*, **5**, 237–59.

Vrij, A. (2004) Why professionals fail to catch liars and how they can improve. *Legal and Criminological Psychology*, **9**, 151–81.

Vrij, A., Mann, S., Kristen, S. and Fisher, R.P. (2007). Cues to deception and ability to detect lies as a function of police interview styles. *Law and Human Behavior*, **31**, 499–518.

Questions for Discussion and Research

1. In the account of how a confession emerged in Box 10.1 what are the various sources of information with which the police are working? How would you set about evaluating that information? What procedures might the police have used in that situation to develop a fuller account of what had happened and the truthfulness of the information given?

2. Lawyers often claim that the evidence of witnesses for the prosecution is more important than the confession of the accused. Do psychological considerations throw any light on this?

3. Suppose a new procedure had been proposed for detecting deception by careful examination of how people organise their desks. How would you set about testing whether this procedure was reliable and valid?

4. What are the strengths and weaknesses of written accounts of the events of a crime when compared with a spoken account?

5. Do the ethical and legal constraints on how police may interview suspects have any implications for the use of confessions in psychological research?

6. Discuss the strategies that you and your friends use to tell convincing lies. How may these interfere with the processes used by investigative psychologists for detecting deception?

7. What do you think the main difficulties will be in setting up a study to examine the conditions under which false allegations of rape are made?

8. Note that most of the procedures dealing with investigative interviewing in the previous chapter are strongly based within police work in Britain whereas the focus on detecting deception and more intensive interview strategies of the present chapter is more typically prevalent in the United States. Why do you think this might be?

9. Box 10.5 lists some websites that present people making false appeals for help in crimes that they have committed themselves. Can you determine any indicators that they are lying?

PART III

Profiling Criminal Actions

Models of Offending Behaviour and Applications of Investigative Psychology

The mob pursuing Mrs M'Dougal

Source: The New Newgate Calendar © The Folio Society Ltd 1960

CHAPTER 11

Acquisitive Crime

In This Chapter

Learning Objectives

When you have completed this chapter you should be able to:

1. Understand the different offending styles in burglary and the types of behaviour that exemplify each, appreciating that:
   (a) the 'Conservative Tragedy' NAS mode manifests as efficient offences focused on maximising material gain;
   (b) the 'Adaptive Adventure' NAS mode produces competent offences in which the offender is aware of and actively manages the risks of his intrusion into the premises in which the theft occurs;
   (c) the 'Integrative Irony' NAS mode manifests as offences focused only on obtaining items to meet the offender's immediate needs, irrespective of other considerations;.
   (d) the 'Expressive Quest' NAS mode produces demonstrative, impactful and potentially confrontational offences.
2. Accept that the modulating facet of offending intensity will be revealed in the degree of exploitation, material and otherwise, that the offender undertakes of the victim's environment.
3. Understand the different offending styles in robbery and the types of behaviour that exemplify each, appreciating that:
   (a) the 'Adaptive Adventure' NAS mode produces highly effective offending behaviour, with the victims managed as 'objects';
   (b) the 'Integrative Irony' NAS mode produces offences that have a desperate, reckless quality – the interpersonal style of treatment of the victims is consistent with the 'victim as person' role described in relation to violent crime;
   (c) the 'Expressive Quest' NAS mode produces dramatic, risky, impulsive offences in which the victim is a vehicle for the offender's demonstration of his dominance.
4. Understand the differences between various types of fraud, and the different psychological processes underlying each.

Synopsis

The many different forms of crime that have as their central process the acquisition of money or goods are explored in this chapter. The NAS model turns out to be useful and reasonably robust in considering these crimes and distinguishing between them. This enables us to see that there are many aspects to these crimes beyond the obvious desire to acquire something of value.

Many offenders commit burglary even if they go on to violent crimes. It may be thought of as the crime that defines a person as being dedicated to a criminal lifestyle. It may therefore be expected to exhibit the full range of modes of interaction that we have found to characterise crimes in general.

The legal distinction between robbery, in which theft involves violence or the threat of violence, and burglary, in which there is no violence, is not as clear-cut in terms of actual behaviour as it is under the law. However, those crimes in which some violence or threat of violence is used to obtain goods or money offer a further range of psychological issues to consider. The active role of interacting with others to acquire money or goods possibly limits the range of styles for this type of crime, in particular making the Tragic, Conservative role less likely.

Fraud moves the form of social interaction a stage further on in complexity from burglary and robbery, but also makes use of knowledge of what is possible, especially for the larger scale frauds carried out by people within or upon businesses. These individuals are less likely to have obvious roots in other forms of criminal activity. It is the context within which they act which is often the most useful key to their characteristics.

Differentiating Acquisitive Crime

The examples in the opening Box 11.1 give a flavour of what happens when offenders are seeking money, often for drugs. In both these cases the offender interacted with the victims.

Box 11.1 Offenders' Personal Narratives

A 33-year-old in prison for robbery:

> I was out drinking, got badly drunk. My mates told me a car had broken down outside. There were three lads in the car. I pretended to be a police officer and said, 'can I see your driving documents' and asked them to get out of the car and empty their pockets. I took their money and left. There was no preparation. I just said I was the police. It would not have happened if I wasn't drunk. When I robbed them I left, but then came back and the police were there. I pushed past them and ran away. A week later they arrested me as one of the police women knew me.

A 22-year-old in prison for robbery:

> We'd make about £500 a day committing robberies, I wasn't even bothered about being caught, and I just needed the money for cocaine. We were doing it every day for a while but it only hit us when we got caught, so that was just me for the next few years. I was working, I was 15 with a full time job . . . my manager introduced me to cocaine and I started stealing from work to fund my habit, so I got sacked and started doing the robberies. I did it with a mate. We robbed people on the street: anybody for anything. I'd take phones off people etc. Then we'd get away and get it sold. We thought it was funny how we did it, we wouldn't just get one phone, we'd nick loads all at once. Now I know it's not funny at all. I got caught coz I stole a phone off a police officer, he was in plain clothes but he ran after me and tackled me to the floor, he was much faster than me.

But some offenders will be careful to avoid dealing directly with their victims, for example by breaking into a warehouse at night. Others will operate at a distance from any form of confrontation or overt intrusion into another's property as in complex frauds. This variety of potential interactions can be thought of as lying along a psychological continuum that reveals the offender's preparedness or propensity to interact with others when committing the crime. At one extreme is robbery, an offence whose success lies in the effectiveness of the direct interaction with victims, although, as in our examples, it can require subterfuge or can just be 'grab and run'. At the other end are those fraud offences in which the gain is achieved not just without any contact but frequently by the offender concealing aspects of his identity from others.

FRAUD   BURGLARY   EXTORTION   AGGRAVATED BURGLARY   ROBBERY
Increasing preparedness to interact →

This continuum draws attention to crucial variations within the broad category of property crimes. So, although the study of the psychological correlates of offence types has tended to compare person-related crimes, typically crimes of violence, with acquisitive crimes, explorations of offender differences within property crimes, relating to their preparedness to interact with implicit or explicit victims is fruitful. One basic hypothesis suggested by some initial work then will be that these differences between different types of property crime will be reflected in offender characteristics relating to interpersonal predisposition and styles of interacting with others (Youngs, 2004).

In more detailed NAS terms, different variants of acquisitive crime represent different modes of functioning. Burglary is the direct management of available external resources to achieve material gain, so is essentially an 'Adaptive Adventure'. Fraud is, at its core, a rejection of normal rules and procedures, the stealing activity hidden from the outside world, understandable as a form of 'Integrative Irony'. Robbery is the manly imposition of the individual's will upon the outside world as a means of acquisition that is consistent with an 'Expressive Quest'. The vindictive exploitation of an external circumstance that characterises blackmail or extortion is an approach to acquisition that emphasises the 'Conservative Tragedy' mode of functioning. The present chapter shows, using the illustrations of burglary and robbery that, within these fundamental modes of functioning, differences in the offending action patterns within a crime type can also be understood in terms of the NAS.

Problems with Typologies

Throughout this book we have kept away from assigning offences or offenders to distinct, separate 'types'. In Chapter 5 this was discussed in relation to identifying 'theme' in crimes and criminal actions. This is a way of avoiding the simple view that a crime or criminal can only be assigned to one of a very limited number of distinct types. This avoidance of thinking of a crime as being one or another 'type' is particularly important when considering the actions in crimes and how offences may be effectively distinguished from each other. It is therefore useful to review the central problems with distinct types.

The key assumption of assigning anything to one type as opposed to any other types is that, within each type, the characteristics that define that specific type are likely to co-occur with one another with regularity. For instance, all those actions that are considered aspects of aggression are going to happen in any crime that is described as 'aggressive'. It is not of much value to speak of crimes being 'aggressive' if the crimes so assigned contained different mixes of aggressive and nonaggressive activity. But in addition it is assumed that specific characteristics of one type do not co-occur with any frequency together with the specified characteristics of another type.

For typologies to have any utility each type needs to have characteristics that are clearly distinct from those of other types. Or, if there is a mix of characteristics belonging to different types, a clear set of criteria would need to be in place to determine how an individual or event is to be categorised. So, if we wish to use only some aggressive behaviours to place a crime in that type, we would need to be clear which they were. For example if verbal aggression was to be ignored and only physical aggression included that would need to be clearly stated. In essence, then, the central test of a typology is to test the hypotheses that (a) the characteristics within each type consistently co-occur with one another and (b) that these characteristics do not co-occur with characteristics of other types. If the patterns of co-occurrences and lack of co-occurrences do not reflect the proposed characteristics of each type then there is no support for the typology.

Therefore one way to test directly if it useful to assign crimes to different 'types' is to examine directly the co-occurrence of characteristics across a large number of cases. A thorough test requires that the frequency of co-occurrence between every pair of characteristics needs to be examined. This is a daunting task if handled in a purely numerical way. But a visual representation of these patterns of co-occurrence can be used to test the primary assumptions directly. Multi-dimensional scaling (MDS) procedures are of value for this because they represent the co-occurrence of variables (offence characteristics, in this case) as distances in a geometrical space. Each characteristic is a point in the space and the further apart any two points the less frequently do they co-occur. The characteristics defining each type are hypothesised to form a distinct region of the MDS space. As we have seen in earlier chapters and will see in the following chapters, it is extremely unusual for any behaviours or other variables used in research to form distinct regions in the MDS space. This indicates that 'pure' types rarely exist. Instead we can identify dominant themes, but there will be actions that can contribute to more than one theme requiring caution in how these themes are interpreted.

Burglary

The identification of differences in offending style and the possibility of investigative inferences this raises, has particular implications in relation to burglary. This is an offence that is found within the criminal histories of most offenders (see Box 11.2). It tends to be common to the earlier offending of many rapists, drugs offenders and violent offenders (Safarik, Jarvis and Nussbaum, 2002; Youngs, 2001). Not surprisingly, then, burglary offenders tend to be a fairly heterogeneous group (see Table 11.1). It is therefore the level of the more detailed behavioural variations within offences that provides the potential for investigative inferences. Offenders from across the board may commit a burglary at one point or another but they will not all commit it in the same way. Indeed, given that many more serious offenders will also tend to be in police databases for burglary offences, models of burglary variation have considerable utility beyond the investigation of burglary.

However, the investigative psychological examination of burglary encounters a number of challenges. The information available is limited. Detection rates for burglary are very low (typically less than 10%), and these only refer to those burglaries that are reported. This suggests that not only are we working with a small subset of all offences but that the offences that are detected may not be a representative subset of all burglaries. Apart from this, police recording procedures often limit the amount of information about what went on in the offence, together with other problems discussed in Chapter 9.

All these challenges are tackled within IP through the use of the thematic differentiation approach, which means that behaviours are taken as indicators of the theme to which they belong. Conceptually, the models developed are models of differentiation and so provide the psychological basis for distinguishing patterns within the range of information that is available (and within the particular context or phenomenon under consideration) rather than stipulating that particular behaviours are fixed indicators of a given offending style. The thematic differentiation approach also reduces many of the problems associated with simply assigning crimes to one of a limited number of types.

Box 11.2 Burglary Key Facts

- Burglary is categorised as a property crime.
- There is a distinction between domestic (break-ins to all inhabited dwellings) and nondomestic burglaries (break-ins to businesses, sheds and outhouses that are not part of the inhabited property).
- Aggravated burglary is where an offender is armed with any kind of weapon at the time of committing the burglary.
- While there are a wide range of burglar characteristics, the typical burglar is a young unemployed male.
- Fifty-two per cent of offenders are known to the victim (2006 British Crime Survey).
- The items that are usually stolen include money, jewellery, electrical goods, mobile phones, computers and related equipment, DVDs/CDs.
- The median cost of burglary per household is £330 (2006 British Crime Survey).
- The police recorded 280 704 domestic burglaries and 302 995 non-domestic burglaries in 2007/08 (British Crime Survey) in England and Wales.

- The 2007/08 BCS estimated that only 64% of domestic burglaries were reported to the police.
- Burglary accounts for 7% of all British Crime Survey crime and 12% of recorded crime (2008 British Crime Survey).
- Around 2.4% of households had experienced a burglary in the last year (2008 British Crime Survey).
- The following factors have been found to influence the decision to offend: need for money, being drunk/drugged up, opportunity and influence of others/friends (Wiles and Costello, 2000).
- There is a strong association between drug abuse and burglary. Wiles and Costello (2000) report that 69% of burglars were hard drug users.
- Factors often cited as important in target selection: The absence of the occupants; target attractiveness; familiarity of the area; proximity of crime location to offender's base; the affluence of an area; visibility and accessibility of the target; and security cues such as alarm systems and window locks.

Table 11.1   Attributes of burglars.

Age	UK: Home Office statistics (%)
	School age: 9
	16–24: 48
	25–39: 28
	40<: 15
	USA: FBI Uniform Crime Reports (%)
	<15: 8.1
	<18: 27
	<21: 45.3
	<25: 58.6
Gender	FBI Uniform Crime Reports (%)
	85.5 Male
	Farrington and Lambert (2007) (%)
	95.4 Male
Race	USA: FBI Uniform Crime Reports (%)
	White: 68.5
	Black: 29.8
	American Indian or Alaskan Native: 1
	Asian or Pacific Islander: 0.7
	Farrington and Lambert (2007) (%)
	89% White
	6% Afro-Caribbean
	4% mixed race
	1% Asian

Modelling Burglary

> A person is guilty of burglary if, having entered a building or part of a building as a trespasser, he steals or attempts to steal anything in the building, or inflicts or attempts to inflict grievous bodily harm on any person in the building.
>
> (UK Theft Act 1968; section 9(1)(b))

Although defined legally in terms of trespass and stealing, consideration of burglary from the perspective of the offender and in psychological terms provides a rather different understanding of this offence. For the offender, burglary is the crossing of psychologically significant physical boundaries in order to gain, in a general sense, from the material wealth there. It differs, then, in psychologically important ways from offences in which particular items are selected and then taken, being a more exploratory and open-ended approach to material gain. It also differs in the general approach to accessing this material gain. Burglars typically adopt an exploratory, adventuring, enquiring and to some extent unknown, risky strategy rather than confrontation and the maintenance of superior physical and psychological force (as in robbery), manipulation and subterfuge (as in fraud), threat (as in extortion) or indeed a battle of wits with security measures and staff (as in shoplifting). This understanding of what burglary represents psychologically as an activity for the offender opens up thinking about what the differences might be in the way offenders tackle the offence.

Consistent with this conceptualisation of exploration and exploitation of what may be available within the external world, burglary represents a fundamentally 'Adaptive' offence in terms of the action system modes of functioning that we have reviewed in earlier chapters. The offence emerges out of the external availability of desired goods; it is a response to, and prompted by, these external cues. The offender is acting directly on the external environment with a central, functional (Adaptive) purpose of obtaining those goods (external impact). The narrative that drives forward the Adaptive mode of functioning is that of 'adventure', an individual negotiating the external world to his tangible fulfilment. The dominant roles acted out are aspects of 'professionalism' including power, mastery and competency. It is against this 'Adaptive Adventure' backdrop that the variations in the offending styles revealed in different burglaries need to be understood.

Psychological Components of Burglary

Most of the work on the classification of burglars and their offences focuses on effectiveness and competency. A recurrent theme in the literature is the level of skill, epitomised by Maguire and Bennett's (1982) notion of the 'first-division burglar' and that is often tied to the circumstances in which the burglary arises. Walsh (1986), for example, distinguishes the Novitiate ('an apprentice learning from a skilled burglar who lacks detailed technical skill') from the Pillager ('an unskilled adult burglar who is triggered into offending by need and fails to plan') and the Breaksman ('A skilled artist ... He will plan ahead ... This burglar will be self-disciplined'). Similarly, Cromwell, Olson and Avery (1991) describe a general scale of professionalism, along which Novices, Journeymen and finally Professionals lie. In the same vein, Merry and Harsent (2000: 48) distinguish between High Craft ('cognitive capability . . . and proactive rather than reactive in quality') and Low Craft ('a comparative lack of planning, knowledge and skills together with a tendency to reactiveness . . .') in the burglary behaviour that they studied.

The assessment of skill in burglary that all these typologies draw attention to is a complex challenge. In part, this is because the sophistication of the offence behaviour will often reflect the skill required rather than the skill potentially available. For example, it is not necessarily appropriate to consider a burglar who exploits a security weakness, such as an open window, as less skilful than one who successfully overcomes a complex alarm system. Why use the skill to overcome the alarm system if the window is open?

The assessment of skill in a burglary is also complex because there is a range of varying ideas about what exactly it represents. In the details of the skill typologies, authors refer variously to planning, technical skill, manual dexterity, proactivity, detection avoidance, access to criminal contacts and value of property stolen. Certainly all of these may be part of a skilful burglary and are consistent with the 'Adaptive' concept of what burglary is about generally. The difficulty is that they reflect a variety of different psychological processes that have differing psychological origins, some being a reflection of experience, others of various combinations of intelligence, cognitive styles and personality characteristics.

It is proposed instead that the psychological concept that can be understood as common to all of these processes is one of degree of focus (Youngs and Canter, in press, c). This is the idea that the observed differences in burglary behaviour will reflect the extent to which the offender is focused on the task of completing a successful, effective burglary. This may manifest in variations in aspects of planning, technical skill and the value of the property stolen. It may also underpin variations in features of burglary such as the degree of superfluous activity or the amount of risk-taking, as well as other features. The common relevance of all of these components to the commission of burglary and so to our understanding of potential variations within this activity lies in the extent to which they indicate the offender's centre of attention is on the task.

Alongside a task-focused distinction, the IP understanding of crime as a social transaction (Canter, 1989) suggests a further psychological distinction that may also be relevant to burglary behaviour. Canter argues that all offending constitutes some form of interaction with the victim, ranging from the explicit interaction that characterises violent crime to an implicit social transaction that he asserts is part of all acquisitional offences, even when the victim is not present at the time of the offence. The existence of an implicit transaction opens up the possibility that sometimes property offences will involve interpersonally-directed actions that are highly significant to the offender. It is an assertion that at its extreme underlies Walsh's (1980) specification of the 'Riddlesmith' burglar who targets individuals who represent a personal obsession. It is also apparent within the pervasive idea, captured by Walsh's (1980) 'Feral Threat' type of burglaries, which are directly malicious acts of vandalism. This notion, that there can be aspects of burglary offending that are an attempt to relate to the victim, is also supported by work on the impact of the offence in which many victims report a sense of interpersonal violation (Bennett and Wright, 1984; Brown and Harris, 1989; Korosec-Serfaty and Bollitt, 1986).

Following this general line of thinking, it is proposed that, in the context of a burglary, an important variation between offenders will lie in the extent to which they are consciously aware of the occupant of the house into which they are intruding (Youngs and Canter, in press, c). The conceptualisation of burglary as essentially 'Adaptive' suggests that it will be this awareness rather than the degree of malice in the interpersonal interaction that is fundamental. It is argued, then, that some offenders will not see the house as somebody's home but rather simply as a building, whereas for others the existence and personal identity of the householders will be more salient. In some cases, this awareness of the victims will produce a desire to have an impact upon them while in others it may manifest as a heightened awareness of the potential risk of the occupants returning.

This awareness of the victims' likely presence represents a second basis for behavioural differences, independent of differences in the degree of focus on the criminal acts. It interacts with the degree of focus to produce distinguishable offending styles to the criminal actions. Within the range of possibilities this generates four rather different thematic emphases that provide a framework for considering burglary.

Offending Styles: A Narrative Action System for Burglary

When considering the differentiation within broad classes of crime the NAS distinctions capture differences in how the offence is committed rather than what type of activity it is. As such, an *external source* of the action will manifest as burglary behaviour that is focused on managing the external environment and the physical execution of the offence. An *internal source* underpinning how a burglary is committed would suggest behaviour that is less concerned with managing the environment and more concerned with the enactment of an individual's personal, expressive objectives, producing extraneous behaviour that may be risky and is not conducive to the burglary. This can be readily understood to have direct parallels to the distinction in the degree of task focus.

In the same way, the 'action system' distinction between an internal or an external desired impact can be interpreted in terms of the interpersonal awareness the offender has of the victim. An *external actualisation* or desired impact requires that the offender has an interpersonal awareness of the victims. This is not required if the behaviour is simply about the benefits for the offender (*internal actualisation*). This model, as with arson offending styles, allows us to interpret burglary in terms of different action system modes. As the section below illustrates, these offending styles can be elaborated by reference to the narrative associated with each mode (Youngs and Canter, in press, c).

The empirical evidence for the presence of these distinguishable action modes is given in an SSA derived from a limited set of variables (Merry and Harsent, 2000). The original authors had worked with a descriptive account of their results but they can now be seen to illustrate a NAS for burglary (Figure 11.1). The figures in brackets indicate the frequencies of occurrence of each action (see Table 11.2 for full action descriptions) across the sample of 60 house burglaries in England.

Figure 11.1 An SSA of burglary actions.

Source: Youngs and Canter, in press, c (derived from Herry and Harsent, 2000).

Conservative Tragedy

The first distinct theme in burglary is found where the offending is highly focused on the job yet there is a lack of conscious awareness of the owners/occupants of the property. The lack of consideration of the people being targeted will accentuate the task-based approach to the burglary further. This will produce streamlined, efficient offences that rely on technical competency rather than any broader strategies or control of the situation for the successful commission of the offence. The combination of this and the psychological irrelevance of the victim will lead to an offending style in which occupied premises are avoided and in which the interaction with the premises is minimal. The focus will be entirely on the material gain that can be obtained so the expectation would be that these offences are characterised by very careful target selection and the taking of high-value goods from them (see Figure 11.1).

The external shaping of the actions inherent in the task-focused approach and the lack of interest in any external impact of the actions on the victims means that this burglary form may be understood as a 'conservative' mode of action system functioning (external source, internal actualisation). The conservative mode draws attention to the relevance of the nature of the internal impact of the action. It suggests an understanding of the offences as the assimilation of external resources internally that will in some way support the continuation of the offender's

Table 11.2   Frequencies of occurrence of burglary actions.

Attribute	Frequency (n = 60)	Percentage
On or near main thoroughfare	57	95
Identifiable property stolen	45	75
Multiple rooms searched	43	71
Forced entry	42	70
Audio-visual equipment stolen	37	61
Entry through window	31	51
More than 5 items stolen	28	46
Value stolen worth £500+	27	45
Objects strewn	25	41
Tool brought to scene and used	22	36
Forensically careless	20	33
Jewellery stolen	20	33
Recorded music stolen	20	33
Cash stolen	20	33
Carrier taken from scene	16	26
Property occupied	14	23
Insecure	14	23
Skilled entry	13	21
Credit cards stolen	10	16
Watches stolen	9	15
Cameras stolen	8	33
Theft without search	7	11
Alcohol	7	11
Entry by climbing	6	10
Secondary insecurity exploited	6	10
Offender drew curtains	6	10
Clocks stolen	6	10
Small electrical items stolen	6	10
Tool from scene used	5	8
House secured from occupants	5	8
Ornaments stolen	5	8
Offender used facilities	4	6
Antiques stolen	4	6
Children's items stolen	4	6
Offender prepared exit	3	5
Malicious damage	3	5

functioning (Shye, 1989). In arson, Canter and Fritzon (1998) suggest that this may take the form of direct personal retaliation offences; the internal sense of revenge this achieves against an external hurt providing psychological support (the resource) for the individual (and his continued effective functioning). In the context of burglary and its essentially adaptive mode, the offences produced will be ones that can be understood very directly as the drawing in of material resources from an external source.

Within the context of burglary then, the focus on the assimilation of external resource will produce a style of offending that is very focused on material gain (Table 11.2). The conservative emphasis on the internal impact of this gain and its role in facilitating continued functioning suggests that these may be understood as offences that are carried out to support the perpetuation of broader, possibly organised criminal activity. This would suggest that one component of this offending style may be a professional, commercial approach to what is taken and possibly the targeting of not just high value but particular types of goods to order.

Reference to the Tragedy narrative linked to a conservative mode enriches understanding of this offending style further. The central thesis of this narrative is that the individual has been wronged or deprived so all that matters now is retaliation. The actions that emerge out of this narrative are vindictive and avenging rather than the defeatism that is more characteristic of Irony. In relation to burglary, a fundamentally Adaptive Activity, this active avenging may take the form of attacking particularly wealthy victims whose affluence accentuates the offender's sense of deprivation. This would mean that the targeting of notably affluent homes and areas may be an integral part of this style of burglary.

Adaptive Adventure

Where the offender is task focused and fully aware of his intrusion into somebody's house, an offending style characterised by precautionary activity would be expected. The Adaptive action system mode that describes these externally guided and externally directed actions is one of directly responding to and handling of the environment that will produce highly effective burglaries. The management of the environment will be through its direct physical modification revealed in burglary actions such as the drawing of curtains during the offence to allow unrestricted exploitation of the house.

As Shye (1989: 354) reminds us, in Adaptive mode the 'energy discharged' through the action on the environment is of no significance so the awareness of the interpersonal intrusion here will not result in the emotionally significant activity seen within the expressive mode. Rather, in these offences this awareness will manifest as an alertness to the potential risks of being discovered by the occupants, seen in offending actions such as the securing of premises against the occupants' return (see Figure 11.1).

The seeking of external reward from a direct exploitation of the environment that characterises Adaptive functioning produces highly instrumental action. In arson, this has been argued to take the form of insurance fraud offences or arsons to conceal evidence of other criminal activity (Canter and Fritzon, 1998). In burglary, the instrumentality of purpose would be revealed in offending actions concerned with maximising the resources drawn off. Unlike conservative offences where predetermined high value types of items only are taken the offending style consistent with the Adaptive mode would be one in which all valuable goods are identified in a very thorough search of the setting.

The Adventurer narrative that is consistent with the Adaptive mode, elaborates understanding of this burglary style further. Within this narrative, the management of external conditions takes the form of mastery and the satisfaction derived from this mastery is emphasised. This would suggest a style of burglary in which the offender's effective environmental management evolves into a domination of the house. This is seen in the offence actions, sometimes misconstrued as malicious, of moving things and turning the house upside-down.

Integrative Irony

The burglaries that emerge out of a lack of awareness of the house as somebody's home yet which also lack a focus on the task, can seem the most bizarre offences, being neither about significant material gain nor about the experience of the intrusion. One way of understanding this activity is suggested by interpreting it in terms of the NAS mode. That is consistent with both the source and locus of effect being internal, as a form of self-adjustment. In other words, the action is an attempt to feel better; a response to a negative internal state.

In some contexts, the integrative mode produces behaviour that is an inwardly directed, self-destructive attempt to draw attention to the emotional distress the individual is suffering. One form, for example, is suicide by arson (Canter and Fritzon, 1998). In the generally Adaptive context of burglary, however, this mode of functioning would be apparent at this 'second-order' level, as offending actions that are simply focused on obtaining what the individual needs to feel better and are about nothing but his or her requirements.

The self-involved functioning that the Integrative mode implies would suggest that the lack of focus in the offence task will be particularly evident in a failure to consider the possibilities for detection, by, for example, stealing identifiable objects, rather than by any actively risky behaviour as in the Expressive mode. In terms of the types of goods stolen, the Integrative emphasis on internal adjustments would suggest that these will be items of immediate gratification for personal use and comfort, such as alcohol (see Figure 11.1).

The irony narrative that animates the Integrative mode develops an underlying story for these offences in which the individual is the powerless victim of a senseless and empty world. This absence of any rules or meaning provides the psychological context that allows the offender to ignore even the most fundamental social codes. It suggests an extension of our understanding of this burglary style to include offending actions that represent abuses of trust (such as the targeting of neighbours' houses and the exploitation of knowledge about their security procedures/weaknesses) and other forms of socially unacceptable behaviour (such as stealing children's items) as indicated in Figure 11.1.

Expressive Quest

A further variant of burglary emerges when the offending is characterised by an awareness of the house as somebody's home along with a lack of focus on the task of committing a burglary. This combination of psychological conditions would be expected to produce a lot of extraneous and superfluous activity within the offence that is related to the experience of the intrusion into another's private personal world.

The Expressive action system mode consistent with this non-task focused (internal source), victim aware (external impact) functioning is one in which the central concern is with impacting on the external world, particularly in a way that 'reflects in one way or another the system's own characteristics' (Shye, 1989: 353). This suggests, then, that the extraneous, superfluous activity will have this particular expressive quality, comprised of actions in which the offender seeks to impact emotionally on the victim, typically through hostility. This may be seen then in actions such as the daubing of graffiti, vandalism or using the bathroom facilities within the house (see Figure 11.1).

The quest narrative suggests a further understanding of this emotional expression in terms of the offender on a heroic, manly mission. This is the burglar who is concerned not with exhibiting detailed technical proficiency, as might be the case for the offender on an Adaptive Adventure, but with demonstrating his manly prowess. This is revealed in risky and physically challenging behaviours such as climbing up the property to enter (see Figure 11.1). This is the style in which the offender will be ready to confront householders directly. Congruent with this theme of uncompromising bravado, the lack of task focus here manifests as carelessness. This is indicated, for example, by leaving footprints or fingerprints (see Figure 11.1).

In sum then different patterns of burglary offending actions can be understood by reference to the different modes of functioning of the narrative action system, such that Adaptive Adventure, Expressive Quest, Integrative Irony and Conservative Tragedy variants of burglary may be identified (Youngs and Canter, in press, c).

The radex structural model of criminal differentiation (see Chapter 5) predicts more marked differentiation of offending styles with increased intensity of offending. In line with the proposition that burglary should be understood in psychological terms as an exploratory, adventuring approach to acquisition that involves the offender in crossing psychologically significant physical boundaries into someone's home, this intensity would be expected to be revealed in the degree of exploitation of the victim's environment. High levels of exploitation will take on different forms depending on the particular NAS emphasis to the offending behaviour. For example within the Conservative Tragedy it may be reflected very directly in the amount of material gain derived from the burglary. There is some indication of degree of exploitation as a modulating facet that is to some extent reflected in the prevalence or rarity of the behaviours (see Table 11.2), on the Merry and Harsent SSA presented here, although future studies with a broader variable set may be able to clarify this further.

Robbery

On the night of 7 November 2000 six men tried to steal the De Beers Millennium diamond collection, worth an estimated £200 million, from the Millennium Dome in London. The robbers were caught literally, red-handed by police lying in wait as the result of a sophisticated operation, as they smashed their way into the dome with a JCB digger equipped with a giant mechanised shovel. The robbery was planned carefully and professionally, in minute detail. It almost succeeded. If it had, as the prosecuting QC Martin Heslop observed; 'it would have ranked as the biggest robbery in the world in terms of value. It could probably be described as the robbery of the millennium'!

(The Millennium Dome Diamond Heist Source: BBC News Website)

Although the Dome Diamond Heist was, of course, a real crime, the Hollywood mythology of the meticulously planned attack by a team of anonymous, masked, ruthless professionals targeting diamonds, gold bullion or cash reserves of unimaginable value does not hold for the majority of robberies. In fact, studies show that very few robbers carry out any extensive planning (3% according to Feeney, 1986), target places that hold vast reserves of cash and valuables (20% in Alison *et al.*, 2000), use direct physical violence (McClintock and

Gibson, 1961) or even wear a prepared disguise (22% in Alison *et al.*, 2000). Table 11.4 shows the general attributes of robbers. Table 11.3 shows the behaviours typical of a sample of robberies studied by Watts (1994). Certainly for the investigative psychologist, what distinguishes this form of offending is not its sophistication and distant professionalism; rather it is the

Table 11.3   Frequencies of robbery offence actions.

Robbery behaviours	Frequency (%)
Instructional language	83
Handgun	65
Disguise (made)	41
Disguise (none)	38
Victim participate (victim forced to assist)	32
Assault (control)	31
Overt security	29
Shotgun	28
Spontaneous threat	22
Disguise (improvised)	20
Floor (instructs/forces victim to floor)	20
Pre-planning	19
Implied knowledge	17
Demeaning language	14
Incapacitate (victim bound/locked/isolated in part of building)	13
Post-event threat	12
Response threat	11
Other weapon (additional)	10
Assault (response)	9
Reassuring (compliance)	7
Assault (gratuitous)	7
Replica	7
Firearm implied	6
Firearm concealed	4
Firearm discharge (threat)	4
Precautions	3
Apology	3
Justification	3
Hostage	3
Scanners	1
Burglary	1
Sexual language	1
Firearm discharge (intent)	1
Firearm discharge (injury)	1
Implied knowledge (personal)	Nil
Insider	Nil
Reassurance (comforting)	Nil
Indecent assault	Nil

Source: We are grateful to Steve Watts for collecting the data used in this analysis.

Table 11.4 Attributes of robbers.

Age	UK: Home Office statistics (%) School age and under: 15 16–24 years old: 71 25–39 years old: 16 40<: 1
	USA: FBI Uniform Crime Reports (%) <15: 5.8 <18: 27.2 <21: 49.4 <25: 64.7
	Metropolitan Police Service About 70% of offenders aged 16–24
Gender	UK: Home Office Statistics 94% Male
	USA: FBI Uniform Crime Reports 88.4% Male
	Metropolitan Police Service 90% Male
Race	USA: FBI Uniform Crime Reports (%) White: 42 Black: 56.7 American Indian or Alaskan Native: 0.6 Asian or Pacific Islander: 0.7
	Barker *et al.* (1993) 2/3 Afro-Caribbean 1/3 White
Home environment/ background	Barker *et al.* (1993) 69% from one-parent families 25% had been in care 66% described childhood as 'happy' 70% living at family home when arrested
Education	Barker *et al.* (1993) average age at which left school: 15 large majority said they never went many suspended from school

preparedness to interact directly with the victim and, importantly, in this interaction overtly pursue a criminal goal.

This distinguishes robbery from other property crime, whether fraud, burglary or shoplifting, in which it is by avoiding the interaction and any contact that the theft is possible. But it also distinguishes the offence from other violent crimes in which, although there will be direct interaction, criminal intent will not be explicitly part of this interaction from the outset, either because the violence is actually generated by the encounter itself or because the intent is deliberately concealed. However, the psychologically interesting preparedness to present directly to another person the overt criminal objective that is central to robbery has led to a misconstrual of the offence as a highly professional criminal activity.

This belief in the fundamental 'professionalism' of robbery has led to an emphasis in the literature on distinguishing robbers and robberies in terms of degrees of professionalism and related concepts (Conklin, 1972; McClintock and Gibson, 1961; Walsh, 1986). For example the four types of robber that Conklin (1972) identifies in his study of 67 imprisoned robbers in Massachusetts are differentiated on the basis of how the offence is instigated and the degree of planning this implies. For his 'professional robbers' the offence is part of a committed criminal activity and so involves considerable skill and planning. He distinguishes these from the offences of the 'addict robbers' who plan to the extent that they select their targets carefully. These are different again from the random, impulsive offences of the 'opportunist robbers' and 'alcoholic robbers'. Walsh's (1986) distinction between the 'planned' robber who focuses on high value impersonal targets and the 'opportunist' robber, whose decision to offend is impulsive and typically precipitated by alcohol or drug taking, is along similar lines.

Yet, from a psychological perspective, the defining feature of robbery as an activity is the willingness to confront victims and take from them directly. As part of this direct confrontation, the offender must be prepared to take and maintain control of the interaction. This demonstrates a readiness by the offender to impose his wishes directly on the outside world. Its success lies in the coherence of the offender's imposition of himself and his wishes upon the victim. In psychological terms then robbery is a highly demonstrative act, in general terms, an 'Expressive' action system mode of functioning. Against this Expressive backdrop, the intensity and drama of this offence demands a confidence and clarity of presentation from the offender; a particularly salient set of narrative roles. An essential feature of this is the approach to the handling and treatment of the victims.

Modelling Robbery

A development of the concepts of planning and professionalism as a way of understanding variations in robbery comes from the NAS framework (Youngs and Canter, in press, c). Given the significance of the direct interaction integral to robbery, components of the role of the victim framework (Canter, 1994) are useful to further elaborate the offender's style of interpersonal treatment of the victim. An initial IP study of 144 armed robbers (Alison et al., 2000) produced the SSA output in Figure 11.2. Although Alison and his colleagues were aware of the narrative implications of their results, the reinterpretation presented in Figure 11.2 shows how directly it does provide empirical support for the NAS and victim role interpretations. This shows a core region of high-frequency variables that define the types of offences considered here: Surprise attacks (47%) on business premises such as petrol stations (47%) by a group of two or more offenders, carrying a firearm (67%) and who verbally instruct the victims to give them money (70%). This sample thus has many parallels to that described by Smith (2003) summarised in Box 11.3. Beyond this general description three regions of behaviours indicating different psychological themes or styles of offending are identifiable.

Box 11.3 Robbery: Key Facts

- 'A person is guilty of robbery if he steals, and immediately before or at the time of doing so, and in order to do so, he uses force on any person, or puts or seeks to put any person in fear of being then and there subjected to force' (Theft Act 1968, s. 8(1)).
- Other terms such as street robbery, street crime or muggings are often considered synonymous with robbery.
- Recorded crime offences distinguish between personal and business robbery. Personal robbery is when the goods stolen belong to an individual or individuals rather than a corporate body, regardless of the location of the property. Business robbery is when the goods stolen belong to a business or other corporate body (such as a bank or a shop), regardless of the location of the robbery.
- An offence of theft from person is recorded when there is no use or threat of force.
- Robbery offenders are more likely to use weapons than other violent offenders. Weapons are used or displayed in 33% of personal robberies (Smith, 2003).
- Robbery accounts for 2% of recorded crime and 3% of British Crime Survey (BCS) crime (included in BCS violence).
- Robberies are most commonly committed by two or more persons acting together (Smith, 2003).
- The police recorded 84 706 robberies in England and Wales in 2007/08 (BCS, 2008).
- Smith (2003) reports that 94% of the offenders are male while female robbers are rare, accounting for only 6% of suspects.
- Smith (2003) found that seven out of ten robberies involved male victims being attacked by male offenders.
- Two out of every five personal robberies involves a victim and an offender under the age of 21 years. Over half of all offenders are between 16 and 20 years old (Smith, 2003)
- Forty-five per cent of robberies recorded by police in England and Wales took place in London.
- Personal robbery is more likely to occur at night. About half of all robberies occur between the hours of 6 p.m. and 2 a.m. (Smith, 2003).
- A large number of robberies occur in open public spaces, streets, footpaths, alleyways, subways and parks.
- Two out of every five personal robberies results in injury of some sort to the victim (Smith, 2003).

Adaptive Adventure: The Professional

Within an Adaptive Adventure style, the activity is responsive to and focused on influencing the environment in order to derive tangible benefits from that environment. The approach

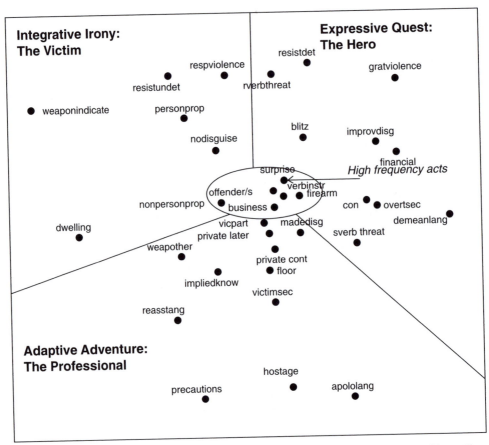

Figure 11.2   An NAS reinterpretation of robbery actions of 144 British armed robbers illustrating three-way NAS classification and core set of behaviours.

Source: Reinterpretation of Alison *et al.* (2000). Youngs and Canter, in press, c.

to this is one of competent control and calm management of the situation. The key role the offender is playing is that of the 'professional'.

The behaviour in the bottom (left) section of the plot can be interpreted in these terms. For example, the offender's access to the private areas of the premises ('Private Cont', 'Private Later') are indications of the emphasis on mastery and control of the event. The focus on competent management is revealed in the act of taking 'Precautions' to secure the property while offending, for example by pulling down blinds and disconnecting the phone, that is similar to the physical modification and control of the house seen in Adaptive Adventure burglary offences. The use of victims to perform tasks that facilitate the offence ('Vict. Part.') highlights a generally efficient approach to offending.

The interpersonal style of interaction here is one in which the victims are 'Objects' (cf. Canter, 1994). They are treated as less than fully human (as indicated here by the action 'Floor'– making victims lie or sit on the floor) so simply to be controlled (for example, 'Victim sec.' – the binding or locking up of victims) or used for some objective purpose (for example, 'hostage' – such as the holding of customers while demands are met).

Integrative Irony: The Victim

The activity that emerges out of a perspective of 'Integrative Irony' is only concerned with, and driven by, the offender's desire to relieve his internal state. It is underpinned by a sense of impotency and meaninglessness. This produces robbery that has a desperate, reckless quality to it; the key role played by the offender is, possibly paradoxically, that of the victim.

The behaviours in the top left area of the plot show the detailed actions that contribute to this theme. There is no attempt by the offender to conceal his identity ('No disguise'), for example. The self-involved desperation drives the offender to continue regardless of any opposition ('Resistundet' – offender's actions not deterred by any resistance or intervention). These are the offenders who, in an internal world without rules and in which nothing matters, will carry out their attacks in people's homes rather than commercial targets.

This 'victim as person' style of interpersonal interaction is consistent with this 'rule-less' mode. It is one in which the robber deals with the victim in a generally aggressive, coercive and abusive manner (Canter, 1994). This approach is indicated in this analysis by a preparedness to steal directly from the people present ('Personprop' – stealing of personal property from victims such as watches and jewellery) and to use violence directly in response to any lack of co-operation/resistance ('Response Violence').

Expressive Quest: The Hero

The central quality of an Expressive Quest style of activity is the attempt to impact on the external world in line with some heroic mission that the offender is pursuing. In robbery this mission may simply be a sense of entitlement. The approach to pursuing this mission is an uncompromising demonstration of his manliness, a demand for recognition. This produces dramatic robberies, as illustrated by behaviours such as a blitz attack ('Blitz' – typically the sudden, immediate use of physical force to initiate the offence) and the targeting of banks and other high security, high value financial targets ('Financial') as seen in the right section of Figure 11.2. The proclivity for risk-taking that is part of an Expressive Quest is clear here in the preparedness to tackle targets with overt, obvious security measures in place ('Overtsec'). The emotional intensity that underpins these robberies is revealed in the impulsiveness of some of the components of this offending style (for example, the use of improvised disguises, 'Improvdisg').

The approach to handling the victims in this style of offending can be better understood through reference to the victim as vehicle mode of interpersonal interaction (Canter, 1994). This is a style in which the victims are used as a means through which the offender can express himself and his anger. The victim as vehicle mode elaborates this offending style then to predict that the expressions of manliness and potency that are key to the Expressive Quest will take the form of demeaning actions (for example, 'Sverb threat' – spontaneous verbal threats; 'Demeanlang' – demeaning language including profanities). The offenders may be excessively violent ('Gratviolence' – acts of gratuitous violence), as a direct demonstration of their dominance of the situation, justified by the notion that they could not stop (seen in the analyses of self-reported roles as discussed in Chapter 6). Interestingly the current analysis indicates the presence of the 'con' or confidence trick approach to initiating the attack is part of this offending style too. This behaviour does support the conceptualisation of this style as one of exploitation of the victim for the offender's expressive ends rather than as a simple 'object' to control.

In sum, then, differences in robbery offending style may be understood in terms of different modes of the NAS. These modes are elaborated by consideration of the role of the victim (Canter, 1994) assigned during the interaction. The empirical analysis drawn from the IP study presented here provides no indication however of the fourth NAS mode in robbery – the Conservative Tragedy. As explained in Chapter 6, a Conservative mode is the polar opposite of the Expressive mode that robbery represents as a broad type of crime. While the Conservative mode is a turning inwards and an internal absorption, the Expressive mode is an outward expulsion. Shye (1989) notes that it is between these two modes that the conceptual distance is greatest. It may be then that robbery is such an overtly Expressive mode of functioning that the radically different Conservative way of acting, although conceptually possible, is not likely to appear within a set of robberies in police records. For example forms of stalking in which demands are made of the victim to feed the stalker's personal gratifications, as discussed in Chapter 12 may be understood as a 'Conservative' form of robbery.

Box 11.4 Criminal Weapon Use in Brazil: A Psychological Analysis

- Study aims: to explore links between the meaning of a weapon, offending behaviour and offenders' personality characteristics.
- Sample: 120 offenders in three prisons in northeast Brazil.
- Methodology: self-reported offending behaviour analysed using smallest space analysis (SSA-I); the FIRO measure of Interpersonal Behaviour (Schutz, 1958) and Eysenck Personality Inventory (Eysenck, 1980).
- Key findings:
  - weapons had emotional/expressive or criminal/instrumental meanings for the criminals
  - offenders for whom the weapons had emotional/expressive meaning were more likely to use stabbing weapons and commit crimes such as rape and murder than those for whom the weapons were simply instrumental
  - offenders for whom the weapons had emotional/expressive meaning report higher FIRO interpersonal tendencies to control, and extraversion scores, than those for whom the weapons were simply instrumental (Lobato, 2000).

Modelling Fraud

The central investigative psychology task of differentiating offending styles in order that inferences can be made about offender characteristics has some particular complexities to it in relation to fraud. On the one hand, fraud represents a very psychologically particular form of criminal activity that often requires no direct interaction with a victim or their property. Rather the central offending actions are ones of avoidance, misrepresentation and concealment of themselves and their identity in some form or another. In line with this there are indications that those offenders who engage in fraud will form a distinct group of criminals tending to specialise in this type of offending (Krambia-Kapardis, 2001). Yet at the same time there are indications that significant proportions of the general population would and do commit fraud offences, especially insurance fraud, when presented with the opportunity to do so (Smith, 2003).

   This would seem to suggest two rather different types of activity, underpinned by the operation of different psychological processes and emerging out of very different contexts. One type of activity would be attributable to individuals who will have similar background characteristics to other property offenders. However, it is hypothesised that they are distinguishable from these other property offenders on variables that indicate their propensity to avoid direct interpersonal interaction. A second group of offenders will be drawn from the general population. Studies suggest these will be males (Krambia-Kapardis, 2001; Smith, 2003) of higher education (Smith, 1983; Wheeler, Weisburd and Bode, 1982) in their 30s and 40s (Krambia-Kapardis, 2001) in professional positions of trust (Smith, 2003).

   As will be appreciated, the characteristics of this second group of offenders describe the typical individual within a given organisation or professional context. Such fraudsters do not have obviously distinct personal qualities. Furthermore, when fraud offences occur within a particular organisation, the investigative challenge is not one of eliciting suspects based on general background characteristics or searches through criminal records, rather it is a case of identifying a culprit within a predefined set of people who could have committed the offence. Interesting work on the relevance of particular personality characteristics that may aid this identification such as hostility towards authority and thrill seeking may be fruitful here (for example, Hogan and Hogan, 1989; Hollinger and Clark, 1983; Jones and Terris, 1983).

   The expectation would be then that these different underlying psychological processes and routes to fraud (see Figures 11.3 and 11.4) produce readily distinguishable patterns of offence behaviour that can be linked to the very different groups of offenders. Certainly initial IP studies of workplace theft/fraud and insurance fraud bear this out (Dodd, 2000; Robertson, 2000), although any assumption that these differences can be understood simply in terms of the seriousness of the offending needs further consideration. As cases such as those of Nick Leeson and Frank Abergale illustrate (Boxes 11.5 and 11.10), in fraud the scale of an offence rather than being an indication of criminal professionalism, as might be the case in burglary or robbery, is often determined by access, opportunity and the authority a person wields within a legitimate role and environment.

   One interesting aspect of fraud is the range of different and continually evolving potential manifestations it can take (see Box 11.7) with new forms such as 'phishing' or receiving a satellite signal without paying, emerging. The 2006 law identifies three broad variants that

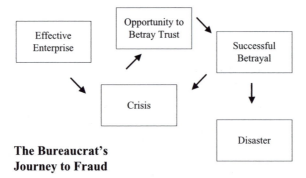

Figure 11.3 The opportunist's (or bureaucrat's) journey to fraud.

Source: Canter (2008).

imply different strategies to the deceit: fraud by false representation, fraud by failing to disclose information and fraud by abuse of position. These psychologically important differences, which are likely to be committed by individuals with somewhat different characteristics, draw attention to interesting aspects of fraud offending for future study. Relatedly, Jackson's (1994) study of identity fraud is intriguing in highlighting a 'duping delight motivation' to the offences he studied. This all points to the psychological significance of the activity that goes beyond a focus on the material gain accrued. As we shall see, this psychological significance is beginning to be explored through examination of the narrative accounts offenders give of their offences.

Differentiating Fraud and Fraudsters

The empirical work on differentiating fraud offence styles and identifying related characteristics follows the broad indication that fraud will emerge out of two rather distinct contexts and be committed by two rather different groups of individuals: the criminal and the opportunist without any other criminal background.

Figure 11.4 The criminal's journey to fraud.

Source: Canter (2008).

Robertson's (2000) study of 88 workplace thefts within a courier and distribution company, delivering items of value, showed this distinction between opportunism and criminality as well as identifying a third group of individuals whose 'theft' was best understood as a product of their lack of commitment to and competency in the job.

Robertson's 'criminal' group often worked with accomplices and targeted those courier vehicles with the highest probability of containing credit cards. They took care to conceal their actions within the workplace and were confident enough to smuggle items out of the factory. These were individuals who had external criminal links and in many cases previous criminal histories. They were younger (twenties and early thirties), unmarried and not likely to have been with the company more than six years. Robertson reports an interesting indication of their criminal sophistication in that approximately half unequivocally denied the activity and a quarter immediately requested a solicitor when confronted.

The 'opportunists', in contrast, stole less valuable items from the courier vehicles, taking them back to the workplace with them to remove their contents. As Robertson (2000: 197) notes, they revealed their lack of criminal sophistication by 'returning debris and torn open items into the traffic stream, or leaving them in corners and alcoves ... in effect a crime scene that over time can build up a pattern enabling the source to be traced.' These individuals often had a longer service record with the company and the group included typically married individuals covering a wider age range, up to some offenders in their mid- fifties. None had pre-convictions and most confessed at least in part upon being confronted. At least some of this opportunistic offending was a response to personal problems so may have some similarities to Weisburd *et al.*'s 'Crisis Responders'.

The third group within this study, 'Responsibility', is best understood as comprising individuals whose crimes were part of irresponsibility at work and a general dysfunctional lifestyle rather than any direct attempt at fraud.

Box 11.5 Case Study: Nick Leeson

Nick Leeson, a former manager of a new operation in futures markets on the Singapore Monetary Exchange (SIMEX), caused the collapse of Barings Bank, the UK's oldest investment bank. Leeson was making unauthorised speculative trades that brought large profits for Barings, earning him big bonuses. But when he ran out of luck he started making losses and used one of Barings' error accounts (accounts used to correct mistakes made in trading), 88888, to hide them. The bank allowed Leeson to be chief trader while also being responsible for settling his trades, jobs that are usually done by two different people. This made it easier for him to hide his losses. In all, $1.4 billion was lost by Leeson's crooked dealing and in 1995 he was arrested in Germany and extradited to Singapore where he was sentenced to six-and-a-half years in prison. He was released from prison in 1999 and returned to the UK. While in prison he published an autobiography, *Rogue Trader*, which was made into a film starring Ewan McGregor. He currently lives in Ireland and is the CEO of Irish football club, Galway United.

Box 11.6 Fraud: Key Facts

- Fraud happens when somebody uses deception to obtain goods, services or money. Fraud is the obtaining of financial advantage or causing of loss by implicit or explicit deception; it is the mechanism through which the fraudster gains an unlawful advantage or causes unlawful loss (Levi *et al.*, 2007).
- The Fraud Act 2006, which replaced the laws relating to obtaining property by deception, obtaining a pecuniary advantage and other related offences, eight in total, that were created under the Theft Act 1978, came into effect on 15 January 2007.
- The Fraud Act 2006 gives a statutory definition of the criminal offence of fraud, defining it in three classes – fraud by false representation, fraud by failing to disclose information and fraud by abuse of position.
- 'Fraud by false representation' is defined by s. 2 of the Act as a case where a person dishonestly makes a false representation, express or implied, which they know to be untrue or misleading.
- 'Fraud by failing to disclose information' is defined by s. 3 of the Act as a case where a person fails to disclose any information to a third party when they are under a legal duty to disclose such information.
- 'Fraud by abuse of position' is defined by s. 4 of the Act as a case where a person occupies a position where they are expected to safeguard the financial interests of another person, and dishonestly abuses that position; this includes cases where the abuse consisted of an omission rather than an act.
- In all the above classes of fraud the person must have acted dishonestly and with the intent of making a gain for themselves or anyone else, or inflicting a loss (or a risk of loss) on another.
- Fraud in the United Kingdom involves at least 2.5 times greater loss than the combined cost of burglary, theft and robbery of individuals (Dubourg and Hamed, 2005).
- A report commissioned in 2007 by the Association of Chief Police Officers (ACPO) estimated the cost of fraud to be at least £13.9 billion a year.
- Plastic card fraud alone cost £535 million in 2007, an increase of more than £100 million over 2006 (figures published by APACS, the UK Payment Industry).
- The average sentence (not time served) for frauds of over £50 000 is 3.05 years.
- The average sentence for the largest frauds (over £50 million) is just over six years.
- Eighty-five per cent of fraudsters are male and 70% are between 36 and 55 years old (KPMG, 2007).

Box 11.7 Forms of Fraud

- Benefit fraud: frauds of various kinds upon the social security system, such as housing benefit fraud.
- Charity fraud: frauds in which donations are stripped from entirely fictitious or unregistered charities, or are embezzled from registered charities.
- Consumer frauds: including lottery/prize scams; rogue dialling and other communications-based frauds; 'dishonest' misdescriptions of products and services; gaming frauds; purchases of goods and services that are not sent by the supplier. Counterfeit intellectual property and products. Items sold as genuine and believed by consumers to be genuine.
- Counterfeit money: a direct loss to the people given counterfeit money.
- Data-compromise fraud: frauds on companies and on individuals (sometimes called 'phishing' and 'pharming') arising from website manipulations; these frauds include the manipulation of corporate websites to make the target believe that the firm is genuine
- Embezzlement: frauds against all businesses, government departments and professional firms by staff that normally either involves accounts manipulation or the construction of false invoices.
- Gaming frauds: this refers to 'fixed' races and other forms of sport upon which spread betting and other gaming wagers have been made.
- Insider dealing/market abuse. This affects the general integrity of the market. These are to be distinguished from 'boiler room' and other stock manipulations in which salespeople convince investors to purchase stock with little underlying value.
- Investment frauds. Three subtypes: (a) frauds in which investors do not believe that investments are authorised, for example, advance fee/some high-yield investment frauds involving 'secret inside information' or 'whisky/champagne' (boiler room scams); (b) frauds in which investors wrongly believe that the investments are regulated; and (c) frauds in which investors correctly believe that investments are authorised.
- Lending fraud: frauds involving lending funds and credit for goods and services, also includes fraudulent bankruptcy, consumer credit and mortgage frauds (which can involve the manipulation of property prices or the overstatement of applicants' income).
- Payment card fraud: frauds on issuers and merchant acquirers of debit, credit and charge cards.
- Pension-type frauds: the employer or third party steals company pensions and National Insurance contributions.
- Procurement fraud: frauds and corruption in the purchasing process, including price fixing rings, abuse of inside information in the construction of tenders or in their application. Tax fraud: failure to pay direct, indirect and excise taxes.

(*Source*: Levi and Burrows 2008: 299–301, Reproduced with permission)

Box 11.8 Fraud – Psychological Theories and Explanations

There have been various attempts to explain fraud and distinguish psychological indicators of the propensity of an individual to commit fraud. In the 1950s criminologist Donald Cressey introduced the theory of the 'fraud triangle', which is the most widely accepted model for explaining why people commit fraud. The fraud triangle suggests that there are three factors that must be present in order for an ordinary person to commit fraud; perceived pressure, perceived opportunity, and rationalisation.

Cressey called the first factor pressure or a perceived nonsharable financial need. Examples of pressures include credit card debts, gambling, desire for status symbols such as a bigger house, nicer car and so forth, and frustration with work.

The second factor, perceived opportunity or the employee's perception that an opportunity to commit fraud exists. The perpetrator must believe that he or she can commit the fraud and not get caught or if he or she gets caught the consequences will not be serious. This opportunity may arise from the company's poor internal controls, loose discipline policy, or some other factor. The third factor is the employee's ability to rationalise the fraud, suggesting to him or herself that it is somehow justified and/or non-criminal.

Duffield and Grabosky (2001) and Krambia-Kapardis (2001) have also have argued that fraud can best be explained by three factors known as ROP (i.e. Rationalisations, Opportunity, and crime-prone Person). The model proposes that the probability of fraud will be a function of these three components.

Box 11.9 Fraud Rationalisations

The third factor of Cressey's Fraud Triangle is rationalisation. Rationalisations provide the fraudster with self-justification for his/her actions. Common rationalisations include the following:

- I was entitled to the money.
- I had to steal to provide for my family.
- I have no other option.
- I was underpaid/my employer had cheated me.
- It's for a good purpose.
- My employer is dishonest to others and deserved to be fleeced.
- It's for the good of the company.
- The scheme is only temporary.
- I was only borrowing the money.
- I am not hurting anyone.

Box 11.10 Case Study: Frank Abagnale

Frank Abagnale remains one of America's most successful fraudsters ever. He cashed $2.5 million passing bad cheques in 26 countries over the course of five years in the 1960s. During this time, he used at least eight aliases to cash bad cheques. Impersonating an airline pilot he flew over a million miles on over 250 flights and to 26 countries, all at Pan America Worlds Airways' expenses. Forging a Columbia University degree he worked as a teaching assistant teaching sociology at a university. For nearly a year he impersonated a doctor, and forging a Harvard University law degree, passed the bar exam of Louisiana and got a job at the office of the state attorney general of Louisiana at the age of nineteen. Eventually, he was caught in France in 1969. In 1974, after he had served less than five years, the US federal government released him on condition that he would help the FBI without pay as an advisor for crimes of fraud. As well as being the subject of a series of books about his experiences, he was the subject of the movie *Catch Me If You Can*, in which he was played by Leonardo Di Caprio. Abagnale still teaches at the FBI Academy more than 30 years on and runs Abagnale and Associates, which advises the business world on fraud, becoming a millionaire through his legal fraud detection and avoidance consulting business.

Box 11.11 Action Box

Below is an example from Robertson's (2000) study of delivery van theft. Which of the narratives does it imply?

'Joe' – Male, Aged 59 with Five Years' Tenure
  Caught stealing from items being carried by the delivery company.
  The matter came to light when empty, torn-open transit packs were found in a public rubbish bin. These were handed into a police station. The company was alerted. Investigators interviewed Joe the next day when Joe outlined some difficulties in his life. His mother had recently died and his wife was unwell. He said that he felt life was getting on top of him, and because of his age, was frightened of losing his job. The company management accepted a recommendation that Joe was clinically depressed, and did not press charges.

(continued)

His work conduct record was exemplary, with virtually no sick absence, and no managerial warnings. His training period had passed without problems, and his personnel file indicated that his immediate supervisors thought well of him. To all appearances, Joe was the model employee.

He had neither formal qualifications nor industrial skills. His previous employment had been for twelve years as a messenger, from which he was provided with a good reference. There was nothing in Joe's background to suggest any criminal experience. His offences were clumsily committed.

(From Robertson, 2000)

Dodd's (2000) work on insurance fraud extended the basic distinction between criminal and opportunistic fraud and fraudsters, specifying four groups: the experienced, sophisticated, opportunist and document abuser (see Figure 11.5). Table 11.5 shows the characteristics of his sample and how he characterised the distinctions between them.

Table 11.5 Insurance fraud and fraudsters.

Experienced	**Sophisticated**
Submits higher claim	Knows the system
Knows the insurance system	Fabricates claim
May be unemployed	Provides secondary address
May be in some financial difficulty	Claims large amount
Opportunist	**Document abuser**
Make use of genuine situation	Knows the system
Exaggeration of claims	Maybe uncooperative
Believe they are entitled to claim	Claim for small amounts

General characteristics of insurance fraudsters (Dodd sample)
Male
Married
About 38 years old
In skilled employment
Owns house
Offers a permanent address
Co-operative during claims procedure
One dependent
Not in financial difficulty
No criminal convictions
Claims around £6,000

Source: Dodd (2000).

Figure 11.5 Types of fraud.

Narratives of Fraud

In some interesting unpublished IP work there are indications that different narrative themes give shape to fraud offences. This work is based on narrative interviews with imprisoned fraud offenders carried out by one of our students Mary Santarcangelo. Analysis of their accounts of their experiences using questionnaires similar to those discussed in Chapter 6 showed that the narrative role themes of 'professional's Adventure', 'Victim's Irony', 'Avenger's Tragedy' and 'Hero's Quest' can be distinguished in the offenders' descriptions of their offences and the events leading up to their offences. A case-study illustration with excerpts from one interview illustrating the offender's key 'professional' role played as part of an Adventure narrative is presented below.

The Professional's Adventure

Fraud value: £2 million – sentenced: 3.5 years:

> About 2 o'clock in the morning, I woke up and I thought of the idea . . . I was to ring up the head office, I had my own firm at the time, and I was to say 'could I buy or could you give me credit for x number thousand of pounds worth of gift vouchers?' And that's how it happened. I told my partner in crime, Jim, and I said 'look would this work?' So we went to the bank, then we went to Company House. We opened up a firm called DEF couriers and then we rang up one particular branch of P&Q and we said 'I'm operations manager for DEF couriers and it's getting towards Christmas my staff', which I have none by the way. 'They've decided this year they'd like P&Q gift vouchers for Christmas.' 'That's wonderful, how much do you want?' I said '£25 000, how do we go about this?' And she said 'well just a moment.' I gave them my bank details and she came back to me said 'just send your courier over with a company cheque with a company letter' and that was all there was to it. We sent the courier over and then we did that to every P&Q in the UK, some less than £30 000 some more, simple as that.'

Adventure

> Oh I loved it, I was the number one! You haven't got no idea how that feels. I valued it too much to describe. I was perceived as Mr Big, the number one, everyone said 'that was a brilliant idea'. My family called me Robin Hood and I gave loads away as well.

A job

I had to get things in operation first. Basically, I had an ordinary account. I went to my bank and said I wanted a business account and they said 'what you want it for?' And I said 'I'm starting my own career firm' and because I've been with them for some time they gave me the business account straight away. They also gave me 18 months of free bank charges, which I wasn't interested in but I got the actual cheques, got the computer going, printed invoices etc. etc., got business lines set up, going to Company House, registered the company so P&Q would check that this company did exist. It all took about four or five days.

Professionalism

And then we hit them. Then I got on the phone ordering, it was like a sort of like a military position because I had couriers working for me but the courier didn't know what I was doing they just thought they were working for me and they were told to collect vouchers. I never banked the money. I used to walk around with a briefcase full of money and I gave it to various people who I could trust. Never banked anything because well you bank it and other people find it. You know when they're looking for confiscation they will find it because if you put so much in the bank the bank wouldn't know where the money come from, they looking for money laundering and all that sort. So didn't get money involved in any of that so I just put it in places where I knew I could get at it.

Satisfaction in Mastery

To be honest, the law didn't know what to do with me because, one it was a legitimately registered company, two it was my bank account, the only crime they possibly could get me was did I knowingly know that the cheque was going to bounce? I could of told them a lie that I expected funds. I didn't steal the cheque book. So first of all P&Q thought about taking a civil action against me but they had to find me first so after two years I tried to do it again and that's when they caught me. HA HA HA.

(Adapted from interview by Mary Santarcangelo, International Research Centre
for Investigative Psychology, IRCIP.)

Summary

The NAS model can be applied to acquisitive crime, providing a framework for understanding within-crime differences in offending style. Adaptive Adventure, Conservative Tragedy, Integrative Irony and Expressive Quest styles are elaborated for burglary and robbery (although conservative tragedy is not found in currently available robbery data).

For burglary, the different NAS modes capture differences in the degree of focus on the task of committing the burglary and in the offender's interpersonal awareness of the premises as belonging to somebody.

For robbery, given the direct interaction with the victim(s) required within this offence, consideration of the Object, Vehicle and Person victim roles (Canter, 1994) associated with the different NAS modes allows further understanding of the offending style differences.

Fraud emerges out of two very different psychological contexts, being committed by two distinct groups of offenders. A broad distinction between opportunistic and criminal fraud offending behaviour can thus be identified. Initial IP studies suggest that, within this, different narrative role emphases underpin different forms of fraud offending.

Further Reading

Books

Bennett, T. and Wright, R. (1984) *Burglars on Burglary: Prevention and the Offender*, Gower, Aldershot.
Canter, D. and Alison, L. (2000) *Profiling Property Crimes*, Ashgate, Dartmouth.
Doig, A. (2006) *Fraud*, Willan, Cullompton.

Articles

Dodd, N.J. (2000) The psychology of fraud, in *Profiling Property Crimes* (eds D. Canter and L. Alison), Ashgate, Dartmouth.
Doig, A. (2000) Investigating fraud, in *The Social Psychology of Crime: Groups, Teams and Networks* (eds D. Canter and L. Alison), Ashgate, Dartmouth.
Farrington, D.P. and Lambert, S. (1994) Differences between burglars and violent offenders. *Psychology, Crime and Law*, **1**, 107–16.
Nee, C. and Meenaghan, A. (2006) Expert decision making in burglars. *British Journal of Criminology*, **46** (5), 935–49.
Yokota, K. and Canter, D. (2004) Burglars' specialisation: development of a thematic approach in investigative psychology. *Behaviormetrika*, **31** (2), 1–15.

Questions for Discussion and Research

1. Find someone who has been involved in petty crime, such as shoplifting sweets of low value, and discuss with them how they felt about doing it.

2. Why do you think ex-robbers are more willing to talk about their crimes than people who have committed rape? Why are there so many autobiographies by gangsters?

3. Why do so many people think it is acceptable to defraud insurance companies?

4. Do the different forms of fraud in Box 11.7 imply different personal narratives for the fraudsters? Or different pathways to fraud as in Figures 11.3 and 11.4?

CHAPTER 12

Sexual Offences

In This Chapter

Learning Objectives

When you have completed this chapter you should:

1. Understand how a violent offender's interaction with the victim provides the core psychological function of violent crime.
2. Recognise that the intensity of the offending in violent crime is revealed in the degree of destruction of the person; of the identity of the individual.
3. Be aware of the variety of offending styles that distinguish rapists.

4. Understand the nature and prevalence of sexual assault on male victims.
5. Be able to discuss the nature of stalking and its relationship to domestic violence.
6. Be alert to the varieties of child abuse and paedophilia.

Synopsis

Rape and other forms of sexual assault appropriately fall within the framework of other violent crimes but because of their special nature and the particular ordure that surrounds them it is fitting to deal with them separately in the present chapter and turn to the broader range of violent crimes in the next chapter.

Crimes against the person run the gamut from brawls to serial murder. Within each of these subsets a variety of styles of offending can be identified. Therefore to understand these crimes and have the basis for making any inferences from offenders' actions it is necessary to clarify the ways in which they differ. These differences derive from the relationship with the victim because of the fundamentally interpersonal nature of the crime. This leads to the realisation that, rather than classifying rapists in terms of the forms of the sexual and emotional gratification the offender seeks, it is useful to examine the role that the offender assigns to the victim in the offender's personal narrative. Three overlapping roles for the victim have been identified, which map on to the NAS.

The offender who thinks of himself as tragically forced by the accidents of fate to seek some sort of redress, operating in a Conservative Action mode, sees his victim as a representative of those on whom he must act vindictively. They are Vehicles for his anger. His sexual crimes will often be extremely violent.

The person who sees himself on an Heroic Quest, acting in an Expressive action mode is using the victim as some representative of a wider set of possible victims. For him the victim is a different sort of vehicle on his heroic quest for recognition. His concern will be to control the victim to achieve his gratification. Such offenders share much with the 'Adventurer', operating in an Adaptive mode. These sexual offenders are focused on obtaining sexual gratification and their victims are little more than Objects to them.

The roles of Vehicle and Object contrast with the roles assigned by offenders who see themselves as Victims, operating in an 'Integrative' Action mode. For them the (actual) victim has very particular significance as a Person (Person Victim role).

This framework of victim roles has relevance across all sexual crimes, including assaults on men and children as well as being important in understanding stalking and related matters of sexual violence.

The Role of the Victim in Violent Crime

The two accounts of an alleged rape in Box 12.1 throw into stark relief the way in which all violent crime emerges out of a relationship and often a relationship that is open to different interpretations by each of those involved. The accounts show that the actions in an assault, whether its focus is solely violent or dominated by sexual activity, are interpreted in terms of the understanding those involved have of each other's roles.

Box 12.1 Rape Accusation

Summaries of two newspaper articles about the same events from the viewpoints of first 'the victim' and then 'the accused' to show the various challenges the police face in collecting information.

Rape Victim Tells of Attack Horror

A care worker who was raped on a tombstone in a Chippenham churchyard has spoken for the first time of her horrific ordeal. The victim, who was 22 years old, was left so traumatised by the attack that she is still terrified to go out, even in daylight and in the company of others, or remain home alone. She felt hatred towards her attacker, stating that, 'he has taken my pride away'.

Having spent the evening of the attack with friends in the Rose and Crown pub in Chippenham, the victim left alone. She reported, 'the next thing I remember is that I was in the churchyard being attacked'. Throughout the attack, she was screaming but was told to 'shut up'. The first person she contacted was her ex-boyfriend. He rang her friends, who were the first ones on the scene, and the police. She reported that, 'after the attack I was in shock and my injuries were so painful that it blocked out a lot of what had happened. But now I feel hurt and I hate the man that attacked me.' She then explained, 'I don't remember much after my friends arrived but I know I was taken to The Royal United Hospital in Bath'. Police are continuing to follow up CCTV footage, forensic evidence and information from the public.

(Exclusive, written by Lily Canter for the *Wiltshire Gazette and Herald*,
26 September 2002)

Rape Case Made Life Living Hell

Labourer Ashley Lawrence said his life has been a living hell since he was wrongly accused of raping a care worker in a churchyard. Once released on bail, Mr Lawrence lost his lodgings, work, and confidence. He reported that he could not believe what had happened to him because he was not a stranger to the victim, and that she had consented to sex. He added that the victim said she didn't know her attacker but she kept changing her story. However, the case against Mr Lawrence was dropped because of a lack of evidence. The Crown Prosecution Service said it could not proceed because there were no independent witnesses and the case was based on one word against another.

(continued)

In her final statement, the victim named Mr Lawrence and admitted to arranging to meet him in the alleyway next to the churchyard. Mr Lawrence described how earlier, in the Rose and Crown pub, the victim 'had basically offered it to me on a plate. She was rubbing herself against me at the bar.' He maintained that he did have sex but 'she knew what she was doing as did I and she consented'. Mr Lawrence stated that they were both a bit drunk and she virtually fell off the gravestone so that might explain some of her injuries. He had been told that the victim fancied him and he realised he was a bit of a bastard for leaving her in the churchyard. Mr Lawrence further stated that the photofit looked nothing like him. However, when he heard that the victim had named him he went to the police station voluntarily.

He added, 'I would definitely not have a one-night stand again. This stigma will always be with me. She has not only ruined my life she has ruined the lives of women who are genuinely raped, because no-one will believe them.' The victim refused to comment on the dropping of the charge.

(Exclusive, written by Lily Canter for the *Wiltshire Gazette and Herald*,
5 December 2002)

If the activity is dominated by sexual behaviour then the issue of consent governs how the actions are interpreted. But even this issue of consent draws on interpretations made by those involved of what roles each is playing in the unfolding drama. Is it the selfish sexual gratification of one individual that is forced on the other? Or do both parties participate in mutually agreed behaviour? Some offending behaviours will be fundamental to central issues that give the activities their meaning, whether it be sex or violence, so will be common to all or most offences. But there will also be different routes to achieving the core purpose that are the key to understanding different offending styles within a crime.

Among the plethora of behaviours that do, or could, occur within any given crime, it is the identification of what the salient features are that characterise offending styles on which investigators must focus. It is the understanding of the psychological basis for the distinctions in offending style that allows the development of theories about which classes of offender characteristics may vary. The diverse roles that the victim is made to play in the offender's personal narrative help in the prediction of what will be consistent across an offender's series and help to answer the many questions about investigative inferences.

Unlike property offending, where intrapersonal issues are implicit and it is broad attitudes towards others in general that may be most pertinent, for crimes against the person the offender's attention must be taken up with relating to the victim. The direct explicitness of this interaction means that the significance of a criminal's actions lies in the meaning that this interaction with the victim has to him.

The Body or the Person?

Clearly in violent crimes, the immediately identifying feature of this interaction with the victim, that is the basis of the offence, is the harm done by the offender to the victim's body.

But in developing our framework for understanding this interaction it is useful to note that in psychological thinking the body is distinguished from the person. The person is the invention of a coherent self that transcends the body, 'an identifiable, unique, sentient human being with a past and an anticipated future' (Canter, 2002). As Canter argues, unlike the reductionist perspectives of evolutionary biology and neuroscience:

> personhood emerges as an entity that has its own forms of complexity which give it qualities that cannot be found in the body alone. They are derived from the history and the anticipated future, the memories and social transactions, social representations and cultural experiences that give any particular person their unique characteristics.

In the context of violent and especially sexually violent crime, greater insight into the fundamental psychological nature of the offence is gleaned through careful consideration of the details of the interaction with the victim. This needs to include then not only the damage to the body but the damage done to the person through the actions on the body.

Offending Intensity in Violent Crime: Destruction of the Person

This leads to the view that the intensity of the offence will be reflected in the strength of the attack on the person, the destruction to the individual's identity. In rape, then, the more extreme offences will not necessarily be those in which the most sexually violating acts are committed on the victim's body. Rather they may be those offences where the violations have the greatest implications for the victim's identity and where the threat and damage extend to other aspects of the victim's self.

In the context of murder, the most extreme attacks will involve not simply the ending of an individual's life but the complete destruction of that person's identity. In these offences, the body is destroyed, the person becoming totally unrecognisable as the particular person he/she was or even as a human being at all. This total depersonalisation may be achieved through extreme violence, particularly towards areas of the body associated powerfully with identity such as the face or the genitals, or by its complete objectification and/or dismemberment.

Strategies for Destruction of the Person

If the core psychological purpose of the offence is drawn from the relationship that the offender imposes upon the victim then clearly a model that will be important in distinguishing offending styles is one that focuses on differences in this interaction. A variety of strategies can be adopted to attack the person. A fundamental psychological distinction underlying these is reflected in the very different forms of murder described by Bolitho (1926) and Katz (1988) in their early writings on the nature of crime and criminals.

Bolitho, writing in the 1920s, identifies 'murder for profit' in which the offence is a means to achieving a distinct end result, often financial gain. In contrast, Katz draws attention to a rather different rage-driven 'righteous slaughter' form of murder that is an act of emotional expression. In the crimes that Katz describes, the offender is interacting directly with the victim and the offence is about the impact on the victim. In the interaction that characterises Bolitho's murder, the effect the offender's actions have on the victim is incidental. In core psychological terms, the underlying distinction here is that the approach adopted in Bolitho's murder is one of ignoring the person while, in contrast, the righteous slaughter that Katz describes is focused on having a direct impact on the victim as a person.

Role of the Victim within the Offender's Narrative

The significance of this interaction and, in particular, of the role assigned by the offender to the victim as a key feature of the offender's criminal narrative is recognised and developed by Canter (1994). Canter argues that violent offenders have an inability to 'create private dramas in which others share centre stage . . . to assign to (victims) an active role in their own or anyone else's life story' (Canter 1994: 246, 241). This inability to allocate normal roles to others leaves a gap in the narratives that these offenders construct. The nature of the role to fill this gap that offenders assume for their victims will then be psychologically revealing, telling us something about the characteristics and experiences of the perpetrator.

In his model of different victim roles, Canter argues that the particular role an offender assigns will be the product of his or her distorted approach to the achievement of the core power and intimacy life narrative themes that, MacAdams (1993) has argued, characterise all life stories. In the context of violent offences this manifests as variations in the way the offender tries to maintain the control he requires to conduct the offence and also in the offender's style of interpersonal treatment of the victim. These produce a complex framework of varying roles assigned to the victim, which Canter simplifies into three main emphases: victim as Object, victim as Vehicle and victim as Person. The particular NAS modes out of which these emerge are described in Chapters 6 and 7.

Object

The victim as Object offences are those crimes in which the offender sees the victim as having very little, if any, human significance or emotions and towards whom he has no feelings. She is not credited with any agency or given any active part in the situation but is simply something for him to act upon, an object.

This approach to the victim runs through offences in which the offender seeks out specific types of sexual target, for example young men, to attack. It is characteristic of the rapist who kills his victim after the sexual attack simply because of the possibility that she could now identify him. At the extremes of the destructive urge, it is the perception of the victim as an object that allows some of the most bizarre criminal acts of mutilation, cannibalism and dismemberment. Canter argues that these most extreme offenders have a lack of contact with human reality that may be reflected in an absence of a normal human existence. Such offenders may be expected to have a history of psychiatric illness and may be diagnosed as psychotic.

Vehicle

A rather different style of offences is those in which the victim is a Vehicle for the expression of the offender's desires and anger. Rather than just being bodies to use, these victims often carry particular meanings by what they represent, possibly symbolising significant people in the offender's life story. In these offences there is sufficient recognition of the humanity of the victim that attacking and exploiting her serves the offender's purpose (Canter 1994). In line with this conceptualisation of the victim, the violence in these offences can be extreme and frenzied – as Canter 1994 puts it 'in the ferocity of the assault the victim is forced to carry the burden of some of the [offender's] anger.' But perhaps in apparent contrast, this style of offending is also often characterised by an initial 'confidence' approach in which the offender is able to draw upon the interpersonal experience and skills that he does typically have to gain access to the victim on some kind of pretence.

The symbolic significance of the victim means that careful selection or targeting will usually be part of the offending actions too. The most extreme and direct examples of this use of violence against others as a vehicle for the expression of the offender's own emotions, however, are spree killings and suicide bombings. In these crimes it is not one particular victim that is targeted but many victims who, as a group, represent a society against which the offender wishes to express his anger.

Person

A large group of violent offences are those in which there is a full recognition that the victim is human, a person. What draws together these crimes is the way they emerge out of a general style of human interaction in which others are to be taken advantage of or abused and violence is the normal, natural strategy for achieving this. In Victim as person offences then, the target is usually that particular person, the victim from whom the offender is trying directly to obtain something, whether this be money, sex or simply to hurt that person as part of an unfolding destructive relationship. Even in those cases where the victim is not a particular, known individual but rather a stranger, there will be an assumption on the part of the offender that the offence is somehow part of a customary interaction between him and the victim (Canter, 1994).

The type of criminal actions that comes out of this approach to the victim can range from the explosive domestic murder or pub brawl to the burglary in which the offender seizes the opportunity to steal sex too, raping the occupant. It may include the murder of an elderly person, which is the result of some local youths' attempt to take advantage of her frailty to steal from her. It may further include the rapes conducted as a form of 'recreation' in which the offender or offenders attempt to relate on a personal level to the victim, or the rapist who assumes the attacks he has perpetrated in fact represents some kind of acceptable intimate contact (Canter, 1994). As Canter notes, the offenders for whom this type of interaction with others is the norm often emerge out of a more general criminal background and community so may well have a lengthy and diverse criminal record.

Interestingly, there is an underlying order to Canter's victim role model that maps broadly on to the well-established distinction between instrumental and expressive aggression as discussed earlier. Within this distinction, expressive aggression is considered to be an attack perpetrated for its own affective ends, whereas instrumental aggression is carried out to facilitate another objective. Although it is often treated as a dichotomous concept, Marshall and Kennedy (2003) lay out diminishing degrees of instrumentality along a continuum from sufficient force, through instrumental gratuitous violence to silence a victim, and expressive violence to sadistic violence. In the same way, the victim role model moves from the highly expressive victim as Person, where the particular quality of the interaction with the victim is central, to the victim as Vehicle role in which the interaction with the victim remains important but only in allowing the offender a more generalised expression. The least expressive role assigned will be the one where, while the interaction with a victim is still the purpose of the offence, the impact on and reactions of this victim are irrelevant to the offender, so the victim is seen simply as an Object.

A general model of offending-style differences is therefore proposed for violent crime based on variations in the role within the criminal's narrative assigned by the offender to the victim (Youngs and Canter, in press, b). Offending styles reflecting a victim as object, victim as Vehicle and Victim as Person role assignment can be described. Quantitative variations in the intensity of the offending are revealed in the strength of attack on the person, the destruction of the individual's identity. This model has a radex structure (see Chapter 5) such that the qualitative differences in the role assigned to the victim emerge more distinctly at higher levels of intensity of the attack on the person. As Youngs and Canter (in press, b) note, this is a model of the basis for differentiation that can be applied across forms of crime that involve a direct interpersonal interaction. The form the victim role styles and the destruction of the person takes will reflect the particular context. A given behaviour can then be understood as part of different offending styles in different classes of offence. The particular NAS modes out of which these detailed victim role assignments emerge are indicated in Figure 12.1.

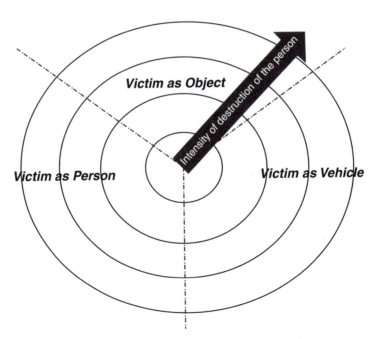

Figure 12.1   A general model of offending style in violent crime.

Differentiating Rape

One of the earliest breakthroughs in IP was the identification of distinct and meaningful styles of offending actions in rape. Rather than all offences being broadly similar, or the combination of behaviours that occurred in any offence being random, there was usually some discernible, dominant theme (Canter, 1994; Canter and Heritage, 1990). It is from an understanding of what those themes are that the possibility of drawing inferences about differences in the perpetrators arises as well as of understanding what will be consistent across offences that allows the linking of crimes by the same offender.

We can move from the general framework of criminal differentiation for violent crime (Figure 12.1) to propose a detailed structure of offending style variations in rape. Specifying the crime actions that will characterise these rape styles requires an understanding of how the different object, vehicle and person victim roles, and the variations in the strength of the attack on the identity of the person, are likely to be evident in the particular context of a rape offence. Some ideas about this can be developed from an understanding of the psychological issues central to rape.

There are a number of motivation classification schemes for rape – typically developed in a therapeutic context and so reflecting differences in rapists rather than offence behaviour patterns – which are nonetheless useful in drawing attention to some of the key issues. Along with the discussions in the literature of what rape is and is not about, these motivation typologies draw attention to at least five psychological processes that may be relevant to rape. One of these is the expression of sexuality (see, for example, Knight 1999) or, as Scully and Marolla (1983) characterise it, 'the impersonal need for an object to satisfy a physical craving.' A second well-established process relevant to rape is the expression of anger and aggression (see, for example, Groth, 1979; Knight, 1999). The assertion of the rapist's power is a third related key feature of rape (see, for example, Douglas *et al.*, 1992; Groth and Birnbaum, 1979), which at its extreme would produce the sadistic motivation described by Knight (1999) and Knight and Prentky (1987). Marshall (1989) refers to a further central motivation as the desire for social contact, part of which may be the expression of the vindictiveness in rape that Knight (1999) identifies. Finally, a general criminal approach, involving the general abuse of, and stealing from, others has been argued to run through many rapes (Rada, 1978; Scully and Marolla, 1983). These are all potential psychological components of a rape offence on which we may predict differences across the object, vehicle and person roles (Youngs and Canter, in press, b).

Object, Vehicle and Person Roles in Rape

Where the offender's approach to the victim is one that assigns her the role of an Object, we would expect the sexuality to take the form of a very self-involved focus on the mechanisms of gratification for the offender, possibly involving an obsessive concern with the victim's particular bodily characteristics. The expression of the sexuality may be exploratory as the offender treats the victim as an object to examine and play with. The anger and social contact components of rape both require an awareness of the victim as an agentic human being so for the object role there will be minimal social interaction with the victim and unnecessary aggression will not be a strong feature of this offending style. In terms of power, it would be consistent with this role for the offender to take a very functional approach to the control of his victim, adopting very direct physical means of controlling her and/or ensuring his identity is protected. The total lack of empathy the offender has for the victim will mean that if it is necessary to control her, the offender will display extreme, although not excessive or frenzied, violence.

When the role assigned to the victim is what Canter refers to as a 'Vehicle', the attack on the victim has symbolic significance so the anger and vindictive social contact components of rape will feature strongly. This may produce excessive, expressive violence targeting meaningful parts of the victim's body as well as verbal abuse or cruelty and manipulative interpersonal interactions. The emotional significance of the victim's reactions means that the sexuality component will be exploitative and demeaning. The expression of power will be highly relevant to this style of rape but on its own, possibly sadistic terms, not as a means of controlling the victim. The criminality component of rape may not be particularly featured here because these offences are primarily concerned with the particular abuse of an individual for what she represents rather than the generalised abuse and stealing that comes out of a broader criminal propensity.

Central to the assignment of a 'Person' role to the victim is the offender's attempt to coerce intimacy from her. This style emerges out of a distorted approach to interpersonal relations in which the attacker is an offender who recognises the human feelings of his victim but for whom normal human interactions are typically abusive, coercive and aggressive. This produces offences in which the aggression required to commit the rape can coexist with features of otherwise normal interactions. In these crimes then the social contact component is important. The offender may attempt to relate to the victim and may display some degree of apparent empathy. Similarly, here the expression of the sexuality component of rape can be straightforward, 'normal' and characterised by attempts at physical intimacy. Neither the power nor the anger processes found in some rapes will be prominent here. In so far as the 'Victim as Person' approach to others does comes out of a generally abusive, criminal style the offender may also be threatening and assault the victim as well as stealing from her where there is the opportunity to do so.

Degrees of Attack of the Person

Within the general model of differentiation for violent offences (Youngs and Canter, in press, b) the intensity of offending behaviour will be a reflection of the strength of attack on the person – that is, on the individual's identity as a human being. In the context of a rape, defined by sexual violation, it is argued that any additional physical aggression against the victim would, as a threat to her fundamental safety, represent an even stronger attack on her as a person. However, the most extreme offences of all will be those that involve direct attacks, beyond the other violations, on the individual's sense of self, privacy and autonomy. In line with this, Canter *et al.* (2003) propose a scale of violations in rape that describes a broadening violation from sexual through to additional physical to further personal violations.

What happens in a Rape?

To be able to identify the specific crime-scene actions that characterise the different offending styles, it is necessary to have an understanding of what actually happens in a rape and how often. Table 12.1 shows a list of the individual behaviours drawn from a content analysis of victim statements across the 66 British stranger sexual assaults examined in Canter and Heritage's (1990) definitive study, with their coding dictionary definitions and percentage of occurrence in the sample.

Table 12.1   Offence characteristics in stranger sexual assaults with frequency of occurrence

1. Confidence approach – The style of approach used by the offender in which any ploy or subterfuge is used in order to make contact with the victim prior to the commencement of the assault: this would include any verbal contact – questions asked, false introductions, story told – 15%.
2. Surprise attack – The immediate attack on the victim, whether preceded by a confidence approach or not, where force is used to obtain control of the victim: force in respect of this variable includes threat with or without a weapon. Violence is for the physical control of the victim, i.e. is exercised against the victim in order to render her available to the offender, but not the actions covered in variable – 67%.
3. Blitz attack – The sudden and immediate use of violence, whether preceded by a confidence approach or not, which incapacitates the victim: typically this is the sudden blow which leaves the victim unable to respond or react to the attack. This variable focuses on the extreme violence of the initial assault, which leaves the victim incapable of reaction – 15%.
4. Blindfold – The use at any time during the attack of any physical interference with the victim's ability to see: this only includes the use of articles and not verbal threat or the temporary use of the offender's hands – 35%.
5. Binding – As above in respect of the use of articles to disable the victim: the categorisation does not include the possible situational effect of partial stripping of the victim, nor the temporary use of manual control of the victim – 26%.
6. Gagging – As above in respect of the prevention of noise: this does not include the manual gagging of victims commonly associated with the attack variables – 23%.
7. Reaction (1) deter/change – One of two reaction variables, to examine how the offender copes with, or reacts to, active victim resistance: the resistance of the victim can be verbal or physical but does not include the act of crying alone. This categorisation addresses the offender and not the victim – 8%.
8. Reaction (2) no difference – as above but this variable categorises those offenders whose action and/or intentions are not changed by victim resistance; the offender will continue the assault against an actively resisting victim – 42%.
9. Language (1) compliments – The first of five variables concerned with the complexities of what is said by the offender to the victim. This is not necessarily the result of verbal interchange but is focused on the style of speech used by the offender, in the nonviolent context. This variable relates to those instances where the offender compliments the victim, usually on some aspect of her appearance – 12%.
10. Language (2) inquisitive – The second language variable categorises the offender's speech in being inquisitive about the victim. This includes any questions asked about the victim's lifestyle, associates etc. There are other variables that deal with the identifying of the victim and the requirement, for example, of the victim to participate in the acts committed against her. This therefore focuses on the questions asked of the victim which are those of a nonsexual nature – 42%.

(Continued)

Table 12.1   Offence characteristics in stranger sexual assaults with frequency of occurrence (*Continued*)

11. Language (3) impersonal – This language variable categorises those aspects of the offender's impersonal/instructive dealings with the victim. The focus is the impersonal style of the offender rather than the categorised differences between personal/impersonal. The personal style of speech will be shown in one or more of the other language variables – 70%.

12. Language (4) demeaning/insulting – a nonviolence language variable that categorises offender's speech with or towards the victim that is demeaning and/or insulting: this would include profanities directed against the victim herself or women in general. The focus of this variable is the insult and not sexually orientated comment – 35%.

13. Victim clothing disturbed – One of two clothing variables: this categorises the offender's removal of the victim's clothing himself. This alternative category, i.e. category 1, includes the act of disrobing carried out by the victim. This act is always at the instruction of the offender and therefore the same category is used in the circumstances of a naked or semi-naked victim. The focus of this variable is on the actions of the offender and can be seen in comparison with the activities of the offender in the second clothing variable (14). It categorises any act of removal by the offender, regardless of whether the victim assisted or not – 70%.

14. Victim clothing cut/torn – This variable addresses the offender's removal of clothing by particular methods. Although there are obvious differences in the tearing or cutting of clothing, this category deals with the offender who is prepared to use an apparently more violent style in his treatment of the victim. Category 1 covers the disturbance of clothing as well as the undressed victim. The focus is on the removal of clothing and not what the offender does with it after removal. 24%.

15. Control weapon – The categories differentiate those offenders who are prepared to display a weapon in order to control the victim – 52%.

16. Demand goods – The variable categorises the offender's approach to the victim that includes a demand for goods or money. Importantly the demand characterised in this context is that which is made in the initial stages of the attack. A later variable deals generally with stealing from the victim (V22) – 26%.

17. Victim participation – verbal – There are two variables dealing with the requirement of the victim to participate in the offence. Both have been found to occur at the instruction of the offender. Those instructions may appear in many forms, therefore this categorisation deals with the offender's requirement that the victim say words or phrases to him at his insistence. The category does not cover the occasions where an offender directs a question to the victim that does not appear to require her to answer – 15%.

18. Victim participation acts – As above, but this is categorised to cover the offender's requirement that the victim physically participate. The acts demanded of the victim are those that may be in association with specific sexual demands made of her but are in addition those sexual acts. Therefore an example may be the requirement made of the victim to kiss the offender, or to place her arms around him. In other words it focuses on the requirements that the victim participate in any act committed against her; in this context the expectation is to differentiate between those offenders who will commit, say, fellatio against the victim and those who commit the same act but accompanied by instructions to do specific acts associated with oral sex – 56%.

19. Disguise – Various disguises can be and are worn by offenders, categorically the definition of them all would result in an unwieldy variable. The category of disguise in this variable, therefore, deals with those offenders who wear any form of disguise – 14%.

20. Instances occur within the attacks, at various times, in which the offender implies knowing the victim. This categorisation records the implication that the offender knew or knew of the victim before the sexual assault – 15%.

Table 12.1   Offence characteristics in stranger sexual assaults with frequency of occurrence (*Continued*)

21. Threat – no report – This is specific categorisation of the verbalised threat made to a victim that she should not report the incident to the police or any other person. This may take many forms however the specific threat against the victim in this context is plain when made – 26%.

22. Stealing – The general category of stealing differentiates those offenders who do steal from those who do not – 44%.

23. Identifies victim – This categorisation covers offences in which offenders take steps to obtain or attempt to obtain from the victim the details that would identify her. This may take many forms including verbal approaches, the examination of personal belongings before or after the actual sexual assault, or indeed the stealing of personal identifying documents following the assault. The act is complete if the offender acts in any way that allows him to imply to the victim that he has, or can, identify her – 27%.

24. Violence (1) control – This categorisation of 'violence to control' identifies the use of force that is more than the physical control of the victim and that, situationally, is not the initial attack to obtain control of the victim. The category in this variable describes the punching, kicking, etc., of the victim in order to reinforce the control the offender is seeking to exercise on the victim – 32%.

25. Violence (2) not control – This categorisation here deals with the offender who is prepared to use excessive violence in retaliation to perceived resistance or, in some cases, the use of violence apparently for its own sake – 26%.

26. Violence (3) verbal – This variable addresses the use of intimidating language in the form of threats to maim or kill which are not necessarily associated with control or resistance. Focus is therefore on verbal violence which is not associated with control or resistance – 23%.

27. Vaginal penetration – This variable covers whether vaginal penetration was achieved or attempted – 83%.

28. Fellatio (1) – This is one of two variables dealing with the forced oral penetration of the victim. The categories of this variable deal only with whether oral penetration was carried out or attempted – 35%.

29. Fellatio (2) in sequence – The second variable of fellatio categorises offenders' requirements that their victims submit to oral penetration and are those whose performance of the act is part of a sequence of sexual acts – 24%.

30. Cunnilingus – This variable deals with the performance of a particular sexual act committed against the victim's genitalia by the offender's use of his mouth. In the present sample there is no sequential variable in this context as to date no cases have been seen where this act is performed alone. There is always some other sexual activity accompanying the act of cunnilingus – 21%.

31. Anal penetration – This is one of two variables dealing with penetration per anus committed against a victim. This categorisation deals only with those cases where the act was carried out. In the present sample categorised cases the penetration is by male organ only. It includes attempts where there is clear indication of intent – 15%.

32. Anal penetration in sequence – The second variable dealing with anal assault: the category addresses anal assault in sequence with other sexual acts – 14%.

33. Apologetic – This is a further language variable to deal with the specific apologetic speech used by an offender, most typically at the end of a sexual assault – 8%.

Canter and Heritage (1990). Reproduced with permission.

Identifying Different Styles of Rape Action

Investigative psychologists work with variables coded according to content dictionaries as shown in Table 12.1, exploring the patterns of co-occurrence across different offences to identify groups of variables that tend to happen in the same offences but not in other offences. In this way, offending styles can be identified. A detailed description of the IP methodological approach first described in detail by Canter and Heritage (1990) is presented in Chapter 5.

Canter and his colleagues have now carried out a number of these studies on different samples and using slightly varying sets of offence variables (for example, Canter and Heritage 1990; Canter *et al.*, 2003). Figure 12.2 shows the patterns of co-occurrence revealed using SSA in the original Canter and Heritage work, interpreted in terms of the victim role model for violent crime (Youngs and Canter, in press, b). The full behaviours indicated by the labels on the plot are described in Table 12.1.

The variables in the bottom right area of the plot describe actions that imply a treatment of the victim as an *object.* The actions are all about the control of the victim, whether through direct verbal instruction ('do not tell') or physical restraints ('binding'). The offence is initiated by the offender suddenly, violently attacking and incapacitating the victim ('blitz') and tearing off her clothes ('torn'), showing the offender's exclusive focus on the victim as a body for his

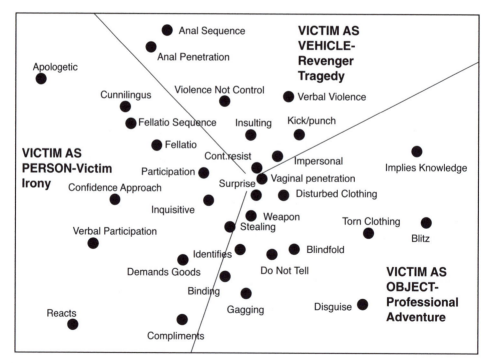

Figure 12.2 Smallest space analysis of 33 rape actions in 66 offences.

Source: Adapted from Canter and Heritage (1990). Reproduced with permission.

gratification. The 'gagging' of the victim is a clear indication of the offender's conceptualisation of the victim as an object with whom he does not seek to interact. The blindfolding of the victims reveals the total lack of empathy these offenders have for their victims as human beings.

The 'Professional Adventurer' narrative out of which this victim role assignment emerges is apparent in a number of the rape actions closely associated with these controlling and objectifying behaviours. The competent mastery that is characteristic of this narrative is clearly shown in the offender's management of the risks of being detected the situation carries by seeking to identify the victim ('identifies') as well as implying that he knows her ('implies knowledge'). The taking of a weapon to the offence and the use of a disguise point to the 'professionalism' that is central to the criminal narratives of these offenders.

The style of interaction underpinning the behaviours in the top area of the plot is consistent with the victim as *vehicle* mode. The actions reveal the offender's use of the victim as a means through which to express his anger and desires. The offender kicks and punches the victim ('kick/punch') and is verbally threatening and intimidating ('verbal violence'). Most tellingly, there is violence that, unlike when the victim is treated as an object, is excessive, beyond that which is required to control ('violence not control'). The exploitation that dominates this interpersonal treatment of the victim is indicated here in the sexually exploitive 'anal penetration' and 'anal sequence' behaviours.

The 'Revenger Tragedy' narrative that underpins this form of victim role can be discerned in some of the actions here. The offender is verbally demeaning and insulting ('insults'), suggesting that his (stranger) victim is a symbolic representation of others who have wronged him. Rather than being deterred by the victim's reactions the offender continues the attack against an actively resisting victim ('cont. resist') implying that this is an anticipated and important part of the offence for him. This points to the vindictive and avenging agenda that is at the heart of the 'Revenger Tragedy' narrative.

The actions in the left of the plot encapsulate a rather different form of interpersonal treatment of the victim as a *person*. The attempt to coerce an intimacy from the victim through the offence is revealed in the apparently bizarre acts of apologising and complimenting the victim ('apologises', 'compliments'). The 'inquisitive' questioning here is a very different way of referring to the victim's background than the threatening, implying of knowledge seen in the victim as object mode. The demands for participation ('verbal participation', 'participation') further point to the desire for intimacy that characterises these offences as well as the offender's awareness of the victim as fully human, a person. The more 'normal' and less physically violent sexual activity seen here is consistent with this distorted attempt at intimacy (for example, 'cunnilingus', 'fellatio').

This desperate attempt to achieve some intimacy reveals the sense of emptiness that runs through the 'Victim Irony' narrative. Consistent with this narrative of a meaningless and rule-less world in which these offenders see themselves as the victims and are ready to take further advantage of the situation by stealing from the victim ('demands goods').

The intensity of offending, argued to be revealed in rape in the extension of the violations beyond the sexual and into other aspects of the victim's self and identity, corresponds to the frequency contours identified here. At the centre of the plot are those behaviours that are the basic violations of the offence, defining the activity (for example, vaginal intercourse, surprise attack, victim's clothing disturbed, impersonal language). There is an increasing breadth of violation as we move out from this core to the lower frequency behaviours. At the periphery we find behaviours that are the most threatening to the victim's sense of safety in the object region (for example, disguise, blitz attack, implies knowledge). In the vehicle region these most extreme violations take the form of sexual acts that are particularly demeaning to the victim's sense of pride and dignity ('anal intercourse', 'anal sequence'). The extreme behaviours in the 'person' region are those that would be the most confusing to the victim ('apologetic', 'reacts', 'compliments'). These subtly imply that she has somehow been complicit in the horrific attack on her. Although not overtly violent or threatening, then, these would be extremely psychologically harmful, undermining her sense of agency and freedom.

Characteristics of Rapists

Investigative psychology studies of rape provide some detailed information on the basic characteristics of rapists as a group of offenders. To be fully useful to investigations further work is needed to clarify the distinctions between rapists and other groups of offenders. Table 12.2 shows the offender characteristics in one of these studies focusing on a sample of 93 stranger rapists in Finland (Häkkänen, Lindlöf and Santtila, 2004).

Table 12.2   Offender characteristics and their definitions

Variable	%	Definition
Arrived by foot	67	The offender arrived at the scene by foot
Intoxicated	54	There was evidence that the offender had been under the influence of alcohol during the attack
Employee	42	The offender was an employee (service-, sales-, care-, building, mechanic-, process-, cleaning-, kitchen-, messenger work, etc.)
Children	30	The offender had children
Criminal history	29	The offender had a criminal history
Student	29	The offender was a student/pupil/conscript
Foreigner	28	The offender was a foreigner/refugee/immigrant
Married	28	The offender was married or cohabited
Income > 1150 Euros	19	The offender's income is on average over 1150 Euros/month
Divorced	16	The offender had previously been married or cohabited
Age > 50 years	14	The offender is over 50 years of age
CHrape	13	The offender had a criminal history of rape
CHtheft	9	The offender had a criminal history of theft
CHassault	8	The offender had a criminal history of assault
Psychiatric patient	8	The offender had previously been diagnosed for mental health issues
Retired	5	The offender was on old-age pension, retired
Sickness pension	5	The offender was on sickness pension
CHdrunk driving	4	The offender had a criminal history of drunk driving

Source: Häkkänen, Lindlöf and Santtila (2004). Reproduced with permission.

The question that arises is how do these characteristics relate to the offending style differences described above? One important study by Knight *et al.* (1998) points the way forward in establishing these A-C links in rape. Knight *et al.* assessed the accuracy of a variety of offending actions in predicting the rapist's classification to one of the Massachusetts Treatment Center rapist types (MTC: R3). These researchers examined the consistency of the crime scene actions to select variables that would be most predictive of the offender types, showing that features such as offence planning, presence of a gun, binding the victim and an excessive response to resistance were particularly consistent across crimes. Knight *et al.* then showed that some of these variables (as well as some variables that were not so consistent) predicted rape offending style. In particular variables relating to using a weapon, medical damage and stabbing were predictive of the expressive aggression domain in the MTC:R3 rapist classification scheme.

Sexual Assaults on Males

Despite indications that it can involve more intense physical injury, a longer offence duration and is more likely to be a gang assault (Kaufman *et al.*, 1980), male sexual assault is markedly less studied than female rape. In part this is because of the difficulties in obtaining information on the offence, which can be due to victim reticence in reporting this crime, but it is also because male sexual assault is often assumed to be an extremely rare offence. Of the work that has been carried out, much appears to support the widely held assumption that this is an exclusively sexual offence that occurs between homosexual men (Stermac *et al.*, 1996). Stermac *et al.*, for example, conclude in their study of 29 sexual assaults self-reported to a crisis centre in Canada, that the most common victims of male sexual assault are young, gay men and the offenders are males with whom the victims are acquainted or in a relationship.

However, an initial IP study by Hodge and Canter (1998) suggests that such indications may be a product of the sampling and that this offence may in fact cover two rather distinct forms of offending activity. Using a form of multidimensional scaling to explore differences in the offences of the 49 offenders they studied, Hodge and Canter (1998) were able to show a clear distinction between homosexual and heterosexual offenders in terms of the offender-victim relationship that characterises the offence. In particular, the offences by heterosexual offenders were all attacks on strangers, while the offences of the homosexual offenders involved young victims, typically less than 25 years old, although there were no differences in offender age.

Further analysis of the differences between these types of incident, led the authors to conclude that there were two distinct forms of male sexual assault. The first, perpetrated by heterosexual men, consisted of stranger attacks, sometimes by gangs, on victims who were vulnerable, irrespective of their age or sexuality. Hodge and Canter argue that these are best understood in terms of control and dominance. A second form, in which young males were targeted, emerged out of some form of existing relationship, in which the offender may be older than the victim and is sexually motivated.

These findings have considerable investigative implications. They provide an initial basis for the police, through understanding the general type of incident, to draw some broad inferences about the likely perpetrator. Importantly, in many cases, these offender characteristics will not be those that may be assumed in a sexual assault on a female.

From a research perspective, a productive way forward that this work suggests may be the consideration of these different types of incidents as separate forms of offending – one of which may have more in common with female acquaintance rape, the other with more general models of violence, including perhaps murder of a sexually sadistic nature. Treating these as different forms of encounter may then be the most effective way to understand detailed offending styles and their implications. The prediction would be that while generic differences in offending style relating to the violent crime model of victim role and offending intensity may hold, these will manifest in rather different particular patterns of offending actions in the distinct subsets of male sexual assault.

Box 12.2 False Rape Allegations

One major aspect of the investigation of rape with which police officers have to deal is the determination of whether an allegation made of rape is genuine or false. This can be an extremely difficult task, as there are often no independent witnesses and the reliability of reports cannot easily be proved as indicated in chapter 10. Psychologists have sought to inform and guide protocol and procedures for dealing with rape allegations by exploring the context and situations under which they may occur.

It is difficult to estimate how frequently allegations that are made of rape are false or inaccurate, with figures varying greatly (Parker and Brown, 2000). Kanin (1994), in his exploration of 45 consecutive, disposed, false rape allegations covering a nine-year period, finds that false rape allegations constitute 41% of total forcible rape cases. Other studies, for example, Theilade and Thomsen (1986), estimate the prevalence of false allegations amongst all rapes reported as less than 10%.

One major problem for research in the area, which may account for the discrepancies in the figures on false rape that have been provided, is the lack of consensus on what constitutes a false allegation and whether false allegations even exist. However, Parker and Brown (2000) identify two main types of false allegation: a deliberate deceptive and intentional fabrication; and falsely held or erroneous memories, delusional states and suggestive influences.

So why might a person allege that they have been raped when they haven't? Kanin (1994) proposes that false rape allegations reflect impulsive and desperate efforts to cope with personal and social stress situations. He suggests that false allegations of rape serve three major functions for the complainants:

1. Providing an alibi – the complainant's need to provide a plausible explanation for some suddenly foreseen, unfortunate consequence of a consensual encounter, usually sexual, with a male acquaintance. These make up 56% of false rape allegations. Example: A married 30-year-old female reported that she had been raped in her apartment complex. During the polygraph examination she admitted that she was a willing partner. She reported that she had been raped as her 'partner' did not stop

before ejaculation, as he had agreed, and she was afraid that she was pregnant. Her husband is overseas.

2. Seeking revenge – this category involves falsifying rape reports as a means of retaliating against a rejecting male. These rejections can range from very evident cases of women who are sexually and emotionally involved with a reciprocating male to those women who see themselves spurned from what was in reality the female's unilateral involvement. These make up 27% of cases, and because the suspect is always identified, these false allegations potentially pose the greatest danger for a miscarriage of justice. Example: A 16-year-old reported she was raped, and her boyfriend was charged. She later admitted she was 'mad at him' because he was seeing another girl, and she 'wanted to get him into trouble'.

3. Obtaining sympathy and attention – although this device seems to be the most extravagant use for which a false rape charge is made, it is also the most socially harmless in that no one is identified as the rapist. Approximately 18% of the false charges clearly served this function. The entire verbalisation of the charge is, by and large, a fabrication without base. Example: an unmarried female, aged 17, had been having violent quarrels with her mother who was critical of her laziness and style of life. She reported that she was raped so that her mother would 'get off my back and give me a little sympathy'.

Marshall and Alison's (2006) study of genuine versus simulated (rather than explicitly false) statements showed that:

- genuine statements tend to report a larger total number of behaviours than simulated statements;
- pseudo-intimate behaviours are reported significantly more often in genuine statements
- some violent behaviours are more frequently reported in simulated incidents
- simulated statements are less behaviourally coherent than genuine statements.

Stalking

Although it has now been designated by law in both the US and Great Britain as a distinct offence type, stalking covers a remarkably diverse set of behaviours (see Box 12.3), that develop over a period of time. It will typically include the offender following, telephoning and threatening the victim. But beyond this the central actions can range from taking or damaging the victim's property, carrying out surveillance of the victim, sending gifts or physical violence. In most stalking cases there is a pre-existing relationship of some sort, often intimate (Meloy, 1996). The offending behaviour often emerges when the emotional tie is severed, particularly if this is done suddenly. In other cases, there is no prior relationship at all and the stalking occurs when the offender comes to blame the victim for some kind of loss or failure.

Box 12.3 Coding Dictionary

The coding dictionary used by Canter and Ioannou (2004) in their study of stalking actions. It shows the range and variety of behaviours that characterise this offence. The figures in brackets show how frequently each behaviour was found in Canter and Ioannou's sample.

- **Variable 1. Phone calls (76%).** The stalker makes phone calls (verbal or silent) or leaves messages on victim's answer phone. This includes any calls at the victim's home, workplace or mobile telephone.
- **Variable 2. Letters sent (46%).** The stalker sends written material to the victim. This includes letters, cards, and electronic mail sent via the Internet.
- **Variable 3. Public defamation (28%).** The stalker leaves offensive, untrue and/or inappropriately personal notes in public about the victim. This includes graffiti.
- **Variable 4. Gifts sent (28%).** This includes gifts sent to the victim at home, at work and/or via another address. Gifts may be left near the victim's home, work, car and/or where the victim will find them. Gifts include flowers, chocolates, photographs, and clothing. Gifts that imply threat, should not be counted here but within 'threatening content' (6). These may include dead animals or parts of animals, the delivery of coffins and/or any other unusual object.
- **Variable 5. Sexual content (32%).** An obscene or sexual content is observed in communications from the stalker. This includes sexual remarks in letters, phone calls and/or e-mails, heavy breathing during telephone calls. Also includes acts such as the stalker throwing underwear at the victim.
- **Variable 6. Threatening content (80%).** Threatening or abusive content is observed in communications from the stalker. This may be within letters, phone calls, e-mails, graffiti, gifts. The threat content may include threats to harm or kill (towards the victim), or indirect threats such as sending severed animal heads or coffins. Direct physical confrontations between the stalker and victim should not be coded here, but under 'threat of violence' (16) or 'violence to victim' (22).
- **Variable 7. Asking personal details (16%).** The stalker asks via letter, phone, email and/or in person for personal details about the victim. This may include questions about what they like to wear in bed (which also should be coded as sexual content), where they live or work, or any similar questions.
- **Variable 8. Offender invites contact (42%).** The stalker indicates via communication that he or she would like/expect to meet the victim, that they expect a future relationship and/or invites the victim to make contact with them. (Any such statement, which includes sexual or threatening contents, should also be coded under the appropriate category.)
- **Variable 9. Reveals knowledge about victim (12%).** The stalker reveals knowledge about the victim via letter, phone, e-mail or directly. This may include knowledge

about the victim's family, workplace, activities, colour of clothing or location at specific times and/or photographs that the victim was unaware of being taken.

- **Variable 10. Steal personal property (24%).** The stalker steals personal property from the victim's house, garden, car or place of work. This may include underwear, photographs or any item belonging to the victim. This category does not necessarily include burglary or trespass.
- **Variable 11. Destroy personal property (32%).** The stalker destroys or attempts to destroy property belonging to the victim or associated with the victim (such as neighbour's car tyres being slashed). Any attempt that could endanger life (i.e. arson) should not be coded here, but under 'threat of violence' (16).
- **Variable 12. Confrontation (52%).** The stalker makes a physically immediate confrontational threat of violence towards the victim. (This may occur separately from or in conjunction with actual violence; however only the immediacy of the threat content should be coded here.) The threat(s) may be verbal, physically with fists, with weapons and/or arson (whereby the victim is physically threatened but not physically harmed).
- **Variable 13. Threat to commit suicide (18%).** The stalker threatens either by correspondence or directly to the victim that he or she will commit suicide if the victim does not satisfy the stalker's request(s).
- **Variable 14. Follows/visits victim (78%).** The stalker follows the victim and/or visits them at their house, estate, place of work or in transit. This may be on foot, via public transport and/or by vehicle. The victim is aware of this behaviour.
- **Variable 15. Surveillance of victim (44%).** The victim may or may not be aware of the following surveillance types (which can become apparent during police investigations, court cases or subsequent discoveries); electronic bugging of their house or telephone, the stalker taking photographs or film of the victim and/or the stalker spying on the victim successfully concealing their activity or without revealing their presence.
- **Variable 16. Access victim's house (46%).** The stalker gains entrance to the victim's house or private estate through illegal entry or 'con' approach (such as getting victim's children to let in stalker as their mother's friend).
- **Variable 17. Abuse to family (10%).** The stalker makes threats, abusive remarks or harasses persons connected to the victim. This may include children, partners, friends, work colleagues and/or neighbours. These may include threats to harm or kill.
- **Variable 18. Violence to victim (42%).** The stalker perpetrates physical violence upon the victim. This may include punching, stabbing or any other kind of physical assault. The act of homicide should be included in this category.
- **Variable 19. Break restraining order (50%).** The stalker breaks a legal restraining order or injunction preventing him or her from contacting the current victim. This offence may not necessarily have been prosecuted.

(continued)

- **Variable 20. Contact after intervention (52%).** The stalker makes contact with the victim after intervention, legal or other, has been carried out.
- **Variable 21. Threat to another (40%).** The stalker threatens to harm or kill persons connected to the victim. This may include relatives, partners or friends.
- **Variable 22. Drive by (14%).** Stalker repeatedly drives by or passes victim's place of residence or workplace. This may occur on foot or in a vehicle.
- **Variable 23. Contacts another (40%).** Stalker contacts a person connected to the victim. This may be in order to elicit information about the victim, to pass on messages to the victim or to threaten, abuse or converse with the receiver of the call.
- **Variable 24. Researching (16%).** Offender researches the victim. This can be done by means of contacting and questioning those connected to the victim, accessing recorded information pertaining to the victim, or surveilling the victim. The knowledge of this research is imparted through correspondence with the victim/others connected to the victim.

The complex and varied nature of this offence has meant that much of the work in this area has focused on classifying stalkers and stalking scenarios. Although exploring rather different samples, from differing perspectives (for example, psychiatric, motivational, contextual, target type) and for different purposes (for example, treatment, dangerousness prediction, sentencing), the variations described by these classification schemes can be understood in terms of just two core psychological dimensions.

One of these relates to differences in the interpersonal distance or the familiarity of the relationship between the offender and the victim he targets. Ritchie's (1994) classification system, for example, distinguishes between celebrity stalking, stranger stalking, acquaintance stalking and ex-partner stalking. Similarly, the scheme Hendricks and Spillane (1993) propose differentiates between domestic, workplace and celebrity stalking, while along the same lines, Wright et al. (1996) distinguish the domestic from the nondomestic stalker.

A second core psychological dimension within many of the typologies relates to the nature of the contact the offender is attempting to impose upon the victim. Harmon et al. (1995) are explicit on this, distinguishing between an 'affectionate/amorous' attachment and a 'persecutory/angry' one. Similar differences in stalking goals are implicit in the psychiatric classifications proposed by both Geberth (1992) and Zona, Sharma and Lane (1993). Geberth's 'Psychopathic Personality Stalker', whom he describes as typically a male from a dysfunctional, violent family background who vandalises the property of a former partner as well as carrying out other aggressive acts such as killing pets is clearly seeking to have an aggressive, destructive impact upon the victims. In contrast, the 'psychotic personality' stalker identified by Geberth, whom he describes as a male or female offender obsessed with a stranger to whom he or she sends letters and gifts as well as continually telephoning and attempting to visit, is trying to achieve a rather different type of contact. Similarly, Zona, Sharma and Lane (1993) 'erotomanic' (see Box 12.3) and 'love obsessional' types are both concerned with the love of their victim, the 'erotomanic' believing he/she already has this, while the 'love obsessional' believes the target could love them if given the opportunity. Zona,

Sharma and Lane's third type, the 'simple obsessional', is again distinguishable from these in terms of the type of contact goal, with this group focused on controlling, rectifying or avenging a prior relationship or situation.

Clearly, typologies of the offenders or general situations from which stalking emerges draw attention to important differences in the contexts and objectives of stalking, although more empirical validation is needed for many of the proposed types. From an investigative perspective however, the central concern will be the likely patterns of development and dangerousness, specifically the particular sorts of threats an offender may pose as well as his likely reactions to victim or police behaviour within different stalking patterns and sequences. This requires a detailed understanding of the way in which particular offending actions are likely to co-occur as well as the psychological processes underlying these and how they may develop.

Offending Styles in Stalking

Canter and Ioannou (2004) report one of the few detailed empirical analyses of styles of stalking behaviour, drawing upon a set of 50 stalking cases which included ex-intimate through to stranger and celebrity relationships, these researchers used the IP content analysis procedure to derive 24 dichotomous behavioural variables. The SSA structure of the patterns of co-occurrence they found across these different actions is shown in Figure 12.3.

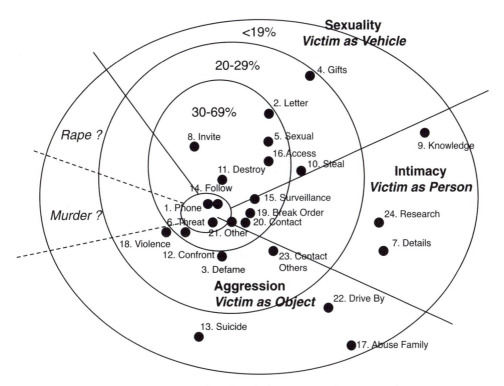

Figure 12.3 Smallest space analysis of stalking behaviours, with Victim Role reinterpretation.
Source: Canter and Ioannou (2004). Reproduced with permission.

Victim as Person

As Figure 12.3 shows, towards the right-hand section of the plot are a group of actions that tend to co-occur within stalking offences. These are associated with researching the victim (researc v24), revealing knowledge (know v9) and asking personal details (detail v7). Also in this broad region, nearer to the centre of the plot (suggesting these actions are less distinct and may sometimes also occur within other stalking patterns) are two further behaviours: Breaking a restraining order (v19) and 'surveillance' (including spying on the victim, bugging or filming with or without the victim's awareness – v15). Canter and Ioannou refer to this clustering as an 'intimacy' pattern, arguing that these actions are a distorted attempt to reduce the interpersonal distance with the victim and to enter into some sort of relationship.

A related way to understand this style of behaviour is in terms of the 'Victim as Person' role within Canter's (1994) 'role of the victim framework (Youngs and Canter, in press, b). This role is one in which, unlike other roles that may be assigned, the offender recognises that he is dealing with a real individual. But in line with a generally abusive style of human interaction, he sees simply taking what he wants as a legitimate way of relating to others. In the context of stalking, then, an activity that may be considered essentially an attempt to force an engagement/relationship with or an impact upon a victim, this victim role is likely to emerge as an attempt to develop a 'normal' personal relationship through a strategy of 'stealing' it; gaining personal, intimate information without consent.

Behaviours such as asking others personal information about the victim or researching her in other ways, as well as direct questions to the victim of an inappropriately personal nature, reveal both an awareness of the victim as an individual and an interest in finding out about her. This is a way of imposing a relationship along with no compunction about invading her privacy.

Victim as Vehicle

In the top section of the SSA plot, the behaviours sending letters (letter v2), sending communications with sexual content (sexual v5), asking the victim to meet (invite v8), entering the victim's house (v16), stealing personal items belonging to the victim (steal v10) and destroying the victim's personal property (destroy v11) together form a second pattern of stalking. As well as the explicit sexual content variable appearing in this region, Canter and Ioannou draw attention to the implicit sexuality and/or potential sexual contact underlying these behaviours. They point out that even the theft and destructive actions in this region differ from other forms of stalking violence in that their focus is on the personal possession of the victim.

This central theme of sexuality and sexual possession can be further elaborated by considering this action pattern in terms of Canter's (1994) 'Victim as Vehicle' role. As outlined, for this style of offending the offender is simply using the victim to express his own desires and/or anger. Because the interaction carries symbolic meaning, the reactions and participation of the victim are significant to the extent that they support the expression of his anger or desires.

In line with the general exploitative approach, the offender may use manipulative or 'con' strategies to facilitate his crime.

Within a stalking context this will emerge in behaviours that are not about the victim and relating to, or even controlling her but are rather concerned with the offender imposing his feelings upon a victim. Typically within stalking this will be his sexual feelings as seen in the sexual content of communications as well as unwanted gifts and letters that reflect anticipated sexual contact. In some cases, where an individual comes to symbolise a failure or misfortune that the offender has suffered, the stalking may revolve around the expression of anger. The relevance of the victim's reactions will produce dramatic actions and attacks on material items that are likely to be personally significant (as seen in the stealing and destruction of personal property variables). Behaviours such as 'Access House', where this access is gained by subterfuge, reveal the offender's general manipulative and exploitative interpersonal style.

Victim as Object

A final area in the bottom half of the plot comprises behaviours concerned with control. Canter and Ioannou identify two forms that this may take. One is a possessive form in which the offender assumes ownership, controlling indirectly by watching the victim and contacting her family and friends. Four behaviours reflect this style: the offender driving repeatedly past the victim's home/work (drive by v22), the offender contacting the victim after some kind of legal or other intervention (v20), the offender contacting someone connected to the victim (contact others v23) and abuse or attacks against the victim's family (abuse family v17). As Canter and Ioannou note 'the contact with those other than the victim is compatible with the claim from a number of researchers that these stalkers see the victim as their property and believe that if they do not "possess" them then no-one will.'

The second form that the control may take is an aggressive/destructive form in which the offender attempts to impose the control directly and will inflict physical or psychological harm to force this. The behaviours indicative of this style that Canter and Ioannou point to on the plot include physically threatening and confronting the victim (confront v12), threats in letters, emails or phone calls (threat v6), actual physical attack on the victim (violence v18) and the offender making defamatory public notices about the victim (defame v3).

Youngs and Canter (in press, b) argue that this general pattern of controlling behaviours, whether through a possessive or aggressive strategy, depicts the manifestation of the 'Victim as Object' mode (Canter, 1994) as would be anticipated in the context of stalking. This offending mode is one in which the offender has a complete lack of empathy for, or simply fails to understand the victim as a human being. Rather she is something without human significance for him to act upon, elicit from and control as required, an object.

Where the general focus of the offending activity is the creation of a relationship with or having some other impact upon the victim, this object role will be revealed in an approach where the offender believes he can simply make this happen. He will assume he can force a 'relationship' by creating and controlling the external conditions as revealed in the behaviours involving contacting and threatening those related to the victim (for example, contacting a person related or connected to the victim (contact others v23) and threatening violence against a person connected to the victim (other v21)) the preparedness to ignore legal actions (contacting victim after an intervention – v20) as well as the monitoring behaviours (repeatedly driving past victim's home or place of work – drive by v22).

The complete lack of empathy that characterises the victim as object offending mode will be revealed in a cruel and socially inappropriate approach as indicated by the public defamation variable (defame v3) here, as well as a failure to comprehend that these actions will be detrimental to his cause. The assumption of control and lack of empathy produce a readiness to use direct physical violence where necessary to manage the victim (violence v18).

Offending Intensity in Stalking

The intensity of offending in stalking is revealed in the intensity of the personal contact the offender seeks with the victim. As predicted by the radex model of criminal differentiation, this form of offending intensity modulates the qualitative differences in victim role assignment. These stylistic variations thus emerge most clearly within the most intense personal contact actions. As in many IP studies, Canter and Ioannou show that this intensity distinction is reflected (inversely) in the frequency of occurrence across their sample.

At the core of the SSA are the actions that occur in over 70% of the cases. Threatening the victim, in essence the key defining act of stalking, occurs in 80% of cases; following or visiting the victim, another key aspect for the event to be regarded as harassment, in 78% of cases, and telephoning the victim in 76% of cases. These three actions thus provide a focus for the whole configuration.

Around these are actions that happen in 30 to 69% of the cases. Farthest from the focus are those that occur in 10 to 20 per cent of the cases. The highest frequency variables that characterise the stalking act and are present in most cases are: the offender phones the victim (phone v1), the offender follows/visits the victim (follow v14) and the offender threatens the victim (threat v6) all of which occur in over 70% of the offences considered.

The facet depicted by these frequency contours can be conceptualised as representing the various stages that occur in contacting the victim. The first stage is telephoning (1), following/visiting (14), and threatening (6). The next stage contained within the 30–69% involves an effort for more contact, the offender tries to come closer to the victim by sending letters (2), making sexual remarks in communication (5), accessing the victim's house (16), inviting contact (8), destroying personal property or belongings of the victim (11), carrying out surveillance of the victim (15), breaking a restraining order (19), confronting the victim (12), contacting the victim after he/she has intervened (20), threatening another person (21), contacting another person (23) and finally by perpetrating physical violence on the victim (18).

A third stage is represented by the 10–29% contour. In this the behaviour becomes even more personal as the offender sends gifts to the victim (4), reveals knowledge about the victim (9), researches the victim (24), asks for personal details (7), defames the victim (3), drives by the victim's place of residence or workplace (22), abuses the victim's family (17), steals personal property (10), and threatens to commit suicide (13).

Activity Box
Box 12.4 Differentiating Paedophilia

The table below shows the offence actions identified within Canter, Hughes and Kirby's (1998) study of paedophilia in this study.

1. Drawing on all the ideas in the generic model of violent crime differentiation, which of these actions would you expect to co-occur across offences?
2. Provide a formal definition of the manifestation of the generic model of violent crime differentiation in paedophilia. How does this differ from the stalking and rape versions of the model?

Variable	Description
Variable 13	The victim was a complete *stranger* to the victim.
Variable 8	The offence was facilitated by the use of *initial force* or a threat of force was used to control the victim.
Variable 14	The offence was committed *outdoors*.
Variable 6	The offender *kissed* the victim on the lips.
Variable 1	The offender *promised* the victim money or other presents and treats.
Variable 11	*Abusive and/or sexually explicit language* was used by the offender during the offence.
Variable 17	The child was *alone* at the time of the offence; this implies that when the offence was committed only the victim and the offender were present.
Variable 3	The offender showed *affection* towards the child through compliments, hugs, or spending time with him or her other than for sexual gratification.
Variable 9	The offender was *not deterred by an adverse reaction* from the victim and carried on to commit the offence knowing that the victim did not consent.
Variable 15	The offence was a *one-off* event and the offender had committed no other indecent acts against the victim prior to being arrested for the current offence.
Variable 2	The offender *reassured* the victim by explaining what he was doing in order to minimise the victim's fear.
Variable 19	Penile-*vaginal penetration* or attempted penetration occurred.
Variable 5	The offender performed *oral sex* on the victim.
Variable 16	The offender was *intoxicated* with alcohol and/or drugs during the offence.
Variable 10	*Threats of violence* were used by the offender to prevent the child from reporting the offence. Such threats often involve telling the child that he or she, or someone for whom he/she cares, will be subjected to violence if the offence is disclosed.
Variable 12	Penile-*anal penetration* or attempted penetration occurred.
Variable 7	*Violence was used beyond the level necessary* to control the victim for gratuitous purposes.
Variable 18	The offender *ejaculated* during the offence.
Variable 4	*Desensitisation* (a.k.a. minimisation) occurred; this involves the lowering of a child's threshold to sexual behaviour and can include the following; allowing the child to observe sexual behaviour taking place physically (i.e. between the offender and the child's mother, or between the offender and other children), or through pictures (i.e. pornographic magazines or video-cassettes), or by physically touching the child – making any indecent action appear as a legitimate mistake.

Activity Box
Box 12.5 Unwanted Sexual Activities on Dates

Percentage of SA Dates Involving Specific Unwanted Sexual Activities

Unwanted sexual activity	Percentage women reporting experiencing activity[a]	Percentage men reporting doing activity[b]
Kissed without tongue contact	3.7	2.2
Kissed with tongue contact	12.3	0.7
He touched her under her shirt (not her breasts)	16.5	4.4
He touched/kissed her breasts through her clothes	24.7	7.3
He touched/kissed her breasts under her clothes	22.6	13.1
He touched her buttocks through her clothes	23.0	4.4
He touched her buttocks under her clothes	19.3	8.0
He touched her genitals through her clothes	28.8	15.3
He touched her genitals under her clothes	28.4	13.9
He performed oral sex on her	9.9	8.8
He forced her to touch him under his shirt	0.8	0.7
He forced her to touch his buttocks through his clothes	1.2	0.7
He forced her to touch his buttocks under his clothes	3.3	1.5
He forced her to touch his genitals through his clothes	2.9	0.7
He forced her to touch his genitals under his clothes	5.8	2.2
He forced her to perform oral sex on him	2.5	4.4
Sexual intercourse	20.6	15.3

Note. Percentages add to more than 100% because more than one unwanted activity often occurred on one date. SA = sexual aggression.
[a]$n = 243$. [b]$n = 137$.

Source: Muehlenhard and Linton (1987).

Summary

- It is proposed that the core psychological purpose of violent crime will lie in the interaction with the victim and the meaning derived from this.
- This psychological purpose is argued to be common to all violent crimes such that a generic model of differentiation based on variations in the offenders' style of interpersonal interaction within an offence can be proposed. This, rather than, for example differences

in the sexual activity in rape or in the overt goal of harassment in stalking, is emerging as the basis of offending style distinctions.

- One framework for these variations in style of interpersonal interaction that is proving productive is Canter's (1994) 'role of the victim' model (Object, Vehicle or Person roles), which has its roots in the core narrative psychology themes of power and intimacy.

- In line with general psychological thinking, the basis for understanding the intensity of the offending actions within violent crime is proposed not in terms of the strength of attack on the body within an offence but the strength of attack on the person. Consistent with the radex of criminal differentiation, the differences in Object, Vehicle and Person styles of offending emerge as the intensity of attack on the person increases.

- The victim role model is a framework for the differentiation of offending activity rather than the specification of particular behaviours. The particular patterns of offending activity that characterise the Object, Vehicle and Person modes have to be understood in terms of the form of criminal activity under consideration. One possibility is that the same action will reflect different modes in different contexts.

- The different Victim Roles emerge out of particular criminal narratives and as such relate to the NAS modes; the Object role is part of a Professional's Adaptive Adventure mode, the Person role is part of a Victim's Integrative Irony mode and different variants of the Vehicle role emerge from the Revenger's Conservative Tragedy and the Hero's Expressive Quest.

Further Reading

Books

Bourke, J. (2008) *Rape: A History From 1860 to the Present*, Virago Press, London.
Groth, A.N. (1979) *Men Who Rape: The Psychology of the Offender*, Plenum, New York.
Horvath, M. and Brown, J. (eds) (2009) *Rape*, Willan, Cullompton.

Articles

Hodge, S. and Canter, D. (1998) Victims and perpetrators of male sexual assault. *Journal of Interpersonal Violence*, **13**, 222–39.
Jordan, J. (2004) Beyond belief? Police, rape and women's credibility. *Criminal Justice*, **4** (1), 29–59.
Porter, L., and Alison, L. (2006) Examining group rape: a descriptive analysis of offender and victim behaviour. *European Journal of Criminology*, **3**, 357–81.
Warren, J., Reboussin, R., Hazelwood, R. R. *et al.* (1998) Crime scene and distance correlates of serial rape. *Journal of Quantitative Criminology*, **14** (1), 35–59.

Questions for Discussion and Research

1. Should rape be treated as a crime that is distinct from other crimes of violence?
2. Why do many aspects of stalking contain strongly sexual components?

3. What sense does it make to consider a 'style' of offending in rape?

4. Would you expect sexual assaults on male victims to be different from those on female victims?

5. Is it appropriate to consider all sex crimes as extreme forms of normal behaviour?

6. What are your experiences of unwanted sexual activity in relationships with others? How might this relate to sexual assaults or stalking? Does the concept of 'date rape' make any sense (cf. Muehlenhard and Linton, 1987)? Consider Box 12.5 in the light of your discussion of these issues.

7. What criminal narratives would you draw on to describe the different styles of stalking offending?

Murder

In This Chapter

Learning Objectives

In this chapter you will learn that:

1. The psychological contexts out of which murders arise can be distinguished in terms of whether the murder was the central aim of the event (expressive murder encounters) or not (instrumental murder encounters).
2. Contract murder takes different forms. These suggest that it is not invariably a professional, organised criminal activity.

3. In the context of serial murder, offending intensity manifests as the extremeness of the dehumanisation and destruction of the person's identity that is inherent within the actions.

4. The generic model of differentiation for violent crime holds for serial murder. Distinct offending styles, reflecting the object, vehicle or person modes of transaction with the victim, emerge within the higher intensity acts as different interpersonal approaches to the dehumanisation and destruction of the victim.

5. The role of victim as object in serial murder is apparent as actions that are explorations of the body, typically post-mortem.

6. The role of victim as vehicle emerges in serial murder as actions that are emotional attacks on or exploitations of the live victim.

7. The role of victim as person in serial murder takes the form of actions that suggest an intimacy on the part of the offender and that recognise the victim as an individual with an identity.

8. The often cited organised-disorganised serial murder typology is not supported by the evidence.

9. Sexual sadism is a poorly defined concept and its relationship to offending behaviour unclear.

Synopsis

Murder can arise in many ways in many different contexts. It is therefore essential to attend to the differences in the events of which murder is part as a first step in identifying offending style differences. Broadly, one can distinguish between expressive encounters where the murder emerges out of an intimate or family interaction, and instrumental encounters where the murder is a subsidiary action to other offending behaviour, typically burglary or rape. The clarification of these context dependent differences in the detailed patterns of offending actions has direct investigative value.

The intensive IP study of serial murder challenges existing frameworks based on speculations about motivations, psychopathology or the organised–disorganised dichotomy. It leads to an understanding of offending-style differences in terms of distorted forms of interpersonal interaction. Patterns of offending actions, as was indicated in relation to sexual offences, can be related to the role assigned to the victim within the offender's criminal narrative. The 'victim as object' role that emerges from a Professional Adventure narrative is argued to underpin a murder style that involves extensive post-mortem exploration of the body. The 'victim as vehicle' role, associated here with the Revenger Tragedy narrative, is revealed in frenzied attacks on and exploitations of the live victim. The 'victim as person' role, derived from a narrative of Victim Irony, is argued to underlie those offending patterns that do recognise the identity of the victim as an individual. The NAS modes that these victim role styles emerge from provide a broader, alternative basis for interpreting these offending differences. In line with the radex model of criminal differentiation, these style variations emerge most clearly at the higher levels of offending depravity, producing distinct styles in these acts that represent the most extreme forms of dehumanisation.

Murder

From an investigative perspective it is significant that, in most murders, the offender will know the victim. Indeed as the offender will typically be a family member, intimate partner or estranged intimate partner, there will often be precursors to murder in domestic violence or stalking activity. The important IP question here, then, rather than the identification of the perpetrator, will be the prediction of when stalking episodes or family violence are going to develop into murder. However, although this violence will very commonly precede a nonstranger murder, very few domestic violence or stalking cases do progress to become murders. What is required, then, is an understanding not simply of the violent behaviour that precedes murder but of the differences between this violence and other violent domestic situations. Yet there are varied developmental paths that lead to murder in domestic violence or stalking. Consequently, nonstranger murder prediction models need to be multidimensional, elucidating different violence escalation routes.

Stranger murders and particularly serial stranger murders, despite their rarity, generate intense reactions and are of great psychological interest because they reflect such an extreme form of human action. They are also of considerable practical import with the cost of the typical stranger homicide investigation in the UK running into the millions of pounds (see Canter, 2003 for accounts of recent major murder investigations). Considerable attention within IP has therefore been directed towards understanding the psychological variations in the ways in which these crimes are committed and what this can tell us about the offenders and also about the psychology of murder itself.

Offending Style in Murder: Understanding the Context of the Encounter

'Murder' is a legal term that is applied to a diverse range of psychological events that happen in a variety of different situations, emerging out of a variety of types of interaction and where the relationship between victim and offender can range from that of strangers to intimate partners. The central psychological purpose of crimes against the person is recognised within IP as being derived from the interaction with the victim (see Chapter 12). Given the range of different types of encounter from which murder can arise, it is clear that at a broad level, the general purpose that the victim as an individual serves for the offender will vary markedly across murder offences, sometimes having a very particular significance, sometimes being entirely insignificant. As Youngs and Canter (in press, b) note, a starting point for understanding more detailed differences in homicide action patterns and the particular role a victim may play for an offender is to distinguish between the psychological contexts of murder encounters.

Expressive or Instrumental Encounters

One distinction in offending style that can be found across many studies is whether or not the murder was the central aim of the event (for example, Salfati and Canter, 1999; Santtila *et al.*, 2001). This is not the issue of whether or not the offender deliberately killed the victim when he attacked, as in legalistic debates relating to questions of intent that distinguish murder from manslaughter, but whether the killing was really incidental to another objective. Salfati and Canter (1999) noted that this distinction reflected Fesbach's (1964) theoretical distinction between instrumental and expressive aggression. For Fesbach some aggression is what he termed 'hostile' in that it is driven by the emotion generated by some attack on or insult against the offender, while other aggression is simply a means to another end, 'instrumental'.

Investigative psychological studies are beginning to show that differences in homicide offending style can be related to a number of different variants of expressive and instrumental encounters (Salfati and Canter, 1999; Santtila, Elfgren and Hakkanen 2001). This work, which has explored samples of diverse single homicide incidents in many different countries, points to four psychological contexts out of which the offence may occur and elaborates some of the particular sets of offending actions these encounters tend to produce.

Expressive murder encounters can take two broad forms. In one form, the offence emerges out of an intimate relationship. These are the crimes that Santtila *et al.* (2001: 380) describe as happening 'where the person of the victim is important to the offender and the killing occurs in response to an insult, physical attack, personal failure or sexual jealousy'. Santtila *et al.* suggest that this psychological context may underlie the 'Expressive: firearm' set of offending actions that they identify. They argue that this pattern of behaviours (body positioning indicating indifference regarding it being found, victim shot and excessive number of shots fired), describes an intensely reactive scenario in which the offender simply goes to the scene armed with a gun, kills and then leaves the victim. It is important to note that this focus on the use of firearms does seem to be a particular artefact of the Finnish sample these researchers studied, given that more than 40% of the adult population in that country owns guns. Indeed, the expressive crime scene theme that Salfati and Canter (1999: 401) describe in similar terms in their UK sample of offences as indicating 'a very emotional attack where the offender is attacking the core representation of that person', comprises a rather different set of offending actions, including multiple wounds and injuries to the face but little care to avoid leaving forensic evidence.

In an investigative context, the starting point for any investigation of a murder scene characterised by these unequivocal (for example, with excessive shots, multiple wounds) and at the same time, unconsidered (for example, with indifferent body 'positioning') offending actions would be the intimate and/or former intimate partners of the victim.

The second variant of the *Expressive murder encounter*, less clearly articulated to date, is one in which a female offender, possibly with a psychiatric diagnosis, attacks a family member as indicated by the Santtila *et al.* (2003) 'Expressive: Blood' characteristics theme. These authors note that female murderers are significantly more likely than males to kill relatives, although they are less likely to use a firearm. Salfati and Canter provide some support for this family variant of the expressive encounter reporting a tendency for female offenders to exhibit the Expressive style they identified. More work is needed to elaborate the detailed offending actions that characterise murders that arise from this and, in particular, how these will differ from the intimate expressive form of homicide.

The research so far indicates that *instrumental murder encounters* can arise out of two broad psychological contexts. One form occurs when the offender has sexually attacked a victim and kills her after this to silence her and avoid later detection. This subset of offences, indicated in crime scene reports by a range of pre-mortem sexual activity, was clear in the homicides that Santtila *et al.* (2001) considered, although it is not yet clear what other offence behaviours such as weapon type or killing method are indicated in this scenario. This form of rape murder has been elaborated by Keppell and Walter (1999) who propose four specific types of offence and offender: the power-assertive rape murder, the power-reassurance rape murder, the anger-retaliatory rape murder and the anger-excitation rape murder. It should be stressed that although these ideas no doubt have some currency and Keppell and Walter illustrate their types with case study examples, these researchers do not provide data analyses to support their assertions so these remain interesting ideas for empirical exploration.

The second form of instrumental murder encounter happens as part of a burglary or other property crime and will typically involve the targeting of vulnerable victims in their homes and manual killing rather than with a weapon (Salfati and Canter 1999). Santtila *et al.* depict these offenders as 'petty criminals leading marginalised lives'. This claim is supported by Salfati and Canter who report relationships between these opportunistic offences and previous offences for theft and/or burglary as well as unemployment. Although these offenders may not be well known to the victim they are likely to be familiar with the area and the victim. They are typically opportunistic individuals taking advantage of known vulnerable targets within their locality.

Salfati and Canter (1999) provide some indications of the offender characteristics which may be associated with Expressive forms of offences (Table 13.1). In line with the consistency principle (Chapter 5), they argue that these characteristics follow the same theme of impulsive violence and interpersonal conflict. This list is a useful starting point but further work is now needed to clarify how these characteristics may differ across the intimate and family murder encounters.

Table 13.1 Offender characteristics – expressive theme

Previous violent offences
Previous offences for public disorder
Previous offences for damage to property
Previous sexual offences
Previous traffic offences
Previous drugs offences
Married at time of offence
Previous marriage
Female offender

Source: Adapted from Salfati and Canter (1999). Reproduced with permission.

The identification of these *Expressive-Intimate, Expressive-Family, Instrumental-Rape* and *Instrumental-Burglary murder* encounters provides a first level of differentiation for defining offending styles in homicide. It highlights the diversity of psychological processes out of which this offence can emerge. Understanding these contexts is a crucial first step in specifying offending styles within homicide because they represent very different types of incident that will tend to produce characteristic ranges of behaviours. With different samples of offences researchers may delineate further encounter types. Interestingly, studies are emerging that indicate that there may be significant cross-national differences in the detailed murder actions that these psychological contexts produce (for example, Salfati and Haratsis, 2001; Santtila *et al.*, 2001).

This is, however, only a starting point in terms of being able to address the core IP questions about the identification of salient criminal actions and the differentiation of offending style in homicide. Further steps are necessary in order to identify consistencies in these actions across serial cases and what offender inferences these will allow. Detailed explorations of the variations in behavioural patterns within each of these contexts are now needed. In this, the prediction would be that distinct patterns that represent different versions of the generic object, vehicle and person offending styles will emerge but that these will be coloured by the psychological context from which they emerge. For example, the intensity of emotion that will inevitably characterise murders within an intimate relationship will tend to produce explosive violence.

Nonetheless, this mapping out of an initial, general basis for distinguishing homicide styles in terms of the psychological context of the encounter can have direct investigative relevance, allowing police to disentangle the likely circumstances of a murder. So, for example, through the exploration of whether or not the violence targets the face, some initial indications can be drawn about the likely involvement of an intimate partner rather than a rapist who killed to protect his identity, for instance. But this work also starts to open up thinking about the psychological processes that may distinguish those unusual murders where the victim is neither known nor the unfortunate, incidental victim of the offender's rape or burglary agenda, but rather where the offender's explicit purpose is the killing of an unknown victim and where the offender is likely to be serial.

Contract Murder

One variant of murder that fits a highly Instrumental interpretation is contract murder. A contract murderer is defined as 'an offender who unlawfully kills an individual on behalf of someone else for financial or material gain' (Crumplin, 2009). The contract killer is distinguished from an assassin whose murder is committed for ideological reasons rather than financial gain. In psychological terms, the concept of contract murder is interesting in that it represents such an extreme form of behavioural instrumentality, the gain being for carrying out the murder directly, the action being entirely premeditated. The expectation would be, then, that both the style of offending behaviour observed in such offences and the offenders who perpetrate these crimes will differ from other murders and murderers.

In an impressive example of the innovative approaches required for data collection in IP (see Chapter 3), Crumplin (2009) provides one of the few empirical examinations of this unusual form of murder. His analysis of 33 cases of contract murder drawn from published sources, predominantly true crime magazines, throws light on what actually happens in these offences that are rather more often represented in fiction and the movies than they are in empirical research. Crumplin content analysed the accounts prepared by journalists for these publications using a content dictionary of 28 items adapted from dictionaries developed at the International Centre for Investigative Psychology for research on general homicide (Holden, 1994; Salfati, 1994). The prevalence of the behaviours and crime-scene actions indicated by these items is shown in Table 13.2. The offenders from this sample were all male with a mean age of 29 years.

Table 13.2 Frequency of crime scene variables in contract murder.

Variable number	Variable name	Frequency	Percentage agreement (interrater reliability)
1	Weapon to scene	30	100
2	Partner	27	100
3	Went to plan	22	100
4	Shot	21	100
5	Head	19	100
6	Found outside	19	100
7	Killed at home	18	100
8	Killed outside	17	100
9	Found at home	17	100
10	Torso injuries	15	100
11	Basic offender error	12	100
12	Stage	8	100
13	Kill day	7	90
14	Panic	7	90
15	Beaten	6	100
16	Neck	6	90
17	Secondary criminal activity (e.g. theft)	6	90
18	Stabbed	5	100
19	Strangled	5	90
20	Face up	5	90
21	Steal property	4	100
22	Forensically aware	4	80
23	Leave weapon at scene	4	100
24	Bound	3	100
25	Overkill	3	90
26	Limbs	2	100
27	Body placed	2	90
28	Body moved	2	100

Source: Crumplin (2009). Reproduced with permission.

The very frequent behaviours help to understand and define the fundamental nature of this offence. Consistent with the general understanding of contract murder, the frequencies indicate that this is typically a premeditated offence, the murderer taking a gun to the scene and the murder being committed by a shot to the head or torso. Perhaps less expected is the finding that almost all such murders are committed with a partner.

Although these core behaviours are common to most contract killings, Table 13.2 does indicate a variety of lower frequency behaviours that may allow the identification of different styles of contract murder. To identify such variations, Crumplin examined the patterns of co-occurrence of these behaviours across the different crimes using smallest space analysis (see Chapter 5). The plot he extracted from this suggested the existence of three themes or offending styles in contract murder that allowed offences to be differentiated beyond the core activities found across most cases.

The first of these he referred to as *criminally sophisticated* behaviours. This style comprised behaviours that indicated experience such as being forensically aware, injuries to the neck, victim killed by strangulation, the victim being killed/found outside, injuries to the head, moving or placing the body and a 'staged' crime scene.

Case Study: Floyd Holzapfel and Bobby Lincoln

Judge Joseph Peel hired Floyd Holzapfel and Bobby Lincoln to kill Judge Curtis Chillingworth in Miami on the night of 14 June 1955. Equipped with guns, adhesive tape, rope, diving weights and gloves, Holzapfel and Lincoln arrived by boat at the Chillingworth's seaside home. Peel had assured his two killers that Judge Chillingworth's wife was not at home, but instructed them to kill anyone else who happened to be there. Holzapfel, wearing a yachting hat to give the impression that he was a sailor in distress, knocked on the door of Chillingworth's house. When the judge opened the door, Holzapfel asked him if he was Judge Chillingworth. When the judge confirmed his identity, Holzapfel produced a pistol and pointed it at him. To Holzapfel's horror the judge called his wife. In turn, Holzapfel summoned Lincoln, who was still in the boat. Having bound the two victims with adhesive tape and ropes, Holzapfel searched the house for cash. He removed some bank notes from the judge's wallet, but left some change as they wanted there to be no hint of a crime. Peel wanted it to look as if the judge had gone for a late night swim and had been swept out to sea. As they headed out to sea Holzapfel strapped the diving weights around Mrs Chillingworth's waist. He picked her up and threw her into the sea. Holzapfel had not expected to kill more than one person but as a precaution he had brought along enough weights for two. Before he could put the weights on Mr Chillingworth, the judge had jumped in to the sea. Holzapfel shouted at Lincoln to hit him. Lincoln failed to stop the judge by hitting him with the butt of a shotgun, so Holzapfel took over. He hit the judge with such force that the butt of the shotgun broke. They did not want to shoot him for fear they would be heard. Holzapfel then took the anchor rope and wrapped it around the judge's neck, cut it and threw the anchor overboard taking the judge with it.

As a young man, Holzapfel had been involved in petty crime, such as bookmaking. Before he met Judge Peel he had carried out a series of armed robberies, all of which netted less than he boasted they did. He had also served at least two jail sentences. Holzapfel's behaviours and the general style of the offence reflected a theme of criminal experience. His control of the victims, although not especially expert, reflected his experience of victim control from his previous armed robberies. Lincoln was a lesser character in the Peel empire; he owned pool bars and ran rackets for Peel. He was not a violent man but had agreed to join the conspiracy through fear for the safety of his family. Lincoln's background and character seem to be evident in his lesser role in the murder.

Crumplin calls the second distinct set of behaviours *aggressive* behaviours. This style includes, for example, overkill, stabbing, beating and injuries to the torso and head. As Crumplin notes, these behaviours are all acts of extreme aggression, epitomised by the overkill variable.

The third offending style Crumplin identified was revealed in *inept* behaviours. He argues these are the kind of behaviours that one might expect to be committed by an inexperienced offender. The variables included here include behaviours that are unnecessary for the successful contract, such as secondary criminal activity and stealing property. They also include variables that indicate an incompetency and inefficiency in the core killing task, such as injury to the torso and limbs, panicking, making a basic error, and the body being left face up.

Case Study: James Arnold and Gary Cagnina

James Arnold and Gary Cagnina were paid to kill Harold Schornick, in 1977 by W. G. Holsinger. They broke into Schornick's house at night. James Arnold had a .22 handgun. They disturbed the residents of the house and it made them panic. Arnold and Cagnina shot Schornick and his housekeeper (who they thought was Schornick). Schornick survived, but his housekeeper died. The two offenders fled. Before the attack the hired killers damaged the car in the Schornicks' garage. The vehicle used to get to and from the scene, which had been sighted in the area, was registered in Arnold's name. It is possible that this inept style of offence is indicative of inexperience and it is hypothesised that this could be due to the offenders having a low level of intelligence, being under the influence of drugs or alcohol, or being young. In fact, Arnold was 17 years old and Cagnina was 20 years old at the time of the offence. Cagnina was a fairly experienced burglar who was known to the police. A bench warrant for Cagnina's arrest was in effect at the time of the offence. Arnold, who actually carried out the shooting, was a heroin addict and was desperately in need of money.

The identification of the aggressive and inept styles here is interesting, suggesting that many contract murders are not part of the professional, organised criminal activity that is often assumed. This concurs with findings that Crumplin established for the cases he examined – contrary to the stereotypical Hollywood depiction of contract murder, in many of these offences the offender will know both the victim and the contractor.

Box 13.1 Smallest Space Analysis of Autographical Accounts of Violence

Justifications for Violence

In an interesting study of the justifications violent criminals give for their actions, Barrett (2001) explored 104 violent incidents drawn from four criminals' autobiographies. She content-analysed these accounts and subjected her variables to a smallest space analysis. Her plot can be reinterpreted as shown below to draw attention to four different types of justification for the violent incidents described in the autobiographies:

- Defence – these are incidents justified by the threat of imminent physical attack against the offender. As can be seen on the plot, this will often have occurred in prison and the offender may not have a weapon readily available so will use his hands.
- Retribution – these are incidents justified by previous harm done to the offender by the victim or his associates, indicated here by the prior contact variables.
- Unintended – these are incidents justified as unintentional, with innocent victims getting hurt. They occur because the victim undermines the offender in a public place such as a bar where there is an audience.
- Disrespect – these are incidents justified by the victim disrespecting the offender. The actions here such as using a gun and the violence occurring indoors suggest the attack is premeditated.

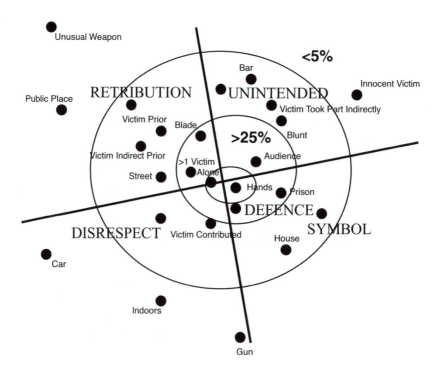

What criminal narratives would you argue underpin these different forms of justification?

Source: We are grateful to Emma Barrett for collecting the data and conducting these statistical analyses.

Serial Murder

Serial killers have become the stuff of myth and legend. They are the mainstay of fictional crime drama and, as noted in Chapter 3, are guaranteed to steal the headlines if they break into fact. They seem to epitomise the essence of evil and to symbolise the darkest corners of the human soul. With such a load resting on the images of people who kill again and again it is perhaps not surprising that the images have been distorted and that fantasy and invention often hide the true facts (see Table 13.3).

Much of the invention about serial killers that passes instead of real knowledge has its origins in the often quoted, but limited, research of the Behavioral Science Unit of the FBI in the 1980s and 1990s. The fascination that Hollywood has with the FBI gave the musings of FBI agents at that time a currency that far outweighs their validity. Leading actors are given scripts that repeat confused and misinformed opinions and as a consequence audiences from Alaska to Zanzibar gain the mistaken impression that what is said with such conviction and apparent authority must be the truth.

Out of this 'Hollywood effect', gracing personal opinion with dramatic illustration and thereby giving that opinion inappropriate validity, have emerged a great range of statements about serial killers, not one of which survives close scientific scrutiny. So, for example, serial killers are thought to be way above average intelligence, they are not thought ever to be of African-American extraction. The phenomenon of serial killing is presented as an almost uniquely American one that had virtually no existence until the last quarter of the twentieth century. Serial killers are claimed only to attack victims of the same ethnicity as themselves and a strongly sexual component is assumed always to be present. Most curiously of all, the complex sets of processes that underlie serial killings are apparently reducible to the simple, if rather ambiguous dichotomy of being 'organised' or 'disorganised'. All of these claims about serial killing are false.

Facts about Serial Killing

The National Center for the Analysis of Violent Crime of the US Department of Justice defines serial murder as 'The unlawful killing of two or more victims by the same offender (s) in separate events' (Morton and Hilts, 2005: 9). It is differentiated from spree killing and mass murder on the basis of the temporal and spatial attributes of the murders; serial murders

Table 13.3 Key findings – serial murder.

Prevalence	Four serial killers active at any one time in the United Kingdom and between 1982 and 1991 there were 196 victims of multicide in England and Wales (Gresswell and Hollin, 1994).
	Serial murder in the US accounted for 1.7% of murders between 1940 and 1985, increasing to a rate of 3.2% between 1970 and 1993 (Jenkins, 1988).
	Hickey (1997) measured long-term trends and conducted one of the most exhaustive measurements of the prevalence of serial murder in the United States. He assembled a historical database going back to 1800 and showed slowly rising trend from 1800 through the 1960s and since 1970 the number of cases increased dramatically. In contrast to the Justice Department's estimate of thousands of victims annually, Hickey enumerated 2526 to 3860 victims slain by 399 serial killers between 1800 and 1995 and 974 to 1398 victims in 1975 to 1995, which is 49 to 70 per year, although his data collection did not involve undetected cases.
	During the 1970s and early 1980s there were about 35 serial killers active in the United States (United States Department of Justice, 1983, cited in Harrower).
	Serial killers are estimated to commit only 1% to 2% of all homicides in the United States. (Bartol, 1995)
	Holmes and DeBurger (1988) claimed that as many as 3,500–5,000 people are victims of serial murder each year in the United States and that serial murderers are responsible for up to two-thirds of unsolved homicides as well as a portion of 'missing persons'. (This claim has been criticised because it is based on attributing all unsolved murders to serial killers.)
	There is an indication that since the 1970s there has been an increase in serial killing (Canter, Missen and Hodge, 1996).
Victim characteristics	Young, vulnerable, Caucasian women; stranger-to-stranger crime (Egger, 1998).
	Females (67%) and Caucasian (71%) and an average of 33 years old. The racial proportions of serial homicide victims are roughly equivalent to the proportion of different races in the US population. Eighty per cent of victims were Caucasian, 16% were African American, and 4% were members of other racial groups (Kraemer *et al.*, 2004).
	Majority are adult strangers, with young women being the most likely victims (Hickey, 1991).
	Prime targets are hitchhikers, women living alone, prostitutes, young children, and the elderly (Levin and Fox) and 24% of serial offenders killed at least one child.
Periodicity	In the great majority of cases, intervals between murders in a series range from a few days to a year or even longer. A common pattern has been for a year or more to elapse after the first killing, which is followed by three or four further murders in a year. The only rule of periodicity that does appear to have some validity is that in the career of each murderer the rate of killing has accelerated over time (Ioannou, 2009).

occurring after a 'cooling-off' period and usually at distinct locations. Mass murder is defined as murder in which there are four or more victims killed at a discrete time and place (Delisi and Sherer, 2006; Fox and Levin, 2003). Spree murder is a single event with multiple victims in multiple locations and an absence of the 'cooling-off' period between murders (Delisi and Sherer, 2006; Fox and Levin, 2003).

Much of the enduring fascination with serial killers centres around attempts to understand how these individuals are created and what motivates their offences. A number of factors have been implicated in the aetiology of serial killing, notably, child abuse (Hickey, 1997), dysfunctional parental relationships (Fox and Levin, 1994) and mental illness (Monahan, 1992). However, as Ioannou (2009) points out, research on these factors indicates correlation not causation and suffers from a lack of a nonoffending comparison group. Furthermore, there are few indications as to why those serial killers who did suffer abuse or are mentally ill went on to murder when the vast majority of such individuals do not.

The central challenge, then, in explaining the cause of serial killing comes from recognition that the development and creation of a serial killer is a process rather than a simple cause-effect mechanism (Canter, 1994). In this regard, the narrative framework offers a potentially fruitful way forward, as discussed in Chapter 6. It may be that this way of construing what happens during one's life, as much as the events themselves, distinguishes those individuals who become violent criminals from those who do not.

Considerable effort has also been directed at understanding the more proximal influences on serial murder. This is often couched in the form of trying to determine the 'motive' of a serial killer. But, as discussed in Chapter 5, there are many difficulties in considering the concept of motive. Indeed, the limited usefulness of understanding motive in an applied investigative context is made clear in the NCVCA report on investigative recommendations for serial murder:

- A serial murderer may have multiple motives for committing his crimes.
- Motive generally may be difficult to determine in a serial murder investigation.
- A serial murderer's motive may evolve within a single murder as well as throughout the murder series
- The classification of motive should be limited to observable behaviour at the crime scene
- Even if a motive can be identified it may not be useful in identifying a murderer
- Utilising investigative resources to discern the motive instead of identifying the offender may derail the investigation
- Investigators should not necessarily equate a serial murderer's motivation with the level of injury.
- Regardless of the motive, serial murderers commit their crimes because they want to. The exception to this would be those few killers suffering from a severe mental illness.

Differentiating Offending Styles in Serial Murder

Although the most extreme and sometimes bizarre of crimes, the IP perspective with its focus on understanding offending within a normal rather than an abnormal framework for behaviour, leads us to the expectation that the general model of differentiation for violent crime in terms of victim role and degree of destruction of the person will hold even for serial murder. This idea that differences in offending style will be based upon the way in which the offender interacts with the victim and the role he assigns to her (Canter 1994), diverges from many frameworks and perspectives on serial killing offending styles. Most experts tend rather to focus on the motivational and psychopathological aspects with all the difficulties this approach generates.

For example, Fox and Levin (1998) distinguish five types of motivation for serial murder (see Table 13.4). Holmes and Holmes' (1998) well-known typology, which is a development of the original work by Holmes and DeBurger (1985), identifies different types of serial killer on the basis of the motivation or compulsion that drives their offences (Table 13.5).

All of these typologies suffer from the weaknesses discussed earlier, so that although each type can usually be illustrated with a telling example, there are many other examples that do not fit neatly into any given type. There are also recurring difficulties with any framework that makes assumptions about the reasons or 'motives' for a crime because these, as has been noted, can be complex mixtures, unknown to the offenders, and are inherently speculative. Nonetheless these typologies are useful in drawing attention to the range of initial internal and external aspects that are relevant to different offences. However to disentangle differences in the underlying psychological themes that produce variations in the patterns of offending actions requires a fuller understanding of the nature of the serial murder activity itself and the psychological components and processes integral to this.

In elaborating this victim as Object, Vehicle or Person framework, Youngs and Canter (in press, b) draw on a number of empirical analyses of the details of what actually goes on and the patterns of actions in this most horrendous of crimes. This allows us to develop

Table 13.4 Examples of motivations for serial murder.

Motivations	Example
Power	Inspired by sadistic fantasies, a man tortures and kills a series of strangers to satisfy his need for control and dominance.
Revenge	Grossly mistreated as a child, a man avenges his past by slaying women who remind him of his mother.
Loyalty	A team of killers turn murder into a ritual for proving their dedication and commitment to one another.
Profit	A woman poisons to death a series of husbands in order to collect on their life insurance.
Terror	A profoundly paranoid man commits a series of bombings to warn the world of impending doom.

Source: Fox and Levin (1998). Reproduced with permission.

Table 13.5 Holmes and DeBurger's types of serial killer.

Visionary: Suffering from a break with reality, the visionary serial killer murders because he has seen visions or heard voices from demons, angels, the devil or God telling him to kill a particular individual or particular types of people. His quick, act-focused killings are seen as a job to be done.

Mission: The mission killer is focused on the act of murder itself. He is compelled to murder in order to rid the world of a group of people he has judged to be unworthy or undesirable.

Hedonistic: This type of sexual killer is subdivided into the following two groups:

    Lust: The lust killer kills for sexual gratification; sex is the focal point of the murder, even after he has killed the victim. This type of murderer derives pleasure from the process of the murderous event. Various acts such as cannibalism, necrophilia, and dismemberment are prevalent in this type of murder

    Thrill: The thrill killer murders for the pleasure and excitement of killing. Once the victim is dead, this murderer loses interest. This type of killing often involves a long process involving extended acts of torture.

Power/control: This killer derives pleasure and gratification from having control over the victim and being considered to be a 'master' at what he does. His motives are the need for power and dominance over another human being. The longer he can extend the process of murder, the greater his gratification.

---

an understanding about how these different victim roles may manifest as styles of offending within serial killing. Understanding these styles of interpersonal interaction is particularly challenging in relation to murder where no information can be obtained directly about the nature of the interaction.

From various analyses of what actually happens in a serial murder a number of distinct themes have been identified. Figure 13.1 presents the SSA results that summarise these drawn from Canter *et al.* (2004). Most striking in all these analyses is the identification of a distinct subset of behaviours to do with the mutilation and *post mortem* exploration and exploitation of the body. In the Canter and Wentink (2004) study this is made up of variables such as 'body parts missing' and thoracic, genital and abdominal mutilations. Canter *et al.* (2004) show that decapitation and dismemberment are also part of this pattern. Hodge's study (in Canter, 2000) describes a similar area of variables including the hacking of the body and missing body parts as well as indications of necrophilia and cannibalism.

Separate from this in both the Canter *et al.* and the Canter and Wentink studies is a subset of frenzied activity indicated by the scattering and ransacking of victims' clothing and belongings as well as the beating and bludgeoning of the victim. In the Hodge study this frenzied area also emerges defined by behaviours such as kicking and frenzied attack. However her inclusion of some different variables in the analysis allows Hodge to elaborate this pattern further, showing that less explosive, more exploitative acts such as torture and blindfolding are also part of this style.

A further subset, distinct from both these regions, emerges across the analyses, although there are only a limited number of variables identified in the studies available. In the Canter *et al.* and the Canter and Wentink studies this area is defined by variables describing the presence of bite marks on the victim, requiring intimate contact from the offender, as well as facial disfigurement (Canter *et al.*, 2004). This more personal involvement is also suggested by

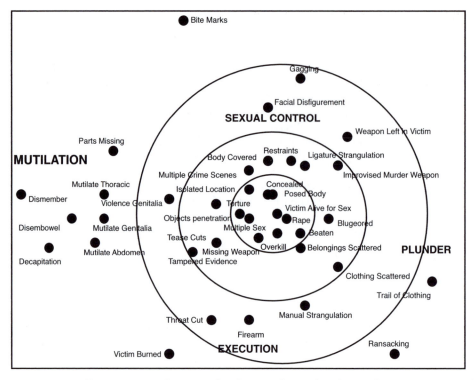

Figure 13.1 Smallest space analysis results for serial murder drawn from Canter *et al.* (2004). For full items see Table 13.9.

Source: Canter *et al.* (2004). Reproduced with permission.

the delineation of an area involving redressing the victim after the attack and, less distinctly, the stealing of personal documents and belongings in the Hodge study.

Object, Vehicle, Person

These distinctions between patterns of mutilation, frenzied attack and personal involvement do seem, even in this most extreme and bizarre form of offending, to reflect differences not along abnormal, bizarre dimensions but in the offender's general style of interaction with the victim that Canter (1994) elucidates. The mutilation and dismemberment activity is readily understood in terms of the 'victim as object' offending style in which the offender does not see the victim as fully human but rather as something to be explored and played with. The assignment of this victim role is further reflected in a complete lack of empathy for, or interest in, the reactions of the victim. In the context of murder this would be revealed in the insignificance of the actual process of killing. Consistent with this the Canter *et al.* study shows a grouping of manual strangulation, throat cutting and use of a firearm behaviours located close to the mutilation activities.

The 'Victim as Vehicle' offending style is one in which the offender is using the victim as a means to express his anger and desires. The victims have some kind of symbolic significance and the offender has an awareness of their reactions, which feed into and facilitate his emotional expression. This mode produces the kind of frenzied, emotional approach to the offence that underlies the ransacking and scattering behaviour grouping identified in the empirical analyses. The extreme violence, beyond that necessary to control the victim, is also part of this process with bludgeoning and beating of the victim. The direct, cruel exploitation through torture, the use of blindfolds, props and specialised offending 'kits' that Hodge also finds as part of this offending pattern, is further consistent with the 'Victim as Vehicle' role interpretation in which the victim's reactions and suffering are fundamental to the offence.

Although comprised of only a few variables at the extremes in these studies, a tentative interpretation of the third theme of 'personal involvement' activity in terms of the 'Victim as Person' role is also possible. In the context of serial murder, this conception of the victim by the offender would be revealed as either acts that involved the offender himself in some kind of intimacy or acts that recognise the victim as an individual, a person with an identity. The 'bite marks' variable is congruent with this interpretation, an act in which the offender uses his mouth, reminiscent of normal forms of intimacy. The act of redressing the victim that Hodge describes, as well as the post-mortem covering of the body described in the Canter *et al.* study, is also consistent with this, suggesting some kind of recognition of her humanity and an attempt to normalise the interaction. Although behavioural examples are few, possibly because this kind of interaction will not be so readily apparent from crime scene evidence, the fact that these acts are clearly distinct from the others does lend support to the 'victim as person' style of offending in serial murder.

The role of 'Victim as Object' in serial murder is most clear in actions that are explorations of the body, typically *post mortem*. The role of 'Victim as Vehicle' is seen in serial murder as actions that are emotional attacks on or exploitations of the live victim. The role of 'Victim as Person' is revealed by actions that suggest attempts at some distorted form of intimacy on the part of the offender and that recognise the victim as an individual with an identity (Youngs and Canter, in press, b).

In line with the general radex of criminal differentiation (Chapter 5), the generic model of violent crime predicts that these differences in Object, Vehicle and Person modes will emerge as increasingly distinguishable styles as the intensity of the actions increases. For violent crime generally this intensity was argued to be the strength of the attack on the person. In the specific context of serial murder the most extreme attacks will be those that exhibit the greatest depravity, going beyond killing to completely destroy and dehumanise the victim and his or her identity as a person.

In both the Canter *et al.* and the Canter and Wentink studies these most destructive acts are the least frequent across the sample. For example, genital mutilation and decapitation occur in 10% and 5% of cases respectively. Similarly, 'bitemarks' on the victim's body are found in 5% of crimes. In contrast, the behaviours that seem to constitute the basic activities of serial killing, rather than forms of additional dehumanisation beyond this, are the most frequent in the studies. This includes acts such as keeping the victim alive during sex acts (91%), vaginal rape (74%) (both of which perhaps reflect the high number of murders related

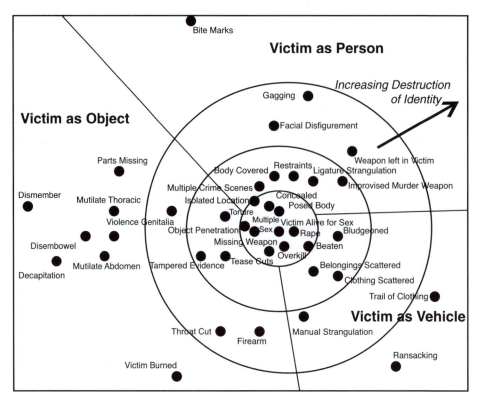

Figure 13.2   Radex of serial murder. For full items see Table 13.9. Youngs and Canter, in press, b.

to sexual activity within the samples studied by Canter and his colleagues here), as well as positioning of the body (75%), removing the weapon (67%) and beating the victim (61%).

As Figure 13.2 shows, the interaction of these variations in victim role and attack intensity produce a model of serial killing in which distinct offending styles reveal the three different victim-role approaches to destruction and dehumanisation. These different offending styles emerge most clearly within the most destructive and dehumanising acts. In the object mode these extreme variants are the complete physical destruction of the body through dismemberment and decapitation. In the vehicle mode these tend to be obliterating attacks on the victim and her belongings. In the person mode, facial disfigurement is an extreme form of interpersonal destructiveness. Interestingly, there are no very rare actions for this mode. This may be because their interpersonal nature is carried out through conversation and other modes of interaction that are not revealed in police records of the crime scene. Variations in offending style are less distinguishable at the core among the behaviours which are fundamental to the offence and important in facilitating its commission. These are behaviours that are, broadly speaking, equally likely to occur in crimes characterised by an object, vehicle or person style of interaction. They also tend to be common to many or most killings by serial killers as indicated by their high frequencies.

The NAS Context of the Victim Role Offending Styles

The generic model of differentiation for violent crime can be shown to hold for serial murder. Distinct offending styles reflecting the object, vehicle or person mode of transaction with the victim emerge within the higher intensity acts as different interpersonal approaches to the dehumanisation and destruction of the victim.

The particular roles assigned to the victim are integral parts of the broader criminal narratives (as described in Chapter 6). The object role emerges out of the 'Professional Adventure' narrative, as part of the offender's focus on control and competent mastery of the event. The person role emerges within an 'Irony Victim' narrative, in which the offender is desperately seeking some kind of intimacy with the victim in a distorted attempt to address his sense of emptiness. Different variants of the 'victim as vehicle' role are assigned to victims within the 'Revenger Tragedy' and 'Heroic Quest' narratives. Here, the variant is most consistent with the 'Tragedy' variant of the victim playing a symbolic role as a target for his vindictive, angry desire for Revenge.

As outlined in Chapter 7, the different narratives imply particular action system modes. An alternative, broader interpretation of the victim role murder offending styles that focused on the overall event rather than the details of the interaction with the victim, is possible then in terms of the NAS model.

The 'Adventure' narrative represents an Adaptive action system mode in which the focus is on the direct exchanges of effort and skill for the acquisition of material gains (external effect), prompted by their availability in the environment (external source of the action). This would be the NAS mode implied by the 'victim as object' style here.

Within the 'Tragedy' Narrative, the behaviour is a retaliation, the offender's response to having been wronged (external source) but the concern, whether the actual target of the action is the self or another, is only with the impact on the self and the individual's internal state (internal effect) so the underlying action system mode is conservative. This would be the NAS interpretation consistent with the 'victim as vehicle' style of murder.

The Irony Narrative is one of generalised impotence and meaninglessness in which nothing makes any sense and there are no rules. The offences characterised by the playing out of this narrative are integrative events (Canter and Youngs in press, b) that seek only to assuage the internal sense of emptiness and need that prompted the action (internal actualisation; internal source). The desperate distorted intimacy seeking 'Victim as Person' style of offending is readily understood as part of this broader Integrative Irony NAS mode.

Victim Role in Single Homicide

Interestingly some work by Fritzon and Ridgway (2001) suggests that the Vehicle, Object, Person model also helps us to understand single, attempted homicide offences. Their smallest space analysis of the offenders' actions in 31 cases, in which the victim of murderous assault survived, reveals three different emphases to the behaviour (see Table 13.6). Their sample consisted of attempted homicide cases from 1986 to 1995, and was collected and supplied by the Malmo Police Force, the third largest police precinct in Sweden. Each of the 93 cases

Table 13.6 Victim, object and person crime-scene actions.

Victim as …	Crime scene actions
Person	Offender makes remarks that imply he knows the victim as a person
	Offender talks to the victim
	Attack occurs at victim's residence
	Offender uses verbal violence against the victim
	Offender uses a weapon to control the victim
	Offence occurs on a weekday
	Offender brings a weapon to the crime scene
	Offender uses a blunt instrument to injure the victim
	Offender uses threats to control the victim
Vehicle	Victim is bound and/or gagged
	Offender employs a single act of violence
	Offender steals objects from the victim.
	Attack occurs at offender's premises
	Offender uses a weapon from the crime scene
	Offender drunk at time offence occurs
	Single wound to one area of the body
	Victim drunk at time offence occurs
Object	Multiple wounds to one area of the victim
	Wounds are located on the victim's torso
	Wounds are located on the victim's face
	Offender insults victim
	Wounds are located on the victim's limbs
	Body is left at scene where crime occurs
	Victim has defence wounds
	Offender changes his behaviour following victim resistance
	Offender starts attacks, stops, and re-starts
	Wounds are located on the victim's head
	Offender uses a sharp object to injure the victim
	Wounds are located on the victim's neck

Source: Fritzon and Ridgway (2001). Reproduced with permission.

involved an offender who had been convicted in a court of law of a single attempted homicide against a single victim.

Alternative Models of Serial Killing

The notion that the overriding differences between offences lie in the style of interpersonal interaction in the crime is at odds with some of the most widely cited ideas about serial killers. One particularly ubiquitous idea that it challenges is the concept of the organised as opposed to disorganised serial killer. This dichotomy, developed by special agents of the FBI as part of their training course at the FBI Academy in Quantico (Ressler *et al.*, 1986a) has passed into popular culture as a definitive way of understanding serial killing.

Ressler *et al.* draw on an interesting consistency principle such that an organised offender leads a planned and orderly life that is reflected in the way he commits his crimes. The organised crime scene reveals evidence of a carefully planned crime, control, use of restraints,

Table 13.7 Offender characteristics of organised and disorganised murderers.

Organised	Disorganised
Good intelligence	Average intelligence
Socially competent	Socially immature
Skilled work preferred	Poor work history
Sexually competent	Sexually incompetent
High birth order status	Minimal birth order status
Father's work stable	Father's work unstable
Inconsistent childhood discipline	Harsh discipline in childhood
Controlled mood during crime	Anxious mood during crime
Use of alcohol with crime	Minimal use of alcohol
Precipitating situational stress	Minimal situational stress
Living with partner	Living alone
Mobility, with car in good condition	Lives/works near crime scene
Follows crime in news media	Minimal interest in news media
May change jobs or leave town	Minimal change in lifestyle

Source: Ressler, Burgess and Douglas (1988).

and use of a weapon he has brought with him and subsequently removed from the crime scene. Consistent with his lifestyle a disorganised offender kills spontaneously and leaves a haphazard crime scene. The disorganised crime scene is characterised by the minimal use of controls or restraints and no attempt to destroy forensic evidence or conceal the body (Ressler, Burgess and Douglas, 1988).

Two important IP studies by Canter *et al.* (2004) and Canter and Wentink (2004) provide direct empirical examinations of these ideas, using the Missen corpus of serial killer data (see Box 13.2). As well as moving on our understanding about the sorts of distinctions that are valid for serial killing, these studies provide useful illustrations of the research methodology that can be utilised to explore and test the hypotheses that are inherent in such classification schemes.

Table 13.8 Crime scene differences between organised and disorganised murderers.

Organised	Disorganised
Offence planned	Spontaneous offence
Victim a targeted stranger	Victim or location known
Personalises victim	Depersonalises victim
Controlled conversation	Minimal conversation
Crime scene reflects overall control	Crime scene random and sloppy
Demands submissive victim	Sudden violence to victim
Restraints used	Minimal use of restraints
Aggressive acts prior to death	Sexual acts after death
Body hidden	Body left in view
Weapon/evidence absent	Evidence/weapon often present
Transports victim or body	Body left at death scene

Source: Ressler, Burgess and Douglas (1988).

Box 13.2 The Missen Corpus: Data for Empirical Studies of Serial Murder

The 'Missen Corpus', named after the researcher who compiled the data, is a large-scale dataset held at the International Research Centre for Investigative Psychology (IRCIP). It contains over 3000 files of data drawn from published accounts of serial killers operating in the United States since 1960. This material consisted of secondary sources of nationally and internationally known US newspapers, periodicals, journals, true crime magazines, biographies, trial transcripts, and case history narratives. All material was verified by cross-referencing a number of reliable sources, and only cases or files where information could be reliably validated were included in the core sample.

The Organised-Disorganised Typology

The first step in this empirical test of the Organised-Disorganised dichotomy (Ressler *et al.* 1986a) is the specification of the variables from within the Canter *et al.* (2004) data set that represent each of the different offending types. These are shown in Table 13.9. makeatother

Within-Type consistency?

Drawing on these variables, the next stage of the analysis is to test the fundamental assumption of any typology: that the variables within a type do indeed co-occur (here, within crime scenes). To test this, Canter *et al.* took pairs of actions hypothesised to occur together within each of the 'organised' and 'disorganised' types and calculated the proportion of the cases when these occurred that they occurred together. This was calculated using Jaccard's coefficient (Jaccard, 1908). This coefficient takes no account of joint nonoccurrence so that when neither behaviour was found within a crime scene this was not treated as evidence that those behaviours were part of the same type. This is a particularly powerful measure of co-occurrence when, as in crime data, there are often many absences of any occurrence and these absences may be due to oversights by those reporting on the crime. Tables 13.10a and 13.10b show these calculations for the six most common behaviours within each of the organised and disorganised types.

The expectation here is that if the organised and disorganised categories are indeed operating as distinct offending types, the relevant behaviours would occur together approaching 100% of the time (as would be indicated by a Jaccard's coefficient of 1.00). Such very high levels of co-occurrence would be particularly anticipated given that the variables selected do not describe behaviours that are likely to be strongly influenced by any situational factors such as the victim's reactions.

Tables 13.10a and 13.10b show that none of the co-occurrences between any behaviour pairs reach this level. Indeed for many of the pairs, the identified action co-occurs in less than 50% of the case. Interestingly, the behaviours within the organised category do show slightly better results for four of the pairings (body positioned and victim alive during sex acts; victim alive during sex acts and weapon taken from scene; victim alive during sex acts and multiple

Table 13.9 Variables from the Missen corpus identified as 'organised' or 'disorganised' crime scenes.

Organised	Disorganised
1. victim alive for sex (91%) - victim was alive when sex acts were performed 2. body positioned (75%) - victim's body was positioned in a deliberate way 3. murder weapon missing (67%) - no murder weapon found 4. multiple crime scene (61%) - separate abduction site, murder site and disposal site 5. body concealed (58%) - body concealed from immediate view at disposal site 6. torture (53%) - offender subjected the victim to acts of torture 7. restraints (40%) - restraints used; includes neck, wrist and leg restraints 8. body covered PM (37%) - victim's body covered by offender post-mortem 9. ligature strangulation (34%) - victim was strangled using some form of ligature 10. firearm used (23%) - evidence of firearm use at the scene 11. tampered with evidence (21%) - offender tampered with evidence that could ID him 12. gagging (16%) - victim had been gagged 13. bite marks (5%) - bite marks present on the victim's body 14. vaginal rape (74%) - victim was vaginally raped 15. overkill (70%) - more violence than necessary for death was used 16. multiple sex acts (66%) - victim/body subjected to multiple sexual acts 17. beaten (61%) - victim's body showed signs of having been beaten 18. body left in isolated spot (54%) - body disposed of in an isolated location 19. belongings scattered (47%) - victim's belongings scattered at the crime scene 20. tease cuts (38%) - superficial knife cuts found on victim's body 21. bludgeoned (38%) - victim struck with heavy blow(s) 22. clothing scattered (36%) - victim's clothing scattered at crime scene 23. object penetration (35%) - offender inserted objects into victim's opening(s) 24. improvised murder weapon (31%) - weapon of opportunity; used item from scene 25. manual strangulation (27%) - victim was manually strangled 26. violence directed at genitalia (23%) - evidence of violent act aimed specifically at genitalia	27. weapon left in victim (19%) - murder weapon left in victim's body post-mortem 28. facial disfigurement (19%) - evidence of violence to face causing disfigurement 29. throat cut (19%) - victim's throat had been cut 30. trail of clothing to murder scene (13%) - trail of clothing led to/from scene 31. ransacking (11%) - crime scene was in a state of disarray 32. genital mutilation (10%) - body showed deliberate mutilation of genitals 33. body parts missing (10%) - one or more body parts missing from the victim 34. thoracic mutilation (9%) - mutilation of the thorax 35. burns on victim (8%) - Burn marks found on victim's body 36. abdominal mutilation (8%) 37. disembowel (6%) - inwards extracted 38. decapitation (5%) 39. dismemberment (3%)

Source: Canter *et al.* (2004). Reproduced with permission.

Table 13.10a Proportion of co-occurrences of most frequent organised features across 100 serial killings.

Organised Characteristics	Victim alive during sex	Body positioned	Weapon missing	Many crime scenes	Body concealed
Victim alive during sex					
Body positioned	0.71				
Weapon missing	0.61	0.54			
Many crime scenes	0.63	0.62	0.58		
Body concealed	0.57	0.58	0.52	0.70	
Torture	0.52	0.58	0.50	0.46	0.46

Source: Canter *et al.* (2004). Reproduced with permission.

crime scenes; and body concealed and multiple crime scenes) being observed at least 60% of the time as would be predicted within the typology. However this may be a function of the high overall levels of occurrence of these variables. 'Victim alive during sex', for example, was found in 91% of Canter *et al.*'s crime scenes, which clearly means that it is highly likely that when other acts predicted to co-occur with this are found, this behaviour will also be observed. What it also suggests is that these high frequency organised variables are also co-occurring with disorganised variables. This is the issue examined in the next phase of the analysis.

Between-Type Discrimination?

Table 13.11 shows the same calculations of proportions of co-occurrence using Jaccard's coefficient but between pairs of organised and disorganised variables. As can be seen, these figures are of the same magnitude as the within-type analyses suggesting that these variables are as likely to be found at a crime scene with variables from the other category of the organised-disorganised typology.

Indeed Canter *et al.* note that the 'disorganised' behaviour of the body being left in an isolated spot co-occurs with the 'organised' behaviour of 'multiple crime scenes' in a higher proportion of cases than any of the within-type pairs they examined.

These analyses taken together suggest that, among these pairs of the highest frequency variables, there is no marked tendency for crime scenes that reveal coherent sets of one type

Table 13.10b Proportion of co-occurrences of frequent disorganised features across 100 serial killings.

Disorganised characteristics	Vaginal rape	Overkill	Multiple sex acts	Victim beaten	Left isolated
Vaginal rape					
Overkill	0.53				
Multiple sex acts	0.69	0.49			
Victim beaten	0.48	0.52	0.44		
Left isolated	0.47	0.43	0.43	0.35	
Belongings Scattered	0.44	0.43	0.35	0.48	0.29

Source Canter *et al.* (2004). Reproduced with permission.

Table 13.11 Relationships between frequently occurring organised and disorganised features.

Disorganised	Organised					
	Alive	Pose	No weapon	Scenes	Conceal	Torture
Rape	0.72	0.64	0.48	0.53	0.50	0.37
Overkill	0.64	0.59	0.65	0.46	0.41	0.54
Sex	0.64	0.60	0.51	0.53	0.49	0.50
Beat	0.58	0.49	0.47	0.39	0.43	0.50
Isolate	0.54	0.57	0.51	0.74	0.72	0.41
Scattered	0.50	0.37	0.37	0.27	0.31	0.35

Source: Canter *et al.* (2004). Reproduced with permission.

of organised or disorganised behaviours and also, notably, that these are not the basis for distinguishing between crime scenes.

Patterns of Behavioural Co-occurrence?

A third phase of the analyses allows the full set of behaviours to be explored and the relationship of every behaviour with every other variable to be considered at the same time. This allows the additional exploration of any overall patterns beyond the pair by pair comparisons that may indicate any relative trends for disorganised or organised clusterings.

This examination is achieved by submitting all the 39 behaviours to the SSA form of multivariate analysis (see Chapter 5). The SSA of the serial killer data from Canter *et al.* (2004) is given in Figure 13.3. It shows, for example, that there is a strong relationship (Jaccard's coefficient = 0.72) between raping the victim ('rape') and keeping the victim alive ('alive'). In contrast, the weaker relationship between scattering the victim's belongings and leaving the body in an isolated spot ('isolated') (Jaccard's coefficient = 0.29) means that these two variables appear farther apart on the plot.

The hypothesis of distinct organised and disorganised types of offending can be tested directly by seeing if the different crime scene actions, stipulated by Ressler *et al.* as belonging to each of these categories do indeed fall within separate regions of the SSA. In contrast, as Canter *et al.* note, if the variables do not fall into two distinct regions of the SSA, the null hypothesis that there is no evidence for the organised-disorganised typology must be accepted.

As Figure 13.3 shows, the 'disorganised' variables (represented by the triangles) are found right across the plot rather than in one distinct region. This suggests that these behaviours are just as likely to be found across all the different empirical forms of serial killing, rather than characterising a distinct type. Within this, the 'organised' variables (represented by the squares) are not separated off as would be expected if this did indeed describe a particular type of murder distinct from the 'disorganised' killing activity. Indeed many of the organised variables occupy the conceptual centre of the plot (along with some 'disorganised' variables), the region of highest frequency behaviours. This suggests that, rather than being one type of serial killing, 'organised' activity is a feature of most offences. In sum then there is no evidence for the disorganised-organised dichotomy of types of serial murder. Indeed it may be suggested that in order to escape detection and carry out a series of murders on strangers some degree

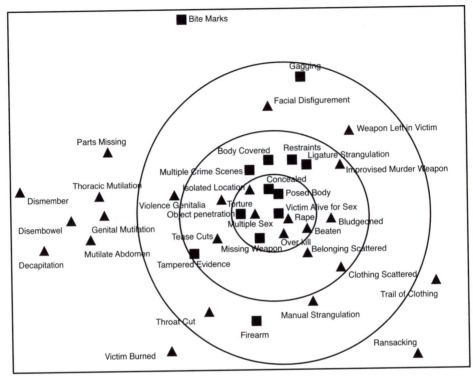

Figure 13.3   Smallest space analysis of the serial killer data from Canter *et al.* (2004). For full items see Table 13.9.

Source: Canter *et al.* (2004). Reproduced with permission.

of what Ressler *et al.* refer to as 'organisation' may be necessary. So it is 'organisation' that characterises serial murders in general.

Canter and Wentink (2004) carried out a similar empirical test of the Holmes and Holmes typology (1998) (see Box 13.3). This analysis, again explored the patterning on an SSA plot of crime scene variables from the Missen Corpus on Serial Killers, selected to represent the different types of visionary, mission, lust, thrill and power/control killing. It showed that the power/control variables did not form a distinct type but were common to most offences. For the mission, lust and thrill types, examination of the plot indicated that while some of the variables from each type were located contiguously in a region as predicted, other behaviours also expected to be part of each of those types were dispersed around the SSA. Interestingly, the visionary variables did form a relatively distinct region, although as Canter and Wentink argue, this grouping is only in respect of variables such as 'bludgeoning', which deal with the offenders' direct physical form of transaction with the victim rather than any particular visionary psychosis or compulsion. There was little evidence here then to support distinct patterns of behaviour corresponding to Holmes and Holmes' hypothesised types of motivation or compulsion.

Box 13.3 Reorganisation of Classification of Serial Killers (Holmes and De Burger's, 1988; Holmes and Holmes, 1998)

Below is a table of key offence actions created by Canter *et al.* from each of the serial killer types. What point are the authors making by organising these in this way?

Feature	Types of Serial Killer					
	Visionary	*Mission*	*Comfort*	*Lust*	*Thrill*	*Power*
Disorganised	X					
Spontaneous	X					
Random	X	X				
Nonspecific	X		X			
Affiliated			X			
Act-focused	X	X	X			
Concentrated	X	X	X	X		
Strangers	X	X		X	X	X
Organised		X	X	X	X	X
Planned		X	X	X		X
Specific		X		X	X	X
Process-focused			X	X	X	X
Nonrandom				X	X	X
Dispersed					X	X

Serial Murder as a Psychological Phenomenon

These studies of the validity of the various schemes for classifying styles of offending in serial killing are important because of what they tell us about the fundamental psychological nature of this phenomenon. Implicit within the organised-disorganised typology is the assumption that serial killing activity can be conceptualised as being primarily about the completion of a task. The essential distinguishing feature is in the approach (organised or disorganised) taken to the achievement of this task. Similarly, within the Holmes and Holmes model of offending differences according to the particular satisfactions derived, is the assumption that in psychological terms serial killing represents a response to or manifestation of a compulsion.

While these may be components of the process, what the evidence suggests, both from the empirical tests of these typologies and in the positive support for the victim role model, is that the key differences lie in the style of relating to the victim. In psychological terms serial killing is an activity best understood, not as the expression of a compulsion or a task the individual is simply seeking to complete but as a distorted form of interpersonal interaction.

Box 13.4 Focus on Muti Murder in South Africa

In South Africa there is a very unusual and quite rare form of homicide that has occurred throughout history, and continues to happen today. These are murders in which body parts are removed from a live victim to be utilised for medicinal purpose, being used on their own or mixed with other ingredients to make 'muti'. The victim will usually die from blood loss or as a result of the injuries. A loose definition of muti murder is murder where the intention is to gather human body parts for use in traditional African medicine (Minnaar, 2001).

The purpose of 'muti' is usually to improve an individual's or community's circumstances, and the process is advocated by a traditional healer who, upon being approached by a client, will commission a third party to harvest the necessary parts. The parts used are believed to contain a person's 'life essence', and traditionally they are taken from a living person as it is believed that they are more powerful in this state.

It is widely believed that muti murder has been practised as part of a subculture of traditional African beliefs for centuries. However, with the arrival of Western criminal justice systems and beliefs, such practices are, for obvious reasons, deemed illegal, and muti murders constitute a proportion of the cases with which police officers in South Africa have to deal. It is difficult to determine the prevalence of such offences, although estimates suggest that there are between 15 and 300 cases occurring in South Africa each year. No figures are available for other countries.

Investigative psychologists like Labuschagne (2004) have been exploring the nature and characteristics of muti murder in order to enable them to effectively be distinguished from other forms of murder, including cult-related or ritualistic homicides and for the practices involved to be understood more clearly. By doing this they are able to inform and guide investigations and provide training and support for police officers dealing with these bizarre homicides.

Sexual Murder

Although it is widely believed that 'a significant motivator for almost all serial killing is sexual' (Douglas and Olshaker 1999: 23) and as the Canter *et al.* (2004), Hodge (1999) and Canter and Wentink (2004) studies described in the last section show, sexual activity certainly does commonly occur in these offences, it is not inevitably part of all serial murders. Serial murders are not all sexual and sexual murders are not all part of a series. Indeed, as Ioannou (2009) points out, some of the most well-known serial killers such as Harold Shipman showed no sexual focus at all to their activities. Further, it is also the case that of those that do involve some sexual activity, this sexual component is not necessarily the central motivation behind the offence.

For example, Grubin (1994: 624) states that

> There are a number of ways in which homicide and a sexual offence may become associated. An offender may murder his victim in order to silence his potential accuser, he may become angry and kill in response to her resistance, he may simply panic, death may be accidental . . . The killing may also be closely bound to the sexual element of an attack. In these cases the offender's control of his victim, and her pain and humiliation become linked to his sexual arousal.

Beauregard *et al.* (2008) also identified this distinction in their review of studies of typologies of sexual murderers. These authors concluded that there were three main categories of sexual murderers: (a) sadistic, (b) anger and (c) detection avoidance. Their 'sadistic' is similar to Grubin's (1994) type of murder in which hurting the victim gives the offender sexual arousal. Along the same lines, Myers *et al.* (1999) distinguish two types of sexual murderers: Vindictive murderers (or displaced anger murderers) who commit homicide out of rage at someone other than the victim. These are the people whom Podolsky (1966) describes as engaging in killing after raping and who Rada (1978) points out rarely derive any sexual satisfaction from the murder. Myers *et al.*'s second type are lust murderers for whom 'aggression and sexuality become fused into a single psychological experience – sadism – in which aggression is eroticized' (Rada 1978: 155) . This work indicates, then, that the co-occurrence of sexual activity and murder can happen in a variety of psychological scenarios.

Sadistic Sexual Murder

Nonetheless, all of these authorities do agree that there is a distinct subset of murderers for whom the aggression is an integral part of the sexual activity. The offender obtains sexual arousal and gratification from controlling and inflicting pain on his victims. As expressed in the detailed, recent Crime Classification Manual (Douglas *et al.*, 2006: 226) definition that has its origins in the experience of FBI agent:

> A sexual sadist is one who has established an enduring pattern of sexual arousal in response to sadistic imagery. Sexual gratification is obtained from torture involving excessive mental and physical means. The offender derives the greatest satisfaction from the victim's response to torture. Sexually sadistic fantasies in which sexual acts are paired with domination, degradation, and violence are translated into criminal action that results in death.

This is in accord with the definition of sexual sadism provided by psychiatric experts. One of the first people to define sexual sadism was Krafft-Ebing (1965: 109). He defined it as 'the experience of sexual, pleasurable sensations (including orgasm) produced by acts of cruelty . . . [it] may also consist of an innate desire to humiliate, hurt, wound or even destroy others.'

The Diagnostic and Statistical Manual of Mental Disorders, American Psychiatric Association (1994: 530) (DSM-IV) indicates that sexual sadism can be recognised from the following: 'Over a period of at least six months, recurrent, intense sexually arousing fantasies, sexual urges or behaviours involving acts (real not simulated) in which the psychological or physical suffering (including humiliation) of the victim is sexually exciting to the person.'

The prevalence of sexual sadism so defined is open to debate. DSM-IV (American Psychiatric Association, 1994) proposes 10% of rapists will be sexual sadists. Other studies give estimates of the number of sexual offenders who are sadists as ranging from 5–10% (Groth, 1979), 45% (Fedora et al., 1992) to 80% (MacCulloch et al., 1983). Allnutt et al. (1996) state that only 5.6% of the 728 sexual offenders they studied met DSM-III-R (American Psychiatric Association, 1987) criteria for sexual sadism; Langevin and Langevin (in Marshall and Kennedy, 2002) claim that 45% of 91 sexual aggressives were sadists (using Clarke Sex History questionnaire). The variety of prevalence rates suggests that the definition and recognition of sexual sadism in practice is very variable and probably rather confused. Certainly, different authors draw on different aspects of the definition and additional aspects to define sadism emphasising variously the degree of victim injury, victim suffering, controlling of the victim or psychological torture through humiliation/enslavement.

One problem that Marshall and Kennedy (2002) draw attention to in this definition of sadism as sexual satisfaction from certain acts/consequences is that satisfaction is subjective, so must be inferred. Indeed, Siomopoulos and Goldsmith (1976: 632) point out that the assumption that there is an identity comprised of enjoying humiliating others, who engage in ritualistic sex acts or who mutilate and kill their sexual victims is a 'gross violation of common sense'.

Furthermore, within published scientific studies, the operation of any link between the mental processes of fantasy and action is questioned. For example, Gosselin and Wilson's (1980) sample of 'sexually variant men' (including a sadomasochistic sample) showed a greater dissociation between fantasies and behaviour than (age-matched) controls, indicating a *decreased* likelihood to act on fantasies among those with the more deviant fantasies. In other words, the claim that fantasies have a clear and distinct link to actions cannot be accepted without challenge, especially for people whose fantasies include violence against others. Indeed studies using phallometry report ambiguous results on what produces arousal in sadists (see, for example, Seto and Kuban, 1996).

In relation to offending behaviour in particular, scientific studies indicate that sadistic preferences cannot be easily or simply identified from the crime scene. For example, McConaghy (1993: 314) concluded after review of the evidence that there is 'no empirical evidence to support the distinction between sadistic and nonsadistic rapists in relation to the use of excessive force'. The link between sadism and offending behaviour is further questioned by Marshall and Darke's (1982) finding that 60% of a random (*not* predominantly sadistic) sample of rapists indicated that their primary goal was to humiliate and degrade the victim. Hill et al. (2006) also report no difference across sexual sadistic versus nonsadistic sexual homicide perpetrators in such apparently sadistic behaviours as mutilation of genitals, face, breasts, abdomen; insertion of foreign objects, amputation, vampiristic or cannibalistic acts, although strangulation and a long offence duration were significantly more common among the sadists. Following their study of test retest reliability and concurrent validity of the MASA sadism measure they developed (with MTC: R3), Knight et al. (1994: 89) conclude that 'achieving reliability and differentiating sadistic motivation from other kinds of violent sexual aggression has proven elusive'. Furthermore in a recent study, Marshall et al. (in press) showed that internationally renowned forensic psychiatrists, all of whom were known for their work on sexual sadists could not agree on who was and was not a sadist. Thus, the link between sadistic preference and actual behaviour is unproven and consequently the identification of this confused concept from a crime scene would present a considerable challenge.

Notwithstanding the problem of the subjectivity in inferring arousal, it is unclear precisely which behaviours are considered central to sadism. Different researchers focus on different behavioural features as central to sexual sadism and make different assumptions about which are the key elements of these that elicit the sexual arousal.

- For numerous authors, the behaviour is motivated by exercising power and control (for example, Brittain, 1970). It is the subjugation of the victim that generates sexual arousal. Gratzer and Bradford (1995) claim that control is the source of satisfaction.
- Other authors refer to the eroticisation of aggression (for example, Abel, 1989), sexual sadists being aroused by gratuitous violence. Groth (1979) proposes that both the act of aggression and the effect it has on the victim (fear and suffering) is arousing for the sexual sadist.
- Others emphasise that it is the pain and suffering of the victim that generates arousal (for example, Yarvis, 1995).
- Psychic distress through humiliation and degradation is given prominence in some discussions (for example, Rada, 1978).

Across this mix of emphases, the central theme that can be given weight is that for a murder to be shown to be a 'sexual murder' in the sense accepted by most experts it has to be demonstrated that controlling the victim and carrying out acts of violence are an integrated component of the sexual arousal and gratification. This has to be distinguished from violence as a means of controlling the victim, or murder to silence a potential witness. It should be noted that such a form of murder is extremely rare within murders. Meloy (2000) estimated that within the United States less than 1% of all homicides could be considered 'sexual homicides'. Given the greater prevalence of all forms of extreme violence in the United States it would be expected that such offences would be much rarer in the United Kingdom.

Despite these difficulties, the recently updated *Crime Classification Manual* developed by the FBI National Center for the Analysis of Violent Crime (Douglas *et al.*, 2006) develop an extensive set of what they refer to as 'Crime Scene Indicators Frequently Noted' for sexually sadistic murders. Although no details are provided of the basis for these claims, the list they provide can be taken as a useful starting point for any serious empirical research:

- The victim being a stranger to the offender.
- Typically being abducted.
- Multiple crime scenes involved; pace of initial encounter, torture and death scene and body disposal site.
- The very nature of this crime, sadism expressed through torture, necessitates a secluded or solitary place for the prolonged period of time the offender spends with the victim. This captivity may range from a few hours to as long as six weeks.

- The offender's residence may be used if it can provide the required seclusion.
- The offender's vehicle will be altered for use in abduction and torture, disabling windows and doors, soundproofing, and installing police accessories.
- Gloves are often worn to avoid fingerprints.
- Secluded sites are selected well in advance.
- The offender undertakes his crime with methodical preparation, and the crime scene reflects this.
- Torture racks or specially equipped torture rooms are constructed.
- Weapons and torture implements of choice are brought to the scene and removed if it is outside.
- Restraints are usually present at the crime scene since they are common to this homicide.
- Sexual bondage, which is the elaborate and excessive use of binding material, unnecessarily neat and symmetrical binding, or binding that enables the victim to be placed in a variety of positions that enhance the offender's sexual arousal is also noted.
- The use of customised modes of torture may be evident, especially at the scene of torture and death, which include electrical appliances, vice grips, pliers, foreign objects used for insertion, and whips.
- Sexual arousal occurs most often with the victim's expression of pain and is evidenced by sexual fluids or possibly defecation at the scene.
- The body is routinely concealed, especially with the more organised offender, who is prepared with shovels, lime and remote burial sites.
- Bodies have also been burned.
- Sometimes inconsistencies are noted, however, as victims have been left where they will be seen by intimates, can be easily found, or disposed of carelessly.
- Occasionally the body may be transported to a location that increases the chance of discovery because the offender wants the excitement derived from the publicity that the body's discovery generates. This is 'staging'. It is possible that there are implications of overkill or depersonalisation for pragmatic reasons, for example, to obscure the victim's identity.
- The offender may also tamper with the crime scene by staging secondary criminal activity (for example; rape-murder, robbery) to veil the primary motive of sadistic murder.

They also note 'Common Forensic Findings':

- The offender engages in sex prior to death.
- Anal rape, forced fellatio, vaginal rape and foreign object penetration (in decreasing order). A majority of offenders forced their victims to engage in more than three of these activities.
- The attack is antemortem because the primary source of pleasure for the sadistic killer is in the pain caused the victim as opposed to the actual sexual act.
- Battery is focused on the sex organs, genitals and breasts.
- Sexually sadistic acts may include biting or overkill to areas with sexual association: thighs, buttocks, neck, and abdomen, in addition to the breasts and genitals. However, injury can be anywhere that causes suffering, for example, the elbow.

- Insertion of foreign objects into vaginal or anal cavities is often combined with the act of slashing, cutting, or biting the breasts and buttocks.
- Evidence of sexual fluids is usually found in the body orifices and around the body.
- If partners are involved, this may be evidenced by differing sexual fluids and pubic hairs.
- Offenders may also urinate on the victim.
- Ligature marks are common as restraints are frequently used, along with blindfolds and gags.
- Sexual bondage is prevalent.
- The fact that the offender usually spends a long time with the victim is evidenced by varying wound and injury ages or varying stages.

A number of studies do show what the key behaviours of sadistic sexual offences are and how commonly these occur. Some of the findings from this work are summarised in Table 13.12.

Offender Characteristics

Murderers

The characteristics of murderers in general, irrespective of the particular offending style, provide an important starting point for any inferences about the type of likely perpetrator in an investigation. Unlike burglary, which tends to be committed by offenders who go on to commit varied types of more serious offences, those individuals who commit murder are relatively distinct from offenders in general. If murderers can be distinguished from other offenders this could allow considerable narrowing down of possible suspects within police databases. Table 13.13 shows the typical characteristics of the homicide offenders drawn out of the criminal records in the study by Salfati and Canter (1999) in the United Kingdom. Salfati and Dupont's (2006) sample of 75 murderers in Canada comprised 76% white offenders, 87% males, 67% had previous convictions and 20% were in a relationship. Hakkanen's (2005) study of murderers who used ligature strangulation reported in her sample of 19 cases, a mean offender age of 34.9 years with a high rate of female offenders (35%) and 63% with a previous criminal history. Her sample were characterised by alcohol dependence (79%) and 47% came from a home where one or both parents abused alcohol.

Serial Murderers' Characteristics

The samples of murderers from which the above information is drawn may include one or two serial offenders although they will be predominantly single homicide offenders. Detailed background information on samples of serial murderers is more difficult to obtain although reported characteristics of these offenders, usually for US serial killers, are summarised in Table 13.14. The Missen Corpus (described in Box 13.2) of 331 American serial killers with 3334 victims provides another source of information on the characteristics of these offenders (see Table 13.15). This, in turn, provides some insights into how these individuals may be

Table 13.12 Prevalence of key behaviours in sadistic sexual offences including murders.

Behaviour/crime scene variable	Gratzer and Bradford (1995) Sadistic (DSM-III R) sexual murderers and sexual aggressors (n = 28)	Marshall, Kennedy and Yates (2002) Sadistic (DSM-III-R/DSM-IV) sexual offenders including 29.3% murderers (n = 41)	Proulx, Blais and Beauregard (2007) Sadistic MTC-R-3 sexual aggressors (n = 43)	Beauregard et al. (2007) Sexual murderers as defined by Ressler et al. (1988) (n = 66)	Dietz, Hazelwood and Warren (1990) Sadistic sexual offenders
Planned offence well/premeditation of crime (%)	82.1		86	27.3	93.3
Torture/coercive acts including torture (%)	78.6	38.9	30.2	19.7	100
Blows resulting in injuries (%)	64.3	61.1			
Selected victim (%)			52.5	39.1	
Unknown victim (%)			83.8		
Mutilation including of erogenous zones (%)			25.6	21.2	83
Psychological torture (humiliation) (%)			53.7	36.4	
Crime lasted more than an hour (%)				47.0	
Tied up/gagged (%)				23.8	87
Sodomy (%)					73
Body hidden/concealed (%)				35.4	65

Table 13.13 Typical characteristics of the homicide offenders.

Variable/characteristic	Salfati and Canter (1999)
Sex of the offender	72% male
Age of offender	Mean = 27 years (range = 15–49)
Offender knew victim	74%
Offender knew/was local to area	79%
Offender married/cohabiting	49%
Offender unemployed	41%
Offender served in armed forces	12%
Offender served prison sentence	40%
Previous conviction: theft	56%
Previous conviction: burglary	45%
Previous conviction: violent personal offences	37%
Previous conviction: damage to property	30%
Previous conviction: disorder	30%
Previous conviction: traffic offences	23%
Previous conviction: vehicle crimes	22%
Previous conviction: possession of drugs	16%
Previous conviction: sexual related offences	12%

Source: Salfati and Canter (1999). Reproduced with permission.

Table 13.14 Offender characteristics of serial killers.

Offender characteristics	Offenders are more likely to be Caucasian than African American but in numbers consistent with the relative proportion of Caucasians and African Americans in the US population (Godwin, 2000; Keeney and Heide, 1994).
	Hickey (2002): 169 American offenders, average age was 28.5 and 85% were white. Half of the offenders were categorised as local and the majority of the victims were strangers.
	Wide variety of educational and occupational backgrounds but the majority were not highly educated and tended to be in unskilled jobs. Almost 60% had a history of prior criminal activity.
	Serial murderers begin their careers of serial homicide at a relatively late age. Most start between the ages of 24 and 40. Have extensive police records, but for petty theft, embezzlement, and forgery, rather than violence (Jenkins, 1988)
	The median age of arrested serial murderers is 36. (Bartol, 1995)
	In a study of 217 American serial murderers Canter *et al.*, (1996) found that 75% had previous convictions and nearly half had been arrested as juveniles
Distances travelled	Median and average home-to-crime distances for American serial murderers were 15 km and 40 km, respectively, whereas the median and average home-to-crime distances for UK serial murderers were 9 km and 18 km, respectively (Lundrigan and Canter 2001)
	Serial murderers offend farther from their homes than do other types of criminals but they still offend relatively close to home
	Serial offenders commit crimes further from their home as the series lengthens (Snook *et al.*, 2005: 150)
	In the sample of 79 serial killers studied, their offence series ranged from two to 24 crimes (mean, 8; SD 4.53) and contained distances from 0 to 845 km (mean, 46.39 km; SD 85.71 km) (Canter *et al.*, 2000)

Table 13.15 Characteristics of 405 perpetrators from the Missen corpus.

Victim-offender relationship	76% strangers
	17% casual acquaintances
	4% friends/casual lovers
	2% spouses/partners
	0.6% in laws
	0.5% other relatives
	0.4% sons (of victims)
	0.1% law enforcement killers
Offender's ethnicity	73.5% Caucasian
	26.5% non-Caucasian (Afro-American 20.4%, Hispanic 3.8%, Jewish 0.68%, Native American 0.91%), South-East Asian/Chinese 0.3%)
Offender's age	<20 years old 9.1%
	20–29 years old 50.6%
	30–39 years old 27.2%
	40–49 years old 12.4%
	50< 0.9%
	Age was calculated from the date of the first homicidal episode in their series; the average age was found to be 27.8 years old (when committed first murder)
Offender's marital status	Single 49.8%
	Married 18.5%
	Divorced 18.3%
	Twice married 7.4%
	Divorced two or more times 5%
	If split to married and single only categories then it is 50% each – 50% were married (when they committed the murders or had been in the past) and 50% single
Offender's criminal history	Armed robbers 20.54%
	Burglars 19.03%
	Sex offenders 16.76%
	Serial arsonists 12.69%
	Sniping incident involvement 9.67%
	Previous homicide 9.7%
	Two or more previous homicides 1.5%
Offender's family background	More than two siblings 60%
	Only child 13%
	One or two siblings 21.2%
	Was first child 59.5%
	Was last child 14%
	Formally or informally adopted 14.1%
	Brought up by grandparents 14.5%
	Mother married three times or more 12.3%
	Living with natural mother only 41.2%
	Living with natural father only 2%

distinguished from single-homicide offenders. One interesting issue for further exploration here will be the question of whether serial murderers are more different from general offenders than single homicide offenders on all aspects of their characteristics or if there are some variables on which the serial killers are actually more similar to the general offending population.

Summary

In most murders the offender will be known to the victim and in many cases the offence will be preceded by domestic violence or stalking scenarios. The key investigative challenge then is differentiating between these scenarios to identify those that may develop into murder.

- The differentiation of offending style in murder requires an understanding of the psychological context from which the incident has emerged. Investigative psychology research suggests that the key distinction between these contexts lies in whether the crime was the central aim of the event (Expressive Murder encounters) or not (instrumental murder encounters). To date, intimate and family-based variants of expressive encounters and burglary- and rape-driven variants of instrumental encounters have been indicated.
- Although most models of serial killing and serial killers propose distinctions in terms of motivation and related psychopathology, the IP approach seeks to understand even this most bizarre and horrific variant of criminal activity as a distorted form of interpersonal interaction.
- As a corollary of this, the generic model of violent crime differentiation of Object, Vehicle and Person roles at high offending intensity levels provides a basis for understanding behavioural differences in serial murders.
- In serial murder, variations in offending intensity are revealed as different levels of dehumanisation and destruction of the identity of the individual.
- Little empirical support can be provided for the organised-disorganised types proposed within this widely known classification of serial killing.
- Sadistic sexual motivation is not part of all serial killing offences nor indeed of all serial murders that involve some sexual activity. A comprehensive understanding of sexual sadism and its recognition in crime scenes remains to be established.

Further Reading

Books

D'Cruze, S., Walklate, S. and Pegg, S. (2006) *Murder: Social and Historical Approaches to Understanding Murder and Murderers*, Willan, Cullompton.

Innes, M. (2003) *Investigating Murder: Detective Work and the Police Response to Criminal Homicide*, Oxford University Press, Oxford.

Leyton, E. (2003) *Hunting Humans*, John Blake, London.

Miethe, T.D., Regoeczi, W.C. and Drass, K.A. (2004) *Rethinking Homicide: Exploring the Structure and Process Underlying Deadly Situations*, Cambridge University Press, Cambridge.

Morton, R.J. and Hilts, M.A. (2005) *Serial Murder: Multi-Disciplinary Perspectives for Investigators*, Federal Bureau of Investigation, National Center for the Analysis of Violent Crime, Quantico, VA.

Proulx, J., Beauregard, E., Cusson, M. and Nicole, A. (eds) (2007) *Sexual Murderers: A Comparative Analysis and New Perspectives*, John Wiley & Sons, Ltd, Chichester.

Articles

Delisi, M. and Sherer, A.M. (2006) Multiple homicide offenders: offence characteristics, social correlates, and criminal careers. *Criminal Justice and Behaviour*, **33**, 367–91.

Fox, J.A. and Levin, J. (2003) Mass murder: an analysis of extreme violence. *Journal of Applied Psychoanalytic Studies*, **5** (1), 47–64.

Myers, W.C., Burgess, A.W., Burgess, A.G. and Douglas, J.E. (1999) Serial murder and sexual homicide, in *Handbook of Psychological Approaches with Violent Offenders* (eds V. van Hassalt and M. Herson), Kluwer Academic, New York.

Salfati, G. (2003) Offender interaction with victims in homicide: a multidimensional analysis of frequencies in crime scene behaviours. *Journal of Interpersonal Violence*, **18** (5), 490–512.

Santtila, P., Hakkanen, H., Canter, D., and Elfgren, T. (2003) Classifying homicide offenders and predicting their characteristics from crime scene behaviour. *Scandinavian Journal of Psychology*, **44**, 107–18.

Stone, M. (1989). Murder. *Psychiatric Clinics of North America*, **12** (3), 643–51.

Wentink, N. (2008) Homicide and serial killing, in *Criminal Psychology* (ed. D. Canter), Hodder Education, London.

Questions for Discussion and Research

1. Under what conditions would you expect a 'contract murder' to exhibit 'expressive' characteristics?

2. Does it make sense to define serial killing in terms of the number of people killed by one offender? What else might be relevant?

3. How could you explain a murder committed by someone who had previously had a blameless, crime-free life? Can you find any examples of such a killer?

4. Why do so many myths about serial killers still exist although research shows they have no validity?

5. What personal narratives and victim roles are implied by the classifications of serial killers provided by (a) Holmes and Holmes, (b) Fox and Levin?

CHAPTER 14

Organised Crime

In This Chapter

Learning Objectives

When you have completed this chapter you should be able to:

1. Understand what is and what is not 'organised' about organised crime.
2. Differentiate the dominant forms of criminal organisations.
3. Distinguish different features of the organisational structures of criminal networks.
4. Recognise the major indexes derived from social network analysis.
5. Be aware of the possibilities for a destructive organisational psychology.

Synopsis

Beyond the consideration of individual criminals or even one-to-one contacts between offenders there is a need to understand how three or more people may be organised in order to carry out illegal activities. Such an understanding comes from an awareness of the many ways in which networks of people may be structured. Various studies of these criminal network structures show that it is rare for them to reflect directly the forms that would be expected for legal organisations. They vary from those in which offenders are only loosely in touch with each other for specific crimes to those that are strongly hierarchical. The variations in the morphology of these networks relate to two crucial dimensions – one that reflects how strong the rules of the organisation are and the other that captures how significant the network is in the life of its individual members. These two dimensions provide a framework for the four dominant modes of the NAS (Narrative Action System).

Social network analysis, which provides mathematical definitions for various aspects of organisational network structures, allows a more precise and detailed study of the properties and vulnerabilities of criminal networks. These studies demonstrate that different forms of criminal activity tend to have different organisational structures. They also reveal that major variations between criminal networks can be identified from measures of their size and the extent to which they have subgroups.

All these considerations provide a basis for exploring how the reciprocal anarchy that characterises most criminal activity may be open to disruption and destruction. This provides the basis for a new application of the theory of organisations that is called 'destructive organisational psychology'.

The Social Nature of Crime

We have seen in earlier chapters that inferences and explanations that relate to interpersonal processes are a crucial aspect of understanding offending. So far, however, we have tended to limit our consideration to one-to-one personal contact. But the awareness that criminality always involves some form of social transaction, and this often includes more than one offender, leads to the exploration of social psychological processes. Our attention is drawn to how groups, teams and networks operate and what the study of them offers to the understanding and investigation of crime.

The description in Box 14.1 gives a taste of the experience of being a member of a criminal gang that is connected to organised crime involved in supplying drugs as well as various forms of violent control and retribution. The claim that being part of such a group has parallels to being in a family is belied by the viciousness of the existence and the claim that he could drop in and out of gang life. It shows, as many researchers (for example, Van Duyne, 1999) have pointed out, that there are usually crucial differences between the networks and organisations in which criminals participate and those of legitimate companies.

Box 14.1 Experience of a Gang Member

One time someone tried to kill me – tried to set me up. A rival gang tried to kill me. I was supposed to meet this girl, but she was not there. I waited for a while and then decided to go home. Then a car pulled up beside me and shot me four times in the chest. I was wearing a bulletproof west. I had two guns on me – I pulled them out and started shooting. I chased them, but crashed into a bus and left the car before the police arrived. I tried to get them after too, but did not get them at the time. When I left the car I went home alone.

My friend died in a car crash just before this incident. That made me more jumpy. I was getting into arguments with the wrong kind of people. When this happened I remember just feeling angry.

They wanted to shoot me, because I shot one of them. A normal man would not do it. I am always looking over my shoulder. That is the cost of being in organised crime – selling drugs.

The gang are like an extended family. Because it is dangerous to be in a gang – you need an extended family to get your back. I have always been in a gang – it was just part of growing up in the area. But it is not always like this – you know 24/7 and 365 days in the year. I am sometimes in and sometimes out of the gang – like it is all about protecting yourself.

Studies of criminal social processes highlight the importance of group structures as well as the social and cultural networks that form the context within which many offences occur. When offences do not involve a sole operator and consist of groups or teams of individuals that, to a greater or lesser extent, have to work together to make the offence possible then, to understand how these crimes are achievable, the implicit and formal organisational networks of which they are a part have to be explored. This is most obvious in what is known as 'organised' crime, typically dealing with the purchase and sale of illegal goods, or 'people trafficking', but it is also a part of all crime that has some financial, or property-related component to it from burglary to major frauds because wherever there are illegal transactions taking place there are networks of interactions. The variety and significance of the structure of these networks needs to be understood in order to investigate them effectively and have some impact on reducing their possibilities for survival.

The recognition of the social and organisational aspects of crime offers a particular perspective for investigations because it requires an analysis of how groups, teams and networks function. This requires forms of analysis that take us beyond considerations of the individual offender and the pattern of interactions between pairs of criminals.

Most organisational psychology has the purpose of determining how social transactions can be facilitated and how organisations can be made more effective. An IP perspective on criminal networks can be seen to have the opposite objective. Investigators are attempting

to incapacitate criminal networks and to weaken the social interactions of criminals. Therefore there is a sense in which such investigators need to turn organisational theory on its
head; learn what factors make an organisation efficient and then see whether the same factors used 'in reverse' can render that organisation unworkable, as we shall see later in this
chapter.

What is Organised Crime?

The term 'organised crime' is a popular one but like most popular labels it assumes more than
it delivers. For although most criminals are involved in some form of contact or cooperation
with others it is rare for there to be in place a strictly hierarchical management structure that
would be recognised as an 'organisation' in the legitimate world. Indeed offenders are often
characterised as 'entrepreneurs' (Hobbs, 1988) who operate outside of any very clear formal
organisational structure.

Many researchers, for example Sarnecki (2001) in his study of delinquent networks emphasise a loose pattern of associations that does not reflect any formal structure like that
which would be expected in a legal organisation. These findings on how criminal networks
operate challenge the popular view, enshrined in fictional portrayals, that criminal networks
are strongly hierarchical with a 'Mr Big' in charge. There is the further possibility that different types of crime require, or encourage, different organisational morphologies with the
hypothesis that the structure of criminal groups may be predicted from knowledge of their
criminal activities. For example, Canter (2000d) [WHICH?] has shown that criminal activity
that benefits from weight of numbers, such as a group of hooligans involved in aggression,
would not require the same degree of structure as a drug distribution network that must
pass products from hand to hand and coordinate the collection of finances. Furthermore,
studies of criminal networks certainly indicate that all criminal networks are not similar to
each other (Passas and Nelken, 1993; Van Duyne, 1996). They differ by the degree or type of
organisation, which may range from loosely connected networks to highly structured groups
(Bourgois, 1985; Potter, 1994).

Relatively little is known about the fundamental ways in which criminal patterns of communication vary from one network to another and how those variations may relate to the
objectives and forms of criminality they support. This is partly, of course, because many of
these networks are secret and difficult to penetrate. When they are penetrated by undercover
agents, those agents are reluctant to give any account of what they have discovered for fear of
helping criminals to protect themselves from undercover penetration in the future. Developments in electronic surveillance techniques are changing this situation, particularly in relation
to present-day terrorism. The disruption of many terrorist networks with subsequent arrests
of their members is improving our knowledge of how those networks operate, as discussed in
the next chapter.

The central finding from all these studies of organised crimes, as with all the other forms
of criminality we have been examining, is that there is an underlying variation in the forms
they can take.

Cultural Ideologies and Criminal Networks

The major variation in the organisation of criminals is the degree of structure. This can vary from minimally structured groups, whose members are only casually and loosely in contact with each other as with football crowds that become violent (Stott and Pearson, 2007) to those that have a clear organisational shape with a clear hierarchy and defined roles, as has been found in some Chinese Triad groups. This quantitative variation from low to high degree of organisational structuring is reflected in a number of different aspects of criminal communication networks and related features of group membership. The closer consideration of these variations helps us to understand the nature of organised crime and provides pointers for investigations.

The word 'structure' has been used to characterise 'form' or 'shape' of an organisation. It is taken to mean the pattern of contacts between the members of the group or network. However, this pattern reflects what Mars (2000) refers to as an ideology or organisational culture.

He provides a framework for the varieties of such cultures that has its roots in the anthropological theories of Douglas (1978), which emphasises two underlying dimensions that Mars (2000) uses to distinguish between the various criminal cultures. One dimension is the extent to which a culture imposes rules and classifications on its members, assigning them to distinct roles within any criminal network. The other is the strength of the group of which a person is a member and how much of the person's life is tied into that group. Combinations of these distinctions help to draw attention to important differences in the social context of which a criminal may be a part. They also help to clarify the significance of that culture for offenders. The task for investigators is to determine where on these dimensions any criminal network actually resides. From such examinations the vulnerabilities of those networks can be revealed.

The dimensions that Mars (2000) describes can be seen to reflect our general action system, where the system is not an individual but one or more people interacting with each other in various forms of social process. The dimension of group power reflects the extent to which the person or the group is the dominant originator of actions. In those organisations that have a lot of controls over their members then their actions are not likely to be initiated by the needs of the members but by the demands of the group. The strength of the hierarchy will determine whether those actions are aimed at satisfying processes within the individual or relate more directly to aspects of the organisational environment. In a strongly hierarchical organisation the outcome of the criminal actions are aimed at supporting the particular role or position of the offender within the hierarchy. In a more loosely structured network the outcome of actions reflect more directly the consequences for the individual. So the action system maps on to Mars' model as shown in Figure 14.1.

At one extreme is the 'alienated' offender. As discussed in earlier chapters, the bizarre thought patterns, self images and extreme behaviours that help to distinguish these offenders are likely to be a product of a personal narrative of alienation, feeling they are victims of the acts of others. These people are typically outside any clear criminal organisation although they

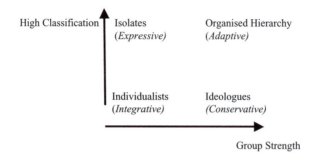

Figure 14.1   Fourfold categories of criminal organisation (from Mars, 2000) with action system interpretation.

may still have contact with other offenders. As we saw in Chapter 11, perhaps paradoxically, fraud is often committed by these sorts of offenders. Spahr and Alison (2004) have shown that of the 481 fraudsters they studied 75% were lone offenders, isolates, who often are struggling with feelings of the need to redress the hurt they have felt from others.

So, Mars' model of criminal cultures helps to show how for some criminals it is the very lack of group strength and clearly defined rules and roles that create the context in which some crimes occur. This is particularly true for the individualists who are distinct from the 'isolates'. As Mars (2000) explains, individualist offenders are often on the periphery of criminal organisations. They act as entrepreneurs (Hobbs, 1988) and use other people as a means to an end. Thus they are likely to lack long-term relationships or be part of enduring criminal activities.

Not surprisingly, then, these individually oriented crimes require rather different investigative strategies from those that are more structurally embedded within organised networks. In relation to the frauds that Spahr and Alison (2004) studied there were a small number of other cases, 14 out of the 481, who had between five and eight offenders per group. These would be part of quite different organisational milieu. They are more likely to be part of an organised hierarchy that operates as professional criminals developing rules and roles for their different members.

The groups that Mars (2000) calls *ideologues* are more likely to act in conservative actions system mode, modifying their structure in response to external threats. This is typical of terrorist groups and others that are indeed driven by ideology rather than by direct acquisitive gain. Mars (2000) gives the interesting example of the IRA whose organisational blueprint found its way into the public domain in 1977. This showed that they had actually changed their strict conventional military structure of a hierarchical battalion because it was too easily infiltrated by informants. Instead they restructured using a cellular structure of groups of four. As Mars (2000: 37) puts it: 'the new system thus combining and maximising organisational finesse and commitment, the attributes and benefits of both hierarchy and ideology.'

At the extreme of this sort of hierarchical organisation is, for example, the US Mafia (Nelken, 1993), which has a high degree of classification and clearly defined ranks. This requires the person to be strongly committed to that group whilst providing for all aspects of his life. The adaptive mode that is typical of this form of organisation does make it very much more in control of its environment than, for instance, an *ad hoc* gang of armed robbers who only come together to carry out one particular crime. This more obviously individualistic group, which is made up of people who are mainly concerned with their own survival is fraught with pressures to maintain the egocentric demands of its members.

But it would be wrong to assume that all criminal hierarchical organisations are the same. A number of researchers have found differentiation in roles and levels of individual power (Donald and Wilson, 2000; McAndrew, 2000; McCluskey and Wardle, 2000) but no rigid hierarchies. This can include important differences in the way in which leadership is exerted within an offending group, as Porter and Alison (2005) have shown for gang rapes. All these studies have revealed that there is much to be explored about the variations in the structure of those criminal networks that do have some structure. These structures may therefore be examined to reveal the varieties of roles available to offenders and the implications they carry for investigations and any offender's identification with criminal activity.

For example Johnston's (2000) examination of the structure of football hooligan groups shows there are differences in levels of 'commitment' to offending depending on the extent to which the individuals identify with the hooligan group. This is manifest in such differences as, for example, the extent to which individuals are prepared to travel to organised fights. The more committed members travel further. So strong are these group processes that fighting is often dictated by the extent to which the individuals feel a part of the 'in' or 'out' group. As Johnston points out, two groups that have recently fought one another may form into a larger group to fight against a jointly perceived more dissimilar, and therefore 'threat' group. Thus persistence and the severity of offending appears to be a product of subtle social processes. Recent research has shown that social identity theory, which explores more deeply the significance of group membership in giving shape to an offender's personal narrative, is of great value in helping to clarify the social psychological processes involved (Stott and Pearson, 2007).

Criminal 'Careers' within Criminal 'Organisations'

The organisational processes that Johnston (2000) describes can be seen in many other forms of offending and have been explored at least since the early ethnographic studies of the 1920s and 1930s (cf. Thrasher, 1927; Whyte, 1956). Many of those studies and more recent explorations, such as Marsh *et al.* (1978), have demonstrated the existence of role differentiation and consequent organisational structure within gangs and teams of offenders. Donald and Wilson's (2000) study of ram raiders, in which a team of offenders attack a shop or bank to steal goods or money, shows that the different roles within a team are derived partly on the basis of the different skills available to and necessary for the purpose of carrying out ram raids. In fact the authors argue that the offence requires such a level of skill that it can only be effectively carried out if it is considered and planned as a professional activity.

Donald and Wilson see no need to draw upon diagnostic or pathological models to explain behaviour but instead develop an argument for group processes as evolving from principles

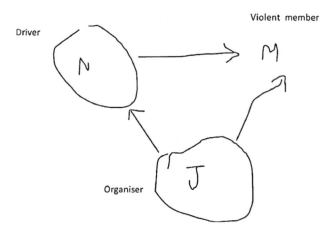

Figure 14.2   Drawing from an armed robbery team member of the group organisation.

Source: McCluskey and Wardle (2000). Reproduced with permission.

of organisational and social psychology. They draw heavily upon Guzzo's (1996) research on work groups. These are defined by the existence of social entities within a larger social system, where tasks are performed as a product of the group not by discrete individuals. Moreover, they note that in ram raiding there are specified roles of which the offenders appear to be well aware.

Indeed, McCluskey and Wardle (2000) reveal from interviews with members of armed robbery teams that these criminals have a clear conception of roles amongst their members and they appear to enjoy these self-descriptions. Figure 14.2 is a diagram actually drawn by a member of an armed robbery presented by McCluskey and Wardle (2000: 257). It shows that there were three very distinct roles: the organiser, the driver and the 'heavy', violent member of the team, who dealt with any threats to their actions. The arrows also show the lines of communication of which their respondent was clearly aware. Katz (1988) has pointed out the value in examining the 'seductive' qualities of the image that certain criminal lifestyles promote. Thus, in denying that they belong to the conventional, non-criminal group, some offenders define themselves as members of an 'out group'. This gives shape to their personal narratives, sometimes as 'outlaws', or as in our opening account in Box 14.1, as a member of a 'family'.

Donald and Wilson (2000) were able to relate the roles offenders' played in criminal gangs to their criminal backgrounds. This enabled Donald and Wilson (2000) to demonstrate that the previous offences of criminals related directly to their roles in the teams. The 'drivers' were more likely to have offences relating to vehicles. The 'heavy' typically had criminal antecedents for violence. The leader of the group, by contrast, was most likely to have been convicted of offences relating to dishonesty. This role differentiation raises the question as to what paths lead criminals into these different positions in criminal organisations. Are there any parallels here to the 'careers' that people follow in legal organisations?

The idea of a criminal career, in which offenders take on different roles in an illegal enterprise and possibly move through those roles over time, is rather different from the notion of 'criminal career' that, for example, Blumstein, Cohen and Farrington (1988) offer. They merely consider the temporal progress of serial criminals in order to establish if there are any defining consistencies to that progress. From a social psychological perspective a career implies changing relationships to the other people with whom the person is working, indeed changes in the person's own understanding of their role in their own narrative. Therefore understanding where an offender is on his career path can assist in understanding his current actions and criminal history, both matters of great significance to police investigations.

This development in a criminal's involvement in crime, as Johnston (2000) has illustrated for football hooligans, may involve more commitment to the 'job' being carried out. For an offender this would imply that they identify with the life of crime, becoming a 'career criminal'. They can come to see significant aspects of themselves as defined by the 'job' they do, namely committing crimes.

Social Network Analysis

The variety of organisational structures apparent for different criminal networks points to the possibility of detailed systematic analysis of the forms and qualities of these structures. This treats individuals as nodes in a network. Information on such networks may have been obtained through observations of known contacts between members, for example from direct observation, telephone bills or monitored telephone calls. Once the pattern of nodes and contacts has been determined it is possible to examine mathematical aspects of the links between those nodes (see, for example, Cole, 2001). With the advent of reliable and easy-to-use computer systems for measuring many different aspects of social networks, known not surprisingly as social network analysis (SNA), such as Ucinet (Borgatti, Everett and Freeman, 1992) this analysis is rapidly gaining popularity to examine empirically the structures of criminal networks (McAndrew, 2000; Swanson, Chamelin and Territo, 1992; Wasserman and Faust, 1994).

Drawing on earlier work by Wasserman and Faust (1997), McAndrew (2000) describes in detail the mathematical possibilities that now exist for describing criminal networks. In doing this he shows that some of the central concepts for describing groups can be very ambiguous unless given mathematical precision. Such precision then allows sensible consideration of crucial investigative questions – for instance, where the vulnerabilities really are in any networks or if the criminal organisation will be fatally wounded if its apparent leader is removed. These analyses also facilitate the monitoring of changes in communication networks and the revelation of just how fluid they are and how difficult it may be to specify their structure.

Seven features of any network may be drawn from McAndrew's extensive (2000) study of criminal networks. The features are summarised in Table 14.1.

Table 14.1 Components of social networks.

1. *Core group* of individuals that co-ordinate operations in a network
2. *Key central figures* that form the core group
3. *Sub-groups* that carry out different activities
4. *Mid-level individuals* that conduct daily operations, liaise with lower-level members and provide protection to the key figures
5. *Isolated individuals* that provide information and resources
6. The *size* of the networks – the number of individuals involved
7. *Chains* are subgroups that are connected to each other with each member only connected to one other

According to McAndrew (2000), how many and which of these features are present in a criminal network is a fruitful indicator of how a network is operating, as well as providing valuable insights into what its strengths and vulnerabilities may be. A group or network that has high values on all of these components could be regarded as very structured. One that was low on them can be seen as just a loose set of independent individuals. There may also be various mixes of the different constituents that would give rise to qualitative differences between the organisation of each group.

Core Group

The presence of a core *group* of individuals that coordinate network activities and are clearly differentiated from other members in the network is perhaps the most recognised structural feature (Dorn, Murji, and South, 1992; Dorn and South, 1990; Johnston, 2000; Lewis 1994; Ruggiero and South, 1995). For instance, although Lewis (1994: 46) described heroin distribution in the United Kingdom from 1970 to 1990 as '. . . composed of complex, articulated, multifaceted series of layered networks which individuals enter and exit according to means and circumstances', thereby showing that this distribution was far from a tidy single, hierarchical organisation, nonetheless he indicated that there were distinctions to be made between a crucial group who lead trade (for example, importers) and other more peripheral members of the network (for example, street dealers). Potter (1994) also pointed to clear differences between leaders and street-level workers in organised crime groups and that these differences were related to age and criminal experience. Hobbs (1997) supported the notion that there are clear differences between leaders and other members in property crime networks. For instance, he labelled core groups in criminal networks as 'hubs', which were made up of entrepreneurs that were distinguished from other members of a network.

Key Central Figures

Related to the notion of a core group is the idea that there are *key central figures* that form the core group (Block, 1978; Bourgois, 1995; Potter, 1994; Reuter and Haaga, 1986; Williams, 1993). In one of the earliest studies of the cocaine trade in New York during the first decade of the twentieth century, Block (1978) reported that drug networks had a core group of people that governed importing, wholesaling and retailing of cocaine. More recent research by Williams (1993) has also found that the small core group that run the upper levels of the wholesale distribution and retail side of the international heroin and cocaine industry consisted of key central figures that are bound by ethnic identity or familial ties. Although to a lesser extent, the existence of a core group has also been evident in stolen property networks. For example, Shover (1991) found that burglary networks were constantly changing in size, yet, a small core of two or three associates emerged when a burglary was required. Similarly, Van Limbergen, Colaers and Walgrave (1989) observed a decline in the intensity of hooligan involvement, whereby the centre of the hooligan group consisted of a number of hard-core members that organise and plan violence.

Subgroups

Often found within a criminal network are *subgroups* of individuals that are responsible for conducting different activities (Block, 1989; Jenkins, 1992; Zhang and Gaylord, 1996). Subgroups were evident in Jenkins' (1992) study of the methamphetamine industry in Philadelphia. He found that the mafia group that controlled the acquisition of chemicals was made up of subgroups of powerful individuals or cliques. Jenkins reported that the subgroups interacted with various other networks within the industry. Subgroups were also found in property networks. A study by Maguire (1982) found that subgroups existed in burglary networks of highly professional thieves. He found that burglars survived by forming small cliques with a high level of secrecy, made up of small pools of mutually trusting members.

Mid-level Individuals

An enduring theme in the analysis of criminal networks is the existence of *mid-level individuals* or intermediaries. Mid-level individuals may be leaders themselves or individuals mediating between 'leaders' and 'workers', thus, providing a safeguard for the key central figures from detection by law enforcement agencies and competing criminal groups. For instance, Potter (1994) found this to be the case with high-risk activities associated with drug dealing. Mid-level intermediaries have also been used as liaisons with other networks. One example noted by Jenkins (1992) was that subgroups in networks were organised around powerful individuals who interacted with other networks in the drug industry.

Bourgois (1995) also demonstrated the similarity between the structure of drug markets and legal enterprises, whereby mid-level individuals or *pseudo-entrepreneurs* were used to discipline the workforce and manipulate the kinship networks to ensure loyalty. Shover (1973) reports that handlers acted as intermediaries between burglars and fences. The handlers often relayed to the burglars what was to be stolen, provided loans to the burglars and communicated with legitimate businessmen. More recently, Hobbs' (1995) ethnographic study of professional criminals in London revealed that handlers continue to play an intermediary role in property crime networks by running storehouses for stolen goods. These mid-level intermediaries have been found to play significant roles in hooligan groups (Van Limbergen,

Colaers and Walgrave, 1989). They called these individuals *stagiaries*, who were younger and less delinquent individuals surrounding the hard core with the aim of becoming part of the core group. Similar to drug and property crimes, the *stagiaries* were likely to protect the core group by being the first to participate in the violence.

Isolated Individuals

The fifth aspect of criminal networks is *isolated individuals*. These individuals play a peripheral role by providing information and resources to a network (Sutherland, 1937; West, 1978). For example, Reuter and Hagga (1986) argued that cocaine shipping would be organised around a few members with peripheral contacts being utilised occasionally to dispose of the drugs as the opportunity arose. Similarly, Shover (1973) found that groups of burglars had external contacts, such as tipsters, fences and handlers that could be utilised to gain sources of information about potential crimes. Although peripheral members have been observed in hooligan networks, peripheral members are not so important for maintaining their structure. For example, Van Limbergen, Colaers and Walgrave (1989) found that peripheral members were ordinary adolescents who were motivated by the macho image and behaviour but did not become involved in the physical violence.

Network Size

The sixth and possibly most important feature of criminal networks is the size of the network. It has been observed that large networks that involve the movement of larger quantities of goods and a greater number of customers require a more sophisticated structure to operate efficiently without detection (Reuter and Haaga, 1986). Bourgois (1995) argued that larger drug networks form a more sophisticated structure because it adds a safety feature, that is, the avoidance of detection for the core group. Similarly Johnston's (2000) study of hooligan groups revealed that hooligan groups varied according to size. She found that higher levels of structure were found in networks with the largest number of members. This accords directly with the considerable literature in organisational psychology that demonstrates the ways in which increases in the size of an organisation are reflected in a wide range of aspects of that organisation. The impact of organisation size is as varied as how much absenteeism and worker turnover it has, or how bureaucratic and inefficient it is (cf. for example Barker and Gump, 1964).

Subgroups as Chains

One further measure was to establish if there were any *subgroups as chains*. This was defined as a number of individuals connected to one core member, having few connections within other members of the group. Subgroups exist when members are connected in a chainlike configuration, rather than clusters, or cliques of highly interconnected members. This is distinct from the *subgroups* variable because subgroups as chains imply a more structured, hierarchical organisation than having subgroups as coherent cliques.

Box 14.2 A typical Social Network Analysis

This is based on telephone records of a network of 22 individuals engaged in a wide variety of crimes.

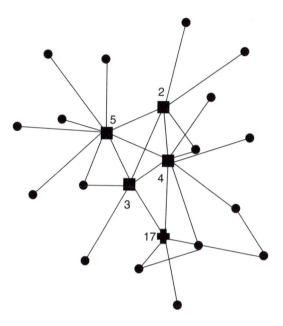

Each point (circle or square) is an individual in the network. Lines represent known associations between these. Numbered squares identify key individuals, showing that individuals 2, 3, 4, 5 and 17 form an inner clique that is crucial for the coherence of the network.

Source: McAndrew (2000).

A Study of Criminal Networks

In order to explore the ways in which these various aspects of criminal networks related to each other and distinguished between different criminal organisations Canter (2004b) studied 12 drug-dealer networks, 11 property crime networks and six hooligan networks by deriving measures of organisational structure relating the six components in Table 14.1.

In order to obtain precise measures of the components of networks Canter (2004b) drew on measures available within UCINET (Borgatti *et al.*, 2002) *Degree, Betweenness, Closeness, Information, Clique, N-clique, K-core* and *Cutpoints and Knots* (see Wasserman, Faust and Iacobucci, 1994 for a comprehensive account of the precise mathematical calculations for this and subsequent measures), which are given more detailed definition in Table 14.2.

These measures allow quantification of the features discussed above. They resulted in the following set of variables:

Table 14.2 Summary of SNA measures.

Degree measures how connected an individual is in a network. Degree is calculated as the number of links that a member has with all other members in the network (Freeman, 1979). The more links an individual has then the more power he or she is considered to have.

Betweenness measures the extent to which an individual acts as an intermediary between all other pairs of points. More specifically, betweenness measures how many times an individual falls on the shortest path between all members in a network (Bonacich, 1987; McAndrew, 2000).

Closeness measures how 'easily' a member can contact all other members with the least number of go-betweens. In other words, the sum of the shortest distance between any two individuals in a network, such that the individual with the smallest sum is considered to have a close relationship to all other individuals in the network.

Information measures of how involved a member is in all possible paths in a network (Stephenson and Zelen, 1989). This measure takes account of the access the individual has to other individuals who are highly connected.

Clique measures the extent to which all individuals in a subgroup in a network are connected to all other members of that subgroup. A clique is thus a subset of individuals that are more closely tied to each other than are other members that are not part of that subgroup. A perfect clique would consist of all members being connected to one another.

N-clique is a more lenient measure that does not require all individuals in a network to be connected with one another. In contrast to a perfect clique (one-clique), a two-clique would be all individuals connected through an intermediary.

K-Core consists of a subgroup of individuals that are connected to each other a little more than they are to others within the network as a whole. All individuals have an equal number of contacts between one another and one more than others in the network do with them (Seidman, 1983).

- *Size* was determined by regarding groups of 15 or more members as large. Those with less than 15 members were defined as small.
- *The key central figures* that indicate the prominence of apparent leaders were determined from the SNA centrality scores. If any individual had a distinctly higher score than anyone else then this group was defined as having a key central figure.
- The presence of a *core group* indicates that one central group is present in the overall communication network. This was determined by looking at the size of the various measures of clique-ness. When some, or all, of the people in a network, had high clique scores together with the highest centrality measures, this was taken as indicating that there was a cohesive subgroup at the core of the network.
- *Mid-level members* exist when individuals are found whose centrality scores, whilst being clearly lower than the *key central figures,* are nonetheless distinctly higher than the rest of the group. Further examination of their position in the network also supports their role as intermediaries.
- *Subgroups* were determined by the presence of cliques and n-cliques. These consisted of one or more groups distinct from the main network but having a connection with the rest of the network.
- *Isolated individuals* exist when there are one or more members who are connected to the network through only one individual. These members are located at the periphery of a network as they only have one connection to any other person within the network.

In order to analyse the relationships between these measures across the 29 groups of offenders Canter (2004b) used a special and rather unusual form of multivariate analysis known as partial order scalogram analysis (Shye, 1978, 1998, 1998). Although it has some analogous properties to SSA, and other multidimensional procedures, it operates on a very different basis. As in other procedures it starts with a set of values (a 'profile') for each case, across all the measures. This profile assumes that all the values have a common meaning. In the present case this can be thought of as increasing social network sophistication. The profile for each entity (here it is the criminal group) is compared with every other. If the change in values across the set of all measures is in the same direction between one profile and another, then these profiles are technically known as 'comparable', allowing them to be put in some common order. The profile with the lower values can be represented as lower on the overall dimension that defines the common meaning for all the measures.

Any profile that has some values higher and some lower when compared with another profile is regarded as qualitatively different and so does not sit on the same overall dimension. This is actually a way of thinking of relationships between entities that have both qualitative and quantitative differences that is part of what is mathematically known as 'order theory', the study of such systems being influenced greatly by the work of Helmut Hasse (1898–1979). He created a way of representing these which became known as Hasse Diagrams (http://en.wikipedia.org/wiki/Hasse_diagram). However such diagrams are difficult to construct and interpret once there are more than three variables with more than three categories each. Therefore Shye (1978) developed a way of working with larger data sets using co-ordinates (Partial Order Scalogram Analysis with Coordinates, POSAC). So although the resulting diagram from POSAC looks rather like those from multidimensional scaling procedures, such that individual cases are represented as points in the space so those closer together share some important properties, the analysis this is based on works directly from the underlying coordinates. The mapping of the cases can be summarised as follows:

> Every pair of profiles is compared, determining whether they are 'comparable' or 'incomparable' (in a technical sense described above). If comparable, it is determined which one is greater. Then profiles are mapped into Cartesian coordinate space of sufficient dimensionality so that the originally observed relations between profiles (incomparability, comparability etc.) are preserved in the new, shorter profiles made up of the new coordinate-values assigned to original profiles. Suppose you observed 7 variables and found that their POSAC-dimensionality of 2 is satisfactory, then the 2 new scores on the two dimensions preserve (almost) all the originally observed comparability relations.
>
> (Shye, personal communication, 2009)

Because of the use of co-ordinates, POSAC is particularly powerful when there is a strong underlying theory with parsimonious variables. So in the present case with the 29 criminal groups in which we are focusing directly on the patterns of social complexity it is a fruitful procedure to use. The resulting Figure 14.3 thus represents each case as a point on the basis of their overall scores on the horizontal and vertical axes. To ease interpretation, the way the different measures of group sophistication relate to the x and y axes, is schematically indicated.

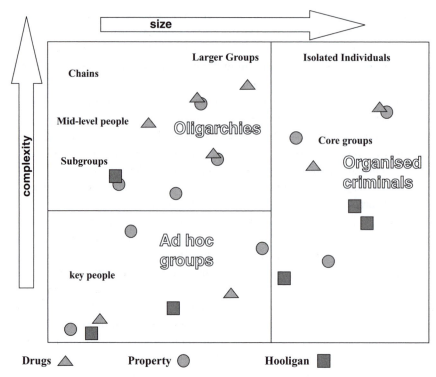

Figure 14.3   A schematic representation of the POSA results reported by Canter (2004).

Source: Canter (2004b). Reproduced with permission.

It shows each of the criminal networks as a point in space such that the closer together they are the more similar their social network profiles are on the seven variables listed in Table 14.1. The variables that describe the groups in each region of the space are indicated and the broad styles of organisation labelled for each region of the space.

Two dimensions create the two dominant axes of Figure 14.3. As anticipated, the size of the network is a crucial feature. The horizontal axis relates to the increasing size of the group. As the size increases so there are more likely to be individuals who act as links between the key central individuals and the rest of the group. Interestingly groups that have all these components may also have isolated individuals who only have contact with the group through one person. So the isolation of individuals can be seen to be partly a product of the largeness of the group attracting people who only have peripheral contact.

The vertical axis relates to an increase in differentiation of the group structure. This moves from the presence of key central figures on to the emergence of core groups that form a sort of 'aristocracy' around these figures then on to the emergence of subgroups linked in as chains to significant figures in the group. At their most differentiated these groups are also likely to have isolated individuals. This helps to show how organisational complexity is reflected in aspects of a hierarchical network that develops from the role of significant interlinked individuals.

These two dimensions assisted in the identification of three broad types of group. The most definitive aspect of the networks appeared as the presence or absence of subgroups:

- *Ad hoc* groups, which are less differentiated in organisational structures that have no subgroups. They are low on both dimensions, with relatively little structure, sometimes with just the presence of key central figures. They tend to be the smallest groups, ranging in size from eight to 22 with a mean of 13 members. In the sample studied they have a preponderance of hooligan groups and property criminals but they do also contain some of the smaller drug networks. These groups are made up of Mars' (2000) individualists, forming loose opportunistic groups that are relatively short lived.
- *'Oligarchies'*, whose communication networks are controlled by a small group of people. These tend to be larger than the *ad hoc* groups, ranging in size from 12 to 32 members with an average of 20 members. In the sample they consisted mainly of drug networks but also contained property criminals and the largest hooligan group in the sample of 32 members. They are Mars' (2000) ideologues with their pattern of subgroups only loosely connected.
- *Illegal organisation* is an appropriate term for those networks that were both complex and large with most forms of differentiation, indicating a management hierarchy. They contained the largest network in the sample of 45 property criminals, with the smallest group being 16 drug dealers. Their average size of 25 members indicates that they typically contain the largest number of people in any group. They are what Mars (2000) labels the 'organised hierarchy'. They are closest to a structure that would be recognisable in a legitimate company. Of particular interest is the fact that they are most likely to attract isolated individuals who would be expected to be operating in the expressive mode. This is a matter for further study but does suggest that these individuals may be attracted to the possibilities provided by being on the fringe of large criminal networks.

These findings indicate that, as has been found in so many studies of organisational size, the number of people involved in any group carries implications for how hierarchical and structured a group needs to be to survive. Apparently once a criminal network grows beyond about ten members it starts to differentiate in various ways. Beyond about 20 members this differentiation becomes more pronounced.

However, size is certainly not the only influence on network morphology. For although none of the groups with less than ten members have any identifiable subgroups and the groups with more than 30 people are all highly differentiated, nonetheless there is a drug oligarchy with only 12 members and, by contrast, a hooligan group of 22 people that appears to be a loose *ad hoc* network. It would appear that the nature of the criminal activity has some relationship to the emergence of more highly structured groups. Hooligan groups really only need to gather at particular sporting events and respond to opportunities for violence. It therefore makes sense that these groups will tend not to need a strong structure until it starts getting quite large, say, beyond 25 people. A drug network, on the other hand, is a form of commercial organisation that needs to obtain goods, distribute them, and obtain financial gain from the transactions. In the present sample once such a group got beyond about 15 people it took on a more differentiated structure, presumably to help manage the transactions involved. The property networks sit between these two in the present sample. This may be because they cover a bigger variety of activities, some closer to the opportunistic actions of hooligans and others closer to the planned management of large drug cartels.

Destructive Organisational Psychology

The consideration of the variations in organisational structure of criminal networks leads to the consideration of how such organisations may be explored and undermined. This requires considerations of where the vulnerabilities of such networks are. These come in the main from the challenges of keeping any clandestine organisation alive.

Organisational Vulnerability: Communication

Organisations are nothing without communications between their members and with their suppliers and 'clients'. Communications are fundamental to the two crucial aspects – objectives and structure. People need to be informed of what the objectives and tasks of the organisation are and to be kept involved in its activities. The assignment of roles and the processes of leadership all depend not only on communications between the different individuals and groups but also on some of those individuals having knowledge of the communication process itself.

Noncriminal organisations constantly battle to maintain and improve the efficiency and effectiveness of their communications. Weaknesses in this aspect of their activities are frequently chronic problems with which they struggle. This is almost invariably their Achilles' heel. For criminals this vulnerability is more parlous. They have to keep their contacts confidential and secret wherever possible. They must even hide any knowledge of who is in contact with whom. This makes them less effective and more prone to confusion and misinterpretation. Therefore many of the vulnerabilities of criminal organisations can be traced to the various weaknesses that emerge from problems generated in aspects of their communication processes.

As messages are passed between more people there are more opportunities for confusions to occur. As a consequence the larger an organisation the more likely are its communication processes to be weak. For a criminal organisation this also means the more opportunity there is for unwanted leaking of information. The implications for law enforcement therefore are to establish the extent of a criminal network as fully as possible. The larger a network the more likely there are to be weaknesses in its communication. These weak links can be used for intelligence sources or as opportunities for disruption.

Further, as we have seen, there is the possibly paradoxical discovery that the larger the organisation the more likely there are to be individuals within it whose connections with the organisation are tenuous. These individuals may well be people who have their own personal difficulties and have not embraced the dominant narrative of the organisation. They will be the ones who are open to influence and persuasion from the outside and may be a route into the central groups that manage the network.

Along with the problems of extended communication, any increase in size also puts greater demands on the mechanisms of control. This is particularly problematic for criminal organisations both because of their need to keep their activities secret and because of the importance that coercion often has in maintaining their activities. Knowing who is doing what is the key to control and furtive communications make this much more difficult to determine.

The problems that increase in size poses for effective control can be better understood by following the implications that organisational leadership requires an understanding of who is communicating with whom. The mathematical implications of this are that the more people involved the more of the organisational effort is required to monitor communication processes themselves. Consequently the less time and energy there is available for the directly 'productive' activities of the organisation.

Therefore, as criminal networks grow, the greater the possibility that 'maverick' offshoots will form that will not be strongly under the power of any 'boss'. These mid-level groups and chains of contacts may wish to bring the downfall of the central group or may be the source of new criminal activities. This proliferation and growth has particularly important policy implications for international law enforcement agencies as it can help them to predict the forms of growth that crime will take as well as providing them with strategic opportunities for intervention.

As organisations become more hierarchical, more of the decisions and information flow passes through central figures. This can be extremely demanding in terms of the time and intellectual resources needed to manage the activities. If there is no delegation then the central figures may lose real knowledge of what is going on in their organisation. If there is delegation their lieutenants become more powerful and able to form stronger subgroups that may challenge the leadership.

A further inevitable component that is the essence of any organisational structure is that the people who make it up will have different but related roles within the activities of the organisation. These roles may be fluid and each may carry out the full range of activities in which the group or network engages, but at any point in time the various tasks that the organisation needs to have done in order to achieve its objectives will have to be divided amongst its members. This process gives rise to differentiation within the organisation and often to the emergence of different groups and subgroups.

Such differentiation itself requires management and guidance. This may be achieved through group discussion and the emergence of a consensus but it often requires some direction from one or more individuals, in a word, leadership.

The notion of leadership, like that of motivation, is a complex and hotly debated one within the realms of organisational theory. The relevance of these debates for the consideration of criminal organisations lies in the attention they have drawn to the many different forms of leadership that any group, team or network requires. Leaders are not required merely to issue instructions. They are needed to devise plans, to obtain knowledge and information as well as to keep people participating in the organisation. Criminal groups, like noncriminal ones, are likely to have different people taking these different leadership roles. This has important implications for how such an organisation may be disabled. Removing the person who has the important information, or who coerces the other members to stay within the group, may be more effective than arresting the person who plans and gives instructions, who may be the most difficult to convict in court.

Reciprocal Anarchy as an Organisational Strategy

Although it can be shown that there is some structure and organisation to most criminal networks it must be remembered that these are often fleeting and casual contacts. As Van Duyne (1999), who spent many years investigating criminal networks, pointed out, even Mafia bosses are unlikely to have an organisational chart on their wall or to recognise structural issues such as those discussed in the present chapter. The clear management positions, strict chains of command and specific roles that would be expected of a legitimate organisation may have some presence in illegal groups but are unlikely ever to be as strong as they are in a National Health Service or Army. All of the pressures and vulnerabilities noted will lead to changes and from time to time collapse and reconstruction in response to the intervention of law enforcement and other changing demands. In general, criminal networks may be regarded as essentially anarchic but in reciprocal contact for the personal benefits of those involved.

It is this anarchic network quality of criminal organisations that makes them so difficult to investigate and destroy. As the IRA found, a strictly structured organisation can be readily understood, described and destroyed by removing crucial individuals. A fluid, flexible, opportunistic pattern of activities can be easily reconstructed if some of its members are removed. Further, no one person will know what a network does or how. Therefore obtaining clear intelligence on the network can be very difficult indeed.

Summary

Most criminals are part of one or more networks of offenders. These are typically loosely linked *ad hoc* groups that have casual contact with each other from time to time, but in some cases they can mirror the hierarchical structures and role assignments of legitimate organisations. These varieties of organisational structure are open to study by social network analysis to reveal important properties of how they operate, drawing attention to the existence of cliques or key individuals in the communication network, or the existence of isolated individuals. All of these aspects of illegal networks reveal potential vulnerabilities that can be targeted by law enforcement agencies in a strategy that may be thought of as 'destructive organisational psychology'.

Further Reading

Books

Abadinsky, H. (1983) *Criminal Elite – Professional and Organised Crime*, Greenwood Publishing Group, Westport.

Canter, D. and Alison, L. (2000) *The Social Psychology of Crime: Groups, Teams and Networks*, Ashgate, Dartmouth.

Hobbs, D. (1995) *Professional Criminals*, Ashgate, Dartmouth.

Knoke, D. and Yang, S. (2008) *Social Network Analysis (Quantitative Applications in the Social Sciences)*, Sage, London.

Levi, M. and Osofsky, L. (1995) *Investigating, Seizing and Confiscating the Proceeds of Crime*. Home Office, Police Research Group: Crime Detection and Prevention Series No. 61.

Wright, A. (2005) *Organised Crime*, Willan, Cullompton.

Articles

Hobbs, D. (1997) Criminal collaboration: youth gangs, subcultures, professional criminals, and organised crime, in *The Oxford Handbook of Criminology* (eds M. Maguire, R. Mogan and R. Reiner), Oxford University Press, Oxford.

Von Lampe, K. (2008) Organized crime in Europe: Conceptions and realities, *Policing: A Journal of Policy and Practice*, **2** (1), 7–17.

Questions for Discussion and Research

1. Consider any network of which you are a part and draw out its organisational structure

   (a) How easy was it to define who is in and who is outside that network?

   (b) How would you characterise the network's structure?

   (c) If for any reason that organisation were made illegal what problems would it face in trying to survive?

2. What problems are there in building up social network patterns from police surveillance? Consider:

   (a) Defining who is in and who is outside the network.

   (b) What the actual communication link implies.

   (c) Whether power only relates to position in the network

   (d) What different linking information may mean and how might you resolve differences in structure that emerge from different types of link – for example, who meets whom, who is related to whom, who speaks on the telephone to whom, who e-mails whom.

3. What difference might the Internet be making to the nature of criminal organisations and how they operate? (Cf. Sharp, 2009 and Computer Crime Research Center, www.crime-research.org/news/14.04.2004/211/, accessed 24 May 2009.)

CHAPTER 15

Terrorism

In This Chapter

Learning Objectives

When you have completed this chapter you should be able to:

1. Understand the variety of terrorist activities and terrorists.
2. Recognise the weaknesses in many explanations of terrorism.
3. Appreciate the value of social network analysis in representing terrorist networks.
4. Be aware of the developing nature of terrorist groups.
5. Discuss the difficulties of disengagement from terrorism.

Synopsis

The wide-ranging nature of terrorist activity, over time and place, makes it clear that terrorism is multifaceted and, as a consequence, no one explanation, theory or discipline will ever fully account for all terrorist activities. Despite the importance of a multidisciplinary perspective on politically or ideologically motivated acts against the state, consideration of the psychological and social psychological processes that lead any given person to commit a terrorist act are central importance.

Consideration of the actions of the individuals involved makes possible the understanding of terrorism as a process that people move through. This draws attention to the mechanisms by which people become engaged in these actions and a need to explore any ideological roots to their actions. The actual nature of their activities also needs to be understood. The particular case of suicidal acts calls for special attention because of the apparent challenges it presents to normal psychological processes of self-preservation.

Terrorism has many parallels with organised crime, with which it also often interacts. There is therefore value in considering the social networks that constitute terrorist groups. The details that have become public about major terrorist networks enable us to see their evolving nature. These illustrate some general principles of organisational development that point to crucial stages in the evolution of a network that have investigative implications.

Disengagement from terrorism is a further process to which attention is drawn when it is considered as a set of individuals involved in an unfolding activity. Part of the difficulty of disengaging is shaking off the social pressures that drew the person into terrorism initially.

The Great Variety of Terrorism

The outrage that the world saw in the destruction of the Twin Towers in New York on 11 September 2001 has become the iconic image of a terrorist attack but terrorist activities have been extremely varied, carried out by many different kinds of people. Those from many different religions, and of no religion, men and women, people under occupation in tyrannies and living freely in democracies, people who have clear objectives and who have vague objectives have participated in some form of terrorist activity.

Terrorism is not something new. Acts of violence with political objectives have always been with us. From the fight against Roman domination of Judea by Zealots in the first century, through the assassins – who were a breakaway faction of Shia Islam – in the thirteenth century, to the Fenians who challenged British rule in Ireland in the nineteenth century, and the anarchists at the beginning of the twentieth century, who contributed to the start of the Great War, and through their writing articulated the notion of 'the propaganda of the deed', there have always been groups who sought to have an impact on public opinion and the stability of governments through attacks on people or buildings that were seen as being of political or ideological significance. Indeed, possibly the most well-known terrorist attack was that associated with Guy Fawkes and his attempt to blow up the Houses of Parliament in 1605. If it had been successful it would have killed the king and most of the English aristocracy.

The historical range of violent political acts is matched by the range of organisations, individuals and groups that are willing to carry them out. Currently the United Nations recognises over 150 organisations around the world as 'terrorist', and the US State Department lists over 50 of them as being active. So the present-day popular assumption that acts of political and/or ideological violence are likely to be related to Islamic belief systems is far from being valid. Indeed, many books on terrorism written before 11 September 2001 made no mention of Islam or *jihad* at all.

The varied nature of terrorist groups is matched by the great variety of acts that they have carried out. Although flying aeroplanes into the Twin Towers on 9/11 is now the most well-known and notorious terrorist action, it is, fortunately, an extremely unusual form of terrorist behaviour. In the 1980s and 1990s kidnapping and the hijacking of airliners, holding the plane and the passengers hostage, were the most widely known forms of terrorism. The bombing campaigns of the IRA, ETA and other political groups were prevalent throughout the latter half of the twentieth century. Other insurgent groups, such as those supporting Sri Lankan independence, have focused on the assassination of key figures. In this regard they have overlapped with organised criminal groups, notably the Mafia, who have killed investigating magistrates.

All of this variety requires a rather different consideration of terrorists than was appropriate for the focus on particular types of crime in earlier chapters. We do need to get some overall summary of the different themes or styles of terrorist actions if at all possible, but this will be less relevant for inferring any characteristics of the people involved than for other criminal activity. The dominant questions revolve around whether these different forms of terrorism help us to understand how people find their way into terrorism. They are also particularly relevant for considering how to interact with individuals when they are engaged in terrorist events such as hijacking or hostage taking, with some indication of the likely outcome of those events.

Difficulties in Studying Terrorists

The study of terrorism is fraught with challenges and problems as listed in Table 15.1.

The first problem is being clear what terrorism is. Broadly speaking, most people agree that terrorism is a serious criminal act aimed at challenging a country and/or creating fear in its public. But there is no legal definition of what it is on which all jurisdictions concur. This is

Table 15.1 Summary of difficulties of psychological studies of terrorism.

1. Defining who is a 'terrorist'
2. Gaining access to terrorists is difficult and time consuming
3. Those available are likely to have 'failed' in some way so unlikely to be representative
4. Accounts of what terrorist say may be just propaganda
5. Confidential security service interviews unlikely to be made public
6. Terrorist groups likely to be very different from each other

in part because it is crime defined very much in terms of its objectives rather than the nature of the actions involved.

Away from these important definitional problems there are serious challenges to uncovering the truth about those who can be identified, by any definition, as terrorists (see Table 15.1). These challenges are somewhat paradoxical in that a major purpose of any terrorist act is to draw attention to the cause and mission of those who perpetrate it. So there is much public attention drawn to these actions and eventually those who are caught for terrorism are subjected to considerable public scrutiny in court and the mass media. However, the only people available for interview, if access can be gained to them, are those who have been detected or captured, frequently through failure to achieve their goals.

Even if access can be gained to these people, what they tell the security services is unlikely to be made public and what they tell the few researchers who have gained access (for example, Merari, 1990; Soibelman, 2004) is likely to be distorted by their own views of their failure and the current incarceration in which they find themselves. However, as Speckhard (2006) shows from her interviews with the families and associates of Chechen suicide bombers, it is important to attempt to gain some understanding of the social and psychological processes involved in these outrages even if there is inevitable bias in the information obtained.

It is also important to point out, as Horgan (2004) does in some detail, that gaining access to people involved in or associated with any form of terrorism may be dangerous and is often a lengthy, drawn-out process. This is one of the reasons why public understanding of terrorists is often so misinformed, making it prey to the political distortions that Danis and Stohl (2009) explore.

Statements made by terrorists, notably those by suicide bombers recorded for broadcast after their death, suffer from similar difficulties. Merari (1990) suggests that the preparation of such a statement is part of the process by which the bomber is tied into the intended act. These 'testaments' are fundamentally propagandist, expressing the received viewpoints of the ideologies which the footsoldiers are following. It is difficult to know from these sources whether the views expressed really do capture the personal perspectives of the individuals carrying out the acts. A clear example is the tape-recording of Mohammad Sidique Khan (2005), one of the 7/7 London bombers, which has been widely broadcast. This is clearly a paraphrasing of the writings of Osama bin Laden and his apologists. It would be expected that such statements would claim international significance and grand motivations for the suicidal act rather than belittling it by reference to personal frustrations or individual experiences.

We must also be careful about generalising from what is known about the psychology of one set of terrorists to all others. Most information comes from very limited sources, typically the IRA or Palestinian terrorists. The changing world scene and evolving social processes, together with the changing opportunities for acts of political violence, also mean that there is unlikely to be one psychology of the terrorist applicable to all places and all times.

Certainly, this is an area of IP for which the search for 'profiles' of a terrorist is of least value. Any such profiles that have been attempted are rather diffuse and of little value in helping to identify individuals. The social and cultural processes turn out to be of much more value in understanding what gives rise to these actions. They are attempts to change social processes and as such are essentially dominated by what we have called 'adaptive' or 'conservative' modes of a criminal 'actions system', dominated by personal narratives of heroic missions and revenge for mistreatment and exploitation in the past.

Box 15.1 Is This an Acceptable Definition of What Constitutes a Terrorist Act?

Consider the 1605 'gunpowder plot' associated with Guy Fawkes. Was that a terrorist plot within this definition drawn from Richardson (2006)? She chose to define terrorism in terms of seven characteristics that any act must have in order to attract that label. The seven crucial characteristics for terrorism from Richardson (2006) are:

1. Politically inspired
2. Violent or threatens violence
3. Communicates a message
4. Act and victim symbolically significant
5. Carried out by substate groups
6. Victim is different from the audience
7. Deliberate targeting of civilians

A Moving Target

In considering the forms of terrorist actions in general a useful starting point is how these actions relate to the opportunities readily available. All crimes evolve and modify in relation to law enforcement and changing opportunities, but this is particularly noticeable for terrorist actions. A consideration of the recorded frequency of terrorist hostage taking and hijacking over the quarter century from the mid 1960s (Wilson, Canter and Smith, 1995) shows how much terrorist acts may vary in relation to the opportunities. Figure 15.1 shows that the frequencies reveal a remarkably regular series of peaks at five-year intervals starting in 1970. The most obvious explanation for this is that it takes the authorities about two-and-a-half years to reduce the opportunities for these sorts of crimes by increasing security and it then takes terrorist groups a further two-and-a-half years to find ways around these new precautions until eventually it is so difficult for them to overcome the safety measures that they change to other forms of action.

The implication of this is that an understanding of the variety of terrorist actions cannot be based simply on the terrorist events that have occurred overall, as was our approach to other crimes. The nature of the event will have a lot to do with the combination of the resources available to the groups and the security controls in place. We have to find a way to a more fundamental structure behind terrorists' actions.

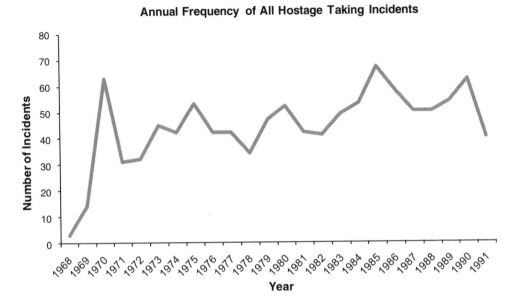

Figure 15.1 Frequency of hostage-taking incidents.

Modes of Terrorism

By their nature, all terrorist acts are an attempt to modify the political or ideological context in which they are operating. But these attempts, as we have seen with all other criminal behaviour, can be dominated by different modes of transaction. We would expect to find these differences in any set of terrorist actions. The actions need to be explored, though, in the context of the particular form of offending otherwise it will be quite confusing to identify the underlying variations. For example, including a bombing campaign within the same exploration as political kidnapping and the assassination of significant authority figures would make the comparison of detailed actions extremely difficult, although research comparing the broad strategies of different terrorist groups could be productive.

If we look at actions in one type of terrorist event, a picture does emerge of the general variations between terrorist actions that offer some possibility of generalisation to other forms of political violence. A study carried out in 1991 by Wilson and Canter for the US army looked at the behaviour of 30 aerial hijackers operating between 1968 and 1979. They worked with reports in the public domain, but drawn heavily from the ITERATE database (Mickolus, 1980), they drew out 29 variables and carried out an SSA (Figure 15.2).

SSA of Hijack Actions

Interestingly in this configuration the high frequency variables are the presence of guns and grenades. It is probably difficult to remember how easy it was to board an aeroplane in the 1970s and how long it took the authorities to make it almost impossible to hijack a commercial

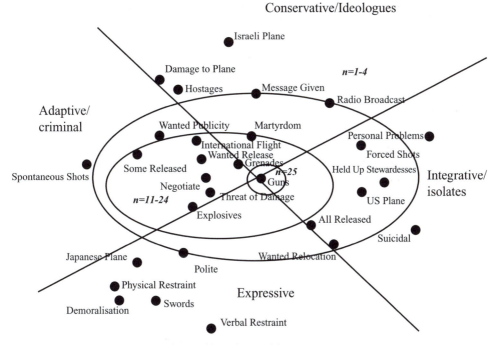

Figure 15.2 Smallest space analysis of hijack variables.

Source: Wilson, M. and Canter, D. (1991) Terrorism: multivariate analysis of hijack attacks. Internal report, Centre for Investigative Psychology, University of Surrey.

airliner in this way. As we move outward from this central control of international flights, on the plot, the differences in the style of the hijack are revealed more clearly.

To the right of the SSA configuration are those individuals who have personal problems, often indicating that they are suicidal. They are operating in an integrative mode like the isolates we identified in criminal groups. It is probably inappropriate to regard these people as terrorists in any strong sense.

To left of the plot are those terrorist groups who are willing to negotiate and may have released some of those on board the flight. They fit our adaptive mode of action, having objectives that are obviously related to publicity. Interestingly these hijackers are likely to have access to explosives and thus possibly to be more embedded within criminal groups.

At the bottom of the plot are the more expressive hijackings that seem to have been typical of Japanese hijackers in this era. The variable 'demoralisation' refers to any actions that the hijackers make to demoralise the passengers and crew, such as preventing them from sleeping. The hijackers are seeking to make the people with whom they are in contact aware of their presence without too clear a focus on the purpose of their actions.

In contrast to the variables at the bottom of the plot are those at the top in which Israeli planes are typically involved. Here a clear message is given and they may well use the aeroplane's radio system to communicate with those outside or to pass messages on to others. These are the people very willing to die for their cause.

The partitioning of this configuration thus draws attention to four broad styles of event which have a recognisable relationship to styles identified in earlier chapters. This should perhaps not be so surprising because the actions being drawn upon do of course have many criminal components. They serve to illustrate that terrorism is not a totally distinct enterprise from all the others we have been considering in this book.

The frequencies on the configuration show a bias towards the more professional adaptive variables. This is to be expected as the organisation involved in taking over a flight implies some sort of planned determination. However, interesting as this analysis is, it is based on a small, unusual sample. It serves more to illustrate what is possible than to provide a definitive account of styles of aerial hijacking.

Explanations for Terrorism

It is tempting to deal with terrorism entirely in terms of political science and social history but while these perspectives have much to contribute they still leave room for more fundamentally psychological approaches. These approaches need, first, to clear away some of the common assumptions about the causes of terrorism and the nature of terrorists.

Is Deprivation a Direct Cause of Terrorism?

In his review of the psychological causes of terrorism, Moghaddam (2005) makes clear that 'material factors such as poverty and lack of education are problematic as explanations of terrorist acts'. He quotes Coogan's (2002) account of the IRA as giving no support to the view 'that they are mindless hooligans drawn from the unemployed and unemployable'. The Singapore Ministry of Home Affairs reported in 2003 that captured Al Qaeda terrorists were not typically from impoverished backgrounds and had reasonable levels of education. Indeed accounts of the people who carried out the 9/11 attacks on New York and Washington showed that they did not come out of refugee camps, ignorant and lacking education (Bodansky, 2001). So a simple-minded analysis proposing that acts of terrorism are the first stages of a people's revolution, being the actions of a downtrodden proletariat that has no other means of bettering its lot, does not have much empirical support.

A slightly more sophisticated argument would be that although an individual has some material comfort, if they live within a repressive regime the deprivation of their liberty is the source of their terrorist zeal. This view is also difficult to support from the facts. As Youngs (2006) makes clear in his analysis of the influence of political repression on the prevalence of terrorism, there is little correlation between relative degrees of political repression and 'radicalism'. He compares various Middle Eastern countries, India and China and the source of revolution in other areas of the world to show that, if anything, repressive regimes serve to keep terrorist activity under control and that those who wish to attack civilians benefit from the freedoms associated with democracy.

Mental Illness and Suicide Bombing

The psychological explanation of suicide bombing is particularly difficult to fathom. It seems to go against all notions of self-preservation unless the person was out of contact with reality. As a consequence, one common view about the psychology of suicide bombers is that they must be 'mad' in some sense of being severely mentally disturbed. However, consideration of the July 2005 bombings in London makes clear that the perpetrators could not have been insane in the usual sense of out of contact with reality, drugged or even highly trained fanatics. The New York aeroplane hijackers similarly indicated a determination and coolness of purpose that is not compatible with a psychosis or other extreme form of mental illness. This accords with the reviews of both Silke (2003) and Moghaddam (2005), who demonstrate that there is no evidence at all that suicide bombers are overtly mentally disturbed.

The five failed Palestinian suicide bombers that Soibelman (2004) had interviewed showed no signs of mental illness and were able to discuss many matters with their interviewers in an apparently rational way. But then, the incidence of overt mental illness in another homicidal group that challenges our understanding of sanity, serial killers, appears to be no greater than in the population at large, such that it is very rare indeed for insanity to be used as a defence (Hickey, 2005). Neither are those possibly more bizarre acts of spree killing, in which a number of people are killed in one onslaught, as in the Columbine School shootings in 1999, or in Hungerford in 1987, or Dunblane in 1996, committed by people with any obvious psychotic illness (Canter, 1995). With hindsight, their acquaintances may claim they were strange people who did not relate well to others but people with diagnosed mental illnesses are far more likely to hurt themselves rather than anyone else.

Far from being disturbed, there is some evidence that those recruiting people to commit these atrocities go to some pains to exclude people who may be mentally unstable. Merari (1990) claims that only a minority of all those who volunteer to be suicide bombers are selected to do so. This is understandable in military terms. A person who was mentally unstable could not be relied upon to focus and follow through with the desired objective and so would weaken the whole operation and put disclosure of its methods at risk.

Brainwashing?

The graphic metaphor for clearing a person of previously held beliefs, washing their brains, in order to insert some alien set of perspectives, has become a further explanation of how people could turn from reasonably well adjusted citizens to violent terrorists. This perspective puts people such as Osama bin Laden and the Hamas leader Sheikh Yassin in roles that have only ever been demonstrated clearly in George Du Maurier's fictional story of the control of the opera singer Trilby by the manipulative Svengali. Many other studies show that in real life it is difficult to demonstrate the possibility of such quasi-occult powers (cf. Heap and Kirsch, 2006, for a review of these issues).

This view of the influence of terrorist leaders also implies a very strong hierarchy, very similar indeed to what would be expected in a rigid military structure. In general, however, as with all illegal groups (Canter and Alison, 2000), especially those spread over a wide geography, it is not possible to maintain the top-down discipline that is *de rigueur* for a standing army.

Instead, what Atran (2004) calls a 'hydra-headed network' is much more likely to be the norm. The evolving structure of such networks is well illustrated by Mullins (2009), and how they can develop into something not far from a business when they involve frequent kidnap activities, is described by Phillips (2009).

In a detailed study of the Al Qaeda network, Sageman (2004) shows just how complex and self-generating terrorist networks can be. These loose networks come about partly because illegal organisations face such challenges to preserving the identification and communication processes that are crucial for the effectiveness of legitimate ones, as discussed in the previous chapter. The indications are that they survive by encouraging and supporting small, independent groups, over which they have very little direct control (Altran, 2004). But this requires that the groups are very much self-defined and self-motivated, rather than being fiercely manipulated by some charismatic leader. In his most recent review, Sageman (2008) takes this a step further and claims that Islamic Jihad is currently, in effect, leaderless.

One important implication of this mechanism of autonomous, self-generating groups as a mechanism for carrying out terrorism is that it can be traced at least to the writings of nineteenth-century anarchists such as Michael Bakunin (cf. Anarchist Archives, 2006) who saw revolution emerging out of spontaneous secret societies who combine together to overthrow the status quo. The intelligentsia were to articulate the disquiet and aspirations of the masses who would then find their own ways into revolution.

Terrorism as Process

In his earlier writing Horgan (2005) had developed the important argument that terrorism is not an act but a process of which a person is a part. Moghaddam's (2005) 'staircase' model of terrorism makes a similar point – a person enters into and becomes part of an ever more involving commitment to violence for political or ideological ends. The framework for this is a mixture of, firstly, recognition that the group with which the terrorist identifies is distinct from and threatened by some other external group and, secondly, that there are culturally remembered or experienced causes of grievance that are nursed by the group to which the terrorist belongs. Ross (2009) reviews the power of these grievances by examining three very different terrorist groups in different parts of the world. He emphasises in particular the roles these grievances play in keeping the group in existence over many years. The grievances become part of the terrorist narrative, which fuels its antagonism. It is not the deprivation or other degrading experiences themselves that are seen as central cause of acts of violence, but the embedding of these in a narrative of victimisation or tragedy.

The Evolution of Terrorist Networks

Organisational and economic processes become an integral part of the survival of terrorist activities leading to an overlap with organised crime. This is particularly true of terrorist groups for whom frequent kidnapping can become a major part of their activities, as Phillips (2009) shows. The requirements of kidnapping lead to the need for many features that would be recognised in any business, although 'warehousing' and 'selling on' take more chilling meanings than in the conventional world of commerce. A particularly important consequence of this is that once such a 'business model' is in place it can have a self-sustaining quality that may mask the original ideological or political intentions. The development of individualist, conservative groups driven by ideologies, as discussed in the previous chapter when examining styles of criminal organisation, can mutate into more structured organised groups whose main task is to survive.

This process draws attention to the fact that terrorists and their networks are no more stable than any other human communication network and are likely to be very volatile. There is therefore value in gaining a better understanding of how they develop and change. Yet, as mentioned earlier, it is often difficult to obtain enough detailed information to build up an effective picture. However, recent terrorist plots have been of such international significance and have been so carefully investigated that a great deal of information about them is emerging. This has been put together by government commissions and is also available through reports of court proceedings in enough detail to allow of careful analysis (Sageman, 2004, 2008).

Drawing on this material, Mullins (2008, 2009) has mapped out the development of the social networks that reflect the group processes involved. In particular he has focused on the foiled 'millennial plot' to bomb Los Angeles International Airport in late December 1999 as well as the 9/11 attack on the Twin Towers. He shows that there were some interesting and important differences between these two groups.

Mullins (2009) points out that the millennial group was primarily criminal. They could be seen as Adventurer 'professionals'. Their commitment to the attack grew out of involvement with a person who had been in terrorist training in Afghanistan. It seems to have been the excitement engendered by the involvement in the group activity that spurred them on.

By contrast the 9/11 group emerged out of religious, ideological commitment. Their activities related directly to the desire to express their anger, to carry through their 'quest' of making an impact on what they saw as their enemy, not unlike the violent offenders we considered in Chapter 13. But in both cases these narratives were shared and evolved through an unfolding development of contacts.

Developing Social Networks

In considering what is known about Islamic terrorist networks Mullins (2009) points out that the importance of social settings such as mosques, youth clubs and gyms has been recognised, for instance in the Report of the Official Account of the Bombings in London on 7 July 2005 (Murphy, 2006). Murphy makes clear that 'Mentors may first identify individuals from within larger groups who may be susceptible to radicalisation; then "groom" them privately in small groups until individuals begin feeding off each other's radicalisation' (Murphy, 2006: 31). Or, as Sageman, (2004) puts it, social bonds precede ideological commitment. As we saw in the previous chapter with organised crime in general, the process of becoming a terrorist derives from spontaneous group interaction with one's peers (Kirby, 2007). Therefore, changes in the structure of terrorist networks are to be expected as these informal groups begin to focus on their destructive goals.

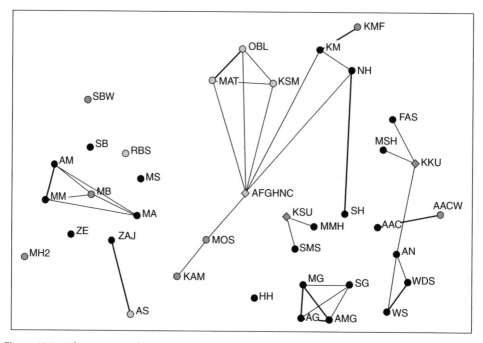

Figure 15.3 The pattern of contacts between the 9/11 terrorist group in early 1996.

Source: We are grateful to Sam Mullins for collecting the data and conducting these statistical analyses.

Mullins (2006, 2009) explored these developments by examining the social networks apparent from various published sources using Ucinet (Borgatti, Everett and Freeman, 2002). In his study of the 9/11 hijackers Mullins reports that, of the nineteen people eventually involved in the attacks in the United States, three came from a group of eight friends based in Hamburg centring around a local community mosque. Most of this Hamburg group of friends had recently migrated to Germany to attend university. Figure 15.3 shows the relatively loose worldwide network of contacts that existed early in this process.

As Mullins (2009: 42) puts it:

> newcomers joined individually and were introduced to the rest of the group, maintaining a full-clique structure but with internal alliances, as particular members shared different levels of similarity and each individual's relationship to the rest of the group was more or less unique.

These processes further increased the group size leading to further elaboration of the contacts and structuring of the network during 1999, as shown in Figure 15.4.

As the group developed role differentiation occurred and the group divided in preparation for action. Some group members made a trip to Afghanistan where they were chosen for 'The Planes Operation' (The 9/11 Commission Report). Mullins (2009: 43) makes the interesting point that: 'although this initial division may have been simply for practical reasons, it was the beginning of a permanent rift, including between the group and their original mentor.'

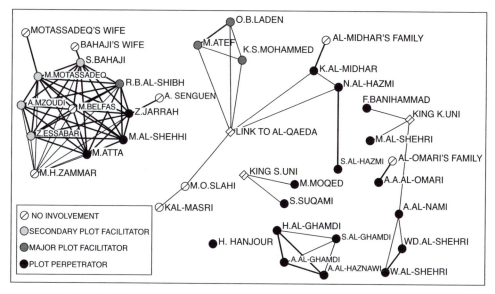

Figure 15.4 Late 1998/early 1999: the Hamburg group (left side of plot) has developed into an extremely cohesive singular unit, committed to violent jihad. Despite this overall cohesion there are still important internal alliances.

Source: Mullins (2008).

The ties within the group that apparently became stronger as the whole network became more segmented did not totally isolate the members from all outside contacts. It is reported that several of the 11 September hijackers requested to contact family in the days leading up to the attack (The 9/11 Commission Report, p. 245) even though they were committed to killing themselves.

Part of the network that emerged for the 9/11 attacks had rather different origins from the 'Hamburg' group, starting their involvement in Saudi Arabia. Rather less is known about this group, but it is clear that by early 2001 they had become a very distinct subset within the overall network as shown in Figure 15.5.

The common commitment to the ultimate attacks enabled the whole network to operate in collusion even though by the time of the attacks they had formed very distinct and relatively independent sub-groups.

The social network diagrams show graphically the way in which these networks form and develop and change. However, they also draw attention to the way in which committed groups, especially those set on a destructive group mission, typically have strong sets of interconnections. This group cohesion helps to strengthen their individual and social identity, providing fertile ground for the building up of their personal narratives.

Disengagement

The developmental perspective on terrorism also throws light on the real possibility of people moving out of these networks and disengaging from terrorist activities. But the intricacies of

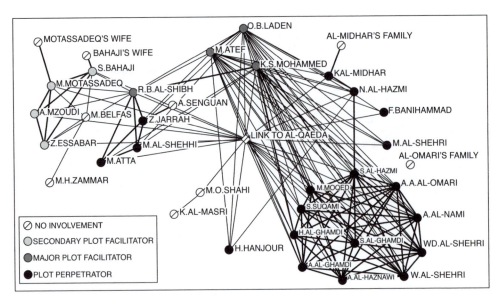

Figure 15.5 Summer 2000 – early 2001.

Source: Mullins (2008).

A permanent rift has set in amongst the Hamburg group as Atta, al-Shehhi and Jarrah train in the US, with bin al-Shibh acting as a vital liaison. Particular friendships are also important within the Saudi group, (right side of plot), and for most, external family ties are severed.

the social processes in which any terrorist is embedded make this especially difficult. Both Horgan (2009) and Moghaddam (2009) have explored the difficulties of disengagement for people whose whole life and subculture have embraced terrorism. In their different ways these two experts show that the problems of disengagement are integrally linked with the processes that lead people into terrorism initially. These can be the bonds of family and kinship, which do emerge as relevant in many terrorist groups (see, for example, Kassimeris' 2009 case study of the Greek N17 terrorist group). As Moghaddam (2009) expresses it, these are people already well up a staircase and so have a long way to get down.

Summary

Terrorism may seem to be a curious form of criminal activity because it is apparently driven by ideological commitment and is defined in terms of its objectives rather than the actions that occur. This makes it a complex mix of activities that can take many different forms. However, it has been possible to demonstrate that, underlying these varieties, many of the processes found in other areas of criminal activity can be discerned. This includes the different modes of action systems as well as the group structures and social network processes that are helpful in understanding organised crime.

However, the prevalence of public accounts of terrorist acts makes it possible to discern, possibly more clearly than with other forms of criminality, that what terrorists do relates very strongly to the opportunities available. The study of terrorism therefore emphasises the dynamic nature of criminal activity and the ways in which it interacts with the social and cultural environment of which it is a part.

The lack of any obvious distinguishing characteristics of terrorists makes the investigative strategies for identifying them exceedingly difficult if the focus is on individual terrorists. However, because people find their way into terrorism through personal contacts and the evolving networks of terrorists, which are crucial for their survival, strategies for keeping people from being radicalised need to connect with the patterns of personal contacts and social networks. Notably investigative strategies have been found to be most productive when they deal directly with the communication and social networks that sustain people's involvement and preparation for acts of political violence. The understanding of these networks and how to disable them is therefore a crucial contribution of IP to the study and investigation of terrorism.

Further Reading

Books

Canter, D. (ed.) (2009) *The Faces of Terrorism: Cross-Disciplinary Explorations*, John Wiley & Sons, Ltd, Chichester.

Horgan, J. (2005) *The Psychology of Terrorism*, Routledge, London.

Razzaque, R. (2008) *Human Being to Human Bomb*, Icon Books, Cambridge.

Sageman, M. (2008) *Leaderless Jihad: Terror Networks in the Twenty-First Century*, University of Pennsylvania Press, Philadelphia, PA.

Articles

Moghaddam, F.M. (2005) The staircase to terrorism: a psychological exploration. *American Psychologist*, **60** (2), 161–9.

Sarangi, S. and Alison, L. (2005) Life story accounts of left-wing terrorists in India. *Journal of Investigative Psychology and Offender Profiling*, **2**, 69–86.

Soibelman, M. (2004) Palestinian suicide bombers. *Journal of Offender Profiling and Investigative Psychology*, **1** (3), 175–90.

Questions for Discussion and Research

1. Is it appropriate to have a special chapter on 'terrorism', or should the offences of violent politically oriented individuals be treated as part of discussions of criminality in earlier chapters?

2. From newspaper reports, Internet searches and consideration of books on terrorism, build up a picture of the sorts of terrorist acts that have been perpetrated by different terrorist groups. What does this tell you about the nature of these groups?

3. How far can we trust published accounts of what terrorists are trying to achieve?

4. What is the difference between terrorists and organised criminals?

5. How do you think terrorism in the twenty-first century has changed from previous centuries?

CHAPTER 16

Investigative Psychology in Action

In This Chapter

Learning Objectives

When you have completed this chapter you should be able to:

1. Understand the ways in which IP can help the police with their enquiries.
2. Evaluate the ways in which the quality of investigative information can be assessed and improved.
3. Outline some of the ways in which IP offers support for effective investigative decision-making.
4. Be able to outline and discuss some of the emerging areas of IP.
5. Understand the six fundamentals of the IP approach to research.
6. Appreciate the wider reaches of IP and the range of areas to which it can be applied.

Synopsis

The major ways in which IP can and is contributing to police investigations are reviewed to summarise previous chapters. This emphasises, first, the value of systematising and presenting visualisations of investigative information and secondly the development of decision support systems that can be an integrated aspect of police activities. Two areas in particular are proving fruitful for such decision support: geographical offender profiling and the linking of cases to a common offender. Both of these will benefit from an increasing amalgamation of spatio-temporal and behavioural information as has been attempted in recent investigative decision support systems.

It has been demonstrated throughout this book that IP is relevant to the full range of offence activity. Some areas that were not reviewed in this book due to lack of space are briefly mentioned: crimes in which written text is a crucial component, equivocal deaths and missing persons. However, what all these considerations reveal is that IP is an approach to real-world problem solving and is thus not solely limited to criminal investigations. It is a valuable approach to any enquiry that has a psychological focus. The six primary tenets of IP are therefore outlined as well as a note of the broader reaches for which it is a relevant and powerful approach to changing the world.

Helping the Police with their Enquiries

Under British law it is very important that there is no hint that a person is assumed to be guilty until the court has issued a verdict. Therefore when a suspect is arrested it is crucial that the police do not indicate that they believe that person to be guilty. As a consequence a form of words was developed that has been widely used whereby, when a suspect was arrested, if the police were asked why he had been taken in for questioning the police would merely say 'he is helping us with our enquiries'. Because of its wide use this turn of phrase now has an

Table 16.1   Relating investigators' questions with psychological input.

Investigators' question	Informed by psychologists' understanding of ...
What type of crime is this?	The differentiation of criminal action
What are the likely characteristics of the sort of individual who might commit a crime such as this?	Investigative inferences
Which of the possible suspects are most likely to have committed the crime?	Investigative inferences
Where is the offender most likely to live in relation to the crime?	Geographical offender profiling
Which other crimes are likely to have been committed by the same perpetrator(s)?	The consistency of criminal action
Are the decisions made during the investigation free from distortion and bias?	Decision-making under stress/ cognitive load
Have the lines of enquiry pursued been determined systematically?	Decision support tools
Can we get the witness to remember more?	How to interview a witness
Can we tell if a suspect is lying?	The detection of deception
Can we tell who wrote something?	Forensic psycholinguistics
Did this crime really happen?	False allegations
Did this person really do the crime they say they did?	False confessions

almost paradoxical meaning but it does show the awareness that a police investigation is an 'enquiry' to which many contributions can be made. It is therefore a useful umbrella under which to summarise the contributions of IP.

As we have seen throughout this book, IP integrates the questions that need to be answered in any investigation with the psychological issues and associated answers that are related to those questions. These are summarised in Table 16.1.

From these broad areas of study, psychologists are increasingly able to formulate answers to, or approaches to answering, a number of the specific questions faced during various stages of an investigation. These contributions are emerging out of the growing number of studies that relate actions to characteristics (the metaphorical $\mathbf{A} \rightarrow \mathbf{C}$ equations). A summary of the emerging results from a few such studies are given in Table 16.2.

Assessment and Improvement of Investigative Information

One of the major classes of contributions psychologists can make to investigations concerns the evaluation and enhancement of the information detectives rely upon to advance their enquiries. This information can be evaluated against the same scientific principles that psychologists would use to evaluate their data in a research study. More particularly psychological research on distortions in recall, whether from normal psychological memory deficiencies or

Table 16.2 Summaries of some studies that demonstrate links between crime scene actions and offender characteristics.

A–C studies	A→C findings
Davies, Wittebrood and Jackson (1997) 210 solved stranger rape cases – logistic regression	85% of stranger rapists have criminal records, which usually contain a mixture of crime types. • If precautions taken to avoid leaving *fingerprints* then a rapist was approximately four times more likely to be a burglar than those who took no such precautions. The latter were approximately three times more likely to be a one-off sexual offender. • The best sign that a rapist had a prior conviction for a sexual offence was *semen destruction*, individuals engaging in this behaviour being approximately four times more likely to have prior convictions for sexual offences than those who did not. • In the absence of *sighting precautions* a rapist was approximately three times more likely to be a *one-off* offender than one who took such precautions. • If a rapist did not take *departure precautions*, then he was nearly three times as likely to be a *one-off* offender and about twice as likely to have prior convictions for drug-related offences as a rapist who was concerned about getting away safely. • Another indication of prior drug-related offences was *theft from the victim.* • If a rapist exhibited the behaviour *reference to the police* he was approximately four times more likely to have been in custody, five-and-a-half times more likely to have a conviction and two-and-a-half times more likely to have a conviction for violence than one who did not. • *Theft from victim* indicated that a rapist was approximately four times more likely to have prior convictions for burglary, and also more likely to have prior convictions for property crime in general or drug-related crime, or to have prior convictions, or have been awarded a custodial sentence, than one who did not. • *Forced entry*, indicated he was over five times more likely to have prior convictions for burglary than one who did not. • Striking the victim two or more times indicated that a rapist was over three times more likely to have prior convictions for violent offences than one who did not. • A *confidence approach* indicated that he was approximately two-and-a-half times more likely to be a *one off* sexual offender, suggesting that serial rapists are more likely to use the surprise approach.
Häkkänen, Lindlöf and Santtila (2004): 100 stranger rapes – correlation	The action theme 'theft' correlated significantly with the characteristics 'criminal/property'.

Table 16.2   *(Continued)*

A–C studies	A→C findings
Knight *et al.* (1998: 46) 116 repeat rapists, 25 serial rapists both from the BSU of the FBI academy, and 254 rapists from the MTC	'Promising predictive results in the domains of adult antisocial and expressive aggression. In addition, the domains of sadism, offense planning and relation with victim showed high internal consistency and good to high cross-crime consistency, suggesting that predictive scales are possible for these domains.'
Kocsis, Cooksey and Irwin (2002) 62 sexual assault cases from Australia – MDS	• Offenders exhibiting a *brutality pattern* tend to be relatively older, have scars and a criminal record and are typically in some form of conjugal relationship. These offenders tend not to collect souvenirs from the crime and typically do not confess to their activities. • The *impulsive and violent offence* style is of young offenders who are unlikely to have any identifiable features or social patterns that come with age (scars, tattoos, a partner). This chaotic pattern seems to represent the actions of a young opportunistic offender who haphazardly embarks on some form of larceny and sexual assault.
Ressler, Burgess and Douglas (1988) – 36 incarcerated murderers – no inferential statistics	Report proposes that offenders exhibiting a particular behavioural theme at the crime scene (i.e. organised or disorganised) are likely to exhibit the same theme in their background.
Salfati and Canter (1999) 82 British single offender single victim solved stranger homicide cases – MDS	• Those with an *Impulsive theme* had previous impulsive offenses, such as sexual offenses, violent offenses and offenses against public order. • The *opportunistic* type of homicide had previous convictions for theft and burglary, being unemployed. They usually know the victim and live close to the crime scene. • The *cognitive theme* related to having served in a professional army and prior prison sentence.
Santtila, Junkkila, and Sandnabba (2005) – 43 serial stranger rape cases – correlations	• Involvement (expressive) offenders were found to reside in the locality where the crime took place. • Involvement (deceptive) offenders were unemployed and likely to have alcohol problems.
Santtila, Häkkänen, Alison and Whyte (2003) 61 male and five female juvenile firesetters (aged 6–17 years) – MDS	• *Expressive–person* tended not to be living with their parents at the time of the offence, being female, and having a diagnosis of depression and a personality or conduct disorder, not having come to the attention of the police and being institutionalised, negative association with a previous conviction for theft. • *Instrumental–person* had a criminal record, specifically for criminal damage and arson. • *Expressive–object* not living with their parents, being institutionalised, had set fires previously, diagnosis of personality disorder, negatively related to a conviction for criminal damage. • *Instrumental–object* indicative of juveniles who tend to offend in groups, more likely to be males living with their parents with cautions by the police as well as previous convictions for theft, burglary and criminal damage.

(Continued)

Table 16.2 (*Continued*)

A–C studies	A→C findings
Santtila, Häkkänen, Canter and Elfgren (2003) – 502 homicides set of single-offender/single-victim Finnish homicides – MDS	• *Instrumental crime scene* (including moving and hiding the body) were associated with instrumental background characteristics and not surrendering immediately to the police and resisting owning up to the crime in police interviews. • *Expressive crime scene* themes were associated with expressive background characteristics, unlikely to deny involvement, for male offenders prior relationship between offender and victim. For female offenders tended to be blood relations of their victims and have psychiatric problems and possible difficulties in long-term relationships. • The general pattern of offender background characteristics bore substantial similarities to Salfati's (2000) findings. The typical homicidal offender was a man who killed a person he knew, in familiar surroundings. He was also likely to lead a socio-economically deprived life.
Youngs (2004) 207 young offenders self-reported offending patterns – MDS	• Overall variations in offence style related more clearly to the 'FIRO' personality scale aspects of interpersonal Control than to interpersonal elements of Inclusion or Openness. • *Property offences*, especially acts of vandalism, tended to be committed by individuals who reported higher levels of control from others (received control) than did person offences. • *Expressive person style* crimes, typically behaviours incorporating violence, or threats thereof, especially where a weapon was involved, reported higher levels of the need for power and dominance (expressed control) in their interpersonal relationships. • Expressive property crimes tended to be individuals for whom other people were felt to be more emotionally open and intimate (received openness) than other offenders.

deliberate attempts at deception, can be applied to assess and offer ways to improve the material the police have (as discussed in Chapters 9 and 10).

In relation to investigative information, psychologists will be concerned with improvements on two components of the scientific data. One of these is the usefulness and detail of the material. The second is its accuracy or validity.

The Usefulness and Detail of the Data

Psychologists can help increase the amount of relevant information that can be drawn out in an investigation by developing processes, especially for police interviews with witnesses or victims, which maximise the information obtained. A number of guidelines for interviews have been developed as discussed in Chapter 9. The best known of these is the 'cognitive interview' developed by Geiselman *et al.* (1985, 1986) but because it has its roots in a strongly experimental, cognitive psychology tradition it has been enriched with other procedures that draw more heavily on interpersonal processes (for example, Shepherd, 2007). Investigative hypnosis has also been used to improve recall of information. However, rather than being a 'special' technique, many experts argue that hypnosis is simply a more intensive form of cognitive interview in which the respondent is helped to relax and concentrate (Wagstaff, 1982).

In an investigation, it is important that the information is operationally useful. Canter (1993) notes that this is a criterion against which 'offender profilers' have often neglected to evaluate the advice they have given to police. An indication of the broad location where an offender could be living is a clear example of information that is useful to an investigator but more subtle material such as how others may regard the offender or his/her likely skills and domestic circumstances may also be of value. On the other hand, as has been noted throughout this book, intensive psychodynamic interpretations of the offender's motivations, that might only become available during in-depth therapeutic interviews, are less likely to be of direct assistance to police investigators.

It is useful to be reminded, as explored in Chapters 9 and 10, that much information comes to the police from talking to people – interviews. But these take many different forms depending on the role of the interviewee in the whole criminal event, witness, victim or suspect. There is also the real possibility that people move between these roles during the course of the investigation. This means that the interviewing skills of investigators have to be subtle and flexible. Police forces are beginning to recognise this but there is still a long way to go as Williamson (2006) discusses.

Decision Support Systems

Throughout this book we have seen the complexity of the police task; the large amount of information that has to be sifted and the difficulties of making effective sense of it. Recognition of these problems is leading to the development of decision support tools that reduce the complexity of the information that needs to be understood and facilitate empirical analyses that can inform the decisions that investigators must make.

It is worth distinguishing between 'expert systems', which were very popular in the 1980s and 1990s but probably owed more to science fiction than science fact, and 'decision support tools'. The former make the decisions as if they were the expert whereas the latter distil and digest the information available and may also do some analysis on it to present investigators with the material in a form that will assist them in making decisions.

The support procedures that are emerging do still need some interpretation from those who know how they work. This has meant that some progressive police forces have set up their own IP units to provide assistance to the police across a range of areas. Boxes 16.1 and 16.2 give the official accounts of these units from the innovative Israeli National Police and the South African Police Service.

The Values of Visualisation

Many decision support tools are based on the fact that human beings can often see patterns between associations and within activities if they can be presented in some visual summary.

Bar charts of frequencies are one common example of this but commercially available software will chart networks of contacts and other sequences of associations or actions. A remarkable series of books by Tufte (1999) that explore the wide range of visualisations of data reveals just what the possibilities are for using visual images to enhance understanding of events and their causes.

Box 16.1 The South African Police Investigative Psychology Unit (IPU)

The IPU was created in 1997 to assist in the investigation of psychologically motivated crimes. At the time the main focus was on serial murder investigations however the focus expanded over the years to include a wide variety of offences. Crimes classified as psychologically motivated typically have no external (for example, financial) motive. These include, but are not limited to: serial murder, serial rape, sexual murders, muti murders, paedophilia, intimate partner murders, child abductions and kidnappings, mass murder, spree murder, equivocal death scenarios (helping determine if a death is as a result of an accident, murder or suicide), and extortion cases. The unit currently consists of four members:

- Commander: Senior Superintendent (Professor) G. N. Labuschagne;
- Superintendent J. H. De Lange;
- Captain E. A. Myburgh;
- SAC III Amanda Swanepoel.

The IPU is situated at SAPS Criminal Records and Forensic Science Services. It provides its services throughout the country to any investigator who needs assistance, irrespective of the unit (for example, Organised Crime, General Detective. etc.).

The members are employed under the Police Act and are therefore regarded as functional police members.

Roles of the Unit

Investigative Support

Assistance is provided upon request from any investigator in the service. The unit acts in an advisory capacity (like consultants) in the investigation of psychologically motivated crimes by providing services such as behavioural analysis (offender profiling), investigative guidance, risk assessments, interviewing of witnesses and suspects, crime-scene analysis, case linkage analysis, and courtroom testimony. The unit's previous experience with such cases is offered to the investigator who most likely has never dealt with a case of a similar nature.

Training

The unit provides training to investigating officers in the identification and investigation of psychologically-motivated crimes. Training is given to various members of the detective service. *Ad hoc* training is given upon request to prosecutors and other interested parties, such as forensic pathologists. Not only does this aid in the identification and successful investigation and prosecution of such crimes, but it also educates investigators as to how and when behavioural analysts can be of assistance.

The unit provides training to SAPS members by means of:

* crime-scene processing unit refresher course;
* serious and violent crime course;
* family violence, child protection and sexual offences course;
* training tours through provinces upon request of a particular province;
* psychologically motivated crimes (PMC) course.

The unit also provides practical training placements to students from overseas universities such as the International Research Centre for Investigative Psychology (IRCIP) in the United Kingdom and Alliant International University in the United States.

Research

This aspect helps understand psychologically motivated crimes better, and therefore aids in the investigative support and training provided. A local understanding of how crimes present themselves is imperative, as foreign research has proved to be of limited use. This has resulted in the SAPS being one of the few law enforcement agencies that has a thorough database of its solved and unsolved serial murders. Suspect details are meticulously recorded for research purposes and for use in offender profiling.

The unit is understaffed so this role is augmented by the use of masters and doctoral students, who research relevant topics as part of their studies.

The unit has close research links with:

* International Research Centre for Investigative Psychology (IRCIP), University of Huddersfield, United Kingdom;
* John Jay College of Criminal Justice, United States;
* Alliant International University, United States;
* University of the Free State, South Africa;
* University of Pretoria, South Africa;
* UNISA, South Africa.

Box 16.2 The Israeli Police Investigative Psychology Unit, Investigative Psychology Section, Division of Identification and Forensic Science

Section head: Chief Superintendent Asher Zan-Ger

General: the Investigative Psychology Section deals with a wide range of topics from the field of behavioural sciences. The section deals with the psychological aspects of criminal investigation while providing services to a variety of investigation and intelligence units of the Israeli Police, as well as other agencies. The section is deployed in five regional laboratories throughout the country. The section also provides professional supervision and support, to the Military Police laboratory at the Israeli Defence Force.

The Functions of the Section

Polygraph Test

Providing polygraph services to investigation units in order to confirm, or to refute the examinees' version (suspect, witness or victim). This is being achieved by deploying different polygraph techniques, according to the investigation needs and purpose of the test. The main techniques that are implemented are: comparison question techniques (CQT), guilty knowledge test (GKT) and screening. The goals of these procedures are to present an investigative indication, reject possible accomplices (by using elimination tests) and to provide a decision support tool, for the continuation of the investigation.

Cognitive Interviews (Memory-Enhancing Technique)

This method is based on a structural questioning technique conducted in a controlled environment, developed by Professor R. Fisher. This procedure uses known psychological models to assist a cooperative eyewitness or victim, to recall as many as possible details regarding the investigated event. Various findings indicate that compared to other questioning methods this procedure provides significant value to the investigation. This technique enables the collection of additional information regarding the crime scene, refuting some investigation leads while providing others. As a rule, this procedure is conducted prior to the assembly of a facial construction procedure for possible suspects, in order to enhance and sharpen the interviewees' memory.

Advising and Assisting Investigation Teams with Psychological Aspects

Collaboration with investigation units, while accompanying an investigation in any given case, in order to contribute from the pool of knowledge and experience accumulated by the section specialists. This knowledge and experience is available to any investigating unit that is interested in an additional point of view regarding the investigated case and in particular, provides references regarding the psychological aspects of those involved in the case.

Offender Profiling

During the years 1999–2004, an Israeli model of offender profiling for four major crimes (murder, rape, sexual assault and robbery), was developed by Shye and Englehard (2004). The model was presented in an illustrative computer software named Crimina. Since 2004, the Investigative Psychology Unit has been experiencing encouraging results with the model. Recently, work is being done to develop a computerised system for offender profiling, based on the suggested model. The system is intended to be integrated with the computerised police system for criminal files management.

Offender profiling is being used for narrowing down and prioritising a list of potential suspects in cases such as serial crimes or in one time criminal events and linking crimes to one possible offender. In cases of a known suspect, recommendations for investigation and arrest strategies are given. Psychological profiling is also constructed in cases such as equivocal death and missing person cases.

Questioning the Vulnerable

Vulnerable interviewees require different conditions and approaches than those required by the general population. This population generally consists of minors and the disabled. These can include those suffering from mental, emotional or cognitive disorders. In such cases, a special approach and different questioning techniques must be employed. In order to produce as many details and with the highest accuracy possible, theoretical knowledge is being applied.

Some decision support tools developed for police work have very little analytic functions at all, being almost entirely ways of visualising the data, notably i2 (www.i2.co.uk). These tools can be productive in summarising a great deal of data and, in association with databases, can improve the search for and access to crucial information but they are very dependent on the skills of the particular user, often referred to in police forces as a crime analyst or intelligence analyst. In the wrong hands these systems can imply a behavioural pattern through the strong visual impact that diagrams produce, when in fact the diagram is a biased emphasis of some peripheral aspect of the criminal behaviour being investigated.

A further level of support to decisions can be made by identifying the salient characteristics of the offences and offenders and by producing summary accounts of them. One widespread application of this use is in the production of maps that indicate the locations where there are high frequencies of crimes, sometimes called criminal 'hotspots'. In these cases the salient characteristics are simply where the crimes have occurred and the description consists of some summary or averaging of the crimes over an area in order to indicate where its geographical focus might be. All description requires some selection, distillation or averaging of information, which is open to distortion, but when it is done validly the description is helpful.

A further level of assistance to police decision makers can be given by carrying out some form of analysis on the crime material, typically looking for patterns of co-occurrences or discriminating nonoccurrences. An example of the former would be the recognition that certain acts of vandalism occur shortly after the end of the school day near to schools. Knowledge from descriptive analyses of the age and backgrounds of offenders prosecuted for vandalism and the geographical hot-spot information could be combined to target possible culprits and introduce other forms of crime reduction. More advanced analysis of the co-occurrence of criminal behaviours could also be used for classifying offenders and generating different investigative strategies for the different forms of offender, as discussed throughout this book.

Offline and Online Use of Information

It is helpful to distinguish between two types of information; the first is information that may be available to a researcher during the course of a scientific study and from which principles may be derived that could be used by investigators. This could include the offender's understanding of what had happened and his/her account of the reasons for the offence. We can think of this as 'offline' information. Much of it may not be admissible in court, such as hearsay accounts of who said what to whom and the speculations of various people about the activities of others. But the information can generate trends that are of relevance to later investigations.

This contrasts, on the other hand, with the 'online' information that the police obtain as part of their investigations, on which they base their inferences for a particular case and which is likely to form at least part of the case they bring to court. In addition to forensic evidence such as DNA, fingerprints, fibres and the like, this will include behavioural evidence on what the offender did during an offence, where he/she did it and to whom.

The crucial point is that rather different demands are made on 'offline' information to those that are made of 'online' information; the former, being oriented to generalisations of broad applicability focus on representativeness and validity. The latter are concerned with the immediate case and lead to analysis of the particularities of that case and how the investigation may be moved forward.

Dragnet and Other Geographical Profiling Systems

The most powerful and widely used decision support systems to find their way into police investigations from IP are those that build on the studies of criminal propinquity and geographical morphology discussed in Chapter 8. These systems have become known as geographical profiling systems because they were labelled that by Rossmo (2000) when he developed the first widely available, commercial system known as Rigel (www.geographicprofiling.com).

Dragnet

In parallel to the development of Rigel, working from related but slightly different principles Canter (2005) produced a flexible research tool that he called 'Dragnet'. The power of this system was revealed in a variety of studies (for example, Canter et al., 2000; Canter and Hammond, 2006), which led to its uptake by a number of police forces around the world.

Current geographical profiling systems, such as Dragnet, work on the basis of adding the probabilities of an offender's home being at any of a series of distances from the scenes of crimes. This provides a 'probability surface' to show the relative likelihood of an offender being based at any of a range of locations within the area of the crimes. This is illustrated in Figure 16.1 for the location of the crimes associated with the 1881 murders that were all linked to the offender known as Jack the Ripper. This analysis is derived from Canter (2005) where a detailed discussion of this analysis is given (also presented on YouTube at http://www.youtube.com/watch?v=QCdskRH-B6s). Canter (2005) also comments on the fact that the Dragnet analysis points to a likely area of residence that is named as a place where the writer of what is known as *Jack the Ripper's Diary* (Harrison, 1993) claims to have taken rooms. Although there is heated debate over the authenticity of the 'diary', many believe it to be genuine.

Another area of debate, although not quite so well informed or heated, is the role of geographical profiling systems in contributing to investigations. What has been appreciated by academics (Snook *et al.*, 2005) is that many of the principles on which geographical profiling systems are based are quite straightforward. This means that in relatively simple cases it is possible for people who understand those principles to make an accurate guess of where the geographical profiling system will place the highest probability of an offender having a base (Snook, Canter and Bennell, 2002; Snook *et al.*, 2005). As Canter (2005) has pointed out,

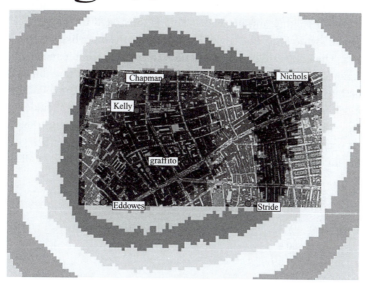

Figure 16.1   Dragnet analysis of 5 murder locations and graffito associated with Jack and Ripper (names are of the victims indicating where their bodies were found).

- An interactive system designed for use on a PC with minimal training, allowing context sensitive modification.
- Developed as a support tool to indicate the likelihood of the offender living at any given location and the implications of linking local crimes.

however, this rather misses the point of geographical profiling systems. They do not indicate a point but a set of regions with degrees of probability indicated. They are reliably based on clear, developing principles and thus provide objective support to investigators who will often have other information to incorporate. Furthermore, in complex cases the simple principles that can be given to people may be inappropriate, but this inappropriateness will not influence a computer system, which draws on rather more subtle analyses.

The Bayesian Approach

Recently the growing availability of large databases of solved crimes has given rise to another approach to determining where an offender may be based that has been attracting a lot of interest. This is a purely statistical procedure, having no connection with psychological theories of offender location choice. This approach is derived from the probabilities of any unknown offender behaving in a similar way to the general pattern of known offenders. For example, if it is known from past solved crimes that offenders who carry out crimes in location A typically live in location B, then it is reasonable to assume that any new, unsolved crime in location A will have been carried out by an offender who lives in location B. By adjusting for the pre-existing random probabilities and using Bayesian probability calculations it is possible to determine the confidence that an offender may live in any given location using this approach. Recent research (Levine, 2009) has shown how powerful this Bayesian approach can be when the appropriate data are available.

The important point to bear in mind with all these approaches is that there is a payoff relationship between validity and precision. This is illustrated by the general 'search cost function' shown in Figure 16.2. The larger the search area the more likely is the offender to be within that area. The important point (as described in detail by Canter and Hammond, 2006) is that the relationship between search area and accuracy is not a concave, linear one. In other words, as illustrated in Figure 16.2, a high proportion of offenders are found by any system within a relatively small portion of the search area. It is because the 'shoulder' illustrated in Figure 16.2 has been found with many data sets for systems such as Dragnet that these systems are regarded as useful and are increasingly used by law enforcement agencies (see Canter and Youngs, 2008b, for examples of the applications of geographical offender profiling).

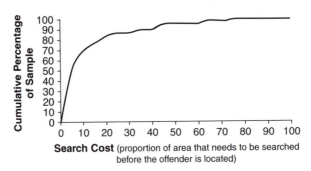

Figure 16.2 The search cost function: the relationship between proportion of sample and frequency of accurate matches.

Interactive Offender Profiling (iOPS)

The major weakness of all current geographical profiling decision support systems is that they are only based on the locations of the crimes. They take no account of the details of the offence actions, they do not integrate directly with police databases on offenders, nor do they connect with the social networks of which much crime is a part. Decision support tools are therefore emerging that go beyond the mere geography of crimes and incorporate a number of powerful analytical functions.

One such decision-support tool is iOPS, an interactive offender profiling system (Canter and Youngs, 2008c) (as illustrated in Figure 16.3). Developed by Canter and colleagues, this integrates large police databases at speed, drawing on the research findings to improve and systematise the investigation process through its ability to:

- link crimes (comparative case analysis);
- prioritise suspects;
- build catalogues of offenders' geo-behavioural profiles;
- generate potential TICs (further offences 'taken into consideration');
- explore co-offending networks;
- indicate locations for intelligence gathering;
- map crimes and perform hotspot analysis.

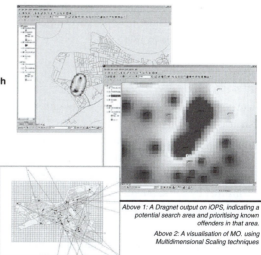

iOPS

A interactive Offending Profiling System

- iOPS is an ArcView 9 based **geo-behavioural profiling** system originally developed for the Metropolitan Police Service

- iOPS has been developed as an **operational system** to aid police work and a powerful **research tool,** using **ArcGIS 9**

- iOPS combines sophisticated crime mapping techniques such as **hotspot analysis** and **geo-coding capabilities** with powerful investigative functionality to **link crimes, prioritise suspects** and to **explore co-offending networks**

- iOPS integrates **large police data sets** at speed and uses this to perform analysis using **Dragnet** to explore spatial behaviour and **Multidimensional Scaling** to examine the structure of M.O.'s.

Above 1: A Dragnet output on iOPS, indicating a potential search area and prioritising known offenders in that area.

Above 2: A visualisation of MO. using Multidimensional Scaling techniques

Above: A co-offender network analysis indicated on a map

Figure 16.3   The IOPS system.

Linking Cases (Comparative Case Analysis)

A crucial aspect of many police investigations is the ability to confidently link crimes to a common offender. This has value for a number of purposes:

- Developing information for offender identification; the more information that can be tied to the same person the more inferences that can be made with some validity.
- Prioritising forensic examination; by knowing crimes are linked there can be an increased awareness of the value of obtaining forensic information from different locations.
- Providing the bases for reviewing the crimes that an offender may be willing to have 'taken into account' if he pleads guilty.
- Opens up the possibility of providing 'similar fact evidence' in court, thereby strengthening the prosecution case.

There are many sources of information that can be drawn on for linking crimes to a common offender. Of course, various forms of evidence from forensic science, such as hair, DNA, fibres, fingerprints and other marks are usually the strongest way of linking crimes. Witness accounts and circumstantial evidence, such as the same credit card being used close in space and time to a series of crimes, can also be very valuable. But in many cases this sort of information is not available and criminal actions need to be explored.

In looking at criminal actions the issues explored in previous chapters come to the fore. These include the need to determine what is salient about the actions as well as the awareness of developmental processes within the offender. The dominant themes of the offences and the narrative actions they imply will also be of great utility. This form of behavioural analysis has been allowed into court in some cases under the rubric of 'similar fact evidence', so it is an area that is growing in importance.

Varieties of Linking Problem

Figure 16.4 illustrates that there is not one simple linking problem. There may be two crimes that it is desirable to link to each other. There may be a number of crimes and the question of whether a further crime has been committed by the same person. There may be a number of crimes that might be related to others that are known to be by the same offender. Finally, there may be a number crimes and the question is raised as to whether any of them have been committed by the same offender.

Each of these different types of linking questions requires different forms of criteria for answering them. For example, if there is a group of crimes that are known to be linked, say with forensic evidence, then it may be possible to determine what behavioural characteristics they have in common. However, if there is a general trawl of many crimes to determine which may be linked, a great deal of refinement may be necessary to ensure that there is no confusion from base rates or other challenges to inference.

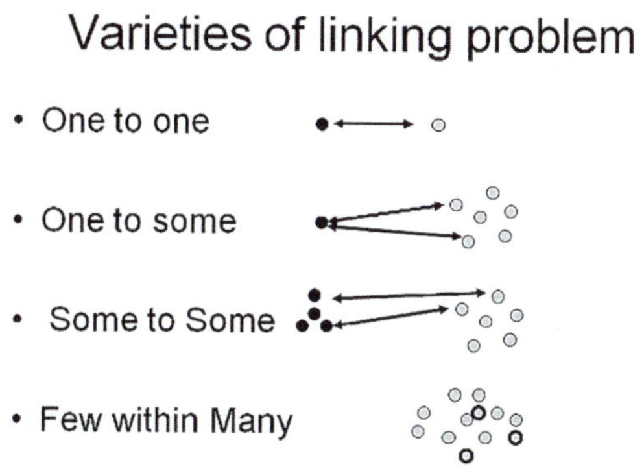

Figure 16.4 Varieties of linking problem.

Beyond 'Yes' or 'No' (Receiver Operator Characteristics)

Any decision choice that requires one of two answers is open to measures of effectiveness depending on the criterion used to generate the decision. This was illustrated for geographical profiling by the search cost function. A directly analogous process is also present for determining whether two crimes may be linked. If a very broad criterion is used, such as the witness seeing a young male running from the crime scene, then very many crimes may be linked. If a very precise, rare criterion is used, such as an elderly man escaping from the scene in a wheelchair, then very few if any other crimes may be linked.

The relationship between the generality of the criterion and its validity has the mixture of possibilities illustrated in Table 16.3. This shows that the judgement can miss cases that are linked or link cases that it should not, as well as validly link cases or validly not link cases. The relative proportions of these possibilities depend on the criteria used; the more effective the criteria the lower the proportions of misses, or false hits. A fruitful way of exploring this is to use what is known as receiver operator characteristics (ROC) (Fawcett, 2006). Bennell and Canter (2002) have shown that ROC analysis can indeed be very helpful in determining criteria for linking cases. They produce ROC curves as shown in Figure 16.5; the larger the area under the curve (AUC), the more effective the criteria.

Table 16.3 Possible decision outcomes in a linking task.

		Reality:		
		Actually linked	Actually unlinked	
	Linked	a	b	$a+b$
		hits	False alarms	
Prediction:		$pH = a/(a+c)$	$pFA = b\,(b+d)$	
	Unlinked	c	d	$c+d$
		misses	correct rejections	
		$pM = c/(a+c)$	$pCR = d/(b+d)$	
		$a+c$	$b+d$	$a+b+c+d=N$

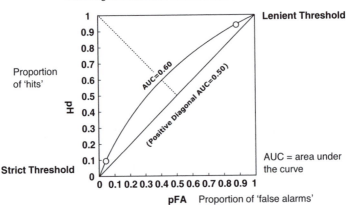

Figure 16.5 A ROC curve.

Approaches to Linking – Multidimensional Scalogram Analysis (MSA)

A number of approaches to behavioural linking of crimes have been explored. These cover a range of methodologies from simply matching cases on key variables through to comparisons against a raft of variables. The problem of just using a set of variables is that, if some of them co-occur, the theme that they represent will be given more weight than those themes that happen to be represented by very few of the variables in the set. Therefore some form of structural analysis is necessary as explored when considering the Radex in earlier chapters.

One approach that uses multivariate analysis is illustrated in Figure 16.6. This was utilised in the actual investigation of a series of rapes in Manchester (Canter, 1995). The police had thought, on the basis of witness descriptions, that the nine rapes were all committed by the same person. The analysis used the procedure of multidimensional scalogram analysis (MSA) whereby each crime is located as a point in space. The closer together any two points the more similar is the profile of actions that occur in those crimes.

The interpretation of Figure 16.6 leads to the view that there was more than one offender and, although there was only DNA available for three of the nine crimes, it was possible to assign the crimes to different offenders on the basis of their behaviour. The line on the plot shows the division that resulted.

The difference in the two offenders seems to relate to two very different narratives. One offender seemed to be very much the committed professional adventurer, who it was predicted (and subsequently found) had a long history of crime and of instrumental violence against women. The other offender seemed to be a much more confused individual whose crimes came out of a difficulty of relating to women.

Various studies have been carried out recently to explore the potential of linking crimes on the basis of behaviour. Woodhams and Toye (2007), for example, have been able to show that there is empirical support for linking crimes on behaviour for serial commercial burglaries. Santtila and Fritzon (2004) showed the fruitfulness of identifying themes in serial and spree

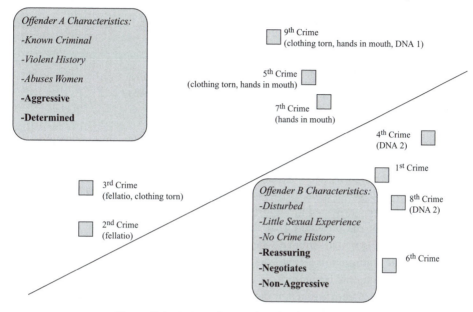

Figure 16.6   MSA solution for nine bedsit rapes.

arson cases for linking those cases. In a literature review Woodhams, Hollin and Bull (2007: 233) claim that:

> in comparison with intra-individual variation in behaviour, inter-individual variation is sufficient for the offences of one offender to be distinguished from those of other offenders. Thus, the two fundamental assumptions underlying the practice of linking crimes, behavioural consistency and inter-individual variation, are supported. However, not all behaviours show the same degree of consistency, with behaviours that are less situation-dependent, and hence more offender-initiated, showing greater consistency.

Two important matters emerge from the growing number of studies of linking crimes. One is the need to go beyond individual behaviours and to look at the underlying themes that characterise criminals' actions. A second, as hinted in the quote from Woodhams, Hollin and Bull (2007) above, is the need to understand what it is about the actions that make them consistent and differentiated enough to be of value for linking. They point to actions being 'less situation dependent' but we need to explore more deeply what it is about offenders' actions that makes them consistent. This may not be as simple as first thought. What if the offender chooses the situation? Some studies have certainly shown that the geographical closeness of offences may be one of the most useful criteria for linking them (Alison, Snook and Stein, 2001; Canter and Youngs, in press, c).

Table 16.4   Action plans for investigative support.

Criteria for linking cases
Distinguish salient features
Identify characteristic patterns
Consider geography
Consider temporal sequence
Incorporate forensics
Recognise offender development

Investigative Support Action Plans

The range of uses of IP does require a systematic approach. Therefore some action plans have been developed that provide a framework for drawing on the issues, theories and methodologies for integrating IP into police work. The basic components that such an action plan particular to crime linking may have are indicated in Table 16.4. More broadly, Table 16.5 shows the issues that need to be considered by an investigative psychologist when examining a crime.

Figure 16.7 shows the procedure that investigative psychologists at the National Police Research Centre in Japan go through when asked to comment on a particular case. This is really a generic summary of all the components of the consideration of criminal actions integrated into a sequential framework.

Box 16.3 is an except from actual flow diagram developed under the supervision of Professor David Canter, by Andreas Mokros and Brent Snook for a police murder investigation in Germany, described in detail in Canter (2005). What is particularly interesting about this flow diagram is that although it was prepared for one specific case the German police found it could easily be adapted and made use of it in subsequent cases without any further contact with its authors.

Table 16.5   Illustrative issues to consider in a crime.

	Base rates	Contingencies	Interactions
Time	When are crimes of this sort committed?	Does the time relate to darkness?	Are others usually around at this time?
Place	Is this place known for crimes?	What access does the place have?	Are there relevant changes to use?
Location	Is this central to the city or a special area?	What else goes on in this area?	What locations does it connect to?
Victim	How vulnerable is the victim?	Was the victim in a 'normal' state?	Was s/he present or implicit?
Guardianship	Was 'guardianship' available?	Did the offender take account of this?	Did anyone observe the offence?
Approach to the crime	How typical is this for crimes of this type	What risks did the offender take?	Was the offender disturbed?
Actions during offence	Is there anything unusual about these?	Did the offender exhibit any special skills?	Did offender react to events at crime scene?
Offender's escape	Was the escape route unexpected?	Was the escape route opportunistic?	Did anyone observe the escape?

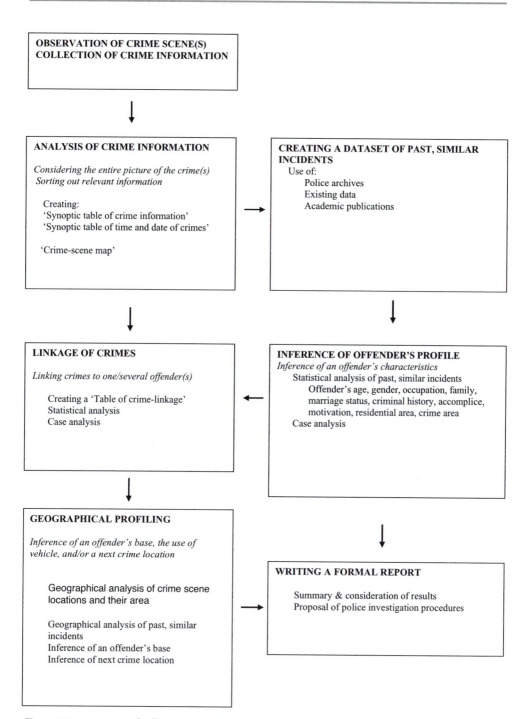

Figure 16.7 Process of offender profiling as used by the Japanese National Police Research Institute, Tokyo.

Box 16.3 A sequence for generating guidance for an investigation (excerpt from an IP Action Plan)

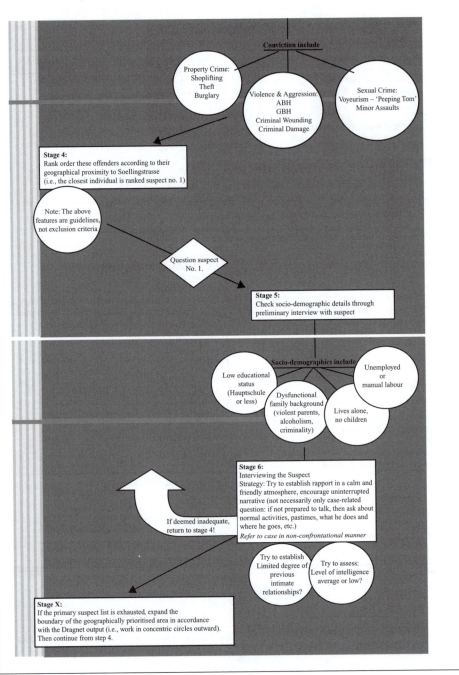

Conviction include

Property Crime:
Shoplifting
Theft
Burglary

Violence & Aggression:
ABH
GBH
Criminal Wounding
Criminal Damage

Sexual Crime:
Voyeurism – 'Peeping Tom'
Minor Assaults

Stage 4:
Rank order these offenders according to their
geographical proximity to Soellingstrasse
(i.e., the closest individual is ranked suspect no. 1)

Note: The above
features are guidelines,
not exclusion criteria

Question suspect
No. 1.

Stage 5:
Check socio-demographic details through
preliminary interview with suspect

Socio-demographics include

Low educational
status
(Hauptschule
or less)

Dysfunctional
family background
(violent parents,
alcoholism,
criminality)

Lives alone,
no children

Unemployed
or
manual labour

Stage 6:
Interviewing the Suspect
Strategy: Try to establish rapport in a calm and
friendly atmosphere, encourage uninterrupted
narrative (not necessarily only case-related
question: if not prepared to talk, then ask about
normal activities, pastimes, what he does and
where he goes, etc.)
Refer to case in non-confrontational manner

If deemed inadequate,
return to stage 4!

Try to establish
Limited degree of
previous
intimate
relationships?

Try to assess:
Level of intelligence
average or low?

Stage X:
If the primary suspect list is exhausted, expand the
boundary of the geographically prioritised area in accordance
with the Dragnet output (i.e., work in concentric circles outward).
Then continue from step 4.

Emerging Areas of IP

As noted in the opening chapters some of the earliest explorations of investigative psychologists related to serial killers and rapists. This has broadened to cover the complete gamut of crimes, from arson to terrorism, by way of fraud and blackmail, child abuse and cyber crime. The field continues to develop ever more rapidly. The following briefly summarises some of the areas not already touched on in previous pages.

Investigative Psycholinguistics

In many cases the actions of interest to an investigation are the written or spoken word. Spoken or written threats, suicide notes, confessions, declarations in wills and a range of other utterances may become part of civil or criminal proceedings or the associated investigations. These reports of what people have said or copies of what people have written may be examined to make any of the inferences that have been considered throughout this book. For example, exactly what the utterances mean, what is likely to happen as a consequence of them, what the characteristics of their author are likely to be, who the author is likely to be, or whether they are genuinely the product of the person who it is claimed produced them. Text offers special potential as evidence. A threatening, extortion letter is a record of exactly what the offender did to commit the crime. As noted in Chapter 9, the letter is the crime scene. There is no need to make sure the witness saw what was happening or to puzzle over the pathologist's report. On the page is a complete record of the relevant criminal actions.

Investigative psychologists have begun to work with (or in some case in rebuttal of) linguists to examine contested, or investigatively significant utterances (as reviewed by Canter, 2000). Psycholinguistic analysis of text is not to be confused with 'graphology', which claims to be able to provide accounts of the personality of an author from the style of his/her actual handwriting. There is no consistent scientific evidence for these claims. Almost invariably the scientific analysis is not concerned with the shape and style of the handwriting but how the person actually expresses him/herself; the words and syntax used.

The questions that investigative psycholinguists are seeking to answer fall into three groups. One set is to do with the identity of the writer. Is this the way in which a known individual expresses themselves? A second set of questions relates to the character of the writer, really trying to answer the same types of questions as graphologists about the traits and personality of the person writing. However, an important aspect of this is whether the author really meant what is implied by the writing. This connects with a third set of questions that falls under the heading of prognosis. What is the writer likely to do under various circumstances?

A particularly interesting example of this is the study of the difference between genuine and false suicide notes. Shneidman, as discussed below, made this part of his exploration of the conditions in which suicide occurs, but in a very interesting and unusual study Gregory (1999) used the MDS technique of POSA (illustrated in relation to criminal networks in Chapter 14) to show that it was possible to distinguish between suicide notes by people who had taken their lives and those written as a simulation. The importance of this analysis relates to those equivocal death cases in which there is some question of whether a death was a suicide or a murder made to look like a suicide (Canter, 2006).

Questions of a writer's identity may be raised about whether the words attributed to a particular author are actually the words of that person or not. This may occur, for example, when a suspect denies that he made the statement attributed to him or her, or in cases of forgery or fraud. To deal with these questioned utterances there have been a variety of attempts to use techniques based on the quantitative examination of language. These approaches are sometimes put under the general heading of 'stylistics', or forensic linguistics, or more generally forensic psycholinguistics. Yet although much is claimed for these procedures by their protagonists the systematic research into them rarely finds any evidence to support even the mildest claims (Aked *et al.*, 1999). Advances in computing techniques may change this (Coulthard, 1994).

One interesting perspective on exploring language-based crimes is the whole matter of plausibility. Studies of what makes a narrative plausible (mentioned in Chapter 10) have been carried out drawing on models of narrative structure (Canter *et al.*, 2003). The possibility of this approach being utilised in the consideration of contested documents remains to be explored.

Psychological Autopsy

One area of IP that draws on many of the theories and methods discussed in earlier chapters relates to those incidents of suspicious death in which the mental state of a deceased person needs to be assessed, as reviewed in detail by Canter (2000). If some evaluation can be made of the sort of person the deceased was, obtaining information from interviews with survivors of the deceased and archival sources about their personality and thought processes, especially as this may throw light on any involvement they themselves had in their death, then it may assist the investigation by carrying out what is sometimes referred to as 'equivocal death analysis' (EDA) or a *psychological autopsy*.

Contributions to equivocal death investigations can range from an essentially informal attempt to reconstruct the thoughts of the deceased to a much more thorough exploration of everything that is known about him/her. For, although such contributions have been made over a period of approximately 40 years there are still no standardised procedures that have been agreed upon for making them. Some of the earliest systematic studies were carried out by Shneidman and Farberow (1970) looking at teenage deaths in Los Angeles. They interviewed relatives, friends, employers, physicians and others, including teachers and in some cases even bartenders, who could provide relevant information in an attempt to reconstruct the deceased's background, personal relationships, personality traits and lifestyle. They sought significant details of the events immediately preceding the death. All of this information was subsequently reviewed by the 'Death Investigation Team' in the Coroner's office resulting in a determination of the mode of death.

The procedure implies a form of corroboration in which as wide a range and variety of sources of information as possible are collected to ensure that the bias inherent in any one source of information does not distort the whole picture.

The problem of bias is especially important, given the weight that may be attributed to the psychologist's opinion about the cause of death. Yet few writers on this process discuss it in any depth. Litman *et al.* (1970) are possibly the most direct in drawing attention to recurring problems. They point out that there is often a lack of information about the individual, particularly information that could be used for a reliable inference regarding his/her psychological state. Secondly, the information may be distorted by the informants. They cite instances of evasion, denial, concealment and even direct suppression of evidence. Indeed, it may be expected that expert advice is required precisely in those situations in which there are doubts and ambiguities surrounding the events of the death. That, after all, is what makes it 'equivocal', so the problems described by Litman *et al.* (1970) are part of the reason why an expert is called in to help. Canter (2000) in his attempts at producing a psychological autopsy noted that the legal process actually disallowed him from talking to some of the key 'witnesses'.

To explore the extent of these biases Otto *et al.* (1993) examined the agreement between reports completed by 12 psychologists and two psychiatrists who reviewed materials that addressed the adjustment and psychological functioning of Clayton Hartwig, suspected of causing an explosion aboard the *USS Iowa* in 1989, which resulted in his own death and that of 46 other sailors. Although broad criteria were adopted, they found only moderate agreement between the findings of the 14 professionals conducting the assessment.

Otto *et al.*'s study was initiated as a reaction against an equivocal death analysis (EDA) carried out by FBI agents into the *USS Iowa* tragedy. The agents had formed the conclusion that Clayton Hartwig had deliberately caused the explosion in an act of suicide. Their opinion was upheld by the initial navy enquiry. However, a number of psychologists were highly critical of the EDA and the way it was carried out (Poythress *et al.*, 1993). Their examination of the facts indicated that the explosion was indeed an accident, a conclusion later supported by the technical evidence and accepted by a US Congress investigation. Poythress *et al.* suggested that the FBI used scientific terms for a process lacking significant scientific methodology, and compounded that problem by failing to sufficiently delineate between 'opinions' and 'facts'.

As so often happens with good ideas in psychology, these contributions to investigations have been used in a variety of situations before they have reached the maturity needed to be safely allowed out of the careful confines of their professional birthplace. Coroners' courts in Los Angeles, considering teenage deaths, are a far cry from enquiries of national significance into explosions on a navy warship. It is perhaps some measure of the readiness with which people in the United States embrace psychology, especially in the forensic context, that the psychological autopsy has already been tested in so many jurisdictions, long before detailed, large-scale studies have been carried out to ensure its effectiveness and to determine the best way of carrying it out.

There can be little doubt that more system and less bias would be an advantage for many enquiries into suspicious deaths and ambiguous fatalities but for this emerging science to survive it is essential that it does not offer more than it can deliver.

As ever the fiction writer may have got there before the scientist, Jonathan Kellerman puts it in his 1990 book *Time Bomb* (quoted by Ogloff and Otto, in press):

'Mr Burden, what is it exactly you think I can do for you?'

'Conduct a psycho-biography. The life and times of Holly Lynn Burden . . . Apply the same tools of scholarship you apply to your research and become the resident expert on my little girl – on what made her tick. Delve as deep as you like. Be unsparing with your questions. Do whatever it takes to get to the root of this mess. Learn the truth, Dr Delaware.'

I took my time answering. His eyes never left me.

'Sounds like you're talking about two separate things, Mr Burden. Reconstructing your daughter's life – what's known as a psychological autopsy. And vindicating her. One may not lead to the other.'

Missing Persons

Much police time can be taken up looking for missing persons, even though no obvious crime may have been committed. This is consequently an area to which IP can contribute. Aspects of it can take the form of a 'psychological autopsy' as discussed above. But there are also obvious geographical issues involved in determining where the missing person might be.

In one of the few empirical studies into this issue Shalev, Schaefer and Morgan (2009) found that 39% of the 70 cases they studies actually travelled less than a mile from where they had last been seen. A substantial 41%, however, travelled abroad. This shows that there are many different processes underlying a person going missing. The way is therefore open to develop a more coherent account of what is the behavioural structure of missing person activities.

Six Fundamentals of IP

Investigative psychology has a broader remit and applicability than just criminal and civil investigations within the framework of legal processes. It focuses on examining existing circumstances and naturally occurring patterns of activity in order to solve problems and provide insight of relevance to policy and decision makers. It is thus investigative in a number of senses but most particularly in the sense that the problems that are tackled have an existence independently of any scientific interest in them.

They do not reach towards the sort of activity that is investigative in the meaning of 'investigative journalism'. Nor are they as full-bloodedly 'investigative' in the sense that Douglas (1976) advocates in his account of 'investigative social research'. He sees the truth of social reality as only open to construction from the active participation of teams of people in the processes they are studying. Investigative psychology uses rather more distant forms of contact with its subject matter than the intense immersion in the setting that Douglas insists is so important. It is also different in focusing on the experience and conceptualisations of individuals and the conceptual systems they draw upon to guide their activities. It is much more influenced by the psychological perspective of George Kelly (1955) and his 'alternative constructionism', than the field research approaches of Garfinkel (1967) and Goffman (1963) that are a major source of Douglas' methodology. The quest is to understand the processes going on within individuals that help to explain their actions in and on the world rather than social processes that are the product of such actions. The other dominant influence is the social science methodologist Louis Guttman (Levy, 1996). In developing his 'facet theory' of research methodology he took the notion of alternative constructionism into fundamental questions of research process. He thus does share with Douglas the view that scientific truth is constructed rather than discovered but he showed how research methodologies can assist that construction.

Investigative psychology is therefore not solely academic in the strict 'Ivory Tower' sense. It may be 'action research' in the sense that it is carried out with the objective of providing direct input to decision processes. It can also be 'consultancy', providing direct guidance to a commissioning client. Studies with more general scientific objectives are frequent as well. What they all have in common, though, is a search for the meanings and psychological structures that characterise people in their daily situations.

In order to provide a framework for understanding the generic nature of Investigative Psychology it is useful to identify six assumptions that underpin the approach. These are given in more detail in Canter (2000).

Assumption One – Researchers Have Styles

The similarity of approaches to different sorts of research problems brings the most basic assumption that there are styles of working. Many research decisions are guided more by what a researcher is comfortable with than by any inviolate logic. Some researchers can only think in terms of standardised questionnaires, others open-ended interviews. Some find the world outside the controlled laboratory to be frightening and mystical. Others start their studies by talking to whomever they can and have their likely results formulated before they start collecting any reportable data. The fundamental assumption of an investigative psychology is that there are effective and ineffective ways of working within any style, not that there are right or wrong ways of doing research.

This can be taken as a pragmatic approach, or even one that is opportunistic in the positive sense of taking advantage of the opportunities provided. But it is also a way of providing a more 'organic' approach to research questions, that Canter (1993) somewhat tongue-in-cheek called 'holistic'. This approach requires the methodology and results to be a natural part of the problem being studied rather than something that is artificially tacked on only to provide scientific credibility. It does demand a flexible approach to carrying out research but one that makes sense to the researcher. It is out of this that a research 'style' emerges.

Learning on the Street Where Research Comes From

The origins of research projects are not often described in academic publications. As a consequence there are some parallels with the way sex was dealt with in Victorian times. Everyone knew it happened but they only found out how and when from private, personal experience. In a similar way, students are not told where research comes from or the processes that give rise to its gestation and birth.

Learned journals implicitly support the myth that research and its findings emerge full-grown from the scientist's loins with no intervention of either God or man. The apparently secret process by which studies are funded, research assistants found, data accessed and a dozen other hurdles surmounted requires many management and financial skills. If it is field-based and/or applied it also requires the support and cooperation of people outside of the research team as well as direct support from a variety of individuals and organisations who are not necessarily experts in psychology, or scientific studies. Many of these people look to the research activity both to contribute to the growing knowledge and understanding of the science and to have direct benefits either in general policy or in relation to actions that will be carried out as a consequence.

Like jazz performers who want to improvise around a new tune, any researchers faced with the challenges of real-world research have to draw upon a set of useful habits that will see them through. These habits have to be grounded in effective scientific procedures and ways of thinking.

Styles Grow out of Classical and Romantic Research Traditions

Canter (2000) has suggested that, just as Gombrich (1950) has argued that the major movements in the arts are reflections of Classical or Romantic traditions, so are the styles of scientific activity. The Classical approach is to see everything as a reflection of pure Platonic forms. Beauty is merely a mirror of some ideal that can never be reached; the serenity of Apollo versus the spontaneity of Dionysius.

In the research tradition the Classical is one in which an ideal structure is defined into which the perfect study should fit. From this perspective the everyday is seen as a reflection of pure, ideal forms, whether it is a statue of Venus or carefully crafted factorially designed experiment. The research tradition that imposes a predetermined scientific structure on how studies should be conducted can be seen as classical in many senses of the word.

By contrast, research that sees the everyday as inherently exquisite, which recognises the need to shape approaches in order to study problems in their own light, can be seen as inherently Romantic. This may result in a series of controlled experiments each examining a different aspect of the central research question, or as ever more focused exploratory studies investigating a range of perspectives on the problem at the end. Indeed, Schneider (1998) has given a rallying call for Romanticism as a basis for a revival in psychology at large. However, there is always a movement between Classical and Romantic traditions in science as much as in the arts.

Assumption Two – Data Speak Theories

There is an important second assumption that emerges from the investigative perspective and the productive tension between Classical and Romantic traditions. This is that data are not enough. Collecting information, for example, about what criminals do in one place or another or recording the number of times a particular behaviour occurs, does not add up to an understanding until some explanatory framework is tested against them. We need to know if our observations of activities reveal important aspects of how people typically deal with those settings. So, an investigative psychology grapples with concepts, models and processes rather than being buried in very extensive data sets or highly complex analyses.

This is another way of expressing what was referred to in earlier chapters, following Burch (2006), as 'going beyond the data'. This is the argument that the essence of science is to build ever more generalisable models or theories so that any finding is not limited to summarising only one data set.

Assumption Three – Theories are Practical

The importance of building theories, possibly paradoxically, grows out of the desire to solve practical problems. This can be clarified by recognising the distinction between engineering and science. Engineering is concerned with making things work and science is concerned with understanding how and why things work the way they do; the move from a scientific finding to an engineering application is not inevitable. It requires special development work. Furthermore, there may be engineering discoveries that defy current scientific explanation. However, the scientific principles have much further reach and potential over a longer timescale than engineering practicalities. Some theories and approaches to theory building have more potential for application than others. Investigative psychology aspires to applicable theories.

Assumption Four – Context Provides Meaning

One principle that is a starting point for interpreting the results of many studies is that a person's actions derive their significance from their context. The caresses of a lover are very different in their significance from the lewd fingerings of a rapist, even though the physical behaviour itself may be identical in both cases. Thus, the context that gives significance to our lives is a function both of variations between people and of variations in the settings and how they interact. This is so fundamental a theoretical assumption that it almost acts as an axiom. It is based on the view that lives are provided with excitement and challenge, or desperation and despair from the transactions between the particular qualities that the person brings to a context and the particular qualities of that context. Furthermore, the context has a place in space and time that provides the basis for its significance and relevance to the person experiencing it. That person also brings his or her position in social space and time to bear on that interpretation. Yet the fact that generations of psychologists have chosen to ignore the importance of physical and temporal context only serves to illustrate how demanding a challenge it presents.

Laboratories are Artificial

Taking account of the natural settings in which human experience takes place poses great demands on both theory and methodology. The problem is that human beings are remarkably adaptable. Indeed environmental adaptability is the primary tool in human evolutionary development. But for psychologists it is a capability fraught with dangers as well as delights. People will develop ways of dealing with any setting, no matter how artificial. As a consequence the cunning inventions of experimental, laboratory-based psychologists may often bring to the surface skills and propensities which are nonexistent in any other situation. They may at best be superficial or minor capabilities that have no strong function outside of the rarefied milieu of the controlled experiment.

It is helpful to elaborate a little further on this devilish invention the 'laboratory experiment'. It is a situation that is characterised by a large number of artificial constraints – artificial in the sense that the constraints are devised by psychologists for the purposes of studying problems that are of interest within the realms of psychology but not necessarily of any significance to anybody else. Constraints in the sense that attempts are made in advance to limit as far as possible all except a very few aspects of the environment that the research participant will experience. There are constraints that limit even more severely the range of responses that the participant will be allowed to generate and that will be measured during the course of the study.

The strength of these controlled experimental studies, it is claimed, is that they allow very clear conclusions to be drawn about the effects that particular aspects of the environment have on particular reactions of the respondent. But, of course, this is precisely their most profound weakness too. They make it extremely difficult to explore and understand how people give shape and meaning to their surroundings and act on it in order to improve their control and subsequent satisfactions. In other words, it is not so much the experimental, scientific precision that is the profound weakness of most experiments but the constipated and restricted models of human beings, their actions and experiences, which are a product of the methods that are used for studying them.

A further problem with the whole concept of the experiment is the way in which it provides a mode of thinking about research that is carried through, unchallenged, into other areas. Field 'experiments' and the whole vocabulary of 'quasi-experimental' design (Campbell, 1978) drag inappropriate models into the study of real-world phenomena. It is much more appropriate to think of these as 'quasi-naturalistic' studies.

This perspective on laboratory studies is part of the stream of psychology that can trace origins in modern times to William James (1890) and in classical times to Aristotle's *De Anima*. This is the view that human beings are best considered in an analogy to Newton's laws of motion. They are naturally in motion unless acted upon in some way to distort and modify that dynamic. Thus, any framework that looks to a person being triggered or stimulated to act in a particular way has ignored the basic principle that people already bring with them to a situation far more than they take away.

This perspective has the further interesting consequence of changing the understanding of any simulated experimental situation or stimuli. The conventional wisdom among psychologists is that it is possible to represent or mirror the 'real world' in the laboratory by creating some sort of surrogate for the actual experience. The IP view is that these representations elicit a particular perspective on the experience, a sort of Brechtian alienation, by which the representation is treated primarily as a symbol rather than as a multimodular reflection of real experience (cf. Scott and Canter, 1997). In other contexts Orne (1962) has drawn attention to what he calls the 'demand characteristics' of any study, which is another way of recognising how artificial is the psychological laboratory.

Social is Fundamental

Although context provides meaning, it is the social aspects of a context that bring it to psychological life. That is why crime has been considered throughout this volume as a fundamentally interpersonal process, not the actions of an isolated, probably abnormal individual. Social processes are thus not superficial additions to fundamental human processes, later chapters in the textbooks of the psyche, but rather they are the fundamental constituents of our world that underlie all purpose and meaning.

Assumption Five – Structures Explain

The search for the meaning of people's transactions with their surroundings, as they experience them in relation to their reasons for being in those locations, presents a fairly complex set of interrelated facets. The research task is to distil the many variables that are possibly relevant into the dominant themes that help to explain the processes under study. This is a task that can be accomplished in many different ways but particularly productive approaches allow the data to reveal their underlying structure while imposing the minimum constraints on that interpretation process.

The crucial idea here is that the meanings that people assign to their actions or that organise their utterances can be established by seeing how those utterances or actions co-occur. It is the patterns of co-occurrences that reveal the underlying meanings of what people say and what people do.

Means are External, Correlations Internal

There is an important and often rarely understood consequence of the search for meaning in patterns of relationships, which also raises questions about whether experimental designs can ever reveal anything of fundamental psychological relevance. The laboratory framework is construed as comparing the average differences between groups that experience the treatment condition and those that experience the control condition. The fundamental assumption is made that the participants in the experiment do not interact with the process of experimentation as such. The treatment and control conditions are regarded as externally created by the researcher. They are assumed to be independent variables. The major statistical analysis of this type of research design is to form some summary of the reactions of each of the subgroups in each of the experimental conditions. These subgroups are summarised, in effect, by calculating their average response. These averages are thus one summary of the overall response of a group to the externally structured constraints provided by the experimenter. It follows that it is extremely difficult to understand the meanings that any given individual brings to a situation by comparing the average responses of subgroups.

By contrast, a correlation actually reveals the patterns of co-variance within individuals summarised as general trends across individuals. So if you know there is a correlation between the amount of violence in a crime and the number of previous convictions the offender has for violence, you know that the person who has been very violent in one crime is likely to have a previous conviction for violence. This is not the case if you assign offenders to 'high violence' and 'low violence' pseudoexperimental groups and compare their means on their number of previous convictions.

Research Processes Interacts with Their Products

This brief consideration of the psychological differences between measures of central tendency and measures of association makes clear that research processes carry direct and profound implications for the sorts of psychological theory that can reasonably be constructed. The way a study is designed and the sort of data that is collected assume something about the qualities of the people being examined. If a theory is going to be about the active interpretations and purpose oriented actions that people bring to their environmental transactions then the study has to explore processes within the person. These will essentially grow out of correlations between aspects of what each participant under study says or does.

Assumption Six – All Methodologies Assume but Some Assume More Than Others

To the casual reader it is the methodology that is the most obvious distinguishing feature of IP; the use of multidimensional scaling techniques (MDS) and the interpretation of multivariate analyses as conceptual structures. These methodologies have been in use for well over half a century but still appear novel to many psychologists and social scientists. This is partly because even applied field researchers are still wedded to experimental models and ways of thinking. They still look back to fashion their research designs on laboratory chemistry as practised in Victorian times rather than, say, modern astronomy or even archaeology, or, within the social framework, areas of system analysis and structural modelling.

The contructivist approach requires a methodology that is rich in many different ways. What people say and what people do as well as the traces that they leave behind and the records that are collected about their actions must all be drawn upon to provide grist for the investigative psychologist's mill. But this multiplicity of multivariate data sources demands modes of analysis that will not destroy the systems and context that we are trying to study. Even at the risk of clarifying the apparently obvious rather than elaborating the remote and arcane, we have to be confident that what we are finding does reflect a fruitful account of what actually occurs rather than merely paying obeisance to some scientific ritual.

This leads to the important assumption that research methodologies, including how the research is organised and the data collected, make fundamental assumptions about the nature of human beings. This is perhaps the most challenging paradox for any psychological research. What we are able to find out about people depends on the way we approach how we will find that out. This self-reflective quality is perhaps the most important assumption of IP.

The Wider Reaches of an Investigative Psychology

The tasks that investigative psychologists face are not uniquely tied into crime and police investigations. Investigative psychology grew out of other areas of applied psychology and has much to offer back to those areas. It is a way of doing psychology that can be extended with value far beyond the criminal domain. For brevity, some of these are listed below:

- Preventing emergencies becoming disasters through the study of human actions in buildings on fire and other emergencies (cf. Canter, 1990; Donald, 1993; Donald and Canter, 1990, 1992).

- Reduction and prevention of crimes through study of criminal decision making and crime location choice.
- Crowd control and public order policing through the study of effective and ineffective crowd control (cf. Stott, 2003; Stott and Drury, 2000; Stott, Hutchison and Drury, 2001).
- Critical incident management through study of actions and decisions during demanding critical incidents (cf. Alison and Crego, 2008).
- Industrial safety through the study of when and where accidents occur and the understanding of the workforce (Donald, 1995).
- Management consultancy.
- Policy formulation.
- Market research through studying consumer conceptualisations and actions.

Conclusions

There has been a long journey from trying to profile the characteristics of a witch through the attempts to fathom the criminal mind of the late nineteenth and twentieth centuries. The experienced detectives, notably at the FBI training academy in Quantico, who drew attention to the possibility of working directly with what occurred in a crime to draw systematic inferences about offenders, pointed the way to a more empirical, scientific basis for psychological and related behavioural science contributions to police investigations. The blossoming of applied psychology into many areas of professional activity laid the foundations for an investigative psychology that goes far beyond the initial speculations about serial killers of 50 years ago.

Over the last decade some of the more firmly established findings and processes in IP have given rise to decision-support systems and training procedures for many areas of investigation. As illustrated in the present chapter some major police forces around the world already have IP units, which although still small are making a significant impact on policing in their own and neighbouring countries.

The contribution of IP to all stages in the law enforcement process and to the full gamut of crimes has also been demonstrated. Psychology and related disciplines need no longer be assigned to the 'hit-and-run' offering of an 'offender profile', which is only relevant to bizarre, extreme crimes. It is now taking its place as of central importance to many aspects of police training and beyond.

A general theory of criminal action is also emerging, which we have called a narrative actions system (NAS). Much of it is still speculative but it does offer the route to ways of thinking about criminals that embrace their own understanding of their actions whilst still focusing on what they actually do. Only future research will tell how fruitful this perspective is.

When he was Defence Secretary, Donald Rumsfeld commented on the challenges faced in the modern world, especially in relation to insurgency and other challenges to the state. His comments are often mocked, but actually map out the challenges that are faced by any discipline that by necessity has to grapple with secret, clandestine and criminal activities:

> . . . as we know, there are known knowns; there are things we know we know. We also know there are known unknowns; that is to say we know there are some things we do not know. But there are also unknown unknowns – the ones we don't know we don't know.

In previous pages we have mapped out what we know about criminals that is relevant to their investigation. We have indicated in many places what we do not know and which therefore provide the basis for a considerable and exciting research effort, but it is also clear that criminality and its investigation is constantly changing. Therefore only the future will reveal what we currently do not know that we do not know.

Further Reading

Books

Alison, L.J. and Crego, J. (2008) *Policing Critical Incidents: Leadership and Critical Incident Management*, Willan, Cullompton.

Canter, D. (ed.) (1990) *Fires and Human Behaviour*, David Fulton, London.

Ebiske, N. (2008) *Offender Profiling in the Courtroom: The Use and Abuse of Expert Witness Testimony*, Praeger, London.

Stott, C. and Pearson, G. (2007) *Football Hooliganism: Policing and the War on the English Disease*, Pennant, London.

Youngs, D. (ed) (in press). The Behavioural Analysis of Crime: Investigative Psychology Studies in Honour of David Canter. Ashgate: Dartmouth.

Articles

Bennell, C. and Canter, D. (2002) Linking commercial burglaries by modus operandi: tests using regression and ROC analysis. *Science and Justice*, **42**(3), 1–12.

Canter, D., Coffey, T., Huntley, M. and Missen, C. (2000) Predicting serial killers' home base using a decision support system. *Journal of Quantitative Criminology*, **16**, 457–78.

Reicher, S., Stott, C., Cronin, P. and Adang, O. (2004) An integrated approach to crowd psychology and public order policing. *Policing: An International Journal of Police Strategies and Management*, **27**, 558–72.

Santtila, P., Zappala, A., Laukkanen, M. and Picozzi, M. (2003) Testing the utility of a geographical profiling approach in three rape series of a single offender: a case study. *Forensic Science International*, **131**, 42–52.

Woodhams, J., Hollin, C.R. and Bull, R. (2007) The psychology of linking crimes: a review of the evidence. *Legal and Criminological Psychology*, **12**, 233–49.

Questions for Discussion and Research

1. If you were asked to contribute to an investigation into people hacking into sensitive computer systems how would you go about it?

2. Why might the courts be reluctant to allow evidence on a 'psychological profile' of the accused?

3. If a criminal were to read this book what effect might it have on how he carried out his crimes? What are the implications of this?

4. What ethical issues need to be considered in working as an investigative psychologist?

5. Reviewing this book as a whole, what are the main principles of IP?

6. What future directions do you think would be most fruitful for investigative psychologists to pursue?

Glossary

A→C equations   A summary of the integrated set of psychological questions at the heart of offender profiling, generated by the exploration of inference, where A are all those actions that occur in and are related to a crime and C refers to characteristics of the offender – the things the police want to know about him (or her) that will lead to identification and conviction. The scientific modelling that would allow inferences to be made about the characteristics from the actions is indicated by the → symbol. This simple symbol enshrines a complex and challenging set of issues.

Acquisitive crimes   Offences that have as their central process the acquisition of money or goods, such as burglary, robbery or fraud.

Action system   A framework for considering the behaviour of any entities that are open to their surroundings, explored by Talcott Parsons and systematised by Samuel Shye.

Actuarial judgements   Those assessments of a person or situation that are based on careful measurements and the resultant statistical relationships. (Contrasting with *clinical judgements*.)

Base rates   The standard rate at which anything of relevance may happen.

Canonical relationships   A mathematical way of thinking about the A→C equations. They have a number of 'predictor' A variables and a number of 'criterion' C variables and thus have a variety of solutions to the equations based on variations in the weightings of the A and C variables.

'Circle hypothesis'   Canter and Gregory's (1994) proposal that offenders are frequently likely to reside within the area circumscribed by their crimes, as defined by a circle with a diameter that is the distance between their two furthermost offences.

Classes of crime   Subgroups of different offence categories, comprising broad offending themes such as 'property offences' or 'crimes against the person'.

Clinical judgements   Instances where a decision based on training and experience forms an opinion about a person or situation rather than objective assessment (contrasting with *actuarial judgements*).

Cognitive interviews   An interviewing procedure developed to assist in the retrieval of detailed and accurate information from eyewitnesses, which makes use of cognitive mechanisms for remembering.

Commuters   Those offenders whose base is not within the circle defined by the diameter of the two furthest crimes. See *circle hypothesis*.

Concept   An internal representation of the nature or extent of a phenomenon.

Consistency
  (a) Whether the salient aspects or features of an offender and/or their crimes are similar from one context, or crime, to another.
  (b) Whether there are similarities in the way an offender commits a crime and the way s/he acts in noncriminal situations.

Contract murderer   An offender who unlawfully kills on behalf of someone else for financial or material gain.

Contingency   The context or circumstance that provides opportunities or limitations on a crime or aspects of it, which may influence what happens or how the actions interact with each other.

Criminal differentiation   Distinguishing between and isolating different groups, subgroups or behavioural styles of offences or offenders.

Criminal narratives   The life stories of offenders and the roles that they perceive themselves as playing during a crime or throughout their lives

Criminal/social network analysis   The process of identifying 'nodes' and links between them in order to determine patterns of association between them, where nodes may be individuals, locations or objects.

Criminal scripts   The roles that a person plays imply that he is following some sort of script that determines the relationships between people and the succession of episodes. In the criminal context these scripts may be drawn upon so that offenders may think that there is a particular way of carrying out a certain crime, depending in part on what they think their role is.

Criteria based content analysis   An approach to the analysis of victim statements or allegations, which may be used to determine their essential nature and which may assist in determining whether or not they are truthful.

Decay function   A mathematical formula of the relationship between the frequency of offending and distance from the home or base of an offender or offenders. The frequencies typically reduce more rapidly the further the distance is from home (it 'decays').

Decision support systems   Procedures (typically software programs or statistical models) designed to help inform investigative decision making within an operational context (for example, to prioritise information in terms of relevance, or to direct lines of enquiry). Distinct from *expert systems*.

Domestic violence   Physical, psychological, sexual, financial or emotional abuse inflicted within a domestic setting, most typically by a partner or spouse.

Domocentricity   The tendency for the spatial distribution of an offender's crimes to be heavily related to, or influenced by, their home and its relative positioning.

Dragnet   A decision support tool designed by Professor David Canter and developed by the International Research Centre for Investigative Psychology, which takes a series of crime locations and applies mathematical functions in order to produce a prioritised probability map, which indicates where the perpetrator of those offences might be most likely to be based. In an operational context Dragnet may be used to focus investigative strategies and help to prioritise lines of enquiry (which is why it is known as a 'decision support tool') but Dragnet is also frequently used as a research tool for studying patterns of offence locations. Dragnet is also known as a 'geographical profiling system'.

Earwitness testimony   Information given in an investigation by a person or persons who witnessed the crime in question occurring and gives an account of what they heard.

Environmental psychology   The study of people's experience and use of the physical environment and of the psychological processes underpinning the ways in which people interact with their surrounding environs.

Equivocal death analysis   Analysis of crime-scene information to determine the cause of death in situations in which there is some doubt of the role of the deceased in their own death. Usually distinguished from *psychological autopsy.*

Expert system   A procedure (typically software) that makes decisions as an expert might. Distinct from a decision support system that assists experts.

Expressive behaviours   Those criminal actions for which the execution of the act itself is the primary aim, such that these behaviours carry rewards of their own; typically direct expressions of some emotion. Not to be confused with the 'expressive' mode of an action system.

Eyewitness testimony   Information given in an investigation by a person or persons who witnessed the crime in question occurring and gives an account of what they saw.

Facets   Mutually exclusive components of an exhaustive classification system. In algebraic terms a facet is a subset of nonoverlapping sets; for example, gender, age and levels of violence are all facets.

False allegation   An untrue complaint of having suffered at the hands of others. Often, but not always, this is an allegation of sexual abuse or harassment.

False confession   Admitting to a crime that confessor has not committed.

Geographical (offender) profiling   The use of the spatial or geographical attributes of a crime to make predictions about likely characteristics of an unknown offender; most typically where that offender might be most likely to reside but also for linking offences to a common offender, predicting future movement patterns and so forth.

Hierarchy of criminality (or hierarchy of criminal variation)   An ordered listing of the scale of criminal actions, ranging from general criminality to precise details of what happens in a crime, which reflects the different levels at which inferences might be made.

'Hollywood Effect'   The process whereby claims or processes are regarded as valid or effective because they have been portrayed in fictional movies.

IEE technique   An approach to 'Improving Interpersonal Evaluations for Law Enforcement and National Security', based on research into emotions and their assumed prevalence when attempting to lie or deceive. The IEE technique emphasises a search for the truth through open questioning.

Inferences (appropriate)   The conclusions drawn from consideration and analysis of investigative information that claim that certain features of a crime and/or criminal are linked. The most obvious example of this is determining likely characteristics of an offender from some knowledge of how a crime was committed.

Instrumental behaviours   Criminal actions that are carried out not for their inherent benefit but rather in order to achieve some secondary goal(s).

Intrinsic statement validity analysis   A procedure that enables assessment of the validity of any claim or accusation from a victim, which uses the principle that deception may be detected on the basis of the coherence of, and consistencies or discrepancies in, victims' accounts of what allegedly happened.

Investigative information   Information that is the starting point for an investigation or for IP research, derived from real-life events.

Investigative psycholinguistics   The psychological examination of contested or investigatively significant utterances or written material, such as extortion letters or suicide notes.

Investigative psychology   The study of offenders and the processes of apprehending them and bringing them to justice. It is concerned with psychological input to the full range of issues that relate to the management, investigation and prosecution of crime, providing a framework for the integration of many aspects of psychology into all areas of police and other investigations.

iOPS   Interactive Offender Profiling System; a decision support system developed at the International Centre for Investigative Psychology which integrates large police databases at speed, drawing on the research findings to improve and systematise the investigation process.

The 'journey to crime'   Offenders' spatial decision making is assumed to relate very strongly to established routes and actual journeys; within this framework emphasis is put on the actual streets and pathways that offenders may follow – a notional 'journey to crime'

Linking   (a) The process of associating behaviours with a certain type of person, or (b) associating crimes that have been committed by the same perpetrator.

Locatedness   The assumption that crimes have a distinct setting that can be drawn upon in modelling and predicting offender spatial behaviour.

'Marauders'   Offenders whose home/base is within the circle defined by the diameter between the two crimes furthest from each other. See *circle hypothesis.*

Mental (imaginary) maps   Internal/cognitive representations that people have of their environments, which influence where and in what ways an individual interacts with their surroundings.

Model   A formal statement of the hypothesised relationships between a set of facets or variables, typically between different aspects of behaviour.

Modulating facets   Those *facets* that play the role of modifying other facets. They have often been found empirically to relate to the frequency of occurrence of variables, but not always. See *radex.*

Modus operandi   An offender's typical 'method of operation'.

Morphology   The pattern or overall geometry of offence distribution.

Multidimensional scaling   A family of statistical procedures that represent the relationship or degree of association between variables as distances between points in a notional space that represents those variables.

Muti murder   Murder where the intention is to gather human body parts for use in traditional African medicine.

Narrative approach A perspective within the social sciences that regards human beings as making sense of their interactions with people and things around through the development of personal stories in which they are the central protagonists.

Narrative Action System model A framework for modelling criminal activity that combines an *action system* framework with a *narrative approach*.

NAS inference model A model providing a generic basis for developing deductions about offenders from information about their offending; an integrated model of crime differentiation and criminal inferences.

Offender profiling The process by which individuals, drawing on their clinical or other professional experience, make judgements about the personality traits, psychodynamics, demeanour, family background, or criminal history of an unknown offender.

Offline information Information that may be available to a researcher during the course of a scientific study, which include the offender's understanding of what had happened and his/her account of the reasons for the offence. Much of it may not be admissible in court, such as hearsay accounts of who said what to whom and the speculations of various people about the activities of others, but the information can generate trends that are of relevance to later investigations.

Online information Information that the police obtain as part of their investigations, which is likely to form at least part of the case they bring to court. In addition to forensic evidence, such as DNA, fingerprints, fibres and the like, this will include behavioural evidence on what the offender did during an offence, where he/she did it and to whom.

Organised crime Offending activity carried out by a number of people who are in contact with each other, each playing different roles so that some form of administrative structure is in place, even though it may be very loose and changing, typically with the intention of monetary gain.

PACE The Police and Criminal Evidence Act; a legislative framework for the powers of police officers in England and Wales to combat crime, which provides codes of practice for the exercise of those powers.

Paedophilia The legal definition of an obsession with children as sex objects. Overt acts, including taking sexually explicit photographs, molesting children, and exposing one's genitalia to children, are all classed as serious crimes.

PEACE An approach to investigative interviewing adopted by the police in England and Wales, which emphasises appropriate preparedness and interpersonal interactions

Polygraph (lie detector) Equipment that measures a number of aspects of the autonomic arousal system and records the variations in these responses over time, originally as a graph (hence poly graph). Typically, heart rate, galvanic skin response and breathing patterns are recorded but the measurement of brain activity is also coming into use. The changes in the emotional response implied by changes in the graphs are taken as possible indicators of lying when it occurs in relation to specific forms of questions.

POSA Partially ordered scalogram analysis; a form of *multi-dimensional scaling* that represents 'types' (i.e. individuals) as points in space, allowing the identification of underlying processes that give rise to differences in types. It can be regarded as an MDS analogy for analysis of variance. Contrasts with *SSA*, which represents variables.

Propinquity   Literally 'nearness'. Used in IP to refer to the closeness of the crime locations to key places in the offender's life, notably their home or base.

Psychological autopsy   An expert analysis of the mental state, and/or personality of a deceased person, assessed, for example, in order to determine whether they had any involvement in their own demise. Usually based on interviews with all who knew the person and any written records the person may have left. Usually distinguished from *equivocal death analysis*.

Radex of criminality   The combination of qualitative and quantitative facets in which the quantitative modify (see *modulating facet*) the qualitative facets. The radex is an empirical discovery for criminal activity and is therefore fruitful in summarising the major ways in which crimes can differ and so helps in the identification of what is *salient* for an offence.

Rational choice theory   The proposition that offenders will make informed choices about where and how to commit their offences, considering available options and weighing up the costs and benefits associated with, for example, different potential crime locations.

Reid technique of interrogation   A suspect interviewing approach in which the principal objective is to gain an admission to the crime. This contrasts with the 'search for the truth', which is the stated objective of many other interviewing procedures (such as *PEACE*).

Reliability   Whether a measure of a given phenomenon produces consistent results across replications under similar conditions.

Robustness   How tolerant a method, measure, or procedure is to being used by different people under difficult circumstances and across a range of situations.

Routine activities theory   The notion that criminal opportunities are encountered and selected as an individual goes about their routine, day-to-day activities.

Safety (buffer) zone   An hypothetical area of decreased offending activity around the home or base of an offender, where the risks associated with being recognised and/or apprehended may be considered higher.

Salience   The significant or important features of offences (typically behaviours), which might be used to distinguish between crimes or criminals, or which might form the basis for investigative inferences.

Sexual sadism/sadistic sexual murder   Offences within which aggression is an integral part of the sexual activity. The offender obtains sexual arousal and gratification from controlling and inflicting pain on his victims.

Signature   Distinct set of actions in a crime that are unique to a criminal.

Smallest space analysis (SSA)   A form of multi-dimensional scaling in which variables are represented as points in a space such that the closer together the ranked distances between the points the closer in ranks are the associations/correlations between the points those variables represent. It is the use of ranks that produce interpretable results in a smaller mathematical space. Raw correlations are used as in other MDS procedures. It is from this property that the term 'smallest space' is derived.

Stalking   The UK Home Office defines stalking as the experience of persistent and unwanted attention that gives rise to fear or threat of violence. It is a form of harassment that in recent years has been reclassified as a crime in its own right. The nature and form that this attention takes can vary greatly and anyone can be a victim.

Styles of offending   Identifiable behaviours that co-occur to form interpretable groupings of criminal action.

System integration   A process in which scientific psychology generates principles and procedures out of which processes can be developed, which then become part of investigative practice.

Temporal buffers   The tendency for serial offenders to keep away from their previous offence locations.

Terrorism   There is no commonly, widely agreed definition of terrorism, but it is usually taken to mean violent action carried out with political objectives.

Theory   A postulation or a collection of general principles that serve as an explanation for a phenomenon, or for a framework for summarising a set of established facts and/or empirical observations.

Types of crime   Classifications of offences that come close to distinctions that underlie the law, such as 'residential burglary', 'armed robbery' and 'homicide'.

Typicality   Actions that can be found in the great majority of the crimes and which can be regarded as characteristic of those crimes. These are usually the aspects of the crime that lead to its definition both in any research context and in law.

Unconscious transference   Eyewitness memory of seeing a person but wrongly assigning that person to a criminal context.

Validity   Whether a theory, principle, method or measure effectively relates what it purports to relate.

Victim as object   A style of offending where a criminal is focused on obtaining some form of gratification and their victims are little more than *objects* to them.

Victim as person   A style of offending where the victim has particular significance as a *person* for the offender

Victim as vehicle   A style of offending in which offenders see their victims as a representative of those on whom they must act vindictively; they are a *vehicle* for the offender's anger.

Voice stress analysis   A procedure that claims to be able to detect lies through recording variations in physical attributes of the voice.

The 'windshield wiper' effect   The hypothesis that the angle subtended from an offender's home between his sites will tend to be acute rather than oblique.

References

Abel, G.G. (1989) Paraphilias, in *Comprehensive Textbook of Psychiatry*, 5th edn (eds H.I. Kaplan and B.J. Sadock), Williams & Williams, Baltimore.

Abelson, R.P. (1981) Psychological status of the script concept. *American Psychologist*, **36**, 715–29.

Adam, J. and Adam, J.C. (1934) *Criminal Investigation: A Practical Textbook for Magistrates, Police Officers, and Lawyers*. Adapted from Hans Gross's System der Kriminalistik, Sweet & Maxwell, London.

Aked, J., Canter, D.V., Sanford, A.J. and Smith, N.J. (1999) Approaches to the scientific attribution of authorship, in *Investigative Psychology Volumes 1: Evidence and Information* (eds D.V. Canter and L.J. Alison), Dartmouth, Aldershot.

Alison, L.J., Barrett, E. and Crego, J. (2007) Criminal investigative decision making: context and process, in *Expertise Out of Context: Proceedings of the Sixth International Conference on Naturalistic Decision Making* (ed. R.R. Hoffman), Lawrence Erlbaum, Mahwah.

Alison, L.J. and Canter, D. (1999) Profiling in police and practice, in *Profiling in Police and Practice* (eds D. Canter and L.J. Alison), Dartmouth, Aldershot.

Alison, L.J. and Crego, J. (2008) *Policing Critical Incidents: Leadership and Critical Incident Management*, Willan, Cullompton.

Alison, L. and Kebbell, M. (2006) Offender profiling: limits and potential, in *Practical Psychology for Forensic Investigations and Prosecutions* (eds M. Kebbell and G. Davies), John Wiley & Sons, Ltd, Chichester.

Alison, L., Rocket, W., Deprez, S. and Watts, S. (2000) Bandits, cowboys and Robin's men: the facets of armed robbery, in *Profiling Property Crimes* (eds D. Canter and L. Alison), Dartmouth, Ashgate.

Alison, L.J., Smith, M., Eastman, O. and Rainbow, L. (2003) Toulmin's philosophy of argument and its relevance to offender profiling. *Psychology, Crime and Law*, **9**(2), 173–83.

Alison, L., Snook, B. and Stein, K. (2001) Unobtrusive measurement: using police information for forensic research. *Qualitative Research*, **1**, 241–54.

Allnutt, S.H., Bradford, J.M.W., Greenberg, D.M. and Curry, S. (1996) Co-morbidity of alcoholism and the paraphilias. *Journal of Forensic Sciences*, **41**, 234–9.

Allport, F.H. and Allport, G.W. (1921) Personality traits: their classification and measurement. *Journal of Abnormal and Social Psychology*, **16**, 6–40.

Allport, G.W. and Postman, L.J. (1947) *The Psychology of Rumour*, Holt, Oxford.

American Psychiatric Association (1987) *Diagnostic and Statistical Manual of Mental Disorders, 3rd edn – Revised*, APA, Washington, DC.

American Psychiatric Association (1994) *Diagnostic and Statistical Manual of Mental Disorders, 4th edn (DSM-IV)*, APA, Washington, DC.

Anarchist Archives (2006) Bakunin's collected works. Available at http://dwardmac.pitzer.edu/Anarchist_Archives/bakunin/BakuninCW.html, accessed, 29 May 2009.

Atran, S. (2004) Mishandling suicide terrorism. *The Washington Quarterly*, **27**(3), 67–90.

Baker, D. and Donnelly, P.G. (1986) Neighborhood criminals and outsiders in two communities. Indications that criminal localism varies. *Sociology and Social Research*, **71**(1), 58–65.

Barker, M., Geraghty, J., Webb, B. and Key, T. (1993) The prevention of street robbery. *Crime Prevention Unit Series No 44*, Home Office Police Department, London.

Barker, R. and Gump, P. (1964) *Big School, Small School: High School Size and Student Behaviour*, Stanford University Press, Palo Alto, CA.

Barrett, E. (2001) Accounts of Violence. Unpublished Masters thesis; University of Liverpool.

Bartlett, F. (1932) *Remembering*, Cambridge University Press, London.

Bartol, C.R. (1995) *Criminal Behaviour: A Psychosocial Approach*, Prentice Hall, Englewood Cliffs, NJ.

Beauregard, E. and Proulx, J. (2002) Profiles in the offending process of non-serial sexual murders. *International Journal of Offender Therapy and Comparative Criminology*, **46**(4): 386–99.

Beauregard, E., Stone, M.R., Proulx, J. and Michaud, P. (2008) Sexual murderers of children: developmental, pre-crime, crime, and post-crime factors. *International Journal of Offender Therapy and Comparative Criminology*, **52**, 253–69.

Begg, P. and Skinner, K. (1992) *The Scotland Yard Files: 150 Years of the CID*, Headline, London.

Benedikt, M. (1881) *Anatomical Studies Upon Brains of Criminals*, William Wood & Company, New York.

Bennell, C., Alison, L., Stein, K. *et al.* (2001) Sexual offences against children as the abusive exploitation of conventional adult-child relationships. *Journal of Social and Personal Relationships*, **18**, 115–71.

Bennell, C. and Canter, D. (2002) Linking commercial burglaries by modus operandi: tests using regression and ROC analysis. *Science and Justice*, **42**(3), 1–12.

Bennell, C., Taylor, P.J. and Snook, B. (2007) Clinical versus actuarial geographic profiling strategies: a review of the research. *Police Practice and Research*, **8** (4), 335–45.

Bennett, T. and Wright, R. (1984) *Burglars on Burglary: Prevention and the Offender*, Gower, Aldershot.

Benneworth, K., Canter, D., Grieve, N. and Nicol, C. (2003) Narrative plausibility: the impact of sequencing and anchoring. *Behavioral Sciences and the Law*, **21**(2), 251–67.

Berg, K. and Godwin, G. (1993) *Monsters of Weimar*, Nemesis Books, London.

Berger, P.L. and Luckman, T. (1991)[1966] *The Social Construction of Reality. A Treatise in the Sociology of Knowledge*, Penguin, London.

Blackburn, R. (1993) *The Psychology of Criminal Conduct*, John Wiley & Sons, Ltd, Chichester.

Blau, T.H. (1994) *Psychological Services for Law Enforcement*, John Wiley & Sons, Inc., New York.

Block, J. (1989) *California Adult Q-set, unpublished measure*, University of California, Berkeley, CA.

Blumstein, A., Cohen, J. and Farrington, D. (1988) Criminal career research: its value for criminology. *Criminology*, **26**, 1–36.

Bodansky, Y. (2001) *Bin Laden: the Man who Declared War on America*, Random House, New York.

Bolitho, W. (1926) *Murder for Profit*, Jonathan Cape, London.

Booker, C. (2004) *The Seven Basic Plots: Why We Tell Stories*, Continuum, London.

Bonacich, P. (1987) Power and centrality: A family of measures. *American Journal of Sociology*, **92**, 1170–82.

Borg, I. and Lingoes, J.C. (1987) *Multidimensional Similarity Structure Analysis*, Springer, New York.

Borgatti, S.P., Everett, M.G. and Freeman, L.C. (1992) *UCINET IV Version 1.62*, Analytic Technologies, Columbia.

Bourgois, P. (1995) *In Search of Respect: Selling Crack in El Barrio*, Cambridge University Press, Cambridge.

Bowlby, J. (1949) The study and reduction of group tensions in the family. *Human Relations*, **2**, 123.

Bradfield, A.L., Wells, G.L. and Olson, E.A. (2002) The damaging effect of confirming feedback on the relation between eyewitness certainty and identification accuracy. *Journal of Applied Psychology*, **87**, 112–20.

Brantingham, P.J. and P.L. Brantingham (1981) Notes on the geometry of crime, in *Environmental Criminology* (eds P.J. Brantingham and P.L. Brantingham), Beverly Hills, Sage Publications, pp. 27–54.

Brigham, J.C., Maass, A., Snyder, L.D. and Spaulding, K. (1982) Accuracy of eyewitness identifications in a field setting. *Journal of Personality and Social Psychology*, **42**, 673–81.

Britt, C.L. (1994) Crime and unemployment among youths in the United States, 1958–1990. *American Journal of Economics and Sociology*, **53**, 99–109.

Brittain, R. (1970) The sadistic murderer. *Medicine, Science and the Law*, **10**, 198–207.

Brown, B.B. and Harris, P.B. (1989) Residential burglary victimisation: reactions to the invasion of a primary territory. *Journal of Environmental Psychology*, **9**, 119–32.

Brown, J. and Canter, D. (1985) The uses of explanation in the research interview, in *The Research Interview: Uses and Approaches* (eds M. Brenner, J. Brown and D. Canter), Academic Press, London.

Bruner, J. (1987) Life as narrative. *Social Research*, **54**(1), 11–32.

Brussel, J.A. (1968) *Casebook of a Crime Psychiatrist*, Bernard Geis Associates, New York.

Buckhout, R. (1974) Eyewitness testimony. *Scientific American*, **231**, 23–31.

Buckhout, R. (1977) Eyewitness identification and psychology in the courtroom. *Criminal Defense*, **4**, 5–10.

Buckley, J.P. (2006) The Reid technique of interviewing and interrogation, in *Investigative Interviewing* (ed. T. Williamson), Willan, Cullompton.

Bull, R. (2002) Police interviewing, in *Criminal Justice Research* (eds I. McKenzie and R. Bull), Ashgate, Aldershot.

Bull, R. and Milne, R. (2004) Attempts to improve police interviewing of suspects, in *Interrogation, Confessions and Entrapment* (ed. G.D. Lassiter), Kluwer/Plenum, New York.

Burch, T.K. (2006) The model-based view of science: an encouragement to interdisciplinary work. *Twenty-first Century Society*, **1**(1), 39–58.

Byford, L. (1981) The Yorkshire Ripper case: review of the police investigation, in D. Canter (2003) *Mapping Murder*, Virgin Books, London.

Campbell, D.T. (1978) Qualitative knowing in action research, in *Experimental and Quasi-experimental Designs for Research* (eds M. Brenner, P. Marsh and M. Brenner), Croom-Helm, London.

Canter, D. (1977) *The Psychology of Place*, The Architectural Press, London.

Canter, D. (1985) *Facet Theory: Approaches to Social Research*, Springer Verlag, New York.

Canter, D. (1989) Offender profiles, *The Psychologist*, **2**(1), 12–16.

Canter, D. (1990) An overview of behaviour in fires, in D. Canter (ed.) *Fires and Human Behaviour*, David Fulton, London.

Canter, D. (1993) The wholistic, organic researcher: central issues in clinical research methodology, in *Curriculum in Clinical Psychology* (eds G. Powell, R. Young and S. Frosh), BPS, Leicester.

Canter, D. (1994) *Criminal Shadows*, HarperCollins, London.

Canter, D. (2000a) Psychological autopsy, in *Encyclopaedia of Forensic Science*, Academic Press, London.

Canter, D. (2000b) Seven assumptions for an investigative environmental psychology, in *Theoretical Perspectives in Environment-Behavior Research: Underlying Assumptions, Research Problems, and Methodologies* (eds S. Wapner, J. Demick, T. Yamamoto and H. Minami), Plenum, New York.

Canter, D. (2000c) Psycholinguistics, In *Encyclopaedia of Forensic Science*, Academic Press, London.

Canter, D. (2000d) Destructive organisational psychology, in *The Social Psychology of Crime* (eds D. Canter and L.J. Alison), Ashgate, Aldershot

Canter, D. (2002) The violated body, in S. Sweeny and I. Hodder (eds) *The Body*, Cambridge University Press, Cambridge, pp. 57–74.

Canter, D. (2003) *Mapping Murder: The Secrets of Geographical Profiling*, Virgin Books, London.

Canter, D. (2004a) Offender profiling and investigative psychology. *Journal of Investigative Psychology and Offender Profiling*, **1**, 1–15.

Canter, D. (2004b) A partial order scalogram analysis of criminal network structures. *Behaviormetrika*, **31**(2), 131–52.

Canter, D. (2005) Confusing operational predicaments and cognitive explorations: comments on Rossmo and Snook *et al*. *Applied Cognitive Psychology*, **19**(5), 663–68.

Canter, D. (2006) The Samson syndrome: is there a kamikaze psychology? *Twenty-first Century Society: Journal of the Academy of Social Sciences*, **1**(2), 107–28.

Canter, D. (2008) The Psychology of Fraud. Internal report to the Centre for Investigative Psychology.

Canter, D. and Alison, L.J. (eds) (1999a) *Interviewing and Deception*, Ashgate, Aldershot.

Canter, D.V. and Alison, L.J. (1999b) The social psychology of crime, in D.V. Canter and L.J. Alison (eds), *The Social Psychology of Crime: Teams, Groups, Networks*, Dartmouth, Aldershot.

Canter, D.V. and Alison, L.J. (2000) *The Social Psychology of Crime: Teams, Groups, Networks*, Dartmouth, Aldershot.

Canter, D. and Alison, L.J. (2003) Converting evidence into data: the use of law enforcement archives as unobtrusive measurement. *The Qualitative Report*, **8**(2), 151–76.

Canter, D., Alison, L.J., Alison, E. and Wentink, N. (2004) The organized/disorganized typology of serial murder: myth or model? *Psychology Public Policy and Law*, **10**, 293–320.

Canter, D., Bennell, C., Alison, L. J. and Reddy, S. (2003) Differentiating sex offences: a behaviourally based thematic classification of stranger rapes. *Behavioural Science and the Law*, **21**, 157–74.

Canter, D.V., Breaux, J. and Sime, J. (1990) Domestic, multiple occupancy and hospital fires, in D.V. Canter (ed.) *Fires and Human Behaviour*, David Fulton Publishers, London.

Canter, D. and Brown, J. (1985) Explanatory role, in *The Psychology of Ordinary Explanations of Social Behaviour* (ed. C. Anataki), Academic Press, London.

Canter, D., Coffey, T., Huntley, M. and Missen, C. (2000) Predicting serial killers' home base using a decision support system. *Journal of Quantitative Criminology*, **16**, 457–78.

Canter, D. and Fritzon, K. (1998) Differentiating arsonists: a model of firesetting actions and characteristics. *Journal of Legal and Criminological Psychology*, **3**, 73–96.

Canter, D. and Gregory, A. (1994) Identifying the residential location of serial rapists. *Journal of the Forensic Science Society*, **34**, 169–75.

Canter, D. and Hammond, L. (2006) A comparison of the efficacy of different decay functions in geographical profiling for a sample of US serial killers. *Journal of Investigative Psychology and Offender Profiling*, **3**(2), 91–103.

Canter, D. and Heritage, R. (1990) A multivariate model of sexual offence behaviour: developments in offender profiling. *Journal of Forensic Psychiatry*, **1**(2), 185–212.

Canter, D., Heritage, R. and Kovacik, M. (1989) *Offender Profiling*, Home Office, London.

Canter, D. and Hodge, S. (2000) Criminal's mental maps, in *Atlas of Crime: Mapping the Criminal Landscape* (eds L.S. Turnbull, E.H. Hendrix and B.D. Dent), Phoenix, Arizona, Oryx Press.

Canter, D., Hughes, D and Kirby, S. (1998) Paedophilia: pathology, criminality, or both? The development of a multivariate model of offence behaviour in child sexual abuse. *The Journal of Forensic Psychiatry*, **9**(3), 532–55.

Canter, D. and Ioannou, M. (2004) A multivariate model of stalking behaviour. *Behaviormetrika*, **31**, 113–130.

Canter, D., Kaouri, C. and Ioannou, M. (2003) The facet structure of criminal narratives, in *Facet Theory: Towards Cumulative Social Science*, (eds S. Levy and D. Elizur), University of Ljubljana, Faculty of Arts, Centre for Educational Development, Ljubljana, pp. 27–38.

Canter, D. and Larkin, P. (1993) The environmental range of serial rapists. *Journal of Environmental Psychology*, **13**, 63–9.

Canter, D., Missen, C. and Hodge, S. (1996) Are serial killers special? A case for special agents. *Policing Today*, **2**(1), 22–8.

Canter, D. and Shalev, K. (2008) Putting crime in its place: psychological process in crime site location, in *Principles of Geographical Offender Profiling* (eds D. Canter and D. Youngs), Ashgate, Aldershot.

Canter, D. and Wentink, N. (2004) An empirical test of Holmes and Holmes' Serial Murder Typology. *Criminal Justice and Behaviour*, **20**(10), 1–26.

Canter, D. and Youngs, D. (2003) Beyond offender profiling: the need for an investigative psychology, in *Handbook of Psychology in Legal Contexts* (eds R. Bull and D. Carson), John Wiley & Sons, Ltd, Chichester, pp. 171–205.

Canter, D. and Youngs, D. (eds) (2008a) *Principles of Geographical Offender Profiling*, Ashgate, Aldershot.

Canter, D. and Youngs, D. (eds) (2008b) *Applications of Geographical Offender Profiling*, Ashgate, Aldershot.

Canter, D. and Youngs, D. (2008c) iOPS: An Interactive Offender Profiling System. In S. Chainey, L. Thompson. Crime Mapping Case Studies. Wiley: Chichester.

Canter, D. and Youngs, D. (in press, a) Psychological explanations of geographical offender profiling. International Research Centre for Investigative Psychology (IRCIP) (internal report, submitted for publication).

Canter, D. and Youngs, D. (in press, b) Villain or hero? The roles offenders play. International Research Centre for Investigative Psychology (IRCIP) (internal report, submitted for publication).

Canter, D. and Youngs, D. (in press, c) A review of investigative psychology methodologies. International Research Centre for Investigative Psychology (IRCIP) (internal report, submitted for publication).

Canter, D. and Youngs, D. (in press, d) A Narrative Action System Model of Criminal Differentiation. International Research Centre for Investigative Psychology (IRCIP) (internal report, submitted for publication).

Capone, D. and Nichols, W.W.J. (1975) Crime and distance: an analysis of offender behavior in space. *Proceedings, Association of American Geographers*, **7**, 45–9.

Cattell, R.B. (1946) *The Description and Measurement of Personality*, Harcourt, Brace & World, New York.

Ceci, S.J., Ross, D.F. and Toglia, M.P. (1987) Suggestibility of children's memory: psycholegal implications. *Journal of Experimental Psychology*, **27**, 38–51.

Cervone, D. and Shoda, Y. (1999) Beyond traits in the study of personality coherence. *Current Directions in Psychological Science*, **8**, 27–32.

Clarke, C. and Milne, R. (2001) National evaluation of the PEACE investigative interviewing course. *Police Research Award Scheme*, Home Office, London.

Clifford, B.R. and Scott, J. (1978) Individual and situational factors in eyewitness testimony. *Journal of Applied Psychology*, **62**, 352–9.

Cohen, L.E. and Felson, M. (1979) Social change and crime rate change: a routine activity approach. *American Sociological Review*, **4**, 588–608.

Coid, J.W. (1992) DSM-III Diagnosis in criminal psychopaths: a way forward. *Criminal Behaviour and Mental Health*, **2**, 78–94.

Cole, S. (2001) *Suspect Identities: A History of Fingerprinting and Criminal Identification*, Harvard University Press, Cambridge, MA.

Coleman, C. and Norris, C. (2000) *Introducing Criminology*, Willan, Cullompton.

Conklin, J.E. (1972) *Robbery and the Criminal Justice System*, Lippencott, Philadelphia.

Coogan, T.P. (2002) *The IRA*, Palgrave, New York.

Cooke, D.J. (1998) Cross-cultural aspects of psychopathy, in *Psychopathy: Antisocial, Criminal and Violent Behaviour* (eds T. Millon, E. Simonsen, M. Birket-Smith, and R.D. Davis), Guilford, New York, pp. 260–76.

Copson, G. (1995) *Coals to Newcastle. Part 1: A Study of Offender Profiling*, Home Office, Police Research Group, London.

Cornish, D.B. and Clarke, R.V. (1986) *The Reasoning Criminal: Rational Choice Perspectives on Offending*, Springer-Verlag, New York.

Costello, P. (1991) *The Real World of Sherlock Holmes: True Crimes Investigated by Arthur Conan Doyle*, Robinson, London.

Coulthard, M. (1994) The use of corpora in the analysis of forensic texts. *Forensic Linguistics*, **1**(1), 27–43.

Cressey, D.R. (1953) *Other People's Money: A Study in the Social Psychology of Embezzlement*, Wadsworth Publishing, Belmont, CA.

Cromwell, P.F., Olson, J. and Avery, D.W. (1991) *Breaking and Entering: An Ethnographic Analysis of Burglary*, Sage, London.

Crossley, M.L. (2000) Narrative psychology, trauma, and the study of self/identity. *Theory and Psychology*, **10**(4), 527–46.

Crumplin, P. (2009) Contract murder, in *Profiling Violent Crime* (eds D. Canter and D. Youngs), Aldershot, Ashgate.

Cutler, B. and Penrod, S. (1995) *Mistaken Identity*, Cambridge University Press, Cambridge.

Cyriax, O. (1993) *Crime: An Encyclopaedia*, Andre Deutsch, London.

Danis, M. and Stohl, M. (2009) Framing Muslim terrorist incidents in the United States and United Kingdom: implications for counterterrorism, in D. Canter (ed.) *The Faces of Terrorism: Cross-Disciplinary Explorations*.

Davies, A., Wittebrood, K. and Jackson, J.L. (1997) Predicting the criminal antecedents of a stranger rapist from his offence behaviour. *Science Justice*, **37**, 161–70.

Deffenbacher, K.A., Bornstein, B.H., Penrod, S.D. and McGorty, E.K. (2005) A meta-analytic review of the effects of high stress on eyewitness memory. *Law and Human Behaviour*, **28**(6), 687–706.

Delisi, M. and Sherer, A.M. (2006) Multiple homicide offenders: offence characteristics, social correlates and criminal careers. *Criminal Justice and Behavior*, **33**(3): 367–91.

Dietz, P. (1985) Sex offender profiling by the FBI: a preliminary conceptual model, in *Clinical Criminology* (eds M.H. Ben-Aron, S.J. Hucker and C.D. Webster), Clark Institute of Psychiatry, Toronto, Ontario, Canada.

Dietz, P. (1986) Mass serial and sensational homicides. *Bulletin of the New York Academy of Medicine*, **62**, 477–91.

Dietz, P., Hazelwood, R. and Warren, J. (1990) The sexually sadistic criminal and his offenses. *The Bulletin of the American Academy of Psychiatry and the Law*, **18**, 163–78.

Dodd, N.J. (2000) The psychology of fraud, in *Profiling Property Crimes* (eds D. Canter and L. Alison), Ashgate, Dartmouth.

Donald, I.J. (1993) Behaviour in fires: preventing disasters. *Health, Safety and Environment Bulletin*, **216**, 5–8.

Donald, I.J. (1995) Psychological insights into managerial responsibility for public and employee safety, in *Handbook of Psychology in Legal Contexts* (eds R. Bull and D. Carson), John Wiley & Sons, Ltd, Chichester.

Donald, I.J. and Canter, D.V. (1990) Behavioural aspects of the King's Cross disaster, in D.V. Canter (ed) *Fires and Human Behaviour* 2nd edn, David Fulton Publishers, London.

Donald, I.J. and Canter, D.V. (1992) Intentionality and fatality during the King's Cross underground fire. *European Journal of Social Psychology*, **22**(3), 203–18.

Donald, I. and Wilson, A. (2000) Ram raiding: criminals working in groups, in *The Social Psychology of Crime* (eds D. Canter and L.J. Alison), Ashgate, Aldershot, pp. 189–246.

Dorn, N., Murji, K. and South, N. (1992) *Traffickers: Drug Markets and Law Enforcements*, Routledge, London.

Dorn, N. and South, N. (1990) Drug markets and law enforcements. *British Journal of Criminology*, **30**(2), 171–88.

Douglas, J. (1976) *Investigative Social Research: Individual and Team Field Research*, Sage Publications, Beverley Hills.

Douglas, J.E., Burgess, A.W., Burgess, A.G. and Ressler, R.K. (1992) *Crime Classification Manual: A Standard System for Investigating and Classifying Violent Crime*. New York: Simon & Shuster.

Douglas, J., Burgess, A.W., Burgess, A.G. and Ressler, R.K. (2006) *Crime Classification Manual: A Standard System for Investigating and Classifying Violent Crimes*, John Wiley & Sons, Inc., San Francisco, CA.

Douglas, J. and Olshaker, M. (1997) *Mindhunter: Inside the FBI's Elite Serial Crime Unit*, Scribner, New York.

Douglas, J. and Olshaker, M. (1999) *The Anatomy of Motive*, New York, Scribner.

Douglas, J., Ressler, R.K., Burgess, A.W. and Hartman, C.R. (1986) Criminal profiling from crime scene analysis. *Behavioral Sciences and the Law*, **4**(4), pp. 401–21.

Douglas, M. (1978) Cultural bias. Royal Anthropological Institute. Occasional Paper No. 35. Reprinted in M. Douglas (1982) *In the Active Voice*, Routledge & Kegan Paul, London, pp. 183–254.

Downs, R.M. and Stea, D. (1977) *Maps in Minds*, Harper & Row, London.

Drummond, D.S. (1976) *Police Culture*, Sage Publications, London.

Duffield, G. and Grabosky, P. (2001) The psychology of fraud. *Trends and Issues in Crime and Criminal Justice*, **199**.

Dugdale, R.L. (1877) *The Jukes: A Study in Crime, Pauperism, Disease, and Heredity*, Putnam & Sons, New York.

Duyne, van, P. (1996) The phantom and threat of organised crime. *Crime, Law and Social Change*, **24**, 341–77.

Duyne, van, P. (1999) Mobsters are human too, in *Profiling in Policy and Practice* (eds D. Canter and L.J. Alison), Ashgate, Aldershot.

Ebbinghaus, H. (1913) *Memory. A Contribution to Experimental Psychology*, Teachers College, Columbia University, New York. (Reprinted Bristol: Thoemmes Press, 1999)

Eckman, P. (2001) *Telling Lies*, Norton, New York.

Edwards, S. (1977) *The Vidocq Dossier: The Story of the World's First Detective*, Houghton Mifflin Company, Boston, MA.

Egger, S.A. (1984) A working definition of serial murder and the reduction blindness. *Journal of Police Science and Administration*, **12**, 348–57.

Egger, S.A. (1998) *The Killers Among Us: An Examination of Serial Murder and its Investigation*. New Jersey: Prentice Hall.

Egger, S.A. (1999) Psychological profiling. *Journal of Contemporary Criminal Justice*, **15**(3), 242–61.

Elaad, E. (1999) A comparative study of polygraph tests and other forensic methods, in *Interviewing and Deception* (eds D.V. Canter and L.J. Alison), Ashgate, Aldershot, pp. 211–31.

Eldridge, J.E. and Jones, J.P. (1991) Warped space: A geography of distance decay. *The Professional Geographer*, **43**(4): 500–11.

Elliot, D.S. and Ageton, S.S. (1980) Reconciling race and class differences in self-reported and official estimates of delinquency. *American Sociological Review*, **45**, 95–110.

Esplin, P.W., Boychuk, T. and Raskin, D. (1988) Application of Statement Validity Analysis. Paper presented at the NATO Advanced Study Institute on Credibility Assessment, Maratea, Italy.

Eysenck, H.J. (1980) *The Causes and Effects of Smoking*, Maurice Temple Smith, London.

Eysenck, M. (1987) Trait theories of anxiety, in *Personality Dimensions and Arousal* (eds J. Strelau and H.J. Eysenck), Plenum Press, New York, pp. 79–97.

Farrington, D.P. (1973) Self-reports of deviant behaviour: predictive and stable? *Journal of Criminal Law and Criminology*, **64**, 99–110.

Farrington, D.P. (1986) Age and crime, in *Crime and Justice* (eds M. Tonry and N. Morris), Chicago, University of Chicago Press.

Farrington, D.P. (1989) Self-reported and official offending in adolescence and adulthood, in *Cross-National Research in Self-Reported Crime and Delinquency*, (ed. M.W. Kelin), Kluwer, Dordrecht.

Farrington, D.P. (1995) The development of offending and anti-social behaviour from childhood: key findings from the Cambridge Study of Delinquent Development. *Journal of Child Psychology and Psychiatry*, **360**, 929–64.

Farrington, D.P., Joliffe, D., Loeber, R. *et al.* (2001) The concentration of offenders in families, and family criminality in the prediction of boys' delinquency. *Journal of Adolescence*, **24**, 579–96.

Farrington, D.P. and Lambert, S. (1994) Differences between burglars and violent offenders. *Psychology, Crime and Law*, **1**, 107–16.

Farrington, D.P. and Lambert, S. (2007) Predicting offender profiles from offence and victim characteristics, in *Criminal Profiling: International Theory, Research, and Practice* (ed. R.N. Kocsis), Humana Press, Totowa, NJ.

Faust, K. (1994) *Social Network Analysis: Methods and Applications*, Cambridge University Press, Cambridge.

Fawcett, T. (2006) An introduction to ROC analysis. *Pattern Recognition Letters*, **27**, 861–74.

Fay, F.J. (1988) *The Police Dictionary and Encyclopaedia*, Charles C. Thomas, Springfield.

Fedora, O., Reddon, J.R., Morrison, J.W. *et al.* (1992) Sadism and other paraphilias in normal controls and aggressive and non-aggressive sex offenders. *Archives of Sexual Behaviour*, **21**, 1–15.

Feeney, F. (1986) Robbers as decision-makers, in *In Their Own Words: Criminals on Crime* (ed. P.F. Cromwell), Roxbury Publishing Co, Los Angeles, CA.

Fesbach, S. (1964) The function of aggression and the regulation of aggressive drive. *Psychological Review*, **71**, 257–72.

Fisher, D. (1999) *The Case for Pragmatic Psychology*, New York University Press, New York.

Fisher, R.P. and Geiselman, R.E. (1992) *Memory Enhancing Techniques for Investigative Interviewing: the Cognitive Interview*, Charles C. Thomas, Springfield, IL.

Fisher, R.P., Geiselman, R.E. and Amador, M. (1989) Field test of the cognitive interview: enhancing the recollection of actual victims and witnesses of crime. *Journal of Applied Psychology*, **74**, 722–7.

Flin, R., Slaven, G. and Stewart, K. (1996) Emergency decision making in the offshore oil and gas industry. *Human Factors*, **38**(2), 262–77.

Fox, J.A., and Levin, J. (1994) *Overkill: Mass Murder and Serial Killing Exposed*, New York, Plenum.

Fox, J.A. and Levin, J. (2003) Mass murder: an analysis of extreme violence. *Journal of Applied Psychoanalytic Studies*, **5**(1), 47–64.

Francis, B., Soothill, K. and Ackerley, E. (2004) Multiple cohort data, delinquent generations and criminal careers. *Journal of Contemporary Criminal Justice*, **20**, 103–26.

Frank, G. (1966) *The Boston Strangler*, New American Library, New York.

Frank, M.G., Yarbrough, J.D. and Ekman, P. (2005) Investigative interviewing and the detection of deception, in *Investigative Interviewing: Rights, Research, Regulation*, (ed. T. Williamson), Willan Publishing, Cullompton.

Freeman, L.C. (1979) Centrality in social networks: conceptual clarifications. *Social Networks*, **1**, 215–39.

Fritzon, K. (2000) The contribution of psychological research to arson investigation, in *Profiling Property Crimes. Offender Profiling Series* (eds D.V. Canter and L. Alison), Vol. 4, Ashgate, Aldershot, pp. 147–84.

Fritzon, K. (2001) An examination of the relationship between distance travelled and motivational aspects of arson. *Journal of Environmental Psychology*, **21**, 45–60.

Fritzon, K. and Canter, D. (1998) Differentiating arsonists: a model of firesetting actions and characteristics. *Legal and Criminological Psychology*, **3**, 73–96.

Fritzon, K., Canter, D. and Wilton, Z. (2001) The application of an action systems model to destructive behaviour: the examples of arson and terrorism. *Behavioral Sciences and the Law*, **19**(5–6), 657–90.

Fritzon, K. and Ridgway, J. (2001) Near-death experience: the role of victim reaction in attempted homicide. *Journal of Interpersonal Violence*, **16**, 679–96.

Frye, H.N. (1957) *Anatomy of Criticism: Four Essays*, Princeton University Press, Princeton.

Furnham, A. and Thompson, J. (1991) Personality and self-reported delinquency. *Personality and Individual Differences*, **12**, 585–93.

Garfinkel, H. (1967) *Studies in Ethnomethodology*, Prentice Hall, Englewood Cliffs, NJ.

Geberth, V.J. (1992) Stalkers. *Law and Order*, October, 138–43.

Geiselman, R.E., Fisher R.P., MacKinnon, D.P. and Holland, H.L. (1985) Eyewitness memory enhancement in the police interview: cognitive retrieval mnemonics versus hypnosis. *Journal of Applied Psychology*, **70**, 401–12.

Geiselman, R.E., Fisher, R.P., Mackinnon, D.P. and Holland, H.L. (1986) Enhancement of eyewitness memory with the cognitive interview. *American Journal of Psychology*, **99**, 385–401.

Gerard, F., Mormont, C. and Kocsis, R.N. (2007) Offender profiles and crime scene behaviours in Belgian sexual murders, in *Criminal Profiling: International Perspectives in Theory, Practice and Research* (ed. R.N. Kocsis), Humana Press/Springer, Totowa, NJ.

Godlewski, J. (1987) Typologia zgwałceń [Typology of rape]. *Psychiatria Polska*, **21**(4), 296–301.

Goffman E. 1963. *Stigma: Notes on the Management of Spoiled Identity*, Prentice Hall, Englewood Cliffs, NJ.

Goodwill, A.M. and Alison, L.J. (2007) When is profiling possible? Offence planning and aggression as moderators in predicting offender age from victim age in stranger rape. *Behavioral Sciences and the Law*, **25**, 823–40.

Goring, C. (1913) *The English Convict*, Darling, London.

Gosselin, C. and Wilson, G. (1980) *Sexual Variations*, Faber & Faber, London.

Gratzer, T. and Bradford, J.M.W. (1995) Offender and offense characteristics of sexual sadists: a comparative study. *Journal of Forensic Sciences*, **40**, 450–5.

Green, E.J., Booth, C.E. and Biderman, M. D. (1976) Cluster analysis of burglary MO's. *Journal of Police Science and Administration*, **4**, 382–8.

Gregory, A. (1999) The decision to die. The psychology of the suicide note. In D.V. Canter and L.J. Alison (eds) *Profiling in Policy and Practice: Offender Profiling Series*, Vol. I, Ashgate, Aldershot, pp. 127–56.

Gresswell, D.M. and Hollin, C.R. (1994) Multiple murder: a review. *British Journal of Criminology*, **34**, 1–14.

Grimm, L.G. and Yarnold, P.R. (1995) *Reading and Understanding Multivariate Statistics*, American Psychological Association, Washington.

Gross, H.G. (1911) *Criminal Psychology*, Little, Brown & Company, Boston, MA.

Gross, H.G. (1934) *Criminal Investigation: A Practical Textbook for Magistrates, Police Officers, and Lawyers*, adapted by John Adam and J. Collyer Adam, Sweet & Maxwell, London.

Groth, A.N. and Birnbaum, H.J. (1979) *Men Who Rape: The Psychology of the Offender*, Plenum, New York.

Grubin, D. (1994) Sexual murder. *The British Journal of Psychiatry*, **165**, 624–9.

Grubin, D. (2004) The role of the polygraph in the assessment and management of risk in sex offenders in the community, in *Sex Offenders in the Community* (ed. A. Matravers), Willan, Cullompton.

Grubin, D., Kelly, P. and Brunsdon, C. (2001) *Linking Serious Sexual Assaults Through Behaviour*, Home Office, Research, Development and Statistics Directorate, London.

Grubin, D., Madsen, L., Parsons, S., *et al.* (2004) A prospective study of the impact of polygraphy on high-risk behaviors in adult sex offenders. *Sexual Abuse: A Journal of Research and Treatment*, **16**, 209–22.

Gudjonsson, G.H. (1984) A new scale of interrogative suggestibility. *Personality and Individual Differences* **5**, 303–14.

Gudjonsson, G.H. (2001) False confession. *The Psychologist*, **14**, 588–91.

Gudjonsson, G.H. (2006) Sex offenders and confessions: how to overcome their resistance during questioning. *Journal of Clinical Forensic Medicine*, **13**, 203–7.

Gudjonsson, G.H., Clare, I.C.H. and Rutter, S. (1995) The relationship between suggestibility and anxiety among suspects detained at police stations. *Psychological Medicine*, **25**, 875–8.

Gudjonsson, G.H. and MacKeith, J.A.C. (1988) Retracted confessions: legal, psychological and psychiatric aspects. *Medicine, Science and the Law*, **28**, 187–94.

Guttman, L. (1954) A new approach to factor analysis: the radex, in *Mathematical Thinking in the Social Sciences* (ed. P.R. Lazarsfeld), Free Press, Glencoe, p. 111.

Guttman, L. (1965) A faceted definition of intelligence, in *Studies in Psychology. Scripta Hierosolymitana* (ed. R. Eiferman) vol. 14, Hebrew University, Jerusalem, pp. 166–81.

Guttman, L. (1968) A general nonmetric technique for finding the smallest coordinate space for a configuration of points. *Psychometrika*, **33**, 469–506.

Guttman, L. (1982) Facet theory, smallest space analysis and factor analysis. *Perceptual and Motor Skills*, **54**(2), 491–3.

Guzzo, R. (1996) Fundamental considerations about work groups, in *Prospective Studies of Crime and Delinquency* (ed. M. West), John Wiley & Sons, Ltd, Chichester, pp. 211–24.

Haber, R.N. and Haber, L. (2000) Experiencing, remembering and reporting events. *Psychology, Public Policy, and Law*, **6**, 1057–97.

Häkkänen, H. (2005) Homicide by ligature strangulation in Finland: offence and offender characteristics. *Forensic Science International*, **152**, 62–4.

Häkkänen, H., Lindlöf, P. and Santtila, P. (2004) Crime scene actions and offender characteristics in a sample of Finnish stranger rapes. *Journal of Investigative Psychology and Offender Profiling*, **1**(1), 17–32.

Hall, H.V. (1983) Guilty but mentally ill: feedback from state attorneys general. *Bulletin of the American Academy of Forensic Psychology*, **4**, 2–8.

Hammond, L., Wagstaff, G.F. and Cole, J. (2006) Facilitating eyewitness memory in adults and children with context reinstatement and focused meditation. *Journal of Investigative Psychology and Offender Profiling*, **3**, 117–30.

Hare, R.D. (1991) *Hare Psychopathy Checklist – Revised*, Multi-Health Systems, Toronto.

Hare, R.D. (1993) *Without Conscience: The Disturbing World of Psychopaths Among Us*, Guilford, New York.

Hare, R.D. (1996) Psychopathy: a clinical construct whose time has come. *Criminal Justice and Behavior*, **23**, 25–54.

Hare, R.D. (2003) *Hare Psychopathy Checklist – Revised*, 2nd edn, Multi-Health Systems, Toronto.

Harman, H.H. (1976) *Modern Factor Analysis*. Chicago, University of Chicago Press.

Harmon, R.B., Rosner, R. and Owens, H. (1995) Obsessional harassment and erotomania in a criminal court population. *Journal of Forensic Sciences*, **40**(2), 188–96.

Harré, R. (1979) *Social Being*, Blackwell, Oxford.

Harrison, S. (1993) *The Diary of Jack the Ripper: The Discovery, The Investigation, The Debate*, Hyperion, New York.

Hazelwood, R.R., Ressler, R.K., Depue, R.L. and Douglas, J.E. (1987) Criminal personality profiling: an overview, in *Practical Aspects of Rape Investigation: A Multidisciplinary Approach* (eds R.R. Hazelwood and A.W. Burgess), Elsevier, New York.

Heap, M. and Kirsch, I. (eds) (2006) *Hypnosis*, Ashgate, Aldershot.

Hendricks, J.E. and Spillane, L. (1993) Stalking: what can we do to forestall tragedy? *The Police Chief*, December, 68–71.

Hickey, E. (1997) *Serial Killers and their Victims*, 2nd edn, Brooks/Cole, Pacific Grove, CA.

Hickey, E. (2005) *Serial Murderers and their Victims*, Belmont, Wadsworth.

Hill, A., Habermann, N., Berner, W. and Briken, P. (2006) Sexual sadism and sadistic personality disorder in sexual homicide. *Journal of Personality Disorders*, **20**(6), 671–84.

Hindelang, M.J., Hirschi, T. and Weis, J.G. (1981) *Measuring Delinquency*, Sage, London.

Hirschfield, A. and Bowers, K. (2001) *Mapping and Analysing Crime Data: Lessons from Research and Practice*, Taylor & Francis, London.

Hobbs, D. (1988) *Doing the Business: Entrepreneurship, the Working Class and Detectives in the East End of London*, Oxford University Press, Oxford.

Hobbs, D. (1995) *Professional Criminals*, Ashgate, Dartmouth.

Hobbs, D. (1997) Criminal collaboration: youth gangs, subcultures, professional criminals, and organised crime, in *The Oxford Handbook of Criminology* (eds M. Maguire, R. Mogan and R. Reiner), Oxford University Press, Oxford.

Hobbs, D. (1988) *Doing the Business: Entrepreneurship, the Working Class and Detectives in the East End of London.* Oxford University Press, Oxford.

Hodge, S. (1999) Canter's Victim Role Model of Serial Murder. Unpublished internal report to the International Research Centre for Investigative Psychology (IRCIP).

Hodge, S.A. (2000) Multivariate model of serial sexual murder. Unpublished work cited in Canter, D. (2000) offender profiling and criminal differentiation. *Legal and Criminological Psychology,* **5**, 23–46.

Hodge, S. and Canter, D. (1998) Victims and perpetrators of male sexual assault. *Journal of Interpersonal Violence,* **13**(2), 222–39.

Hogan, J. and Hogan, R. (1989) How to measure employee reliability. *Journal of Applied Psychology,* **74**(2), 273–9.

Hollinger, R.C. and Clark, J.P. (1983) *Theft by Employees,* Lexington Books, Lexington, MA.

Holmes, R.M. and DeBurger, J. (1985) Profiles in terror: the serial murder. *Probation,* **49**, 29–34.

Holmes, R.M. and DeBurger, J. (1988) *Serial Murder,* Sage, Newbury Park.

Holmes, R.M. and Holmes, S.T. (1996) *Profiling Violent Crimes: An Investigative Tool,* Sage Publications, London.

Holmes, R.M. and Holmes, S.T. (1998) *Serial Murder,* 2nd edn, Sage, Thousand Oaks, CA.

Hooten, E.A. (1939) *The American Criminal: An Anthropological Study,* Harvard University Press, Cambridge, MA.

Horgan, J. (2004) The case for first-hand research, in *Research on Terrorism: Trends, Achievements, Failures* (ed. A. Silke), Frank Cass, London.

Horgan, J. (2005) *The Psychology of Terrorism,* Routledge, London.

Horgan, J. (2009) Disengagement from terrorism, in *The Faces of Terrorism: Cross-Disciplinary Explorations* (ed. D. Canter).

Howlett, J., Hanfland, K. and Ressler, R. (1986) The violent criminal apprehension program. *FBI Law Enforcement Bulletin,* **55**, 14–18.

Huff, C.R., Ratner, A. and Sagarin, E. (1986) Guilty until proven innocent: wrongful convictions and public policy. *Crime and Delinquency,* **32**, 518–44.

Huizinga, D. and Elliot, D.S. (1986) Reassessing the reliability and validity of self-report measures. *Journal of Quantitative Criminology,* **2**, 293–327.

Hull, C.L. (1943) *Principles of Behavior.* New York, Appleton Century Croft.

Hunter, J.M. and Shannon, G.W. (1985) Jarvis re-visited: distance decay and service areas of mid-19th century asylums. *Professional Geographer,* **37**(3), 296–302.

Huss, M.T. and Weaver, K.A. (1996) Effect of modality in earwitness identification: memory for verbal and nonverbal auditory stimuli presented in two contexts. *The Journal of General Psychology,* **123**, 277–87.

Inbau, F.E. and Reid, J.E. (1962) *Criminal Interrogation and Confessions,* Williams & Wilkins, Baltimore.

Ioannou, M. (2006) Hero or villain: criminals' emotional experience of crime. University of Liverpool, UK. Unpublished doctoral dissertation.

Ioannou, M. (2009) Serial murder, in *Violent Crime: Clinical and Social Implications,* (ed. C. Ferguson), Sage Publications, Thousand Oaks, CA.

Jaccard, P. (1908) Nouvelles recherches sur la distribution florale. *Bulletin de la Société Vaudoise des Sciences Naturelles,* **44**, 223–70.

Jackson, J. (1994) Fraud masters: professional credit card offenders and crime. *Criminal Justice Review,* **19**(1), 24–55.

James, W. (1890) *The Principles of Psychology,* Vol. 1, Dover, New York.

Jarvis, E. (1850) The influence of distance from and proximity to an insane hospital, on its use by any people. *The Boston Medical and Surgical Journal,* **42**, 209–22.

Jenkins, P. (1988) Serial murder in England 1940–1985. *Journal of Criminal Justice*, **16**, 1–15.

Jenkins, P. (1992) The speed capital of the world: organizing the methamphetamine industry in Philadelphia 1970–1990. *Criminal Justice Policy Review*, **6**(1), 17–39.

Jenkins, P. (1994) *Using Murder: The Social Construction of Serial Homicide*. Aldine De Gruyter, New York.

Johnston, L. (2000) Riot by appointment: an examination of the nature and structure of seven hard-core football hooligan groups, in *The Social Psychology of Crime* (eds D. Canter and L.J. Alison), Ashgate: Aldershot.

Jones, J.W. and Terris, W. (1983) Predicting employees' theft in home improvement centres. *Psychological Reports*, **52**, 187–201.

Junger-Tas, J. and Marshall, I.H. (1999) The self-report methodology in crime research. *Crime and Justice: A Review of the Research*, **25**, 291.

Kanin, E.J. (1994) False rape allegations. *Archives of Sexual Behavior*, **23**(1), 81–92.

Kassimeris, G. (2009) Case study: The November 17th Group – Europe's last revolutionary terrorists, in D. Canter. (ed) *The Faces of Terrorism: Cross-Disciplinary Explorations*.

Kassin, S.M., Tubb, V.A., Hosch, H.M. and Memon, A. (2001) On the 'general acceptance' of eyewitness testimony research: a new survey of the experts. *American Psychologist*, **56**(5), 405–16.

Katz, J. (1988) *Seductions of Crime: Moral and Sensual Attractions in Doing Evil*, Basic Books, New York.

Kaufman, A., Divasto, P., Jackson, R., *et al.* (1980) Male rape victims: non-institutionalised assault. *American Journal of Psychiatry*, **137**, 221–3.

Kebbell, M.R., Milne, R. and Wagstaff, G.F. (2001) The cognitive interview in forensic investigations. A review, in *Psychology and Law in a Changing World: New Trends in Theory, Practice and Research* (eds G.B. Traverso and L. Bagnoli), Reading, Harwood, pp. 185–97.

Kebbell, M.R. and Wagstaff, G.F. (1999) *Face Value? Evaluating the Accuracy of Eyewitness Information*. Home Office: Police Research Series. Home Office, London.

Kelly, G.A. (1955) *The Psychology of Personal Constructs*, Routledge, London.

Keppel, R. (2004) (ed.) *Offender Profiling*, Thomson, London.

Keppel, R.D. and Walter, R. (1999) Profiling killers: a revised classification model for understanding sexual murder. *International Journal of Offender Therapy and Comparative Criminology*, **43**(4), 417–37.

Keppel, R.J. and Weis, J. (1993) Time and distance as solvability factors in murder cases. *Journal of Forensic Sciences*, **39**(2), 286–401.

Keppel, R.D., Weis, J., Brown, K.M. and Welch, K. (2005) The Jack the Ripper Murders: a modus operandi and signature analysis of the 1888–1891 Whitechapel murders. *Journal of Investigative Psychology and Offender Profiling*, **2**(1), 1–21.

Kind, S. (1987) *The Scientific Investigation of Crime*, Forensic Science Services, Harrogate.

Kinsey, A.C., Pomeroy, W.B. and Martin, C.E. (1948) *Sexual Behaviour in the Human Male*, W.B. Saunders, Philadelphia, PA.

Kirby, A. (2007) The London bombers as 'self-starters': a case study in indigenous radicalization and the emergence of autonomous cliques. *Studies in Conflict and Terrorism*, **30**, 415–28.

Kitchen, R.M. (1994) Cognitive maps: what are they and why study them? *Journal of Environmental Psychology*, **14**(1), 1–19.

Klein, M.W. (1984) Offence specialisation and versatility among juveniles. *British Journal of Criminology*, **24**, 185–94.

Kleiner, M. (1999) The psychophysiology of deception and the orienting response, in *Interviewing and Deception* (eds D.V. Canter and L.J. Alison), Ashgate, Aldershot, pp. 183–208.

Knight, R.A. (1999) Validation of a typology for rapists. *Journal of Interpersonal Violence*, **14**, 303–30.

Knight, R.A. and Prentky, R.A. (1987) The developmental antecedents and adult adaptations of rapist subtypes. *Criminal Justice and Behavior*, **14**(4), 403–26.

Knight, R.A., Prentky, R.A. and Cerce, D.D. (1994) The development, reliability, and validity of an inventory for the multidimensional assessment of sex and aggression. *Criminal Justice and Behavior*, **21**, 72–94.

Knight, R.A., Warren, J.I., Reboussin, R. and Soley, B.J. (1998) Predicting rapist type from crime scene characteristics. *Criminal Justice and Behavior*, **25**, 46–80.

Kocsis, R.N., Cooksey, R.W. and Irwin, H.J. (2002) Psychological profiling of offender characteristics from crime behaviors in serial rape offences. *International Journal of Offender Therapy and Comparative Criminology*, **46**, 144–69.

Kocsis, R.N. and Irwin, H.J. (1997) An analysis of spatial patterns in serial rape, arson and burglary: the utility of the circle theory of environmental range for psychological profiling. *Psychiatry, Psychology and Law*, **4**(2), 195–206.

Koehn C.H., Fischer R.P. and Cutler B.L. (1999) Using cognitive interviewing to construct facial composites, in *Interviewing and Deception* (eds D. Canter and L. Alison), Ashgate, Darmouth.

Kohnken, G., Thurer, C. and Zorberbier, D. (1994) The cognitive interview: are the investigators' memories enhanced too? *Applied Cognitive Psychology*, **8**(11), 13–24.

Korosec-Serfaty, P. and Bollitt, D. (1986) Dwelling and the experience of burglary. *Journal of Environmental Psychology*, **6**, 329–44.

Kraemer, G.W., Lord, W.D. and Heilbrun, K. (2004) Comparing single and serial homicide offences. *Behavioural Sciences and the Law*, **22**, 325–43.

Kramer, H. and Sprenger, J. (1971) *The Malleus Maleficarium*, Dover Publishing, New York.

Krafft-Ebing, R. von. (1965) *Psychopathia Sexualis*, Stein & Day, New York. (Original work published in 1886.)

Krambia-Kapardis, M. (2001) *Enhancing the Auditor's Fraud Detection Ability: An Interdisciplinary Approach*, Peter Lang, Frankfurt am Main.

Kretschmer, E. (1925) *Physique and Character*, Harcourt, New York.

Labuschagne, G. (2004) Features and investigative implications of muti murder in South Africa. *Journal of Investigative Psychology and Offender Profiling*, **1**, 191–206.

Lamers-Winkelman, F. (1999) Statement validity analysis: its application to a sample of Dutch children who may have been sexually abused. *Journal of Aggression, Maltreatment and Trauma*, **2**(2), 59–81.

Langer, W.C. (1943) *Psychological Profile of Hitler*. Declassified Documents of the Office of Strategic Services. Accessed from the National Archives, Washington, D.C.

Langer, W.C. (1972) *The Mind of Adolf Hitler: The Secret Wartime Report*, Basic Books, New York.

Le Beau, J.L. (1987) The journey to rape: geographic distance and the rapist's method of approaching the victim. *Journal of Police Science and Administration*, **15**, 129–36.

Lee, R.M. (2000) *Unobtrusive Methods in Social Research*, Open University Press, Maidenhead.

Leibowitz, H.W. (1985) Grade crossing accidents and human factors engineering, *American Scientist*, **73**, 558–62.

Leo, R., Costanzo, M. and Shaked, N. (2009) Psychological and cultural aspects of interrogations and false confessions: using research to inform legal decision making, in *Psychological Expertise in Court: Psychology in the Courtroom*, (eds D. Kraus and J. Lieberman), Ashgate, Aldershot.

Levi, M. and Burrows, J. (2008) Measuring the impact of fraud: a conceptual and empirical journey, *British Journal of Criminology*, **48**(3), 293–318.

Levine, N. (in press) Introduction to the special issue on Bayesian journey-to-crime estimation, *Journal of Investigative Psychology and Offender Profiling*.

Levy, S. (ed.) (1994) *Louis Guttman on Theory and Methodology: Selected Writings*, Dartmouth Publishing, Aldershot.

Levy, S. and Guttman, L. (1975) On the multivariate structure of well-being, *Social Indicators Research*, **2**(3), 361–88.

Lewis, R. (1994) Flexible hierarchies and dynamic disorder, in J. Strang and M. Gossop (eds), *Heroin Addiction and Drug Policy: The British System*, Oxford University Press, Oxford.

Liebow, E. (1982) *Dr Joe Bell: Model for Sherlock Holmes*, Bowling Green State University Popular Press, Bowling Green, OH.

Lingoes, J. (1973) *The Guttman-Lingoes Non-Metric Program Series*, Ann Arbor, Michigan, Mathesis Press.

Litman, R.E., Curphey, T., Shneidman, E.S. *et al.* (1970) The psychological autopsy of equivocal deaths, in *The Psychology of Suicide* (eds E.S. Shneidman, N.L. Farberow and R.E. Litman), Science House, New York.

Little, B.R. (1983) Personal projects: a rationale and method for investigation. *Environment and Behavior*, **15**(3): 273–309.

Lobato, A. (2000) Criminal weapon use in Brazil: a psychological analysis, in *Profiling Property Crimes* (eds D. Canter and L.J. Alison), Ashgate, Dartmouth, 107–45.

Loftus, E.F. (1976) Unconscious transference. *Law and Psychology Review*, **2**: 93–8.

Loftus, E.F. (1979) *Eyewitness Testimony*, Harvard University Press, Cambridge, MA.

Loftus, E.F. and Burns, T.E. (1982) Mental shock can produce retrograde amnesia. *Memory and Cognition*, **10**(4): 318–23.

Loftus, E.F., Loftus, G.R. and Messo, J. (1987) Some facts about weapon focus. *Law and Human Behavior*, **11**, 55–62.

Lombroso, C. (1876) *The Criminal Man (L'Uomo Delinquente)*, Hoepli, Milan.

Lombroso, C. (1911) *Crime: Its Causes and Remedies*, Little & Brown, Boston.

Lombroso, C. and Ferrero, G. (2004) *Criminal Woman, the Prostitute, and the Normal Woman*, Duke University Press, London.

Lombroso-Ferrero, G. (1911) *Criminal Man*, Patterson Smith Publishing, Montclair, NJ.

Lombroso-Ferrero, G. (1972) *Criminal Man: According to the Classification of Cesare Lombroso*, Patterson Smith Publishing, Montclair, NJ.

Lundrigan, S. and Canter, D. (2001) A multivariate analysis of serial murderers' disposal site location choice. *Journal of Environmental Psychology*, **21**, 423–32.

Lynch, K. (1960) *The Image of the City*, MIT Press, Cambridge, MA.

MacCulloch, M., Snowden, P., Wood, P. and Mills, H. (1983) Sadistic fantasy, sadistic behavior, and offending. *British Journal of Psychiatry*, **143**, 20–9.

Maguire, M. (1982) *Burglary in a Dwelling*, Heinemann, London.

Marks, J. (2002) *What it Means to be 98% Chimpanzee*, University of California Press, Berkeley.

Mars, G. (2000) Culture and crime, in *The Social Psychology of Crime* (eds D. Canter and L.J. Alison), Ashgate, Aldershot.

Marsh, P., Rossee, E. and Harré, R. (1978) *The Rules of Disorder*, Routledge & Kegan Paul, London.

Marshall, B.C. and Alison, L.J. (2006) Structural behavioural analysis as a basis for discriminating between genuine and simulated rape allegations. *Journal of Investigative Psychology and Offender Profiling*, **3**, 21–34.

Marshall, W.L. (1989) Intimacy, loneliness and sexual offenders. *Behavioral Research in Therapy*, **27**, 491–503.

Marshall, W.L. and Darke, J. (1982) Inferring humiliation as motivation in sexual offenses. *Treatment of Sexual Aggressives*, **5**, 1–3.

Marshall, W.L. and Kennedy, P. (2003) Sexual sadism in sexual offenders: an elusive diagnosis. *Aggression and Violent Behaviour: A Review Journal*, **8**, 1–22.

Marshall, W.L., Kennedy, P., Yates, P. and Serran, G. (2002) Diagnosing sexual sadism in sexual offenders: reliability across diagnosticians. *International Journal of Offender Therapy and Comparative Criminology*, **46**(6), 668–77.

Maruna, S. (1999) Desistance and development: the psychosocial process of 'going straight'. *British Society of Criminology Conference Selected Proceedings*, **2**, 1–25.

Maruna, S. (2001) *Making Good: How Ex-Convicts Reform and Rebuild Their Lives*, American Psychological Association Books, Washington, DC.

McAdams, D. (1988) Biography, narratives and lives: an introduction. *Journal of Personality*, **56**, 1–18.

McAdams, D. (1993) *The Stories We Live By*, Guilford Press, New York.

McAdams, D., Josselson, R. and Lieblich, A. (2006) *Identity and Story: Creating Self in Narrative*, APA Books, Washington, DC.

McAndrew, D. (2000) The structure of criminal networks, in *The Social Psychology of Crime* (eds D. Canter and L.J. Alison), Ashgate, Aldershot.

McClintock, F.H. and Gibson, E. (1961) *Robbery in London*, Macmillan, London.

McCluskey, K. and Wardle, S. (2000) The social structure of robbery, in *The Social Psychology of Crime* (eds D. Canter and L.J. Alison), Ashgate, Aldershot.

McConaghy, N. (1993) *Sexual Behavior: Problems and Management*, Plenum Press, New York.

McLeod, J. (1997) *Narrative and Psychotherapy*, Sage, London.

McNally, R.J. (2003) *Remembering Trauma*, Harvard University Press, Cambridge, MA.

Meaney, R. (2004) Commuters and marauders: an examination of the spatial behaviour of serial criminals. *Journal of Investigative Psychology and Offender Profiling*, **1**(2), 121–37.

Meehl, P.E. (1996) *Clinical versus Statistical Prediction: A Theoretical Analysis and a Review of the Evidence*. Jason Aronson: Northvale, NJ. (Original work published 1954.)

Meloy, J.R. (1996) Stalking (obsessional following): a review of some preliminary studies. *Aggression and Violent Behavior*, **1**(2), 147–62.

Meloy, J.R. (2000) The nature and dynamics of sexual homicide: an integrative review. *Aggression and Violent Behavior*, **5**, 1–22.

Memon, A. and Stevenage, S. (1996) Interviewing witnesses. *Psycoloquy*, **7**(6).

Memon, A., Wark, L., Holley, A. *et al.* (1997) Eyewitness performance in cognitive and structured interviews. *Memory*, **5**, 639–55.

Merari, A. (1990) *Special Oversight Panel on Terrorism Hearing on Terrorism and Threats to US Interests in the Middle East*, http://www.armedservices.house.gov/schedules, accessed 11 November 2005.

Merry, S. and Harsent, L. (2000) Intruders, pilferers, raiders and invaders: the interpersonal dimension of burglary, in D. Canter and L. Alison (eds) *Profiling Property Crimes*, Ashgate, Dartmouth.

Mickolus, E.F. (1980) *Transnational Terrorism: A Chronology of Events, 1868–1969*, Aldwych Press, London.

Mikkelsen, E.J., Gutheil, T.G. and Emens, M. (1992) False sexual abuse allegations by adolescents and children: contextual factors and clinical sub-types. *American Journal of Psychotherapy*, **46**, 566–70.

Mills, C.W. (1940) Situated actions and vocabularies of motive. *American Sociological Review*, **5**, 904–13.

Milne, R. and Bull, R. (1999) *Investigative Interviewing: Psychology and Practice*, John Wiley & Sons, Ltd, Chichester.

Milne, R. and Bull, R. (2002) Back to basics: a componential analysis of the cognitive interview. *Applied Cognitive Psychology*, **16**, 743–53.

Milne, R. and Bull, R. (2003) Interviewing by the police, in Carson, D. and Bull, R. (eds) *Handbook of Psychology in Legal Contexts*, John Wiley & Sons, Ltd, Chichester.

Minnaar, A. (2001) Witchpurging and muti murder in South Africa: the legislative and legal challenges to combating these practices with specific reference to the Witchcraft Surpression Act (No. 3 of 1957, amended by act No. 50 of 1970). *African Legal Studies*, **2**, 1–21.

Mischel, W. (1968) *Personality and Assessment*, John Wiley & Sons, Inc., New York.

Moghaddam, F.M. (2005) The staircase to terrorism: a psychological exploration. *American Psychologist*, **60**(2), 161–9.

Moghaddam, F.M. (2009) De-radicalization and the staircase from terrorism, in D. Canter (ed.) *The Faces of Terrorism: Cross-Disciplinary Explorations*, in press.

Mokros, A. and Alison, L. (2002) Is profiling possible? Testing the predicted homology of crime scene actions and background characteristics in a sample of rapists. *Legal and Criminological Psychology*, **7**, 25–43.

Monahan, J. (1992) Mental illness and violent behaviour: perceptions and evidence. *American Psychologist*, **47**, 511–21.

Morton, R.J. and Hilts, M.A. (2005) *Serial Murder: Multi-Disciplinary Perspectives for Investigators*, Federal Bureau of Investigation: National Center for the Analysis of Violent Crime, Quantico, VA.

Moston, S., Stephenson, G.M. and Williamson, T.M. (1992) The incidence, antecedents and consequences of the use of right of silence during police questioning. *British Journal of Criminology*, **32**, 23–40.

Muehlenhard, C.L. and Linton, M.A. (1987) Date rape and sexual aggression in dating situations: incidence and risk factors. *Journal of Counseling Psychology*, **34**(2), 186–96.

Muller, D. (2000) Criminal profiling: real science or just wishful thinking? *Homicide Studies*, **4**(3), 234–64.

Mullins, S. (2006) The small-group psychology of terrorism: a dynamic network approach. University of Liverpool. MSc Dissertation.

Mullins, S. (2008) Criminal groups and networks, in *Criminal Psychology*, (ed. D. Canter), Hodder Education, London, pp. 133–44.

Mullins, S. (2009) Terrorist networks and small-group psychology, in *The Faces of Terrorism: Cross-Disciplinary Explorations*, (ed. D. Canter).

Munsell, A.H. (1912) A pigment color system and notation. *American Journal of Psychology*, **23**, 236–44.

Murphy, P. (2006) *Report of the Official Account of the Bombings in London on 7th July 2005*. The Stationery Office, London.

Murray, K. (1985) Life as fiction. *Journal for the Theory of Social Behaviour*, **15**(2), 173–87.

Myers, W.C., Burgess, A.W., Burgess, A.G. and Douglas, J.E. (1999) Serial murder and sexual homicide, in V. van Hassalt and M. Herson (eds), *Handbook of Psychological Approaches with Violent Offenders*, Kluwer Academic, New York.

Naka, M., Itsukushima, Y. and Itoh, Y. (1996) Eyewitness testimony after three months: a field study on memory for incidents in everyday life. *Japanese Psychological Research*, **38**(1), 14–24.

Nee C. and Meenaghan, A. (2006) Expert decision making in burglars. *British Journal of Criminology*, **46**(5), 935–49.

Nelken, D. (1993) *White-Collar Crime*, Dartmouth, Aldershot.

Neumann, C.S., Vitacco, M.J., Hare, R.D. and Wupperman, P. (2005) Reconstructing the 'reconstruction' of psychopathy: a comment on Cooke, Miche, Hart and Clark. *Journal of Personality Disorders*, **19**, 624–40.

Newton, M. (2000) *The Encyclopaedia of Serial Killers*, Checkmark Books, New York.

Nye, F. and Short, J. (1957) Scaling delinquent behaviour. *American Sociological Review*, **22**, 326–31.

O'Donohue, W. and Bowers, A.H. (2006) Pathways to false allegations of sexual harrassment. *Journal of Investigative Psychology and Offender Profiling*, **3**(1), 47–74.

Ogloff, J. and Otto, R.K. (1993) Psychological autopsy: clinical and legal perspectives. *St Louis University Law Journal*, **37**, 607.

Orel, H. (1991) *Sir Arthur Conan Doyle: Interviews and Recollections*, Palgrave Macmillan, London.

Orne, M.T. (1962) On the social psychology of the psychological experiment: with particular reference to demand characteristics and their implications. *American Psychologist*, **17**, 776–83.

Otto, R.K., Poythress, N., Starr, L. and Darkes, J. (1993) An empirical study of the reports of APA's Peer Review Panel in the Congressional Review of the *USS Iowa* incident. *Journal of Personality Assessment*, 422–5.

Overbeck, J. (2005) Beyond admissability: a practical look at the use of eyewitness expert testimony in the federal courts. *New York University Law Review*, **80**, 1895.

Parker, A. and Brown, J. (2000) Detection of deception; statement validity analysis as a means of determining truthfulness or falsity of rape allegations. *Legal and Criminological Psychology*, **5**, 237–59.

Parsons, T. and Shils, E. (eds) (1951) *Toward a General Theory of Action*, Harper & Row, New York.

Passas, N. and Nelken, D. (1993) The thin line between legitimate and criminal enterprises: subsidy frauds in the European Community. *Crime, Law and Social Change*, **19**(3), 223–43.

Pearse, J.J. (2006) The interrogation of terrorist suspects: the banality of torture, in *Investigative Interviewing*, (ed. T. Williamson), Willan, Cullompton.

Peters, D.P. (1988) Eyewitness memory and arousal in a natural setting, in *Practical Aspects of Memory: Current Research and Issues* (eds M.M. Gruneberg, P.E. Morris and R.N. Sykes), Chichester, John Wiley & Sons, Ltd.

Phillips, E. (2009) Terrorist aspects of kidnap for ransom, in *The Faces of Terrorism: Cross-Disciplinary Explorations* (ed. D. Canter).

Phillips, M.R., McAuliff, B.D., Kovera, M.B. and Cutler, B.L. (1999) Double-blind photo array administration as a safeguard against investigator bias. *Journal of Applied Psychology*, **84**(6), 940–51.

Phillips, P.D. (1980) Characteristics and typology of the journey to crime, in *Crime: A Spatial Perspective* (eds D.E. Georges-Abeyie and K.E. Harries), Columbia University Press, New York.

Pinizotto, A.J. and Finkel, N.J. (1990) Criminal personality profiling: an outcome and process study. *Law and Human Behavior*, **14**(3), 215–33.

Piquero, A.R., Farrington, D.P. and Blumstein, A. (2003) The criminal career paradigm, in *Crime and Justice: A Review of Research* (ed. M. Tonry), University of Chicago Press, Chicago, vol. 30, pp. 359–506.

Plutchik, R. and Contel, P. (1997) *Circumplex Models of Personality and Emotions*, American Psychological Association, Washington, DC.

Podolsky, E. (1966) Sexual violence. *Medical Digest*, **34**, 60–3.

Polkinghorne, D. (1988) *Narrative Knowing and the Human Sciences*, State University of New York Press, Albany, NY.

Porter, L. and Alison, L. (2004) An interpersonal model of sexually violent gang behaviour. *Aggressive Behaviour*, **30**, 449–68.

Porter, L.E. and Alison, L. (2005) The primacy of decision-action as an influence strategy of violent gang leaders. *Small Group Research*, **36**(2), 188–207.

Porter, L.E. and Alison, L. (2006) Examining group rape: a descriptive analysis of offender and victim behaviour. *European Journal of Criminology*, **3**, 357–81.

Potter, G. (1994) *Criminal Organizations: Vice, Racketeering, and Politics in an American City*, Waveland, Prospect Heights, IL.

Powers, P.A., Andriks, J.L. and Loftus, E.F. (1979) Eyewitness accounts of males and females. *Journal of Applied Psychology*, **64**, 339–47.

Poythress, N., Otto, R.K., Darkes, J. and Starr, L. (1993) APA's expert panel in the Congressional Review of the USS Iowa Incident. *American Psychologist*, January, 8–15.

Proulx, J., Blais, E. and Beauregard, E. (2007) Sadistic sexual offenders, in J. Proulx, E. Beauregard, M. Cusson and A. Nicole (eds), *Sexual Murder: A Comparative Analysis and New Perspectives*, John Wiley & Sons, Ltd, Chichester.

Quincey, V.L., Rice, M.E. and Harris, G.T. (1995) Actuarial prediction of sexual recidivism. *Journal of Interpersonal Violence*, **8**, 512–23.

Rada, R.T. (1978) *Clinical Aspects of the Rapist*, Grune & Stratton, New York.

Raskin, D.C. and Esplin, P.W. (1991) Statement validity assessment: interview procedures and content analysis of children's statements of sexual abuse. *Behavioural Assessment*, **13**, 265–91.

Rattner, A. (1988) Convicted but innocent: wrongful conviction and the criminal justice system. *Law and Human Behaviour*, **12**, 283–9.

Reiser, M. (1982) Crime-specific psychological consultation. *The Police Chief*, March.

Ressler, R.K., Burgess, A.W. and Douglas, J.E. (1988) *Sexual Homicide: Patterns and Motives*, Lexington, Lexington, MA.

Ressler, R.K., Burgess, A.W., Douglas, J.E. *et al.* (1986a) Sexual killers and their victims: identifying patterns through crime scene analysis. *Journal of Interpersonal Violence*, **1**, 288–308.

Ressler, R.K., Burgess, A.W., Douglas, J.E. *et al.* (1986b) Murderers who rape and mutilate. *Journal of Interpersonal Violence*, **1**, 273–87.

Ressler, R.K. and Shachtman, T. (1992) *Whoever Fights Monsters*, St Martin's Press, New York.

Reuter, P. and Haaga, J. (1986) *The Organization of High-Level Drug Markets: An Exploratory Study*, RAND, Santa Monica.

Rhodes, W.M. and Conly, C. (1981) Crime and mobility: an empirical study, in *Environmental Criminology* (eds P.J. Brantingham and P.L. Brantingham), Sage Publications, Beverley Hills.

Rich, E.G. (1935) *Vidocq: The Personal Memoirs of the First Great Detective*, Houghton Mifflin Company, Cambridge, MA.

Ritchie, J.H. (1994) *The Report of the Inquiry into the Care and Treatment of Christopher Clunis*, HMSO, London.

Roam, D. (2008) *The Back of the Napkin: Solving Problems and Selling Ideas with Pictures*, Portfolio, London.

Robertson, A. (2000) Theft at work, in *Profiling Property Crimes* (eds D. Canter and L. Alison), Ashgate, Dartmouth.

Rose, H. and Rose, S.P.R. (2000) *Alas, Poor Darwin: Arguments Against Evolutionary Psychology*, Jonathan Cape, London.

Ross, D.F., Ceci, S.J., Dunning, D. *et al.* (1994) Unconscious transference and mistaken identity: when a witness misidentifies a familiar but innocent person. *Journal of Applied Psychology*, **84**(6), 918–30.

Ross, J. (2009) The dynamics of terrorism and terrorist groups, in *The Faces of Terrorism: Cross-Disciplinary Explorations*, (ed. D. Canter).

Rossmo, D.K. (2000) *Geographic Profiling*, CRC Press, Boca Raton, FL.

Ruggiero, V. and South, N. (1995) *Eurodrugs: Drug Use, Markets and Trafficking in Europe*, UCL Press, London.

Rumbelow, D. (1987) *The Complete Jack the Ripper*, Penguin, London.

Sageman, M. (2004) *Understanding Terror Networks*, University of Pennsylvania Press, Philadelphia, PA.

Safarik, M.E., Jarvis, J.P. and Nussbaum, K. (2002) Sexual homicide of elderly females: linking offender characteristics to victim and crime scene attributes. *Journal of Interpersonal Violence*, **17**(5), 500–25.

Sageman, M. (2008) Leaderless Jihad: terrorist networks in the twenty-first century. *Policing*, **2**(4), 208–9.

Salfati, C.G. (1994) Homicide: a typology, University of Surrey, UK, unpublished MSc dissertation.

Salfati, G. (2000) The nature of expressiveness and instrumentality in homicide. *Homicide Studies*, **4**(3), 265–93.

Salfati, C.G. and Bateman, A.L. (2005) Serial homicide: an investigation of behavioural consistency. *Journal of Investigative Psychology and Offender Profiling*, **2**, 121–44.

Salfati, C.G. and Canter, D. (1999) Differentiating stranger murders: profiling offender characteristics from behavioral styles. *Behavioral Sciences and the Law*, 391–406.

Salfati, C.G. and Dupont, F. (2006) Canadian homicide: an investigation of crime-scene actions. *Homicide Studies*, **10**(2), 118–39.

Salfati, C.G. and Haratsis, E. (2001) Greek homicide: a behavioural examination of offender crime scene actions. *Homicide Studies*, **5**(4), 335–62.

Santtila, P., Canter, D., Elfgren, T. and Häkkänen, H. (2001) The structure of crime scene actions in Finnish homicides. *Homicide Studies*, **5**, 363–87.

Santtila, P., Häkkänen, H., Alison, L. and Whyte, C. (2003) Juvenile firesetters: crime scene actions and offender characteristics. *Legal and Criminological Psychology*, **8**, 1–20.

Santtila, P., Häkkänen, H., Canter, D. and Elfgren, T. (2003) Classifying homicide offenders and predicting their characteristics from crime scene behavior. *Scandinavian Journal of Psychology*, **44**, 107–18.

Santtila, P., Häkkänen, H. and Fritzon, K. (2003) Inferring the characteristics of an arsonist from crime scene actions: a case study in offender profiling. *International Journal of Police Science and Management*, **5**, 1–15.

Santtila, P., Junkkila, J. and Sandnabba, N.K. (2005) Behavioural linking of stranger rapes. *Journal of Investigative Psychology and Offender Profiling*, **2**(2), 87–103.

Sarangi, S. and Youngs, D. (2006) Spatial patterns of Indian serial burglars with relevance to geographical profiling. *Journal of Investigative Psychology and Offender Profiling*, **3**(2), 105–15.

Sarnecki, J. (2001) *Delinquent Networks: Youth Co-offending in Stockholm*, Cambridge University Press, Cambridge.

Schaefer, E. (1959) A circumplex model for maternal behavior. *Journal of Abnormal and Social Psychology*, **59**, 226–35.

Schaefer, E. (1997) Integration of configurational and factorial models for family relationships and child behavior, in *Circumplex Models of Personality and Emotions* (eds R. Plutchik and H. Conte), American Psychological Association, Washington, DC.

Schmalleger, F. (2004) *Criminology Today*, 3rd edn, Prentice Hall, New Jersey.

Schneider, K. (1998) Toward a science of the heart: romanticism and the revival of psychology. *American Psychologist*, **53**(3), 277–89.

Scott, M.J., and Canter, D. (1997) Picture or place? A multiple of landscape. *Journal of Environmental Psychology*, **17**, 263–81.

Scully, D. and Marolla, J. (1983) *Incarcerated Rapists: Exploring a Sociological Model*, final report for the Department of Health and Human Services, NIMH, Rockville, MD.

Serin, R.C. and Amos, N.L. (1995) The role of psychopathy in the assessment of dangerousness. *International Journal of Psychiatry and Law*, **18**, 231–8.

Seto, M.C. and Kuban, M. (1996) Criteria-related validity of a phallometric test for paraphilic rape and sadism. *Behaviour Research and Therapy*, **34**, 175–83.

Shalev, K., Schaefer, M. and Morgan, A. (2009) Investigating missing person cases: how can we learn where they go or how far they travel? *International Journal of Police Science and Management*.

Shapiro, D. (2002) Renewing the scientist-practitioner model. *The Psychologist*, **15**(5), 232–34.

Shapland, J.M. (1974) Self-report delinquency in boys aged 11–14. *British Journal of Criminology*, **18**, 255–66.

Sharp, A.M. (2009) Cyberterrorism: The emerging worldwide threat, in *The Faces of Terrorism: Interdisciplinary Perspectives* (ed. D. Canter), John Wiley & Sons, Ltd, Chichester.

Sheldon, W. (1954) *Atlas of Men*, Macmillan, London.

Shepherd, E. (2007) *Investigative Interviewing: The Conversation Management Approach*, Oxford University Press, Oxford.

Sherman, C. (2003) *A Rose for Mary: The Hunt for the Real Boston Strangler*, Northeastern University Press, Boston.

Sherman, L.W., Gartin, P.R. and Buerger, M.E. (1989) Hotspots of predatory crime: routine activities and the criminology of space. *Criminology*, **27**, 27–55.

Shneidman, E.S. and Farberow, N.L. (1970) Sample psychological autopsies, in *The Psychology of Suicide* (eds E.S. Shneidman, N.L. Farberow and R.E. Litman), Science House, New York.

Shoda, Y. (1999) Behavioral expressions of a personality system: generation and perception of behavioral signatures, in *The Coherence of Personality: Social–Cognitive Bases of Consistency, Variability, and Organization* (eds D. Cervone and Y. Shoda), Guilford Press, New York.

Shoda, Y., Mischel, W. and Wright, J.C. (1994) Intra-individual stability in the organization and patterning of behavior: incorporating psychological situations into the idiographic analysis of personality. *Journal of Personality and Social Psychology*, **67**, 674–87.

Shover, N. (1973) The social organisation of burglary. *Social Problems*, **20**, 499–514.

Shover, N. (1991) Burglary, in *Crime and Justice: A Review of Research* (ed. M. Tonry), University of Chicago Press, Chicago.

Shye, S. (1978) Achievement motive: a faceted definition and structure analysis. *Multivariate Behavioral Research*, **13**, 327–46.

Shye, S. (1985a) Smallest space analysis, in *International Encyclopedia of Education* (eds T. Husen and T.N. Postlethwaite), Pergamon, Oxford, pp. 4602–8.

Shye, S. (1985b) Non-metric multivariate models for behavioural action systems, in *Facet Theory: Approaches to Social Research*, (ed. D. Canter), Springer Verlag, New York.

Shye, S. (1989) The systemic life quality model: a basis for urban renewal evaluation. *Social Indicators Research*, **21**, 343–78.

Shye, S. (1998) Modern facet theory: content design and measurement in behavioral research. *European Journal of Psychological Assessment*, **14**(2), 160–71.

Shye, S. (1999) Facet theory. *Encyclopedia of Statistical Sciences, Update*, Vol. 3. John Wiley & Sons, Inc., New York, 231–9.

Shye, S., Elizur, D. and Hoffman, M. (1994) *Introduction to Facet Theory: Content Design and Intrinsic Data Analysis in Behavioural Research*, Sage Publications, London.

Shye, S. and Engelhard, M. (2004) *Profiling Offenders and Crime Scenes*, The Van Leer Jerusalem Institute, Jerusalem. (Report submitted to the Israel Ministry of Public Security, Bureau of the Chief Scientist)

Silke, A. (2003) The psychology of suicidal terrorism, in *Terrorists, Victims and Society* (ed. A. Silke), John Wiley & Sons, Ltd, Chichester.

Siomopoulos, V. and Goldsmith, J. (1976) Sadism revisited. *American Journal of Psychotherapy*, **30**(4), 631–40.

Smith, C. (1993) Psychological offender profiling. *The Criminologist*, **24**(4), 224–50.

Smith, R.G. (2003) Corporate crime in the digital age. *Corporate Misconduct eZine*, vol. **1**, issue 1. Available at http://www.aic.gov.au/publications/other/2003-03-corporate.html, accessed 31 May 2009.

Snook, B., Canter, D. and Bennell, C. (2002) Predicting the home location of serial offenders: a preliminary comparison of the accuracy of human judges with a geographic profiling system. *Behavioural Sciences and the Law*, **20**, 109–18.

Snook, B., Zito, M., Bennell, C. and Taylor, P.J. (2005) On the complexity and accuracy of geographic profiling strategies. *Journal of Quantitative Criminology*, **21**(1), 1–26.

Soibelman, M. (2004) Palestinian suicide bombers. *Journal of Investigative Psychology and Offender Profiling*, **1**, 175–90.

Soothill, K., Francis, B., Sanderson, B. and Ackerley, E. (2000) Sex offenders: specialists, generalists – or both? *British Journal of Criminology*, **40**, 56–67.

Spahr, L. and Alison, L. (2004) US savings and loan fraud: implications for general and criminal culture theories of crime. *Crime, Law and Social Change*, **41**, 95–105.

Spearman, C. (1904) The proof and measurement of association between two things. *The American Journal of Psychology*, **15**(1), 72–101.

Speckhard, A. (2006) Defusing human bombs: understanding suicide terrorism, in *Psychology and Terrorism* (eds J. Victoroff and S. Mednick), IOS Press, Amsterdam.

Sporer, S.L., Read, D., Penrod, S. and Cutler, B. (1995) Choosing, confidence and accuracy: a meta-analysis of the confidence-accuracy relation in eyewitness identification studies. *Psychological Bulletin*, **118**(3), 312–27.

Stead, P.J. (1953) *Vidocq: A Bibliography*, Staples Press, New York.

Steller, M. and Kohnken, G. (1989) Criteria-based content analysis, in *Psychological Methods in Criminal Investigation and Evidence* (ed. D.C. Raskin), Springer-Verlag, New York.

Steller, M., Wellerhaus, P. and Wolf, T. (1988) Empirical validation of criteria based content analysis. Paper presented at NATO Advanced Study Institute on Credibility Assessment, Maratea, Italy.

Stephenson, G.M. (1992) *The Psychology of Criminal Justice*, Blackwell, Oxford.

Stephenson, K. and Zelen, M. (1989) Rethinking centrality: methods and applications. *Social Networks*, **11**, 1–37.

Stermac, L., Sheridan, P.M., Davidson, A. and Dunn, S. (1996) Sexual assaults of adult males. *Journal of Interpersonal Violence*, **11**, 52–64.

Stone, M. (1989) Murder. *Psychiatric Clinics of North America*, **12**(3), 643–51.

Stott, C. (2003) Police expectations and the control of English soccer fans at 'Euro2000'. *Policing: An International Journal of Police Strategies and Management*, **26**, 640–55.

Stott, C. and Drury, J. (2000) Crowds, context and identity: dynamic categorization processes in the 'poll tax riot'. *Human Relations*, **53**(2), 247–73.

Stott, C., Hutchison, P. and Drury, J. (2001) 'Hooligans' abroad? Inter-group dynamics, social identity and participation in collective 'disorder' at the 1998 World Cup Finals. *British Journal of Social Psychology*, **40**, 359–84.

Stott, C. and Pearson, G. (2007) *Football Hooliganism: Policing and the War on the English Disease*, Pennant, London.

Stuesser, Lee (2005) Experts on eyewitness identification: I just don't see it. *International Commentary on Evidence*, **3**(1), Article 2. Available at http://www.bepress.com/ice/vol3/iss1/art2, accessed 31 May 2009.

Sugden, P. (1995) *The Complete History of Jack the Ripper*, Robinson, London.

Sutherland, E. (1937) *The Professional Thief*, University of Chicago Press, Chicago.

Sutherland, E.D. and Cressey, D.R. (1974) *Criminology*, J.B. Lippincott, Philadelphia, PA.

Sutherland, E.H., Cressey, D.R. and Luckenbill, D.F. (1992) *Principles of Criminology*, 11 edn, General Hall, Dix Hills, NY.

Swanson, C.R., Chamelin, N.C. and Territo, L. (1992) *Criminal Investigation*, 5th edn, McGraw-Hill, New York.

Szondi, L. (1952) *Introduction to the Szondi Test: Theory and Practice*, Grune & Stratton, New York.

Tabachnick, B.G. and Fidell, L.S. (1983) *Using Multivariate Statistics*, Harper & Row Publishers, New York.

Talbot, E. (1898) *Degeneracy: Its Causes, Signs, and Results*, Walter Scott, New York.

Tallis, F. (2008) *Fatal Lies*, Arrow Books, London.

Tamura, M. and Suzuki, M. (2000) Characteristics of serial arsonists and crime scene geography in Japan, in *Forensic Psychology and Law: Traditional Questions and New Ideas* (eds A. Czederecka, T. Jaskiewicz-Obydzinska and J. Wojcikiewicz), Institute of Forensic Research, Krakow, Poland.

Tate, C.S., Warren, A.R. and Hess, T.M. (1992) Adults' liability for children's lie-ability: can adults coach children to lie successfully? In *Cognitive and Social Factors in Early Deception* (eds S.J. Ceci, M.D. Leichtmen and M. Putnick), Lawrence Erlbaum Associates, Hillsdale, NJ.

Teton, H. (1989) Offender profiling. In W. Bailey (ed.) *The Encyclopaedia of Police Science*, Garland Publishing, New York.

Teton, H. (1995) Offender profiling, in *The Encyclopedia of Police Science*, 2nd edn (ed. W.G. Bailey), New York, Garland Publishing.

Thaler, R.H. and Sunstein, C.R. (2008) *Nudge: Improving Decisions About Health, Wealth, and Happiness*. Yale: Yale University Press.

Theilade, P. and Thomsen, J.L. (1986) False allegations of rape. *Police Surgeon*, **30**, 17–22.

Thrasher, F. (1927) *The Gang: A Study of 1,313 Gangs in Chicago*, University of Chicago Press, Chicago.

Tolman, E.C. (1948) Cognitive maps in rats and men. *Psychological Review*, **55**, 189–208.

Tufte, E.R. (1999) *The Visual Display of Quantitative Information*, Graphics Press, Cheshire, CT.

Tullett, T. (1987) *Clues to Murder*, Bodley Head, London.

Tully, B. (1999) Statement analysis: review of developments and research, in *Interviewing and Deception* (eds D. Canter and L. Alison), Offender Profiling Series, Vol.1, Ashgate, Dartmouth.

Turner, S. (1969) Delinquency and distance, in *Delinquency: Selected Studies* (eds T. Sellin and M.E. Wolfgang), John Wiley & Sons, Inc., New York.

Turvey, B. (1999) *Criminal Profiling: An Introduction to Behavioural Evidence*, Academic Press, San Diego, CA.

Undeutsch, U. (1989) The development of statement reality analysis, in *Credibility Assessment: A Unified Theoretical and Research Perspective* (ed. J. Yuille), Proceedings of the NATO-Advanced Study Institute, June 1988, Maratea, Italy, Kluwer Academic Publishers, Dordrecht (NL).

Van Koppen, P.J. and Jansen, R.W. (1998) The road to robbery: travel patterns in commercial robberies. *British Journal of Criminology*, **38**(2), 230–46.

Van Limbergen, K., Colaers, C. and Walgrave, L. (1989) The societal and psycho-sociological background of football hooliganism. *Current Psychology Research and Reviews*, **8**, 4–14.

Vorpagel, R.E. (1982) Painting psychological profiles: charlatanism, charisma, or a new science? *The Police Chief*, 156–9.

Vrij, A., Leal, S., Granhag, P.A. *et al.* (2008, published online) Outsmarting the liars: The benefit of asking unanticipated questions. *Law and Human Behavior.* Available at http://www.springerlink.com/content/u254472301p4242m/fulltext.pdf, accessed 31 May 2009.

Vrij, A. and Mann, S. (2001) Telling and detecting lies in a high-stake situation: the case of a convicted murderer. *Applied Cognitive Psychology*, **15**(2), 187–203.

Vygotsky, L. (1978) *Mind in Society: The Development of Higher Psychological Processes*, Harvard University Press, Cambridge, MA.

Wagstaff, G.F. (1982) Hypnosis and witness recall: a discussion paper. *Journal of the Royal Society of Medicine*, **75**, 793–7.

Walsh, D. (1980) *Break-Ins: Burglary from Private Houses*, Constable, London.

Walsh, D. (1986) *Heavy Business: Commercial Burglary and Robbery*, Routledge & Kegan Paul, London.

Warren, J., R. Reboussin, Hazelwood, R. *et al.* (1998) Crime scene and distance correlates of serial rape. *Journal of Quantitative Criminology*, **14**(1), 35–59.

Wasserman, S. and Faust, K. (1997) *Social Network Analysis: Structural Analysis in the Social Sciences*, Cambridge University Press, Cambridge.

Wasserman, S., Faust, K. and Iacobucci, D. (1994) *Social Network Analysis: Methods and Applications*, Cambridge University Press, Cambridge.

Watts, S. (1994) Robbers and robberies: behavioural consistencies in armed robbers, and their interpersonal narrative constructs. University of Liverpool. MSc Dissertation:

Weale, R.A. (1982) *A Biography of the Eye: Development – Growth – Age*, H.K. Lewis, London.

Webb, E.J., Campbell, D.T., Schwartz, R.D. and Sechrest, L. (1966) *Unobtrusive Measures: Non-reactive Research in the Social Sciences*, Chicago: RandMcNally.

Welch, K. and Keppel, R.D. (2006) Historical origin of offender profiling, in *Offender Profiling* (ed. R.D. Keppel), Thompson Custom Publishing, Mason, OH.

Wells, G.L. (1993) What do we know about eyewitness identification? *American Psychologist*, **48**(5), 553–71.

Wells, G.L. and Olson, E.A. (2003) Eyewitness testimony. *Annual Review of Psychology*, **54**, 277–95.

Wells, G.L., Small, M., Penrod, S. *et al.* (1998) Eyewitness identification procedures: recommendations for line-ups and photospreads. *Law and Human Behaviour*, **22**, 603–47.

West, W.G. (1978) The short term careers of serious thieves. *Canadian Journal of Criminology*, **20**, 169–90.

Wheeler, S., Weisburd, D. and Bode, N. (1982) Sentencing the white collar offender: Rhetoric and reality. *American Sociological Review*, **47**, 641–59.

Whyte, W.H. (1956) *The Organisation Man*, Doubleday, Garden City, NY.

Wiles, A. and Costello, P. (2000) *The 'Road to Nowhere': The Evidence for Travelling Criminals*. Home Office Research Study, 207, Home Office, London.

Williams, P. (1993) The international drug trade: an industry analysis. *Low Intensity Conflict and Law Enforcement*, **2**(3), 397–423.

Williamson, T. (1993) From interrogation to investigative interviewing: strategic trends in police interviewing. *Journal of Community and Applied Social Psychology*, **3**, 89–99.

Williamson, T. (2006) *Investigative Interviewing: Rights, Research, Regulation*. Willan, Cullompton.

Wilson, A. and Donald, I. (1999) Ram raiding: criminals working in groups, in *The Social Psychology of Crime: Teams, Groups, Networks. Offender Profiling Series Vol III* (eds D.V. Canter and L.J. Alison), Ashgate, Aldershot.

Wilson, M. and Canter, D. (1991) A theory of inference derivation for qualitative data: development and test with application to criminal and terrorist detection, University of Surrey, Guildford (report to US Army – DAJA45-88-C0021).

Wilson, M.A., Canter, D. and Smith, A. (1995) *Modelling Terrorist Behaviour. Final Report*. U.S. Army Research Institute, Alexandria, VA.

Wilson, M. and Smith, A. (2000) Rules and roles in terrorist hostage taking, in *The Social Psychology of Crime: Groups, Teams and Networks* (eds Canter, D.V. and Alison, L.J.), Dartmouth: Ashgate.

Woodhams, J., Hollin, C.R. and Bull, R. (2007) The psychology of linking crimes: a review of the evidence. *Legal and Criminological Psychology*, **12**, 233–49.

Woodhams, J. and Toye, K. (2007) An empirical test of the assumptions of case linkage and offender profiling with serial commercial robberies. *Psychology, Public Policy, and Law*, **13**, 59–85.

Wright, J.A., Burgess, A.G., Burgess, A.W. *et al.* (1996) A typology of interpersonal stalking. *Journal of Interpersonal Violence*, **11**(4), 487–502.

Wrightman, L.S. (2001) *Forensic Psychology*, Wadsworth, Belmont, CA.

Yarmey, A.D. (1984) Age as a factor in eyewitness memory, in *Eyewitness Testimony* (eds G.L. Wells and E.F. Loftus), Cambridge University Press, London.

Yarmey, A.D. (1986) Verbal, visual, and voice identification of a rape suspect under different levels of illumination. *Journal of Applied Psychology*, **71**, 363–70.

Yarmey, A.D. (1993) Adult age and gender differences in eyewitness recall in field settings. *Journal of Applied Social Psychology*, **23**, 1921–32.

Yarvis, R. (1995) Diagnostic patterns among three violent offender types. *Bulletin of the American Academy of Psychiatry and Law*, **23**, 411–19.

Youngs, D. (2001) Specialisation in offending behaviour. University of Liverpool. Unpublished doctoral dissertation.

Youngs, D. (2004) Personality correlates of offence style. *Journal of Investigative Psychology and Offender Profiling*, **1**(1), 99–119.

Youngs, D. (2008) Contemporary challenges in investigative psychology: Revisiting the Canter Offender Profiling Equations, in *Psychology and Law: Bridging the Gap* (eds D. Canter and R. Zukauskiene), Ashgate, Aldershot.

Youngs, D. (ed.) (in press). The Behavioural Analysis of Crime: Investigative Psychology Studies in Honour of David Canter. Ashgate: Aldershot, UK.

Youngs, D. and Canter, D. (in press, a) A radex framework for offender specialisation. International Research Centre for Investigative Psychology (IRCIP) (internal report, submitted for publication).

Youngs, D. and Canter, D. (in press, b) Victim role assignments by violent offenders. International Research Centre for Investigative Psychology (IRCIP) (internal report, submitted for publication).

Youngs, D. and Canter, D. (in press, c) A Narrative Action System Model of Acquisitive Crime. International Research Centre of Investigative Psychology (IRCIP) (internal report, submitted for publication).

Youngs, D., Canter, D. and Cooper, J. (2004) The facets of criminality: a cross-modal and cross-gender validation. *Behaviourmetrika*, **31**, 99–111.

Youngs, R. (2006) *Democracy and Security in the Middle East*, Fundación para las Relaciones Internacionales y el Diálogo Exterior, Madrid. Available at http://www.fride.org/publication/58/democracy-and-security-in-the-middle-east, accessed 12 May 2009.

Yuille, J.C. (1984) Research and teaching with police: a Canadian example. *International Review of Applied Psychology*, **33**, 5–23.

Yuille, J.C. and Cutshall, J.L. (1986) A case study of eyewitness memory of a crime. *Journal of Applied Psychology*, **71**, 291–301.

Zhang, S. and Gaylord, M. (1996) Bound for the Golden Mountain: the social organization of Chinese alien smuggling. *Crime, Law and Social Change*, **25**(1), 1–16.

Zona, M.E., Sharma, K.K. and Lane, J. (1993) A comparative study of erotomanic and obsessional subjects in a forensic sample. *Journal of Forensic Sciences*, **38**(4), 894–903.

Index

Note: Page numbers in italics refer to figures and tables. The abbreviation IP is used for Investigative Psychology.